Karen Lapp

REAL ESTATE FINANCE

Real estate finance

1981   *Seventh edition*

WILLIAM B. BRUEGGEMAN, Ph.D.
Corrigan Professor of Real Estate
Edwin L. Cox School of Business
Southern Methodist University
Real Estate Consultant

LEO D. STONE, M.B.A., J.D.
Professor Emeritus of Business Finance
College of Administrative Science
The Ohio State University
Certified Public Accountant
Chartered Financial Analyst
Member of the Ohio Bar

AMBITION !

RICHARD D. IRWIN, INC.   *Homewood, Illinois   60430*
IRWIN-DORSEY LIMITED   *Georgetown, Ontario   L7G 4B3*

© RICHARD D. IRWIN, INC., 1954, 1961, 1965, 1969, 1973, 1977, and 1981

ISBN 0-256-02444-8
Library of Congress Catalog Card No. 80–84359

Printed in the United States of America

1 2 3 4 5 6 7 8 9 0 D 8 7 6 5 4 3 2 1

Preface

This edition represents a major effort to preserve the values inherent in the sixth edition, yet to give the new text a significant thrust into the area of decision making in the financing of real estate. Whereas the major strength of previous editions was probably the depth and extent of treatment of institutional aspects of the financing process, an equally great contribution of this edition may be in the development of student or professional skills in dealing with problem situations related to the textual discussion. Many additions in this edition should assist in the attainment of that objective. Major changes include a chapter on alternative mortgage instruments, including an analysis of adjustable interest rate and adjustable payment mortgages that have been either authorized for use or proposed for use since the last edition of this text. A considerable expansion in the analysis of income-producing property has been undertaken in Part Three. More material has been included on valuation, financial analysis, investment analysis and taxation, and financial leverage. Also, with the addition of three new chapters, a more complete treatment is given to real estate syndication, sale-and-leaseback financing, and strategies in financing and investment.

This new edition also includes more material on lending policy and a discussion of the Depository Institutions Deregulation and Monetary Control Act of 1980 which will cause major changes in the mortgage market and in the structure of financial institutions in the United States during the coming decade. This material has been incorporated into Part Four of the text.

Finally, Part One continues to provide the legal characteristics and financial implications of the use of the principal instruments involved in financing real estate and Part Five, "Government and Real Estate Finance," summarizes the principal FHA and VA programs; the functions of the Federal National Mortgage Association, the Government National Mortgage Association, and the Federal Home Loan Mortgage Corporation in the secondary mortgage market; and the Farmers Home Administration as an aid to rural economic interests and housing.

This edition is designed for both academic and professional use. Its goal is not only to provide a basic orientation in commonly used instruments and institutional structures and policies but also to develop problem-solving capabilities in all areas of general discussion.

The authors responsible for this revision want to express their appreciation to their reviewers for many helpful comments and constructive suggestions. In particular, they are grateful to William M. Shenkel of the University of Georgia, Stephen D. Messner and T. Gregory Morton of the University of Connecticut at Storrs, Jeffrey D. Fisher of Indiana University, Wade Ragas of the University of New Orleans, Carroll Melton of the U.S. League of Savings Associations, and Gary Fisher of AmeriCare Corporation of Dallas, Texas. They also acknowledge the assistance of Ms. DWayne Roberts in the preparation of the revised manuscript. The authors also acknowledge their great debt to the late Henry E. Hoagland, who wrote the first edition of this text and set the tone of the editions that have followed. He was a distinguished pioneer in real estate education. His absence is deeply felt.

William B. Brueggeman
Leo D. Stone

Contents

Introduction

The practice of financing real estate dates back to the earliest history of man. The durability and immobility of land have always made it an ideal security to support credit extension. Before World War I and the Great Depression of the 1930s, however, mortgage debt financing tended to carry an evil connotation: it should be extinguished at the earliest opportunity.

Since the mid-1930s and particularly after World War II, real estate credit has been accepted as a moral and often necessary means of achieving the goal of home ownership. The criterion for becoming a buyer of housing today relates to a person's ability to carry the financing, not the extent of his or her savings. Similar principles have applied in the financing of commercial and industrial properties to support our population demands.

In addition to sheer growth in volume of activity, dynamic changes in policies, techniques, and institutional patterns during the 1960s and 1970s have made the area of real estate financing hard to fathom and even more difficult to describe. The recent historically high interest rates sent shock waves throughout the institutional structures and management, causing new attitudes toward old policies. This is evidenced by the appearance of adjustable interest rate and adjustable payment mortgages and equity participation mortgages. Scarcities of funds in thrift institutions, brought on by extensive disintermediation by the public prompted passage of the Depository Institutions Deregulation and Monetary Control Act of 1980, which will have a significant impact on financial intermediaries in the coming decade. Then, most recently, the disastrous impacts of the economic recession on developers, real estate investment trusts, commercial banks, and others have left their traumatic

1

marks. These trends are taken into account, and the development and characteristics of the new business forms are discussed in this edition.

When one of the blind men in a Hindu fable sought to describe an elephant, he said the beast is like a rope. This man had felt only its tail. Another, who had stroked its ear, thought the elephant to be like a fan. So students who read real estate finance topics tend to become lost in a maze of individual bits of information. The purpose of this text is to isolate and deal with the major problems in a discrete order.

Thus it is that Part One discusses the instruments of real estate finance and characteristic legal problems created by their use. In this part of the text, the discussion is particularly detailed and comprehensive, to develop an awareness of the dangers of a little knowledge, a sense of the great variety and flexibility of financing tools, and an appreciation of the need for professional expertise to operate in the field.

Part Two includes material on the mathematics of finance, which is the cornerstone of much of the analysis done in real estate analysis and mortgage lending, and an in-depth discussion of residential mortgage finance. In the latter case, material is provided on loan underwriting, disclosure requirements, and a separate chapter is provided on adjustable rate and adjustable payment mortgages.

Part Three reviews the many analytic factors involved in the financing and investment decision-making process, together with the most commonly used specialized varieties of financing techniques. The purpose of this discussion is to advance the reader's technical abilities to participate in the decision-making process in such matters as borrowing or lending, owning or leasing, and evaluating sources of funds. To achieve that objective, the reader is provided with extensive coverage on valuation, financial leverage, investment analysis, risk analysis, construction and development financing, real estate syndication, as well as material on strategies that can be considered when financing an investment in real estate.

Part Four, in order, considers the general structure of the mortgage market, the significance of savings and loan associations, mutual savings and commercial banks, life insurance companies, real estate investment trusts, syndicates, and mortgage bankers as sources of funds. Some history of each institution has been considered essential to an understanding of its position as a source of funds today—to give a perspective of its philosophy and predilections. Beyond that, discussion of the general nature and limitations of its operations is designed to give a sense of its potentiality as a source of funds.

Part Five seeks to put in their place the expanding roles of the federal government in its various approaches to assistance in the financing of real estate. Particularly because of the magnitude of the housing programs and the importance of the federal support of secondary mortgage markets, financial terms and practices in all markets are affected by government action.

Instruments used in real estate finance: Legal and financial considerations

Legal nature of real estate mortgages

1

The most common method of financing the purchase of real estate is by borrowing and pledging the real estate acquired as security for the loan. Under this arrangement the terms of the borrowing are set forth in a promissory note signed by the borrower, and the terms governing the nature of the pledge are established by a mortgage signed by the borrower, also known as the *mortgagor*. The lender is termed the *mortgagee*.

The mortgage note or bond

The mortgage note or bond must meet certain legal requirements to be enforceable. It must be a written instrument committing an obligor (borrower) to pay a specific sum to an obligee (lender or someone in his behalf) under specific terms. A default clause will provide that the holder of the note may proceed against the borrower personally for breach of obligations undertaken under terms of the note and also for breach of mortgage covenants incorporated by reference. The note must be properly executed and voluntarily delivered and accepted. The parties must have contractual capacity. This note may be written separately or may be made a part of the mortgage. If written separately, it may be copied into the mortgage. In either event the note is the primary obligation of the mortgagor. The mortgage merely represents the security to protect the noteholder in case of default. If the lender were sufficiently confident that the borrower would always be able to meet his obligations, no mortgage would be necessary. The note constitutes all the evidence of the debt that is needed.

In fact, in case of default the mortgagee may elect to disregard the mortgage and sue on the note. The judgment awarded him as the result of the suit on the note may be attached to other property owned by the mortgagor which, through sale, may enable the mortgagee to recover the amount of his claims more readily than if he foreclosed his mortgage. Should the mortgagee elect to do so, he may take double-barreled action against the mortgagor simultaneously. He may bring suit in a court of law praying for relief on the note and at the same time enforce his foreclosure rights in a court of equity. Unless one of these suits results in a decision which completely satisfies his claim, the other is not affected. Since, however, such simultaneous suits are not likely to produce either more speedy or more complete results than one of them, simultaneous suits are seldom resorted to.

Just as a debt could be evidenced without a mortgage, so is it possible to have a mortgage without a note. The mortgagee could agree to leave the mortgagor free from any form of personal liability. Such an arrangement would not affect the validity of the mortgage. If the mortgagor undertakes no personal liability, the mortgagee must look to the security alone to provide the means of satisfying his claims.

Because of recent practices, it is recommended that the note not only be a separate instrument from the mortgage but that its terms be omitted from the mortgage. Reference to the note in such terms as to identify it without stating its terms is sufficient to fix the mortgage as its security. By this means the rate of interest, the terms of repayment, and so forth, are not made matters of record. A common form of reference to the note in the mortgage mentions a "certain promissory note of even date herewith in the principal sum of (amount here filled in) with interest from date at the rate therein specified." Consequently, competitors of the mortgagee who might take advantage of the knowledge they could gain from the record for raiding purposes are denied this privilege.

Definition of mortgage

A standard law treatise on mortgages says: "A real estate mortgage is a lien on an interest in the land, created by a formal agreement, by a transfer of such interest, to secure the payment of money or the performance of some other act."[1] The National Conference on Uniform State Laws has defined a mortgage as "any form of instrument whereby a lien is created upon real estate or whereby title to real estate is reserved or conveyed as security for the payment of a debt or other obligation." As will be noted from both of the above definitions, the essential point is their application to an interest in real estate in the form of an agreement which establishes a lien against the particular interest in question.

---

[1] H. T. Tiffany, *A Treatise on the Modern Law of Real Property* (Chicago: Callaghan & Co., 1939), p. 912. Treatise is updated to current years by supplements.

A "lien" as used in these definitions is a legal right to have a debt or obligation satisfied out of the specifically identified property of the debtor. The mortgage delineates the nature of the lien.

Interests covered

Because "interest in real estate" covers a wide variety of possibilities, "mortgage" must be considered equally broad in its applications. In general, we are accustomed to think of the mortgage in relation to full ownership. In addition, it may cover any interest in real estate that is a proper subject of sale, grant, or assignment.[2] Whether, as a matter of sound business judgment, mortgagees would be willing to lend money against these lesser interests is quite another question.

In addition, mortgages are used to protect obligations that are more or less independent of the property mortgaged. For example, a mortgage on a home may be used to protect a line of credit to be used for business purposes, to assure the payment of an annuity, to guarantee an agreement by A to support B during the latter's lifetime, to make sure that some contract will be fulfilled, and so forth.

Minimum contents of mortgage

Whether a printed form of mortgage instrument is used or an attorney draws up a special form, certain subjects must always be included. These are:

1. Appropriate identification of the mortgagor and mortgagee.
2. Proper description of the liened property.
3. Covenants of seizin and warranty.[3]
4. Provision for release of dower by the mortgagor.

The proper names of both mortgagor and mortgagee should be used with great care. If possible, the mortgagor should use the same form of name by which he is known as the lawful owner of the property. In case there has been a change of name since the property was acquired, either through marriage or otherwise, this fact should be shown in the records to avoid future confusion. Likewise the proper and correct name of the mortgagee is important, whether an individual or a corporation is involved.

In like manner the description of the property which serves as security for the loan should be the legal description as recorded in the public records. While

---

[2] This means that rents, dower interests, an estate for years, the rights of a remainderman, reversion rights, life estates, the interest of an heir or devisee (subject to the debts of the decedent), an option in a lease, and improvements apart from the land are all proper bases for mortgages so far as legal theory is concerned.

[3] A *covenant* is a promise or binding assurance. *Seizin* is the state of owning the quantum of title that is being conveyed.

this is not an absolute requirement, it can save future confusion. In any event, the property must be described in such terms that there can be no reasonable doubt about its identification. The mortgagee is usually given the right to transfer his interests to his heirs and assigns (successors and assigns in the event that the mortgagee is a corporation).

As a practical matter, the covenant of seizin and warranty may give the mortgagee paper protection against the mortgagor, but no substantial protection in case the mortgagee depends too much upon this clause. For example, such a clause commonly reads as follows: "The mortgagor covenants that he is lawfully seized of the above described premises in fee simple, and has good right to bargain and sell the same; and that the same are free from all encumbrances whatsoever; and that he will warrant and defend said premises, with all the appurtenances thereto belonging, against all lawful claims or demands."[4] A breach of this covenant by a financially irresponsible mortgagor might result in a worthless judgment in favor of the mortgagee and against the mortgagor. Nevertheless, it is well to include this clause and then to determine the seizin part of it by an independent check of the records. If this is done, the warranty part assumes less importance. However, an occasion in which the covenant of seizin and warranty may become important arises when the mortgagor later acquires a title of which he was not seized when he executed the mortgage on the property. By his covenant he is estopped from denying the full effect of his mortgage grant as a conveyance, and the subsequently acquired title inures to the benefit of the mortgagee.

Dower is the interest in a husband's real estate given by law to the widow for support after his death. The common law counterpart of the dower right running in favor of the husband as a widower is called *curtesy*. In many states a statutory allowance from the decedent's estate is now made in lieu of dower and curtesy. The formalities of execution in this regard are governed by local law. In states following the common law tradition the dower clause should be observed if the mortgagor is married. If not, the mortgage should show his unmarried status.

Many states have taken statutory measures to simplify and clarify mortgage forms. By statute the covenants considered essential to the protection of the mortgagee are deemed to be incorporated in the instrument if it conforms to statutory requirements.

Other important clauses

As a part of the total loan agreement there are several important protective provisions for one or the other party in common use. These include:

1. Acceleration clause.
2. Subordination clause.

---

[4] *Fee simple* describes an absolute and complete title to real estate.

3. Insurance clauses.
4. Prepayment privilege.
5. Assignment of mortgage with an estoppel certificate.
6. Future advances.
7. Defeasance clause.
8. Other provisions.

Acceleration clause. Most modern mortgages contain an acceleration clause. In effect this permits the mortgagee, in case of default by the mortgagor, to declare the full amount of the obligation due and payable immediately. In other words, even though the terms of the mortgage give the mortgagor 20 years within which to amortize the principal amount of the loan, in monthly installments or otherwise, the acceleration clause in the mortgage gives the mortgagee the right to demand payment of the full amount of the debt should the mortgagor fail to meet a specified small number of payments. Although legally any default will authorize the holder to make use of the acceleration clause, this is rarely done on default in a single payment. Most holders seek to avoid foreclosure, and a forbearance of 60 to 90 days is common.

Also, it should be remembered that the acceleration clause merely represents an option available to the mortgagee. He may use it or not as he sees fit. Whether or not he exercises his rights under it usually depends upon a combination of factors, including his estimate of the amount of cushion of value left in the property to protect his lien, the circumstances which resulted in the default, the attitude and intentions of the mortgagor, the state of the real estate market, the presence and amount of junior liens, and a variety of other conditions. As a general rule, the mortgagee would prefer to help the mortgagor solve his financial problems rather than to take advantage of the first opportunity to exercise his option under an acceleration clause.

Sleeper clause. There is another type of acceleration clause, no longer in common use, that has been given the not too complimentary name of sleeper clause. This is a clause that permits acceleration at the expiration of some period of time, say, three years, even though the mortgagor is not in default. Since the average mortgagor does not read the fine print carefully, or does not grasp its significance, he is not aware of the authority of the holder to accelerate the debt and demand payment in full. Later, at a most inconvenient time, he may awake in dismay to the acceleration of the full debt when he has promptly met all of his obligations. Such a clause is outlawed by the regulations of the Federal Housing Administration and the Veterans Administration, but it may still be found in conventional loan mortgages.

Acceleration upon transfer. Still another type of acceleration clause included in some mortgages gives the mortgagee the right to declare the unpaid balance of the debt due and payable in case the mortgagor sells his property to someone not acceptable to the mortgagee. Even the FHA at one time included in one mortgage form the following clause: "If there shall be any change in the ownership of the premises covered hereby without the consent of the Grantee, the entire principal and all accrued interest shall become due and payable at the election of the Grantee, and foreclosure proceedings may be instituted thereon." The justification for such a clause is that since the mortgagee takes pains to measure the moral hazard of the borrower before he makes the loan originally, he should have the same opportunity to examine and evaluate the moral hazard of any person who assumes the mortgage.

Absence of acceleration clause.   Failure to include any acceleration clause in a mortgage means that a default occurs only in the part of the debt that is matured and unpaid. The remainder of the debt cannot be said to be in default because it is not yet due. Consequently, the mortgagee may find that he is permitted to sue only for the matured and unpaid part of the debt. This would suggest a succession of suits as additional installments of the debt fall due, if they remain unpaid. Under these circumstances an appeal to a court of equity would probably result in a decree of foreclosure and sale, subject to the unmatured part of the debt.

Some statutes come to the rescue of the mortgagee at this point, permitting him to bring foreclosure suit, involving the entire amount of the debt to date but omitting any consideration of unmatured interest. Public policy as represented in such statutes assumes that the mortgagee would rather realize his principal and accrued interest at the time of foreclosure sale than to wait until unmatured interest has accrued.

Subordination clause.   In the disposal of unimproved land, a variety of practices are followed. In one that is frequently used, the seller transfers title, taking back a purchase-money first mortgage as part payment for the land. Since such a sale is likely to be to a builder who needs a construction loan to finance the improvements which he plans to place on the land, it follows that such a loan must be given priority over the purchase-money mortgage. The well-informed subdivider is not likely to accept a second mortgage which permits just any first lien to take precedence over it. In such a case, an unscrupulous purchaser might take advantage of the seller and simply borrow money with the land as security for a first mortgage which would have priority over the purchase-money second mortgage.

The more common practice would be to make the purchase-money mortgage a first mortgage in form but include a subordination clause which agrees that it shall become a junior lien if and when a construction loan is obtained for the purpose of financing the structure to be built upon the land. As a result, the original first lien purchase-money mortgage becomes a junior lien. This the subdivision company seller willingly agrees to because it will be to its advantage in selling additional building sites to encourage all the construction possible in its locality.

Insurance clauses.   Every mortgage should (and most of them do) contain provisions for insurance of the property as protection to both mortgagor and mortgagee. The exact nature of the insurance varies with geography, the nature of the property, and the experience of the parties. Fire insurance is standard. Extended coverage is commonly used. Rent insurance and other less well-known types are not as generally needed.

Mortgage clause. The mortgage clause is commonly included as a rider in insurance policies against properties that are mortgaged. Under it, both mortgagor and mortgagee are protected, "as their respective interests may appear." This usually means that the interest of the mortgagee is taken care of first, with the remainder applicable to the interest of the mortgagor. Incidentally, the application of this division may not be as simple as it appears. Depending upon a variety of factors, including the age of the building, the neighborhood in which it is located, and the extent of the damage by fire or otherwise, the major interest of the mortgagee may be to use the proceeds of insurance to liquidate his claims. Meantime, the mortgagor may prefer to use such proceeds to repair or rebuild the damaged structure.

The mortgagee should require the mortgagor to keep the property insured (the forms of insurance should be specified, although sometimes they are left to be determined from time to time by the mortgagee) and to give the mortgagee the right to insure if the mortgagor does not, adding the cost of insurance to the claims of the mortgagee. In addition, the latter has the independent right to carry such insurance on the property as he sees fit. He is never permitted to collect more than the amount of his interest. Also, standard policies protect the rights of the mortgagee, regardless of the defenses that may be set up against the mortgagor. Even where the mortgage makes no mention of insurance, the mortgagee has the right to purchase insurance on his own account for an amount not in excess of his mortgage claims. In such case he must bear the cost of such insurance.

It is a common practice for the insurance policies to be kept by the mortgagee. By this means he is always in a better position to check on the kinds and amounts of insurance in force, whether or not the premiums have been paid, and whether the carriers are acceptable to the mortgagee according to the terms of the mortgage.

Prepayment privilege. Mortgages are expected to prescribe the manner of the payment of the debt which they secure. If this is included only in the note or bond—which may not be reproduced in the body of the mortgage—the effect is the same as if such statement were made a part of the mortgage. By mutual agreement the debt may be paid and the mortgage released at any time before the maturity date. In the absence of mortgagee consent, the debtor has no right to insist upon payment before maturity. Even though the full amount of the debt—including full interest to the date of maturity—be tendered to the mortgagee, he is not bound to accept it before the due date of the mortgage.

In recent years most mortgages, on residential properties in particular, have included prepayment clauses. Some are unqualified in character, giving the debtor the right to prepay any or all of the debt at any time. Some provide that prepayment must take place at the time any regular installment of the debt is due. Some provide limited prepayment privileges—for example, not to exceed 20 percent of the principal amount of the debt in one calendar year. Others set a preliminary period of time within which prepayment privileges may not apply. For example, it may be stipulated that no prepayment will be accepted during the first two years after the execution of the mortgage.

In some mortgages, prepayment penalties are fixed in the instrument. The mortgagee may reserve the right to extract a penalty of three months' interest in case the mortgage is redeemed within three years. Since this is an option, the mortgagee may not see fit to take advantage of it. Or the mortgage may provide that if it is redeemed from the proceeds of another mortgage to a different mortgagee, a penalty for prepayment may apply. Regardless of penalty clauses in mortgages, their use frequently depends upon competitive conditions at the time prepayment is planned.

Assignment of mortgage with an estoppel certificate.   Since a mortgage is considered to be an asset owned by its holder, it follows that he may dispose of it as he would any other asset. The person who acquires it should make sure that he succeeds to the rights of the original mortgagee. This process is known as an assignment. In the absence of an agreement to the contrary, the right of assignment does not require the consent of the mortgagor. Presumably his rights and obligations are not affected. He merely owes the assignee instead of the assignor.

In order to make sure that an agreement reached in the assignment of a mortgage states exact facts, estoppel certificates are sometimes used to prevent subsequent representations about a different set of facts. For example, if A is about to purchase from B a mortgage on property owned by C, A would be better protected if he obtained a written statement from C, showing the unpaid balance of the mortgage. Otherwise, representations made by B might be intentionally or unintentionally erroneous. Or a verbal statement by C might later be denied and C might produce evidence to show that the amount owed by him is less than A thought it was. The estoppel certificate protects the purchaser of the mortgage.

A covenant in the mortgage commonly requires the mortgagor to give the required estoppel certificate within a certain time upon proper request. This assures availability of information necessary to support the assignment.

Future advances.   Since a mortgage provides security to protect an obligation, this obligation may take the form of an executory contract as well as a debt already in existence. While it is expected that a mortgage will always state the total amount of the debt it is expected to secure, this amount may be in the nature of a forecast of total debt incurred in installments. In other words, a mortgage may cover future as well as current advances. For example, a mortgage may be so written that it will protect several successive loans under a general line of credit extended by the mortgagee to the mortgagor. In case the total amount cannot be forecasted with accuracy, at least the general nature of the advances or loans must be apparent from the wording of the mortgage.

From one of the mortgagor covenants of a mortgage form in common use, the following quotation indicates the intent of the mortgagor and the mortgagee on this subject:

> That the mortgagee or legal holder of this mortgage may make future advancements for the repair, restoration and improvement of said buildings, and that the amount of funds so advanced may be added to the then unpaid balance on said loan and bear interest as provided by the terms of the original note, and shall be secured by and subject to all of the terms of this mortgage deed.

One excellent illustration of a mortgage for future advances (sometimes called an open or open-end mortgage) takes the form of construction loans. Here the borrower arranges in advance with a mortgagee for a total amount— usually definitely stated in the mortgage—which will be advanced under the mortgage to meet the part of the costs of construction which the owner of the property does not expect to meet from his own capital funds. As the structure progresses, the mortgagor has the right to call upon the mortgagee for successive advances on the loan.

Intervening liens.   One problem that is always faced by a mortgagee when the mortgage provides for future advances has to do with the priority of intervening liens. Suppose, for example, that a construction mortgage has been duly executed and recorded, and a first advance has been made. Suppose also that before a second advance is due, a junior lien of some kind is filed against the property. If now a second advance is made under the original mortgage, does it take precedence over the intervening junior lien? Here again there is considerable confusion because of a variety of court decisions, some of which conflict with others made under similar conditions.

A general rule seems to sanction the idea that if the mortgage contract makes the future advances obligatory if stipulated conditions are met by the mortgagor, then the mortgagee may make the future advances regardless of the existence of intervening liens. This rule seems to govern even though the obligatory nature of the advances is not spelled out in the mortgage but is dependent upon a definite oral agreement. When the mortgage mentions future advances, however, junior lienors are at least on notice of the probable superior lien of the senior mortgagee. The junior lienor may still wish to pursue the subject further to try to determine if a contract for future advances actually exists.

Where there is no definite contract requiring the mortgagee to make future advances, court decisions may follow at least two paths. One leads to the conclusion that the mortgagee is protected in the priority of his future advances, even though he does not take the trouble to search the record for intervening liens. However, if he has notice outside of the record that such junior liens exist, he is bound by their priority over his future advances. This seems to be the prevailing rule. The other path leads to a different conclusion. In a minority of cases, the courts hold that before discretionary future advances are made by the mortgagee, he must search the record and be bound by any intervening liens that he finds there.

Use of the open-end mortgage is not limited to application of the newly borrowed funds to improving the mortgaged property. Increasing the lien under such a mortgage can also provide economical financing of other unusual family obligations, such as purchase of a new car, medical care, or education for the children.

What is particularly desired in an open-end mortgage is to secure future advances without running the risk of making such advances junior to intervening liens. In recent years numerous states have passed legislation pointing in this direction.

Defeasance clause.   The characteristic of a mortgage deed that, above all others, distinguishes it from an absolute conveyance is the defeasance clause. This is the clause that gives the mortgagor the right to redeem his property upon payment of his obligations to the mortgagee. A typical defeasance clause reads:

> Provided always however, that if the mortgagor shall pay unto the said mortgagee the moneys provided for in and by said note or notes and this mortgage shall well and truly keep, observe and perform, comply with and abide by each and every one of the stipulations, agreements, conditions and covenants thereof as and when required thereby, then this deed and the estate hereby created shall cease and be null and void, otherwise the same shall remain of binding force and effect.

This clause is usually made a part of the mortgage, even though it frequently takes the form of an afterthought added at the end of a document which reads quite differently. It may assume the character of a separate instrument, with no mention of it within the body of the mortgage. If a separate instrument is used for this purpose, the protection of all concerned is best served if mortgage and defeasance instrument are treated as one document, even to the extent of having them recorded at the same time.

Other provisions.   An additional covenant should define the mortgagor's obligation to pay all taxes, assessments, and water charges. In addition, the presence of a receiver clause often protects the mortgagee against losses occasioned by delays in the foreclosure process. It permits prompt court appointment of a receiver for the benefit of the mortgagee to take over the management of the property from the mortgagor in default. This action reduces the risk of loss of rents collected from the property and improper handling by the owner while the default persists. Other covenants may be included to protect the mortgagee in event of governmental intervention requiring that the property be modernized, radically modified, or demolished. Escalator clauses, providing for limited increases in interest rate at the option of the mortgagee, and variable rate mortgage provisions, tying interest rate changes to general interest rate fluctuations, are discussed as special forms of mortgages in Chapter 2.

Forms of notice

To protect the mortgage lienholder against the claims of subsequent creditors of the mortgagor, proper notice should be given of the lienholder's prior claim. This notice may take the form of:

1. Recording into a public record.
2. Some form of actual notice.
3. Mortgagee in possession.

Recording of mortgages. Public records provide opportunities for the protection of holders of estates in real property and at the same time place upon them obligations to make use of them. By recording a mortgage we simply mean having it copied by a public official into a public record kept for that purpose. Indexes and cross-indexes are used for convenience in the use of the records and are usually considered to be a part of the record. The first recording act in the United States was passed in Massachusetts Bay Colony in 1634. Other colonies soon followed the example of Massachusetts.

Records are usually kept in the county (or township in some states) where the property is located. If the property is located in more than one county, a record should be made in the proper public office in each county concerned. Before the mortgage is made a part of the record it must be "admitted to record." By this is meant that all formalities peculiar to the locality must be observed. These peculiarities attain significance for anyone who is required to search the records to discover the quality of title to a piece of real estate. Unless the searcher knows what to look for and where to find it, he may waste much time and still fail to reach his goal.

A mortgage record is expected to speak for itself. If errors appear in it, they can be corrected. If the errors result from the carelessness of the recording agents, they can be corrected without too much trouble. But if the errors appearing in the record are also in the documents recorded, changes can be made only as the result of a suit to reform the record.

Because time is of the essence in settling disputes where priorities of liens are concerned, it becomes a matter of very great importance to have the time of acceptance for record show not only the day but the exact hour and minute. It should be noted that the time that governs is not the time of spreading the mortgage upon the records. Instead it is the day, hour, and minute that shows the act of accepting the mortgage for record. This means that anyone searching the records should include in his search mortgages accepted for record but not yet recorded.

When a property is transferred from one party to another with new financing involved in the transaction, the new deed is usually filed as of one instant of time, a senior, or first, mortgage as of a couple of minutes later, and a second mortgage, if any, as still later, in order to show the proper order of claims. For purchase-money mortgages, however, the deed and the mortgage should be filed for record simultaneously. The record should show no gap between them.

Purpose of recording.   As between the mortgagor and the mortgagee, recording is usually not necessary. Recording is not essential to the validity of a mortgage unless the statutes of the state require it. For example, in Maryland a mortgage must be filed within six months of its execution or it is not a valid lien.

The act of recording creates no rights that did not exist before. But it does give notice of their existence. And it does put all other parties in a position where they are obligated to search the record or take the consequences of their negligence. In other words, a recorded mortgage protects its holder by giving him priority over the subsequent acts of the mortgagor. In general, the priority of successive liens is determined by the time of accepting them for record.

Since records are available for those entitled to make use of them, failure to take advantage of the opportunities offered may result in loss to the mortgagee. In most states junior lienors of record without notice of the existence of a senior mortgage may acquire priority of lien over an unrecorded senior mortgage. Likewise, judgments, which are statutory liens upon property that the debtor presently owns or may later acquire title to, may take precedence over unrecorded mortgages. Even subsequent recordation of an antecedent mortgage lien will not affect the order of priority.

Other forms of notice.   Since the purpose of recording a mortgage is essentially to put on notice all those having a possible interest in the property that it already has a lien against it, other forms of notice may accomplish the same purpose. This means that an unrecorded mortgage would maintain its priority over all subsequent lienors if they knew of its existence and effect. Whenever the mortgagee knows of possible complications arising from his failure to have his mortgage recorded, he can counteract this failure by letting others know about his lien.

Even though the mortgagee takes no positive action to warn others of his lien, one form of notice is usually considered adequate where it obtains. Interested parties are usually put on notice to ascertain the nature of the interest held by the party in possession of the property. The mortgagee would seldom be in possession. Since the mortgagor would usually possess the property and even occupy it, he could easily deceive others about the absence of an unrecorded mortgage, should he care to do so. In inducing another party to grant a loan with mortgage security, he might become involved in later trouble even though a much needed loan would serve a present purpose.

Discharge of debt cancels lien

Since the mortgage lien is currently considered to be merely security for an obligation, it necessarily follows that any discharge of the debt will cancel the lien of the mortgage. Whether the debt be paid in cash, by a valid check, by accumulation of rents collected by the mortgagee in possession, by the proceeds of an insurance policy, by an offset of counterclaims, or in any other lawful manner, the effect is the same. Even forgiveness of the obligation by the mortgagee or any part of it in consideration for meeting the remainder will constitute a termination of the lien. Acceptance of less than the full amount obligated will not necessarily result in a cancellation of the lien unless the mortgagee is willing voluntarily to grant a release to the mortgagor. Obviously the latter should always insist upon a release in such form that it may be used to cancel the lien of record. In exceptional cases it may be necessary for the mortgagor to resort to court action to obtain a release of the mortgage.

Canceled mortgage is dead.   A mortgage which has been canceled cannot be revived. As long as the mortgage is kept alive its lien may be extended beyond its stated maturity by agreement between the mortgagor and the mortgagee. In such case it is not necessary for the extension agreement to be spread upon the record. As long as the original mortgage remains on the record it serves notice to all that it is there to protect the unpaid claims of the mortgagee. But once the lien of the mortgage is discharged, a new instrument is required to protect new or different claims of the mortgagee.

Legal theories of mortgages

There are two general theories of the legal effect on title when a property is mortgaged. These are the title theory and the lien theory.

Title theory.   The title theory of mortgages is one of our heritages from England. Under it, the title to the land rests with the mortgagee. Those who adhere to it take the mortgage deed seriously enough to conclude that title and the right of possession actually pass from the mortgagor to the mortgagee at the time the mortgage is executed. Even if the mortgagor retains physical possession of the land, he does so at the sufferance of the mortgagee, who can dispossess the mortgagor at any time. Since the mortgagor is not admitted to own any estate in the land so long as it is mortgaged to another, he can be dispossessed by that other even without notice. Since the real owner is the mortgagee, he is obligated to observe and to be held liable for all covenants that run with the land. Under this theory, the mortgagor, by virtue of the terms of the mortgage, retains the right to revest title in himself and thereby regain the right of possession if he should meet his obligations to the mortgagee on the due day.[5]

In the United States this theory, in the states where it still prevails, has been subjected to several modifications. From the standpoint of the mortgagee, his liability to observe the covenants that run with the land has been largely abandoned. The mortgagor, meantime, has been given more protection by the provision that so long as he abides by the terms of the mortgage he cannot be dispossessed. It is only when he defaults in his obligations that possession of the land may be passed to the mortgagee.

Lien theory.   This theory developed somewhat later than the title theory. Its use has now become the prevalent one in this country. The lien theory adheres more directly than the title theory to the idea that the mortgage merely provides security to protect the obligations that are due the mortgagee. It grants neither title nor the right of possession to the mortgagee. Indeed, even after a default by the mortgagor, the latter can retain possession of the land unless he voluntarily surrenders it in accordance with the terms of the mortgage.

The exceptions to the above rule apply in those cases where a court may decree that the mortgagor shall turn possession over to a receiver, pending the completion of arrangements for a foreclosure sale of the security behind the mortgage. Since not all states recognize the need or desirability of receivers for this purpose, the mortgagor may retain possession until dispossessed as a result of the sale.

Although the difference between the two theories may be material, the results now tend to lead to the same destination. The right of the mortgagee in title-theory states to take possession of his property upon default by the mortgagor is likely to be circumscribed by terms and procedures. This is not unlike the denial of the right of possession to the mortgagee, except with consent of the owner, in lien-theory states until the ownership of the property is determined as the result of the foreclosure sale. The major significance of the legal theories relates to the mortgagee's rights to possession or rents under conditions not covered by the mortgage terms or the statute.

One cannot distinguish from the typical mortgage forms whether they are for a title-theory or a lien-theory jurisdiction. They tend to follow historic title-theory verbiage in all cases.

Equity of redemption

At common law, absolute title passed to the mortgagee if payment was not made at due date, called law day. To ease the pain of application of this rule,

---

[5] States espousing the title theory, at least in part, include Alabama, Arkansas, Connecticut, Illinois, Maine, Maryland, Massachusetts, Mississippi, New Hampshire, New Jersey, North Carolina, Ohio, Pennsylvania, Rhode Island, Tennessee, Vermont, and West Virginia.

courts of equity, whose primary function has always been to offset harsh, inadequate, or unfair applications of the common law, developed a set of equitable principles to give the mortgagor a better chance at repaying his debt and retaining his property.[6]

The result of the substitution of equity for rigid rules was an extension of time for redemption. Hence the name "equity of redemption." Early decrees for this purpose fixed the time to which the equity of redemption must conform. Only after this time extension expired and the mortgagor failed to meet his obligations did the mortgagee obtain an unqualified title. In fact, courts of equity became overzealous in recognizing the equity of redemption. This position radically limited the effectiveness of the mortgage as a security instrument until the courts developed the decree of foreclosure, whereby a forfeiture of the equity of redemption could be declared under appropriate conditions.

In this exercise of this equity of redemption, the mortgagor possesses the absolute right to recover the property mortgaged upon the payment of all obligations due the mortgagee, plus all costs and expenses incurred in connection with the foreclosure suit and sale. This right may be exercised at any time before the actual confirmation of sale. It applies regardless of the form of foreclosure action.

The mortgagee is given the right to foreclose upon a breach of contract by the mortgagor. As a reciprocal right, the mortgagor may redeem his property upon meeting his obligation. The equity of redemption constitutes an estate in the land. The mortgagor may not be estopped from exercising it; nor may he be bargained out of it except upon fair terms. By agreement, the parties at interest may extend the time for redemption. This will not affect the rights of intervening interests who also possess the right of redemption—for example, those of a junior mortgagee. Any purchaser of the equity of redemption has the same rights under it as the mortgagor.

Who share in equity of redemption.   Not only the mortgagor but others possess rights to the equity of redemption. Those who share in these rights

---

[6] The development of the courts of equity (or chancery) came along to supplement the common law courts in England, where the historical causes of action derived principally from Roman law were interpreted in a rigid and inelastic way, usually limiting remedies to money damages only. Often, special procedures—such as requirements that certain acts be performed or not be performed (injunctive processes), or that special waiting periods be accorded debtors to avoid undue harshness (equity of redemption), or that property interests be split between a legal title holder and a beneficial owner (a trust)—are necessary to accomplish appropriate ends. A system of equitable principles operates to fill this void, and the courts of equity enforce these principles by judicial decree. The jurisdiction of courts of equity extends only to areas where remedies at common law have been deemed inadequate. The U.S. courts have followed the English precedents. Many years ago separate equitable tribunals were generally abolished. Today, both legal and equitable remedies are administered by the same judge and may be granted in the same action. It is a matter of terminology that when the application of an equitable principle is adjudicated the judge is said to be sitting as a court of equity and when a legal matter is being considered he is sitting as a court of law.

include holders of dower and curtesy interests and all junior lienors. This is another reason for joining all of these interests in foreclosure suits. If they or any of them are not joined, any foreclosure decree does not affect their interests. If they are joined, they must be given their day in court. Failure to protect their interests on such occasion will result in having such interests cut off by the foreclosure decree. Since the interests of all such claimants are of the same nature as that of the mortgagor, they must be protected in the same way—pay up or lose. Any party who shares in the equity of redemption with the mortgagor may protect his interests by meeting the obligations of those whose claims are superior to his own. On occasion this can be accomplished by compromise or by agreement to keep the prior claim alive.

Statutory redemption distinguished.   The equity of redemption is a right confirmed by a court of equity. It ceases when the property is sold at foreclosure sale. In about half of the states there is, in addition, a legal right to redeem, granted mortgagors by statute, which becomes effective at the time of foreclosure sale and runs for varying periods of time thereafter. The longest period permitted is two years. Statutory redemption is a right granted to the owner having an equity of redemption before foreclosure and to all junior lienholders, including judgment creditors. Usually the law provides one period of time for the mortgagor, with a succeeding period for junior lienors. The amount required for redemption covers the sale price, interest to the date of redemption, and expenses. At the expiration of the time permitted for statutory redemption, this right too is cut off.

Meantime the purchaser has only a tentative title. He may not even receive a deed as evidence of his interest, but only a certificate of purchase. His chances of losing his title by redemption by a claimant protected by statutory redemption depend upon a combination of circumstances. Near the top of the list of such circumstances is the price he paid for the property at foreclosure sale. If he paid approximately all the property is worth, his chances of losing the property are certainly less than if he paid much less than it is worth on the open market or than it may become worth during the period when the statutory redemption is effective.

Deed of trust

By reason of the historical development of the law, in some jurisdictions real estate is commonly financed by a deed of trust instead of a regular mortgage. The parties to a loan secured by a deed of trust are three in number. The *borrower* (creator of the trust) conveys the title of the property to be used as security to *a trustee* who holds it as security for the benefit of *the holder of the note* executed by the borrower when the loan was made. The conveyance is by deed, but the transfer is accompanied by a trust agreement, either as a part of the deed or in addition to it, setting forth the terms of the security arrangement and giving the trustee a power of sale in event of default.

The deed of trust is commonly used in Alabama, Arkansas, California, Colorado, District of Columbia, Delaware, Illinois, Mississippi, Missouri, Nevada, New Mexico, Tennessee, Texas, Utah, Virginia, and West Virginia. Deeds of trust are not used extensively in other states because their courts have held that any conveyance of real estate given to secure a debt is a mortgage, irrespective of the form of the instrument used. Such an interpretation greatly restricts the trustee's power of sale, often requiring the expense and delay of a court process up to and including foreclosure. States imposing this restriction have sought to assure that a reasonable sale price and all other appropriate benefits are obtained for both borrower and note holder before the property is sold.

Where the deed of trust is used according to its terms, in case of default the trustee is authorized to foreclose the borrower's equity by a sale of the property at public auction, after proper advertisement, He must account to both parties for the proceeds of the sale. Each is entitled to his share as his interest may appear, after expenses of the sale, including compensation to the trustee, have been met. The action is normally more expeditious than where a mortgage is used.

Deed of trust and mortgage compared.   The deed of trust is such a mixture of trust and mortgage law in concept that anyone using it should act under the counsel of a local real estate lawyer. In general, however, the legal rules surrounding the creation and evidence of the debt in the form of a note, rights of the borrower left in possession, legal description of the property, creation of a valid lien on after-acquired property, and recording are the same for both mortgages and deeds of trust. Similarly, a property subject to a deed of trust may be sold subject to the deed of trust either with or without an assumption of the debt by the purchaser. The assignment of the lender's rights is similar to assignment of a mortgagee's interest except that an assignment under a deed of trust need never be recorded. The original recording of the trust deed gives notice of the lien on the real estate, and only the trustee can release this lien by an appropriate act of reconveyance. In event of failure or refusal of a trustee to execute a reconveyance when the borrower repays his debt, the trustee may be forced to act by legal process. In fact, the trustee can be removed and a successor appointed by the noteholder without recourse to court or execution of a conveyance if the trust deed provides for such action.

In California, where deeds of trust and mortgages are used side by side, several distinctions are made between the two instruments. Whereas a mortgage may be discharged by a simple acknowledgment of satisfaction on the record, a reconveyance of title is considered necessary to extinguish a deed of trust. Under a deed of trust, an assignee of a creditor cannot sell the security property because his assignor did not have the power of sale to transfer; only the trustee has this power. Where a mortgage is used, however, if it contains a power of sale, the assignee of the note can himself exercise the power of sale if he has the assignment acknowledged and recorded.

Some states do not require reconveyance to extinguish a deed of trust. Instead, the secured beneficiary of the trust (noteholder) signs a request for release of deed of trust, which is presented by the borrower to the trustee together with the canceled note and the deed of trust. The trustee issues a release of trust, which is then recorded at the appropriate office of public records for the county.

Deeds of trust are also commonly used in connection with corporate mortgages. In these cases trustees are assigned the title to property to be used as security for a group of mortgage bondholders. By qualifications and experience, professional trustees can be expected to represent a group of bondholders better than they could represent themselves individually.

Questions

1 What legal requirements must be met if a mortgage note is to be enforceable?

2 Against what property of the mortgagor may the holder of a real estate mortgage note proceed in event of default?

3 What real estate interests may be mortgaged?

4 What items should always be covered in the mortgage instrument?

5 How important is the covenant of seizin and warranty in a mortgage?

6 What purpose is served by an acceleration clause in a note?

7 What is a sleeper clause as related to accelerations provisions in a mortgage note? Is this type of clause defensible?

8 What is the purpose of each of the following:
   a. Subordination clause.
   b. Insurance clause.
   c. Prepayment clause.

9 How are estoppel certificates used?

10 What problems do subsequent lienholders create for first mortgagees holding open-end mortgages permitting future advances? What precautions may be taken to preserve the highest priority?

11 What is the effect of recording a mortgage on notice requirements to third parties?

12 What differences in the nature of the mortgage security do you find between the title-theory and lien-theory states?

13 What parties share in the equity of redemption and what rights does it give them?

14 What is the effect of a right to statutory redemption on the value of the mortgage security to the mortgagee?

15 How does a deed of trust differ from a mortgage?

Case problems

1   Smith mortgaged his real estate to Jones. Jones has not recorded the mortgage. To what extent is it valid?

2   A holds the legal title to Brownacre. B holds A's note and an unrecorded mortgage on Brownacre. Under his mortgage rights, B has gained possession of Brownacre upon default in payments due on the note. A assigns his title to C, who lives in another state and has never seen the land. What are C's rights?

3   Black borrowed from Green and gave him a note and mortgage on his office building. As further security, Black then executed a deed conveying title to the building to Green and delivered it to the First National Bank to be held in escrow with instructions for delivery to Green in case Black should default in his mortgage payments. Black defaulted, and the deed was delivered to Green. Black then sought to cure his default on the basis of his rights under the equity of redemption. May he do so?

4   *a.*   Sedgewick arranged for an open-end mortgage loan from the Second National Bank in amounts up to $50,000. The loan was closed, and Sedgewick drew down $30,000 initially. Three months later he drew the remaining $20,000. What is the position of the bank with regard to the possibility of intervening liens?

    b.   Assume there was no definite agreement for future advances between Sedgewick and the bank at the time the initial $30,000 loan was closed. Would your answer be different?

Kinds and special forms of mortgages

2

Three kinds of mortgages

There are essentially three kinds of mortgages in common use:

1. Those between individuals that take the legal form.
2. Equitable mortgages that are treated similarly to legal mortgages by judicial construction, although they take the form of different documentation.
3. Collective mortgages.

First, when the term *mortgage* is used, it is generally assumed that it means the kind of financial instrument discussed in the preceding chapter. As such it is presumed to constitute the first private lien against the real estate which is used to secure it. Generally, only certain public claims, such as real estate tax and assessment liens, take precedence over first or prior lien mortgages. Mortgages are often classified by their special characteristics. Several of these types of mortgages will be identified in this chapter.

Second, there are equitable mortgages, frequently given too little attention even by those whose business interests involve first mortgages. For this reason they are defined herein with some care.

Third, what may be classed as "collective" mortgages are commonly known as mortgage bonds. They are collective in the sense that instead of a single mortgagee there may be many beneficial owners of one mortgage. The nature of such bonds is discussed briefly in this chapter.

Identifying characteristics of legal form mortgages

As previously stated, it is common practice to identify mortgages by their significant provisions or characteristics. Important among these characteristics are repayment patterns, interest rate provisions, or type of security provided.

Repayment patterns. The most basic distinction between loan repayment patterns is that between straight term and amortized loans. Under the term loan, only interest payments are made prior to the terminal date of the loan. The entire principal of the loan is payable at the note maturity date. Where a loan is amortized, periodic payments including some reduction of principal along with interest due are made over the life of the loan. The effective borrowing costs under these repayment patterns are discussed in Chapter 7.

Straight term mortgages. Prior to the Great Depression of the early 1930s, most mortgages were for a straight term. They were usually of short duration, three to five years, often rolled over into a new mortgage of similar terms. Lenders were not yet aware of the implications of an illiquid, unamortized debt. That awareness came with the epidemic of insolvencies of mortgage lending institutions during that depression when panic-stricken savers withdrew their funds from savings accounts on a massive scale. The federal government, through its assistance programs of the 1930s and thereafter, was an instrumental force in promoting general acceptance of the amortized mortgage.

Amortized mortgages. Most mortgage loans today are set up to pay off the principal debt fully along with interest by periodic payments (usually monthly) over the life of the loan. In this way the lender enjoys the benefit of a constantly improving loan-to-value ratio in his security, since the property probably will not decline in value as rapidly as the amount owed on the loan is reduced. At the same time, the borrower is building his ownership interest in the property and gradually eliminating the danger of being unable to cope with the debt incurred to finance the property.

Partially amortized mortgages. Where a mortgage is only partially paid off during the contractual period of the loan, an unusually large sum, called a balloon payment, is due at maturity. Partially amortized loans were authorized for national banks in 1935 and have been used commonly since that time in situations where refinancing of the unamortized debt is contemplated at the end of the original loan period.

Recent high interest rates have pressed borrowers beyond their capacity to amortize a loan over, say, 15 to 20 years. This may be the maximum period for which the lender will be willing to set his loan. The lender, however, may be willing to accept a monthly payment to include the interest plus an amortization amount based on a 30-year maturity. He may then provide that the note becomes due and payable in the amount of the unpaid balance at the end of 15 years. Thus, the borrower has substantially lower amortization payments over the 15 years, but he is faced with a substantial balloon payment at the end of the 15th year. He hopes, of course, that he can refinance under satisfactory terms, but there is a chance that he cannot.

Graduated payment mortgages. One of several recent innovations in home financing is the graduated payment mortgage (GPM). Approved in 1978 by the Federal Home Loan Bank Board for its constitutent federally insured savings and loan associations and mutual savings banks, this mortgage payment plan is designed primarily for young people with increasing income expectations. It provides for relatively low monthly payments during the first few years, with higher payments later when the earning power of the borrower is expected to be greater.

A conventional $50,000 30-year loan at 10 percent, for example, costs $439.00 a month. Under a popular GPM plan insured by the Federal Housing Administration, monthly payments begin at $333.52, increase each year an average of about $28.00, level off in the sixth year at $478.81 a month, and remain there for the rest of the mortgage life. Although the delay in principal reduction causes the interest costs of the GPM to exceed those for conventional borrowing over the life of the loan, the lower monthly payments in the earlier years may make feasible a home purchase the otherwise would be out of the question. Effective borrowing costs under GPM plans are discussed in detail in Chapter 9.

Flexible loan insurance program mortgages. An extension of the GPM is the flexible loan insurance program (FLIP). Under this type of GPM, part of the borrower's down payment goes into an interest-bearing savings account. The interest and principal from that account is drawn on to make up the difference between the reduced monthly payment and the payment level required under a conventional payment program. Federal savings and loan associations, as well as numerous other institutions, have been authorized to make FLIP loans, and application of the concept is spreading.

Under a current plan, on a $50,000 FLIP loan for 30 years at 10 percent with a $10,000 down payment (one half placed in the savings account to defray part of loan payments), the actual monthly payments would start at $290.86 the first year and, after increasing by steps through five years, would level off at $438.79 in the sixth year. GPM financing has been touted as a great assist to first-time home buyers. More recently, however, with house prices skyrocketing, second- and third-time buyers have been finding the easier payment schedules extremely attractive.

Renegotiable rate mortgages. An additional alternative, called the renegotiable rate, or rollover, mortgage, has recently come into use. Under this arrangement the amortization period of the loan is long term, often 30 years, but the maturity of the note will be in 3 to 5 years. When the note matures, the interest rate is renegotiable on the basis of prevailing interest rates at that time or of an acceptable index of money costs. In-depth analysis of this alternative is presented in Chapter 9.

Shared-appreciation mortgages. High interest rates have spawned a new arrangement of considerable promise called a shared-appreciation mortgage.

The lender agrees to lower the interest rate by as much as 40 percent (thus, for example, 14 percent becomes 8.5 percent) in exchange for the same proportion of market appreciation in the mortgaged house, payable when the house is sold. In case the house is not sold and the appreciation realized within 10 years, by some agreements, the homeowner must have the property appraised and pay the lender his share of the market gain at that time. Although home buyers may be reluctant to share home owner-ship gains with their lender, they must realize that on their own they would not have been able to buy as large a home, if any at all, and that the additional gains have been made possible because of the lender's funds advanced at a sacrificial rate of interest.

Reverse annuity mortgages. As an additional financing option for retired persons, the Federal Home Loan Bank Board has endorsed the reverse annuity mortgage (*RAM*). Under this plan, older borrowers with spare equity in their homes may increase their mortgage and use the additional loan proceeds to buy a lifetime annuity from an insurance company. After loan interest is deducted automatically and sent to the lending institution, the remainder is paid to the borrower to provide additional income. The loan is repaid from the sale of the house at the borrower's death.

This plan is presently in a tentative stage. One version of the reverse mortgage that has been written does not carry an insurance element allowing the borrower to remain in his home as long as he lives. In such a case, he could use up the proceeds of his increased loan, find he could not afford the bigger payments, and suffer having his home sold away from him while he is still in need of it. Obviously, the plan is more appealing when inflation rates are at their highest, but most retirees are ill equipped to embark on speculative ventures, especially involving the provision of their future shelter. Cost and benefit considerations of *RAM* financing are considered in detail in Chapter 9.

Budget mortgage. Another concession to the need to tailor monthly mortgage payments to the debt-paying capacity of the mortgagor is the budget mortgage. The connotation of this term is that the monthly payment made to the lender includes sufficient amounts, in addition to principal amortization and interest, to meet premium payments for required insurance coverage and real estate taxes. The stability of the required payment covering these principal housing expenditures tends to normalize the borrower's budget. By the same token, the lender has the use of the funds held in escrow as they build up to meet the periodic payments to the insurer and the taxing authorities. In some instances, payment schedules may be adjusted for seasonality of income flow or some predictable irregularity in the debt-paying ability of the borrower that might throw the mortgage into default if not taken into account.

Interest rate provisions. Mortgages may be identified by the manner in which the interest on the note is calculated as well as by repayment pattern. In fact, the latter is usually affected by the way the interest is charged.

There are three principal ways in which the interest rate is stated. It may be as (1) a straight rate, (2) a straight rate with an escalator clause, or (3) a variable rate. Additional benefits paid to mortgage lenders on income-producing property may take the form of equity participations, or "kickers." These are discussed in Chapters 11 and 12.

Straight interest rate. Historically, it has been common practice for the mortgagee to commit its loan to a fixed rate of interest calculated without change on the unpaid principal balance owed over the life of the loan. This is the rate with which nearly everyone is familiar, stated as the *nominal* or *contractual* rate in the mortgage note or bond.

With the increased volatility of interest rates, institutional lenders have found it necessary to pay higher amounts to savers to induce them to place or leave their savings on deposit to fund outstanding mortgage loans. Hence, interest escalator clauses and variable rate mortgage plans (particularly in California) have come into use.

Escalator clause. An interest escalator clause gives the mortgagee, at his option, the right to raise the interest rate on the loan at any time after a specified interval, or upon the happening of a certain condition, regardless of the debt-paying experience of the mortgagor. This clause is not designed to give the borrower a right to a rate reduction in event interest rates decline or conditions otherwise become more difficult for him to make his payments. It is a one-way street.

One of the paradoxes of real estate finance is the use of the escalator clause against mortgagors in default. For example, the mortgage may be written to provide for 10 percent interest but with a proviso that in case of default in two successive installment payments, the rate shall be increased, at the option of the mortgagee, to 11 percent. While it is recognized that this is a penalty clause to prevent default, nevertheless it seems a bit odd to tell the mortgagor, "If you can't pay 10 percent we shall charge you 11 percent."

The opposite policy is sometimes written into a mortgage in order to reach the same goal as does the escalator clause. The mortgage may be written at a rate of 11 percent. Then the borrower is told, "So long as you make regular payments without default, we will charge you only 10 percent. In other words, we will allow you a bonus of 1 percent for living up to your contract." Or this kind of clause may provide in addition that while the mortgagee reserves the right to charge the contract rate of 11 percent at some future time, he will not make the change during the first two (or three) years and then only after notice of the change of 30 to 90 days. The psychological effect upon the borrower of starting with a bonus which may later be eliminated, instead of assessing a penalty, seems to favor the substitute plan.

Variable rate mortgage plans. When the mortgage interest rate may be raised or lowered over the life of the loan in accord with the variation of some other financial rate, the borrower has what is known as a variable interest rate mortgage. Commonly used reference series are the Federal Reserve discount rate, the prime rate for bank borrowers, the Federal Home Loan Bank Board series of effective mortgage rates, a bond rate, or some other indicator of current money costs. In California, where the variable rate mortgage is commonly used, the Federal Home Loan Bank Board of San Francisco prepares a weighted average of the cost of funds (principally savings and borrowed money) of the savings and loan associations in its district. This index is released semiannually at the end of June and December. To protect against extremes in interest rate fluctuation, upper and lower limits are also often established by the rate variation formula.

From the lender's point of view, variable rate mortgages add considerable attractiveness to long-term lending at times of rapid shifts in capital market money rates. By this plan, the mortgage achieves increased flexibility in portfolio earnings. Furthermore, with interest rates subject to adjustment the mortgage more nearly retains its par value in the secondary market in times of rising money costs.

Along with these advantages, the lender must accept certain drawbacks. The flexible interest rate injects an element of uncertainty into cash flow projections that affect the valuation process and marketability of the mortgage. If the mortgage interest rate is changed, it should be clear whether the monthly debt-service payments will be raised or lowered without changing the maturity date, or the monthly payments held constant and the maturity date altered. A second problem for the lender created by variable interest rates arises out of increased uncertainty of gross earnings on his loan portfolio. In a period of declining interest rates, coverage of dividends or interest costs on savings accounts or time deposits may be jeopardized. There are also obvious problems in loan servicing and customer relations associated with every change in rate.

So long as both fixed and variable rate options are open, the borrower will avoid variable plans in periods of low interest rates and surplus available funds, but will seek them out when the opposite condition of high interest rates and tight money exists. The lender will move in the opposite direction. The only way to avoid this counteractive expression of preferences would be for variable mortgage plans to become universally adopted to the exclusion of fixed rate plans.

There are many unanswered questions concerning the social impact of the variable rate mortgage. To what extent will it attract new money sources to finance real estate? How will it fare in an inflationary economy? Will the borrower ultimately be better or worse off under a variable rate mortgage? For the most part, only experience will provide us with answers.[1]

Security characteristics.   Mortgages may be referred to in terms of their security characteristics. These references are used to identify such instruments as (1) the purchase-money mortgage, (2) the package mortgage, (3) the blanket mortgage, and (4) the junior mortgages.

---

[1] For an insightful article on the variable rate mortgage, see James H. Boykin and John S. Philips, "The New Challenger: The Variable-Rate Mortgage," *Real Estate Review,* Summer 1978, pp. 83–87.

Purchase-money mortgage. The most logical source of credit for a real property buyer is often the seller. If the seller is willing to take back a credit instrument as part of the purchase price, in most states he has the advantage of a lien of especially high priority. Any mortgage given by a buyer to secure payment of all or part of the purchase price of land is called a purchase-money mortgage. As such it must be differentiated from mortgages given to secure a loan from a third party for the purchase of land. If it is executed and recorded simultaneously with the deed which conveys title to the property, it takes precedence over judgments, other mortgages, liens, and all other debts of the mortgagor. If the mortgagor should anticipate a purchase of land by placing a mortgage against it before the deed and purchase-money mortgage are executed, the latter would take precedence over the former even though the former were made a matter of record first. The recorded mortgage could have no effect until the mortgagor obtained title to the land. By the time he did so, it would be encumbered by the purchase-money mortgage.

Purchase-money mortgages retain their priority even when written in the name of a third party at the request of the vendor of the real estate. This third person may even provide the funds with which to purchase the property. For the protection of the mortgagee, it is well to state in the mortgage that the mortgage is accepted as a part of the purchase price of the property. A purchase-money mortgage can represent either a senior or a junior lien against the property used as security.

Package mortgage. The growing popularity of practices of selling in one package not only the land and the structure erected thereupon but all the fixtures needed for full enjoyment makes necessary a reexamination of what is meant by "fixtures." Tradition has included in the meaning of this term three concepts, each of which is capable of flexibility of definition: (1) A fixture must be annexed to and made a part of the real estate. (2) It must be appropriate to the part of the real estate to which it is attached. (3) It must be intended by the party making the annexation that it shall become and remain a part of the real estate. All that remains is to determine the meaning of *annexation, appropriate,* and *intention.*

Under the package mortgage concept, both the borrower and the lender sanction the financing of many items of personal property, such as ranges, refrigerators, cooling and ventilating systems, automatic washers and dryers, and garbage disposal units for homes and motels, as a part of the realty. Similarly, personal property particularly adapted to the use of commercial and industrial buildings may be covered under the real estate mortgage.

The added items are annexed to the security for the real estate mortgage by enumerating, immediately following the land description in the mortgage, the things that are sought to be included, but about which there may be some doubt as to legal coverage. This enumeration is then followed by a declaration that such articles "are and shall be deemed to be fixtures" and are to be considered in all respects as a part of the real estate which serves as security for the mortgage.

In event there is some doubt that the recitals will adequately incorporate the personal property as security under a real estate mortgage, it may be possible to protect the lender by filing a copy of the mortgage at the appropriate office of public record for security instruments protected by personal property, as well as at the recorder's office for real estate mortgages. Legal counsel is helpful at this point.

At least six arguments are advanced in favor of the use of package mortgages. From the purely financing point of view, the arguments in favor of packaged mortgages are: (1) The borrower deals with one lender only. He need not worry about a variety of monthly payments to cover parts of the same property. (2) Payments for the equipment are distributed over a longer repayment period. Instead of allowing a few months or, at most, a few years for purchasing the equipment, this financing covers essentially the same period of time as the financing of the main property. (3) The interest rate on the mortgage loan, which in this case covers equipment also, is always lower than the carrying charges on installment sales. (4) The payments may be made uniform throughout the life of the loan. As an alternative, where several items of equipment are purchased on the installment plan, the monthly payments required will be very heavy for several months or a few years. In some cases a middle position is agreed upon with the monthly payments on the package mortgage somewhat larger for the first ten years of the mortgage term. Even then they would be less than under installment purchases. (5) Since the cost of the equipment is merged with the cost of the real estate, the amount of the down payment attributable to equipment alone is less than if the equipment were purchased separately. (6) The mortgagee can better control the total amount of monthly payments by the mortgagor.

Blanket mortgage. As the name suggests, a blanket mortgage covers several pieces of real estate as security. Several sets of circumstances give rise to its use. Subdividers sometimes give a blanket mortgage as part payment for acreage. As each lot is sold, it is released from this mortgage by agreement with the mortgagee according to a schedule of release credits. Normally the amount of cash required to be paid to the mortgagee would be considerably more than the ratio of the number of lots to the amount of the mortgage. For example, if 500 lots are covered by a $1,000,000 mortgage, it might require a payment of $4,000 instead of $2,000 to obtain a release of one lot from the mortgage. Blanket mortgages in connection with land development loans are considered in specific detail in Chapter 12.

Sometimes an owner of various pieces of real estate needs to borrow more than any one property can produce by the use of a mortgage. Several properties are included as security for a blanket mortgage. As lump-sum payments, agreed upon in advance or at the time of payments, are made on the unpaid balance of the debt, one by one the properties are released from the mortgage.

A third practice commonly used by some mortgagees follows a pattern like this: A wishes to purchase B's unencumbered property for $80,000. A hopes to dispose of his own property, presently mortgaged for $20,000 and priced at

$60,000. Instead of making sure of the sale of his own property first, he contracts to buy B's property, putting up $20,000 in cash and offering both properties as security for a blanket loan of $80,000. The new mortgagee pays off the mortgage on A's property and has a first lien on both. The proceeds from the sale of A's property are applied to the blanket mortgage, securing a release of A's property so that it may be sold to C. The remainder of the debt is then owed by A against the property formerly owned by B as security.

Still another use of the blanket mortgage enables an individual to refinance mortgaged properties in which he has a substantial enough equity to support additional borrowing, to provide a down payment for the purchase of an additional property. For example, suppose an apartment owner has Green Building worth $150,000 with a mortgage of $60,000 and Gray Building worth $200,000 with a mortgage of $100,000. He wishes to buy Red Building for $240,000 and to raise his down payment by refinancing Green and Gray properties. His lender will take a blanket mortgage for $400,000 on all three properties. If other terms are satisfactory, the owner can use the combined borrowing power to pay off the $60,000 and $100,000 individual mortgages and provide the total funds requirement for the purchase of Red Building.

Corporate mortgages are frequently of a blanket character. In addition to specific property named in the mortgage as security, arrangements such as "after-acquired" property clauses and "general" mortgages carry the blanket connotation.

Junior mortgages.   In simple real estate financing transactions, such as those involving single residences, the character of the mortgage structure is easily defined. The senior or prior mortgage is usually called a first mortgage. All others are given the class name of junior mortgages. In any particular situation, there may be one or more junior mortgages or none at all. One junior lien, usually called a second mortgage, is sometimes used to bridge the gap between the price of the property and the sum of the first mortgage and the amount of money available to the purchaser to use as a down payment.

Traditionally, second mortgages are short term and carry a higher rate of interest than first mortgages. They frequently cause trouble for mortgagors who are unable to pay them off at their early maturity date. Such mortgagors are then at the mercy of the holder of such paper, who may consent to renew the mortgage for another short term in consideration for the payment of a stiff renewal fee. While the mortgagor is struggling to reduce his first mortgage balance, he is faced with successive heavy renewal charges and high interest rates for junior mortgages.

In other cases, second mortgages may run for somewhat longer periods of time—perhaps as long as five years. Since there is no "business" of second mortgage lending that is organized into financial institutions, the pattern of lending depends in every case upon local conditions and the demands of those individuals who are willing to take the risks that accompany this type of lending. Where second mortgages represent the advance of money needed to bridge the gap between the amount of the purchase price of the property and the sum of the amount of equity funds of the purchaser and the amount available on a first mortgage, the mortgagee who advances the money and takes a second mortgage as security is likely to be an experienced, shrewd person who takes pains to protect his own interests. At the same time he does make possible the purchase of property that would otherwise not be placed at the disposal of a purchaser who cannot finance the purchase otherwise. If, on the other hand, the second mortgage is a purchase-money mortgage needed to enable the seller to dispose of property that he might otherwise be required to hold longer than he wishes, the terms of the second mortgage may be somewhat more to the liking of the purchaser.

The second mortgage reads like a first mortgage, except that it is expected to make reference to and accept the priority of the first mortgage. Unless the mortgagor is careful in writing the second mortgage, he may elevate the priority of the second mortgage to that of a senior lien upon the event of redemption of the first mortgage.

The best way for the mortgagor to protect himself against this contingency is to include in the second mortgage instrument a waiver clause committing the holder of the second mortgage to waive its priority, not only over an existing first mortgage but over any succeeding first mortgage written for an amount not in excess of the amount of the existing first mortgage. This is commonly known as the lifting clause, since it permits the mortgagor to lift the first mortgage and replace it with another one without disturbing the junior status of the second mortgage. For the protection of the holder of the latter, the lifting clause should contain the limitation that the new first mortgage shall not be for a greater amount than the one it replaces, carried at the time the second mortgage was executed.

Other junior liens, subsequent in priority to second mortgages, are sometimes used. For example, suppose that a contractor purchases a building site, financing it through a first mortgage containing a waiver clause in favor of a construction mortgage. With the execution of the latter, the earlier first mortgage becomes a second mortgage. Suppose that the sum of these two is $50,000. Suppose also that a purchaser of the property at $70,000 has only $10,000 for a down payment. The contractor may see fit to accept the $10,000 in cash, take back a purchase-money third mortgage for $10,000, and sell the property to the purchaser who assumes the first and second mortgages. That means a pretty heavy load of junior mortgage financing for the purchaser to carry.

Two topics pertaining to discounts are also considered here: (1) junior mortgage discounts and (2) different use of discounts.

1. Junior mortgage discounts. Because of the greater risks accepted by those who hold junior mortgages, it is expected that they shall bear rates of interest commensurate with the nature of the risks assumed. Laws against usury, if applied strictly, would interfere with some of the practices surround-

ing the use of the junior mortgages. These laws are frequently circumvented by discount operations. For example, suppose that a single residence valued at $50,000 carries a first mortgage of $35,000. Suppose also that a prospective purchaser has only $10,000 available as a down payment. In order for the vendor to realize the additional $5,000 required to complete the price of $50,000, it may be necessary for him to take a second mortgage for $5,500 or even $6,000. He will then hope to sell this second mortgage for at least $5,000. The discount enjoyed by the purchaser will enhance the effective interest rate which he realizes on his investment.

This does not mean that two prices will be quoted for the property, one for cash and the other involving a second mortgage. As a matter of fact, if the seller hopes to realize $50,000 from the sale, he will probably ask more. He will then consider offers submitted upon the basis of financing arrangements, among other considerations. While the purchaser of such a property may not realize it, he will probably pay several hundred dollars more for it if a second mortgage is used as a part of the purchase price.

2. Different use of discount. Sometimes discounts on junior mortgages are used in a way different from that mentioned above. Suppose that A sells his property to B, reluctantly taking back a purchase-money junior mortgage for $5,000. Suppose that B is not financially responsible and has difficulty in keeping up his payments. Since he is unable to meet the mortgage principal at its maturity date, it is informally extended. In other words, A does not press for payment for fear that he will have the property back on his hands when he has no use for it any longer.

Along comes C, who is willing to take over the property from B and to assume the first mortgage, provided that something can be done to reduce the second mortgage. A might be very glad to discount the mortgage 50 percent in order to get $2,500 cash and to be relieved of the worry of trying to make occasional collections from B. Or if C is a shrewd bargainer and is known to meet his financial obligations promptly and without fail, A might even be talked into canceling $2,500 of his second mortgage in return for the assumption of the other $2,500 by C.

Equitable mortgages

In addition to regular mortgages which are readily identifiable as such, common practice sanctions the use of a variety of financial arrangements which are really mortgages even though they carry some other label. These are called equitable mortgages. A few examples will suffice to indicate possibilities in this direction.

Absolute conveyance of title. What appears to be an outright conveyance of title to a property by the use of a deed may be construed to be a mortgage if the parties to the deed intended it to be merely security for a debt. Even though no written evidence of the debt exists, oral evidence, if it be clear, convincing, and unequivocal, will be sufficient to determine the true character of the transaction. Even presumedly innocent purchasers of the property in question may not rely solely upon the record of sale rather than the mortgage against the property if they have notice of the facts. This apparent transfer of title is usually construed to be an equitable mortgage instead.

Likewise, a sale of property with an option to repurchase may be construed to be an equitable mortgage. If it is a bona fide sale, the option must be exercised according to the terms of the option, including its date of expiration. Otherwise, the rights of the seller to repurchase cease to exist. On the other hand, if the option to repurchase can be held to be a mortgage in fact if not in form, the seller can exercise the option any time before foreclosure sale becomes effective. Generally this is the case when the seller has an option to buy the property back at a purely nominal value or for an amount substantially less than market value. In case of doubt, a court may construe the sale as a mortgage.

A third example is provided by the circumstances which result in an advance of funds to purchase property which is to become the security for a regular mortgage. While this is not a common practice, it occurs occasionally. For some reason it may not be feasible for the cancellation of one mortgage to take place simultaneously with the placing of a new one. Hence a friend of the purchaser may advance the money, knowing that his loan will soon be secured by a regular mortgage, the terms of which have no doubt been subject to previous discussion and agreement. Until this regular mortgage becomes effective, the creditor has an equitable mortgage against the property.

Vendor's lien. Another form of equitable mortgage is the vendor's (or grantor's) lien. When a trusting vendor transfers title to property in return for only part of the payment agreed upon, the property in question is considered to be an implied security for the payment of the remainder of the purchase price. At best, this is an unsatisfactory method of transferring title, since an innocent third party who may not know of the unpaid balance, if it does not show on the record, may acquire title to the property free of the vendor's lien.

For his own protection the vendor may do one of two things: (1) He may take back a purchase-money mortgage even though it is to remain in effect only a short time. (2) He may recite in the deed that there is an unpaid remainder which the vendor proposes to protect. Such a recital will be notice to all of the presence of an equitable mortgage. The purchase-money mortgage and, where recognized by statute at least, the second form of protection will give the vendor priority over both dower interests and judgment liens.

Vendee's lien. Whenever a purchaser of real estate advances any part of the purchase money before he receives title to the property, he does so on his faith in the integrity of the seller. Should the seller or vendor violate this confidence and fail to convey title according to the terms of the sale contract, the vendee would have an equitable mortgage against the property. The right is enforceable in equity in the same manner that vendors' liens are enforceable.

This situation may arise when a purchaser of real estate signs a preliminary contract and shows his good faith by the tender of a binder check for a part of the purchase price. In case the vendor keeps the binder payment but fails to consummate the deal according to its terms, the vendee will have an equitable mortgage claim against the property.

Land contracts upon which payments have been made may also be construed to be in the nature of equitable mortgages. This is commonly the case where the buyer has built up a substantial equity in the purchased property and the contractual terms brought to bear in event of his default would result in unduly harsh treatment. These contracts are discussed further in Chapter 5.

Debts of decedent.   Debts of a decedent constitute a lien against whatever property he may possess at the time of his death. These are again in the nature of equitable mortgages. They follow the property, but the purchaser of such property is not bound to assume personal responsibility for their payment if he does not care to do so. He may be asked to assume them as a part of the bargain when the purchase of the property is arranged. The purchaser usually cannot claim that he did not have notice of such debts, since the records of the estate will be a necessary part of public records which should be searched before purchase is consummated. Difficulties may arise, however, where additional estate tax assessments are made by governmental authorities upon audit of tax returns long after the property has passed to a new purchaser. The purchaser's examination of the records of the estate should take contingent liabilities fully into account.

Priority of equitable mortgage.   Depending upon the circumstances in each particular case, an equitable mortgage may or may not enjoy high priority. Liens of record at the time an equitable mortgage is established would normally take precedence. Generally speaking however, an equitable mortgage will enjoy priority over unsecured creditors. Vendors' liens and long-term land contracts are now commonly accepted for record.

Collective mortgages—real estate bonds

In following this discussion of real estate bonds, the reader should not be confused by the subject of notes or bonds which evidence the primary form of obligation behind a real estate mortgage. As pointed out earlier in this text, the mortgagor is expected to execute a promissory note which is sometimes called a bond. Then he pledges the real estate as security to ensure the payment of his note. When we speak of real estate bonds at this time, we have quite a different meaning in mind. Real estate bonds constitute a series of notes. For example, if the amount to be borrowed is $500,000, instead of issuing one note for that amount the mortgagor, through the use of a deed of trust, will perhaps mortgage the property to a trustee. Against this are issued perhaps 300 bonds each carrying a face value of $500 and 350 bonds each carrying a face value of

$1,000. Bonds of less than $500 have been used occasionally but are not very popular because of the high cost of floating them. The costs of engraving, accounting, and so on, are as much for a $100 bond as for a $1,000 bond. By the use of bonds a broad market for participation in real estate financing is tapped.

Students of corporation finance will recognize that corporate bonds issued for whatever purpose are commonly secured by a mortgage on corporate real estate and equipment. The characteristics of mortgage bonds described herein are generally applicable to such bonds. Of particular concern to students of real estate, however, are bonds used in real estate finance, or real estate bonds.

The use of real estate bonds has had an interesting history. In the early days of financing even larger properties, dependence rested almost entirely upon single mortgages. Then a recognition of a sizable market for participation in this type of financing among small investors resulted in the development of real estate bonds. During the decade of the 1920s in particular, this form of financing was very popular. Indeed, it was so popular that it overreached itself and many investors lost heavily on purchases of real estate bonds. The common use of leasehold bonds, whose exact character was not generally understood by those who bought them, added to the losses when the dark days of the 1930 depression brought with them wholesale defaults of such bond issues.

The popularity lost by real estate bonds in the 1930s did not recover until the late 1960s and early 1970s. Several factors account for this. One is undoubtedly the recollections of those who lost heavily on their purchase. Another is the decline of demand for new money for this type of real estate mortgage financing. Relatively few new office and hotel/motel buildings were constructed between the early 1930s and the late 1950s. It was not until the early 1960s that the construction of such properties took a substantial upturn. During the early years of the resurgence, particularly, financing for construction of this type was mainly provided by mortgages privately placed with large institutional investors, especially insurance companies. At that time, the participation of the small investor in such a venture was likely to be limited to subordinated debentures.[2] In the late 1960s, however, real estate investment trusts specializing in mortgage portfolios became a significant factor in construction loan financing.[3] A number of these trusts utilized bonds secured by mortgages to varying degrees, many as debentures looking to the mortgage asset base for credit support, as a basic part of their capital structure. Such bonds were often issued with privileges of convertibility into equity shares or

---

[2] Subordinated debentures are unsecured bonds that rank behind senior debt with respect to claims to assets. They are thus similar to ownership capital. They are different, however, in that the interest paid on them is deductible for income tax purposes while dividends or other returns to equity capital investors are not. Furthermore, the debentures can be paid back, or retired, without the tax implications attendant upon withdrawal of capital funds.

[3] See further treatment of real estate investment trusts, Chapter 21.

with warrants attached. By 1975 the real estate bond investor's experience had come full cycle. In the rigors of a deep recession, with wholesale defaults on mortgages in the real estate investment trust portfolios, the trusts stood hard-pressed to meet their obligations to their short-term creditors and over the longer term the bond obligations became risky.

In more recent years, the whole real estate investment trust industry has suffered upheaval, with many trusts going through reorganization or bankruptcy. The bonds of these trusts have fared according to their priorities and, again, have not proven to be a good investment.

Municipal bonds in real estate finance. In one area, in particular, real estate bonds have become increasingly important. They are a valuable tool for the government-assisted financing of residential housing. These bonds are backed by the credit of the issuing or guaranteeing government agency and do not rely on mortgage security for their ultimate safety.

There are two major programs now active. Since 1937, bonds have been used as a form of direct government support to local public housing authorities. In addition, recently, the U.S. Housing and Community Development Act of 1974 authorized issuance of municipal bonds to finance housing projects supported by a qualified (Section 8) subsidy from the Department of Housing and Urban Development (HUD). It has been estimated that bonds issued under the 1974 authority may have totaled in excess of $2 billion for 1979, for the benefit of 300 to 400 municipalities. The legal bases and limitations of these bonds will be discussed in detail in Chapter 23.

In summary, the interest received on municipal bonds is exempt from federal income tax and possible state income tax as well. The term *municipal* extends to state and other local governmental agencies for income tax purposes. This exemption allows these bonds to be marketed at a lower contract interest rate because the investor can keep all of the interest net of tax. The bond proceeds may, therefore, be loaned by an intermediary of the municipal agency to qualified residents, usually elderly or low- to moderate-income home buyers, at a preferential interest rate. For example, the city of Denver sold $50 million of bonds whose proceeds were loaned to home buyers by a participating savings and loan association at a rate about three percentage points lower than conventional (nonsubsidized) loans.

Offsetting the enthusiasm of those home buyers who are fortunate enough to receive the subsidized mortgages is the criticism that a host of such bond offerings may flood the municipal market and render impossible the financing of projects more traditionally considered appropriate for these funds, such as airports or fire stations. Savings institutions that have not participated with the bond-issuing agency have felt that they are victims of unfair competition. Some critics assert that the income limits for loan applicants are too high; for example, $40,000 in Chicago and no limits at all in Duarte, California, and Milwaukee where areas are being revitalized. Others urge that the effect is to drive home prices even higher.

Parties to the bond issue.   As in all other bond issues, usually three parties are concerned; the issuing corporation or agency, the trustee, and the bondholder. Their rights and responsibilities are established by the contractual provisions contained in the *bond certificate* and the *trust indenture*, also known as the *deed of trust.* Although separate instruments, the bond certificate and the trust indenture are treated as one, and are mutually incorporated by reference.

The bond certificate.   The bondholder receives as evidence of his claim a certificate specifying the primary requirements governing the repayment of the principal debt and interest thereon. Subjects covered may include (1) the amount of the bond and of the total bond issue presently for sale and reserved for future offer; (2) maturity date and interest rate; (3) option to redeem outstanding bonds, with dates and call premiums; (4) call dates and premiums for sinking-fund purposes; (5) conditions for making changes in indenture, and vote of bondholders needed to sanction such changes; (6) negotiability and registration of individual bonds; (7) acceleration in case of default; (8) immunity of shareholders from personal liability on the bonds; and (9) corporate seal and signatures of officers. Then follows the form of coupon attached to the bond, the form of the trustee's authentication, and the form of registration of the bonds.

The bond certificate also serves as evidence of the right of its holder to participate in the rights created by the trust indenture. In this way he becomes the beneficiary of the duties and responsibilities running between the bond issuer and the trustee as well.

The trust indenture.   It would not be practical for a corporation to issue a mortgage to each of many bondholders or for the bondholders to assert their rights on an individual basis. Hence the trust indenture was developed to charge a trustee as a representative of bondholders collectively to deal directly with the bond issuer in their behalf.

In the deed of trust the borrowing corporation or agency and the trustee, usually a large commercial bank with a trust department, are carefully identified. Next in order is the recitation of the authority of the borrower to borrow money and to issue bonds as evidence of such indebtedness.

Where real estate is used as security, its description will be set forth under several captions. These include legal, as well as physical, descriptions of buildings and other tangible property. Intangibles, such as patents, copyrights, trademarks, licenses, and good will, are also incorporated as security.

The definitions section of the indenture includes numerous formal definitions of such terms as *trustee, bond, outstanding, current assets, current liabilities, funded indebtedness,* and *net income.* Under the subject of the particular covenants to which the company subscribes appear the following items: to pay all debts as they come due; to maintain the corporate existence of the obligor and preserve its rights; to conduct the business in an efficient and proper manner; to restrict dividends so long as the bonds are outstanding; to give no prior liens, except that purchase-money mortgages may be issued for an amount not to exceed a fixed percentage of the cost of fixed assets acquired thereby; to restrict subsidiary operations according to a detailed formula set forth in the indenture; not to guarantee obligations of other corporations; not to make loans to officers, directors, or stockholders; to restrict compensation of officers and directors according to terms of the indenture; to render proper accounting; to keep specified amounts of insurance; and to restrict expansion programs to a relationship to net assets as set forth in the indenture.

Sinking-fund provisions of real estate bond issues usually give the issuing company considerable leeway. The required deposit may be a low minimum, such as 2 percent of the original amount of the bond issue annually. Additional deposits will normally be related to annual net corporate income, with a maximum regardless of the net earnings. In lieu of cash, the mortgagor may deposit bonds of this issue, or any combination of cash or bonds. When it is advantageous to do so, the trustee may use sinking-fund cash to retire the bonds.

Where a government-subsidized municipal bond is issued, of course, the trust indenture must vary to meet the needs of the governmental housing authority and its instrumentality, the recipient of the loan proceeds (whether a project developer or a disbursing loan intermediary for home buyers), and the trustee. If a construction loan is involved, such disbursement controls as are imposed by the governmental agency will be delineated. If several uses of the proceeds are identified, instructions must be included to cover allocation of bond proceeds. The trustee must also be advised in regard to investing otherwise idle proceeds, handling debt-service funds, and establishing all proper reserves.

Default on bonds.   Where bonds are secured by real estate mortgages, when default occurs, either the trustee or the holders of the contractually required percentage of the outstanding bonds may file notice with the borrower that the bonds are due and payable immediately. If the borrower makes up all defaults at any time before a judgment is entered in favor of the bondholder, the default is considered cured and the trustee may rescind the declaration of default. In the meantime, upon a declaration of default, the trustee may enter the property, exclude the borrower from possession, and manage the property as if it were owned by the trustee. The trustee may sell the estate, as an entirety or in such parcels as the trustee and the holders of a majority of the bonds may determine. As an alternative, the trustee may foreclose the indenture or use any other remedy available to it to protect the interest of the bondholders.

The indenture provides that should any part of the security be taken over by the exercise of eminent domain or otherwise, the proceeds must be paid to the trustee for the benefit of bondholders. However, should the borrower wish to use these funds to acquire new land or to construct buildings, it may do so. Meantime, the trustee has the right to contest any award and may charge to the borrower any costs incurred in such contest. In case such proceeds are not used for the purchase of land or the construction of buildings to be used in the business, they may be used by the trustee to redeem bonds outstanding. In such case the pattern of bond redemption set forth elsewhere in the indenture is followed.

Questions

1 What are the three principal kinds of mortgages and how are they basically different in derivation?

2 Distinguish between a straight term and an amortized mortgage. Why is the amortized mortgage in more common use today?

3 Identify each of the following and what its purposes are:
   a. Partially amortized mortgage with balloon payment.
   b. Graduated payment mortgage.
   c. *FLIP* mortgage.
   d. Reverse annuity mortgage.
   e. Budget mortgage.
   f. Package mortgage.
   g. Blanket mortgage.

4 Distinguish between a variable rate mortgage and a mortgage containing an interest rate escalator clause. What are the advantages and disadvantages of each?

5 What is a purchase-money mortgage and how is it different in effect from a mortgage given to secure a loan from a third party for the purchase of land?

6 How are junior mortgages most commonly derived?

7 Why are discounts such an important factor in the junior mortgage market?

8 Would you recognize an equitable mortgage by the form of the instrument on which it is based? Why or why not?

9 What is a vendor's lien and how may a vendor protect it? Answer the same question for the vendee's lien.

10 Review briefly the financial history of real estate bonds.

11 What protective covenants would you expect to find in the bond indenture?

12 How may eminent domain proceedings or other forms of involuntary conversion of mortgaged property affect the underlying security, and how should the bond indenture deal with these possibilities?

13 What are the responsibilities of the trustee to bondholders protected by the trust indenture?

14 Recently a considerable portion of long-term real estate financing has been done by subordinated debentures. What are the advantages of this form (*a*) to the borrower and (*b*) to the investor? What are the disadvantages?

Case problems

1 Jones bought land from Smith with funds provided by Hancock. Hancock advanced the funds on Jones's oral promise to give him a mortgage on the land once he acquired

the title. Jones then refused to execute a mortgage in favor of Hancock. What is Hancock's position?

2 X Corporation had mortgage bonds outstanding with an after-acquired property clause providing for the extension of the mortgage lien to all real property subsequently acquired. X Corporation bought a real estate parcel from Y, giving back a purchase-money mortgage. Which lien has priority?

Mortgage default and adjustments

3

Two major kinds of events take place when a mortgage loan is repaid in a manner other than by full compliance with the contemplated plan of repayment. A default may occur or adjustments in the terms or changes in the parties may take place which raise new legal and financial problems. Part 1 of this chapter deals with the problems of default, and Part 2 considers special questions raised by the introduction of mortgage adjustments.

PART 1: MORTGAGE DEFAULT

What constitutes default?

An ordinary dictionary definition of a *default* is "a failure to fulfill a contract, agreement, or duty, especially a financial obligation." From this it follows that a default in a mortgage contract can result from any breach of the contract. The most common is the failure to meet an installment of the interest or principal payments. But failure to pay taxes or insurance premiums when due may also result in a default which may precipitate a foreclosure action. Indeed, some mortgages make specific stipulations to this effect. Even a failure to keep the security in repair may constitute a technical default. We speak of this as a technical default because it would seldom result in an actual foreclosure sale. It might be difficult for the mortgagee to prove that the repair clause in the mortgage had been broken unless the property showed definite evidence of the effects of waste.

From another point of view, default is defined first in the breach of the letter of the contract and then in the attitude of the mortgagee. By this is meant that

43

even though there is a breach of contract, the mortgagee may see fit to ignore it or to postpone action in doing something about it. In case of default accompanied by abandonment, the probabilities are that the mortgagee will act quickly to protect his interests against vandalism, neglect, and waste. If, on the other hand, the mortgagor is a man of good character, has generally met his obligations promptly in the past, wishes to retain his interest in the property, and is only temporarily unable to meet his obligations, a default is not likely to be declared by the mortgagee for an indefinite period.

A form of default definition reads as follows:

> It is agreed that time is of the essence of this contract and that in the event of default in payment of any monthly installment or any part thereof for a period of sixty days after the same is due and payable as herein provided, or in the event of failure to pay when due all the premiums and renewals on the insurance policies on said real estate, and to pay when due all the taxes, assessments or other charges that may be levied, assessed or charged by any public authority on said real estate or the interest of this Association in said real estate or the interest of this Association in this note, or in the event of a breach of any covenant or condition in the mortgage given to secure this note, then the whole of the principal and accrued interest on this note, shall at the option of the holder hereof become immediately due and payable without demand or notice, and the undersigned do hereby specifically waive such demand or notice, and the filing of any action on this note shall be deemed to be an exercise of said option. Any failure to exercise said option shall not constitute a waiver of the right to exercise the same at any other time.

Foreclosure

When we speak commonly of *mortgage foreclosure* we are using language loosely. What is really foreclosed is the mortgagor's equity of redemption. When the equity of redemption merely takes the position that a mortgagor in default should have more time in which to meet his obligations, this could become unfair to the mortgagee unless some provision is made to limit the amount of time at the disposal of the mortgagor. Hence, as an offset to the equity of redemption, the mortgagee was given the right to foreclose it or cut it off.

In practice, most mortgagees are not anxious to take property from mortgagors. The Federal Housing Administration and Veterans Administration, for example, have established policies of forbearance in the enforcement of mortgages serviced in their behalf. Mortgagees prefer to collect the amounts owed them and are likely to be lenient and patient when circumstances warrant it. Seldom does the mortgagee insist upon the exact letter of his contract. Nor does he rush into court to insist upon his full pound of flesh. But after patience and leniency have been extended to delinquent mortgagors, eventually a settlement seems necessary. Then foreclosure proceedings are started. Incidentally, it is interesting to see how frequently a delinquent mortgagor gets off the delinquent list by paying up past-due obligations as soon as foreclosure proceedings are started.

Strict foreclosure. Although it has generally been eliminated by statue as a form of remedy, a strict foreclosure may be accomplished by equity court action. In other words, in some cases the mortgagee may ask that the mortgagor's right of redemption be completely cut off and that unqualified title be vested in the mortgagee. If this is done, the mortgagor loses all rights in the property if he does not redeem it before foreclosure becomes effective. After the equity court gives the mortgagor one last chance to meet his obligations, he is thereafter barred from troubling the mortgagee about the property mortgaged—if he fails to make good. However, the court may not relieve him of his obligations. He may still be held for any part of his obligations that cannot be satisfied by the forfeiture of his claims against the property.

Alternatives to strict foreclosure. In lieu of strict foreclosure, the mortgagee possesses two types of remedies to protect his interests in case of default by the mortgagor: (1) He may sue in a court of law on the debt, obtain judgment, and execute the judgment against property of the mortgagor. In this case, execution is not limited to the mortgaged property. It may be levied against any of the mortgagor's property not otherwise legally exempt from execution. (2) He may bring a foreclosure suit in a court of equity and obtain a decree of foreclosure and sale. This remedy relates only to the mortgaged property, seeking to have those values applied to satisfy the debt. This second option is the one most commonly used.

If the mortgagee elects to sue on the debt, any intervening liens entered between the date of execution of the mortgage and the date of judgment on the debt must be taken into account. They cannot be frozen out, as they could be under foreclosure sale. On the other hand, since a judgment against the debtor can be executed against any property owned by him, it may be advantageous for the mortgagee to sue on the debt rather than foreclose.

Sale of property. Even though the mortgagor who defaults in his obligations and thereby faces foreclosure of his equity of redemption is unable to take advantage of his time extension, he is currently considered to have rights which should be protected in ways never contemplated in early mortgages. He is presumed to have an equity which can be realized only in the marketplace. Hence, currently, equity courts called upon to grant the mortgagee the right of foreclosure accompany their decision with a decree of sale to determine whether or not there is anything left for the mortgagor. Where a sale is decided upon, this of course represents a departure from the strict foreclosure rule.

If such sale realizes a price high enough to meet the expenses of the sale and the claims of the mortgagee and still leave a balance, this balance goes to the mortgagor. The demands of other claimants will be considered later. While foreclosure of the mortgagor's equity of redemption and sale of the property may be undertaken in two separate actions, at the present time they usually go together in practice.

In determining the amounts to be accounted for at a foreclosure sale, it must be remembered that the mortgage secures not only the principal amount of the debt but all lawful interest as well. The interest to be accounted for includes not only all amounts unpaid up to the time of foreclosure but all amounts accruing after default up to the date of the decree of sale.

The advertising of the sale, the place where it takes place, and the method of sale by a county sheriff, a referee, an auctioneer, or a master are all matters that are governed by local practice. While details differ, the results are approximately the same in all localities.

Fixing a price.   Mortgage foreclosure sale emanates from the assumption that a public auction is a satisfactory way to realize the best possible price in selling property. Hence, in some jurisdictions the highest bidder gets the property irrespective of its cost, the amount of liens against it, or any other consideration. The mortgagee is usually the successful bidder. He can use his claims as a medium of exchange in the purchase—except for costs which must be paid in cash. Others must pay cash for their purchases, unless the successful bidder can arrange with the mortgagee to keep his lien alive. As a consequence, frequently only the mortgagee makes any serious bid for the property. In some states his right to bid is protected by statute, while in others the court of equity recognizes this method of protecting the mortgagee's interests. In the absence of either statutory permission or approval by the equity court, a mortgagee who buys the security for his claims may run some risk. However, this issue is academic, since it is inconceivable that a court of equity would refuse to grant the mortgagee the right to protect his interests in this manner.

In a few states an upset price is fixed in advance of the sale. By this is meant that an appraisal by agents of the court fixes a value for the property that must be reached in the bidding or the court will refuse to confirm the sale. This is not a common practice. In any event, the court of equity is expected to determine that the price realized at the foreclosure sale is adequate before it is confirmed. But adequacy is a flexible concept. Even though the court may have some doubt about it, it may question whether a subsequent sale would produce a price as high as the highest one offered at the first sale.

Nevertheless, a judicial sale may be a poor method of realizing the true value of the property. Recognizing this, the court must exercise its best judgment in viewing the offers made for the property at the foreclosure sale. Hence, while every offer made by a prospective purchaser is irrevocable and may not be withdrawn, the court is not bound to accept any offer made. At the outset the court may condition its confirmation by providing, for example, that the price paid must be sufficient to pay all expenses of the sale and the debts of the mortgagor.

It would be quite difficult for the court to fix the price that the property must bring at the foreclosure sale. On the one hand, the court is interested in doing justice to the mortgagor. Since a deficiency judgment may be decreed in case the mortgagee is not completely satisfied from the proceeds of the sale, the lower the price, the larger the deficiency judgment. On the other hand, the mortgagee's rights must be protected also. If the court should attempt to insist upon too high a price, no sale would be effected, and hence the mortgagee would receive no satisfaction of his claims.

Nature of title at foreclosure sale. The purchaser of property at a foreclosure sale is, in effect, the purchaser of the rights of the mortgagor whose interests are cut off by the sale. Even though the sale is conducted under court procedure, the court makes no representation concerning the nature of the title. Certainly there is no implication that a title passed by a court carries any suggestion of full warranty. Any defects that may have been applicable to the title as it was held by the mortgagor will continue with the title as it passes to the purchaser at foreclosure sale. If a junior lienor's interests have been omitted in the suit for foreclosure, his claims will not be cut off by such suit. As long as lienor claims are not satisfied, the purchaser, instead of acquiring a fee simple unencumbered, stands in the position of a mortgagee in possession of his security.

Parties to foreclosure suit.   When the holder of a senior mortgage brings suit to foreclose the equity of redemption, he must join in the suit all who share the mortgagor's interest. These include not only junior mortgage holders but judgment creditors, a purchaser at an execution sale, and a trustee in bankruptcy, if any. Failure to include all of these might improve their position with the foreclosure of the senior lien. For example, should the senior mortgagee become the successful bidder at the foreclosure sale, and should a junior lienor of record be not joined in the suit, it is possible that when the senior mortgagee takes title to the land, the junior mortgagee may acquire the position of a senior lienor. To make sure of the avoidance of this possibility, every foreclosure action should be preceded by a careful search of the record to discover all junior lien claimants who should be joined in the foreclosure suit.

Should any junior lienor think that he has an equity to protect, he has the right to purchase the property at a foreclosure sale, paying off or otherwise providing for the interests of the claimants whose liens are superior to his. This might be the case, for example, if the senior mortgagee has a $50,000 lien on a property that a junior mortgagee with a $10,000 lien considers to be worth more than $50,000. If the junior lienor does not bid for the property, the senior mortgagee may bid it in for $50,000 (in the absence of other bidders) and cut off the junior lienor's equity, causing him loss. By taking over responsibility for the senior mortgage, the junior lienor could bid up to $60,000 for the property without providing additional funds. It is not uncommon for a senior claimant to agree in advance upon the method of settlement of his claims. This may include an agreement to renew the senior mortgagee's claims, either with or without a reduction in their amount.

The purchaser at the foreclosure sale takes over the property free of the lien of the mortgage being foreclosed, but also free of all holders of junior liens who have been joined in the foreclosure action. If the senior mortgage holder or a third party purchases the property at a foreclosure sale, all such junior liens are of no further force or effect.

Sometimes it will be to the advantage of the mortgagor to purchase at the foreclosure sale rather than cure the default. Because of the time lag between default and foreclosure sale, the value of the property may have declined to the point that the foreclosing mortgagee would prefer that the mortgagor retain ownership and possession. Thus, a property originally worth $100,000 may now be worth $70,000 but carry an $80,000 first mortgage. The lender may prefer to have the borrower refinance the property and buy it at foreclosure sale for $70,000 rather than that he (the lender) take on the responsibilities of ownership. The lender might seek to recover his loss by another route.

It should be noted, however, that if the mortgagor purchases property at such a sale, all liens against it will remain alive; except, of course, such liens as are satisfied from the proceeds of the sale. There is one exception to this rule. If the mortgagor borrowed the money with which to purchase the property, the lender comes in ahead of the liens wiped out by the sale.

If a junior lienholder brings suit for foreclosure, he should not join the senior lienholder in the suit. Instead, he should sue subject to the senior lien. By this means he is not obligated to pay off the senior lienholder. He may prefer to keep the senior mortgage alive. The holder of the senior lien may join the action voluntarily, and sometimes does so to make sure that his interests are fully protected. He may wish to have determined by the court the amount due him to be assumed by the purchaser. Or, should there be any question about the order of priority of his lien, he may join the foreclosure action to have this question answered. Again he may have a side agreement with the junior lienor to continue his mortgage unchanged in amount. In case the junior mortgage holder plans to buy the property at the foreclosure sale, he may prefer to pay off the senior lien as well. This must be done with the consent of the lienholder if he is not a party to the suit. This practice represents a redemption of the senior mortgage and follows the English maxim of "Redeem up, but foreclose down." This concept is fairly obvious. It simply means that the junior mortgagee must honor the prior position of the senior mortgagee, but he may wipe out liens junior to his. For example, say a property now worth $100,000 is encumbered as follows:

First mortgage, A....................	$90,000
Second mortgage, B.................	20,000
Third mortgage, C..................	10,000
Total mortgage liens...........	$120,000

In a foreclosure action, mortgagee B has a buying power of $110,000 without raising additional funds if he is able to keep the first mortgage undisturbed or if he refinances it. If he buys the property at the foreclosure sale for not over $110,000, the third mortgage lien will be completely cut off by foreclosure.

Holders of junior liens which are destroyed in a foreclosure action are entitled to have the surplus of sale price over senior mortgage claims applied to their claims. If there is no surplus, then they are entitled to a judgment for the full amount of their claims. From that time on, they are merely general, unsecured creditors of the mortgagor, unless the latter should own other real estate to which such judgments would attach.

Effect of foreclosure on junior lienors

If a senior mortgage holder brings foreclosure suit and joins junior claimants in the suit, the question arises, "What happens to the claims of those cut off by the foreclosure sale?" As indicated above, any surplus remaining after satisfying the costs of foreclosure and the claims of the senior lienor is distributed according to the priority rights of junior claims. Sometimes the distribution of this surplus is not as simple as it sounds. Frequent disputes concerning the order of priority require action by a court of equity to establish the order of settlement.

Where there is no surplus, or where it is insufficient to meet all claims, the holders of such claims still maintain their rights to pursue the mortgagor on whatever personal obligation he has incurred in establishing their interests. This legal right may or may not result in satisfaction of claims to their holders. It may acquire only nuisance value to rise up and plague the mortgagor at some future time should he ever recover his economic status sufficiently to make pursuit of claims against him worthwhile.

Deficiency judgment

While a sale of the mortgaged property may result in a surplus to which the mortgagor is entitled, it may, on the contrary, be consummated at a price that fails to satisfy the claims of the mortgagee. Since equity courts have arrived at the conclusion that the mortgagor is entitled to the surplus, they have followed this with the correlative decision that any deficit should constitute a continuing claim by the mortgagee against the mortgagor. This is known as a deficiency judgment. Since all mortgages involve one or more specific properties—which must be accurately described in the mortgage—the mortgagee must look to such property to provide primary security for his claim.

Deficiency judgments are unsecured claims—unless the mortgagor owns other real estate—and take their place alongside other debts of the mortgagor. Unlike the mortgage from which such judgment springs, the latter gives the holder no right of preference against any of the non-real estate assets of the debtor. Hence the value of deficiency judgments is always open to serious question. This is true in part because of the ways by which they can be avoided or defeated.

A debtor seeking to avoid the deficiency judgment may plan accordingly. Since such judgments could be attached only to real estate which the debtor holds or may acquire in the future, the devious debtor may see to it that he does not acquire any future real estate interests; or if he does so, he will be careful to have the titles recorded in names other than his own.

In some quarters there is considerable sentiment in favor of legislation to abolish deficiency judgments altogether, leaving the mortgagee with only the property to protect his claims. Several states strictly limit the applicability of deficiency judgments.

It should be noted that a deficiency judgment is always entered against the person of the mortgagor or his successor. Hence, it cannot be entered unless he is personally served as a part of the proceedings for foreclosure and sale.

Significance of possession

A little thought will show the significance of the right of possession after default but before a foreclosure sale. If the mortgagor is in lawful possession, he is not accountable to the mortgagee for either the disposition of the proceeds of the mortgage or the income which he may derive from the property while he possesses it. Even where it is evident that the security is inadequate to protect the obligations due the mortgagee, this rule is not relaxed. An honest mortgagor may continue to enjoy normal income until he is dispossessed lawfully as the result of a foreclosure sale. A dishonest or, shall we say, a resourceful mortgagor can find means of increasing normal income substantially, perhaps at the expense of the mortgagee. Such mortgagors are called *milkers.*

Hence the only way for the mortgagee to protect his interest adequately is to obtain possession and, through it, control over the property and its potential income. If he can get possession, he can better protect the property against waste. Even though waste committed by the mortgagor while in possession may decrease the value of the security and correspondingly increase the amount of the deficiency judgment, this may not result in collection by the holder of the judgment of amounts to offset the effects of the waste.

Rent clauses, calling for the direct assignment of rental income to the mortgagee or his representative in case of default, are not adequate substitutes for possession. If the mortgagor feels that he has little at stake in his equity of redemption, he may lose interest in collecting the income which he has agreed in the mortgage to turn over to the mortgagee. Or income may be so difficult to define that it disappears entirely. It may not be in the nature of rent, but of net income from business operations. If the mortgagor's financial affairs are in such condition that it is impossible for him to keep up the contractual payments on his mortgage, his ability to produce any net income from his business may have reached the vanishing point.

For these and other less obvious reasons, the significance of possession becomes quite apparent. Mortgage foreclosure is essentially a time-consuming process. Until the foreclosure sale is completed, the mortgage continues to be only a security device limited by its terms.

Meantime, unrecoverable wastes may occur, and income may flow into channels which lead away from the mortgagee's interests rather than toward them. Deficiency judgments may be in perfect legal form, but also may be perfectly worthless in the recovery of funds that might have been diverted to the mortgagee had he been in possession pending foreclosure sale of the mortgaged property. On the other hand, the rent assignment clause in a mortgage may be so drawn that in effect it virtually gives the mortgagee possession of the property upon default and until the foreclosure sale is confirmed.

While the mortgagee is in possession, he may find it necessary or desirable to spend money for repairs or improvements on the property. Subsequently, he may be called upon to demonstrate that these expenditures were needed to protect his interests. Even though he benefits therefrom, there will be little difficulty in adding such costs to the previous claims of the mortgagee. But if the expenditures merely cause the property to look better, he may have difficulty in recovering such expenditures.

However, the mortgagee in possession is required to render an account annually to the equity court, showing the amount of his receipts from the operation of the property and their disposition. In general, these receipts must be applied first to expenses of operation—including necessary repairs—then to interest accruals, and finally to a reduction in the principal balance. This requirement for an annual reduction in the principal balance is called an annual rest. Its purpose is to prevent the mortgagee from having free use indefinitely of funds collected from the use of the property.

Taxes in default

Payment of taxes is an obligation of the mortgagor. As such, taxes constitute a prior lien against the security. Transfers of title always take into account accrued but unpaid taxes. Mortgages commonly contain tax clauses giving the mortgagee the right to pay taxes not paid regularly by the mortgagor. The amounts so paid are then added to the claims of the mortgagee. While the lien of taxes gives tax-collecting authorities the right to foreclose in case of default, such right is seldom exercised on first or even second default. Instead, the taxing authority from time to time may pursue an alternative policy of selling tax liens with deeds to follow. Since they constitute superior liens prior to the claims of mortgagees if the taxing authorities have observed statutory procedure, and since they customarily carry high effective rates of interest, the mortgagee may prefer to save the accumulation of high interest as a prior claim by paying delinquent taxes and adding them to his claims.

If foreclosure becomes necessary, the mortgagee includes all taxes paid by him. Usually at the time of a foreclosure sale the purchaser is expected to pay all delinquent taxes, thus making the tax status of the property current.

Tax sales. In the preceding section we discussed the relation of delinquent taxes and mortgages. Where there is no mortgage against the property or where the mortgagee does not act to protect his interests against tax liens, it is expected that sooner or later pressure will be brought by taxing authorities to collect delinquent taxes. In effect, if not in form, the procedure followed is intended to parallel that in the foreclosure of mortgages. The time interval between the date of delinquency and the sale date varies from 20 days to 18 months. At the time of sale the purchaser receives a tax certificate, which is then subject to redemption in nearly all states. The period of redemption is usually two or three years. If the property is not redeemed by the delinquent taxpayer within this period, the purchaser at the tax sale is then entitled to receive a deed to the property.

In the absence of bidders at a tax sale—as might occur in periods of depression or in the sale of inexpensive vacant land—the property usually reverts to the state, the county, or some other local governmental unit. Such reversions do not in all cases enrich the new owner or provide the means of meeting delinquent tax obligations. Either the property may be practically worthless, as the complete absence of private bidders suggests, or the governmental unit may neglect to take steps to realize the best price that can be obtained from its disposition. States and local units are notoriously careless in their housekeeping habits in this area.

Tax titles. Tax titles are usually looked upon as weak evidences of ownership. The interest of the tax collector is to find someone willing and able to pay taxes for someone else in return for a claim against the property. The collector is not greatly concerned about passing good title. There is no suggestion of warranty. In addition to any defects in title irrespective of delinquent taxes, the unconcern of the tax collector may in turn result in added clouds on the title. Among the latter the following may occur: (1) Because of inaccurate description of the property or incorrect records of ownership, the notice of sale may be defective. (2) The property owner may have been denied his day in court. (3) The line of authority for the sale may not be clear. (4) Irregularities and carelessness, even in minor procedural matters, may give rise to an invalidation of the tax sale.

All of these depend in part upon the recuperative powers of the delinquent taxpayer. If he has lost interest in the property, or if he lacks the financial resources to protect his interests, he may interpose no objections that will interfere with the plans of the purchaser at the tax sale. Nevertheless, the risk is great enough to suggest caution and due attention even to minor details before purchasing tax liens.

Sale of property which has reverted to the state or some other governmental unit involves fewer complications than sale of tax liens with a tax deed to follow. Because of this, it appears that much confusion could be avoided if the governmental unit would follow a procedure that includes these steps: (1) retain tax liens until the end of the redemption period; (2) foreclose unredeemed liens; and (3) sell titles to lands so acquired, giving good title therefor.

Other remedies for default

In addition to the remedies previously discussed, there may be other appropriate courses of action: These include:

1. Receivership.
2. Power of sale.
3. Foreclosure of deeds of trust.
4. Foreclosure by entry.

Receivership. Frequently a mortgage contains a clause which permits the mortgagee to have a receiver appointed to protect his interests in case of a default. Even though the statute makes no specific provision for the appointment of a receiver, it may result from an agreement written into the mortgage or may be agreed upon at the time of default. The receivership should be looked upon merely as an interim device for temporary control pending the consummation of a foreclosure sale. As such, it takes the place of a mortgagee in possession. While it is preferable to have a disinterested, impartial person appointed as a receiver, the mortgagor may serve in this capacity if the mortgagee consents.

Where a receiver is appointed, he is recognized as the direct representative of the mortgagee. He is not expected to represent all creditors of the mortgagor. Even when the mortgagee has the right to ask for the appointment of a receiver, he may not see fit to exercise it. The most common motives for the use of receivers are the desire to conserve already inadequate security and the fear of waste which may cause the security to depreciate in value before a foreclosure sale can be arranged. "Waste" means any condition that results directly in a diminution in the value of the property. It may be due to intentional destructive tactics or to neglect of needed repairs. A serious hole in the roof may be just as injurious as acts of vandalism. Sometimes, also, the relationship between mortgagor and mortgagee may play its part. If the former should show any indication of resisting the plans of the latter, a receiver may be used to take possession away from the mortgagor.

If the property over which the receiver assumes jurisdiction happens to be the mortgagor's home, the receiver may not ask the mortgagor to vacate the property immediately. Instead, he may determine reasonable rent for it and give the mortgagor the privilege of continuing to occupy the property, pending foreclosure sale, as long as he pays the rent asked of him. In general, there is a tendency to permit the mortgagor in default to occupy his home until the foreclosure sale takes place.

When the right of the mortgagee to have a receiver appointed is written into the mortgage instrument, the mortgagee sees to it that the right is as inclusive as possible. One such clause reads in part as follows:

> In the event of any breach of the terms or conditions of this mortgage or the note which this mortgage secures, the holder of this mortgage shall be entitled to the appointment of a receiver of the rents, issues, and profits of said premises, without regard to the value of the mortgaged premises as security for the amount due, or the solvency of any person or persons liable for the payment of the amount due, and without notice to any party, and in the event of any such default herein described, such rents and profits are hereby assigned to the holder of this mortgage as further security for the payment of said indebtedness.

Power of sale.   As a substitute for a foreclosure sale, the statutes of about a third of the states permit the use of the power of sale, provided it is written into the mortgage. A power of sale is a provision permitting the lender, in the event of the borrower's default, to sell the mortgaged premises after merely giving statutory notices. Even though the procedure of satisfying a mortgagee's claims is supposed to be faster and more economical where the power of sale is exercised, the use of this practice is not always followed, even in the states that have legislated on the subject. Some state statutes prohibit its use. A few undertake to regulate the manner of its use. Where the deed of trust is in use, the power of sale must be exercised by the trustee. One reason it is not always used is that whenever questions arise that do not produce the same answers for both mortgagor and mortgagee, resort must be had to a court of equity. Then follows foreclosure sale as described above. One question about which there may be a disagreement is the exact amount of the indebtedness. Questions even may arise concerning the fairness of the manner in which the sale is conducted.

Another complication in the use of the power of sale arises when the mortgagee may wish to buy the property. In the absence of statutory permission, the mortgagee may not purchase the property either directly or indirectly. If the mortgagee prefers to bid on the property at its sale, he should follow the foreclosure route.

While the mortgagee may dispose of his interest in a mortgage at private sale, the power of sale must be exercised only in public, and the successful bidder must pay cash. Proceeds of the sale go first to pay the expenses of the sale, then to apply on the claims of the senior mortgagee. Any surplus is applied successively to the claims of junior lienors, then to the mortgagor. If there is a deficiency instead of a surplus, the mortgagee is entitled to bring suit for a deficiency judgment.

The notice of the sale must state the total amount claimed by the mortgagee. Unless the statute so requires, no special notice need be sent to holders of junior liens. They are supposed to look out for their own interests. The mortgagor, on the other hand, is entitled to special notice of the sale. This is so because a power of sale may not cut off or impair his equity of redemption. This is his right up to the time of the actual sale of the property.

The purchaser under power of sale acquires the same kind of title that would be available to him where foreclosure proceedings are used. He merely succeeds to the type of interest which the mortgagor held. In effect, he receives a special warranty deed.

Some laws tend to abolish deficiency judgments where power of sale is used. In other cases the statutes place limits upon the amount of deficiency judgments by providing that such judgment may not be greater than the difference between the amount claimed by the mortgagee and the fair value of the property, instead of the amount realized at the sale. The burden of proof for establishing the fair value usually rests upon the mortgagee.

First by emergency statutes during the depression of the 1930s and later by permanent statutes, some states—including New York—have taken the position that a mortgagee may not take advantage of a depressed real estate market, use his power of sale to dispose of the property at a price that represents less than its long-term value, and saddle the mortgagor with a correspondingly large deficiency judgment. The mortgagee may not even anticipate such a situation and use a waiver of this mandatory law which he requires the mortgagor to sign at the time the mortgage is executed.

Sometimes mortgagees use the foreclosure sale in preference to the power of sale because they fear that questions may be raised about the marketability of the title if the land is sold under power of sale. Such questions are predicated upon the existence of some irregularity in connection with the sale that might result in its nullification. The same doubts are not usually present when title passes as a result of a foreclosure sale.

Foreclosure of deeds of trust. It has generally been held that when money is raised with a deed of trust given as security the creditor cannot bring a foreclosure action. Instead, he relies upon the trustee to exercise the powers conferred directly by the trust instrument. In California, however, the trustee has a statutory option to foreclose by suit and decree. Foreclosure is also commonly available, without the necessity of a statute, when judicial aid is required to determine parties' rights, as where it is necessary to have an accounting, adjust setoffs, ascertain the amount due in event of dispute, or establish whether the debt is really in default. Sometimes there are junior liens and their relative priorities are unclear. In such cases the trustee may sue to foreclose. Once the matter has been brought within the jurisdiction of the court the property may then be sold by an officer of the court, as in foreclosure proceedings, rather than by the trustee.

A right of redemption exists after a mortgage foreclosure sale, but not after a trustee's sale under a deed of trust. If the holder of the deed, however, elects to foreclose it in the same manner as a mortgage, the debtor has the same rights of redemption as though a mortgage had been executed in the beginning. In the event that a receivership becomes necessary, properly drawn trust deeds usually give more protection than mortgages. This is true because under an ordinary mortgage the receiver cannot acquire possession until foreclosure and then he must return the property to the mortgagor after the foreclosure sale until the redemption period runs. On the other hand, where a trust deed is used, the receiver may take possession under its terms and retain it until the property is turned over permanently to the purchaser at the sale.

Foreclosure by entry. In several New England states foreclosure by peaceful entry is permitted, provided all formalities are observed. These include the requirement that the entry must be without the opposition of the mortgagor. If it is opposed, resort must be had to judicial proceedings, which means that it soon develops into a foreclosure sale. The entry must be made in the presence of witnesses who can testify to its peaceable nature. And a certificate of entry reciting the action taken by the mortgagee must be properly recorded. Even where foreclosure by entry is used, the mortgagor is protected by a right of recovery of the difference if the security is more valuable than the debt. In addition, the mortgagor enjoys the statutory right of redemption where foreclosure by entry is used. The statutes allow a period varying from one to three years after entry before the right of redemption is cut off.

Also, in some New England states the mortgagee may foreclose by writ of entry. This kind of action partakes of some of the characteristics of equity proceedings. After the amount of the debt is judicially determined, the mortgagor in default is given a definite period of time within which to meet his obligations. If he fails, or is unable to take advantage of this opportunity, the mortgagee is put in possession of the property. He then occupies the same position as if he had foreclosed by peaceable entry as described in the preceding paragraph.

Under both of these plans of foreclosure the mortgagor is allowed a statutory right of redemption varying from one to three years. A long period of redemption may interfere with the plans of the mortgagee in disposing of the property. For this reason foreclosure sales are frequently resorted to even though foreclosure by peaceable entry or by writ of entry is available to the mortgagee.

PART 2: MORTGAGE ADJUSTMENTS

Need for mortgage adjustments

As pointed out previously, mortgage contracts are so drawn as to indicate definite penalties to follow any breach therein. Our most heartrending melodramas would have lost much of their appeal except for their recitals of the dire consequences which follow a failure to keep up mortgage payments on the old homestead. Nevertheless, experience testifies that in spite of provisions for prompt action in case of a default in mortgage payments, many such commitments are not met in strict accordance with the letter of the contract. Instead, whenever mortgagors get into financial trouble and are unable to meet their obligations, adjustments rather than demands for the proverbial pound of flesh are likely to follow. Some of these adjustments best meet the needs of the mortgagee, to be sure. Others are accepted at times when strict adherence to the letter of the contract would give the holder of the mortgage a financial advantage. Various types of mortgage adjustments are discussed in the pages that follow. These adjustments include:

1. Voluntary conveyance.
2. Assumption of mortgage.
3. Purchase of mortgage by grantor.
4. Extension agreements.
5. Release of mortgage.
6. Recasting of mortgages.

Voluntary conveyance.   On the theory that the mortgagor is a free agent, he may sell his equity to the mortgagee at any time after the mortgage becomes effective. Such sale must be conditioned upon the appearance of a new form of consideration—not present before—and complete freedom from fraud or duress. Because there are so many ways of taking advantage of a distressed mortgagor and of freezing out those with junior claims against him, the burden of proof governing the absence of fraud or duress usually rests upon the mortgagee.

For example, suppose that the mortgagor is unable to meet his obligations and faces foreclosure of his equity. In perfect good faith and to save time, trouble, and expense, the mortgagee may make or accept a proposal to take title from the mortgagor upon paying a nominal sum to the latter for his equity. Suppose also that shortly thereafter the former mortgagor's fortunes improve; or suppose that depressed real estate values recover sharply. The former mortgagee may face a suit for recovery on the ground that he used duress to wrest title from the mortgagor. He might have difficulty in proving his honest intentions and in demonstrating that at the time of the purchase, he paid the fair value of the mortgagor's equity. At that time the property might have possessed little or no value over and above the amount of the mortgage.

Where such voluntary conveyances are used, the common practice in lien states would include a warranty deed from mortgagor to mortgagee. A quitclaim deed would probably suffice in title states. In either event the mortgagor should insist upon a release to make sure that he is no longer bound under his note and mortgage. Otherwise, he may find that he has sacrificed his equity and still is under financial obligation to the mortgagee.

In addition to the legal questions involved in voluntary conveyances, the mortgagee frequently faces very practical financial issues as well. If there are junior liens outstanding, they are not wiped out by a voluntary conveyance. Indeed, their holders may be in a better position than before if the title to the property passes into stronger hands. Unless in some manner these junior liens may be lifted from the property in question—possibly by agreement with their holders to transfer them to other property owned by the mortgagor or even on occasion to cancel them—the mortgagee may find it necessary to foreclose instead of taking a voluntary conveyance. By this means he has a lawful method of becoming free from the liens of the junior claimants.

Assumption of mortgage. It has been pointed out that a mortgage is essentially security for a personal debt. The mortgagor is expected to sign a note which accompanies or becomes a part of the mortgage. By agreement, it is possible for the mortgagor to obtain release from his personal obligation after he assumes it; or if the mortgagee consents, he may be relieved of such obligation at the time the mortgage is executed. This would be an unusual type of agreement for the mortgagee to become a party to, but it would be one that would find sanction at law because it is a matter of voluntary agreement, resulting in a contract.

When the mortgagor transfers his rights to another, the question arises, "Does the grantee undertake to relieve the mortgagor of his personal obligation?" If this is the intention of both parties, the assumption of the obligation by the grantee may accomplish the purpose. The deed, after reciting the nature of the mortgage which encumbers the property, will contain a clause to the effect that the grantee assumes and agrees to pay the amount of the obligations owed to the mortgagee, as part consideration of the conveyance of title. Where an assumption is undertaken by the grantee, it should be couched in such language that there should be no doubt about his intent.

An assumption agreement takes the form of a contract of indemnity. It undertakes to shift the responsibility for the payment of the debt from the shoulders of the grantor to those of the grantee. Thereafter the grantor stands in the position of surety for the payment of the debt.[1] However, such an arrangement binds only the parties to it—the grantor and the grantee. Since the mortgagee is not ordinarily a party to such an agreement, he is not bound by it. As a consequence, he may still hold the original mortgagor and every grantee in the chain of title who has assumed the personal obligation of the debt. He may see fit to release the original mortgagor and any subsequent grantee. Occasionally questions are raised about the ability of the mortgagee to reach back of any nonassuming grantees. Some courts seem to take the position that nonassumption interrupts the right of the mortgagee to hold all assuming grantees in the chain of title.

Release of grantor from assumed debt. When a mortgagor owning property grants that property to another and the grantee assumes the grantor's mortgage, the lender may or may not release the grantor from personal liability for the mortgage debt. The decision of release will depend on the value of the property as security, the grantee's financial capabilities, and other factors affecting the lender's attitudes toward the transaction. As a mortgagee, he cannot be expected to release an antecedent mortgagor if the result will be to

---

[1] A *surety* is a person who binds himself to pay a sum of money or to perform another act in behalf of another.

increase the credit risk. In the absence of a release from the mortgagee when a mortgaged property is transferred, there is always one way for the grantor to obtain release from an assumed mortgage—that is, to sell the property free and clear of all encumbrances, letting the grantee do his own financing. Even this proposal is based upon two assumptions: (1) that the mortgage contains a prepayment clause, permitting the grantor to pay off at his discretion; and (2) that the grantee has access to funds that will permit him to refinance the mortgage.

Sometimes even where there is no provision for prepayment, the grantor may still prefer to get the grantee to do his own financing, provided that the grantor can prepay the loan without too great a penalty. If the grantee will accept a loan from the same mortgagee, there may be little or no penalty. In such case, the old mortgage may be continued with a release granted to the grantor. In many instances, particularly in a tight money market, it is not convenient for the grantee to refinance the mortgage. In such case it is futile for the grantor to insist upon selling the property free and clear. The grantee may be willing but unable to purchase on those terms.

"Subject to."   In contrast to the assumption of the personal obligation to pay the debt, the grantee may refuse to accept this responsibility. In this case he takes title "subject to" the mortgage. So long as he thinks it will be to his advantage—assuming his continuing financial ability—he will keep up payments on the mortgage and observe its other covenants. Under normal conditions, if he purchased the property at a fair price, it will be to his advantage to avoid default on the mortgage as the best means of protecting his own equity.

But should the grantee reach the conclusion that it will no longer be to his advantage to make further payments, or should be become financially unable to do so, he may default in his payments. By so doing, he runs the risk of losing whatever equity he has in the property. He cannot be held personally liable for the debt. The mortgagor and all subsequent assuming grantees are still personally liable and may be held for any deficiency judgment.

It is not ordinarily to the advantage of the grantor to sell property subject to the mortgage. He would much prefer that a responsible grantee assume it instead. But there are occasions when the most advantageous sale can be made subject to the mortgage. Indeed, in some situations the only buyer insists upon such an arrangement. If the mortgagor is about to default and expects to lose his property anyhow, he loses little by finding some prospective purchaser willing to take a chance on the recovery of the value of the property in question. Milkers frequently take title subject to the mortgage.

In case of a gift of property encumbered by a mortgage, the donee takes the property subject to the mortgage. Since he does not acquire the property as the result of a contract, he is not required to make any commitment that would bind him personally to pay the debt. Again this rule is subject to exceptions. If the gift is conditioned upon the willingness of the donee to assume personal responsibility for the debt of the donor that is secured by the mortgage, then, of course, the donee assumes the mortgage rather than takes title subject to it.

Purchase of mortgage by grantor.   Not all defaults result in foreclosure actions. Sometimes the mortgagee will approach a financially responsible grantor—or the original mortgagor—for the purpose of giving him a chance to take action that does not involve a foreclosure suit and resulting deficiency judgment. By demonstrating to him that the present grantee has defaulted and that a foreclosure is imminent, he may induce the grantor to follow an alternative course for the purpose of protecting his own interests. One course open to him is to purchase the mortgage—perhaps through a nominee—thus keeping the mortgage alive. By this means he may preserve his right of indemnity against the grantee. By temporizing, through a reduction of installments or otherwise, he may hold the mortgage until the grantee recovers his financial health or until depressed real estate values are improved.

The purchaser may find it to his advantage to secure a voluntary conveyance from the grantee at the same time he purchases the mortgage. Or he may secure an agreement to repossess the property—leaving the question of ultimate title unsettled until a later date. Of course, if he should purchase the mortgage and secure a voluntary conveyance from the grantee without giving a release in return, he could in effect own the property and still hold the right of indemnity against the grantee should his nominee foreclose the mortgage. Since the grantee faces foreclosure and deficiency judgment anyhow, he would probably be no worse off if he followed the plan outlined above.

Extension agreements.   Occasionally, at the maturity of a mortgage or in anticipation of it, the mortgagor may seek permission from the mortgagee to extend it for a succeeding period of time. In responding to such a request the mortgagee may need to pursue several lines of inquiry before arriving at a conclusion. Certainly he should know the condition of the security. Has it been reasonably well maintained, or does it show the effects of waste and neglect? He should determine the existence of intervening liens and their effect upon an extension agreement. Should there be no intervening liens, he has nothing to worry about from this source. But if any exist, will the extension of an existing mortgage which has matured amount to a cancellation of the old mortgage and the making of a new one? If so, will this advance the priority of intervening liens? In most cases the answer to these questions is probably in the negative.

What about the surety status of grantees in the chain of title who have assumed the mortgage? Will an extension of time for the payment of the debt secured by the mortgage terminate such sureties? The best way for the mortgagee to protect himself against the possibilities implied in these questions is to secure the consent of such sureties to the extension. As parties to it they can have no grounds for opposing it. But if they are not made parties, and particularly if changes in the terms of the mortgage through the extension agreement tend to increase the obligations for which the sureties are expected to be bound, then care should be exercised that those sureties who refuse to sign the agreement may not be released by the extension agreement. Perhaps the threat of foreclosure and the placing of a deficiency judgment on the record against them may be used to force an agreement to make them parties to the extension.

The exact nature of an extension agreement depends upon the bargaining position of mortgagor and mortgagee. Since the use of extension agreements is limited to term loans, it is probable that the original loan has not been greatly reduced. If the mortgagor can refinance the loan on more favorable terms, he will probably not apply for an extension agreement. This will suggest that in most cases the mortgagee occupies a more favorable position than the mortgagor in dictating terms of the extension agreement. As a consequence, he may eliminate some clauses in the original mortgage, such as prepayment privileges, which favored the mortgagor. He may make changes that favor the mortgagee, such as an increase in the interest rate. The changes made will perhaps be tempered by his ability to secure approval of the extension agreement by previous grantees whom he wishes to hold along with the present grantee. Frequently the latter has no choice but to accept whatever terms are offered to him. The previous grantees may protest and make the granting of the extension agreement uncertain because of their unwillingness to accept harsher terms than they had once been held to.

Alternative to extension agreement. As an alternative to an extension agreement, the mortgagee may agree informally to a temporary extension, without making any changes in the record. If the mortgagor is unable to meet all of the obligations of the mortgage payments, these too may be waived, in whole or in part. For example, the fact that the question of such an agreement is raised is probably proof that the mortgagor cannot pay the matured principal of the loan. Therefore, some informal arrangement may be made to permit him to retain possession of the property in return for meeting monthly payments which may or may not include principal installments. In general, if such an informal agreement is reached, the amounts demanded will be adjusted to the payment capacities of the borrower.

The use of such an alternative to a definite extension agreement may serve the temporary needs of both mortgagor and mortgagee. If the latter feels that the security amply protects his lien, he can afford to be lenient in helping the mortgagor to adjust his financial arrangements during a difficult period. If the mortgagor also feels that he has a real equity in the property, he will wish to protect it if at all possible.

Release of mortgage. The impact of mortgages may be released by various practices—intentional and otherwise. We have just indicated that intermediate grantees who refuse to sign extension agreements may be released from their liabilities under a mortgage if the mortgagee nevertheless persists in granting an extension of time to the assuming grantee. If the mortgagee voluntarily releases the grantee who has assumed the debt, that act probably releases all grantors as well. Since they stand merely in the position of sureties, the mortgagee must exhaust his claims against the assuming grantee before he can proceed against the sureties. If the mortgagee settles with the grantee for less than the whole debt and thereby releases him from the mortgage, this act releases all grantors as well. Whether the mortgagee collects a part of the debt from the assuming grantee or none at all, if he refuses to bring action on the amount owed he cannot thereafter bring action against any of those who act as sureties on the debt.

Partial releases are of quite a different character. They are quite common. If the mortgage is secured by more than one parcel, the time may come when the owner desires the release of one parcel, either for the purposes of sale or otherwise. The same principle applies when collateral other than real estate is put up to help secure the loan. When the debt is reduced sufficiently to justify the release of this added collateral, a formal release will usually be granted by the mortgagee. The amount of reduction required for this purpose may be written into the mortgage at the time it is executed. Or, if the mortgage covers only one parcel, a sale of a portion of it—provided the remainder is not unduly decreased in value as a result of the sale—will usually be permitted by a release of the lien of the mortgage upon the portion sold. It should be noted, however, that where the debt has also been secured by intermediate grantees who stand in the position of sureties, a release of the lien on any part of the real estate described in the mortgage, or of any collateral security, without the consent of the sureties will immediately discharge them from their whole obligation unless a partial release has been provided for in the mortgage instrument.

Recasting of mortgages. Once a mortgage is executed and placed on record, its form may change substantially before it is redeemed. It may be recast for any one of several reasons. Although the mortgage may contain no provision for future advances, they may be made nevertheless by mutual agreement of mortgagor and mortgagee. If there are no intervening liens, nothing further is required than to change the amount of the obligations that the mortgage secures. The result may be recorded only on the books of the mortgagee without changing the record of the mortgage. If the original note and mortgage call for a lesser amount than the unpaid principal plus the advances, a change in the mortgage may be required to give the mortgagee full protection.

If a patient mortgagee permits the amount of the debt to increase because of delinquency, this too may call for a recasting of the mortgage. Again the subjects of intervening liens and of total debt must be considered. Or should multiple properties be offered as security for the original mortgage, any request for release of any of the original security from the lien of the mortgage must take into account possible changes in the mortgage.

Where a monthly payment direct reduction loan plan is used, with a level monthly payment throughout the life of the mortgage, the time will come when the unpaid balance is but a fraction of the original loan. At that time the mortgagor may request a recasting of the mortgage to provide for a reduction in the interest rate or in the monthly payments, or both. Possessed of a seasoned mortgage and a favorable experience with the mortgagor, the mortgagee is not likely to brush aside such a request. He would probably reduce the monthly payments gladly, since that enables him to keep a good investment for a longer period of time. He may agree to some reduction in the rate of interest more reluctantly. But if the mortgage contains prepayment privileges, he will probably lose it through refinancing by a competitor unless he makes reasonable concessions to the mortgagor. Again, rather than lose the investment he will probably prefer the change in interest rates. A windfall into the lap of a mortgagor may enable him to make a substantial reduction in his real estate loan and to justify an immediate request for a recasting of his mortgage as outlined above.

Recasting of mortgages to admit interests not present at the time the mortgages were executed is sometimes necessary. For example, the mortgage may make no provision for an easement of a public utility company which requires access to the rear of the site covered by the mortgage. Since the installation of the services of the utility will add to rather than subtract from the value of the security, the mortgagee will usually be glad to approve the change. Nevertheless it will require a recasting of the mortgage to the extent indicated.

Power of attorney

In many business transactions it is common for one party to authorize another to act for him without any formal written instrument being required for this purpose. But in authorizing most acts that involve decisions concerning real estate rights, such authorization must be in writing. This writing is commonly known as a power of attorney. The principal who gives the power may be anyone, including a corporation, competent to execute real estate instruments. The agent who receives the power can be any natural and competent person or may be a corporation such as a bank or trust company. When used in connection with transactions involving real estate finance, the power given the agent should be set forth specifically in the instrument. A power of attorney should be made a matter of record so that the signature on the mortgage, for example, of someone other than the owner of the property may not cloud the title. Powers of attorney are subject to revocation by the principal and are generally terminated as a matter of law upon his death or insanity. Such a power does not terminate upon the death or insanity of the principal, however, when his agent, or attorney in fact, has a "power coupled with an interest," as where there has been such a transfer of title, or legal or equitable interest, in property to the attorney in fact that he can exercise the power in his own name.

Questions

1 What is meant by mortgage foreclosure and what alternatives are there to such action?

2 What special procedures are necessary to determine a proper bid for property available through a tax sale?

3 What advantages may be gained by providing for the appointment of a receiver in event of default by the borrower on a mortgage loan?

4 Why is it that some state statutes prohibit the use of a power of sale written into the terms of a mortgage?

5 How valuable to the mortgagee is the right to obtain a deficiency judgment?

6 Should the deficiency judgment be abolished? Why or why not?

7 May a foreclosure sale sometimes be desirable even though the mortgagee would prefer a voluntary deed? Why?

8 What special advantages does a mortgagee have in bidding at the foreclosure sale incident to his own proceedings? Is this arrangement fair?

9 When a mortgagor assigns his property and his obligations under his note and mortgage on the property to another, how is the mortgagee affected?

10 How may a mortgagor obtain a release from liability on a note and mortgage on real estate when the obligations under such note and mortgage have been assumed by another?

11 What dangers are encountered by mortgagees and unreleased mortgagors when property is sold "subject to" a mortgage?

12 In general, how may the surety status of a grantee in the chain of title, who has assumed the mortgage, be affected by an extension of the existing mortgage?

13 How is a partial release used in a mortgage?

Case problems

1 Mortgagor owns a property. A holds a first mortgage against it and B holds a second mortgage. Mortgagor defaults on his mortgage payments. A forecloses without joining B in the action? The property is sold at the foreclosure sale to C. What are B's rights?

2 In case 1 above, what would your answer be if B's lien were not recorded?

3 The Guardian Insurance Company holds a note from X and a first mortgage on a real estate parcel owned by X to secure it. X sold his property to Y and Y assumed the mortgage. The insurance company did not give X a release from his debt. Subsequently, Y missed required payments and the note became overdue. After some negotiating, the insurance company extended the note payment date and restructured the loan at a higher rate of interest. What is X's position at this stage of the transaction?

4 Green held a mortgage against the real property of Grey. Green assigned his mortgage to Brown, who did not record the assignment. Green died. His executor, ignorant of the assignment, brought foreclosure proceedings at which the property was sold to Black. What is Black's position?

Land contracts, leases, and land trust certificates

4

PART 1: LAND CONTRACTS

Meaning

One form of real estate finance that has been commonly used over the years is the land contract. In some respects it has been treated like an unwanted stepchild, in spite of its usefulness. The term *land contract* is more frequently used in real estate offices than among members of the legal profession. There it is recognized—if at all—under a variety of aliases including real estate contract, installment sales contract, agreement to convey, and contract for deed. From one point of view, the latter term is well chosen. The land contract is accurately described as a contract for a deed. But the implications of that concept are not always properly observed.

Perhaps one of the reasons this form of financing has been somewhat neglected is that in many cases the members of the legal profession have little part in its use. They may take a major part in its aftermath but frequently are bypassed when the contract is signed.

Informality surrounding use

The above statement suggests that the drafting of land contracts is too often left to laypersons. This is true. The circumstances surrounding the drawing up of land contracts are exceedingly informal. Both vendor and vendee approach the subject with a lack of attention to details that is absent in transactions involving much less responsibility on the part of all concerned. In his eagerness to economize, the vendee may consider the services of an attorney to represent his interests an unnecessary cost.

Under the land contract, the vendor retains the title in his name. So far as the deed record shows, he is still the owner of the property. But the land contract or contract for deed is supposed to tie the hands of the vendor in future transfers of title to make sure that he or his assigns must transfer it finally to the vendee or his heirs or assigns.

The land contract may be used as a substitute for either a vendor's lien or a purchase-money mortgage. Like the former, it is often a fragile type of evidence of the vendee's equity and would normally not be preferred for a long period of time over the purchase-money mortgage, if the latter is available. In states, however, that have long redemption periods during which the vendee has the right to possession and to collection of rents even though in default, sellers of land may refuse to give a deed and take back a mortgage until a very substantial part of the purchase price has been paid.

Uses.   In general, land contracts are used when:

1. The buyer does not qualify for long-term mortgage credit.
2. The property is ineligible for mortgage credit from institutions.
3. Mortgage money is unavailable, as in rural areas.

In some circumstances, contract terms are more liberal than mortgage terms. For this reason, land contracts are used extensively (1) in the sale of vacant lots under exceedingly liberal credit arrangements with the vendor and (2) in the sale of improved property in which the purchaser usually has only a small amount for a down payment and depends upon his future income, often from the property itself, rather than his capital accumulations to liquidate his obligations to the vendor.

Sale of vacant lots.   In the sale of vacant lots where the purchaser makes a small down payment—frequently no more than enough to cover the salesperson's commission—land contracts find common use. Since the default ratio in such sales has been exceedingly high, it is difficult to visualize any other form of financing that is equally practical. Certainly it would not be expected that the development company which sells the lot on a very small down payment should transfer its title to the purchaser and take back a purchase-money mortgage to account for the remainder of the purchase price. Much of its activities would involve foreclosure suits under such circumstances because of the frequent defaults by purchasers of vacant lots.

Partly because of these defaults, land contracts used by development companies are so drawn that they place major emphasis upon the protection of the vendor. The printed forms used in such cases contain the information required to fit the lots being sold and require but few items to be filled in at the time of sale. Purchasers who buy the lots put implicit trust in the seller and almost never even think about asking a member of the legal profession to inspect the contract to determine whether or not it protects their interests.

Sale of improved property. As in the case of the sale of vacant lots, with improved property acquired with only a small down payment or none at all, the vendor can scarcely afford to give a deed and take back a purchase-money mortgage in light of the cost of recovery of the property in event of failure of the purchaser to meet his obligations. Defaults in this use of land contracts often take place, but they are not nearly as common as with the sale of vacant lots.

The type of improved property—frequently for residential use—which becomes subject to sale under a land contract frequently possesses some major disability that makes its disposal in the ordinary way difficult. The neighborhood may be questionable, the structure may be old, the arrangement of the rooms may leave something to be desired, the market for the property may be sluggish, and so forth. This element of major disability may not necessarily be present, but it frequently is. Any type of property can use the land contract should the vendor and vendee agree. But where disabilities are present, the seller must seek a purchaser whose amount of available capital is so small that he cannot be too choosy in his purchase. Likewise, the purchaser must seek a seller who is attracted by only a small down payment or none at all.

A number of investors have used the land contract–low down payment combination as a means of acquiring control of large amounts of income property (largely residential) with little capital. During the post–World War II period until the late 1960s and early 1970s—a period of general housing scarcity—the consistency of rental incomes produced excellent opportunities for rapid estate building. The deals were structured so that the income streams from the property supported the financing and maintenance requirements. Interest costs and depreciation allowances largely negated the taxability of the income, thus providing a tax-sheltered, highly leveraged investment. At the same time, with strong inflationary forces acting on the total property value, the investor found his depreciation more than offset by inflation. The recent serious recession has seriously impaired many investment programs of this nature and, of course, has cast doubt on the advisability of such thinly financed future ventures, certainly unless the investor has iron-clad escape clauses in his contract to cover unexpected adversity.

Essentials of land contracts

Because of the informality surrounding the use of land contracts and, as a result, the frequent failure to give attention to matters that might later create headaches for both vendor and vendee, a major portion of the remainder of this chapter will deal with the essentials of land contracts required to protect both parties. The subjects discussed represent actual practices where more than ordinary attention is given to essential details of the contents of land contracts.

Vendor and vendee. Assuming that the property which is to be the subject of the land contract is owned by one person, several questions arise about signatures to the contract on his account. Is it sufficient for him to sign for himself, or should his spouse sign also? Since it is a contract for deed, the latter to be delivered when the requirements of the land contract have been fulfilled, it is always safest to have the spouse sign also. Her failure to do so might give her a valid excuse for refusing to release her dower interest when it comes time to transfer title by deed. So far as the intent of the vendor is concerned, his signature alone could indicate that.

Shall the purchaser be indicated in the land contract as the vendee, or shall the contract indicate that he and his spouse are to be considered as joint tenants, with the right of holding the title later in the two names rather than one? Without undertaking at this time to answer this question, let us state that it at least merits greater consideration than it usually receives. If only one name is to be indicated as the vendee, shall the spouse sign the contract along with the vendee? Again caution would recommend both signatures. While the spouse probably has no dower interest in a land contract, one never knows what a court of equity might decide on a subject not too well defined in either law or equity. It is freely admitted that there appears to be less reason for the spouse of the vendee to sign than for the spouse of the vendor to sign. If nothing else is gained, however, the signature of the former is likely to impress her more with the seriousness of the obligation the vendee is undertaking.

Description of property.   Inclusion of the legal description of the property avoids complications. Since this kind of description must later appear in the deed at the time title passes, it is better to start with it in the land contract. In the absence of this type of description, the property must be so described that its identification is certain without too much expense or difficulty. It is never sufficient to attempt to describe a property by street number alone. In addition to complications that may arise even at the date of sale, street numbers are sometimes changed. This may create additional unnecessary complications that are easily avoided at the outset.

Existing mortgage.   Should there be a mortgage of record against the property at the time the land contract is drawn up, it will of course give its holder a prior lien over the contract. Likewise, a subsequent mortgage of record without notice of the existence of the land contract would normally take precedence over the contract. Either one of two policies may be followed in making payments to the mortgagee under an antecedent mortgage: (1) The vendor may continue to make the payments, perhaps using the land contract installments for this purpose. (2) The vendee may agree to make the payments directly to the mortgagee. Perhaps the vendee will assume the mortgage, thereby accepting personal responsibility for it.

In any event, the mortgage should be accurately described in the land contract with sufficient particularity to make sure that the vendee understands its terms. While, for his own protection, he should have the record of the mortgage carefully studied by someone acquainted with such matters, this is seldom done. The amount of the mortgage, its due date, the method and manner of payments, and so on, should all be set forth in the land contract; or at least by reference to the record they should be made a part of the contract. In order to make sure of his own protection in regard to the amount of the unpaid balance of the debt, the vendee should secure from the mortgagee a statement of such balance, together with a statement of any unpaid installments and any other pertinent information that will help the vendee see the whole picture. Such information should be calculated as of the date of the contract.

In case the vendor expects to continue to make the payments on the mortgage, the contract should give the vendee the right to pay directly any amounts due or that may become due in the future but may not be paid on time by the vendor. Any payments so made should apply on the debt of the vendee to the vendor. Since the mortgage represents a lien prior to that of the vendee, any default by the vendor that could result in a foreclosure sale could thereby jeopardize the position of the vendee.

The vendee should also be given the similar right to pay taxes, insurance premiums, or other obligations of the vendor if his neglect to pay these as they fall due could interfere with the rights of the vendee. In all such cases the amounts so paid should be credited against the debt of the vendee.

Insurance clause.   Upon taking over possession of the property, the vendee acquires an interest in any insurance on it. It will be to the interest of the vendor to require the vendee to pay the cost of this type of protection. While it is common practice to state in the contract that the "insurance now in force shall be continued," this hardly gives the vendee a very intelligent picture of the amount of protection from this quarter. In case the vendor is not insurance-minded, he may be carrying insufficient coverage. Of course the vendee can check with the carrier to learn the kinds and amounts being currently carried. In addition, he may wish to add to the amount or provide other types of insurance protection at his own expense.

At the time the contract is signed, insurance carriers should be notified so that they can add the vendee to their policies, to be indemnified along with the vendor in the case of loss, "as their interests may appear." If the carrier is not notified of the change in ownership of the property, it may refuse to pay for the loss if it occurs. Incidentally, these interests not only are separate but they may be in conflict in case of serious loss covered by insurance. Since the vendor usually dictates the terms of the land contract, he will probably provide that in case of destruction or serious damage to the structure he shall have the option to apply the insurance proceeds to the liquidation of the unpaid balance of the debt or to the replacement or repair of the building. If the former policy is followed, any surplus will go to the vendee. If the latter policy is chosen, arrangements must be made to make up any deficit of repair or replacement expenditures over the amount of insurance recovery.

Rights of tenants.   Land contracts should spell out in detail the rights of tenants in possession of any part of the property. In addition, the vendee should check with the tenant to find out if the term of his lease, the amount of rent for which he is obligated—including a statement of prepayments or delinquencies—and all other pertinent facts conform to the representations made by the vendor. The latter might not be dishonest. Even though honest, he can be mistaken. There may even be conflicts of interests between tenant and landlord which should be resolved before the vendee becomes a party to them or has his interests affected by them.

Upon investigation the vendee may decide that he would be well advised not to go through with his part of the land contract if he finds that the rights of the tenants would interfere too seriously with his own plans. It is always better to discover these rights before, rather than after, the contract is signed. If any tenant rights are to be bought off, this is better taken care of before, rather than after, the contract is executed. Even though the tenant's rights have expired, the time and expense of dispossessing him are factors to be taken into account.

If the tenant is not in possession of the property and the vendee has no notice of his rights, he is not bound by them. The tenant in such case would still have recourse against the vendor, but he could not lawfully interfere with the interests of the vendee.

Payments under land contract.   Even the questions arising concerning the payments to be made under the land contract by the vendee to the vendor cannot be simply stated as so many dollars per month, with nothing further said about them. The time and place of making such payments should be carefully defined. The down payment may have been made in the office of a real estate broker, in the directors' room of a local bank, and so forth. It is probable that future payments are not expected to be made at the same place. The rate of interest should be stated specifically, including any change of rate that may be contemplated during the life of the contract.

The contract should outline in detail just what the payments cover. If the monthly payments include interest, this should be stated. If, in addition, they include something for taxes, insurance, and so on, this too should be specifically stated. The contract should leave no doubt about the time and manner of distributing the ingredients of monthly installments. For example, is interest to be credited monthly or semiannually? Will the tax payments be held by the vendor as a trustee, or will they be credited against the unpaid balance of the principal each month and then added again to the principal each half year as the taxes are paid by the vendor?

What about prepayments? Is the vendee permitted to make prepayments as his resources permit? If so, at what times and in what amounts? No doubt the vendor will ordinarily be glad to encourage prepayments in order to increase his security. Nevertheless, the details concerning them should be included in the land contract in clear form so that all parties will understand them. Will prepayments provide a cushion against possible future defaults? If so, in just what manner will they operate? These questions can and should be answered in the contract at the time it is executed.

Mortgage clause.   Whether or not there is a mortgage against the property at the time the land contract is executed, it is customary to provide that the vendor shall be permitted to mortgage the property for an amount not to exceed his equity. In such case the mortgage is given priority over the land contract. This provision enables the vendor to get at least part of his money out of the property should he care to do so. Presumably the interests of the vendee would not be adversely affected even in case of default on the mortgage by the vendor, since the rate of interest and terms of repayment on the mortgage are not likely to be more burdensome than those on the land contract.

However, if the contract does contain a mortgage clause, it should be couched in such terms that there can be no grounds for future disputes about its meaning. So far as possible, all features of the mortgage should be detailed in the contract. Since the interest rate which will govern such financing a few years hence cannot be accurately forecast at the time the contract is executed, it is sufficient to provide that the rate shall be that amount obtainable in the market at the time the mortgage is sought. Care should be exercised to prevent placing ahead of the vendee's interest any mortgage terms that would be unusually difficult for him to meet should the vendor default on the mortgage.

If care is exercised in drafting the mortgage clause in the land contract, and if later the vendor gets into trouble because he has failed to observe the requirements of the contract, the vendee should not be made to suffer. For example, suppose that the contract contains a prepayment clause giving the vendee the right to make advance payments as he sees fit. Suppose also that subsequently the vendor takes out a mortgage which gives him no prepayment privilege. He might easily find himself in a position where the amount of the outstanding mortgage exceeds his equity in the property, constituting a violation of his contract. If he gives prepayment privileges to the vendee, he should make sure that he receives prepayment privileges in his mortgage.

Another type of mortgage clause is frequently made a part of land contracts. The vendor may agree that when the amount of the indebtedness to him has been reduced a stipulated amount—say 25 percent—he will deed the property to the vendee and take back a purchase-money mortgage for the remainder. This clause may be inserted both as a means of providing a continuing investment for the vendor and as a further assurance to the vendee that he can obtain title to the property upon reaching a stipulated goal. The form of this clause should leave the vendee in a position to accept this option if he sees fit or to arrange some other alternative plan of financing instead. He might even prefer to continue the land contract, even though he has the right to have title transferred to his name.

If this type of mortgage provision is inserted in the land contract, its terms should be in such detail that there can at least be no doubt about the nature of the mortgage to be written at a future date. It is probable that the vendor—as an inducement to the purchase of the property—would agree at the time of executing a contract upon mortgage terms somewhat more liberal than could be obtained in the open market. Such liberality should not be nullified at a later time by giving the vendor an opportunity to hide behind indefinite or vague terms in the mortgage clause.

Provision for deed.   As noted above, the vendee looks forward to the time when he will hold title to the property purchased under a land contract. The contract should definitely stipulate the conditions under which deed will be available to the vendee and the kind of deed to be used. Presumably it will be a full warranty deed. If so, the contract should so state. If not, the nature of the deed to be used should be set forth without equivocation.

It is not sufficient for the vendee to take the word of the vendor that a deed will be forthcoming. Before signing the contract, the vendee should make sure, as the result of a proper search of title, of the exact nature of the vendor's interest in the property. In other words, the vendee wants assurance that the vendor has good title. If he has not, he cannot pass it on to the vendee. Then the vendee should be protected against interests which refuse to join the vendor in passing title. For example, it is elementary that the spouse should sign the contract, thereby committing herself to sign away her dower interest when the proper time comes. Her refusal to do so might make it impossible for the vendor to pass good title to the property. Suppose that a life estate in the property exists in the name of someone other than the vendor and his spouse. In such a case the owner of this estate also should sign the contract or in some other manner should indicate his willingness to release his life estate at the time the deed is called for.

Since the vendor may see fit to dispose of his interests in the land contract before title to the land passes to the vendee, the latter is properly concerned with several features of the vendor's assignment of his interests. In the first place, he wants to make sure that the assignee understands the exact nature of the contract and that no new interpretation will be placed upon its provisions.

Then he is concerned with another question which may be very vital to his interests: Will his deed, if and when he is entitled to receive it, be signed by the original vendor, or can an assignee be substituted for him? If the latter is permissible, a second question follows: Would it be possible for the vendor to pass title to a grantee, known to be financially irresponsible, by the use of a special warranty deed which gets the grantor out from under any responsibility for the character of the title? If so, even though the vendee under the contract receives a full warranty deed from the assignee, he does not get the full warranty deed which he thought he was to get when he executed the contract.

While the vendor should not be restricted in his disposal of his interest, it should be stated in the contract that both the vendor and his assigns must give a full warranty deed in passing their interest along to someone else. To protect the assigns of the vendee, provision should be made in the contract that the deed may pass either to the vendee or to his assigns. While it is generally assumed that a deed shall be accompanied by an abstract of title brought down to date—or whatever substitute is common in the community—this should be definitely stated in the contract.

Restrictions upon assignment by vendee. There are occasions when the vendor prefers to place restrictions upon the right of the vendee to assign his interests in a land contract. For example, suppose that the vendor knows about the thrifty habits and the housekeeping ability of the vendees. He may be willing to sell them a piece of property because he feels sure that they will take good care of it and will make every effort to live up to their contract obligations. At the same time the vendor might be quite unwilling to sell the property, under the same terms and conditions, to a specific friend of the vendee. What is to prevent the vendee from assigning his interest in the land contract to this friend? Perhaps he signed the contract in the first instance for this purpose; or perhaps such an assignment is an afterthought and is planned without knowledge that the vendor distrusts the new vendee.

At the time the contract is executed, the vendor can restrict the negotiability of the vendee's interests by the insertion of a clause providing that the vendee may not assign such interests without the consent of the vendor. In the event of a dispute over the application of such a clause to a specific case, the courts would probably look to the reasonableness of the vendor's refusal to approve an assignment as the basis for a decision. It is not probable that the vendor could use his veto power, without justification, to the financial injury of the vendee.

In any event the right of prepayment clause would undoubtedly protect the vendee against prejudicial vetoes by the vendor if the property could be financed in any other manner. Refusal of the vendor to sanction a proposed assignment could be nullified by paying him the amount of the unpaid balance of the debt, thereby canceling his interest in the property.

Failure to pass title. As stated above, unless the vendee makes sure of using all precautions to protect his interest at the time he executes the contract, he may find that when the time comes to secure title, the vendor is unable to transfer title to him. For example, his wife may not release her dower interest. Unless she has agreed to this in effect at the time she signed the land contract, she cannot be forced to do so. The vendor may find that he cannot secure the release of a life estate; there may be an indestructible contingent remainder-man's interest; and so forth. Consequently, the vendor cannot give the vendee a good merchantable title. Since he cannot perform his part of the contract, a suit for specific performance is fruitless.

Here is another place where the vendee needs competent legal advice to know his interests and the best manner of protecting them. Otherwise he may be "bought off" by the vendor at a price that is too low. Since he cannot sue for specific performance, he can bring action for damages. He should be able to recover whatever he has paid on the principal of the debt and the cost of improvements made with the consent of the vendor, and perhaps also an amount representing any increase in value that the property has enjoyed since his execution of the contract.

Since land contracts frequently contain penalty clauses against default by the vendee, it would not be amiss to include a stipulation to the effect that in case of default by the vendor, a penalty of a stipulated amount shall be paid by him to the vendee. In the absence of such a provision in the contract, his chances of collecting a penalty through court action are not good.

Improvements directed by vendee.   The land contract usually provides that no major improvements or physical changes will be made in the property without the consent of the vendor. The reason for such a provision is obvious. Before the vendee has built up a substantial equity in the property, he might wish to make major changes which would please his peculiar tastes but might not be acceptable to a subsequent purchaser, in case the vendee defaults on his contract. Even the removal of trees and shrubs might result in a decrease in the value of the property. Therefore, any major change should be subject to a veto by the vendor, at least until the vendee has built up a substantial equity.

Should this clause be omitted from the contract or should it be violated by the vendee, the cost of any improvements directed by the vendee could not be assessed against the interest of the vendor without his authorization. As a consequence, a mechanic's lien would attach to the interest of the vendee only. In case the vendee's interest was later forfeited before the mechanic's lien had been attached, no lien would continue. The person filing the mechanic's lien must thereafter look to the vendee for satisfaction. In case the vendee directs and the vendor authorizes the improvement, the whole property could be held as security for any mechanic's liens that might be properly filed subject, of course, to prior liens.

Recording of land contracts.   State laws provide for the recording of conveyances of land and instruments affecting title. Land contracts generally are considered instruments affecting title and are consequently admissible to record. Recording land contracts is not essential to their validity; it merely gives notice of their existence to third parties.

In some cases the contract contains a stipulation that it shall not be recorded. This is included at the instance of the vendor who receives only a small down payment or none at all. If such a contract is recorded and there is an early default, clearing the record may take time and involve expense to the vendor. Even so, such a contract is occasionally recorded, in violation of its terms. This does not invalidate the contract. It may subject the vendee to a suit for damages if the vendor suffers loss by being unable immediately to effect a sale to another buyer who refuses to take title with the cloud of the recorded contract against it, and who is unwilling to wait upon the purchase until the record can be cleared. Probably such a right of suit for damages would seldom be exercised.

On the other hand, failure to record land contracts against vacant lots because of small down payments affords the vendor a particularly good opportunity to take advantage of the vendee, should he care to do so. The complete absence of possession by the vendee, or of any evidence of it, makes it easy for the dishonest vendor to sell the land and deliver good title to a third party, even though the vendee be not in default.

If, however, the vendee makes a substantial down payment, or as he builds up an equity with subsequent payments, he may feel safer if his contract is recorded. Under either of these sets of circumstances, the recording of the contract should meet with little opposition from the vendor. However, immediate and continued possession of the property by the vendee will normally serve as a satisfactory substitute for a record of the contract. All parties who might wish to acquire a lien prior to the claims of the vendee are put on notice to determine by what right the vendee occupies the property. Physical possession is not necessary to protect the rights of the vendee if sufficient evidence of possession exists to warrant a further inquiry by other parties.

Judgments and land contracts.   Since judgments against a debtor become a lien against any real estate held in his name from the instant of entry of the judgments upon the record, the vendee of a land contract should make sure that there are no unsatisfied judgments on the record at the time the contract is executed. If there are, they probably have preference over the land contract. As to judgments filed after the contract becomes effective, it appears that the vendee is not chargeable with notice of such entry. Consequently, he runs little risk by continuing to make his payments to the vendor. The judgment creditors can best reach the vendor's interest in these payments through court action. Through garnishment or equity proceedings, judgment holders could probably secure a diversion of such payments to a liquidation of their claims.

Complications sometimes result in conflicts between land contracts and mechanic's liens. Because mechanics generally have from 30 days to 6 months in which to file their liens, the vendee should inspect the property before signing a land contract to determine if there is any evidence that work has recently been done or material delivered that might give rise to a mechanic's lien. If so, receipts from those who did the work or supplied the materials might be a necessary precaution against prior claims. In case the vendee finds that he is responsible for mechanic's liens that were not accounted for in the contract, he may pay them, obtain a discharge of the liens from the record, and take credit for his payments on the debt. If he is not personally responsible for them, he can disregard them, since his claims would precede theirs.

Default and foreclosure

Because of the frequency with which land contracts are not completely executed in accordance with their provisions, consideration of what happens in event of default and foreclosure is particularly important. Courts in the application of principles of equity will often interpret provisions of land contracts in a manner somewhat at variance from what the contract would seem to provide.

Default by vendee. Because of the informality surrounding the execution of land contracts, the inexperience of the vendee, and the common absence of legal counsel to advise him, the vendee frequently interprets the contract to be a kind of option. He assumes that if he decides to default on his contract, all he needs to do is forfeit his rights under it and walk away from it. He may find that conditions established by his signature on the contract are not quite this simple. To be sure most land contracts specifically provide that at the option of the vendor a default by the vendee may result in the forfeiture of the rights of the latter. In addition, the vendor reserves the right to retain as liquidated damages any amounts paid by the vendee, including any improvements to the property made by him.

The vendor may not see fit to exercise this option. If he thinks the unpaid portion of the debt exceeds the value of the property, and if he thinks the vendee is financially responsible, he may insist that the contract be lived up to. As an alternative, he may insist upon a cash settlement as the price of releasing the vendee from his contract. Depending upon the vendee's experience and the nature of advice available to him, the amount of cash demanded may not bear too definite a relationship to the amount of loss presumably suffered by the vendor.

If the vendee has had experience with such questions or if he has competent legal advice, he may decide not to forfeit any equity he may have in the property without a struggle. Even though he has technically violated the contract by defaulting in his payments, he may insist upon retention of possession of the property and may actively resist any effort on the part of the vendor to dispossess him. He too may do a little bargaining and agree to vacate and release the vendor only upon consideration that the vendor pay him a substantial sum of money—perhaps the amount by which the vendee has reduced the principal amount of the debt.

While negotiations are in progress, the vendee continues in possession of the property. Depending upon a combination of circumstances, including the pulse of the real estate market, the attitude of the vendee toward committing waste, and the forecast of a favorable or unfavorable decision in a court of equity, the vendor may be willing to pay a persistent vendee in default something to purchase a release from the contract. Perhaps the amount paid may even be considered by the vendor as a price of ridding himself of a nuisance. Even without such nuisance payment, something may be paid even though the vendor expects to suffer a loss, if he thinks that the vendee is financially irresponsible.

Loss of payments under land contracts. Under a long-term land contract, regular payments over a considerable period of time may have reduced the original indebtedness substantially. Since it is customary to stipulate in the contract that in case of a default on the part of the vendee all payments made may be retained by the vendor in lieu of liquidated damages, on the face of it appearances seem to indicate that a default might nullify all the equity the vendee has built up in the property. Because if appealed to, courts of equity may construe a land contract as an equitable mortgage, it is not clear what rights the vendee may possess in relation to payments already made.

Foreclosure sale. Failing to dispossess a vendee in default, either by a request for observance of the forfeiture clause in the land contract or by an offer of compensation for release from the contract, the vendor may pursue his rights in a court of equity. Since the law on the subject is not well defined, the equity court may render any one of several decisions. It may grant the vendor the relief he prays for, decree that the forfeiture clause in the contract be made effective, and dispossess the vendee from the property. It may even render judgment against the vendee for any installments in default.

As an alternative, it may determine that the vendee still has an equity in the property which he is entitled to recover by continued occupancy of the property for a period of time—fixed in the decree—sufficient to absorb or live up this equity. In other words, without any additional payment, the court may grant the vendee what amounts to free rent for a determined period of time. At the end of that period the vendor is entitled to recover possession of the property unless a new agreement is reached with the vendee in the meantime.

As a second alternative, the court of equity may decree that the land contract is in effect an equitable mortgage. As such it must be foreclosed like other mortgages to determine what disposition shall be made of the proceeds of the sale. Where such an alternative is followed, the procedure from then on follows the path taken by mortgage foreclosure and sale of the security, discussed elsewhere in this text. In general, courts of equity tend to protect the interests of the vendee in default so long as there appear to be reasonable grounds in his favor.

Strict foreclosure of land contracts. In some cases the rule of strict foreclosure is applied to land contracts. In other words, even after default a court of equity may fix a time within which the purchaser under a land contract may pay up his indebtedness to the vendor if he can find an alternative method of financing the deal. Failing to finance the property within the time fixed by the court may be followed by a complete loss of equity by the vendee, leaving the vendor with undisputed and unqualified title to the property. Except in times of extremely tight money, the vendee who is entitled to financial assistance will probably be able to find it. If his equity is so thin that no one will be willing to take the risks involved in assisting him, even a foreclosure sale would result in no recovery for him. If, on the other hand, he has a substantial equity in the property and cannot find someone willing to finance him, he should be able to find a purchaser for his equity, enabling him to enjoy some recovery of previous outlays. If he fails to make use of either of these possibilities, strict foreclosure may follow.

Market for land contracts

In general, the market for land contracts is limited to their sale to individuals acquainted with this type of real estate financing. They know the nature of the risks involved and usually are financially able to bear them. Occasionally a financial institution, such as a savings and loan association, buys them. In such case precautions are taken to protect the purchaser against loss. For example, suppose that a property owner disposes of his real estate at a price of $40,000, accepts a down payment of $3,000, and takes back a land contract for $37,000. If he is sufficiently anxious to raise cash, he may make a deal somewhat as follows: He may sell his contract to a financial institution—with or without a discount—and agree to keep $10,000 on deposit with the purchaser as supplemental security. Usually when the contract balance is written down to $24,000 or when the vendee under the contract is able to finance his property by some other means, the deposit will be released and the vendor permitted to obtain unrestricted possession of the net selling price of his property.

PART 2: LEASES

Meaning of lease

A lease represents a commitment by one party—called the *lessor*—to turn over to another party—called the *lessee*—the use of real estate in return for rent or other consideration. In general, there are two broad classes of leases. The short-term lease leaves the financing and the management in the hands of the lessor. He is expected to supply not only the use of real estate but the necessary services required to make the real estate usable, such as janitor and elevator services. Even though such an arrangement between lessor and lessee might continue indefinitely, this type of lease is considered short term. Since such a lease presents no problems of financing that are peculiar to the fact that real estate uses are subject to rental payments, we shall not be concerned in this chapter with short-term lease financing.

The other type of lease, usually covering a longer period of time than the one just described (though actually it might be for a shorter period) is a type of real estate transaction in which the lessee takes over the management—and frequently the financing of the property. The lessor gives up to the lessee the operation and maintenance of the property. The rent paid represents a net return upon the investment, unless it includes in addition an amount needed to pay taxes in case the lessee does not assume them also. If a building already exists on the site leased, it will probably be purchased by the lessee. Or it may be obsolete or inadequate for the purposes of the lessee. In either case the building will be demolished and will be replaced by a building constructed for and financed by the lessee. Where the lessee constructs and finances the building, its ownership and disposition at the termination of the lease should be specified in the lease.

Complex nature of long-term leases

One of the subjects that give rise to conflicts of interests between real estate brokers and attorneys is: Who should take responsibility for drawing up long-term leases? Lawyers contend that they know best how to protect the interests of all parties concerned because there are so many possibilities for error unless all legal angles are properly explored. Few would dispute the existence of many possible legal complications. On the other hand, real estate brokers contend that most of the questions to be settled in drafting long-term leases involve business practices with which the lawyer may not be fully acquainted. Some years ago the National Association of Realtors® canvassed its members who dealt in long-term leases to determine what questions were encountered in lease negotiations. The results of the study showed that there were 350 such questions, which could be grouped into 44 convenient classes. Probably others would now be added if the study were repeated.

The answer to the controversy mentioned above seems quite obvious. Long-term leases are so important to both lessor and lessee that both real estate brokers and lawyers should be asked to make their contributions to the drafting process. Even though divided responsibility may produce further controversy, the interests involved are too important to risk giving the drafting responsibility to one not acquainted with all angles of the subject.

Provisions of long-term leases

In addition to giving the identity of the property and of the parties to the lease, the long-term lease should deal with the following: (1) The subject of improvements has many facets. If the lessee takes over the existing improvements, by purchase or otherwise, maintenance, replacement in case of fire or other cause of damage, erection of new improvements by lessee, ownership of improvements at the expiration or earlier termination of the lease, and so on— all need careful definition in the lease. (2) Then, of course, rents and their payment; insurance—kinds and amounts; purchase options; renewal privileges; rights of the parties in case of forfeiture of lease by lessee; condemnation proceedings—total or partial—and their consequences for both parties; taxes, present and future—all should be carefully spelled out in the lease so that there can be no reasonable grounds for disagreement later.

Rentals on long-term leases

Flat rentals—sometimes called fixed—are agreed upon in advance to pay the same amount each year for the life of the lease. A succession of flat rentals for predetermined periods of time receives the name "graded or step-up rentals." For example, the rent may be $4,000 a year for the first five years, $5,000 a year for the next ten years, and $6,000 annually thereafter. Conceivably the succeeding periods could carry step-down instead of step-up rentals. In case there is doubt in the beginning about the amount to be charged for succeeding periods, the rent for the first period only may be fixed in the lease.

For later periods, the standards for rent escalation may be set by reappraisal or by index. Under the reappraisal method, an adjusted rental is established on the basis of the new valuation of the property. When an index method is used for the adjustment, the question always arises concerning the appropriateness of the index. The U.S. Bureau of Labor Statistics Consumer Price Index ("cost-of-living" index) is commonly used. A wholesale price or a cost of construction index tends to have greater sensitivity and might be a more representative measure. The implicit price deflator published by the Department of Commerce in the *Survey of Current Business* has much to commend it. This is the index that is divided into the gross national product in current dollars to convert it to constant dollars. It is designed to correct for the effect of inflation (or deflation) in the prices of all goods and services. Use of such an index tends to treat the parties to the lease as if prices are generally stable.[1]

In any case, limits to the amount of change for any one adjustment period are usually contained in the terms. For times when fair rentals or other interpretations of the lease provisions cannot be resolved by the parties, the properly drafted lease provides for arbitration.

The rental provisions sometimes stipulate for a percentage participation in the tenant's revenues in addition to a fixed rental amount. This participation may be quoted in terms of gross or net revenues and it may start from the first dollar or after the tenant has realized a certain amount free of participation. Percentage participations are generally associated with tenants whose rentals support the financing of leasehold improvements.

Advantages to lessor

The lessor may prefer to lease his property for a long term rather than sell it. The possible advantages that may accrue to the lessor are: (1) The amount of the principal is fixed for the term of the lease. (2) The lessee assumes most of the responsibilities of managing the property. (3) All new capital expenditures, such as the cost of the erection of a building, are borne by the lessee. (4) The

---

[1] See further William M. Shenkel, "The Case for Index Leases," *Journal of Property Management,* July/August 1975, pp. 156–61.

rate of return is presumably fixed for the life of the lease. This is subject to limitations that will be discussed below. (5) By leasing the property instead of selling it, the lessor may save taxes. His income is spread over a long period of time as against a larger capital gains tax in case of sale.

Another type of advantage presumably accruing to the lessor is the improvement in his position from the investment in the building by the lessee. A vacant site, having only potential use, is a more speculative holding than the same site after it has been improved by a suitable structure. This added investment by the lessee not only provides the basis for a return to the lessor, but it assures the latter that the return will not be defaulted by the lessee except under the most dire circumstances. Since a default in the rental payment may result in the forfeiture of the building to the lessor, the lessee will not permit such a default if he can possibly avoid it.

The lessor may prefer to continue his investment in the real estate as against the acquisition of cash for which he has no satisfactory alternative use immediately. The lessor may also feel that by leasing his property, he is, in effect, receiving a higher price for it than if he sold it.

Advantages to lessee

When a lessee prefers to hire the use of property owned by another instead of buying it, he hopes to gain the following advantages: (1) His capital investment is reduced, thereby making his funds available for other uses. (2) In case his capital is limited, the lease makes unnecessary the large loan that would be required to finance the purchase of the property. (3) The speculative advantages which may result in an increase in the use value of the property may accrue to the advantage of the lessee who pays a flat rental during its life. If the rent is $6,000 a year for the life of the lease and later becomes worth $10,000 a year, the lessee gets the advantage.

On the other hand, the owner may insist upon a sale even though the lessee might prefer a long-term lease. In such a case perhaps both interests can be served by finding a third party willing to buy the property provided the long-term lease is consummated. Or the same results could be attained if the original parties entered into the lease, and subsequently the lessor disposed of his fee underlying the lease. He might be able to realize a higher price after the new building is completed. Particularly is this true if he effects the sale through the use of land trust certificates, described later in this chapter. Of course, if he insists upon a sale rather than a lease, he is on safer ground to follow the first practice suggested above.

Long-term lease covering land only

Often, long-term leases cover land values only. The lessee is then expected to build a building on the site or replace one already in existence. All construction arrangements should be anticipated in the lease. The rent on such long-term leases is usually net to the lessor, with the lessee obligated to pay taxes, maintenance costs, and so on. As assurance that a building arranged for in the lease will be built, the lessor frequently requires a bond for his protection until the building is erected. All improvements to the land revert to the lessor at the expiration or other termination of the lease, in the absence of arrangements to the contrary.

Financing the leasehold

The right of the tenant to use the property during the term of the lease is called his leasehold. Irrespective of the value of any improvements that he may add to the property, this right may acquire value. In some instances the value has been very large. For example, suppose that a site was leased for 99 years, renewable forever, at $6,000 per year, at a time when this rent measured the current value of the land use. Suppose that through a shift of business districts or otherwise, the rental that could be obtained from this site increased to $50,000 per year. The owner of the lease would enjoy a profit of $44,000 per year in perpetuity, should this new value continue. The present value of this annuity of $44,000 per year would measure the value of the leasehold as such. In case of a reappraisal rental arrangement, to be applied at intervals throughout the life of the lease, the lessor rather than the lessee would enjoy the fruits of any increment in value that might accrue. Hence the leasehold as such would never acquire any substantial value.

In addition to whatever value the leasehold acquires, the lessee usually owns the building erected upon the site, so long as he meets his obligations to the lessor. He may have purchased the building originally from the lessor or, more commonly, he may have caused it to be erected at his expense. In either event, it requires financing. To obtain the funds for this purpose it has been customary for the lessee to issue a leasehold mortgage. Although the mortgage constitutes a first lien on the leasehold and the building, the value of this lien may be obscure to the uninitiated. Underlying this lien is the land lease requiring that the lessee meet his obligations to the land lessor. Should the lessee default in meeting these obligations, the leasehold mortgage may become worthless.

Because of the junior position of the holder of the leasehold mortgage, he will insist upon various protections. Since his resources are necessary to finance the building, the erection of which adds needed protection to the interests of the lessor, he looks to the latter for protection in turn. He wants to be sure of ample notice before action to cancel a lease on account of a breach by the lessee. The mortgagee may elect to succeed to the position of the lessee in such case by keeping up rental payments and by meeting other obligations to the lessor. He much prefers to finance a building under a lease where any increments of land value accrue to the benefit of the lessee instead of the lessor. Reappraisal leaseholds are very difficult to finance for this reason.

The mortgagee also prefers that the lease include a purchase option at a price not too greatly in excess of the value of the land at the time the mortgage is executed. An option at a fantastic price is no option at all. One at a reasonable price enables the lessee, or if necessary the mortgagee, to purchase the fee as a measure of protection at a future time. The lessor's desire to retain this investment in the property may be tempered by the necessity for granting a purchase option as the price of enabling the lessee to secure the financial assistance required to construct the building. As noted above, the lessor's interest is better protected by the presence of the building. The lessee will be well advised to make sure that the terms of the lease will enable him to finance the building before he signs the lease.

In addition to a purchase option, a renewal option is favored by mortgagees. This is particularly true if the lease is about to expire. The shorter the term of the lease, the less likelihood of financing the leasehold. For example, if the lease has only two years to run to maturity, no mortgagee would advance to the lessee more than he was sure of realizing during two years by subtracting from the assured net return from the use of the property all rents, taxes, and other carrying charges for which the lessee is obligated. If there is a renewal clause, it extends the potential life of the lease, unless its terms are unacceptable.

Joining lessor in financing building

Because it is not always easy to secure leasehold financing necessary to pay the cost of constructing an expensive building on a vacant site, particularly in a financial market that is not accustomed to the use of mortgages against leaseholds, it has become increasingly common for the lessee to enlist the cooperation of the lessor in financing the construction. If the lessor is willing to let the mortgage cover the value of the land as well as that of the building, funds from an institutional lender become much more readily available.

This type of financing is accomplished by means of an arrangement whereby the landowner agrees to subordinate his interest in the land to that of the lender's mortgage. The arrangement is called a *subordinated ground lease,* or, sometimes, a *subordinated fee.* Although the landowner does not sign the note to the lender, in event of foreclosure, by virtue of his subordination of his underlying fee interest, the owner forfeits his interest in the property to the lender. From the standpoint of the lender, this structuring of the priorities provides the equivalent of a fee ownership security and therefore an unimpaired basis for a loan.

For obvious reasons, landowners have long shied away from such subordinations. After all, why should the owner risk the loss of his property for the benefit of the lessee-developer? In the last few years, however, it has become apparent that both the lessee-developer and the lessor-owner may benefit from a subordination. More lenders are interested in having an unimpaired lien on the fee for reasons of legality or policy, and most are more generous in their loan appraisals. The developer can, therefore, more nearly optimize his project and respond to the lessor-owner by paying him higher land rentals, likely including a participation in revenues generated above certain minimum levels. Furthermore, it has been made more apparent to the landowner that if he were to develop the project on his own (assuming that he had the expertise), he would have to put up the land in any case, becoming personally liable for the debts of the venture. Under the leasing arrangement, the owner's maximum exposure is the loss of the land.

Problems in financing the underlying fee

There is a recognized conflict of interest between financing the leasehold and improvements thereon and financing the fee underlying the leasehold. Any protections which the lessor sacrifices in making the lease may be necessarily yielded as a condition to securing the signature of the lessee; but at the same time such sacrifices may decrease the value of the interest of the lessor. Should the lessor subsequently find it necessary or desirable to finance his fee in any manner, the terms of the lease will be carefully scrutinized by the party furnishing the finances. For example, a reappraisal lease or even one that provides for a graded rental would normally be more favorable to the interests of the lessor than would one calling for level payments throughout the life of the lease. On the other hand, where the land value is declining rather than increasing, flat rentals might be preferred by the lessor if they reflect at least current land values. This would be exceptional. In like manner purchase options are not always favored by those who finance the fee.

The fee underlying the lease can be financed in either of two ways. Under a favorable lease to a responsible tenant, the value of the fee is determined by the terms of the lease and by the level of interest rates in the financial markets. The latter may become very important. Omitting any speculative advantages which the fee owner may enjoy, a fee worth $100,000 when its rent would be capitalized at 8 percent would drop to $80,000 if the capitalization rate became 10 percent. Of course, one factor which helps to determine the capitalization rate is the credit rating of the lessee.

Like any other real estate interest, the fee underlying a long-term lease can be mortgaged. This mortgage, as a lien upon the senior interest in the real estate, constitutes a prior claim which takes precedence over the lease and consequently over leasehold mortgages or bonds. As an alternative to a mortgage, the fee owner may assign his interests to any purchaser. The assignee would necessarily take title subject to any claims against the fee of which he has notice. Presumably he would have notice of both the long-term lease and of any mortgage against it. Since the fee involves less risk than the leasehold, it follows that financing the fee is much easier than financing the leasehold. In many instances, rates of return upon fees underlying leaseholds are comparable to rates of return upon government bonds.

Financing subleases

A long-term sublease is sometimes financed in a manner similar to that described above for long-term leases. So far as the mortgagee is concerned, his interest is primarily in some questions that would call for answers if he became interested in financing a long-term lease. The difference between financing leases and financing subleases is important and may become the governing factor. In financing the lease, the mortgagee is interested in measuring the difference between the value of the land and building on the one hand and the capitalized rent to the owner on the other. In financing subleases, the latter element would be replaced by the capitalized rent paid to the sublessor instead of to the owner.

The term *sandwich* lease arises out of the case where lessee A subleases to party B. A is then sandwiched between the property owner and B. The value of A's lease is the present value of the excess of his rent claim from B over his rent obligation to the owner. Thus, if A leases from the owner for $5,000 annually and subleases to B for $12,000 annually, the net leasehold income to A is $7,000. If the correct capitalization rate for this investment in light of all the risks and conditions is 10 percent, the leasehold is worth ($7,000 ÷ .10) $70,000.

Valuation of leaseholds. The crucial part of the lending decision where a leasehold is the basis of security lies in its appraisal value. This value is largely dependent upon the type of lease, the correctness of appraisal techniques, and the prevailing costs of money in the capital markets.

Types of leases. In appraising commercial property for lending purposes, the type of lease used is a matter of prime importance to the lender. Of the many types in use, the most common only will be mentioned here. In the net lease the tenant contracts to pay all operating expenses, taxes, and insurance. A modification of this form places the burden of taxes and insurance upon the lessor. At the other extreme, some percentage leases provide for a fixed minimum rent regardless of the amount of business done, while others have no such minimum.

The appraiser must study the type of lease used in order to determine what stabilized income to expect. In the net lease to a financially responsible tenant, the amount to be expected is most easily calculated, particularly if the rent is fixed for the life of the lease. Even where it is graded, the amount is easily ascertainable if the steps are definitely set forth in the lease as to both time and amount of rent changes. While the net lease may hold down the income accruing to the holder of the equity, it probably best suits the needs of the lender on a mortgage against the property. Next to this type, the lender will probably prefer the percentage lease with a minimum guarantee.

PART 3: LAND TRUST CERTIFICATES

Meaning

One method of financing long-term leases that has had considerable vogue in some sections of the country, particularly during the decade of the 1920s, is the use of land trust certificates. This plan of financing did not originate at that time. It is simply an application of the much older idea of the Massachusetts trust. In effect it provides for the ownership of a parcel of land by a number of owners, each of whom owns one or more land trust certificates. Other names used to designate such certificates of ownership are fee ownership certificates, certificates of equitable ownership, participation certificates, and ground rent certificates.

The manner in which such certificates are used follows a pattern somewhat as follows: The owner of a business site leases it to a financially responsible tenant. The latter agrees to build a suitable building on the site. Let us assume that the annual net rental is to be $21,000 a year. If $1,000 is sufficient to pay the fee for managing the project in the interest of the owners of the site, $20,000 remains to pay for the use of the land. Capitalized at 10 percent, the indicated value of the site is $200,000. With the lease to a financially responsible tenant as security, the owner then proceeds to sell the site, vesting legal title in a managing trustee. Equitable title will rest with the owners of the land trust certificates. These certificates typically might have a face value of $1,000 each and pay an annual return of $100.

Land trust certificates have been used also where the owner of the land and the building decides to use money for some other purpose by selling its land, leasing it back, and returning ownership of the building. The same process will be followed as if the seller of the land and the lessee were two different parties.

Financing the building.   Where land trust certificates are used to finance the site, they become the senior lien against the entire property. The building can be financed with leasehold bonds, debenture bonds, equity funds, or any combination of these types of securities. In any event, the financing of the building will place the contributors of the funds needed for this purpose in the position of junior claimants.

Rental trust certificates

A financing device similar to land trust certificates has been given the name *rental trust certificates.* The legal ownership of leases and subleases is vested in a trustee. Against such ownership, certificates of beneficial interest are sold, usually in denominations of $500 or $1,000. They represent fractional parts in an undivided estate in the leases and subleases. The trustee collects all rents due under the leases and subleases. Quarterly payments are made to the holders of the rental trust certificates. Payments up to a certain percent a year are considered to be a return on the investment. Any payments over this amount are considered to represent amortization of the investment. Before making any distribution, the trustee deducts from the rentals received any expenses incurred by him, plus his own fees. Rental trust certificates simply represent a means of distributing the ownership of leases and subleases among a sizable number of people.

Questions

1 What is a land contract?

2 Under what circumstances are land contracts commonly used?

3 When a vendee on a land contract acquires property subject to a mortgage which was placed on the property by the vendor, what precautions should the vendee take with regard to future borrowing by the vendor where the property may be used as security?

4 What provisions should be made for a deed where property is purchased under a land contract? Might an escrow arrangement be established to the advantage of the vendee?

5 What alternative remedies does a seller under a land contract have in event of default in payment of the purchase price by the buyer?

6 What problems arise when a purchaser under a land contract wishes to make major improvements to the premises?

7 What are the advantages and disadvantages to the use of land contracts as a means of achieving control over large amounts of investment real estate?

8 What principal advantages may a property owner hope to gain by becoming a lessor on a long-term lease? What are the disadvantages?

9 What principal advantages may a long-term lessee hope to gain by becoming a tenant as opposed to buying a land site outright? What are the disadvantages?

10 What are the flat rentals? Step-up rentals? Percentage leases?

11 What limitations do rental escalation clauses impose on tenants who might desire to utilize leasehold values as security to finance property improvements?

12 What is a sandwich lease and how does it derive value? May it become a vehicle for speculation?

13 If you were a lending officer of a financial institution, what principal conditions and provisions would you expect to find present before you would accept a long-term lease as security for a loan to the lessor?

14 Should a long-term lessor require bond to ensure that the lessee will complete his undertaking to construct a building on a land parcel?

15 What are land trust certificates and what purposes do they serve in financing real estate? Rental trust certificates?

Case problems

1   Vendee X installed new plumbing fixtures in a building which he is buying under a land contract. No provision was made in the contract regarding improvements, and Vendor Y did not consent. Plumber Z made the improvements. What right, if any, does Z have to enforce a mechanics' lien?

2   B entered into a land contract to purchase real estate from S. The purchase price was to be paid over a ten-year period by monthly amortization. At the end of five years, B defaulted, failing to make his required payments. The contract provided that in event of default for a period of 30 days the seller could declare a forfeiture under the contract and repossess the property. If the courts should consider the land contract an equitable mortgage, what might be the rights of B and S?

3   A sound property in an older neighborhood can be bought on a land contract. It is a 12-unit apartment building that has the following estimated income and expenses:

Income:

Seven five-room apartments @ $40 per week		$ 280
Five four-room apartments @ $35 per week		175
Rental income per week		$ 455
Annualized ($455 × 52)		$23,660
Less: Vacancy allowance		1,660
Estimated effective gross rental		$22,000

Expenses:

Utilities	$5,000	
Insurance	500	
Real estate taxes	1,500	
Maintenance—furniture and fixtures	1,500	
Maintenance—other	1,000	
Management	1,000	10,500
Estimated net cash receipts before financing		$11,500

a.   Assuming the purchase price is $90,000, compute the net cash flow in relation to the cash investment required for the first year of ownership under the following conditions (disregarding depreciation and income taxes):*

	Condition A	Condition B
Down payment of investor	$ 7,000	$15,000
Land contract @ 9% annual interest	83,000	75,000
Annual payment required on contract	9,500	8,000

b.   In further analysis, compute taxable income to the investor assuming a depreciation charge of $4,500 annually and an effective income tax rate of 35 percent.

c.   Under both conditions *a* and *b,* what would be the investor's yield for the first year (1) on an accounting statement basis and (2) in terms of cash flow after taxes? Consider the impacts of the following on this kind of financing: (1) size of down payment, (2) tax shelter, (3) inflation, and (4) kinds of risk.

    * Net cash flow is equal to net cash receipts before financing minus payment on land contract.

4   White and Black are investors. White holds leasehold mortgage bonds whose proceeds were used to finance an office building on the land parcel. Black holds land trust certificates. Who has the senior security?

5   Brown has leased land from Green for 50 years at $3,000 annually. He has constructed a warehouse building on the site at a cost of $100,000. He estimates the life of the building at 50 years with no salvage value.

   a.   Assuming his only costs are land rentals and depreciation, how much must Brown earn in warehouse rentals if he expects to earn 10 percent on his initial investment?

   b.   If he earns a net rental income of $25,000 applicable to these factors during the first year and this income may reasonably be expected to continue, what would be a reasonable asking price for his leasehold interest should he choose to put it up for sale?

6   The High Stick Hockey Club sold its sports arena to Hughes Howard for $4 million. Howard paid $1 million in cash and gave a $3 million mortgage at 9 percent interest per annum. The annual payment on the mortgage was agreed to be $306,000, all excess over interest to be applied in reduction of the mortgage obligation. The club then leased back the arena for 25 years at a net annual rental of $440,000. Howard then sold the underlying land to a religious foundation for $800,000 cash and leased it back from the foundation for $80,000 per year. The arena is estimated to have a 25-year life, and Howard expects to be taxed on his net income at an overall 50 percent rate.

   a.   What is Howard's cash flow before income tax?*

   b.   Compute the effects of the transaction on Howard's taxes for the first year.

   c.   Evaluate the deal for Howard.

   * "Cash flow" is equal to the annual rental income reduced by annual payments for ground rents and mortgage financing.

Validation of title

5

Evolution of assurance of good title

In the evolution of assurance of good title upon which real estate finance must be based, several significant steps can be traced. In some instances even today, title passes with no assurance of the validity of title other than the trust placed by the purchaser in the seller. To save expense, deeds are occasionally accepted without reference to the records. A series of old deeds, showing an unbroken chain of title for a long period of time, may accompany the new deed and may be accepted by the grantee as sufficient evidence of title, particularly if the grantor is a well-known citizen whose word is usually trusted. This course is not recommended. The few dollars saved may be poor compensation for much larger losses that may be suffered, perhaps through no intent of the grantor.

In earlier periods of our history and even in rural communities today, the above course of action may be supplemented by a more or less careful search of the records by a local lawyer who may have some acquaintance with the recording processes in his community. As a matter of fact, even though he is a general practitioner rather than a specialist in real estate law, he may be able to render satisfactory service because of his acquaintance with the peculiarities of the recording system and with the parties involved in the real estate transaction. The results of his researches may be stated orally to his client, may be included in a letter to him, or may be couched in the phrases peculiar to the more formal title "opinion." Where the grantee acts upon the recommendations of his lawyer, he substitutes his trust in him for his former trust in the vendor. For the small fee charged, the lawyer cannot be expected to be held responsible for errors in judgment, if any. Gross negligence on his part or willful intent to take advantage of his client are proper grounds for damage suits.

If the attorney discussed above should "abstract" from the record the salient points upon which he bases his opinion and should pass these along to his client as evidence to support his conclusions, he might well call his report an abstract and title opinion. As this abstracting process became more formal, it not only summarized some parts of the record but copied verbatim some other parts. Thus was born the abstract system which forms the basis of title opinions in many sections of the country. Abstracts are never official documents enjoying the importance attributed to legislation and court decisions. Instead, they represent some presumably competent individual's concept of what parts of the records are significant in searching title to real estate. From the date of earliest land records, abstracts attempt to include all actions of importance that may affect the quality of title to the land in question. In addition to identifying maps, abstracts deal with deeds, mortgages, releases, taxes, leases, judgments and other liens, wills, pending suits, and a variety of other items.

The development of the abstract system tended to separate record search and title examination. Abstract companies and young attorneys are assigned the duty of continuing an abstract once it has been developed. Normally the abstract is passed along with the deed to the grantee. When he in turn becomes a grantor, he is responsible for having the abstract brought down to date by the use of tail sheets that deal with anything that affects the title to the property since the abstract was last continued. When this service has been performed, the abstract is then turned over to the attorney for the new grantee, who bases his opinion of title upon his examination of the abstract. Again he advises his client—orally, by letter, or by a more formal opinion—of his conclusions. His opinion may recite specific items that lead him to question the validity of title or that he thinks his client should know about, even though he concludes that the title is merchantable. As before, the attorney who passes upon title is not expected to guarantee its quality.

The next stage in the evolution of assurance of title makes use of the certificate of title, a little-used plan in most sections of the country today. This is a form of title opinion by which the author may again combine the search of the records with a statement of his conclusions based thereon. The searcher may use the abstract or he may bypass it. In any event he issues to his client a statement in the form of certificate of title, the legal status of which is not always clearly defined. Is a certificate any different from an opinion? Does the author assume any different responsibility when he says, "I certify"? Partly because of the uncertainty surrounding this issue, the certificate is not commonly used.

Nature of abstract

Recorded instruments constitute the basic evidence of title to real estate. The records are official and are treated as such. An abstract, on the other hand, is not an official document. It may be a full and complete copy of every pertinent record, or it may be a short form or synopsis type, often called a *bobtailed abstract*. Its purpose is to furnish all the material information contained in the original documents and records from which it is compiled so that they may be studied as completely as if the originals were under inspection. The abstract should show the inception and foundation of the title, together with its devolution to the date of examination. The abstract should document the incidents of the land, its divisions and subdivisions, all adverse claims and titles, liens or charges, and every other matter of record that may affect the title. Although an abstracter is not required to go beyond the record, he may do so if he becomes aware of an item that may have a bearing on the quality of the title.

Abstracts usually include reference to the source of the original title from the government. City and town plats are usually included if such are in existence. All legal actions pending that may affect the title should be noted. Easements and restrictions are carefully noted, since they run with the land. Likewise, zoning and other regulatory ordinances governing the use and occupancy of the real estate and the improvements permitted to be placed upon the land are important parts of abstracts. The status of taxes is always important.

An abstracter—whether a firm specializing in such activities or a lawyer who takes on abstract work incidentally—is responsible only for an accurate portrayal of original documents and records affecting title. Any mistakes in recording or in indexing legal documents will be carried into the abstract without identifying them as mistakes. The abstract makes no pretense of disclosing hidden title hazards. Among the latter may be one or more of the following: (1) forged deeds in the chain of title, (2) deeds by minors or other incompetents, (3) deeds by grantors who represent themselves as single persons when in fact they are married, (4) claims of unknown or forgotten heirs, (5) mistakes in recording legal documents, (6) falsification of records, (7) errors in indexing of records, (8) birth or adoption of a child after a will is made, (9) deeds delivered after death of grantor, (10) impersonation of true owners of land by others not having title to it, and so forth.

When abstracts were first used, they were made by public officers who had charge of the records. In a dozen or so states it is still the law that when called upon to do so and when compensated according to a schedule of fees, the public official will check the records for specific findings requested of him. Public records are open to the public. Their use by outsiders is not subject to a charge by the public official who is not called upon to make a search of any part of the records.

Legal definition of abstract.   The Supreme Court of Illinois has defined an abstract as follows:

> In a legal sense, a summary or epitome of the parts relied on as evidence of title and it must contain a note of all conveyances, transfers or other facts relied on as evidence of the claimant's title, together with all such facts appearing on record as may impair the title. It should contain a full summary of all grants, conveyances,

wills and all records and judicial proceedings whereby the title is in any way affected and all encumbrances and liens of record and show whether they have been released or not.[1]

Lack of uniformity.   In many areas there is a lack of uniformity in the practices of abstracters. In general, there are no standard requirements which govern the operations of those who profess to be expert in making or in continuing abstracts. Trade associations have done much to raise standards; but unfortunately those who need the benefits of trade association contacts most are those who expose themselves to the practices of others least frequently. Some abstracters have little investment in plant and depend entirely upon the use of public records when their services are sought. Even here they may not be too careful or too wise in the use of information available to them. Such abstracters are sometimes known in the trade as *curbstoners.* Others have a great deal invested in what are known in the trade as *title plants.* These consist of tract indexes, miscellaneous indexes, suit and judgment dockets, plats, maps, takeoffs, and photostatic, photographic, and microfilm equipment. The results of abstracts vary widely, owing to differences in the experience, care, and ingenuity of those who do the work.

Short-term abstracts.   In some cases a practice of using what has come to be known as *short-term* abstracts has sprung up. Suppose, for example, that a plot of ground is being subdivided and that the abstract of title up to the time of subdivision has been so carefully drawn that no attorney or other local interested party will question the title. The abstracts of the lots into which the plot is subdivided begin with the date of the subdivision. Therefore they are called short-term abstracts. They may even serve all local needs quite acceptably. Outside agencies, such as out-of-state insurance companies which may later be called upon to finance a property located in the subdivision, may refuse to base their decisions upon such short-term abstracts. The cost of revising the abstract or of adding to it at a later date may be considerable.

Abstracter's certificate.   At the end of the abstract there should be the certificate of the abstracter, showing the nature of his work, the records searched, and the contents of the abstract. If the abstract does not purport to cover some records, that fact should be stated unequivocally. For example, if the certificate states that the records of the county treasurer, the county clerk, the county recorder, and the clerk of the local courts only have been searched, then any loss occasioned by the failure to include any records from the federal court could not be assessed against the abstracter. However, the certificate of the abstracter cannot protect him if it is couched in vague or obscure language. If he certifies that his searches have revealed no encumbrances, this will be interpreted to mean that there are no encumbrances against the property whose title is at stake.

---

[1] 244 Ill. 363, 91 N.E. 475, 135 Am. St. Rep. 342.

A typical abstract certificate reads as follows:

> We hereby certify that the foregoing Abstract of Title, consisting of 116 sections, was collated by us from the records of Franklin County Ohio: and we believe the same contains every instrument of record in said County, in any way affecting the premises described at title page, as shown by the respective indexes to said records.

Legal opinion of title

A lawyer studies abstracts for the purpose of arriving at an expert opinion of the character of the title. In his study of a specific abstract, the lawyer is generally limited to the evidence presented in the abstract. If it has been carefully compiled and recently brought down to date, any further study of the primary records would disclose no new evidence about the title so far as the records are concerned. The lawyer who renders an opinion about a real estate title is not asked to insure the title. The fee he is paid for examining it will not warrant his assumption of this risk. Based upon his study of the abstract and/or the record, the opinion he gives is his best judgment concerning the character of the title.

The lawyer cannot be expected to take responsibility for any defect in title not disclosed by the records. Any responsibility borne by the lawyer is based upon proof of his negligence or of his lack of professional skill. Either would be difficult to prove. There is always room for honest differences of opinion among competent lawyers on such questions as interpretations of wills and probable outcome of litigation affecting land titles.

Defects in records.   Titles may be defective in many ways. Shortcomings may include defects in execution; defective descriptions; tax liens and judgments; encumbrances not covered by escrow instructions; and miscellaneous errors, including potential mechanics' liens and defective proceedings of various types. Any one of these defects may carry with it a potential liability of the warrantor of the title for large dollar amounts.

Development and meaning of title insurance

It was to cure the inadequacies of title validation purely by abstract and legal opinion that title insurance was developed. Title insurance does all that both a carefully drawn abstract and a well-considered opinion by a competent lawyer are expected to do. In addition, it adds the principle of insurance to the above services and undertakes to spread the risk of unseen hazards among all who benefit from it. It must start with careful analysis of the records. The plant of the commercial title company may be even more complete than the public records. Then there must be skilled technicians to examine all evidence of the title to determine its character. If the conclusions warrant, the title company will back up its opinion about the title to a given piece of property by assuming the risk that is not disclosed in the records or in its own files.

What title insurance is supposed to add to the abstract system and the opinion of skilled lawyers may be classified as follows: (1) definite contract liability to the premium payer; (2) ample resources to back up this liability; (3) reserves sufficient to meet losses; (4) supervision by an agency of the state in which the title insurance company operates; and (5) protection to the policyholder against financial losses that may show up at any future time because of title defects of any kind, disclosed or hidden.

Types of title insurance policies

The title insurance policy commonly arises with the passage of title from a seller to a purchaser. The policy issued covers the purchaser and his heirs. It is purchased with a single premium normally based on the full price paid for the property, and the policy purports to protect the owner of the property and his heirs forever. There is no statute of limitations that restricts the enforceable life of the policy. If the property is sold again, however, a new policy must be taken out for the new buyer if he is to have insurance coverage.

There are two types of title insurance policies in common use. The first type guarantees that the title is good. The second type insures not only that the title is good but also that it is marketable.[2] The most commonly used title policy forms were developed by the American Land Title Association (ALTA). There are two forms of owners' policies: ALTA Form A-1970 and ALTA Form B-1970. Form A insures a good title but does not insure marketability. Form B insures both a good and marketable title. Thus, Form A might not give adequate coverage to a buyer where the seller acquired title by adverse possession, for example, and did not establish it by court record, or where a defective deed in the sellers chain of title needs reformation. Uncollectible damages could arise to an insured under a Form A policy where a buyer from him might refuse his deed on grounds that his title is not marketable. Under Form B he would be protected. Form B is customarily used, although in some states, including Florida, Indiana, and Illinois, Form A is the more common policy issued. New York, Texas, and a few other states require special forms.[3]

A second class of insured is the mortgagee. The mortgagee policy insures the status of the lien and the mortgage. Since the interest of the mortgagee in the land is terminated when his money has been repaid, the mortgagee policy

---

[2] A *marketable title* has been defined as "one that can again be sold to a reasonable purchaser, a title that a man of reasonable prudence, familiar with the facts and apprized of the questions of law involved, would in the ordinary course of business accept." *Siedel* v. *Snider*, 241 Iowa 1227, 44 N. W. 2d 687 (1950).

[3] William A. Thau, "Protecting the Real Estate Buyer's Title," *Real Estate Review*, vol. 3, no. 4 (Winter 1974), pp. 71–83. See also Marvin C. Bowling, Jr., "The ALTA Loan Policy—Have You Read Paragraph 3(a)?" *The Mortgage Banker*, vol. 34, no. 5 (February 1974), pp. 28–33.

expires when the mortgage is paid off or canceled. If as a result of foreclosure the mortgagee becomes the owner of the real estate, the mortgagee policy becomes an owner's policy as of the date of change of title. Because the mortgagee policy is expected to run for a shorter period of time than an owner's policy, it is usually somewhat cheaper.

The risk rate for owners' policies is commonly $3.50 per $1,000 up to $50,000 and becomes progressively lower as the insured amount increases. For amounts over $15,000,000, the rate is $1.25 per $1,000. Mortgage premiums run $2.50 per $1,000 up to $50,000 and become as low as $1 per $1,000 on amounts in excess of $15,000,000. The minimum premium on an owner's policy is $10, and on a mortgage policy, $7.50. These rates prevail in about half the states. In other states and areas special rates apply. These rates are often under the surveillance of the state insurance commission. They tend to be somewhat higher in areas where the loss experience has been bad. Premiums charged are for insurance only and do not cover examination cost, record search, abstract, or closing expenses. In some localities reissues of title insurance policies on the same property, but to different policyholders, are reduced to 50 or 75 percent of the original premium.

It is customary to write two policies on the same property. For example, if A purchases a property for $80,000, he will probably want a title insurance policy for that amount. If he mortgages his property for $50,000 to B, a separate policy for $50,000 will be written to protect B's interest. If the insurance company should pay a loss claim to the mortgagee for his $50,000 interest, the owner's policy would normally be reduced by this amount.

Where an owner's policy and a mortgage policy covering the same property are issued simultaneously, there is some saving in premium. The rates applicable to the owner's policy are the regular owner's rates, but the premium for the mortgage policy is generally a nominal amount, often $7.50, for an insurance coverage not in excess of the owner's policy.

A third class of policy, less common than the other two, should be mentioned. The leasehold policy is written in favor of the lessee to protect his interest in the property during the term of his lease.

Full coverage demanded.   Title insurance companies usually demand that the policy covering the title to a parcel of real estate be written for the full value of the property, in case the owner's policy is used, or for the full amount of the mortgage, in a mortgagee's policy. The reason for insistence upon full coverage is quite obvious. For example, suppose that an owner of a $50,000 property requested a title insurance policy for only $10,000. It is quite probable that any losses that might be suffered would fall within the $10,000. Consequently, the insurance company would, in effect, be giving 100 percent protection but would be collecting a risk premium on only 20 percent of the value of the property.

Extra fees.   In general, title insurance companies will not insure a title unless they think it is good. Therefore they do not make a practice of charging extra fees to cover unusual hazards. If unusual hazards are present, they must be cleared up before the title will be insured. There are occasional exceptions to this rule. Tax titles are not liked by many insurance companies. When they are presented for insurance, sometimes an extra fee is charged. Likewise, temporary hazards are sometimes compensated for by extra fees. For example, during depressions, many voluntary deeds are given to save foreclosure costs and resulting deficiency judgments. Since there is always a question as to whether a court of equity may frown upon such deeds at a subsequent time, an extra and unmeasurable hazard is created which is sometimes the occasion for an extra fee. Other extra hazards may result from any one of several causes. For example, an unreleased though presumably paid mortgage may cause future trouble.

Expansion of coverage.   In areas where title insurance is commonly used, there appears to be developing a tendency to look to the title insurance policy to protect the purchaser of or the lender against real estate from any hazards that might in any manner affect the character of the title. As a result, title insurance in such cases tends to become indemnity insurance as well. The specific hazards which may be covered by such expanded coverage include the following:

1.   Loss resulting from mechanics' liens.
2.   Loss resulting from violations—present or prospective—of covenants or conditions that limit the use to which the real estate may be put. Included among these covenants and conditions are:
    a.   Those which govern the type and cost of improvements.
    b.   Those which prohibit the manufacture or sale of intoxicating liquors.
    c.   Setback limitations.
3.   Loss resulting from improvement encroachments.
4.   Loss resulting from the presence and use of easements, which use might result in damage to buildings, trees, shrubbery, and so on.
5.   Loss resulting from rights of tenants holding property under unrecorded leases, including rent prepayments.

Lenders rather than owners are responsible for the tendency toward expansion of coverage of title insurance policies. This is an outgrowth of the increased marketability of real estate mortgages. If a lender in one section of the country purchases a mortgage on real estate located in a different section, it is natural to expect the lender to seek all possible protection against future potential losses; hence the urge to expand the liabilities placed upon the title company.

Meeting added hazards.   In cases where the expanded coverage of title insurance policies—by the use of riders covering the added risks discussed in the preceding section—creates added burdens for the title insurance companies, means are sometimes used to minimize the risks. For example, to protect against losses resulting from mechanics' liens, the title insurance company may take over some of the functions of the lender. It may insist upon paying out the funds provided by the lender. In this manner it can follow prudent practices in making sure that all bills are paid to the proper people, thus avoiding the possibility of losses resulting from mechanics' liens. In such case the title insurance company would assume the responsibility of checking all subcontract bids against the plans and specifications to make sure that the money supplied by the lender, plus the equity funds provided by the owner, will be sufficient to pay all costs of construction. Such service takes the title insurance company far afield from the business of strict title insurance but helps to get business that might otherwise go to competitors.

To protect title insurance companies against possible losses due to reversions, various plans are followed. One plan that has gained some popularity is to require the mortgagor to deed his property to a trustee who in turn leases it to the mortgagor. The lease contains a cancellation clause which may become effective immediately upon the violation of any of the lease terms, such as prohibition against the manufacture or sale of intoxicating liquor. By invoking such a cancellation clause, the trustee could effectively prevent loss to the title insurance company. The lease would bind not only the original mortgagor but all grantees who hold under him.

Exceptions. Since the title insurance policy is a contract between the insurer and the insured, it may contain such terms and conditions as are agreed upon between the contracting parties. Consequently, any exceptions become matters of great importance. They should be plainly stated in such manner as to make them clear to all concerned. Among the exceptions most commonly found in title insurance policies are: (1) the rights of tenants or others in possession of the property, which are not matters of record and which are not ordinarily found in the plant of the insurance company; (2) any questions which may arise on account of easements, party walls, encroachments, and those that might be disclosed by a survey of the property whose title is insured; (3) laws, government acts, or regulations, including zoning ordinances, restrictions governing use and occupancy of the property, and so on; (4) current taxes and assessments; (5) unrecorded liens; and (6) special conditions which may apply to a particular title and be written into the policy insuring it.

While there is a tendency to standardize title insurance policies, exceptions are frequently subject to bargaining and adjustment. If the insurance company thinks it runs little risk in so doing, it may agree to eliminate some restriction or exception to which the prospective policyholder makes strenuous objection. In other cases, a survey of the property as a condition of insurance will usually result in the elimination of the survey exception.

Binder of commitment. A prospective purchaser of a parcel of real estate may wish to make sure of his status as owner if and when he consummates the purchase. Until he becomes the owner he cannot have the title insured in his name. Likewise, a mortgagee who is approached to make a loan with the real estate as security prefers to know his status before he agrees to make the loan. In either case a binder (called a commitment in some areas) is used to recite the title insurance company's findings concerning the character of the title to the date of the binder. The binder also recites the acts which must be performed and the requirements which must be met before the title insurance policy can be written. When all necessary instruments have been drawn and recorded, the policy will become effective, assuming that no new complications have arisen to create doubts about the character of the title. Usually the time during which the binder takes the place of the policy is short. In unusual cases, such as a delay caused by inability to close a deal because one grantor cannot be easily and quickly located, the time may be longer.

If there are defects in the title which the insurance company insists must be cured before a title policy will be written, they will usually be noted in the binder. In other words, the binder states that the specified defects must be cured and that when they are so taken care of, the policy will be executed.

Losses under title insurance. In effect, title insurance consists of two parts: (1) a determination of ascertainable facts about the character of the title before insurance is granted and a willingness to stand behind such determination; and (2) a wager against the happening of an unascertainable event—beyond the control of the insurer and the insured—which will have an adverse effect upon the title. The primary purpose of the insurance company is so to conduct its investigations that no serious question can be left unanswered under the first heading outlined above. This does not mean that absolute perfection of title is insisted upon as a prerequisite to its insurance. Minor irregularities that are not likely to cause serious difficulty are frequently overlooked. If the latter were to be corrected by the insured before title was accepted for insurance, much business would be lost because the insured would conclude that if a title must first be perfected in all details, it probably would not need to be insured.

Torrens system

Under the Torrens system, the state supervises and arranges for an assurance of title. In effect, the state undertakes two obligations: (1) upon application, to determine the character of title of a specific property, at the expense of the applicant; and (2) by a system similar to title insurance, to guarantee the character of title insofar as the resources in the insurance reserve are sufficient for that purpose. In Hawaii no reserve has been established, but the general credit of the state is pledged to protect against loss. Twenty states have had legislation permitting use of the Torrens system, but 8 states have since repealed it, leaving only 12 with registration statutes still on their books. Only Hawaii, Illinois, Massachusetts, and Minnesota make substantial use of it. The other states in which use is permitted are Colorado, Georgia, New York, North Carolina, Ohio, Oregon, Virginia, and Washington.

The major purpose of the Torrens system is to create and to maintain a merchantable title to land. Before such a title is created, any adverse claims must first be determined and dealt with. In defense of his plan Torrens stated that his purpose was to "simplify, quicken, and cheapen the transfer of real estate and to render titles safe and indefeasible." Specific advantages claimed for the Torrens system include: (1) It substitutes the greater certainty of an official adjudication of title for the uncertainty of unofficial examinations and opinions. (2) It cheapens the cost of title transfer by avoiding the necessity for repeated examination of title whenever a title is transferred. (3) It speeds up the process of title transfer. (4) It avoids the increasing accumulation of title evidence over the years which makes future determination of titles increasingly more difficult and expensive.

Most of the arguments against its use are really against its introduction. The inconvenience and expense of initial registration are cited. Further, it is pointed out that permission of the court must be obtained to remove property from the system once it is registered, and the court must issue an order directing registration of heirs and devisees in case of descent. A major weakness has been the failure of government to provide adequate assurance funds to back up registered titles. This objection could be overcome once a system was under way sufficiently to build a fund large enough to cover the risk to the registrant of title defects not dealt with by registration.

The Torrens law has been in successful operation in Cook County (Chicago), Illinois, since 1897. Registration of titles requires about three months and a modest fee is charged to cover filing of application, examination of title, publication, and issuance of the first certificate of title. To this cost must be added to the payment of .1 percent of the value of the land to be paid to the indemnity fund and to defray abstract charges. Since 1897 the total charges against the fund on account of errors have averaged only about 3 percent of the payments into the fund. The cost of transfer of registration, after the original issuance of the certificate of title, is a nominal set fee irrespective of the value of the property.

Without title registration, reliance must be placed on attorneys' opinions and title insurance for protection from losses because of defective titles. It is apparent that strong vested interests find great advantage in continuation of this mode. These interests have exerted such forces that the movement toward title registration has subsided.

Influence of large investors.   The trend toward nationalizing the market for real estate mortgages has had its effect upon the increasing demand for real estate title insurance. Any absentee owner of a mortgage prefers to play safe by asking that titles to real estate on which he holds titles be insured. Large institutional investors recognize that the greatest risk assumed in the acquisition of federally underwritten real estate mortgages may be in the mortgagor's title. Government insurance is conditioned upon the ultimate ability of the approved mortgagee to offer, in exchange for the government debentures for which the law provides, a foreclosed title satisfactory to the FHA. This condition, in effect, requires of investors in FHA mortgages that they have positive assurance of a good and marketable title, for anything less may result in the nullification of the government insurance upon which the investors depend for protection in event of the mortgagor's delinquency. In general, only with title insurance does the investor have positive protection against financial loss because of unmarketability of titles and indemnification for losses in event the FHA declines to accept titles for causes which can be amply covered in an insurance policy. Investing in mortgages without title insurance protection involves an assumption that the mortgagee, or his assignee, will be able to obtain government debentures in exchange for foreclosed properties; but, too late, the investor may discover that his assumption is false. For these reasons, most corporate investors regard federally underwritten loans as safer when the title is insured. The secondary market for these loans, therefore, is also a primary title insurance market. Life insurance companies, savings banks, savings and loan associations, and commercial banks almost always require title insurance in these circumstances. A similar practice is followed by the federal agencies that are active in the secondary market. Although neither the FHA nor the VA insists upon title insurance as a prerequisite to federal underwriting of mortgages, even small institutional lenders, including local banks and savings and loan associations, may require title insurance if they contemplate resale of a mortgage in the national market. While abstracts may satisfy local needs, title insurance will probably produce a more ready sale should the holder of the mortgage wish to dispose of it later.

Surveys

One important feature of real estate financing that is frequently overlooked is the need for an accurate survey of the property to be financed. Before a mortgage loan is disbursed, it may be desirable to make sure that it is protected by the right property as security. Surveys serve other purposes also. For example, should a request for a partial release of security be presented at any time, a survey will show whether the remaining security is what it is supposed to be. Easements can scarcely be granted safely without a survey. Finally, if the mortgage should for any reason become involved in court proceedings, a survey is almost essential before decisions can be relied upon.

Errors sometimes discovered by surveys include the following: (1) The building which affords the chief security for the mortgage loan may not even be located on the land described in the title. It may be on an adjoining lot instead. (2) Buildings, particularly garages, encroach upon adjacent lots and even upon alleys and streets. (3) Buildings on adjacent lots encroach upon the land described in the title to the property being financed. (4) There may be a material surplus or deficiency of land or its measurements as described in the title. (5) While the building may be located on the proper lot, it may be so situated as to violate setback lines prescribed in the title. (6) Easements may be improperly located or improperly used. (7) Conveyances may not properly describe the property intended to be used as security for the mortgage loan.

Once a proper survey is conducted by a competent engineer or surveyor and a map is submitted by him as evidence of his findings, the next step is to determine what, if anything, is to be done about his findings. If no irregularities are found and if the survey conforms in all respects to the title to the land, so much the better. If inconsequential irregularities are found, they may be disregarded by the lending institution. In some cases it may be best to insist upon corrections before mortgage funds are disbursed. Finally, in some instances, admittedly small in number, the findings of the survey may cause the lending institution to refuse to make the loan.

Surveys of commercial and industrial real estate which is offered as security for mortgage loans are generally more imperative than surveys of residential property. This is true for two reasons. In the first place, much greater amounts of money are usually involved so that the risk of a mistake is correspondingly greater. In the second place, much more of the land area—even up to 100 percent—is covered by the building. As a result, encroachments upon adjoining property are much more common. Where encroachment consists only of use for flower beds, hedges, and so forth, corrections are easily made. Even secondary buildings such as garages can be moved if necessary. But the encroachment of a major building is much more serious. It cannot be moved if it covers 100 percent plus of the land area it is expected to occupy. Its owner may be forced to purchase the "plus" area, perhaps at a holdup price.

Questions

1   What is an abstract of title?

2   How does an attorney's opinion or certificate that a title is good, based on review of an abstract, differ in effect from title insurance?

3   What is the Torrens system, and why is it not more widely used?

4   What is the legal responsibility of an attorney for an opinion which he has rendered stating that he considered the title good and unencumbered when it later appears that the title was defective when the opinion was given?

5   In what ways does title insurance render benefits which are not available to a person relying solely on the abstract system and an attorney's opinion?

6   What types of title insurance policies are in common use?

7   What difference do you see between insurance that the title is "good" and that it is "good and marketable"?

8   How important would you consider the loss experience factor to be in establishing premiums paid by the insured?

9 How has nationalizing the market for real estate mortgages affected the title insurance business?

10 What needs do surveys fulfill in title validation?

Case problems

1 *a.* Smithers was married in the Hawaiian Islands during World War II. In 1948 he acquired land in a stateside jurisdiction that requires release of dower rights upon disposition of real property. He did not disclose his marriage, although it remained intact, and he sold the land in 1970 without release of dower to Bumstead. Bumstead has now sold the property to you. Evaluate the relative advantages of an attorney's review of the abstract and title insurance.

b. Develop as many fact patterns as you can under which an attorney's opinion might give you less protection as a buyer or lender than title insurance.

2 Assume that you as an owner receive a title insurance policy with typical coverage. Give three examples in which you might not be protected by the insurance.

PART TWO

Mortgages and residential financing

The interest factor in financing

6

Financing the purchase of real estate usually involves borrowing on a long- or short-term basis. Since amounts borrowed are usually large in relation to prices paid for real estate, financing costs are usually significant in amount and weigh heavily in the decision to buy property. Because financing costs are important in borrowing decisions, individuals involved in real estate finance must understand how these costs are computed and how various provisions in loan agreements affect financing costs and mortgage payments. Familiarity with the "mathematics of finance" is essential in understanding simple mortgage payment calculations, how loan provisions affect financing costs, and how borrowing decisions affect investment returns.

This chapter provides an introduction to the mathematics of finance. It forms a basis for concepts discussed in financing single-family properties, income-producing properties, and in funding construction and development projects. These topics are included in chapters immediately following. Although the subject matter of mathematics sometimes appears burdensome and difficult, this chapter and the succeeding one will provide a fundamental approach to problem solving. From the concrete applications and illustrations in these chapters, the necessity of an understanding of these subjects will become readily apparent to anyone who seeks to achieve professional levels of competency in the field of real estate finance.

Compound interest

Understanding the process of compounding in finance requires the knowledge of only a few basic formulas. At the root of these formulas is the most elementary relationship of simple compounding. For example, if an individual makes a bank deposit of $10,000 that is compounded at an annual interest rate of 6 percent, what will be the value of the deposit at the end of one year? In examining this problem, one should be aware that any compounding problem has *four* basic components. These are:

1.   An initial deposit, payment, or investment of money.
2.   An interest rate.
3.   Time.
4.   Value at some specified future period.

In our problem, the deposit is $10,000, interest is at an annual rate of 6 percent, time is 1 year (12 months), and value at the end of the year is what we would like to know. We have, then, four components, three of which are known and one for which a solution is desired.

Compound value. In the preceding problem, we would like to determine what value will exist at the end of one year if a *single* deposit or payment of $10,000 is made at the *beginning* of the year and the deposit balance earns a 6 percent rate of interest. To find the solution some terminology must be introduced:

P_0 = deposit or principal at the beginning of the year
i = annual interest rate
I = dollar amount of interest earned during the period
P_n = principal at the end of n periods
n = time

In this problem then, P_0 = $10,000, i = 6 percent, n = 1 year, and P_n, or the value after one year, is what we would like to know.

Value after one year can be determined by examining the following relationship:

$$P_n = P_0 + I_1$$

or the principal, P_n, at the end of one year equals the deposit made at the beginning of the year, P_0, plus interest, I_1, earned in the first period. Since P_0 = $10,000, by determining I_1, the ending value P_n will be known. Since we are compounding annually, P_n is easily determined to be $10,600 which is shown in Exhibit 6–1.

Multiple periods. To find the value at the end of two years, the compounding process can be continued by taking the value at the end of one year, $10,600, and making it the deposit at the beginning of the second year and compounding again. This is shown in Exhibit 6–2.

From Exhibit 6–2 it can be seen that a total value of $11,236 has been accumulated by the end of the second year. Note that in the second year, not only is interest earned on the original deposit of $10,000 but *interest is also earned on interest* ($600) earned in the first year. Hence, in the second year,

EXHIBIT 6–1
Compound interest calculation (one year)

$$P_0 \times i = I_1$$
$$\$10,000 \times .06 = I_1$$
$$\$600 = I_1$$

Value at the end of one year, $n = 1$ year, is determined as:

$$P_0 + I_1 = P_n$$
$$\$10,000 + \$600 = \$10,600$$

or value can be determined as:

$$P_0(1 + i) = P_n$$
$$\$10,000(1 + .06) = P_n$$
$$\$10,600 = P_n$$

EXHIBIT 6–2
Compound interest calculation for two years

$$\$10,600 \times .06 = I_2$$
$$\$636 = I_2$$

and value at the end of two years, or $n = 2$ years, is now:

$$\$10,600 + I_2 = P_n$$
$$\$10,600 + \$636 = \$11,236$$

interest is also earned on interest. This "interest on interest" concept is really the *essential* idea that must be understood in the compounding process and is the cornerstone of all financial tables and concepts in the mathematics of finance.

From the computation in Exhibit 6–2, it should be pointed out that the value at the end of year 2 could have been determined directly from P_0 as follows:

$$P_n = P_0(1 + i)(1 + i)$$
$$P_n = P_0(1 + i)^2$$

In our problem then, when $n = 2$ years:

$$P_n = P_0(1 + i)^2$$
$$P_n = \$10,000(1 + .06)^2$$
$$P_n = \$10,000(1.123600)$$
$$P_n = \$11,236$$

From this computation, value at the end of two years, or $11,236, is identical to the result that we obtained in Exhibit 6–2. Being able to compute P_n directly from P_0 is a *very important relationship* because it means that the ending value, or value for *any* deposit or payment left to compound for any number of periods, can be determined directly from P_0 by simple multiplication. Therefore, if we want to determine the compound value of a deposit made at the end of any number of years, we can find the solution with the *general formula for compound interest,* which is:

$$P_n = P_0(1 + i)^n$$

By substituting the appropriate values for $P_0, i,$ and n, P_n can be determined for any desired number of years.

Other compounding intervals. In the preceding section the discussion of compounding applied to cases where funds were compounded only *once per year.* Many saving accounts, bonds, mortgages, and other investments provide for monthly, quarterly, or semiannual compounding. Because we will be dealing with mortgage loans extensively in later chapters, which almost exclusively involve monthly compounding, it is extremely important that we consider these other compounding intervals.

In dealing with compounding periods other than annual compounding, a simple modification can be made to the *general formula for compound interest.* Recalling from above, the *general formula is:*

$$P_n = P_0(1 + i)^n$$

where n = time, i = interest rate, and P_0 = deposit. To change this general formula for *any* compounding period desired, we divide the interest rate i by the desired number of compounding intervals *within one year.* We then increase n, number of time periods, by multiplying by the desired number of compounding intervals within one year. For example, let k be the number of *intervals within one year* that compounding is to occur and let n equal the number of years in the general formula above for more frequent compounding. This would result in the following:

$$P_n = P_0(1 + i/k)^{n \cdot k}$$

Hence, in the above problem if interest were earned on the $10,000 deposit at an annual rate of 6 percent, *compounded monthly,* to determine the value at the end of one year, where k equals 12, we would have:

$$P_n = \$10,000(1 + .06/12)^{1 \cdot 12}$$
$$P_n = \$10,000(1.06168)$$
$$P_n = \$10,616.80$$

If we compare the results of monthly compounding with those of annual compounding, we can immediately see the *benefits* of monthly compounding. If our initial deposit were compounded *monthly,* by the end of the year we would have a value of $10,616.80 as opposed to a value of $10,600.00 when *annual* compounding was used. Another way of looking at this result is to compute an annual yield on both investments assuming that $10,000 is deposited at the beginning of the year and that all proceeds are withdrawn at the end of the year. For the deposit that is compounded monthly, this is done as follows:

$$\frac{P_n - P_0}{P_0} = \text{Annual yield}$$

$$\frac{\$10,616.80 - \$10,000.00}{\$10,000} = 6.168\%$$

The result can be compared to the annual yield obtained when *annual* compounding is used, or:

$$\frac{\$10,600 - \$10,000}{\$10,000} = \text{Annual yield} = 6\%$$

From this comparison, we can clearly conclude that the annual yield is higher when monthly compounding is used. This comparison should immediately point out the difference between computing interest at an *annual rate of interest* and computing interest at the same *annual rate of interest, compounded monthly*. Both deposits are compounded at the same annual rate of interest (6 percent); however, one is compounded 12 times at a monthly rate of $(.06 \div 12)$, or .005, on the ending monthly balance, while the other is compounded only once, at the end of the year at the rate of .06.

From the above analysis, one result should be very clear. Anytime the annual interest rate offered on two investments are *equal*, the investment with the *more frequent compounding interval* within the year will *always* result in a higher annual yield. Indeed, in our example above we could say that a 6 percent annual rate of interest *compounded monthly* provides an *equivalent annual yield* of 6.168 percent.[1]

Some other investments offer semiannual, quarterly, and daily compounding. In these cases, the basic formula for compound interest is modified as follows:

Compounding interval	Modified formula
Semiannually, $k = 2$	$P_0(1 + i/2)^{n \cdot 2} = P_n$
Quarterly, $k = 4$	$P_0(1 + i/4)^{n \cdot 4} = P_n$
Daily, $k = 365$	$P_0(1 + i/365)^{n \cdot 365} = P_n$

Use of compound interest tables. Finding a solution to a compounding problem involving many periods is very awkward because of the amount of

---

[1] Because of this fact, many savings institutions that compound savings *monthly* quote an annual rate of interest but immediately point out that if funds are left on deposit for one year, a higher *equivalent annual yield* will be earned.

multiplication involved. To provide a shortcut for finding solutions to compound interest problems, a series of *interest factors* has been developed in tables in Appendix A and Appendix B at the end of this textbook. Appendix A contains interest factors for selected interest rates and years based on the assumption of *annual compounding intervals.* Appendix B contains interest factors for selected interest rates and years based on the assumption of *monthly compounding intervals.* These two compounding periods were chosen because they represent the compounding intervals that are most frequently used throughout this textbook.[2]

In both appendixes, the interest factors used for compounding single deposits are contained in column (1), *Amount of $1 at compound interest.* Essentially, these interest factors have been computed from the general formula for compound interest for annual compounding and from the formula as modified for monthly compounding for various combinations of *i* and years.

To familiarize the student with the use of these tables, interest factors (now referred to as *IF*) for the compound value (*CV*) of $1 for various interest rates are shown in Exhibit 6–3. These factors for annual compounding have been

EXHIBIT 6–3
Amount of $1 at compound interest (column 1, Appendix A)
Annual compounding factors

	Rate				
Year	6%	10%	15%	20%	25%
1	1.060000	1.100000	1.150000	1.200000	1.250000
2	1.123600	1.210000	1.322500	1.440000	1.562500
3	1.191016	1.331000	1.520875	1.728000	1.953125
4	1.262477	1.464100	1.749006	2.073600	2.441406
5	1.338226	1.610510	2.011357	2.488320	3.051758

taken directly from column 1 in each table for respective interest rates contained in Appendix A.

In the problem discussed earlier, we wanted to determine the ending value of a $10,000 deposit compounded at an annual rate of 6 percent after one year. Looking to the 6 percent column in Exhibit 6–3 to the row corresponding to one year, we find the interest factor 1.060000. This interest factor when multiplied by $10,000 gives us the solution to our problem.

$$\$10,000(IFCV, 6\%, 1 \text{ yr.}) = P_n$$
$$\$10,000(1.060000) = \$10,600$$

---

[2] More complete tables for these and other compounding intervals such as quarterly, semiannual, daily, and so on, can be computed with an electronic calculator or may be found in *Thorndike Encyclopedia of Banking and Financial Tables* (Boston: Warren, Gorham & Lamont, Inc., 1973), with supplements.

The interest factor for the compound value of $1, at 6 percent for one year (abbreviated as *IFCV*, 6%, 1 yr.), is 1.060000, which is the same result that we would obtain if we computed $(1 + .06)^1$ or 1.06 from the general formula for compound interest. In other words:

$$(IFCV, \; 6\%, \; 1 \; yr.) = (1 + .06)^1 = 1.06$$

The interest factors in the tables in Appendix A allow us to find a solution to any compounding problem as long as we know the deposit (P) and the interest rate (i), and the number of periods (n) over which annual compounding is to occur.

Question: What would be the value of $5,000 deposited for four years compounded at an annual rate of 10 percent?

Solution: $5,000($IFCV$, \; 10\%, \; 4 \; yrs.) = P_n$

$$\$5,000(1.464100) = \$7,320.50$$

As was the case with the interest factors for annual compounding, interest factors for *monthly compounding* for selected interest rates and years have been computed from the modified formula $P_0(1 + i/12)^{n \cdot 12}$ and are compiled in tables contained in Appendix B at the end of this textbook. To familiarize the student with these tables, interest factors for selected interest rates and periods have been taken from column 1, *Amount of $1 at compound interest*, from tables in Appendix B and are shown in Exhibit 6–4.

EXHIBIT 6–4
Amount of $1 at compound interest (column 1, Appendix B)
Monthly compounding factors

Month	Rate		
	6%	7%	8%
1.	1.005000	1.058330	1.006670
2.	1.010025	1.011701	1.013378
3.	1.015075	1.017602	1.020134
4.	1.020151	1.023538	1.026935
5.	1.025251	1.029509	1.033781
6.	1.030378	1.035514	1.040673
7.	1.035529	1.041555	1.047610
8.	1.040707	1.047631	1.054595
9.	1.045911	1.053742	1.061625
10.	1.051140	1.059889	1.068703
11.	1.056396	1.066071	1.075827
12.	1.061678	1.072290	1.083000

Year	6%	7%	8%	Month
1.	1.061678	1.072290	1.083000	12
2.	1.127160	1.149806	1.172888	24
3.	1.196681	1.232926	1.270237	36
4.	1.270489	1.322054	1.375666	48

In our earlier problem, we wanted to determine the value of a $10,000 deposit that earned interest at an annual rate of 6 percent, *compounded monthly.* This can be easily determined by selecting the appropriate interest factor from the 6 percent column for 12 months, or 1 year, in Exhibit 6–4. That factor is 1.061678. Hence, to determine the value of the deposit at the end of 12 months, or 1 year, we have:

$$\$10,000(MIFCV, 6\%, 12 \text{ mos.}) = P_n$$
$$\$10,000(1.061678) = \$10,616.78$$

In other words, the interest factor for a 6 percent rate of interest *compounded monthly* for one year $(MIFCV, 6\%, 12 \text{ mos.})$ is 1.061678, which is the same result that we would obtain if we expanded $(1 + .06/12)^{1 \cdot 12}$ by multiplying, or:

$$(MIFCV, 6\%, 12 \text{ mos.}) = (1 + .06/12)^{1 \cdot 12} = 1.061678$$

At this point note the use of the capital letter M in our abbreviation for the monthly compound interest equation. Instead of writing $(1 + .06/12)^{1 \cdot 12}$, then expanding the equation to obtain the monthly interest factor, we simply indicate that a *monthly* interest factor should be obtained from Appendix B when we use the abbreviation $(MIFCV, 6\%, 12 \text{ mos.})$. When M is *not* included in the abbreviation, *annual compounding is assumed* and those annual interest factors should be obtained from Appendix A.

Hence the interest factors in column 1 in the tables contained in Appendix B allow us to find a solution to any monthly compounding problem as long as we know the deposit (P), the interest rate (i), and the number of months or years over which compounding is to occur.

Question: What would be the value of a single $5,000 deposit earning 8 percent interest, *compounded monthly,* at the end of two years?
Solution: $\$5,000(MIFCV, 8\%, 2 \text{ yrs.}) = P_n$
$$\$5,000(1.172888) = P_n$$
$$\$5,864.44 = P_n$$

Present value

In the preceding section dealing with compounding, we were concerned with determining value at some time in the *future;* that is, we considered the case where a deposit had been made and compounded into the *future* to yield some unknown *future value.*

In this section we are interested in the problem of knowing the future cash receipts for an investment and trying to determine how much should be paid for the investment at *present.* The concept of *present value* is based on the idea that money has *time value.* Time value simply means that if an investor is offered the choice between receiving $1 today or receiving $1 in the future, he will always choose to receive the $1 today. This is because the $1 received today can be invested in some opportunity and will earn interest, which is preferable to receiving only $1 in the future. In this sense, money is said to have *time value.* Hence, in determining how much should be paid today for an investment that is expected to produce income in the future, an adjustment called *discounting* must be made to income received in the future to reflect the time value of money. The concept of *present value* lays the cornerstone for calculating mortgage payments, determining the effective cost of mortgage loans, and finding investment and appraised values, all of which are very important procedures in real estate finance.

A graphic illustration of present value. An example of how discounting becomes an important concept in financing can be seen from the following problem. Suppose an individual is considering an investment that promises a cash return of $10,600 at the end of one year. In the investor's evaluation, this investment should yield an annual rate of 6 percent. The question to be considered here is how much should be offered or paid today if $10,600 is to be received at the end of the year *and* the investor requires a 6 percent return compounded annually on the amount invested?

The problem can be seen more clearly by comparing it to the problem of finding the compound value of $1 discussed in the first part of this chapter. In that discussion we were concerned with finding the *future value* of a $10,000 deposit compounded monthly at 6 percent for one year. This comparison is depicted in Exhibit 6–5.

EXHIBIT 6–5
Comparison of compound value and present value

		Month												
		1	2	3	4	5	6	7	8	9	10	11	12	
Compounding at 6%	$10,000 —————————————————————→													Compound value (?)
Discounting at 6%	Present value (?) ←—————————————————————													$10,600

Note from Exhibit 6–5 that when *compounding* we are concerned with determining the *future value* of an investment. With *discounting,* we are concerned with just the *opposite* concept, that is, what *present value* or price should be paid *today* for a particular investment assuming a desired rate of interest is to be earned.

Since we know from the preceding section that $10,000 compounded annually at a rate of 6 percent yields $10,600 at the end of one year, $10,000 would be the *present value* of such an investment. However, had we not done the compounding problem in the preceding section, how would we know that $10,000 equals the present value of the investment? Let us again examine the compounding problem we considered in the previous section. To determine compound value, recall the general equation for compound interest:

$$P_n = P_0(1 + i)^n$$

In our present value problem P_0 becomes the unknown because P_n, or the value to be received at the end of one year, $n = 1$ year, is $10,600. Since the interest rate (i) is known to be 6 percent, P_0 is the only value which is not known. P_0, the present value or amount we should pay for the investment today, can be easily determined by rearranging terms in the above compounding formula as follows:

$$P_n = P_0(1 + i)^n$$
$$P_0 = P_n \div (1 + i)^n$$
$$P_0 = P_n \times \frac{1}{(1 + i)^n}$$

In our problem, then, we can determine P_0 directly by substituting the known values into the above expression as follows:

$$P_0 = P_n \times \frac{1}{(1 + i)^n}$$

$$P_0 = \$10,600 \times \frac{1}{(1 + .06)^n}$$

$$P_0 = \$10,600 \times \frac{1}{1.06000}$$
$$P_0 = \$10,600 \times .943396 \text{ (rounded)}$$

$$\text{Present value} = P_0 = \$10,000$$

Note that the procedure used in solving for the present value is simply to multiply the ending value, P_n, by 1 divided by $(1 + i)^n$. We know from the previous section on compounding that in our problem $(1 + i)^n$ is $(1 + .06)^1$ or $(IFCV, 6\%, 1 \text{ yr.})$ which equals 1.06. After dividing 1.06 into 1, the factor .943396 results. This last result is important in present value analysis because it shows the relationship between compound value and present value.

Because we have seen from Exhibit 6–5 that the *discounting process* is an opposite process from compounding, to find the present value of any investment is simply to compound in reverse sense. This is done in our problem by taking the inverse of the interest factor for the compound value of $1 at 6 percent, $1 \div 1.06$ or .943396, which we abbreviate as $(IFPV, 6\%, 1 \text{ yr.})$, and multiplying it by the *ending value* of our investment to find the *present value* of the investment. We can now say that $10,600 received at the end of one year, when discounted by 6 percent, has a present value of $10,000. Alternatively, if an investment is offered which promises $10,600 to us after one year and we want to earn a 6 percent return on our investment, we should not pay more than $10,000 for the investment (it is on the $10,000 present value that we earn the 6 percent interest).

Use of present value tables.   Since the discounting process is the reverse of compounding, and the interest factor for discounting $1 \div (1 + i)^n$ is simply the inverse of the interest factor for compounding, a series of interest factors has been developed that enables us to solve directly for present value (PV) instead of having to multiply out the term $(1 + i)^n$ and to divide the result into 1 each time we want to discount. In fact, all of that work has been done for us and compiled in column 4 in tables included in Appendix A, *Present value reversion of $1,* for both annual and monthly compounding. Exhibit 6–6 contains a

EXHIBIT 6–6
Present value reversion of $1 (column 4, Appendix A)
Annual discounting factors

			Rate		
Year	5%	6%	10%	15%	20%
1	.952381	.943396	.909091	.869565	.833333
2	.907029	.889996	.826446	.756144	.694444
3	.863838	.839619	.751315	.657516	.578704
4	.822702	.792094	.683013	.571753	.482253
5	.783526	.747258	.620921	.497177	.401878
6	.746215	.704961	.564474	.432328	.334898

sample of these *IFs* to be used for discounting, taken directly from column 4 in tables for selected interest rates in Appendix A.

In our problem we want to know how much should be paid for *n* investment with a future return of $10,600 to be received at the end of one year if the investor demands an annual return of 6 percent. The solution can be found by selecting the (*IFPV,* 6%, 1 yr.) or going to the 6 percent column in Exhibit 6–6 and selecting the present value interest factor for one year, or .943396. The $10,600 future value can now be multiplied by .943396 resulting in a *present value (PV)* of $10,000.

Question: How much should be paid *today* for a real estate investment that will return $20,000 at the end of three years, assuming the investor desires an annual return of 15 percent interest on the amount invested?

Solution: $20,000(*IFPV,* 15%, 3 yrs.) = PV
$20,000(.657516) = PV
$13,150.32 = PV

The investor should pay no more than $13,150.32 for the investment promising a return of $20,000 after three years if he wants to earn a 15 percent return on investment.[3]

Because we can use the *discounting process* to find the present value of a future amount when *annual* compounding is assumed, we can also apply the same methodology assuming *monthly discounting* is required. For example, in our illustration involving monthly compounding, the future value of $10,000 when interest was earned at an annual rate of 6 percent *compounded monthly* was $10,616.80. An important question to be considered by an investor would be how much should be paid today for the future value of $10,616.80 received at the end of one year, assuming that a 6 percent return *compounded monthly* is required?

We could solve for the answer directly by finding the reciprocal of the formula used to compound monthly, $1 \div (1 + i/12)^{1 \cdot 12}$, and multiplying that result by the future value of $10,616.78 to find the present value (PV). However, following the procedure used in annual discounting, a series of factors have been developed that eliminate the computation of interest factors for monthly compounding. These factors, assuming a *monthly* discounting process, are contained in column 4 in tables contained in Appendix B at the end of this textbook. A sample of factors for selected interest rates and years are shown in Exhibit 6–7.

In our problem, then, we want to determine the present value (PV) of $10,616.80 received at the end of one year assuming a desired rate of return of 6 percent, *compounded monthly*. By going to the 6 percent column and the row corresponding to 1 year (12 months) and selecting the interest factor .941905, we can now multiply $10,616.80 × .941905 = $10,000 and see that $10,000 is the maximum one should be willing to pay today for the investment.

Question: How much should an investor pay to receive $12,000 three years (36 months) from now, assuming that an annual return of 9 percent *compounded monthly* is desired?

Solution: $12,000(*MIFPV*, 9%, 3 yrs.) = PV$
$12,000(.764149) = $9,169.79$

The investor should pay no more than $9,169.79 for the investment, or the present value (PV) of the investment is $9,169.79. (The reader should again note the use of *M* in our abbreviation which designates monthly discounting).

Compound value of an annuity.   The first section of this chapter dealt with finding the compound or ending value of a *single* deposit or payment made only once, at the beginning of a period. An equally relevant consideration

---

[3] There is an accepted convention in finance that if one refers to a simple percentage return on investment, annual compounding or discounting is always assumed. If one refers to monthly compounding, it should be designated as an annual rate of interest *compounded monthly*.

EXHIBIT 6–7
Present value reversion of $1 (column 4, Appendix B)
Monthly discounting factors

Month	Rate 6%	7%	8%	9%	
1......	.995025	.994200	.993377	.992556	
2......	.990075	.988435	.986799	.985167	
3......	.985149	.982702	.980264	.977833	
4......	.980248	.977003	.973772	.970554	
5......	.975371	.971337	.967323	.963329	
6......	.970518	.965704	.960917	.956158	
7......	.965690	.960103	.954553	.949040	
8......	.960885	.954535	.948232	.941975	
9......	.956105	.948999	.941952	.934963	
10......	.951348	.943495	.935714	.928003	
11......	.946615	.938024	.929517	.921095	
12......	.941905	.932583	.923361	.914238	
Year					Month
1......	.941905	.932583	.923361	.914238	12
2......	.887186	.869712	.852596	.835831	24
3......	.835645	.811079	.787255	.764149	36
4......	.787098	.756399	.726921	.698614	48

involves a *series* of equal deposits or payments made at *equal intervals*. For example, assume deposits of $1,000 are made at the end of each year for a period of five years and interest is compounded at an annual rate of 5 percent. What would be the value at the end of the period for series of deposits plus all compound interest?

In this case the problem involves *equal deposits* made at *equal time intervals*. This series of deposits or payments is defined as an *annuity*. Since we know how to find the answer to a problem in which only one deposit is made, it would be logical, and correct, to assume the same basic compounding process applies when dealing with annuities. However, this is only a *partial solution* to the problem since we are dealing with an annuity, or series of deposits which occur annually.

To compute the sum of all deposits made in each succeeding year and include compound interest on deposits only as they occur, the general formula for compound interest must be expanded as follows:

$$S_n = P(1 + i)^{n-1} + P(1 + i)^{n-2} + \cdots + P$$

In this expression, S_n is the compound value of an annuity,[4] or the sum of all deposits, P, compounded at an annual rate (i) for n years. The important thing

---

[4] The formula shown here is the formula for an *ordinary annuity* which assumes all deposits are made at the *end* of each year.

to note in the expression, however, is that each deposit is assumed to be at the *end* of each year and is compounded through year n. In our example, since we are dealing with a series of $1,000 deposits made over a five-year period, the first $1,000 deposit would be compounded for four periods ($n - 1$), the $1,000 deposit made at the beginning of the second year would be compounded for three periods ($n - 2$), and so on until reaching the last deposit P. The last deposit is not compounded because it is deposited at the end of the fifth year.[5]

To compute the value of these deposits, a solution like the one shown in Exhibit 6–8 could be constructed. Note that each $1,000 deposit is com-

EXHIBIT 6–8
Compound value of an annuity of $1,000 per year at 5 percent annual compounding (column 1, Appendix A)

Year	Deposit			IF		Compound value
1................	$1,000 ×	(*IFCV*, 5%, 4 yrs.)	=	$1,000 × 1.215506	=	$1,215.51*
2................	1,000 ×	(*IFCV*, 5%, 3 yrs.)	=	1,000 × 1.157625	=	1,157.63*
3................	1,000 ×	(*IFCV*, 5%, 2 yrs.)	=	1,000 × 1.102500	=	1,102.50
4................	1,000 ×	(*IFCV*, 5%, 1 yrs.)	=	1,000 × 1.050000	=	1,050.00
5................	1,000 × 1.000000		=	1,000 × 1.000000	=	1,000.00
			Also	1,000 × 5.525631	=	5,525.63*

* Rounded.

pounded from the end of the year in which the deposit was made to the end of the next year. In other words, as shown in our expanded formula above, the deposit at the end of year 1 is compounded for four years, the deposit made at the beginning of the second year is compounded for three years, and so on. By carrying this process out one year at a time, the solution, or $5,525.63, is determined when the compounded amounts in the extreme right-hand column are added.

Although the compound value of $1,000 per period, S_n, can be determined in the manner shown in Exhibit 6–8, careful examination of the compounding process reveals another, easier way to find the solution. Note that the $1,000 deposit occurs annually and never changes; that is, it is *constant*. When the deposits are *constant*, it is possible to sum all of the individual IFs as 5.525631. By multiplying $1,000 by 5.525631, a solution of $5,525.63 is obtained, as is shown in Exhibit 6–8 at the bottom of the right-hand column.

Use of compound interest tables for annuities. Because the IFs in Exhibit 6–8 can be added, a series of new interest factors has been developed for various interest rates in column 2 of Appendix A, *Accumulation of $1 per*

---

[5] The reader should be aware that this formulation is different from the one used in the previous edition of this book. Previously we used the formula for an *annuity due*, which assumes deposits are made at the beginning of the year.

period. A sample of these factors, now referred to as *IFCVa, i%,* yrs., has been taken directly from column 2 in Appendix A and compiled in Exhibit 6–9 (the reader should note the use of the small letter *a* after *IFCV* which designates that the series of deposits being considered is an *annuity* and not the deposit of a single amount).

EXHIBIT 6–9
Accumulation of $1 per period (column 2, Appendix A)
Annual compounding factors

Year	5%	6%	10%	15%
1	1.000000	1.000000	1.000000	1.000000
2	2.050000	2.060000	2.100000	2.150000
3	3.152500	3.183600	3.310000	3.472500
4	4.310125	4.374616	4.641000	4.993375
5	5.525631	5.637093	6.105100	6.742381
6	6.801913	6.975319	7.715610	8.753738
7	8.142008	8.393838	9.487171	11.066799
8	9.549109	9.897468	11.435888	13.726819

In the problem at hand, to determine the compound value of $1,000 deposited annually at 5 percent for five years, note that if we go to the 5 percent column in Exhibit 6–9 and obtain the *IF* that corresponds to five years, we can find the solution to our problem as follows:

$$P(IFCVa,\ 5\%,\ 5\ \text{yrs.}) = S_n$$
$$\$1,000(IFCVa,\ 5\%,\ 5\ \text{yrs.}) = S_n$$
$$\$1,000(5.525631) = S_n$$
$$\$5,525.63 = S_n$$

This solution, or $5,525.63, corresponds to the solution obtained from the long series of multiplication carried out in Exhibit 6–8.

Question: What would be the value of $800 deposited each year for six years, compounded at 10 percent interest after six years?
Solution: $800(*IFCVa*, 10%, 6 yrs.) = S_n
$$\$800(7.715610) = S_n$$
$$\$6,172.49 = S_n$$

The same procedure used for compounding annuities for amounts deposited or paid *annually* can also be applied to *monthly annuities.* A very simple modification can be made to the formulation used for annual annuities by substituting $i/12$ in place of i and letting n represent months in the annual formulation presented above as follows:

$$S_n = P(1 + i/12)^{n-1} + P(1 + i/12)^{n-2} + \cdots + P$$

However, in this formulation, n represents *months* and the deposits or payments P are constant in amount and also occur *monthly*. Hence the interest factors used to compound each monthly deposit may be added (as they were for annual deposits in Exhibit 6–8) and a new series for compounding monthly annuities can be developed. This has been done for selected interest rates and years. The factors for compounding monthly annuities are contained in column 2 in Appendix B at the end of this textbook.[6]

Question: An investor pays $200 *per month* into a real estate investment which promises to pay an annual rate of interest of 8 percent *compounded monthly*. If he makes consecutive monthly payments for five years, what will be the compounded value after five years?

Solution: $\$200(MIFCVa, 8\%, 60 \text{ mos.}) = S_n$
$$\$200(73.476856) = S_n$$
$$\$14,695.37 = S_n$$

Hence, in this case the value of these payments earning interest at an annual rate of 8 percent *compounded monthly* can be found by multiplying the *monthly annuity* times the interest factor for the accumulation of $1 per period in column 2 in Appendix B, or $\$200 \times 73.476856 = \$14,695.37$.

Present value of an annuity. In the preceding section, our primary concern was to determine the compound value of an annuity, or constant payments received at equal time intervals. In this section we want to consider the *present value* of a *series* of annual receipts as the investment produces income over time. Since an investor may have to consider a series of income payments when trying to decide whether or not to invest, this is an important problem.

Recalling from the earlier section dealing with the present value of a single receipt, or ending value, P_n, we took the basic formula for compounding interest and rearranged it to determine the present value of an investment as follows:

$$P_n = P_0(1 + i)^n$$
$$P_0 = P_n \div (1 + i)^n$$
$$\text{Present value} = P_0 = P_n \times \frac{1}{(1 + i)^n}$$

To consider the present value of an *annuity*, defined as A_n, we need only consider the sum of individual present values for all receipts. This can be done by modifying the basic present value formula above as follows:

$$A_n = R \frac{1}{(1 + i)^1} + R \frac{1}{(1 + i)^2} + \cdots + R \frac{1}{(1 + i)^n}$$

Note in this expression that each receipt, R, is discounted for the number of years corresponding to the time at which the funds are actually received. In

---

[6] As was the case with annual compounding, this formulation assumes that deposits are made at the end of each month, or that an ordinary annuity is being compounded.

other words, the first receipt would occur at the *end* of the first period and would be discounted only one period, or $R \times 1 \div (1 + i)^1$. The second receipt would be discounted for two periods, or $R \times 1 \div (1 + i)^2$, and so on.

Assuming an individual is considering an investment which will provide a series of annual cash receipts of $500 for a period of six years, and the investor desires a 6 percent return, how much should be paid for the investment today?

We can begin by considering the present value of the $500 receipt in year 1 as shown in Exhibit 6–10. Note that the present value of the $500 receipt is

EXHIBIT 6–10
Present value of $500 per year, discounted at 6 percent annual discounting

Year	Receipt		IF*	Present value
1	$500 × (IFPV, 6%, 1 yr.) = $500 ×	.943396 =	471.70
2	500 × (IFPV, 6%, 2 yrs.) = 500 ×	.889996 =	445.00
3	500 × (IFPV, 6%, 3 yrs.) = 500 ×	.839619 =	419.81
4	500 × (IFPV, 6%, 4 yrs.) = 500 ×	.792094 =	396.05
5	500 × (IFPV, 6%, 5 yrs.) = 500 ×	.747258 =	373.63
6	500 × (IFPV, 6%, 6 yrs.) = 500 ×	.704961 =	352.48
		Also: 500 × 4.917324 =	2,458.66†

* Column 4, Appendix A.
† Rounded.

discounted for one year at 6 percent. This is true because the first year's income of $500 is not received until the *end* of the first period and our investor only wants to pay an amount today (present value) which will assure him of a 6 percent return on the amount he pays today. Therefore, by discounting this $500 receipt by the interest factor in column 5 for one year in the 6 percent tables in Appendix A, or .943396, the present value is $471.70.

Note that the second $500 income payment is received at the end of the second year. Therefore, it should be discounted for two years at 6 percent. Its present value is found by multiplying $500 by the interest factor in column 5 in the 6 percent tables for two years, or .889996, giving a present value of $445. This process can be continued for each receipt for the remaining three years as shown in Exhibit 6–10. The present value of the entire series of $500 income payments can be found by adding the series of receipts discounted each month in the far right-hand column, which totals $2,458.66.

However, as also shown in Exhibit 6–10, since the $500 series of payments is *constant*, it is possible to *add* all interest factors to obtain one interest factor that can be multiplied by $500 to obtain the same present value.[7] The sum of all interest factors for 6 percent in Exhibit 6–10 is 4.917324. When 4.917324

---

[7] Determining these interest factors amounts to adding the interest components $1 \div (1 + i)^1 + 1 \div (1 + i)^2 + \cdots 1 \div (1 + i)^n$ from the modified formula for the present value of an annuity, A_n, presented above.

is multiplied by $500, the present value, $2,458.66, found in the lengthy series of multiplications in Exhibit 6–10, is again determined.

Use of present value of an annuity tables. Because the interest factors in Exhibit 6–10 may be summed, as long as the income payments are *equal* in amount and received at *equal* intervals, this combination obviously takes a lot of work out of problem solving. The sums of *IFs* for various interest rates now referred to as (*IFPVa, i%,* yrs.) have been compiled in table form and are listed in column 5, *Present value ordinary annuity $1 per period,* in the tables in Appendix A.

To familiarize the student with discounting annuities, Exhibit 6–11 has been developed showing the *IFs* for the present value of $1 per period (annuity).

EXHIBIT 6–11
Present value of ordinary annuity $1 per period (column 5, Appendix A)
Annual discounting factors

Year	5%	6%	10%	15%
1	.952381	.943396	.909091	.869565
2	1.859410	1.833393	1.735537	1.625709
3	2.723248	2.673012	2.486852	2.283225
4	3.545951	3.465106	3.169865	2.854978
5	4.329477	4.212364	3.790787	3.352155
6	5.075692	4.917324	4.355261	3.784483
7	5.786373	5.582381	4.868419	4.160420
8	6.463213	6.209794	5.334926	4.487322

These *IFs* were taken directly from column 5 in the tables contained in Appendix A for a sample of interest rates. In our problem, then, we want to determine the present value of $500 received annually for six years assuming an annual rate of return of 6 percent is desired. How much should an investor pay for this total investment today and be assured of earning his desired return? We solve this problem by looking at Exhibit 6–11, finding the 6 percent column, and looking down the column until the *IF* in the row corresponding to six years is located. The *IF* is 4.917324. We can now solve the following:

$$\$500(IFPVa, 6\%, 6 \text{ yrs.}) = A_n$$
$$\$500(4.917324) = A_n$$
$$\$2,458.66 = A_n$$

This solution corresponds to that obtained in Exhibit 6–10.

Question: An investor has an opportunity to invest in a rental property which will provide net cash returns of $400 *per year* for three years. The investor believes that an annual return of 10 percent should be earned on this investment. How much should be paid for the rental property?

Solution: $400(*IFPVa*, 10%, 3 yrs.) = A_n
$400(2.486852) = $994.74

No more than $994.74 should be paid for the investment property. If the investor pays $994.74, a 10 percent return will be earned on the investment. (The reader should again note the use of the small letter *a* after *IFPV*, indicating an *annuity* is being evaluated.)

Based on the logic used above in discounting annuities paid or received annually, the same procedure can be applied to cash receipts paid or received monthly. In this case the formula used to discount annual annuities is simply modified to reflect monthly receipts or payments and the discounting interval is changed to reflect monthly compounding, for example:

$$P(1 + i/12)^1 + P(1 + i/12)^2 + \cdots + P = A_n$$

where in the above formulation payments (P) occur monthly, the exponents represent months, and A_n represents the present value of an annuity received over *n months.*

As was the case with annual discounting, computation of the present value of an annuity can be very cumbersome if one had to expand the above formula for each problem he faced, particularly if the problem involved cash receipts or payments over many months. Hence a series of interest factors have been developed by expanding the above formula for each monthly interval and adding the resulting interest factors as was done with discounting annual annuities in Exhibit 6–10. These factors are contained in column 5 in tables in Appendix B, and like the annual tables the column is labeled *Present value of ordinary annuity of $1 per period;* however, the period in this case is one *month.* A sample of these factors for given interest rates and years has been taken directly from column 5, Appendix B, and included in Exhibit 6–12. Hence, if an investor wanted to know how much should be paid today for an investment that would pay him $500 at the end of each month for the next 12 months and he wanted to earn an annual rate of 6 percent *compounded monthly* on his investment, the solution can be easily determined by consulting Exhibit 6–12. Looking to the 6 percent column and dropping down to the row corresponding to 12 months, the factor 11.618932 is found. Multiplying $500 by 11.618932 results in $5,809.47 or the amount that the investor should pay today if he desires a 6 percent rate of return compounded monthly.

Question: A real estate partnership predicts that it will pay $300 per month to its partners over the next six months. Assuming the partners desire an 8 percent return compounded monthly on their investment, how much should they pay?

EXHIBIT 6–12
Present value ordinary annuity of $1 per period (column 5,
Appendix B)
Monthly discounting factors

		Rate		
Month	6%	7%	8%	
1	.995025	.994200	.993377	
2	1.985099	1.982635	1.980176	
3	2.970248	2.965337	2.960440	
4	3.950496	3.942340	3.934212	
5	4.925866	4.913677	4.901535	
6	5.896384	5.879381	5.862452	
7	6.862074	6.839484	6.817005	
8	7.882959	7.794019	7.765237	
9	8.779064	8.743018	8.707189	
10	9.730412	9.686513	9.642903	
11	10.677027	10.624537	10.572420	
12	11.618932	11.557120	11.495782	
Year				Month
1	11.618932	11.557120	11.495782	12
2	22.562866	22.335099	22.110544	24
3	32.871016	32.386464	31.911806	36
4	42.580318	41.760201	40.961913	48

Solution: $\$300(MIFPVa, 8\%, 6 \text{ mos.}) = A_n$
$\$300(5.862452) = A_n$
$\$1,758.74 = A_n$

Accumulation of a future sum

The previous two sections have dealt with compounding and discounting single payments and annuities. However, in some instances, it is necessary to determine a series of payments necessary to accumulate a future sum, taking into account the fact that such payments will be accumulating interest as they are deposited. For example, assume we have a debt of $20,000 that must be paid off at the end of five years. We would like to make a series of equal annual payments (an annuity) at the end of each of the five years such that when we accumulate all deposits, plus interest, we will have $20,000 at the end of the fifth year. Assuming that we can earn interest on those deposits at the rate of 10 percent per year, how much should each annual deposit be?

Basically, we are dealing with accumulating a future sum in this case, which from Exhibit 6–5 indicates that we will be compounding a series of deposits, or an annuity, to achieve that future value. Hence, we can work with the procedure for determining future values by compounding as follows:

$$P(\textit{IFCVa}, 10\%, 5 \text{ yrs.}) = \$20,000$$
$$P(6.105100) = \$20,000$$
$$P = \$20,000 \div 6.105100$$
$$P = \$3,275.95$$

This computation merely indicates that when compounded at an annual interest rate of 10 percent, the unknown series of equal deposits (P), will result in the accumulation of \$20,000 at the end of five years. Given the interest factor for compounding an annual annuity (*IFCVa*) from column 2 in Appendix A or 6.105100, we know that the unknown deposit, P, when multiplied by that factor will result in \$20,000. Hence, by dividing \$20,000 by the interest factor for compounding an annual annuity, we can obtain the necessary annual payment of \$3,275.95. The result tells us that if we make deposits of \$3,275.95 at the end of each year for five years, and each of those deposits earns interest at an annual rate of 10 percent, a total of \$20,000 will be accumulated at the end of five years.

In examining the above computation, we can see that dividing \$20,000 by 6.105100 is equivalent to multiplying \$20,000 by (1 ÷ 6.105100), or .163797, and the same \$3,275.95 solution results. This latter factor, or .163797, is referred to in real estate finance as a *sinking-fund factor* which is used in problems such as the one we are dealing with as well as other applications in real estate. These *sinking-fund factors* (or reciprocals of interest factors for compounding annuities) have been computed and are contained in column 3 in Appendix A for *annual* deposits (the reader should check for the factor .163797) and Appendix B for *monthly* deposits. In the latter case, if we wanted to know what *monthly payments* would be necessary to pay off the \$20,000 debt at the end of five years, taking into account that each deposit will earn an annual rate of 10 percent compounded monthly, we can easily solve for the solution by multiplying \$20,000 × 0.12914 (the sinking-fund factor, column 3, Appendix B), and we would obtain \$258.28 per month as the required series of deposits.

Determining yields on investments

Up to now, this chapter has demonstrated how to determine future values in the case of compounding and present values in the case of discounting. These two topics are important in their own right. They have also provided tools for determining an equally important component used extensively in real estate financing, that is, calculating *rates of return* or *investment yields*. In other words, the concepts illustrated in the compounding and discounting processes can also be used to determine rates of return or yields on investments, mortgage loans, and so on. These concepts must be mastered since procedures used here will form the basis for much of what follows in succeeding chapters.

In the prior sections of this chapter, we have concentrated on determining the *future value* of an investment made today when compounded at some *given* rate of interest, or the *present investment value* of a steam of cash returns received in the future when discounted at a *given* rate of interest. In this section we are concerned with knowing what an investment will cost today and what the future stream of cash returns will be, but not knowing what yield or rate of return is earned if the investment is made.

Yields on single receipts.   In many cases investors and lenders are concerned with the problem of what rate of compound interest will be earned on an investment. To illustrate the investment yield concept, assume an investor has an opportunity to buy an unimproved one-acre lot for $5,640 today. The lot is expected to appreciate in value and will be worth $15,000 after seven years. What *annual rate of (return) interest* (or investment yield) would be earned on the $5,640 investment in the property if it were made today, held for seven years, and sold for $15,000?

To solve for the unknown interest rate, we can formulate the problem as follows:

$$\$15,000 \times \frac{1}{(1 + i)^n} = \$5,640$$

In other words, we would like to know the rate of compound interest (i) that can be substituted in the above expression that will make the $15,000 return equal to the $5,640 investment outlay, or present value, today. The interest rate can be determined by first solving for the *interest factor* as follows:

$$\$15,000 \ (IFPV, \ ?\%, \ 7 \text{ yrs.}) = \$5,640$$
$$(IFPV, \ ?\%, \ 7 \text{ yrs.}) = 5,640 \div \$15,000$$
$$(IFPV, \ ?\%, \ 7 \text{ yrs.}) = .376$$

From the above calculations the *interest factor* is .376, but we still do not know the *interest rate* (i). However, we do know that the time period over which the investment is to appreciate in value is seven years. Because *IFPV* is .376 and the term of investment is seven years, by consulting the interest tables in Appendix A, we can easily find the interest rate. Since the cash return of $15,000 is a *single receipt,* we need only to locate an *IF* for the *present value reversion* of $1 equal to .376 in column 4 in the row corresponding to seven years for some interest rate. We begin the search for the interest rate by choosing an arbitrary interest rate, say, 5 percent. Looking to the 5 percent table in Appendix A we see the *IF* in column 4 for seven years is .710681, which is larger than .376. Moving to the 10 percent table, the *IF* for seven years is .513158, which is lower than the *IF* at 5 percent but comes closer to the *IF* we are looking for. Continuing this trial and error process, by looking to the 15 percent table we see that the *IF* in column 4 for seven years is .376, therefore the interest rate we desire is 15 percent.[8] We know this is the correct interest factor because $15,000 × .376 = $5,640. This proves that 15 percent is the annual yield on this investment.

What does this interest rate mean? It means that if the $5,640 investment is made today, then held for seven years and sold for $15,000, this would be equivalent to investing $5,640 today and letting it *compound annually* at an interest rate of 15 percent. This fact can be determined with the following computation:

$$\$5,640 \ (IFCV, \ 15\%, \ 7 \text{ yrs.}) = P_n$$
$$\$5,640 \ (2.660) = \$15,000 \text{ (rounded)}$$

This calculation simply shows that $5,640 compounded annually at an interest rate of 15 percent for seven years is $15,000. Hence, making this investment is equivalent to earning a rate of return of 15 percent. This rate of return is sometimes referred to as the *investment yield,* or as the *internal rate of return.*

The internal rate of return integrates the concepts of compounding and present value. It represents an interest rate equivalent for an alternative investment earning interest compounded at some annual interest rate. In other words, if an investor is faced with making an investment in an income-producing venture, *regardless of how the cash returns are patterned,* the internal rate of return provides a guide or comparison for the investor. *It tells the investor what compound interest rate the return on an investment being considered is equivalent to.* In our example of the unimproved one-acre lot, the 15 percent yield or internal rate of return is *equivalent* to making a deposit of $5,640 and allowing it to compound monthly at an annual interest rate of 15 percent for seven years. After seven years the investor would receive $15,000, which includes the original investment of $5,640 plus all compound interest. With the internal rate of return known, the investor can make an easier judgment as to whether or not the investment should be made. If the 15 percent return is adequate, it will be made; if not, the investor should reject it.

The concepts of the internal rate of return or yield, present value, and compounding are indispensable tools that are continually used in real estate finance and investment. The reader should not venture beyond this section without firmly grasping the concepts explained. These concepts form the basis for the remainder of this chapter and the chapters which follow.

Yields on investment annuities. The concepts just illustrated for a single receipt of cash (when the unimproved lot was sold) also apply to situations

---

[8] Even though the interest factor we are seeking was .376 and the one selected was .375937, for all practical purposes the two *IF*s are close enough for a very accurate solution. When searching for an *IF* in column 4, if the first three decimal places are the same, this is usually adequate in solving a problem. There will usually be some differences in *IF*s due to rounding which can be safely ignored past the third decimal place.

where a *series* of cash receipts is involved. Consequently, a yield or internal rate of return also can be computed on these types of investments.

To illustrate, suppose an investor has the opportunity to make an investment in real estate costing $3,170 that would provide him with cash income of $1,000 at the end of each year for four years. What would be the investment yield, or internal rate of return, that the investor would earn on the $3,170 invested? In this case we have a series of receipts that we wish to discount by an unknown rate which will make the present value of the $1,000 annuity equal the original investment of $3,170. We can express our problem as follows:

$$R \; (IFPVa, \; ?\%, \; 4 \; \text{yrs.}) = A_n$$
$$\$1,000 \; (IFPVa, \; ?\%, \; 4 \; \text{yrs.}) = \$3,170$$
$$(IFPVa, \; ?\%, \; 4 \; \text{yrs.}) = \$3,170 \div \$1,000$$
$$(IFPVa, \; ?\%, \; 4 \; \text{yrs.}) = 3.170000$$

This procedure is similar to solving for the yield or internal rate of return on single receipts discussed in the preceding section except that we are dealing with an annuity here (note the use of the small letter *a* after *IFPV* in our abbreviated formula). As before, with this procedure we solve for the interest factor for a four-year period for the still unknown interest rate. To determine what the interest rate is, one must search the tables in Appendix A (column 5) in the four-year row until a factor very close to 3.1700 is found.[9] A careful search reveals that the factor will be found in the 10 percent tables (the reader should verify this). Hence, based on this procedure, we have determined that the investment yield or internal rate of return (*IRR*) on the $3,170 invested is 10 percent. A more in-depth analysis of what the internal rate of return or investment yield means is presented in Exhibit 6–13.

It should be noted from Exhibit 6–13 that when the investment yield or internal rate of return (*IRR*) is computed, two characteristics are present. One is the recovery of capital in each period, and the other is interest earned in each period. In other words, when the *IRR* is computed based on the $3,170 investment and the $1,000 received each year, implicit in the *IRR* computation is the full recovery of the $3,170 investment plus interest compounded annually at 10 percent. Hence the 10 percent *investment yield is really rate of compound interest* earned on investment from year to year. Of the total $4,000 received during the four-year period, total interest earned is $830 and $3,170 is capital recovery.[10]

---

[9] When dealing with annuities, accuracy is acceptable in most situations if interest factors are rounded to the fourth decimal place. However, in mortgage lending or where very large sums are involved, it is advisable to consider the entire six decimal places.

[10] The reader may be wondering what is happening to the $1,000 received each year. It is assumed that those dollars are being reinvested in an alternative investment earning the same *IRR* as the investment producing the $1,000 series of payments.

EXHIBIT 6–13
Illustration of the internal rate of return (*IRR*) and components of cash receipts

	Year			
	1	*2*	*3*	*4*
Investment (balance)	$3,170	$2,487	$1,736	$ 910
IRR or yield at 10%	317	249*	174*	91*
Cash received.	$1,000	$1,000	$1,000	$1,000
Less: Cash yield at 10%	317	249	174	90*
Recovery of investment.	$ 683	$ 751	$ 826	$ 910
Investment (beginning of year).	$3,170	$2,487	$1,736	$ 910
Less: Recovery of investment	683	751	826	910
Investment (end of year)	$2,487	$1,736	$ 910	0

* Rounded.

A similar application can be made in cases where *monthly* cash annuities will be received as a return on investment. For example, assume that an investor makes an investment of $51,593 to receive $400 at the end of each month for the next 20 years (240 months). What would be the annual rate of return, *compounded monthly,* earned on the $51,593 invested? The solution can be easily determined with the following procedure:

$$R \ (MIFPVa, \ ?\%, \ 20 \ \text{yrs.}) = A_n$$
$$\$400 \ (MIFPVa, \ ?\%, \ 20 \ \text{yrs.}) = \$51,593$$
$$(MIFPVa, \ ?\%, \ 20 \ \text{yrs.}) = \$51,593 \div \$400$$
$$(MIFPVa, \ ?\%, \ 20 \ \text{yrs.}) = 128.9825$$

As was the case with finding the *IRR* for investments with annual receipts, we find the interest factor for the present value of an ordinary annuity of $1 per month for 20 years for an interest rate compounded monthly (note the *M* in our shorthand notation), which is 128.9825. Looking to column 5 in Appendix B, in the 20-year row for various interest rates, we find that the interest rate that corresponds to that factor is 7 percent. Hence the *IRR* is 7 percent compounded monthly on the $51,593 investment. Both the recovery of $51,593 plus $44,407 in interest is embedded in the stream of $400 monthly cash receipts received over the 20-year period.

A note on linear interpolation

In the previous two examples involving yields on single receipts and annuities, the interest factors computed in each case were easily found in either Appendix A or B because they corresponded to an interest rate for which tables are provided. Because it is possible only to include a small number of tables for interest rates in a textbook such as this one, in many cases when interest factors are computed, tables for the *exact* interest rate that corresponds to the interest factor computed may not be contained in the book. In that event, a procedure known as *linear interpolation* must be used to solve for the interest rate.

For example, assume that an investor can purchase a vacant lot for $5,000 today and expects to sell it five years from now for $9,000. What would be the internal rate of return? Assuming the investor wants the investment yield or internal rate of return expressed in terms of an annual rate of compound interest, we set the problem up as follows:

$$\$9,000 \ (IFPV, \ ?\%, \ 5 \ \text{yrs.}) = \$5,000$$
$$(IFPV, \ ?\%, \ 5 \ \text{yrs.}) = \$5,000 \div \$9,000$$
$$(IFPV, \ ?\%, \ 5 \ \text{yrs.}) = .555555$$

From this calculation, we obtain the interest factor of .555555 that corresponds to some rate of interest for a five-year period. Since this involves a single receipt of cash ($9,000), we use column 4 in Appendix A to find the appropriate factor. However, the interest factor is not contained in any of the available tables; hence, the need for interpolation. A careful examination of the available tables shows that the interest factor we are seeking falls *between* the factor found in the 12 percent table (.567427) for five years and the factor found in the 15 percent tables (.497177). Hence, we know that because the interest factor we are looking for (.555555) falls between the factors at 12 percent and 15 percent, our yield must also be between 12 percent and 15 percent. The question is how do we find it? We proceed as follows:

$(IFPV, \ 12\%, \ 5 \ \text{yrs.}) = .567427$		$(IFPV, \ 12\%, \ 5 \ \text{yrs.}) = .567427$	
$(IFPV, \ 15\%, \ 5 \ \text{yrs.}) = .497177$		Desired $IF = .555555$	
A. Difference $= \underline{.070250}$		B. Difference $= \underline{.011872}$	

1. Ratio of $B \div A = .011872 \div .070250 = .17$ (rounded).
2. Difference in interest rates $15\% - 12\% = 3\%$.
3. Multiply ratio of $B \div A$ times the difference in interest rates and add to the base (lower) interest rate or

$$(.17 \times 3\%) + 12\% = \underline{12.5\%}$$

Note that in using this procedure we first express B, which is the difference between the desired interest factor and the base interest factor, as a proportion of A or the difference in interest factors for the entire range (12%–15%). We then assume that the internal rate of return falls between 12 percent and 15 percent in that same proportion. Hence, in this case the internal rate of return would be 12.5 percent.

The procedure just used in the case of a single receipt also can be applied for annuities received either monthly or annually. For example, assume an investor purchases an interest in a real estate venture for $13,860 which will provide a $300 *monthly* cash return over the next five years. What would be the internal rate of return (expressed as an annual rate compounded monthly) in this case? The problem can be solved as follows:

$$\$300 \ (MIFPVa, \ ?\%, \ 5 \ \text{yrs.}) = \$13,860$$
$$(MIFPVa, \ ?\%, \ 5 \ \text{yrs.}) = \$13,860 \div \$300$$
$$(MIFPVa, \ ?\%, \ 5 \ \text{yrs.}) = 46.200$$

Because we are dealing with a *monthly annuity* we want to search for the present value interest factor in column 5 in tables contained in Appendix B. A search of those tables reveals that the interest factor we are seeking (46.200) falls between factors contained in the 10 percent and 11 percent tables. From this point we can interpolate as follows:

$(MIFPVa, \ 10\%, \ 5 \ \text{yrs.}) = 47.065369$	$(MIFPVa, \ 10\%, \ 5 \ \text{yrs.}) = 47.065369$
$(MIFPVa, \ 11\%, \ 5 \ \text{yrs.}) = \underline{45.993034}$	Desired $MIFPVa = \underline{46.200000}$
Difference $= \ \ \underline{\underline{1.072335}}$	Difference $= \ \ \underline{\underline{.865369}}$

$$(.865369 \div 1.072335) \times 1\% = \ \ .81$$
$$\text{Add:} \ \ \ \underline{10.00\%}$$
$$IRR = \ \underline{\underline{10.81\%}}$$

Hence, based on our interpolation procedure using factors from column 5, Appendix B tables, we find that the internal rate of return is 10.81 percent, or 10.8 percent rounded. From this result, we can say that investing $13,860 in this venture is equivalent to earning an annual rate of 10.8 percent interest, compounded monthly.[11]

Linear interpolation—a note of caution. Solutions obtained using linear interpolation are subject to some error. This is because the assumption of proportionality between interest rates and interest factors is not exact.[12] The extent of the error depends on the range in interest rates chosen for interpolation. When the range chosen is very small, the error will be small, and vice versa. Hence, when the reader desires a very exact solution to a problem, tables with very small differences in interest rates should be chosen, or a solution should be obtained with an electronic calculator.

---

[11] This procedure can also be used for annual annuities. For annual receipts, factors from Appendix A would be substituted in place of those from Appendix B.

[12] This is because interest factors are based on some form of the exponential relationships for compound interest $(1 + i)^n$, which for any percentage change in i will not result in a proportional percentage change in the interest factor.

Space limitations do not permit the inclusion of numerous tables in Appendixes A or B. The accuracy of desired solutions has influenced the tables we have chosen to include in this book. For example, as can be seen from Appendix A, the differences between interest rates generally range from 2 percent to 5 percent, while in Appendix B, the differences are generally 1 percent. This is because Appendix B will be used extensively in the chapters dealing with *mortgage lending* where a *high degree of accuracy is desired.* Tables in Appendix A, however, will be used in *investment analysis* where we make many estimates in such things as annual rent, expenses, and appreciation in property values. Hence, because of the many uncertainties involved, the *degree* of accuracy in *computation* is not as important when determining internal rates of return on investment projects, which are subject to many more variable influences. In these cases, slightly larger interpolation errors are acceptable.

Questions

1   What is the essential concept in understanding compound interest?

2   How are the interest factors in column 1, Appendix B, developed?

3   Based on the material in Chapter 6, what general rule can be developed concerning maximum values and compounding intervals within a year? What is an equivalent annual yield?

4   What does the time value of money mean? How is it related to present value? What process is used to find present value?

5   How does discounting, as used in determining present value, relate to compounding as used in determining future value? How would present value ever be used?

6   What are the interest factors in column 4 in Appendix A? How are they developed?

7   What is an annuity? How is it defined? What is the difference between an ordinary annuity and an annuity due?

8   When evaluating the present value of an uneven series of receipts, why can't interest factors for annuities be used? What factors must be used to discount a series of uneven receipts?

9   What is a sinking-fund factor? How and why is it used?

10   What is linear interpolation? What is the basic assumption made when it is used? What error should the user be concerned with when using this technique?

11   What is an internal rate of return? How is it used? How does it relate to the concept of compound interest?

Case problems

1   Jack Samuels makes a deposit of $7,000 in a bank account. The deposit is to earn interest annually at the rate of 5 percent for a period of five years.

a. How much will Mr. Samuels have on deposit at the end of five years?

b. Assuming the deposit earned a 5 percent annual rate of interest *compounded monthly,* how much would he have at the end of five years?

c. In comparing (*a*) and (*b*) above, what are the respective equivalent annual yields? (Hint: Consider the value of each deposit after one year only.) Which is the better alternative?

2   Ms. Bette Schmidler has the option of making a $5,000 investment that will earn interest either at the rate of 6 percent compounded semiannually or 5½ percent compounded quarterly. Which would you advise? (Again, consider one year only.)

3   Roger Starbuck is considering the purchase of a lot. He can buy the lot today and expects the price to rise to $20,000 at the end of six years. He believes that he should earn an investment yield of 10 percent annually on his investment. The asking price for the lot is $11,000. Should he buy it?

4   An investor can make an investment in a real estate development and receive an expected cash return of $20,000 after eight years. Based on a careful study of other investment alternatives, he believes that a 10 percent annual return *compounded monthly* is a reasonable return to earn on this investment. How much should he pay for it today?

5   An investor can deposit $2,000 at the end of each year for the next 15 years and earn interest at an annual rate of 6 percent. What will be the value of the investment after 15 years?

6   Jason Smith deposits $500 at the end of each month in an account which will earn interest at an annual rate of 9 percent compounded monthly. How much will he have at the end of five years?

7   Arco Supreme is considering an investment which will pay $1,000 at the end of each year for each of the next 15 years. It expects to earn an annual return of 15 percent on its investment. How much should the company pay today for the investment?

8   Easy Mark has the opportunity to make an investment in a real estate venture with Swampland Enterprises. Swampland is expecting to pay investors $750 at the end of each month for the next six years. Mark believes that a reasonable return on his investment should be 12 percent compounded monthly.

a. How much should he pay for the investment?

b. What will be the total sum of cash he will receive over the next six years?

c. Why is there such a large difference between (*a*) and (*b*)?

9   The Gee Bee Corporation is evaluating an investment that will provide the following returns at the end of each of the following years: year 1, $10,000; year 2, $6,000; year 3, $0; year 4, $9,000; and year 5, $3,500. Gee Bee believes that it should earn an annual rate of 15 percent on its investments. How much should Gee Bee pay for this investment?

10   Starstrek Enterprises has a loan of $60,000 coming due eight years from now. It wants to make annual payments into a sinking fund which will earn interest at an annual rate of 6 percent. What will the annual payments have to be? Suppose that Starstrek makes *monthly* payments earning interest at 6 percent compounded monthly. What would those payments have to be?

11   The Landco Development Company is considering the purchase of an apartment project for $20,000. Landco estimates that it will receive $5,000 at the end of each year for the next seven years. If it purchases the project, what will be its internal rate of return? If the company insists on a 10 percent return on investment, is this a good investment?

12   Arcane Corporation is considering the purchase of an interest in a real estate syndication at a price of $40,000. In return, the syndication promises to pay $360 at the end of each month for the next 20 years (240 months). If purchased, what would Arcane's internal rate of return, compounded monthly, be on its investment? How much total cash would be received on the investment? How much is total profit and how much is capital recovery?

13   The Henry Stabler Company is making an investment in a real estate venture that will provide returns at the end of the next three years as follows: year 1, $8,000; year 2, $9,000; and year 3, $10,000. The company wants to earn a 12 percent annual return on its investment. How much should it pay for the investment? How does Stabler know that he is earning an annual rate of 12 percent on his investment? Now assume Mr. Stabler wanted to earn an annual rate of 12 percent compounded monthly. How much should be paid?

Mortgage loans: Payment patterns and effective borrowing costs

7

In the previous chapter, concepts in compounding, discounting, and the procedure for determining yields were introduced as a foundation for what follows in this chapter and for much of the material in succeeding chapters. The major objective of this chapter is to illustrate payment patterns for various kinds of mortgage loans and to provide techniques for determining the effective cost of borrowing under varying conditions in loan agreements. Common practices found in real estate finance include charges such as loan discount or origination fees, prepayment penalties, and prepaid interest. In addition, various amortization or loan repayment schedules can be agreed on by the borrower and lender to facilitate financing a particular real estate transaction. Since these provisions often affect the cost of borrowing, effective borrowing costs are stressed heavily in this chapter. Many provisions illustrated here are commonly encountered in real estate transactions and should be understood by individuals buying and financing property or by anyone providing counsel in the area.

Loan payment patterns—fixed interest rate loans

Many possible loan payment patterns may be agreed upon by a borrower and lender depending on the circumstances surrounding the real estate transaction being financed. It is safe to say, however, that three loan payment patterns dominate in practice: (1) the fully amortized, constant payment mortgage loan; (2) the partially amortized, constant payment loan; and (3) the demand loan. In this section we consider all three payment patterns in sequence.

Fully amortized, constant payment mortgage loans

The most common loan payment pattern used in real estate finance is the fully amortized, constant payment mortgage loan. This type of loan payment pattern is used extensively in financing single-family residences and is also used in long-term mortgage lending on income-producing properties such as multifamily apartment complexes and shopping centers. This payment pattern simply means that a level of constant monthly payment is calculated on an original loan amount, at a given rate of interest, for a given term. Each payment includes interest and some repayment of principal. At the end of the term of the mortgage loan, the original loan amount or principal is completely repaid, or fully amortized, and the lender has earned a fixed rate of interest on the *monthly loan balance.*

To illustrate how the monthly loan payment calculation is made, assume that an individual wishes to purchase a property which costs $40,000. He or she would like to borrow $32,000 for a period of 30 years. After negotiating with ABC Savings and Loan Association, a loan commitment is obtained for $32,000 for 30 years at an interest rate of 9 percent. What will be the monthly mortgage payment on this loan, assuming it is to be fully amortized ("paid off") at the end of 30 years? Based on our knowledge of discounting annuities from the preceding chapter, the problem is really no more than finding the present value of an annuity and can be formulated as shown in Exhibit 7–1.

EXHIBIT 7–1
Determining constant monthly payments—fully amortized mortgage

Monthly payment × (*MIFPVa*, 9%, 30 yrs) = $32,000
Monthly payments × 124.281866 = $32,000
Monthly payment = $32,000 ÷ 124.281866
Monthly payment = $257.48

From the point of view of the *lender* the loan represents an *investment* of $32,000 today (present value) on which an annual rate of 9 percent interest *compounded monthly* must be earned. What must the series of constant monthly payments (annuity) be to repay fully the $32,000 over the 30-year period and also to earn the lender an annual return of 9 percent compounded monthly? When discounted by the lender at 9 percent, the monthly mortgage payments of $257.48, yields a present value of $32,000 as shown in Exhibit 7–1. Consequently, monthly payments of $257.48 must be made to pay off the loan in 30 years and to earn the lender a 9 percent rate compounded monthly.

Returning to the calculation of the monthly mortgage payment in Exhibit 7–1, we should give particular attention to the following step in the solution:

$$\text{Monthly payment} = \frac{\$32,000}{124.281866}$$

$$= \$32,000 \times (1 \div 124.281866)$$
$$= \$32,000 \times .008046 \text{ (rounded)}$$
$$= \$257.48$$

Note that dividing the *IF* 124.281866 into $32,000 is identical to multiplying $32,000 by (1 ÷ 124.281866), or .008046 (rounded). This simple fact enables us to simplify calculations of this kind considerably.

Standard mortgage loan constants.   Since multiplying is always faster and more convenient than dividing, particularly when decimals are involved, a series of new interest factors, or *loan constants,* has been developed for various interest rates and loan maturities. These loan constants enable a simple multiplication to be made ($32,000 × .008046 = $257.48) to determine monthly mortgage payments, rather than the more awkward division ($32,000 ÷ 124.281866). The factor used for multiplication in our example, .008046, is the *loan constant* for 30 years at 9 percent. In Appendixes A and B to this textbook, column 6 is titled *Installment to amortize $1.* This means that a factor multiplied by the original principal gives the payments necessary to *amortize,* or pay off, principal and earn interest on the unamortized loan balance at a given interest rate over a prescribed number of years. It is customary to refer to this factor as the *loan constant* in mortgage lending, although the factor does have other application in real estate. Factors are provided for loans requiring annual payments (Appendix A) and for monthly payments (Appendix B) in those tables. Given an interest rate and term of a loan, one can find the appropriate loan constant by looking down column 6 and finding the factor in the row corresponding to the number of years for which the loan is to be made. The loan constant can then be multiplied by any beginning loan amount to obtain the monthly mortgage payment necessary to amortize the loan fully by the maturity date.

Exhibit 7–2 provides a sample of monthly loan constants for various interest rates and loan maturities. Returning to our problem of finding the monthly mortgage payment for a $32,000 loan made at 9 percent for 30 years, by locating the 9 percent column and looking down until we find the row corresponding to 30 years, we see that the loan constant in that position is .008046. This constant multiplied by $32,000 results in the monthly mortgage payment of $257.48.

Analysis of principal and interest.   To examine this payment pattern in more detail, it should be obvious that the sum of all mortgage payments made over the 30-year (360 months) period is $257.48 × 360, or $92,693. This amount is far greater than the original loan of $32,000. Why are the total

EXHIBIT 7–2
Monthly mortgage loan constants (column 6, Appendix B)

Years	Months		7%	8%	9%	10%
		Rate				
5	(60)		.019801	.020276	.020758	.021247
10	(120)		.011611	.012133	.012668	.013215
15	(180)		.008988	.009557	.010143	.010746
20	(240)		.007753	.008364	.008997	.009650
25	(300)		.007068	.007718	.008392	.009087
30	(360)		.006653	.007338	.008046	.008776

payments so much higher than the amount of the loan? The reason for this relationship is shown in Exhibit 7–3.

The pattern developed in Exhibit 7–3 shows in month 1 a beginning mortgage balance, or loan principal, of $32,000. The monthly payment, which

EXHIBIT 7–3
Loan amortization pattern, $32,000 loan at 9 percent interest for 30 years

Month	(1) Beginning loan balance	(2) Monthly payment	(3) Interest (.09/12 or .0075)	(4) Principal reduction	(5) Ending loan balance
1	$32,000.00	$257.48	$240.00	$ 17.48	$31,982.52
2	31,982.52	257.48	239.87	17.61	31,964.90
3	31,964.90	257.48	239.74	17.74	31,947.15
4	31,947.15	257.48	239.60	17.87	31,929.27
5	31,929.27	257.48	239.47	18.01	31,911.26
6	31,911.26	257.48	239.33	18.15	31,893.11
↓	↓	↓	↓	↓	↓
358	761.00	257.48	5.71	251.77	509.23
359	509.23	257.48	3.82	253.66	255.57
360	255.57	257.48	1.92	255.56	-0-
Totals	—	$92,693	$60,693	$32,000	—

was calculated to be $257.48, includes interest of $240.00 in the first month. Interest is determined by multiplying the beginning loan amount of $32,000 by (.09/12), or the annual rate of 9 percent divided by 12 months to obtain a monthly compound interest factor (.0075). The difference between $257.48 (column 2) and $240.00 (column 3) gives the amount of loan amortization or principal reduction (column 4) of $17.48 during the first month. The beginning loan balance $32,000 less the principal reduction in the first month, $17.48, gives the balance at the end of the first month of $31,982.52, which provides the beginning balance for the interest calculation in the second month. This process continues through the 360th month, or end of the 30th year, when the loan balance diminishes to zero.

The initial, relatively low, principal reduction shown in column 4 in Exhibit 7–3 results in a high portion of the early monthly payments being interest charges. Note that the ending loan balance after the first six monthly payments (column 5) is approximately $31,893.11; thus only $106.89 has been amortized from the original balance of $32,000 after six months. Interest paid during the same six-month period totals $1,438.01. The reason for such a high interest component in each monthly payment is that the lender earns an annual 9 percent return (.0075 monthly) on the outstanding loan balance. Since the loan is being repaid over a 30-year period, obviously the loan balance is reduced only very slightly at first and monthly interest charges are correspondingly high. Exhibit 7–3 goes on to show that the pattern of high interest charges in the early years of the loan reverses as the loan begins to mature. Note that during the last three months of the loan, interest charges (column 3) fall off sharply and principal reduction increases (column 4).

Interest, principal, and loan balance illustrated. To illustrate the loan payment pattern over time, Exhibit 7-4 shows the relative proportions of interest and principal in each monthly payment over the 30-year term of the

EXHIBIT 7–4
Mortgage payment pattern (approximately)

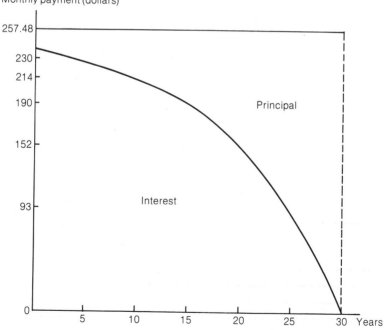

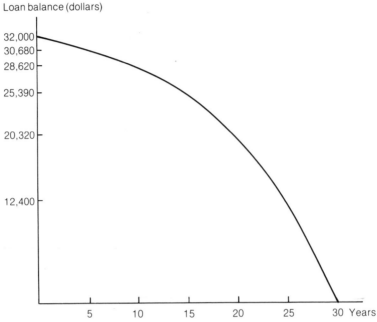

EXHIBIT 7–5
Loan balance pattern (approximately)

loan. Exhibit 7–5 shows the rate of decline in the loan balance over the same 30-year period. It becomes clear from Exhibit 7–4 that the relative share of interest as a percentage of the total monthly mortgage payment declines very slowly at first. Note in Exhibit 7–4 that halfway into the term of the mortgage, or after 15 years, interest still comprises approximately $190 of the $257.48 monthly payment. Exhibit 7–5 shows that after 15 years the loan balance is approximately $25,390. Mortgage payments of $46,346 ($257.48 × 180 months) have been made through the 15th year, with only $6,610 ($32,000 – $25,390) of the loan having been repaid at that point. This pattern reverses with time. Note in Exhibit 7–4 that after 25 years, interest comprises only $93.00 of the $257.48 monthly payment and the loan balance has declined sharply to $12,400 as shown in Exhibit 7–5.

Determining loan balances. A useful tool in mortgage lending is the ability to determine the balance on a fully amortized loan at any time. Most mortgage loans are repaid before they mature. In fact, even though most loans are made for terms of 25 or 30 years, statistics gathered on a national basis indicate that they are usually repaid within 5 to 10 years after they are made. Therefore it is very important to know what the loan balance will be at any point in time when financing real estate.

To illustrate, let us return to the previous example of the $32,000 mortgage loan made at 9 percent interest for a term of 30 years. After ten years, the borrower decides to sell the property and to buy another one. In order to do so the existing loan must be paid off. How much will have to be repaid to the lender after ten years? The solution to this problem can be determined in two ways. First, one can simply find the present value of the $257.48 payments at the 9 percent contract rate of interest for the 20 years remaining until maturity. For example:

$$\$257.48(MIFPVa, \ 9\%, \ 20 \ yrs.) = \text{Mortgage balance}$$
$$257.48(111.144954) = \$28,617.60$$

The unpaid balance after ten years is $28,617.60. This exercise also points out another interesting fact. Because the $257.48 payments include interest and a reduction of principal each month by removing all interest from all remaining payments, then it follows that only the principal can remain. Discounting the $257.48 monthly payments at an annual rate of 9 percent compounded monthly amounts to removing interest from these payments. Hence, after removing interest by discounting, we ascertain that the unamortized or unpaid balance must be $28,617.60.

An alternative method for finding mortgage balances at any time in the life of a mortgage is to divide the interest factor for the accumulation of $1 per period (S_n) from column 2 in Appendix B for the year in which the balance is desired by the factor for the *original term* of the mortgage, then subtract that result from one. To illustrate, our example:

$$1 - [(MIFCVa, \ 9\%, \ 10 \ yrs.) \div (MIFCVa, \ 9\%, \ 30 \ yrs.)] = \text{Percent mortgage balance}$$
$$1 - (193.5143 \div 1830.7435) = 89.43\%$$

This is a more general formula that can be used regardless of the original dollar amount of the loan or payments because it gives a solution in percentage form. In this case we determine that 89.43 percent, or $28,617.60, of the original loan balance ($32,000) is still outstanding. This solution is the same as the result we obtained by discounting.

To assist the reader in finding loan balances more quickly, a series of *loan balance factors* have been included in Appendix C at the end of this textbook. These factors are useful for constant *monthly payment* loans with original terms of 25 years or 30 years only, which are very common maturity periods for loans. The factors in the columns should be converted to percentages and multiplied by the original loan balance to obtain the loan balance for the year desired. Hence, in our example we would go to the 9 percent column for a 30-year loan and obtain the factor for 10 years, or .8943. This factor should be multiplied by the original loan amount $32,000, to obtain the outstanding balance of $28,617.60.

For loans with maturities different from 25 or 30 years, no loan balance factors in table form are provided. Hence, in those cases the two computational procedures described above should be used to find loan balances. Also, for loans requiring *annual* rather than *monthly* payments, outstanding balances may be found using the same computational procedure. However, interest factors from Appendix A must be used.

Loan closing costs and effective borrowing costs—fully amortized loans. Understanding loan closing costs is interesting and vital for professionals associated with the real estate industry. Closing costs are incurred in many types of real estate financing, including residential property, income property, construction, and land development loans. Closing costs can generally be placed in one of three categories: statutory costs, third-party charges, and additional finance charges. These categories are discussed more fully in Chapter 8; however, they are briefly reviewed here in order to point out their relationship to effective borrowing costs.

Statutory costs and third-party charges. When a mortgage loan is closed between borrower and lender, certain charges for legal requirements pertaining to transfer taxes, recording of the deed and mortgage, as well as other fees required by state and local law, are usually charged to the borrower. These charges are made for services performed by governmental agencies for the borrower and consequently *do not* provide income to the lender. Since these statutory charges do not provide income to the lender, they generally should not be included as additional finance charges as they do not affect the cost of borrowing. These charges by law would have to be paid even if a property was bought for cash and no financing was involved.

Third-party charges generally include charges for services such as legal fees, appraisals, surveys, pest inspection, and title insurance, to mention a few. Like statutory charges, these charges would generally occur even if cash was used to buy a property. If a loan is made, charges for these services may be collected by the lender but are in turn paid out to third parties; hence, they do not constitute additional income to the lender. As such, they are not charges associated with financing the real estate being purchased.

Additional finance charges. Another category of closing costs which does affect the cost of borrowing is additional finance charges levied by the lender. These charges constitute additional income to the lender and as a result must be included as a part of the cost of borrowing. Generally, lenders refer to these additional charges as *loan origination fees*. Such fees are intended to cover expenses incurred by the lender for processing loan applications, preparation of loan documentation and amortization schedules, obtaining credit reports, and other expenses which the lender believes should be recovered from the borrower. Sometimes these charges are itemized separately in the loan closing statement, and sometimes they are grouped under the general category of loan origination fees. These fees are generally the "fixed cost" element of originating mortgage loans. Lenders usually charge these costs to borrowers when the loan is closed rather than charging higher interest rates. This is because if the loan is repaid soon after closing, the additional interest earned by the lender as of the repayment date may not be enough to offset the fixed costs of loan origination.

Another item, which may be itemized separately or included in the overall category of loan origination fees, is *loan discount*.[1] This charge also represents an additional finance charge, but its primary purpose is to raise the yield on a mortgage loan. In the context of real estate lending, loan discounting amounts to a borrower and lender negotiating the terms of a loan based on a certain loan amount. The lender then discounts the loan by actually disbursing an amount of funds less than the contract loan amount to the borrower. Payments made by the borrower, however, are based on the contract amount of the loan. For example, assume a borrower and lender agree on a $40,000 loan at 10 percent interest for 20 years. The lender actually disburses $39,000 to the borrower by including a loan discount charge of $1,000. The borrower is required to repay $40,000 at 10 percent interest for 20 years. Since the borrower actually receives $39,000 but must repay $40,000 plus interest, it is clear that the effective borrowing cost to the buyer is greater than 10 percent.

Why do practices such as discounting exist, since any additional lending costs could be recovered by the lender by charging the borrower a higher interest rate? Many reasons for these practices have been advanced. One reason given by lenders is that mortgage rates tend to be somewhat "sticky" in upward and downward moves. This means that if the prevailing rate is 10 percent and market pressures push upward on rates, rather than one lender making a move to perhaps 10.25 percent, 10 percent may still be quoted as the loan rate but a higher origination fee (or loan discount if itemized separately) may be charged. This practice will be continued until the lender is sure that all competition is charging 10.25 percent. Although charging extra fees may amount to the same thing as charging an effective rate of 10.25 percent, lenders prefer this practice to increasing the interest rate. In this case it is obvious that a higher origination fee is used primarily to adjust the interest rate charged rather than to recover additional expenses associated with the loan.

Another reason for this practice may stem from the fact that conventional lenders compete with lenders making FHA-insured loans. Contract interest rates on FHA-insured loans are regulated by the Secretary of the Department of Housing and Urban Development. Changes in rates allowed on FHA-insured loans tend to lag behind those of conventional lenders (i.e., those lenders who make loans without FHA insurance). Consequently, when a borrower shops around for a mortgage loan, a rate may be quoted based on an FHA-insured loan, which is regulated, and it may well be lower than the market rate on conventional loans. So rather than quote a higher rate of

---

[1] Lenders in some areas of the country refer to loan discount as "discount points" or simply "points." In conventional mortgage lending, the borrower usually pays this charge, which adds to financing costs. When FHA and VA mortgages are involved, however, the seller of the property pays the discount points. In this chapter we are concerned with conventional lending situations where the borrower pays the loan discount as a part of origination fees.

interest, conventional lenders may quote the same rate as lenders making FHA-insured loans and "make up the difference" between the current actual market rate and the regulated FHA rate by charging a loan discount or origination fee.[2]

Another reason for loan discount fees is that lenders believe that in this way they can better tailor their return on the loan to the risk they take. For example, some riskier loans may require more time and expense to process and control than others. Since this may not be fully anticipated by the lender when the loan application is made, an interest rate may be quoted on the loan with the understanding that any "extraordinary" charges will be passed on to the borrower with a higher origination or loan discount fee.

The practice of using loan origination and discount fees has historically prevailed throughout the lending industry. It is important to understand (1) that these charges increase borrowing costs, and (2) how to include them in computing effective borrowing costs on loan alternatives when financing any real estate transaction.

Origination fees and borrowing costs. To illustrate loan origination fees and their effects on borrowing costs in more detail, consider the following problem: A borrower is considering the purchase of a $50,000 property and would like to finance it with an 80 percent, or $40,000, fully amortized loan for 30 years. A lender is contacted who is willing to make the $40,000 loan at 10 percent interest for 30 years. The borrower inquires whether any loan origination fee will be charged. The lender indicates that an origination fee of 2 percent of the loan amount will be charged. What is the effective interest rate on the loan?[3]

We structure the problem by first determining the amount of the origination fee or 2% × $40,000 = $800. Second, we compute the monthly mortgage payments based on $40,000 for 30 years at 10 percent. The loan constant from column 6, for 30 years, in the 10 percent tables in Appendix B is .008776. The monthly mortgage payments will be $40,000 × .008776, or $351.04. Now we can determine the effect of the origination fee on the interest rate being charged as follows:

Amount actually loaned:
Contractual loan amount $40,000
Less: Origination fee   800
Net cash disbursed $39,200

Amount to be repaid:
Based on $40,000 contractual loan amount,
$351.04 for 30 years.

---

[2] It may appear that if this practice is followed by conventional lenders, a borrower will be better off with an FHA-insured mortgage because it usually carries a lower, regulated interest rate. This will not necessarily be true because a lender making FHA-insured loans also charges a discount fee, or "points," which must be paid by the seller of a property. Although this fee is usually recovered by the seller of a property in the form of a higher selling price to the buyer, the lender will still quote the fixed FHA rate to the borrower (buyer).

[3] The effective interest rate referred to here is the effective cost to the borrower. However, the effective interest rate also means the internal rate of return or investment yield to the lender.

In other words, the amount actually disbursed by the lender will be $39,200, but the *repayment* will be made on the basis of $40,000 *plus interest* at 10 percent compounded monthly, in the amount of $351.04 each month. Consequently, the lender earns a yield on the $39,200 actually disbursed, which must be greater than 10 percent. To solve for the effective interest cost on the loan we proceed as follows:

$$\text{Monthly payment} \times (MIFPVa, ?\%, 30 \text{ yrs.}) = \text{Amount disbursed}$$
$$\$351.04 \times (MIFPVa, ?\%, 30 \text{ yrs.}) = \$39,200$$
$$(MIFPVa, ?\%, 30 \text{ yrs.}) = \$39,200 \div \$351.04$$
$$(MIFPVa, ?\%, 30 \text{ yrs.}) = 111.668$$

Using the procedure in the previous chapter, when solving for yields on investment *annuities,* this calculation results in an interest factor of 111.668. We know that the loan will be outstanding for a period of 30 years. Therefore, to find the actual interest cost of this loan we want to locate an interest factor in column 5 for 30 years in Appendix B that equals 111.668. A close inspection of Appendix B reveals that the interest factor that we are looking for falls between factors in the 10 percent and 11 percent tables. To find a more exact interest rate we must *interpolate* to find the solution as follows:

$(MIFPVa, 10\%, 30$ yrs.$) = 113.951$		$(MIFPVa, 10\%, 30$ yrs.$) = 113.951$
$(MIFPVa, 11\%, 30$ yrs.$) = \underline{105.006}$		Desired $MIF = \underline{111.668}$
Difference, 1% $= \underline{\underline{8.945}}$		Difference $= \underline{\underline{2.283}}$

$$(2.283 \div 8.945) \times 1\% = .26\%$$
$$\text{and } 10\% + .26\% = 10.26\%, \text{ or } 10.25\% \text{ (rounded)}$$

Hence, from the above calculation we can see that the effective cost of the loan, assuming it is outstanding until maturity, is approximately 10.25 percent, compounded monthly. This yield is obviously higher than the contract, or *nominal,* rate of interest as specified in the note or mortgage.[4]

We should also point out that this computation forms the basis for a very widely used rule of thumb in real estate finance; that is, for every 2 percentage points in origination fees charged the borrower, the effective cost to the borrower, or investment yield earned by the lender, increases by *approximately one quarter of a percent above the contract rate.* Note that in our solution we obtained an effective rate of 10.25 percent. Hence, if our loan is originated with a 4 percent fee to the borrower, the effective rate will increase to approximately 10.5 percent, assuming the loan remains outstanding until maturity. However, most loans, on the average, are "prepaid," or paid off long before maturity. Hence, this rule of thumb, while helpful, generally provides an underestimate of the effective cost (yield) of most mortgage loans.

---

[4] The interest rate specified in the note is sometimes referred to as a *nominal rate* because it does not take account of financing fees charged to the borrower.

Truth-in-lending requirements and the annual percentage rate.   Because of problems involving loan discounts and the potential abuse by some lenders of charging high fees to unwary borrowers, Congress passed a federal Truth-in-Lending Act.[5] As a result of this legislation, the lender must disclose to the borrower the annual percentage rate being charged on the loan. Calculation of the annual percentage rate (*APR*) is generally made in the manner as shown in the preceding example. The annual percentage rate in this case would be disclosed at closing to the borrower as 10.25 percent. The *APR*, then, does reflect origination fees and treats them as additional income, or yield, to the lender regardless of what costs, if any, the fees are intended to cover.[6]

Origination fees and early repayment—fully amortized loans.   An important result of origination fees and early loan payment must now be examined in terms of the effect on interest cost. In this section it will be shown that when origination fees are charged and the loan is paid off before maturity, the effective interest cost of the loan increases even further than when the loan runs for the full term.

To demonstrate this point, we again assume our borrower obtained the $40,000 loan at 10 percent for 30 years and was charged an $800 or 2 percent loan origination fee. At the end of *five years,* the borrower decides to sell the property. The mortgage contains a "due on sale clause"; hence the loan balance must be repaid at the time the property is sold. What will be the effective interest cost on the loan as a result of both the origination fee and early loan repayment?

To determine the effective interest cost on the loan, we first find the outstanding loan balance after five years to be .9657 (10 percent column, balance, 30-year loan, Appendix C) × $40,000 = $38,628. To solve for the yield to the lender (cost to the borrower) we proceed by finding the rate at which to discount the monthly payments of $351.04 and the lump-sum payment of $38,628, so that the present value we compute equals $39,200, or the amount actually disbursed by the lender.

This presents a new type of discounting problem. Here we are dealing with an annuity in the form of monthly payments for five years and a loan balance, or single lump-sum receipt of cash, at the end of five years. To find the yield on this loan we proceed as follows:

$$\$351.04(MIFPVa, \ ?\%, \ 5 \ yrs.) + \$38,628(MIFPV, \ ?\%, \ 5 \ yrs.) = \$39,200$$

This formulation simply says that we want to find the interest rate (?*i*%) that will make the present value of both the $351.04 monthly annuity and the

[5] See Regulation Z of the Federal Reserve Board, 12 C.F.R., sec. 226, as amended, 1977.

[6] Generally the *APR* disclosed to the borrower is the effective interest rate computed under the assumption that the loan will be outstanding until maturity, rounded to the nearest one-quarter percent. If the reader desires greater accuracy in these computations, consult *Computational Procedures Manual for Supplement I to Regulation Z of the Federal Reserve Board: Calculator Instructions,* Office of the Comptroller of the Currency, February 1978.

$38,628 received at the end of five years equal to the amount disbursed. The student should take special note that the two interest factors used in the above formulation are *different*. One factor (*MIFPVa*) is used to discount the monthly *annuity* and the other (*MIFPV*) is used for discounting *single receipt,* or loan balance. Hence, we cannot use the method of dividing the monthly annuity into the disbursement to find an interest factor as we did above. This is because we also have the loan balance of $38,628 which must be taken into account. How do we solve this problem? The answer is by trial and error; that is, we must begin choosing interest rates, then select the interest factors for five years corresponding to (*MIFPVa*) in column 5 and (*MIFPV*) in column 4, then multiply these factors by the cash payments and determine whether or not the calculated present value is equal to $39,200. When we have found the interest rate that gives us a present value of $39,200, we have the solution we want.

The trial and error process referred to is not as ominous as it may seem. Some careful thought about the problem tells us that because financing fees are being charged, the yield we are seeking must be higher than the contract interest rate of 10 percent compounded monthly. Also, careful thought will lead us to conclude that the yield is going to be greater than 10.25 percent. This is because as computed above, the 10.25 percent yield would be earned by the lender if the loan were repaid at the end of 30 years. Because the loan is being repaid over 5 years, the origination fee of $800 is being earned over 5 years as opposed to 30 years; hence, the effective interest cost to the borrower (yield to the lender) will be higher than 10.25 percent. How much higher? Probably not more than 11 percent. This is because, based on our rule of thumb, it would take a fee of about 8 percent to increase the yield from 10 percent to 11 percent over 30 years, and since we are dealing with a 2 percent origination fee, it is very unlikely that the yield would be in excess of 11 percent, even after only 5 years. Therefore we will use the interest factors at 10 percent and 11 percent and interpolate for the solution as follows:

1. Discounting at 10%: $351.04(47.065369) +
                    $38,628(.607789)   = $40,000

    Discounting at 11%: $351.04(45.993034) +
                    $38,628(.578397)   = 38,487

    Difference = 1%   Difference = $ 1,512

2. Desired present value = $39,200.
3. Difference in *PV* @ 10 percent and desired *PV,* or:
                    $40,000 − $39,200 = $800
4. Interpolating: $800 ÷ $1,512 × 1% = .53
    and: 10% + .53 = 10.53%

The student should note that we have employed a slightly *different* form of interpolation than was used in Chapter 6. This approach must be used anytime two or more different cash flow patterns, such as an annuity and a single receipt, are encountered in a problem in which the yield must be determined. Also, it should be noted that when the cash flows are discounted at 10 percent, the original $40,000 balance is determined. This detail can be eliminated in future computations.

From the above analysis, we can conclude that the *effective yield* (or effective interest cost) that we have computed to be approximately 10.53 percent, is higher than *both* the contract interest rate of 10 percent and the 10.25 percent yield computed assuming that the loan was outstanding until maturity.[7] This is because the $800 origination fee is earned over only 5 years instead of 30 years. Earning this $800 fee over 5 years as opposed to 30 years is equivalent to earning a higher rate of compound interest on the $39,200 disbursed. Hence, when this additional amount earned is coupled with the 10 percent interest being earned on the monthly loan balance, this increases the yield to 10.53 percent.

Another point to be made here is that the 10.53 percent yield is *not* reported to the borrower as being the "annual percentage rate" required under the Truth-in-Lending Act. This is because neither the borrower nor lender knows for certain that the loan will be repaid ahead of schedule. Therefore, 10.25 percent will still be reported as the annual percentage rate and 10 percent will be the contract rate, although the actual yield to the lender in this case is 10.53 percent. It should be remembered that the annual percentage rate (*APR*) under Truth-in-Lending requirements never takes into account early repayment of loans. The *APR* calculation takes into account origination fees, but always assumes the loan is paid off at maturity.[8]

Relationship between yield and time.   Based on the preceding discussion, we can make some general observations about the relationship of mortgage yields and the time during which mortgages are outstanding. The first observation that we should make is that the effective interest cost on a mortgage will always be equal to the contract rate of interest when no finance charges are made at the time of loan origination or repayment. This follows because, as we saw in Exhibit 7–3, the level payment pattern assures the lender of earning only a given annual rate of interest, compounded monthly, on the monthly outstanding loan balance. Hence the outstanding mortgage balance can be repaid at anytime and the lender's yield (borrower's cost) will *not be affected*. It will be equal to the contract rate of interest.

The second observation that we should make is that if origination or

---

[7] Many lenders refer to yields computed assuming a loan is outstanding until maturity as "the yield to maturity." When early repayment of a loan occurs, the yield computed is sometimes referred to as the "yield to prepayment."

[8] It has also been suggested that lenders use origination fees rather than charging higher interest rates when loans are made because most loans are repaid early. By using origination fees, the effective yield to the lender will be higher; however, the *APR* disclosure will not reflect the higher yield if loan repayment occurs early. The borrower may not be aware of this possibility. Hence, one can see the importance of the methodology being presented here.

financing fees are charged to the borrower, the following occurs: (*a*) the effective yield will be higher than the contract rate of interest and (*b*) the yield will *increase* as repayment occurs sooner on the life of the mortgage. These relationships can be explained by referring to Exhibit 7–6. The two

EXHIBIT 7–6
Relationship of mortgage yield, financing fees, and time (10% mortgage, 30-year maturity)

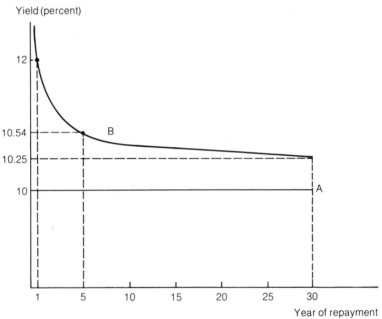

curves, *A* and *B*, shown in the exhibit, represent the mortgage yield pattern under two assumptions. Curve *A* represents the effective yield, or cost, when *no financing fees* are charged to the borrower. In our previous example, then, the yield would remain at 10 percent, or equal the contract rate of interest, regardless of when the loan is repaid; hence, the horizontal line over the range of 0 to 30 years. Curve *B* represents a series of loan yields computed assuming that a 2 percent origination fee is charged to the borrower and assuming that the loan is prepaid *each year* prior to maturity. In our example, then, we should note that the yield earned by the borrower is approximately 12% if the loan is repaid one year after closing and that it diminishes and eventually equals 10.25 percent after 30 years, per our calculation in the preceding section. Hence, we can again conclude that if financing fees are charged to the buyer, the effective yield to the lender (cost to the borrower) can range from one that is extremely high if repaid, say, after one year (the yield in that case would be approximately 12 percent), to a yield that would be considerably lower if held to maturity, or 10.25 percent.

Prepayment penalties. Many borrowers mistakenly take for granted that a loan can always be prepaid in part or in full anytime before the maturity date. This is not the case; and if the mortgage note is silent on this matter, the borrower must negotiate the *privilege* of early repayment with the lender. However, many mortgages do provide that an explicit penalty can be paid by the borrower should the borrower desire to prepay the loan.

One rationale for a prepayment penalty is that the lender may be trying to recover a portion of loan origination costs not charged to the borrower at closing. This may have been done by the lender to compete for the loan by making initial closing costs lower for the borrower. Another reason for prepayment penalties is that the lender has agreed to extend funds for a specified time, 30 years in our present example. Early payment from the lender's view may represent an unanticipated inflow of funds that may or may not be readily reinvested in periods when mortgage rates are stable, or are expected to decline. In recent years, however, with continued increases in mortgage interest rates, most lenders have been delighted when early payments occurred, as they have been able to loan funds out again at higher rates of interest. This argument is now somewhat questionable. Another reason for such penalties is that they are not included in the computation of the APR, hence they are not included in the APR disclosure to the borrower. Some argue that borrowers may not be able to determine the effect of these penalties on borrowing costs and that penalties merely represent a technique used by lenders to increase yields. Because of this, some states have begun prohibiting the enforceability of prepayment penalties to individuals financing residences, if the loan has been outstanding more than some minimum number of years. Also in areas where penalties are allowed, lenders will waive them if the buyer of a property agrees to originate a new loan with the same mortgagee.

Because of the widespread use of penalties, we want to know the effective mortgage loan yield (interest cost) when *both a loan discount fee and a prepayment penalty* are charged on the loan. This combination is used with considerable frequency in practice; consequently, one should be familiar with the combined effect.

To illustrate, we consider both the effects of the 2 percent loan discount *and* a 2 percent prepayment penalty on the outstanding loan balance for the $40,000, 30-year loan with a contract interest rate of 10 percent used in the preceding section. We assume the loan is repaid early, at the end of five years, and would like to determine the effective interest cost to the borrower (yield to the lender). To solve for the yield, mortgage funds actually disbursed in this case will be $40,000 less the origination fee of $800, or $39,200. Taking the loan discount fee into account, we want to find the discount rate, which when used to discount the series of monthly payments of $351.04, plus the outstanding loan balance of $38,628 and the prepayment penalty of $773 (2 percent of $38,628), or a total of $39,400, will result in a present value equal to the amount of funds actually disbursed, $39,200. This is done as follows:

$$\$351.04(MIFPVa, \ ?\%, \ 5 \ yrs.) + \$39,401(MIFPV, \ ?\%, \ 5 \ yrs.) = \$39,200$$

Following the same thinking used in the previous sections, we note that the likelihood of a 2 percent origination fee and a 2 percent prepayment penalty increasing the effective cost of this loan beyond 11 percent, compounded monthly, is unlikely; therefore we discount using the monthly interest factors at 10 percent and 11 percent and interpolate as follows:

A. Discounting at 10 percent:

$$\$351.04(47.065369) + \$39,401(.607789) = PV$$
$$\$40,468 = PV$$

B. Discounting at 11 percent:

$$\$351.04(45.993034) + \$39,401(.578397) = PV$$
$$\$38,934 = PV$$

1. Difference in interest rates $= 1\%$
2. Difference in PV $= \$1,534$
3. Difference in PV in (A) $= \$40,468 - \$39,200 = \$1,268$
    and desired PV
4. $\$1,268 \div \$1,534 \times 1\%$ $= .83$, adding $10\% + .83\% = 10.83\%$

From the discounting procedure used above we see that with a 2 percent origination fee, early payment in the fifth year and a 2 percent prepayment penalty, the effective yield on the loan will increase to about 10.83 percent.

In this case the APR will still be disclosed at 10.25 percent which reflects the loan discount only, not the prepayment penalty, and assumes the loan is repaid at the end of 30 years. The actual yield computed here is 10.83 percent which is a marked difference from both the loan contract rate of 10 percent and the disclosed APR of 10.25 percent.

Charging fees to achieve yield. In the preceding examples, we have developed the notion of the effective interest cost primarily from the borrower point of view. However, we should consider how fees are determined by lenders in establishing a competitive investment yield (the reader should note that effective interest cost and investment yield are the same concepts; hence, we use them interchangably).

Lenders generally have other alternatives in which they can invest funds. Hence, they will determine available yields on those alternatives for given maturities and weigh those yields and risks associated with those alternatives against yields and risks on mortgage loans. Similarly, competitive lending terms established by other lenders establish yields that managers must consider when establishing loan terms. By continually monitoring alternatives and competitive conditions, management establishes loan offer terms for various categories of loans, given established underwriting and credit standards for borrowers (underwriting standards are discussed more in the next chapter). Hence a set of terms designed to achieve a competitive yield on categories of loans representing various loan to property value ratios (70 percent loans, 80 percent loans, etc.) are established for borrowers who are acceptable risks. These terms are then revised as competitive conditions change.

To illustrate, if based on competitive conditions in the mortgage market and yields available on alternative investments, managers of a lending institution believe that a 9.5 percent yield is competitive on 80 percent mortgages with terms of 25 years and expected prepayment periods of 10 years, how can they set terms on all loans made in the 80 percent category to assure a 9.5 percent yield? Obviously, one way would be to originate all loans at a contract rate of 9.5 percent. However, management may also consider originating the loans at 9 percent interest and charging origination fees or prepayment penalties, or both, to achieve the required yield. Why would a lender do this? Because (1) they have fixed costs to recover and (2) competition may be originating loans at a contract rate of 9 percent.

To illustrate how fees for all loans in a specific category can be set, we consider the following formula:

$$MLC(MIFPVa, 9.5\%, 10 \text{ yrs.}) + MLB(MIFPV, 9.5\%, 10 \text{ yrs.}) = ND$$

where:

MLC = monthly loan constant factor at a *9 percent* contract rate for *25 years*
MLB = loan balance factor for a *25-year* loan, after *10 years,* at *9 percent*
ND = net disbursement (unknown) as percent of total loan

Substituting values for a 9 percent, 25-year loan in the above expression, we have:

$$.008392(77.281211) + .8274(.388190) = ND$$
$$.9697 = ND$$

The result we obtain, or ND = .9697, means that the net disbursement at loan closing should be 96.97 percent, or 97 percent (rounded), of the loan amount. This means that if a 3 percent origination fee is charged (100% − 97%) and the loan is repaid in ten years, management will have the 9.5 percent yield, compounded monthly, that it desires.

The above formula can be used for any loan category for which a solution is desired. The application used here was for the 80 percent loan category. However it should be noted that the numerical value of 80 percent does not appear in the formula. Hence, it is usable for all 9 percent, 25-year loans.

Further, if managment wants to charge a 1 percent prepayment penalty fee, how could this be dealt with in the formula? By simply increasing the loan balance factor (LB) by 1 percent, from .8274 to .8374, the necessary origination fee can be determined as follows:

$$.008392(77.281211) + .8374(.388190) = ND$$
$$.9736 = ND$$

The origination fee necessary now will be 100% − 97.36%, or 2.64 percent, if a 9.5 percent yield is desired over the ten-year period. This formula is very useful in considering the impact of various influences in "loan pricing." Changes can be easily made to contrast interest rates, prepayment assumptions, penalties, and other influences. Further, these relationships are especially important to management when attempting to "tailor" sets of loan terms on very large loans on commercial and other income-producing properties, where small changes in terms can be critical to making the loan.

Partially amortized constant payment loans

These loans, sometimes referred to as *balloon loans,* are different from fully amortized loans in that because of a specific financial objective, the borrower and lender agree that the loan will *not* be completely amortized, or paid off at maturity.

For example, assume an investor wants to borrow $2,000,000 to finance a proposed office building. The lender agrees that it is definitely a sound project; however, interest rates have recently moved up very *sharply* to record levels. Based on projections of income after operating expenses, the building will produce $230,000 per year upon completion. However, based on price escalator clauses in lease agreements with very high-quality tenants, the income should rise over the next five years to a level of about $290,000. Based on current mortgage interest rates, the lender must charge 12 percent for a 25-year loan, which would result in a mortgage payment of $21,064 or $252,768 per year on the $2,000,000 loan. Because these payments cannot be met from project income immediately upon completion, the lender may agree to somewhat lower mortgage payments that can be met from current income. For example, the lender may agree to monthly payments of, say, $19,000 per month, or $228,000 per year, which the investor could make from current income; however, the lender could insist on a loan maturity of *five years.* At that time interest rates may have stabilized, or fallen, and building income will be up to $290,000 at that time. Of course the lender would have to (1) be convinced that the project is sound and one considered to be a good investment, and (2) believe that the sharp increase in interest rates is only temporary. Further, the lender will probably have to be provided with other collateral (e.g., other real estate, personal assets) by the borrower, before such a loan is approved.

Assuming such a loan is approved, what will be the loan balance to be refinanced after five years? Will an arrangement like this affect the lender's yield? To answer these questions we first determine the loan balance to be refinanced after five years. This can be easily done by discounting the stream of $19,000 monthly payments at the desired 12 percent interest rate and relating that result to the $2,000,000 loan disbursement, then solving for the unknown mortgage balance as follows:

$$\begin{aligned}
\$2,000,000 &= \$19,000(MIFPVa,\ 12\%,\ 5\ \text{yrs.}) + \\
&\quad \text{Loan balance}\,(MIFPV,\ 12\%,\ 5\ \text{yrs.}) \\
&= \$19,000(44.955038) + \text{Loan balance}\,(.550450) \\
&= \$854,146 + \text{Loan balance}\,(.550450) \\
\$1,145,854 &= \text{Loan balance}\,(.550450) \\
\$1,145,854 \div (.550450) &= \text{Loan balance} \\
\$2,081,668 &= \text{Loan balance}
\end{aligned}$$

This formulation simply recognizes that the present value of the monthly payments plus the present value of the loan balance must equal the original loan balance of $2,000,000 when discounted at 12 percent. Even though the loan balance after five years is unknown, when its present value is added to the present value of the monthly payments, the sum must equal $2,000,000.

From the above computation, we can see that the loan balance or balloon payment required after five years would be $2,081,668, which is _greater_ than the original loan balance of $2,000,000. This is because the $19,000 monthly payment made during the five-year period is not enough to cover interest requirements at 12 percent. Consequently, the investor is actually borrowing more over the five-year period. The $2,081,668 would have to be either paid back or refinanced after five years. As to the lender's yield over the five-year period, because no points or prepayment penalties are being charged, it would still remain at 12 percent, compounded monthly. If such charges were made, given the $19,000 monthly payments and the loan balance of $2,081,668, the effective yield could be easily computed.

Another application of a balloon mortgage occurs when the lender requires the borrower to "rollover the loan" before maturity, in the hope that interest rates will rise in the interim. For example, in periods when financing is becoming tight, a project may be able to carry its mortgage payment requirement; however, the lender may be able to require that the loan be refinanced by making the loan maturity _shorter_ than the amortization schedule. In other words, a lender may provide $2,000,000 at 12 percent for _15_ years. However, the debt service will be computed based on a _25_-year _amortization schedule,_ making the debt service $21,064. Because the maturity of the loan is 15 years, while the amortization schedule is 25 years, there will be a balance to be repaid or refinanced after _15 years._ That balance is simply the present value of $21,064 per month for the *remaining* 10 years (25 years less 15 years) beyond maturity or:

$$\$21{,}064(MIFPVa,\ 12\%,\ 10\ \text{yrs.}) = \text{Loan balance}$$
$$\$21{,}064(69.700522) = \$1{,}468{,}172$$

Hence the borrower will have to repay or refinance (rollover) the $1,468,172 loan balance at the end of 15 years, at what the lender hopes is a higher interest rate.

A final application of a partially amortized loan is the case where the borrower and lender agree on what the *balloon payment* will be at some point in the future in which case the monthly payments must be determined to provide the lender with the required yield. For example, assume that an individual owns a group of rental income properties with a total appraised value of $500,000. These properties are free and clear of debt. The owner is interested in acquiring some attractively located unimproved land that might be profitably developed over the next ten years. If the individual does not develop it, the land could be sold to another developer after it appreciates in value. To finance the acquisition of this land, which will cost $250,000, the buyer decides to borrow against the rental income properties, which are presently free of debt, by obtaining a mortgage loan. A lender is found willing to lend $250,000, or 50 percent of the appraised value of the rental properties, for ten years. This coincides with the time that the borrower thinks it will take either to develop or to sell the land acquired for a gain.

Two conditions are encountered in this situation which make the use of a partially amortized loan possible. The first condition is that the borrower is borrowing only 50 percent of the appraised value of the rental properties, thereby providing the lender with collateral value ($500,000) considerably over the loan amount ($250,000). Second, since the unimproved land will not provide any monthly income to help pay the mortgage loan, the income from the rental property being used as collateral must ultimately be used to make the mortgage payments. The borrower does not wish to use a large amount of income from the rental properties to pay off a mortgage loan on the undeveloped property; he may expect to develop or sell the undeveloped property in ten years at a large profit. Under such conditions, the borrower may be able to obtain a partially amortized mortgage loan from the lender. In this way, the expected cash inflow from the sale or development of the property will coincide with repaying the large loan balance due on the mortgage. To illustrate further, assume the lender agrees to lend $250,000 for ten years; however, after negotiation the borrower and lender agree that the loan balance must be paid down to 85 percent of the original balance, or $212,500, at the end of ten years. At that time the property will either be sold or the deal will be refinanced. In this instance, we know that a balloon payment of $212,500 will be required after ten years and we know the original amount of the loan, or $250,000. Assuming the lender desires a 10 percent return (compounded monthly) on the loan, what will the *monthly payments* have to be over the ten-year period? To solve for the solution, we simply set the problem up as follows with *MP*, or the mortgage payment, as the unknown.

$$\$212,500(MIFPV, \ 10\%, \ 10 \ yrs.)$$
$$+ \ MP(MIFPVa, \ 10\%, \ 10 \ yrs.) = \$250,000$$
$$\$212,500(.369407) + MP(75.671163) = \$250,000$$
$$MP(75.671163) = \$250,000 - \$78,499$$
$$MP = \$171,501 \div 75.671163$$
$$MP = \$2,266$$

Note in this case that regardless of what *MP*, or the mortgage payment, is, when it is discounted and added to the present value of the balloon payment, both must equal $250,000. In other words, all cash payments received from the borrower must be just enough to return to the lender the $250,000 plus the ten percent interest compounded monthly. By discounting the balloon payment at 10 percent and subtracting from the original loan balance, the amount to be made up by the monthly payments, after discounting, is determined.

Demand loans and short-term real estate financing

This section deals with payment patterns and yield determination on loans used under special circumstances when short-term borrowing is necessary. Circumstances that may require short-term financing include interim borrowing by someone who has contracted to buy a new property while waiting to sell his present property, borrowing for minor property improvements that an owner wants to pay off in a short period of time, and borrowing on a short-term basis while waiting for a decline in long-term interest rates to refinance long-term rates. The reasons a borrower may desire interim real estate financing are numerous. Successful professionals involved in real estate finance must be aware of a wide variety of financing patterns. Sometimes a combination of short-term and long-term financing techniques is required to complete a transaction.

Demand loans—interest-only monthly payments. Demand loans[9] differ greatly from fully amortized and partially amortized loans. With demand loans, in most cases no monthly amortization of loan principal is involved and the full amount of loan principal is repaid at maturity. Monthly payments are usually made on these loans, but they are *interest-only* payments and generally do not include any repayment of loan principal. To illustrate the use of a demand loan, consider an individual who wants to borrow $10,000 for a period of one year to make an improvement on a property. A loan with a bank

---

[9] The term *demand loan* arises from the fact that the loan is short term in nature and may include a provision that the loan is callable or must be repaid to the lender on demand, or without notice.

is negotiated at 9 percent interest with interest-only payments to be made monthly and full repayment of the $10,000 principal at the end of one year. How much will the monthly payment be? What will be the actual yield to the lender?

Since no amortization of principal occurs on this loan, the monthly payments are simply *interest only* and are calculated as $10,000 × .09/12 = $75 per month. Therefore, 12 monthly payments of $75 plus one lump-sum payment of $10,000 will be made at the end of the 12th month. The yield to the lender is effectively 9 percent. This is obvious since the full amount of the loan principal is outstanding for one year with no prepayment penalties or origination fees and interest is assessed at an annual rate of 9 percent compounded monthly.

Prepaid interest—demand loans. A practice peculiar to demand loans, which is frequently used by banks, is a requirement that all interest on term loans be prepaid when the loan funds are disbursed. Since all interest is prepaid, there are usually no monthly payments. Only one payment is made at the end of the loan period.

The practice of requiring interest to be prepaid is similar to charging an origination fee in terms of its effect on loan yield. To illustrate the use of prepaid interest, let us assume that the borrower in our previous $10,000, 9 percent, one-year loan example is required to prepay all interest. In other words, $10,000 × .09 = $900, or $75 × 12 months = $900, will be prepaid at closing. The actual amount disbursed will be $9,100 at closing, and the amount repaid will be $10,000 at the end of the first year with no monthly payments between the two points in time. The effective yield in this case is found by discounting the lump-sum repayment of $10,000 made at the end of the year by an interest rate such that the computed present value equals the amount actually disbursed, of $9,100. This can be done as follows:

$$\$10,000(IFPV, ?\%, 1 \text{ yr.}) = \$9,100$$
$$(IFPV, ?\%, 1 \text{ yr.}) = .91$$

This computation results in an *IF* of .91. To determine the effective interest cost to the borrower, we consult the *annual* interest tables in Appendix A because only one annual payment is required in this case. Looking at one-year factors in column 4, we find that .91 falls very close to an annual rate of 10 percent (rounded). Interpolating between 8 percent and 10 percent provides a yield of 9.89 percent which stands in contrast to the contract, or nominal rate of 9 percent. The *APR* disclosed to the borrower in this event would also be 9.89 percent.

In the event of early repayment, if there is no provision for a rebate of interest, the investment yield to the lender (effective cost to the borrower) rises sharply. For example, if the loan were repaid after six months, the 9.89 percent yield increases to 19.78 percent, or 9.89% × (12 mos. ÷ 6 mos.), which is significantly higher than the 9 percent contract or nominal rate.

Short-term loans with add-on interest. Another category of short-term loans widely used in mobile home and home improvement financing is the add-on interest installment loan.[10] This loan gets its name from the fact that simple annual interest is computed at what is called an "add-on rate" and is then added on the amount borrowed. That amount is then divided by the number of monthly payments corresponding to the number of periods the loan will be outstanding.

To illustrate, assume a loan of $10,000 is made for 2 years with add-on interest of 8 percent for 24 months. Payments will be equal to add-on interest of $10,000 × 8% for 2 years or $1,600 plus the loan amount of $10,000, or $11,600, divided by 24 months. This results in payments of $483.33 per month. However, the borrower does not have full use of the $10,000 for two years because part of the loan is being repaid in the $483.33 monthly payments. Hence the effective interest cost to the borrower in this case is:

$$\$483.33(MIFPVa, \ ?\%, \ 2 \ \text{yrs.}) = \$10,000$$
$$(MIFPVa, \ ?\%, \ 2 \ \text{yrs.}) = \$10,000 \div \$483.33$$
$$(MIFPVa, \ ?\%, \ 2 \ \text{yrs.}) = 20.690$$

Looking to column 5 in our monthly interest tables in Appendix B, we find that the factor 20.690 falls between 14 percent and 15 percent for a two-year period. Interpolation provides an annual yield of approximately 14.75 percent compounded monthly, which must be disclosed to the borrower.

When these loans are repaid before maturity, state regulations generally require a rebate of interest. When computing the rebate of interest in most types of installment lending, a procedure known as the "rule of 78's" is usually used. This simply amounts to an approximation to the interest that the lender has *not* earned as of the date of repayment. This approximation is formulated as follows:

$$\frac{S(S + 1)}{N(N + 1)} \times \text{Original unearned interest} = \text{Rebate}$$

where (S) is the number of installments *remaining* when repayment occurs and (N) is the original number of installments. Hence, in our previous example, if the installment loan were repaid after 15 months, of the original 24 months, 9 months would remain. Substituting, we have:

$$\frac{9(9 + 1)}{24(24 + 1)} \times \$1,600 = \$240$$

Hence the borrower would obtain a rebate of $240 from the final installment. The final installment would be equal to 9 × $483.33, or $3,383.31. Hence the final net payment would be $3,383.31 − $240, or $3,143.31. It should be

---

[10] This type of loan is also used for automobile financing and various consumer loans.

noted that in this particular example, when early repayment occurs and the rebate is made, the lender's yield is approximately equal to the effective yield of 14.75 percent compounded monthly, which was previously computed. However, because the rule of 78's is only an approximation for finding rebates, the borrower usually gets a smaller rebate than that to which he is entitled. This is particularly true as length of the loan period increases. For more exact solutions, the rebates should be determined by discounting payments received by the *APR* and subtracting that result from the amount originally loaned. The difference will equal the proper final net installment.[11]

Questions

1 What are the major differences between fully amortized, partially amortized, and demand loans?

2 What does the term *amortization* mean?

3 Why are the monthly payments in the beginning months of a fully amortized mortgage loan comprised of a higher proportion of interest when compared to principal repayment?

4 What are loan closing costs? How can they be categorized? Which of the categories influence borrowing costs and why?

5 When a loan is repaid early, does this ever affect the effective interest cost to the borrower?

6 Why do lenders charge origination fees, especially loan discount fees?

7 What are the Truth-in-Lending Act and the annual percentage rate (*APR*)?

8 Does the annual percentage rate (*APR*) always equal the effective borrowing cost?

9 With respect to demand loans, differentiate between interest-only and prepaid interest requirements. How might each type of payment pattern affect the cost of borrowing?

10 What pattern does the effective interest cost on a fully amortized constant payment loan follow over time when loan origination fees are charged?

11 Describe an installment loan with add-on interest. If this type of loan is repaid before maturity, what method is used to rebate unearned interest to the borrower?

Case problems

1 Ms. Alice Cooper makes a fully amortized mortgage loan for $80,000 at 10 percent interest for 25 years. What will be the monthly payment on the loan?

2 John Brown made a 30-year mortgage loan 5 years ago for $30,000 at 8 percent interest. He would like to pay down the mortgage balance by $5,000.

---

[11] For additional discussion, see Edward A. Dyl and Michael D. Joehnk, "Prepayment Penalties Inherent in the Rule of 78's—A Truth in Lending Issue," *Journal of Bank Research,* Spring 1977, pp. 16–21.

a. Assuming he can reduce his monthly mortgage payments, what will the new mortgage payment be?

b. Assuming the loan maturity is shortened, what will the new loan maturity be?

3   James Doe wants to buy a property for $60,000 and obtains an 80 percent loan for $48,000. A lender indicates that a $48,000 loan can be obtained for 25 years at 10 percent interest; however, a loan origination fee of $1,000 will also be necessary for Doe to obtain the loan.

a. How much will the lender actually disburse?

b. What is the effective interest cost to the borrower assuming that the mortgage is paid off after 25 years (full term)?

c. What is the annual percentage rate (*APR*) which the lender must disclose to the borrower?

d. If Doe pays off the loan after five years, what is the effective interest charge? Why is it different from the *APR* in (*c*)?

e. Assume the lender also imposes a prepayment penalty of 1.5 percent of the outstanding loan balance if the loan is repaid within eight years of closing. If Doe repays the loan after five years, what is the effective interest cost now? Why is it different from the *APR* in (*c*)?

4   A lender is considering what terms should be allowed on a loan to Charles Good. Current market terms are 9 percent interest for 25 years, and the loan amount Good has requested is $30,000. The lender believes that extra credit analysis and careful loan control will have to be exercised in this as Good has never borrowed such a large sum before. In addition, the lender expects that market rates will move upward very soon, perhaps even before the loan with Good is closed. To be on the safe side, the lender decides to extend a loan commitment to Good for $30,000 at 9 percent interest for 25 years; however, he wants to charge a loan origination fee to make the mortgage loan yield 9.5 percent. What origination fee should be charged? What if the loan is expected to be repaid after ten years?

5   First City Life Insurance Company and Glen Road Development Company are negotiating a loan on an office tower that is located in a growing downtown area. The loan will be for $2.5 million and will carry an interest rate of 11 percent. Glen Road has convinced First City that debt-service requirements for the first three years will be too high in relation to the income generated from the property; however, lease contracts will be renegotiated with tenants over that period. Based on current market trends, by the end of the third year, rents should be more than adequate to cover debt-service requirements. First City agrees that $24,000 per month will be adequate for the first three years of the loan, and the loan balance will be refinanced at prevailing interest rates at that time. What will be the loan balance after three years?

6   Acme Landowner is considering the purchase and development of a large tract of land. It and Exchange Life Insurance Company enter into an interim loan agreement which will enable Acme to acquire the land and develop it within the next five years. At the end of five years, when development is to occur, an additional loan will be made for development costs. In the meantime, the land acquisition will cost $5,000,000 with Acme borrowing $2,500,000 from Exchange at 10 percent. The loan will require a balloon payment of $2,300,000 at the end of five years. What will the interim monthly

payments be for Acme? If a 2 percent origination fee were charged to Acme, what would be Exchange's yield?

7   A borrower makes a short-term demand loan for $5,000 at 9 percent for one year. Monthly, interest-only payments are to be made with the $5,000 principal due after one year.

   a.   What will the monthly payments be on such a loan?

   b.   What is the effective interest rate?

8   A borrower makes a short-term demand loan for $5,000 at 8 percent for one year. All interest is to be prepaid at closing, and principal is due after one year.

   a.   What is the amount of prepaid interest?

   b.   What is the effective interest rate on this loan?

   c.   What is the effective interest rate if the loan is repaid after ten months? Is it higher or lower than the *APR?*

9   Ms. Sally Swift makes a loan for $20,000 at 9 percent for ten years to buy a mobile home. The lender informs her that add-on interest will be charged and monthly payments will be equal to total principal and interest prorated over 12 months.

   a.   What will the monthly payments be?

   b.   What will the effective interest rate be? The *APR?*

   c.   If the loan is prepaid after seven years, what will the interest rebate be based on the "rule of 78's"?

   d.   (Optional) If the *APR* is used in (*c*) instead of the "rule of 78's", what will be the rebate?

Financing residential properties

8

This chapter deals with the process of seeking long-term conventional mortgage financing for owner-occupied residential properties.[1] The topics included are not only intended to provide a description of steps one might pursue in obtaining financing but also to provide insights into borrowing and lending risks. In addition, alternatives which commonly confront the borrower in deciding how much to borrow, given different interest rates and loan repayment patterns, are considered in detail. Finally, special financing considerations which frequently confront borrowers after closing, such as refinancing, selling on assumption, and using second mortgages, are included in the appendix to this chapter. Many concepts in this chapter form a basis for discussing the material in the next chapter, which deals with income-producing properties.

Basic concepts in loan risk analysis

Underwriting. The process involved in evaluating a loan by assessing its risk before approval and closing is referred to as *underwriting*. This function is usually performed by a loan officer at a financial institution such as a savings and loan association, commercial bank, mutual savings bank, or mortgage banking company, where a borrower may seek funds. The loan officer performs this function based on an analysis of (1) a loan application submitted by the borrower and (2) the characteristics of the property. This analysis is made also in the context of a lending policy, or guidelines, which a particular

---

[1] Practices relating to FHA and VA mortgages are considered in Chapter 23.

institution specifies. In deciding whether a loan application should be accepted or rejected, the loan officer follows some fundamental concepts in loan risk analysis.

Evaluation of the borrower.   One major concern of the lender is the risk associated with the borrower himself. Since loan conditions require repayment in future periods, the lender must consider the borrower's ability to repay the loan based on present financial condition as well as probable future financial condition. In making the loan analysis the lender may require, as part of this application, basic information on the makeup of the household, a statement of present income, occupations of members of the household, a list of personal assets such as automobiles, savings, stocks, bonds, or life insurance in force, and approval by the applicant to obtain a credit report verifying any of the information in the application.

Borrower income.   As to borrower income, some general policy guidelines are commonly employed by lenders concerning how high income must be in relation to the loan amount sought and the borrower's ability to meet monthly mortgage payments. These guidelines are used as credit standards, which are applied to a credit applicant as a risk indicator. Since the primary concern of the lender is the risk that the borrower will default on the loan, both present and future income are used to gauge the ability of the borrower to repay the loan. Whether a borrower can make monthly payments while at the same time leaving enough "cushion," or excess income, to make normal consumption expenditures over the period of the loan is of primary importance to the lender. However, more emphasis is placed on the current financial status of the applicant as most loan defaults usually occur within three years from closing, due to the borrower's inability to make timely payments.

Commonly employed guidelines used to determine how high income should be in relation to monthly mortgage payments and property value have been developed through statistical studies that show historically what the average household in the United States spends on housing consumption. These guidelines are as follows:

a. Total monthly mortgage payments, including a monthly allowance for property taxes and hazard insurance, generally should not exceed 25 percent of the borrower's gross monthly income.

b. Total monthly mortgage payments *plus* monthly estimates of utilities, repairs, and maintenance should not exceed 35 percent of gross monthly income.

c. Total monthly payments in (*a*) and (*b*) plus installment obligations should not exceed 50 percent of gross monthly income (installment obligations include payments that must be made on purchases or loans for ten consecutive months).

d. The value of the dwelling generally should not be more than approximately two and one half times the borrower's gross annual income.

e. The borrower's credit experience must be rated as good, per a credit report or investigation.

f. Job and income stability must be considered in light of mortgage payment and installment obligations.

g. Guidelines (*a*) to (*f*) must also be considered with respect to the borrower's existing assets in savings accounts, life insurance, and other assets.

In implementing these guidelines, it should be kept in mind that they are *general statements of policy, not hard and steadfast rules.* Loan policy serves as a *guide* for evaluating many average households seeking credit; however, there may be circumstances peculiar to a particular borrower's financial condition that necessitate *exceptions* to the general policy.

Underwriting standards—illustrated. To illustrate the application of loan underwriting standards, if a borrower's income is presently $2,000 per month, or $24,000 per year, underwriting guidelines may indicate that the maximum monthly mortgage payment should not exceed $500, or 25 percent of monthly gross income, for this borrower. Total fixed installment payments, including monthly mortgage payment, should not exceed $700, or 35 percent of gross income. The value of the dwelling being financed should be in the general range of $60,000, or two and one half times annual gross income. Many lenders find that exceeding these limits for the "average" borrower may cause overextension of credit and eventual default on the mortgage loan.

It must be stressed that underwriting guidelines are intended for the average borrower, with average income and family size. If an applicant has a higher than average income, a proportionally greater amount can generally be borrowed with no substantial increase in risk of default. This is true because as income rises over the average, outlays for living essentials are easily made and more income can be used for discretionary purchases, saving, and investing. Additional housing generally becomes one of the discretionary purchases. On the other hand, if an applicant's income is below average, essential outlays for food, clothing, and so on, usually take up a greater percentage of income. Hence, any excess for saving is generally low, and consequently the quidelines are more strictly enforced.

Problem areas in underwriting. Additional questions immediately arise concerning underwriting guidelines. To begin with, the lender will request that the applicant sign a request for verification of income from an employer. In cases where there is only one employed individual in the household, this generally presents no problem; however, if there are two individuals employed, the question of what constitutes income arises. The general rule applied by the lender takes a long-run viewpoint, that is, whether both individuals will remain employed indefinitely, or at least until the income of one is sufficient to meet the monthly mortgage payments. This question often presents difficulty when the value of the property and the corresponding loan amount being requested are high in relation to the income of only one of the income earners. Obviously, a judgment by the lender as to the future stability of the joint incomes will have to be exercised. Generally, if both parties have been employed for several consecutive years, there is a greater likelihood of future income stability. Or, if the intent of one of the parties is to end employment after a given number of years, and this individual is presently employed in a professional activity that lends to employment stability, both incomes may be included for the time both expect to remain employed. An estimate may then be made as to what the primary worker's total income will be at the time the other party ceases employment.

Additional problems in defining or estimating future income arise with individuals whose incomes are strongly affected by general economic conditions. For example, in the case of self-employed individuals, the lender will request evidence of recent income experience. In many cases, construction workers, commission salespersons, or individuals who earn a considerable portion of their income by working overtime fall into a category where seasonality or changing economic conditions cause fluctuations in income. Assessment of future income in these cases is sometimes difficult, as averages must be relied on over the year. The lender will look closely at the applicant's saving behavior and installment credit purchases to determine how well the household budgets income over seasonal or cyclical periods when current income may be low.

Other considerations. It goes without saying that qualitative considerations enter into any underwriting process dealing with the analysis of granting mortgage credit. An applicant's credit history, which can be obtained from a credit report, relating to installment buying, attitude toward prompt payment of obligations, and any past overextension of credit buying resulting in default or delayed payments, will weigh heavily in the judgment of the loan officer. In addition, future installment buying is considered by the lender to the extent possible. For example, if the property being financed is a first-time home purchase by the applicant, consideration of possible additional purchases for furnishings for the property and the ability of the borrower to carry both the mortgage payment and the installment note accompanying additional purchases must be taken into account. Other anticipated purchases which are unrelated to the housing purchase, such as automobiles, must also be taken into account by the borrower. All of these purchases are considered by the lender in establishing the borrower's ability to carry the amount of mortgage credit being sought.

Other assets of the applicant also play an important role in the rating loan quality by the lender. The rating is improved if the applicant has demonstrated a consistent ability to save as evidenced by savings accounts or investments in other property, ownership of life insurance (cash value), purchase of securities, and the like, as well as the ability to carry the obligations associated with the acquisition of these assets. For example, an older applicant whose remaining life expectancy is less than the term of the mortgage being sought may be granted a loan with the desired maturity, even though it exceeds the years of life expectancy remaining, if adequate life insurance exists to pay off the mortgage loan in the event death occurs before the loan is repaid. In most cases, the lender will request that the applicant sign a request allowing other financial institutions, investment companies, and credit agencies to disclose to the lender the nature and amount of the applicant's assets. These could include stocks, bonds, savings accounts and any recent activity in the accounts.

While income and credit capacity form much of the basis for risk analysis by the lender, recent federal regulations have limited the extent to which lenders may obtain information or make inferences concerning a loan applicant's background. Regulation B of the Board of Governors of the Federal Reserve System provides guidelines that lenders must comply with when gathering information about potential borrowers. A summary of the major guidelines that must be followed by lenders is provided below:

a.   The use of sex, marital status, race, religion, age, or national origin in a credit underwriting procedure is prohibited.

b.   Creditors may not inquire into birth control practices or into childbearing capabilities or intentions, or assume, from her age, that an applicant or an applicant's spouse may drop out of the labor force due to childbearing and thus have an interruption of income.

c.   A creditor may not discount part-time income but may examine the probable continuity of the applicant's job.

d.   A creditor may ask and consider whether and to what extent an applicant's income is affected by obligations to make alimony or child support or maintenance payments.

e.   A creditor may ask to what extent an applicant is relying on alimony or child support or maintenance payments to repay the debt being insured; but the applicant must first be informed that no such disclosure is necessary if the applicant does not rely on such income to obtain the credit. Where the applicant chooses to rely on alimony, a creditor shall consider such payments as income to the extent the payments are likely to be made consistently.

f.   Applicants receiving public assistance payments cannot be denied access to credit. If these payments and security provided for the loan meet normal underwriting standards, credit must be extended.

g.   An individual may apply for credit without obligating a spouse to repay the obligation, as long as underwriting standards of the lender are met.

h.   A creditor shall not take into account the existence of a telephone listing in the name of an applicant when evaluating applications. A creditor may take into account the existence of a telephone in the applicant's home.

i.   Upon the request of an applicant, creditor will be required to provide reasons for terminating or denying credit.

Evaluation of the property. The second half of the underwriting process leading to acceptance or rejection of a loan request deals with the characteristics of the property being financed. These characteristics include the property's value and future trends in that value, which invariably include other characteristics such as property values in the neighborhood, local public services, property taxes, and location of the property within the neighborhood and its proximity to major work centers in the community.

Property appraisals. Since the loan being applied for will be used to finance a residential property, the lender must make an estimate of the property's present value, as it will serve as collateral value for the loan in event the borrower defaults. This estimate of value is usually made by an experienced appraiser on the staff of the lending institution or by an independent fee appraiser.[2] In any event, the appraised value, and not necessarily the agreed sales price between the buyer and seller of a property, serves as the basis for the amount to be loaned.

Market comparison appraisals. In making residential property valuation estimates, one method of appraising commonly used is referred to as the *market comparison,* or market, approach. It is an appraising technique which employs data compiled on comparable properties recently sold in the same area as the property being appraised. The sources of data used by the appraiser are usually recent sales prices known from previous appraisals. Other sources of data are real estate transfer documents which are on file in the county courthouse and which indicate how much transfer tax or transfer fees were paid at the time comparable properties were sold. Since transfer fees or taxes in an area are sometimes proportional to the sales price paid by a buyer, the sales price is easily determined. For example, if the transfer fee charged in a particular county or state is .1 percent (.001) of the sales price and the transfer fee shown on the transfer document is $33, then the price paid by the buyer was $33 ÷ .001, or $33,000.

Whether tax data from transfer documents or other sources of sales data for comparable properties are used in estimating value, the appraiser must be sure that the transactions used were made at arm's length between buyer and seller. Obviously, a sale between relatives would not be desirable for use as a comparable sale. In addition, when arriving at estimated value, adjustments must usually be made by the appraiser for minor differences in physical and locational characteristics between the property being appraised and comparable properties. These adjustments are necessary because normally no two properties are exactly alike; they differ in living area (square footage), lot size, age, condition, or location. After compiling all of the relevant comparable sales prices and adjustments, the appraiser reports an estimated property value.

---

[2] An independent fee appraiser is generally an MAI (member of the American Institute of Real Estate Appraisers) or an SRA (member of the Society of Real Estate Appraisers). Independence here means that the appraiser has no vested interest in the transaction at hand and therefore he can give an independent estimate of value.

Cost appraisals.   A second approach commonly used in appraising residential properties is the *cost* approach to valuation. When used by appraisers, this method basically takes into account the cost of the lot and the cost of physical components in the structure based on a detailed inventory. For new structures the cost approach is generally a reliable technique for value estimation. When the property being appraised is not new, the appraiser must estimate the current reproduction cost of the structure and deduct an estimated allowance for depreciation from the reproduction cost.[3] The cost approach is difficult to use in many cases. If no recent comparable properties have been sold, however, use of the comparable sales approach is precluded and reliance on the cost approach is necessary.

Residential property appraisals—illustrated.   To provide more insight into what variables may be included in both the cost and market comparison approaches to appraising residential property, Exhibit 8–1 illustrates a standardized appraisal form presently used by many lenders.[4] Note that page 1 of Exhibit 8–1 requires a detailed description of neighborhood characteristics and physical components of the structure being appraised. In addition to the description, a qualitative judgment must be made by the appraiser as to the desirability of the neighborhood and condition of the structure with appropriate comments required as to undesirable neighborhood conditions and whether the unit is in need of structural repair.

Page 2 of Exhibit 8–1 contains the basic requirements necessary for completion of a cost approach and a market comparison approach to value. At the top of page 2 of Exhibit 8–1, the cost approach must be determined by costing out the square-footage reproduction of the unit, then adding the value of amenities (such as air conditioning, carpeting, built-in equipment, etc.). From the reproduction value is subtracted an estimate of any depreciation due to physical deterioration, design or functional obsolescence, and economic obsolescence because of neighborhood deterioration (traffic, location of undesirable industries nearby etc.). After amounts have been assigned to all of the categories, the remaining figure is the value estimated by use of the cost approach.

The middle portion of the second page of Exhibit 8–1 contains the data requirements for the market approach. Note that this appraisal form requires at least three properties comparable to the subject property to complete the appraisal. A detailed comparison of physical attributes for each comparable property, as well as its sale price and location, are included in the estimate of value for the subject property. The appraiser then judges whether increases or

---

[3] For a description of various methods used in appraising residential property, see Alfred A. Ring, *The Valuation of Real Estate,* 2d ed. (Englewood Cliff, N.J.: Prentice-Hall, Inc., 1970).

[4] This form is a part of the required mortgage documentation for any lender desiring to sell mortgages in the secondary mortgage market to the Federal Home Loan Mortgage Corporation or the Federal National Mortgage Association. Both of these corporations are discussed in detail in Chapter 24.

EXHIBIT 8-1
Residential appraisal report

RESIDENTIAL APPRAISAL REPORT

File No.

To be completed by Lender

Borrower			Census Tract	Map Reference

Property Address

City		County	State	Zip Code

Legal Description

Sale Price $	Date of Sale	Loan Term	yrs	Property Rights Appraised	☐ Fee	☐ Leasehold	☐ DeMinimis PUD

Actual Real Estate Taxes $	(yr) Loan charges to be paid by seller $	Other sales concessions

Lender/Client _____ Address _____

Occupant _____ Appraiser _____ Instructions to Appraiser _____

NEIGHBORHOOD

						Good	Avg.	Fair	Poor
Location	☐ Urban	☐ Suburban	☐ Rural						
Built Up	☐ Over 75%	☐ 25% to 75%	☐ Under 25%	Employment Stability		☐	☐	☐	☐
Growth Rate ☐ Fully Dev.	☐ Rapid	☐ Steady	☐ Slow	Convenience to Employment		☐	☐	☐	☐
Property Values	☐ Increasing	☐ Stable	☐ Declining	Convenience to Shopping		☐	☐	☐	☐
Demand/Supply	☐ Shortage	☐ In Balance	☐ Over Supply	Convenience to Schools		☐	☐	☐	☐
Marketing Time	☐ Under 3 Mos.	☐ 4-6 Mos.	☐ Over 6 Mos.	Adequacy of Public Transportation		☐	☐	☐	☐

Present Land Use ___% 1 Family ___% 2-4 Family ___% Apts ___% Condo ___% Commercial

Recreational Facilities ☐ ☐ ☐ ☐

___% Industrial ___% Vacant ___%

Adequacy of Utilities ☐ ☐ ☐ ☐

Change in Present Land Use	☐ Not Likely	☐ Likely (*)	☐ Taking Place (*)	Property Compatibility	☐ ☐ ☐ ☐

(*) From _____ To _____

Protection from Detrimental Conditions ☐ ☐ ☐ ☐

Predominant Occupancy	☐ Owner	☐ Tenant	___% Vacant	Police and Fire Protection	☐ ☐ ☐ ☐

Single Family Price Range $ ___ to $ ___ Predominant Value $ ___

General Appearance of Properties ☐ ☐ ☐ ☐

Single Family Age ___ yrs to ___ yrs Predominant Age ___ yrs

Appeal to Market ☐ ☐ ☐ ☐

Note: FHLMC/FNMA do not consider the racial composition of the neighborhood to be a relevant factor and it must not be considered in the appraisal.

Comments including those factors, favorable or unfavorable, affecting marketability (e.g. public parks, schools, view, noise) _____

SITE

Dimensions _____ = _____ Sq. Ft. or Acres ☐ Corner Lot

Zoning classification _____ Present improvements ☐ do ☐ do not conform to zoning regulations

Highest and best use: ☐ Present use ☐ Other (specify) _____

	Public	Other (Describe)	OFF SITE IMPROVEMENTS		Topo	
Elec.	☐		Street Access:	☐ Public ☐ Private	Size	
Gas	☐		Surface		Shape	
Water	☐		Maintenance:	☐ Public ☐ Private	View	
San.Sewer	☐		☐ Storm Sewer ☐ Curb/Gutter		Drainage	

☐ Underground Elect. & Tel ☐ Sidewalk ☐ Street Lights **Is the property located in a HUD Identified Special Flood Hazard Area?** ☐ No ☐ Yes

Comments (favorable or unfavorable including any apparent adverse easements, encroachments or other adverse conditions) _____

IMPROVEMENTS

☐ Existing ☐ Proposed ☐ Under Constr. No. Units ___ Type (det, duplex, semi/det, etc.) ___ Design (rambler, split level, etc.) ___ Exterior Walls ___

Yrs. Age: Actual ___ Effective ___ to ___ No. Stories ___

Roof Material	Gutters & Downspouts ☐ None	Window (Type):	Insulation ☐ None ☐ Floor
		☐ Storm Sash ☐ Screens ☐ Combination	☐ Ceiling ☐ Roof ☐ Walls

☐ Manufactured Housing

BSMT

Foundation Walls	___% Basement	☐ Floor Drain	Finished Ceiling ___
	☐ Outside Entrance	☐ Sump Pump	Finished Walls ___
	☐ Concrete Floor	___% Finished	Finished Floor ___

☐ Slab on Grade ☐ Crawl Space Evidence of: ☐ Dampness ☐ Termites ☐ Settlement

Comments _____

ROOM LIST

Room List	Foyer	Living	Dining	Kitchen	Den	Family Rm.	Rec. Rm.	Bedrooms	No. Baths	Laundry	Other
Basement											
1st Level											
2nd Level											

Finished area above grade contains a total of ___ rooms ___ bedrooms ___ baths. Gross Living Area ___ sq. ft. Bsmt Area ___ sq. ft.

INTERIOR FINISH & EQUIPMENT

Kitchen Equipment: ☐ Refrigerator ☐ Range/Oven ☐ Disposal ☐ Dishwasher ☐ Fan/Hood ☐ Compactor ☐ Washer ☐ Dryer

HEAT: Type ___ Fuel ___ Cond. ___ AIR COND: ☐ Central ☐ Other ___ ☐ Adequate ☐ Inadequate

Floors	☐ Hardwood	☐ Carpet Over ☐				Good	Avg.	Fair	Poor
Walls	☐ Drywall	☐ Plaster ☐		Quality of Construction (Materials & Finish)		☐	☐	☐	☐
Trim/Finish	☐ Good	☐ Average ☐ Fair ☐ Poor		Condition of Improvements		☐	☐	☐	☐
Bath Floor	☐ Ceramic	☐		Rooms size and layout		☐	☐	☐	☐
Bath Wainscot	☐ Ceramic	☐		Closets and Storage		☐	☐	☐	☐

PROPERTY RATING

Special Features (including energy efficient items) _____

Insulation—adequacy ☐ ☐ ☐ ☐

Plumbing—adequacy and condition ☐ ☐ ☐ ☐

Electrical—adequacy and condition ☐ ☐ ☐ ☐

ATTIC: ☐ Yes ☐ No ☐ Stairway ☐ Drop-stair ☐ Scuttle ☐ Floored

Kitchen Cabinets—adequacy and condition ☐ ☐ ☐ ☐

Finished (Describe) ___ ☐ Heated

Compatibility to Neighborhood ☐ ☐ ☐ ☐

CAR STORAGE: ☐ Garage ☐ Built-in ☐ Attached ☐ Detached ☐ Car Port

Overall Livability ☐ ☐ ☐ ☐

No. Cars ___ ☐ Adequate ☐ Inadequate Condition ___

Appeal and Marketability ☐ ☐ ☐ ☐

Yrs Est Remaining Economic Life ___ to ___ Explain if less than Loan Term

FIREPLACES, PATIOS, POOL, FENCES, etc. (describe) _____

COMMENTS (including functional or physical inadequacies, repairs needed, modernization, etc.) _____

FHLMC Form 70 Rev. 10/78   ATTACH DESCRIPTIVE PHOTOGRAPHS OF SUBJECT PROPERTY AND STREET SCENE   FNMA Form 1004 Rev. 10/78

EXHIBIT 8–1 (continued)
Valuation section

VALUATION SECTION

Purpose of Appraisal is to estimate Market Value as defined in Certification & Statement of Limiting Conditions (FHLMC Form 439/FNMA Form 1004B). If submitted for FNMA, the appraiser must attach (1) sketch or map showing location of subject, street names, distance from nearest intersection, and any detrimental conditions and (2) exterior building sketch of improvements showing dimensions.

COST APPROACH

Measurements	No. Stories	Sq. Ft.
x x =		
x x =		
x x =		
x x =		
x x =		
x x =		

Total Gross Living Area (List in Market Data Analysis below) _____

Comment on functional and economic obsolescence: _____

ESTIMATED REPRODUCTION COST – NEW – OF IMPROVEMENTS

Dwelling _____ Sq. Ft. @ $ _____ = $ _____
_____ Sq. Ft. @ $ _____ = _____
Extras _____ = _____
_____ = _____
Special Energy Efficient Items _____ = _____
Porches, Patios, etc. _____ = _____
Garage/Car Port _____ Sq. Ft. @ $ _____ = _____
Site Improvements (driveway, landscaping, etc.) = _____
Total Estimated Cost New = $ _____

	Physical	Functional	Economic	
Less Depreciation $	$	$	= $ ( )

Depreciated value of improvements = $ _____
ESTIMATED LAND VALUE = $ _____
(If leasehold, show only leasehold value)

INDICATED VALUE BY COST APPROACH $ _____

The undersigned has recited three recent sales of properties most similar and proximate to subject and has considered these in the market analysis. The description includes a dollar adjustment, reflecting market reaction to those items of significant variation between the subject and comparable properties. If a significant item in the comparable property is superior to, or more favorable than, the subject property, a minus (-) adjustment is made, thus reducing the indicated value of subject; if a significant item in the comparable is inferior to, or less favorable than, the subject property, a plus (+) adjustment is made, thus increasing the indicated value of the subject.

MARKET DATA ANALYSIS

ITEM	Subject Property	COMPARABLE NO. 1		COMPARABLE NO. 2		COMPARABLE NO. 3	
Address							
Proximity to Subj.							
Sales Price	$	$		$		$	
Price/Living area	$	$		$		$	
Data Source							
	DESCRIPTION	DESCRIPTION	+(-)$ Adjustment	DESCRIPTION	+(-)$ Adjustment	DESCRIPTION	+(-)$ Adjustment
Date of Sale and Time Adjustment							
Location							
Site/View							
Design and Appeal							
Quality of Const.							
Age							
Condition							
Living Area Room Count and Total	Total ¦ B-rms ¦ Baths	Total ¦ B-rms ¦ Baths		Total ¦ B-rms ¦ Baths		Total ¦ B-rms ¦ Baths	
Gross Living Area	Sq.Ft.	Sq.Ft.		Sq.Ft.		Sq.Ft.	
Basement & Bsmt. Finished Rooms							
Functional Utility							
Air Conditioning							
Garage/Car Port							
Porches, Patio, Pools, etc.							
Special Energy Efficient Items							
Other (e.g. fireplaces, kitchen equip., remodeling)							
Sales or Financing Concessions							
Net Adj. (Total)		☐ Plus; ☐ Minus	$	☐ Plus; ☐ Minus	$	☐ Plus; ☐ Minus	$
Indicated Value of Subject			$		$		$

Comments on Market Data _____

INDICATED VALUE BY MARKET DATA APPROACH $ _____

INDICATED VALUE BY INCOME APPROACH (If applicable) Economic Market Rent $ _____ /Mo. x Gross Rent Multiplier _____ = $ _____

This appraisal is made ☐ "as is" ☐ subject to the repairs, alterations, or conditions listed below ☐ completion per plans and specifications.

Comments and Conditions of Appraisal: _____

Final Reconciliation: _____

Construction Warranty ☐ Yes ☐ No Name of Warranty Program _____ Warranty Coverage Expires _____

This appraisal is based upon the above requirements, the certification, contingent and limiting conditions, and Market Value definition that are stated in

☐ FHLMC Form 439 (Rev. 10/78)/FNMA Form 1004B (Rev. 10/78) filed with client _____ 19 ____ ☐ attached.

I ESTIMATE THE MARKET VALUE, AS DEFINED, OF SUBJECT PROPERTY AS OF _____ 19 ____ to be $ _____

Appraiser(s) _____ Review Appraiser (If applicable) _____ ☐ Did ☐ Did Not Physically Inspect Property

FHLMC Form 70 Rev. 10/78 Forms and Worms 315 Whitney Ave. New Haven, CT 06511   REVERSE   FNMA Form 1004 Rev. 10/78 decreases in value should be made to the comparable properties when attributes are compared with the property being valued, before arriving at a value. Finally, the appraiser reconciles the value estimated using the cost approach and the value estimated using the market approach before making a best estimate of the value of the property.

Property appraisal and sale price. It should also be pointed out that the sale price of a property agreed on between a buyer and seller may not always correspond to the lender's appraised value. For example, if a buyer and a seller agree on a price of $42,000 for a property and the appraised value obtained by the lender comes in at $40,000, the lender will generally use the $40,000 as the value on which the loan will be based, unless there is convincing evidence to change it.[5] In this case, the lender obviously thinks the buyer is overpaying for the property and, therefore, is unwilling to use the sale price as a basis for the loan. This concept is important because if the buyer is applying for a 90 percent loan, the lender may be willing to lend 90 percent of $40,000, or $36,000, with the buyer making a down payment of ($42,000–$36,000) $6,000. If the property had been appraised at $42,000, the loan would be $37,800 and the down payment, $4,200. Consequently, the buyer will have to make a down payment $1,800 higher simply on the basis of the difference in appraisals.

Carried to an extreme, if the sale price agreed on were $50,000 and the lender based the 90 percent loan on the sale price, $45,000 would be loaned and the buyer would make a $5,000 down payment. If the buyer defaulted shortly thereafter and the loan was foreclosed, resulting in a sale for only $40,000, the lender would lose $5,000 and the buyer would lose the $5,000 down payment. The upshot of this analysis is that the lender wants to be sure that the appraised value is accurate, for if too large a loan is made as a result of a poor value estimate, the lender stands to lose in the event a buyer defaults on the loan.

Property values over time. A cardinal rule followed by lenders is that the value of a mortgaged property should never fall below the outstanding loan balance at any time during the life of the mortgage. In other words, the lender wants to be assured that the market value of the property will always be high enough to assure that the loan balance will be recovered in the event of default by the borrower. As has already been seen in Exhibit 7–2 in Chapter 7, the outstanding loan balance for a fully amortized loan declines over the loan period. This pattern is reproduced in Exhibit 8–2.

An important consideration in the mind of the underwriter is the possible pattern value that a given proprety will follow *over time.* Exhibit 8–2 depicts two hypothetical patterns that a property could follow. In the case of property value A, it is clear that the risk of loss for the lender in the event of default would be slight since the property is *appreciating* in value. The value pattern A

---

[5] An independent appraisal obtained by the buyer or seller may reveal an aspect of the property overlooked by the lender, and because of the oversight, the lender may be willing to change the estimate. However, if no independent appraisal is obtained by the buyer or seller, the lender's appraised value is likely to stand, regardless of what the buyer pays for the property.

EXHIBIT 8–2
Relationship between property value and loan balance

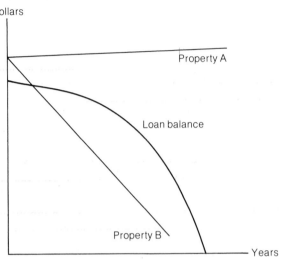

is always higher than the loan balance in each period over the term of the loan. Because of the protection afforded to the lender by the rising property value, if the household's income is adequate, the loan would undoubtedly be granted.

In the case of pattern B shown in Exhibit 8–2, however, it is clear that since the property value is declining over time, the borrower would not extend the amount of credit being sought. Note that pattern B actually *falls below* the loan balance during the life of the loan. The lender could adjust the loan terms by lending substantially less for a shorter time period so that the loan balance curve would be lower in the first place and so that the loan would mature sooner. However, since the risk of value decline appears extremely great to the lender, chances are that the loan would not be made regardless of the amount and the terms.

Factors influencing property value trends. What factors influence property values over time? A number of influences must be considered by a lender when making this determination:

1. Income of households in the contiguous neighborhood.
2. Quality of public services delivered in the form of schools, police and fire protection, recreational facilities, road maintenance, water and sewer service; property taxes associated with provision of public services.
3. Location relative to major employment centers, shopping centers, and other frequented activities.
4. External influences, including industrial plants, sewer plants, heavy traffic patterns, and other negative sources of pollution, noise, and so on.
5. Positive external influences such as green areas, parks, and other amenities.

While this list does not exhaust all considerations, it covers the major categories investigated by lenders when evaluating property value trends. The first consideration listed, income of residents in the area, cannot be overemphasized. Income is the primary determinant of the demand for housing and what households spend on housing. This expenditure includes not only outlays for acquisition of housing but also expenditures for maintenance, repair, and improvements and other housing services. Obviously, higher income households will demand more housing services than lower income households. Consequently, the level of maintenance, repair, and so on, is strictly a function of income. The condition, and hence the value, of a property will reflect the outlays made on these services over time. Income of households in a given area also "spills over" into the demand for public services, particularly schools and educational services as listed in the second category above. Demand for these services also increases with income and reinforces the stability of property value in any given area.

Locational factors, such as distance to work, shopping, and so on, obviously affect travel time and cost outlays by households. Higher income households are generally willing to pay a premium for good accessibility to reduce travel time and fuel costs. Finally, other locational factors, such as proximity to negative external influences like air pollution, may require higher maintenance expenditures. Consequently, it is easier for households living adjacent to these negative influences to allow property to decline than to keep it up. On the other hand, nearness to positive external influences, such as parks and green areas, generally acts as a catalyst for households to maintain housing quality.

Borrower considerations in financing

While the lender is concerned with both property and borrower characteristics when evaluating a loan, the borrower also has options to consider when making financial decisions. One question in the mind of the borrower is how much financing should be applied for. This question may be easily answered for buyers of residential property for the first time who have managed to save just enough for a minimum down payment. For many households, however, the question of how much to borrow must be considered in relation to other investments that may be undertaken with available funds. A second question deals with returns on yields that might be realized from an investment in housing due to possible appreciation in value and tax considerations, and how that return is affected by borrowing.

Housing serves two purposes for the borrower. The more obvious purpose is shelter and attendant amenities. A less obvious one is investment. Anyone familiar with real estate investment knows of the rapid price appreciation in housing that has occurred in recent years. The major causes of this increase have been rising incomes and inflationary pressures; hence the homeowner has come to look on housing as an excellent inflation hedge with which to preserve the economic value of personal assets. Consequently, when a borrower considers the purchase of a property, its investment dimensions should be considered as well as how much borrowing is desirable.

   Analysis of financing alternatives.   We begin by considering the question of how much to borrow. In determining how much to borrow, the buyer of a property may be faced with several options. For example, assume a borrower is purchasing a property for $50,000 and faces two possible loan alternatives. One lender is willing to make an 80 percent loan, or $40,000, for 25 years at 9.5 percent interest. Another lender is willing to lend 90 percent, or $45,000, for 25 years at 10 percent. How should the borrower compare these alternatives?

   To analyze this problem, emphasis should be placed on a basic concept called the incremental or marginal cost of borrowing. Based on the material in the preceding chapter, we know how to compute the effective cost of borrowing for one specific loan. However, it is equally important in real estate finance to be able to compare financing alternatives, or situations in which the borrower can finance the purchase of real estate in more than one way or under different lending terms.

   In our problem at hand we are considering differences in loan terms. A loan can be made for $40,000 for 25 years at 9.5 percent interest, or $45,000 can be borrowed for 25 years at 10 percent interest. Because there are no origination fees, we know from the preceding chapter that the effective interest cost for the two loans will be 9.5 percent and 10 percent, respectively. However, an important cost that the borrower should compute is how much is being paid to acquire the incremental or additional $5,000 should he choose to take the $45,000 loan over the $40,000 loan? At first glance the reader may think that because the interest rate on the $45,000 loan is 10 percent, the cost of acquiring the additional $5,000 is also 10 percent. This is *not* so. Careful analysis of the two loans reveals that when compared to the $40,000 loan available at 9.5 percent interest, if the borrower wants to borrow the additional $5,000, he must not only pay 10 percent interest on the $5,000 but he must also pay an *additional* .5 percent interest on the first $40,000 borrowed. This increases the cost of obtaining the additional $5,000 considerably. The effective cost of borrowing the additional $5,000 can be determined as follows:

Differences in amount borrowed and annual interest cost:		
Alternative I:	$40,000 × 9.5% =	$3,800
Alternative II:	45,000 × 10% =	4,500
Difference	$ 5,000	$ 700

Marginal cost: $700 ÷ $5,000 = 14%

Hence, if our borrower desires to borrow the additional $5,000 with the $45,000 loan, the cost of doing so will be 14 percent, or a rate considerably higher than 10 percent. This cost is sometimes referred to as the *marginal* or *incremental cost of borrowing*.

Why is the marginal cost idea so important? It is important because it tells the borrower what rate of interest must be earned on equity funds not invested in a property because of the larger amount borrowed. In other words, by obtaining a larger loan ($45,000 versus $40,000), this means that $5,000 less will be required as a down payment from the borrower than would have been the case had the $40,000 loan been made. Hence, unless the borrower can earn 14 percent interest or more on the $5,000 not invested in the property, he would be better off with the smaller loan of $40,000. He would save the equivalent of 14 percent in interest costs if he did so. Also, if the borrower could obtain a second mortgage for $5,000 at a rate less than 14 percent, this may be a better alternative than a 90 percent loan. Therefore, the marginal cost concept is also an opportunity cost concept in that it tells the borrower the minimum rate of interest that must be earned, or the maximum amount that should be paid, on any additional amounts borrowed. We should also note that in this example, the incremental cost of borrowing will remain 14 percent even if the loan is repaid before maturity. However, if origination fees or prepayment penalties are included as a condition of obtaining either or both alternatives, the incremental cost will depend on when the loan is repaid.

The incremental cost of borrowing—further considerations. It should be apparent that the incremental borrowing cost concept is extremely important when deciding how much should be borrowed to finance a given transaction. In the preceding section, the two alternatives considered were fairly straightforward with the only differences between them being the interest rate and the amount borrowed. In most cases financing alternatives under consideration will have *different* interest rates as the amount borrowed increases, and possibly *different* loan maturities. Also, loan origination fees will usually be charged on the loan alternatives. Financing alternatives with these characteristic differences are considered in this section.

The first case we wish to consider is the incremental cost of borrowing when loan origination fees are charged on the two 25-year loan alternatives. For example, if an $800 origination fee is charged on the $40,000 loan and a $1,200 fee is charged on the $45,000 loan, how does this affect the incremental cost of borrowing? These differences can be easily included in the cost computation as follows:

Differences in amounts borrowed and payments:

	Loan	−	Fees	=	Net amount disbursed	Loan	×	Loan constant	=	Monthly payments
Alt. I	$40,000	−	$800	=	$39,200	$40,000	×	.008737	=	$349.48
Alt. II	45,000	−	1,200	=	43,800	45,000	×	.009087	=	408.92
			Difference	=	$ 4,600			Difference	=	$ 59.44

Computing the marginal cost we have:

$$\$59.44(MIFPVa,\ ?\%,\ 25\ \text{yrs.}) = \$4,600$$
$$(MIFPVa,\ ?\%,\ 25\ \text{yrs.}) = \$4,600 \div \$59.44$$
$$(MIFPVa,\ ?\%,\ 25\ \text{yrs.}) = 77.388964$$

Note that because of the differences due to the loan origination fee, we must compute the marginal cost of the $4,600 based on the discounting or present value procedure discussed in the previous two chapters. In this formulation we want to find an annual rate of interest, compounded monthly, that makes the present value of the difference in mortgage payments, or $59.44, equal to $4,600, or the incremental amount of loan proceeds received. As seen from above, we have computed the monthly *interest factor* for the $59.44 annuity to be 77.388964. Looking to column 5 in Appendix B in this textbook, we see that this factor falls between the 25-year factors in the 15 percent and 20 percent interest rate tables. We can interpolate to find the incremental cost as follows:

	MIFPVa, column 5		
15%	78.074336	IF at 15%	78.074336
20%	59.578715	Desired IF	77.388964
5% difference	18.495621	Difference	.685372

$$(.685372 \div 18.495621) \times 5\% = .19$$
$$\text{Add: } 15\% + .19\% = 15.19\%$$

Hence, we can see that the marginal cost increases to about 15.2% (expressed as an annual rate of interest compounded monthly) when the effects of origination fees are included in the analysis.

We should note that when origination fees are charged, the marginal or incremental cost of borrowing increases if the loan is repaid before maturity. For example, if in the above problem, the loan were repaid after ten years, the incremental cost would increase to about 15.5 percent.[6] Also if prepayment penalties apply in cases where early payoff occurs, this increases the marginal cost of borrowing.

Differences in maturities.   In the above examples, the loan alternatives considered had the same maturities, that is, 25 years. How does one determine the incremental cost of alternatives that have different maturities as well as different interest rates? Do differences in maturities materially change results? We examine these questions by changing our previous example and assuming

[6] The reader should note that when computing the incremental cost of borrowing when early repayment occurs, the differences in loan balances in the year of repayment, in addition to the differences in monthly payments, must be discounted to present value.

that the $45,000 alternative has a 30-year maturity as well as a higher interest rate. How would the analysis be changed? We first must compute the following information:

	Loan	Payments years 1–25	Payments years 25–30
Alternative I.	$40,000	$349.48	-0-
Alternative III.	45,000	394.92	$394.92
Difference	$ 5,000	$ 45.44	$394.92

In this case we compute the monthly payment for a $45,000, 30-year loan at 10 percent interest ($45,000 × .008776), or $394.92. However, there are two differences in the series of monthly payments relevant to our example. For the first 25 years, should Alternative III be chosen over Alternative II, the borrower will pay an additional $45.44 per month. For the final 5-year period, or years 25 through 30, the difference between payments will be the full $394.92 payment on Alternative III because the $40,000 loan would be repaid after 25 years. Hence the incremental cost must be computed by considering the payment differences as two annuities as follows:

$$\$45.44(MIFPVa, \ ?\%, \ 25 \ \text{yrs.}) +$$
$$\$394.92(MIFPVa, \ ?\%, \ 30 \ \text{yrs.} - 25 \ \text{yrs.}) = \$5,000$$

In the above formulation, it should be noted that the second annuity of $394.92 must be discounted over the period running from year 25 through year 30. Hence, when discounting to find a present value equal to $5,000, the interest factors corresponding to the interest rate chosen for discounting must be the "net" factor of difference corresponding to that time interval. In finding the solution to the above problem we should note that the second annuity of $394.92 is not paid until year 25; hence, its influence on the present value of the combined annuities will be very slight.[7] Hence, we can approximate the incremental cost as follows: ($45.44 × 12) ÷ $5,000 = 10.9% and proceed by discounting by 11 percent:

$$\$45.44(102.029044) + \$394.92(105.006346 - 102.029044) = PV$$
$$\$45.44(102.029044) + \$394.92(2.977302) = PV$$
$$\$5,812 = PV$$

The solution we obtain in this case is below the $5,000 present value we are seeking; so the discount rate must be increased. A rough estimate of 13 percent

---

[7] This can be seen by the "net" factor used to multiply the second annuity, in the solution which follows. This also demonstrates that the present value of amounts received in the future are worth far less than amounts received early in the life of an investment.

should be an adequate rate of discount to bring the solution closer to the desired present value of $5,000. Discounting we get:

$$\$45.44(88.665428) + \$394.92(90.399605 - 88.665428) = PV$$
$$\$45.44(88.665428) + \$394.92(1.734177) = \$4,714$$

Interpolating between 11 percent and 13 percent (not shown) results in a solution of approximately 12.5 percent. Hence the marginal or incremental cost of borrowing the $5,000 for a period of 30 years versus 25 years, given the interest rate increase from 9.5 percent to 10 percent will be about 12.5 percent. This compares to the incremental cost of 14 percent in the previous example, where no points were charged and both maturities were 25 years. The reason the marginal cost is lower in this case is that the funds are being extended for 30 years as opposed to 25 years and the interest rate on the $45,000 loan remained the same.

We should point out that if the loan is expected to be repaid before maturity, both the difference in monthly payments and loan balances in the year of repayment must be taken into account when computing the marginal borrowing cost. Also, should any origination fees be charged, the incremental funds disbursed by the lender should be reduced accordingly.

Tax considerations—borrower. The final consideration by the borrower to be developed here deals with federal income taxes. One advantage that ownership of residential property affords a borrower lies in the deductibility of interest charges on mortgage loans in determining federal income tax liability.

To illustrate how federal income taxes provide an incentive to borrow, we consider a borrower in a 35 percent tax bracket. We assume that $40,000 is borrowed for a period of 25 years at 8 percent interest. The effects of federal income tax on the financing cost can be seen as follows:

Annual mortgage payments: $308.80 × 12 =		$3,705.60
Less principal reduction:		
Initial mortgage balance	$40,000	
Less: Mortgage balance year 1	39,476	
Principal reduction		−524.00
Total interest payments year 1		$3,181.60
Total interest payments year 1		$3,181.60
× marginal tax rate		.35
Tax reduction due to mortgage interest		$1,113.56
Monthly mortgage payment		$ 308.80
Less: Tax reduction restated on a		
monthly basis ($1,113.56 ÷ 12)		92.80
Average aftertax monthly payment		$ 216.00

In this case, for a borrower in a 35 percent tax bracket, it can be seen that the effect of the $3,181.60 interest deduction is equivalent to a reduction in mortgage payments during the first year by an average of $92.80 per month, or from $308.80 to $216.00. This provision obviously reduces the cost of borrowing and adds to the incentive to utilize mortgage financing.

Residential real estate closings

The initial loan application, completed by the borrower and submitted for evaluation by the lender, does not represent a binding contract. Normally it represents a mechanism to gather information concerning the loan, the borrower, and the property. After negotiation between the borrower and lender, if the loan application is approved, the lender will issue a *loan commitment.* The loan commitment is binding and details the loan amount and the terms on which the lender is willing to lend. The commitment usually carries an expiration date, setting the time by which the borrower must accept the terms of the loan offer or lose the commitment.

Borrowers may seek a loan commitment from many different lenders to ascertain what the most competitive terms are among them. The extent to which a borrower wants to utilize financial leverage is based on personal assets, incremental borrowing costs, rate of return on alternative investments available, and tax considerations. All of these factors will influence the amount of loan applied for. The lender will be considering the borrower's income, credit standing, and ability to repay the loan, as well as the property characteristics, in judging how much should be loaned, for how long, and at what interest rate. The borrower and lender ultimately agree on the amount of loan and terms of payment satisfactory to each.

After the loan commitment has been accepted by the buyer, the usual next step is for all interested parties to gather, execute, and exchange the documents necessary to make settlements and close or complete the transaction.[8] Generally, such closings are attended by (1) buyer and seller (perhaps each with legal counsel), (2) any real estate brokers involved, and (3) the settlement agent. The settlement agent is usually a representative of a title insurance company if such insurance is being purchased, or a representative of the lender if no title insurance is purchased.[9] The purpose of the closing, then, is to make final settlement between buyer and seller of costs, fees, and prorations associated with the real estate transaction prior to the transfer of title.

To summarize the many sources, disbursements, charges, and credits associated with the closing, a *settlement* or *closing* statement is prepared by the settlement agent. This statement summarizes the expenses and fees to be paid by the buyer and seller, and it shows the amount of funds that the buyer must

---

[8] For an excellent discussion of loan closings and the Real Estate Settlement and Procedures Act of 1974, see Paul Barron, *Federal Regulation of Real Estate: The Real Estate Settlement and Procedures Act* (Boston: Warren, Gorman & Lamont, 1975).

[9] In many cases a real estate broker or an attorney for the buyer or seller may act as the settlement agent with a letter of instructions from the lender.

pay and the amount of funds that the seller will receive at closing. Before illustrating the closing statement, a summary of some of the costs associated with real estate closings is presented.

Fees and expenses. Expenses associated with loan closings must be paid either by the buyer or the seller depending somewhat on custom in a particular lending area. There is no generally established practice in the area of expense settlement, and in many cases payment of any, or all, expenses is negotiated between buyer and seller. What follows is an identification of various expenses associated with real estate closings, followed by an illustration of a settlement statement.

Financing costs. These charges, called loan origination fees, are generally paid to the lender and are made in connection with services performed by the lender when underwriting and approving the loan. Sometimes many of these services are performed by the lender without charge, depending on how competitive the market for mortgage loans is at the time. During periods when ample funds are available for lending, lenders may not charge for some services; when funds are scarce, however, lenders may charge for all services performed in connection with a loan. What follows is an extensive list of possible charges that may be made by the lender.

1. Loan application fee. Charge made for processing the borrower's loan application.
2. Credit report fee. Charge made for compilation of the borrower's credit statement.
3. Attorney's fees. For preparing loan documents—mortgage/note; also for examining title documents presented to the lender.
4. Property inspection and property appraisal fee required by the lender. (This does not include fees for appraisals desired by the buyer or seller. Those fees are usually paid directly by the buyer and seller outside of the closing.)
5. Fees for property survey/photos when required by the lender.
6. Fees for preparation of loan amortization schedule by the lender for the borrower.
7. Loan discount points. Additional charge paid to the lender to increase the loan yield (per discussion in the preceding chapter).

Prorations, escrow costs, and payments to third parties

Property taxes, prorations, and escrow accounts. Because the dates on which property taxes are due to a particular governmental unit rarely coincide with the loan closing date, a portion of the taxes that come due at the next collection date is paid by the seller at closing. In other words, the buyer pays taxes only from the date title to the property is transferred. For example, if a county collects taxes on January 1 and July 1 of each year, and the loan closing date is April 1, the seller should pay one half of the taxes (January through March), which will be due on July 1. A *proration of taxes* is usually made at closing by deducting the seller's share of taxes from the purchase price paid by the buyer. In this way the seller pays the buyer for taxes up until the closing date.

Depending on the loan-to-value ratio in the transaction, the lender may require that an *escrow account* be established into which is deposited prorated taxes from the seller, and into which the borrower pays a monthly share of property tax along with the monthly mortgage payment. These funds are accumulated until taxes are due; then a disbursement is made by the lender to pay the tax bill when due. This provision assures the lender that no tax liens will be established on the property as a result of the borrower's failure to pay property tax, and it is usually required in cases where the loan-to-value ratio exceeds 80 percent.[10]

Private mortgage insurance. This insurance may be purchased by the borrower to reimburse the lender for any loss in the event of *loan default*. In conventional lending transactions this insurance is usually required by federal or state regulations on loans made in excess of 80 percent of value. Premiums are paid to a private insurer who in turn makes a settlement for any loss to the lender if the borrower defaults. Generally this insurance is taken out by the borrower for the number of years of amortization necessary to reduce the loan balance to 80 percent of value. For example, if an 85 percent loan is made initially, the term of insurance coverage would be equal to the number of years necessary to amortize the loan balance down by 5 percent.[11] The cost of such insurance can range from .25 to 2.75 percent of the loan balance annually, depending on the excess over 80 percent borrowed and the maturity period of the loan. Premiums are usually added to the monthly mortgage payment and collected by the lender who makes the disbursement to the private insurer. For loans made at 80 percent of value or less, this insurance is usually not purchased.[12]

Hazard insurance and escrow accounts. Hazard insurance against property damage is required by the lender as a condition for making the loan and the mortgage usually carries a provision to that effect. For loans made in excess of 80 percent of value, however, the lender usually requires the establishment

---

[10] When the loan-to-value ratio is less than 80 percent, the borrower often takes responsibility for payment of taxes when they become due. However, depending on the circumstances, a lender may require a property tax escrow for loans which are less than 80 percent of value.

[11] In periods when housing values are rising, it may be in the borrower's best interest to have the property reappraised by the lender after a few years. If values have gone up high enough since the outstanding loan balance has been amortized down somewhat, the loan-to-value ratio may have fallen to 80 percent or below and the mortgage insurance may be canceled.

[12] Private insurance is applicable to conventional mortgage loans only, not to FHA-insured mortgage loans. FHA mortgage insurance is discussed in Chapter 23. For a brief discussion of private mortgage insurance policies, practices, and charges, see Rod L. Reppe, "Why Residential Lenders Like Mortgage Guaranty Insurance," *Real Estate Review* (Fall 1973); also, see Chapter 18.

of an *escrow account* for pro rata payments made by the borrower toward the next annual premium due on the policy renewal date.[13] In other words, the lender collects monthly installments equal to one twelfth of the annual premium, along with the mortgage payment, and credits the insurance payment to the borrower's escrow account. When the policy renewal date arrives, the lender then disburses the 12 monthly payments which have been accumulated to the property insurance company. In this way the lender is certain that the property is always insured against damage. This in turn insures the loan collateral.

Mortgage cancellation insurance. Mortgage cancellation insurance is usually optional, depending on whether the borrower desires it. Essentially, it amounts to a declining term life insurance policy which is taken out at closing and runs for the term of the mortgage. Since, with a fully amortized mortgage, the outstanding loan balance declines as monthly payments are made, the insurance coverage also declines with the loan balance. In the event of the borrower's death, the insurance coverage is equal to the outstanding loan balance. The mortgage loan is repaid with insurance proceeds. Premiums are usually paid monthly, being added to the monthly mortgage payment. The lender then disburses those payments to the life insurance company. Although mortgage cancellation insurance is usually bought at the borrower's option, if the borrower's age is a critical factor in the lender's loan analysis, purchase of such insurance may be necessary to obtain the loan.

Title insurance, lawyer's title opinion. Premiums are charged by the title insurance company to search, abstract, and examine title to a property and to issue an insurance policy that indemnifies the buyer against loss arising from claims against the property. Attorneys may perform a similar service for a fee and render an opinion as to the validity of the title held by the seller and whether it is merchantable. Normally the full premium/fee for the insurance policy/abstract opinion is paid at closing. Depending on the policy of the lending institution and government regulations, either title insurance or an attorney's opinion is required as a condition for granting a loan.

Release fees. Release fees are associated with paying off outstanding liens, such as the seller's mortgage lien, mechanics' liens, and so on, and for services rendered by third parties in negotiating and obtaining such releases.

Attorney's fee. When incurred by the buyer or seller, legal fees may be paid directly by each party outside of the closing or may be included in the closing.

Pest inspection certificate. A pest inspection may be made at the insistence of the lender or buyer. In some states, such as Florida, an inspection is required before title is transferred. The inspection fee may be paid directly or included in the closing settlement.

---

[13] When loans are made for less than 80 percent of value, the borrower generally takes responsibility for making insurance payments. The lender usually requires no escrow account or monthly installments. At closing the borrower usually needs only to show evidence of an insurance binder or a statement from the insurance company that the property is insured.

Real estate commission. When a seller of a property engages the service of a real estate agent to sell a property, the seller usually pays the commission for such service, generally at the closing.

Statutory costs. Certain costs are imposed by a local or state government agency and must be paid before deeds can be recorded. These include:

1. *Recording fees.* Fees paid for recording of the mortgage and note in the public records.
2. *Transfer tax.* A tax usually imposed by the county on all real estate transfers.

Miscellaneous costs

Prepaid items. Prepayments generally involve interest on the mortgage loan from the closing date to the time during the month when the borrower begins making regular mortgage payments. For example, if the closing date is January 20 and the borrower wants regular payments to begin on March 1, twelve days of interest will be prepaid at closing (January 20–January 31 inclusive). Regular monthly payments will begin on March 1 covering the loan balance outstanding during the month of February.

The Real Estate Settlement and Procedures Act (RESPA). From the preceding discussion of settlement costs, it is apparent that with the many possible fees and disbursements involved in a residential real estate closing, the event can become a fairly complex undertaking. Because of the lack of buyer sophistication in real estate transactions and because of past abuses in the form of exorbitant closing and referral fees charged mainly to buyers, Congress passed Public Law 95–533, known as the Real Estate Settlement and Procedures Act of 1974 (which became effective June 20, 1975) and Public Law 94–205 (effective January 1976) which amended the 1974 act. These laws established federal control over settlement and closing procedures in transactions involving the purchase of residential real estate. This control is clearly for consumer protection, and its express purpose, as stated in Section 213 of the 1974 act, is to effect certain changes that should result in:

1. More effective advance disclosure of settlement costs.
2. Elimination of kickbacks or unearned fees.
3. A reduction in the amount of escrow placed in accounts by homeowners.
4. Modernization of local land title records and information.

Coverage of the act. The act, as presently constituted, affects any residential purchase involving a federally related loan. By "federally related" is meant any financial institution accepting federal deposits, having federal deposit insurance, or making or dealing in federally insured mortgage loans. In essence, *virtually all residential real estate transactions are covered under this act.* However, mobile home loans, purchases of vacant land, home improvement loans, refinancing of existing loans, and the purchase of property with the intent to resell in the ordinary course of business generally do not fall under provisions of the act. RESPA does apply, though, to mortgage assumptions (sales subject to existing mortgages) and to refinancing if a change in the interest rate or other loan conditions is provided for by the lender, or if the lender charges an assumption or other fee in excess of $50 to approve the transaction.

Requirements under the act. Although RESPA includes many provisions, only those directly associated with the closing are covered here.[14] The essential aspects of RESPA fall into six areas which are used here to facilitate discussion. These areas are:

1. Consumer information.
2. Advance disclosure of settlement costs.
3. Title insurance placement.
4. Prohibition of kickbacks and referral fees.
5. Uniform settlement statement.
6. Advance inspection of uniform settlement statement.

Consumer information. Under provisions in RESPA, lenders are required to provide prospective borrowers with an information booklet containing information on estate closings and RESPA when a loan application is made. This booklet contains information provided by the U.S. Department of Housing and Urban Development. It provides a description of closing costs and contains various illustrations designed to inform a prospective buyer/borrower of the nature of the costs. It describes the function of the parties usually involved in a real estate transaction, as well as fees likely to be charged by lenders. It also provides information on the responsibility of all parties engaged in the closing under RESPA provisions.

Advance disclosure of settlement costs. At present the lender is required to provide to the borrower, at the time of application, good faith estimates of certain closing costs for which information is available. The lender must provide information on the basis of actual costs known at that time, or estimates based on past experience in the locality in which the property is located.

The estimates provided by the lender generally cover costs in the following categories: (*a*) title search, (*b*) title examination and opinion, (*c*) title insurance, (*d*) attorney's fee, (*e*) preparation of documents, (*f*) property survey, (*g*) credit report, (*h*) appraisal, (*i*) pest inspection, (*j*) notary fees, (*k*) loan closing service fee, and (*l*) recording fees and any transfer tax. These items carry fairly standard charges and are usually easy for a lender to estimate.

The lender is encouraged to provide information regarding a second group

---

[14] For a much more detailed treatment of RESPA, see Paul Barron, *Federal Regulation of Real Estate.*

of costs when the application is made, but is not required to do so. This second group of costs include (*a*) loan origination fees; (*b*) loan discounts; (*c*) mortgage insurance application fees; (*d*) assumption/refinancing fees; (*e*) mortgage insurance and hazard insurance premiums; and (*f*) any escrow deposits for hazard insurance, mortgage insurance, and real estate taxes. These costs vary somewhat with time and, depending on companies used by the borrower for insurance, and so on, are more difficult for a lender to estimate at the time of application. However, these costs must eventually be estimated by the lender if the loan application is approved. As will be discussed below, this second group of costs, along with any necessary revisions in the good faith estimates on costs disclosed at the time of application, must be made available for inspection by the borrower one day before the loan is closed.

Title insurance placement.   Under RESPA, a seller may not require that a buyer use a specific title company as a condition of sale. This regulation is aimed primarily at developers who may have obtained a very favorable title insurance rate on undeveloped land, with the understanding that after development, buyers would be required to place the title insurance with the same company. This part of the act prohibits such requirements and insures the freedom of the buyer to place title insurance with any title company.

Prohibition of kickbacks and unearned fees.   Under RESPA, no person can give or receive a kickback or fee as a result of a referral. If any person refers a buyer-borrower to any specific party involved in the closing (lender, title company, attorney, real estate broker, appraiser, etc.) and receives a fee for the referral, receipt of such a fee violates the act.[15] RESPA also prohibits fee splitting by parties associated with the closing unless fees are paid for services actually performed. This latter part of RESPA has probably caused more confusion than any other provision of the act because of the vagueness of the term *services actually performed.* However, the intent was to prohibit any circumvention of payments that would have been normally called referral fees by simply splitting fees.

Uniform settlement statement.   Under RESPA provisions, a uniform settlement statement must be used by the settlement agent at closing. The responsibility for preparation of this statement lies with the lender, and it must be delivered to the borrower and seller at closing. Other closing statements, such as a company form, can also be used for closing purposes, if desired, but the uniform statement must be completed.

This statement is uniform in the sense that the same form (shown in Exhibit 8–3) must be used in all loan closings covered under RESPA. This form, coupled with the information booklet received by the borrower when the loan application is made, which defines and illustrates costs on a line-by-line basis,

---

[15] This simply means that a person must actually perform some service to earn a fee. For example, attorney's fees, cooperative real estate brokerage fees, and title company closing fees are paid for service performed. However, a referral by a real estate broker or lender to a title company, where a kickback, commission, and so on, is paid by the title company, is prohibited.

Exhibit 8–3

Buyer: George and Alice Smith
100 Dirt Road
Anytown, USA

Seller: Ralph and Pearl Brown
200 Heavenly Drive
Anytown, USA

Lender: ABC Savings and Loan Association
Anytown, USA

Settlement agent: Land Title Company
Anytown, USA

Loan commitment date: March 10

Advance disclosure date: March 19

Actual settlement date (closing date): March 20

I. Buyer and seller information:
   a. Purchase price $80,000.00
   b. Deposit 1,000.00
   c. Real estate tax proration (taxes due January 1 and July 1,
      $1,500 per year, $750 per half; taxes unpaid by seller,
      January 1–March 20 or 78 days/365 days × $1,500 = $320.55) 320.55
II. Buyer/borrower and lender information:
   a. Amount of loan (11% interest, 25 years, conventional loan) 64,000.00
   b. Prepaid interest March 20–31 (12 days) or
      (11% × $64,000 ÷ 365 = $19.29 a day) 231.48
   c. Property tax escrow (amount accrued since January
      [$320.55] plus 2 months additional escrow @ $125 month) 570.55
   d. Loan origination fee (2%) 1,280.00
III. Transactions between buyer/borrower and others:
   a. Title insurance fees (Land TItle Co.), $335; survey
      endorsement, $10; notary charge, $5 . . . . 350.00
   b. Recording fees (deed, $10; mortgage, $15) 25.00
   c. Real estate transfer tax 400.00
   d. Larry Lawyer—attorney fee 100.00
IV. Transactions between seller and others:
   a. Land Title Company—closing fee 75.00
   b. Release statement—seller's mortgage 5.00
   c. Payoff—seller's mortgage (Anytown State Bank) 21,284.15
   d. Real estate brokerage fee (6%) (Anytown Realty Co.) 4,800.00
   e. Connie Counsel—attorney fee 100.00
   f. Pest inspection (Anytown Pest Co.) 20.00

should enable the borrower to make a better judgment concerning the reasonableness of closing costs to be paid.

Advance inspection of uniform settlement statement. Not only must a uniform settlement statement which details all closing costs be used at the closing, but the borrower has the right to inspect this statement *one day prior to closing.* At that time, information on the additional closing costs not required to be disclosed when the loan application is made must be disclosed to the borrower. These costs include those in the second category mentioned earlier, such as loan origination fees, loan discount, fees for mortgage insurance application, any assumption or refinancing fees, any prepaid mortgage or hazard insurance premiums, escrow deposits, and prepaid interest.

All of these costs must be disclosed to the extent that they are known to the lender on the day prior to closing. Also, the good faith estimates of other closing costs made when the loan application was completed by the borrower must be revised, if necessary, to reflect actual costs at that time. Both groups of costs must be entered on the uniform disclosure statement for inspection by the borrower, unless the borrower waives right of inspection. This can be done by the borrower signing a statement waiving this right. If the borrower inspects the closing statement and agrees to all of the closing charges, the next step is to close the loan the following day.

The intent of RESPA can be summarized at this point by observing that with the information booklet, with advance disclosure of some closing costs, and with the right of a borrower to inspect the uniform settlement statement *prior* to closing, the borrower is able to shop around for the most competitive loan terms *and* closing costs. Any costs that are not understood by the borrower can be better explained and the borrower is in a better position to judge whether closing costs are excessive and can be obtained from another lender on better terms.

Closing statement—example.   To illustrate the development of the uniform settlement statement required under RESPA, we consider the example that follows. The property, located at 200 Heavenly Drive, has been contracted for purchase at a price of $80,000 and scheduled for closing on March 20. Data pertinent to the transaction are detailed in Exhibit 8–3. The buyer has asked for and received an advance disclosure of settlement costs on a form exactly like the one shown in Exhibit 8–4. Since the disclosure was made by the lender one day prior to closing, accurate information was available on all costs and fees associated with the closing. Therefore, it is assumed in this example that the advance disclosure estimate and final disclosure of settlement cost statements are the same. Recall that they do not necessarily have to be identical since estimates are made on the advance disclosure. Recall also that some items, for example, attorney's fees, pest inspection, and so on, may be paid outside of the closing. In addition, the lender is not requiring private mortgage insurance on the conventional loan, nor is a hazard insurance escrow account to be established as the borrower has presented an insurance binder evidencing a prepaid, one-year hazard insurance policy. The borrower has elected not to purchase mortgage cancellation life insurance; however, the borrower has agreed to establish a property tax escrow account with the lender for payment of property taxes due on July 1 and has agreed to pay a monthly installment equal to one twelfth of estimated annual taxes.

EXHIBIT 8–4

A. U.S. DEPARTMENT OF HOUSING AND URBAN DEVELOPMENT DISCLOSURE/SETTLEMENT STATEMENT	B. TYPE OF LOAN		
	1. ☐ FHA 2. ☐ FMHA 3. ☐ CONV. UNINS.		
	4. ☐ VA 5. ☐ CONV. INS.		
	6. FILE NUMBER	7. LOAN NUMBER	
If the Truth-in-Lending Act applies to this transaction, a Truth-in-Lending statement is attached as page 3 of this form.	8. MORTG. INS. CASE NO.		

C. NOTE: This form is furnished to you prior to settlement to give you information about your settlement costs, and again after settlement to show the actual costs you have paid. The present copy of the form is:

☐ ADVANCE DISCLOSURE OF COSTS. Some items are estimated, and are marked "(e)". Some amounts may change if the settlement is held on a date other than the date estimated below. The preparer of this form is not responsible for errors or changes in amounts furnished by others.

☐ STATEMENT OF ACTUAL COSTS. Amounts paid to and by the settlement agent are shown. Items marked "(p.o.c.)" were paid outside the closing; they are shown here for informational purposes and are not included in totals.

D. NAME OF BORROWER	E. SELLER	F. LENDER
George and Alice Smith 100 Dirt Road Anytown, U.S.A.	Ralph and Pearl Brown 200 Heavenly Drive Anytown, U.S.A.	ABC Savings and Loan Anytown, U.S.A.

G. PROPERTY LOCATION	H. SETTLEMENT AGENT	I. DATES	
200 Heavenly Drive Anytown, U.S.A.	Land Title Co.	LOAN COMMITMENT 1-10-81	ADVANCE DISCLOSURE 3-19-81
	PLACE OF SETTLEMENT 100 North Street Anytown, U.S.A.	SETTLEMENT 3-20-81	DATE OF PRORATIONS IF DIFFERENT FROM SETTLEMENT

J. SUMMARY OF BORROWER'S TRANSACTION		K. SUMMARY OF SELLER'S TRANSACTION	
100. GROSS AMOUNT DUE FROM BORROWER:		400. GROSS AMOUNT DUE TO SELLER:	
		401. Contract sales price	80,000.00
101. Contract sales price	80,000.00	402. Personal property	–
102. Personal property	–	403.	
103. Settlement charges to borrower (from line 1400, Section L)	2,607.03	404.	
104.		Adjustments for items paid by seller in advance:	
105.		405. City/town taxes to	–
Adjustments for items paid by seller in advance:		406. County taxes to	–
		407. Assessments to	–
106. City/town taxes to		408. to	
107. County taxes to		409. to	
108. Assessments to		410. to	
109. to		411. to	
110. to		420. GROSS AMOUNT DUE TO SELLER	80,000.00
111. to		NOTE: The following 500 and 600 series sections are not required to be completed when this form is used for advance disclosure of settlement costs prior to settlement.	
112. to			
120. GROSS AMOUNT DUE FROM BORROWER:	82,607.03		
200. AMOUNTS PAID BY OR IN BEHALF OF BORROWER:		500. REDUCTIONS IN AMOUNT DUE TO SELLER:	
		501. Payoff of first mortgage loan	21,284.15
201. Deposit or earnest money	1,000.00	502. Payoff of second mortgage loan	
202. Principal amount of new loan(s)	64,000.00	503. Settlement charges to seller (from line 1400, Section L)	5,350.00
203. Existing loan(s) taken subject to		504. Existing loan(s) taken subject to	–
204.		505.	–
205.		506.	–
Credits to borrower for items unpaid by seller:		507.	–
		508.	–
206. City/town taxes to		509.	–
207. County taxes 1-1-81 to 3-20-81	320.55		
208. Assessments to		Credits to borrower for items unpaid by seller:	
209. to		510. City/town taxes to	–
210. to		511. County taxes 1-1-81 to 3-20-81	320.55
211. to		512. Assessments to	–
212. to		513. to	
220. TOTAL AMOUNTS PAID BY OR IN BEHALF OF BORROWER	65,320.55	514. to	
300. CASH AT SETTLEMENT REQUIRED FROM OR PAYABLE TO BORROWER:		515. to	
		520. TOTAL REDUCTIONS IN AMOUNT DUE TO SELLER	26,954.70
301. Gross amount due from borrower (from line 120)	82,607.03	600. CASH TO SELLER FROM SETTLEMENT:	
302. Less amounts paid by or in behalf of borrower (from line 220)	(65,320.55)	601. Gross amount due to seller (from line 420)	80,000.00
		602. Less total reductions in amount due to seller (from line 520)	(26,954.70)
303. CASH (☒REQUIRED FROM) OR (☐PAYABLE TO) BORROWER:	17,286.48	603. CASH TO SELLER FROM SETTLEMENT	53,045.30

HUD-1A REV. 6-75 AS & A. (1323)   SPECIAL FORM OMB No. 63-R 1501

EXHIBIT 8–4 (continued)

L. SETTLEMENT CHARGES		PAID FROM BORROWER'S FUNDS	PAID FROM SELLER'S FUNDS
700.	SALES/BROKER'S COMMISSION based on price $ 80,000.00 @ 6 %		
701.	Total commission paid by seller Division of commission as follows: Anytown Realty Co.		4,800.00
702.	$ to		
703.	$ to		
704.			
800.	ITEMS PAYABLE IN CONNECTION WITH LOAN.		
801.	Loan Origination fee 2 %	1,280.00	
802.	Loan Discount %		
803.	Appraisal Fee to		
804.	Credit Report to		
805.	Lender's inspection fee		
806.	Mortgage Insurance application fee to		
807.	Assumption/refinancing fee		
808.			
809.			
810.			
811.			
900.	ITEMS REQUIRED BY LENDER TO BE PAID IN ADVANCE.		
901.	Interest from 3-20-81 to 3-31-81 @ $19.29 /day	231.48	
902.	Mortgage insurance premium for mo. to		
903.	Hazard insurance premium for yrs. to		
904.		yrs. to		
905.			
1000.	RESERVES DEPOSITED WITH LENDER FOR:		
1001.	Hazard insurance mo. @ $ /mo.		
1002.	Mortgage insurance mo. @ $ /mo.		
1003.	City property taxes mo. @ $ /mo.		
1004.	County property taxes mo. @ $125.00 /mo. plus proration $320.55	570.55	
1005.	Annual assessments mo. @ $ /mo.		
1006.		mo. @ $ /mo.		
1007.		mo. @ $ /mo.		
1008.		mo. @ $ /mo.		
1100.	TITLE CHARGES:		
1101.	Settlement or closing fee to Land Title Co.		75.00
1102.	Abstract or title search to		
1103.	Title examination to		
1104.	Title insurance binder to		
1105.	Document preparation to		
1106.	Notary fees to		
1107.	Attorney's Fees to		
	(includes above items No.:)		
1108.	Title insurance to Land Title Co.		350.00
	(includes above items No.:)		
1109.	Lender's coverage $		
1110.	Owner's coverage $		
1111.			
1112.			
1113.			
1200.	GOVERNMENT RECORDING AND TRANSFER CHARGES		
1201.	Recording fees: Deed $ 10.00 ; Mortgage $ 15.00 Releases $5.00	25.00	5.00
1202.	City/county tax/stamps: Deed $; Mortgage $	400.00	
1203.	State tax/stamps: Deed $; Mortgage $		
1204.			
1300.	ADDITIONAL SETTLEMENT CHARGES		
1301.	Survey to		
1302.	Pest inspection to Anytime Pest Co.		20.00
1303.	Connie Counsel – Attorney		100.00
1304.	Larry Lawyer – Attorney	100.00	
1305.			
1400.	TOTAL SETTLEMENT CHARGES (entered on lines 103 and 503, Sections J and K)	2,607.03	5,350.00

The Undersigned Acknowledges Receipt of This Disclosure Settlement Statement and Agrees to the Correctness Thereof.

_____   _____
        Buyer or Agent   Seller or Agent

NOTE: Under certain circumstances the borrower and seller may be permitted to waive the 12-day period which must normally occur between advance disclosure and settlement. In the event such a waiver is made, copies of the statements of waiver, executed as provided in the regulations of the Department of Housing and Urban Development, shall be attached to and made a part of this form when the form is used as a settlement statement.

HUD-1B (5-75)   AS & AS (1323)

Based on the preceding information, which shows how the seller and buyer have agreed to split costs and fees and financing costs, the statement detailing actual settlement costs is shown in Exhibit 8–4. Note that on the basis of the summary of all costs and expenses, the buyer will have to provide $17,286.48 at the time of closing. This represents the purchase price of $80,000 less the $64,000 amount borrowed, less the $1,000 deposit paid to the seller, plus $2,607.03 which represents financing charges, settlement costs, and escrow requirements detailed on the second page of Exhibit 8–4. The seller will receive a check from the lender for $53,045.30 which represents the $80,000 sale price less the $21,284.15 mortgage balance owed, less $5,350 which represents the $4,800 real estate commission and the seller's share of settlement costs, detailed on the second page of Exhibit 8–4.

Federal truth-in-lending requirements.   In addition to disclosure requirements affecting settlement costs under RESPA, disclosure requirements under the federal Truth-in-Lending Act, dealing with finance charges, has been a requirement affecting lenders since 1968.[16] The truth-in-lending provision, like the RESPA legislation, is intended to provide the buyer/borrower with disclosure of financing costs and is not intended to regulate financing costs or interest rates. In addition to the disclosure of costs, the Truth-in-Lending Act requires the computation of the effective loan yield (cost) on a given loan according to an actuarial method as prescribed by the act. This effective loan yield (cost) is called the annual percentage rate (APR), and its computation was demonstrated in the preceding chapter in connection with mortgage yields when origination fees were considered.

Coverage and requirements of truth in lending.   Transactions that fall under RESPA requirements will generally be covered by the Truth-in-Lending Act. Under provisions of the act, the lender must disclose to the buyer/borrower information in six vital areas associated with the loan closing, and this information must be included in a uniform truth-in-lending statement (see Exhibit 8–5).

Finance charges and prepaid finance charges.   Finance charges are generally interpreted to mean interest; however, certain other categories of charges must be included as finance charges and must be disclosed to the borrower. These items include:

a.   FHA or private mortgage insurance *required* by the lender.
b.   Mortgage cancellation insurance when *required* by the lender, unless the borrower is informed of the nature and cost of the insurance and the lender obtains, in writing, from the borrower a statement that he desires the coverage.

---

[16] Public Law 90–321 (1968) as amended. Development of specific regulations and supplementation under the act were charged to the Federal Reserve Board, which issued Regulation Z in 1968.

EXHIBIT 8–5
Federal truth-in-lending disclosure statement

I.	A.	Cash price (contract sales price)			$ 80,000.00
		1. Less any cash down payment	$ 16,000.00		
		2. Less any trade-in	$ –0–		
		3. Total down payment			$ 16,000.00
	B.	Equals unpaid balance of cash price			$ 64,000.00
	C.	Plus any other amounts financed:			
		1. Property insurance premiums	$ –0–		
		2. _____	$ –0–		
		3. Total other amounts financed			$ –0–
	D.	Equals unpaid balance			$ 64,000.00
	E.	Less any prepaid finance charges:			
		1. Origination fee or points paid by borrower	$ 1,280.00		
		2. Loan discount or points paid by seller	$ –0–		
		3. Interest from 3/20/81 to 3/31/81	$ 231.48		
		4. Mortgage guaranty insurance	$ –0–		
		5. _____	$ –0–		
		6. Total prepaid finance charge			$ 1,511.48
	F.	Equals amount financed			$ 62,488.52
II.	The *finance charge* consists of:				
	A.	Interest (simple annual rate of 11%)	$124,178.00		
	B.	Total prepaid finance charge (I. E. 6.)	$ 1,511.48		
	C.	_____	$		
	D.	Total *finance charge*			$125,689.48
III.	A.	The *annual percentage rate* on the amount financed is . . . . (rounded)			11.25%
	B.	If the contract includes a provision for variation in the interest rate, describe: None			

IV. The repayment terms are 300 monthly installments of $627.26 beginning on the 1st day of May 1981 and due on the 1st day of each month thereafter.

V. The finance charge begins to accrue on: April 1, 1981

VI. In the event of late payments, charges may be assessed as follows: After 30 days, interest will be assessed at 11% on all amounts due.

VII. (Use either A or B as appropriate)
A. Conditions and penalties for prepaying this obligation are: None

B. Identification of method of rebate of unearned finance charge is: None

VIII. Insurance taken in connection with this obligation: None

IX. The security for this obligation is: 1st mortgage on property located at 200 Heavenly Drive, Anytown, USA (Zip)

c. Property insurance when *required* by the lender, unless the borrower acknowledges in writing that he is aware of the cost of such insurance and that he can obtain such insurance from any supplier he desires.

Prepaid finance charges must be treated as a cost of borrowing and include:

a. Loan application fees or fees charged by the lender to evaluate and compile data on a loan applicant.
b. Loan commitment fees or a fee charged by lenders for issuing a loan commitment whether the loan is accepted or refused by the borrower.
c. Loan origination fees including discount points charged by lenders to increase loan yields, usually paid by borrowers in conventional loan transactions.
d. Discount points, or fees charged by lenders to raise the yield on FHA/VA loans, paid by the seller.
e. Escrow charges (not to be confused with the escrow reserve for future payments), or a charge made by the lender for establishing an escrow account.
f. Prepaid interest, or interest due the lender from date of closing until the beginning of the period covered by the first mortgage payment.
g. Any prepaid FHA or private mortgage insurance premiums.
h. Assumption fees, or charges levied against the borower by the lender when an existing mortgage is assumed rather than making a new loan when a property is purchased.
i. Preparation of an amortization schedule by the lender and charged to the borrower.

Both categories—finance charges and prepaid finance charges—are treated as part of loan costs and must be included in determining the effective cost of the loan, or *APR,* by deducting such charges as they are paid over the life of the loan. For example, interest charges and mortgage insurance fees occur over the life of the loan and will be included as they are paid. However, prepaid finance charges generally occur at the time of closing and will be deducted from the amount actually borrowed by the buyer. (This process will be illustrated in the section that follows on the annual percentage rate.)

Other closing costs and statutory fees. These items are specifically excluded from the determination of finance charges as they are legal fees and are customarily present in any real estate transfer. They generally provide no income or return to the lender. Costs in these categories include:

a. Title search, opinion, or title insurance costs.
b. Preparation of deeds, settlement statements, and loan documents.
c. Escrow accounts and funds accumulated for future payment of taxes, insurance, water, sewer, and so on.

d.   Appraisal fees, credit reports, notary fees.

e.   Transfer taxes, deed recording, and so on.

Charges financed by lender.   Any fees, insurance, or payments made to third parties connected with the loan closing, which the lender agrees to finance, must be included in determining financing costs. To illustrate: If the first year's hazard insurance premium is borrowed by the buyer, interest charges on this loan are also included with mortgage interest in computing the effective cost of the loan.

The annual percentage rate.   This requirement simply specifies that the lender will disclose to the borrower the amount actually financed by the lender, the dollar amount of finance charges made by the lender, and the resultant actual percentage interest rate charged, termed the annual percentage rate (*APR*).

To show how the disclosure is made on the uniform federal truth-in-lending statement, the preceding loan closing is again used as an example in Exhibit 8–5. Referring back to Exhibit 8–4, which illustrated the uniform loan closing disclosure statement under RESPA, the necessary information can be gathered for completion of the truth-in-lending portion of RESPA requirements. Looking down Exhibit 8–5, it can be seen that the unpaid loan balance (item I–D) is straightforward in our example, since there were no trade-ins or items in addition to the purchase of the property financed by the lender. Hence the unpaid balance is $64,000 and represents the contractual amount to be repaid by the borrower.

In determining how much the borrower will have for actual use, or the amount actually financed, various deductions must be made from the unpaid loan balance when necessary. In our example there was a loan origination fee of $1,280 charged by the lender and prepaid interest in the amount of $231.48, leaving the amount financed at $62,488.52. In other words, the lender is actually financing $62,488.52; however, the borrower has contracted to repay $64,000 plus 11 percent interest over a time of 25 years. Other prepaid items such as loan application fees, assumption fees, commitment fees, discount points, and other items discussed in connection with prepaid finance charges will also be deducted, when appropriate, in the determination of the amount actually financed.

Another required disclosure to the borrower under the truth-in-lending statement is the actual dollar amount of finance charges (Section II, Exhibit 8–5). This is simply determined as total interest to be paid over the mortgage term plus prepaid finance charges. Total interest payments are easily determined in our example by first computing the monthly mortgage payment for the $64,000 loan amount, at 11 percent for 25 years, or $64,000 × .009801 = $627.26, then by multiplying the monthly payment of $627.26 × 300, or the number of monthly payments to be made over the life of the loan (12 × 25 years). This product shows that total dollars to be paid by the borrower over the life of the loan are $188,184. The contract loan amount is $64,000. Therefore the amount of interest collected by the lender over 25 years is $188,184 − $64,000, or $124,178. When the $1,511.48 in prepaid finance charges is added to the interest to be collected by the lender over the term of the loan, the total dollar finance charge of $125,698.48 is determined. Item C under Section II in Exhibit 8–5 also provides for additional charges for FHA insurance and private mortgage insurance premiums, when appropriate, which represent additional finance charges paid over the life of the mortgage loan.

Section III in Exhibit 8–5 deals with the determination of the annual percentage rate (*APR*) which is the true rate being charged on the loan by the lender. This computation has been demonstrated in the preceding chapter. It is carried out as follows:

$$\$627.26(MIFPVa, \ ?\%, \ 25 \ \text{yrs.}) = \$62,488.52$$
$$(MIFPVa, \ ?\%, \ 25 \ \text{yrs.}) = \quad 99.6214$$

Looking to the monthly interest tables provided in the Appendix B, and considering interest factors in column 5 for 25 years for various interest rates, we see that in the 12 percent tables, the *IF* is equal to 94.946551; the interest factor at 11 percent is 102.029044; hence we know that the *APR* lies between 11 percent and 12 percent. Interpolation shows that the effective yield is 11.34 percent. However after rounding to the nearest ¼ percent, the *APR* disclosed to the borrower will be 11.25 percent.[17] This interest rate is obviously higher than the 11 percent contract interest rate that appears on the note accompanying the mortgage.[18]

Method of repayment, late payments, and prepayment penalties. Disclosure requirements under truth in lending also provide that in the time intervals allowed for loan repayment, interest penalties for late payments, and prepayment penalties must be fully disclosed. In our example, such disclosures are illustrated in Sections IV through VII of Exhibit 8–5. However, if a loan is not fully amortized but involves unequal payments as might be the case with a construction loan, a variable interest rate loan, or a partially amortized loan, either a loan repayment schedule disclosing what portion of each payment is interest and principal or a full explanation of how interest is to be computed and any terms and conditions for refinancing must be included.

Security interests. The fact that a lien will be placed on real property must be clearly disclosed. The property that is being made subject to the lien must be described, usually by attaching a copy of the mortgage or note to the truth-in-lending statement.

---

[17] It should be recalled that the 11.34 rate is the true rate assuming the mortgage loan is repaid after 25 years. If repaid earlier, the true yield on the loan will be *greater* than 11.34 percent. In addition, prepayment penalties are not included in the computation of the *APR;* hence, if the loan is prepaid during the penalty period, this will also serve to increase the cost of the loan.

[18] Tables have been compiled by and are available from the Federal Reserve System to provide the *APR* for various loans, given the contract interest rate and prepaid finance charges.

Special types of residential financing

Condominiums.   Many buyers of residential properties have come to know the concept of condominium property ownership. The term *condominium* means individual ownership of one-family units within a multifamily structure (such as a high rise) or complex (such as a planned unit development). This ownership is coupled with an individual ownership interest in the land and common areas (halls, recreation facilities, etc.) which are a part of the condominium development. In other words, the owner of a condominium unit owns the unit and has an ownership interest in all common areas. The ownership interest in the common areas is usually determined by either (1) the ratio of the value of an owner's unit to the total project value or (2) the ratio of square footage contained in an owner's unit to the total square footage in a project. This ownership interest also determines the extent to which each owner must contribute to operating the owners' association which is the legal entity created to operate and manage the common areas within the development.

For a condominium to be created, most states have provided that certain statutory requirements be fulfilled. In Ohio, for instance, the condominium statute provides for a declaration containing:

1. A legal description of the land.
2. The name of the condominium property, including the word *condominium*.
3. Purposes and restrictions in the use of the property.
4. A plot or floor plan of the building, including principal materials and the number of stories, basements, and units therein.
5. Unit designation, together with access areas.
6. A description of the common areas and facilities, and the percentage of the total interest appertaining to each unit.
7. A statement that each owner shall be a member of a unit owners' association which shall be established for the administration of condominium property.
8. Designation of the person to receive service of process for the unit owners' association.
9. A method for amending the declaration, requiring approval of not less than 75 percent of the voting power.

The declaration must be filed with the county recorder and the county auditor.

The unit owners' association is operated by a board of managers duly elected by the membership. This board normally provides for the prompt repair of common areas, assessment of common expenses, and the distribution of common profits. A lien upon an individual unit is provided for failure of a member to pay his properly allocated share of common expenses. Common profits, like losses, are assigned to the unit owners according to their percentages of interest in the common areas and facilities as set forth in the declaration. These percentages also determine members' voting strength in the unit owners' association.

There are features associated with condominium ownership that many buyers find attractive. The primary advantages include maintenance and repair being performed by professional management, retention of the tax deductibility of interest enjoyed by single-family owners, possible lower costs of construction when compared to single-family units of the same size, location in highly desirable areas that would not be affordable if a single-family detached unit were considered, to name a few.

With respect to financing, there is not much difference between financing a single-family unit and a condominium unit. Both require a mortgage loan commitment and a down payment and are closed in a similar fashion. The uniform statement of settlement and truth-in-lending requirements detailed in this chapter contain many of the same closing costs. The primary differences between financing condominium units and single-family units lie in the underwriting process that is performed prior to the loan commitment and the annual or monthly fee charged for management and maintenance of the condominium, in addition to the monthly mortgage payment.

One area in underwriting loans on condominiums that sometimes causes difficulty for lenders and borrowers lies in the appraisal of the interest in common areas owned with the purchase of a single unit. This problem is not too difficult to resolve if the unit is purchased when the development is new because cost data for the entire development can be relied on to some extent in establishing the value of a buyer's interest in common elements. However, when the development has been converted from an apartment complex and a unit is being sold, the lender may be very cautious in accepting an appraisal containing a value for the interest in common elements. This is because the entire development may have to be appraised in order to establish the value of an owner's interest in them. This is very difficult to do, and lenders will consider such appraisals carefully.

The lending institution making individual mortgage loans to prospective buyers of condominium units will be very cautious in examining the declaration on file with the county recorder and the bylaws governing the operation of the condominium owners' association. For example, of importance to the lender are the conditions in the owner association bylaws that restrict sales to tenants. An agreement may specify that buyers of condominiums must be retired, or over a certain age. This restriction in the lender's view may decrease the future marketability of the unit and, therefore, increase the lending risk.

Other areas of vital concern to the lender, particularly when the condominium project is a new one, are:

1. *Provision for maintenance costs.* A statement of the amount of the monthly operating fee and what services are covered must be presented to the lender. Most lenders know what "normal" fees should be from loans

previously made and by continuous updating of information from condominium management companies. Any attempt by a developer of a condominium project to sell units while quoting buyers abnormally low operating costs will be frowned on by the lender. This practice will ultimately lead to the dissatisfaction of the buyer and poor future marketability of units.

2. *Voting control of the owners' association during development or until all units are sold.* During the period when initial sales of condominium units are made, the developer retains voting control because most of the units are yet to be sold. Consequently, if sales slow down or the developer becomes financially troubled, expenditures on maintenance may be deferred in an attempt to save operating cash and to keep the monthly maintenance fee low to attract other buyers. This can be a source of irritation to previous buyers, and should the development become known to have poor management, it may make for even poorer marketability. Hence, many lenders require that voting control of the owners' association be relinquished by the developer after a reasonable time period so that present individual owners may safeguard their investment.

3. *Added expansion.* When a loan on a condominium unit is being considered, the lender will want to see the *entire* development plan of the project, or additional phases of expansion expected to be completed by the developer. This is important because rapid expansion may result in overuse of existing recreational facilities and other common areas and make for poor future marketability. The lender wants to be sure that common facilities are adequate to service the entire number of occupants, both present and future.

4. *Ownership of recreation and vital common areas.* Some developers of condominiums have been known to *retain* ownership of a few vital facilities such as a swimming pool or sewerage plant within a development. These facilities are then leased to the owners' association *after* all units are sold. Sometimes the lease payments are extremely high and raise the monthly fee paid by individual owners. Most lenders will refuse to lend in such a case and will require that these facilities be a part of each buyer's ownership interest in all common areas. In this way, a developer cannot take advantage of owners after units are completed and sold.

5. *Escrow provisions for down payments.* Since many buyers of condominiums make purchase commitments before units are actually constructed, they should require that down payments made on units when the loan is closed be placed in an escrow account until the units are completed. If funds are not placed in escrow and if a developer uses these funds to complete the project and then defaults, buyers will have a difficult time recovering down payments. The developer should have adequate funds from construction and development loan commitments obtained before construction and should not have to resort to using down payments to complete construction.

6. *Conversions.* When an apartment complex is being converted to condominium ownership, extreme caution should be exercised by the lender to

ensure that the physical layout and quality of construction is suitable for conversion. Potential problem areas that may arise include common heating and cooling plants and any common utility metering, as assessment of operating and repair costs may prove to be controversial among owners. Other problems include lack of adequate insulation, electrical outlets, laundry facilities, appliance hookups, storm doors and windows, to mention a few items that affect the marketability of the units.

Cooperatives. To combat high rents following World War I and at intermittent intervals since that time, cooperative apartments have been promoted in some American cities, notably Chicago, Los Angeles, New York, and Philadelphia. The pattern of their financing is as follows: First, there is organized a corporation whose assets consist of the land and building that constitute the apartment. Then as large a mortgage as possible is obtained, with the land and building as security. Each apartment is assigned a price dependent upon the arrangement, the relative location, the number and size of rooms, and so on. The purchaser of each apartment secures the right to use it so long as he meets his obligations to the corporation, together with a percentage of stock that represents the purchase price. The total amount of stock issued is expected to be sold for an amount sufficient to make up the difference between the net proceeds of the mortgage and the total cost of the project. The cost here includes cost for land, construction, selling, and profit to the promoters.

If the building to be used for the cooperative venture is already in existence, the financing follows the pattern just outlined. If the building is not yet built, the promoter may prefer to play safe by selling the blueprints instead of the building. In other words, he has plans drawn for the proposed building and selects a site for its location. Then salespersons sell apartments from the plans, making sure to get substantial down payments, 25 percent or more, but giving a contract for purchase which enables the promoter to return the deposit should he decide not to go through with the deal. If it is found that the venture is not likely to attract enough buyers, he can abandon or postpone the construction. If, on the other hand, buyers are sufficiently numerous to justify completion of the program, construction will proceed. The remainder of the buyer's commitment, above the down payment, will be due at some future date, perhaps at the time of possession.

The blueprint plan assumes complete ownership by all who occupy apartments in the project. It is sometimes designated as the 100 percent plan. In addition, a modification of this plan, variously designated as semicooperative, group ownership, joint ownership, 40 percent plan, and so on, is sometimes financed by only a portion of the tenants with the remaining units rented to nonowners. Under either the 100 percent plan or any variation of it, the ground floor may be used for stores. These stores may be included in the cooperative scheme or may be rented separately at whatever they will bring in the market.

Types of ownership of cooperative apartments. The three common types of ownership of cooperative apartments are trust, corporate, and individual. In the trust type, legal ownership is in the name of a bank or trust company. Purchasers of units are given certificates of beneficial interest or participation certificates. The ownership of such a certificate carries the right to lease a unit in the building. The lease defines the rights and obligations of its owner, including any restrictions upon sale and transfer, subletting rights, and so forth. Management of a trust type of apartment ownership may be vested in the trustee or otherwise, as defined in the agreement.

In the corporate type of ownership, title rests with the corporation of which the purchasers are shareholders. Management is determined by the board of directors. Here also restrictions may be placed upon the sale of stock and the transfer of leases by those originally entitled to them. The stock is frequently pledged with the directors of the corporation as additional assurance that its owners will meet their obligations to the corporation. This practice parallels the pledging of certificates with the trustee—in the previous type described above—for the same purpose.

In the third type of cooperative ownership, individuals have title to the units assigned for their use. Ownership may take one or two forms: tenancy in common or condominium. Under the tenancy in common type of ownership, the purchaser receives by deed an individed interest in the whole with the right to occupy a particular unit. Under the condominium concept, the purchaser acquires by deed a fee simple title to a specific unit and common ownership of the public areas and the underlying ground. Tenancy in common has many of the disadvantages of the traditional cooperatives. Condominiums have recently received numerous statutory assists and are becoming increasingly popular. Prior to 1963 only six states had condominium laws on their books. Now this form of ownership is generally accepted.

Questions

1 What does underwriting mean in real estate lending?

2 What are some standard guidelines used in underwriting residential mortgage loans?

3 What are the differences between the cost and market comparison approaches to appraising property?

4 Why are lenders concerned with the value of a property over time in addition to its present appraised value?

5 What does the incremental, or marginal, cost of borrowing mean?

6 Should borrowers always choose to maximize the amount borrowed as much as possible?

7 What is a loan commitment?

8 What are loan origination fees? List various types.

9 What is an escrow account? What does proration of property taxes mean?

10 What is private mortgage insurance coverage? Why is it used? How does it differ from mortgage cancellation insurance and hazard insurance?

11 What is the Real Estate Settlement and Procedures Act? What is its intent?

12 What are requirements under RESPA? Discuss the process of disclosure of settlement costs from loan application to loan closing. What types of fees and conditions are prohibited under RESPA?

13 What is the Truth-in-Lending Act? How does it affect real estate lending? What must be disclosed under the uniform truth-in-lending statement?

14 When a person buys a condominium, what is being purchased? What is the condominium declaration?

15 What are lenders especially cautious about when underwriting mortgage loans in condominiums?

Case problems

1 Ms. Sally Strutter is considering the following loan alternatives to finance the $60,000 house she would like to purchase. Loan A can be made for 80 percent of value, $48,000, at 9 percent for 25 years. Loan B can be made for 90 percent of value, or $54,000, at 9.5 percent for 25 years.

   a. What should be the monthly mortgage payments under Alternatives A and B?

   b. What is the marginal or incremental cost of borrowing the additional $6,000 under Alternative B?

   c. If the property were held only ten years, would this change the answer in (*b*)?

   d. How would the answer in (*b*) change if a 2 percent origination fee is charged on the 80 percent loan and a 4 percent fee is charged on the 90 percent loan?

2 Referring back to problem 1, assume a new loan, Alternative C, can be obtained for $54,000 at 9.5 percent for 30 years. Comparing Alternatives A and C:

   a. What would be the monthly mortgage payments under Alternatives A and C?

   b. Assuming the property is expected to be held only ten years, what would be the marginal cost of borrowing the additional $6,000 under Alternative C?

   c. If the property were held for 15 years, would the answer in (*b*) be different? Explain. Do not work out a solution.

3 On August 20, Mr. and Mrs. Newton decided to buy a property from Mr. and Mrs. Oldton for $100,000. On August 30, Mr. and Mrs. Newton obtained a loan commitment from ABC Savings and Loan for an $80,000 conventional loan at 10 percent for 25 years. The lender informs Mr. and Mrs. Newton that a $1,600 loan origination fee will be required to obtain the loan. The loan closing is to take place September 22. In addition, escrow accounts will be required for all prorated and prepaid property taxes and hazard insurance; however, no mortgage insurance is necessary. A breakdown of expected settlement costs has been provided by ABC Savings and Loan when Mr. and Mrs. Newton inspect the uniform settlement statement required under RESPA on September 21 as follows:

I. Buyer and seller information:
  a. Purchase price. $100,000.00
  b. Deposit paid by Newton's to Oldton's (paid in
      escrow to ABC Savings and Loan) 1,000.00
  c. Real estate tax proration (taxes due to
      county January 1 and July 1, $800 per year,
      $400 per half) (July 1–September 22 unpaid
      by seller) 83 days or (83/365 × $800) 181.77
II. Buyer/borrower and lender information:
  a. Amount of loan 80,000.00
  b. Prepaid interest (regular monthly payments
      to begin on November 1) from closing through
      September = 9 days [(.10 × $80,000) ÷ 365] × 9 . . . . 197.26
  c. Property tax escrow—2 months required. 133.33
  d. Hazard insurance escrow—2 months or $20 required 20.00
  e. Loan origination fee 1,600.00
III. Transactions between buyer/borrower and third parties:
  a. Title insurance fee (Landco Title Co.). 300.00
  b. Recording fees—mortgage and deed 25.00
  c. Real estate transfer tax. 200.00
  d. Barry Barrister—attorney 100.00
IV. Transactions between seller and third parties:
  a. Landco Title Co—closing fee. 60.00
  b. Release statement—seller's mortgage 5.00
  c. Payoff—seller's mortgage (XYZ State Bank) 15,215.00
  d. Real estate brokerage fee (6% Plain Deal Realty). 6,000.00
  e. Linda Lawyer—attorney 100.00
  f. Pest inspection 20.00

On September 21, Mr. and Mrs. Newton again inspect the uniform settlement statement as required under RESPA and none of the estimates has changed. Complete the closing statement using an approach similar to that used under RESPA.

a.   What are the amounts due from the borrower and due to the seller?

b.   What would the disclosed annual percentage rate be as required under the Truth-in-Lending Act?

APPENDIX: SPECIAL CONSIDERATIONS—
RESIDENTIAL FINANCING

Sometimes, years after a real estate transaction has been closed, individuals are faced with decisions involving various aspects of their mortgage loan. For example, many individuals may be thinking of paying a part of their loan off early, of refinancing their loan, or possibly of selling their house on the basis of a mortgage assumption. This section deals with some of the decisions borrowers may face during the time over which they are paying off an existing loan and includes a framework through which various alternatives which confront them may be analyzed.

Loan refinancing

On occasion, an opportunity may arise for an individual to refinance a mortgage loan at a reduced rate of interest. Indeed, during the period of rapidly rising interest rates encountered in 1979 and early 1980 and the reverse pattern during 1980, some opportunities for refinancing existed, and many borrowers took advantage of it.

To illustrate the fundamental relationships in any refinancing decision, at least three ingredients must be known: (1) terms on the present outstanding loan, (2) new loan terms being considered, and (3) any charges associated with paying off the existing loan or acquiring the new loan (such as prepayment penalties on the existing loan or origination and closing fees on the new loan). To illustrate, assume a borrower makes a mortgage loan for $40,000 at 10 percent interest for 30 years. After five years, interest rates fall and a new mortgage loan is available at 9.5 percent for 25 years. The loan balance on the existing loan is $38,628, and a prepayment penalty of 1 percent must be paid on the existing loan. The lender who is making the new loan available also requires an origination fee of $800 plus $15 for incidental legal fees for recording, and so forth, if the new loan is made. Should the borrower refinance?

In answering this question, we must analyze the costs associated with refinancing and the benefits or savings which all accrue due to the reduction in interest charges, should the borrower choose to refinance. The costs associated with refinancing are as follows:

Cost to refinance:
Prepayment penalty: 1% × $38,628 = $ 386
Origination fee, new loan   800
Recording, etc., new loan   15
                                          $1,201

Benefits from refinancing are obviously the interest savings that result from a lower interest rate. Hence, if refinancing occurs, the monthly mortgage payment under the new loan terms will be lower than payments under the existing mortgage. Monthly benefits would be $13.55 as shown:

Monthly savings due to refinancing:
Monthly payments, existing loan, $40,000, 10%, 30 years $351.04
Monthly payments, new loan, $38,628, 9.5%, 25 years. 337.49
Difference in monthly payments . . . . $ 13.55

The issue faced by the borrower now becomes whether or not it is worth investing, or paying out, $1,201 (charges for refinancing) to save $13.55 per month over the term of the loan. Perhaps the $1,201 could be reinvested in a more profitable alternative? To analyze this question, we should determine what rate of return is earned on the investment of $1,201 for 25 years, given that $13.55 per month represents the return. This is easily done as follows:

$$13.55(MIFPVa, ?\%, 25 \text{ yrs.}) = \$1,201$$
$$(MIFPVa, ?\%, 25 \text{ yrs.}) = \$1,201 \div \$13.55$$
$$(MIFPVa, ?\%, 25 \text{ yrs.}) = 88.635$$

Referring to Appendix B, we want to find the *IF* in column 5 for 25 years for some interest rate which is equal to 88.635. A search reveals that the 13 percent table shows an *IF* in column 5 equal to 88.665 for 25 years. Therefore, we know that the yield on our $1,201 dollar investment, with returns (savings) of $13.55 per month over 25 years, would be equivalent to earning approximately 13 percent per year. If another alternative equal in risk cannot be found which provides a 13 percent annual return, the refinancing should be undertaken.

Early repayment—loan refinancing. One additional point must be made concerning refinancing, however, if the property is not held for the full 25 years. In that event, monthly savings of $13.55 do not occur for the entire 25-year term and therefore the refinancing is not as attractive. To demonstrate, if we assume the borrower plans to hold the property for only ten more years after refinancing, is refinancing still worthwhile? To analyze this alternative, note that the $1,201 cost will not change should the refinancing be undertaken; however, the benefits (savings) will change. The $13.55 monthly benefits will be realized for only ten years. In addition, since the refinanced loan is expected to be repaid after ten years, there will be a difference between loan balances on the existing loan and the new loan, due to different amortization rates.

Loan balance, 15th year—existing loan*............	$32,664
Loan balance, 10th year—new loan†..............	$32,320
Difference.....................................	$ 344

  * Based on $40,000, 10 percent, 30 years, prepaid after 15 years.
  † Based on $38,628, 9.5 percent, 25 years, prepaid after 10 years.

The new calculation comparing loan balances under the existing loan and under the new loan terms shows that if refinancing occurs, the amount saved because of a lower loan balance is $344, should the new loan be made. Hence, total savings in the event of refinancing would be $13.55 per month for ten years, plus $344 at the end of ten years. Do these savings justify an outlay of $1,201 in refinancing costs? To answer this question, we compute the return on the $1,201 outlay as follows:

$$13.55(MIFPVa, ?\%, 10 \text{ yrs.}) + \$344(MIFPV, ?\%, 10 \text{ yrs.}) = \$1,201$$

Because the loan is repaid early and the monthly savings of $13.55 will not be received over the full 25-year period, the yield must be below the 13 percent yield computed in the previous example. Using the trial and error approach with different interest rates, we will finally choose 9 percent and discount as follows:

$$\$13.55(79.941693) = \$1,083$$
$$\$344(.407937) = \underline{\quad\quad 140}$$
$$\text{Present value} = \underline{\underline{\$1,223}}$$

We see that when discounting at 9 percent, the solution $1,223 is very close to the desired present value, or investment, of $1,201. Now we know the yield earned due to refinancing in this case will be slightly higher than 9 percent per year for the ten-year period.

Obviously, this return is lower than the 13 percent computed assuming the loan was repaid after 25 years. This is true because the refinancing cost of $1,201 remained the same, while the savings stream of $13.55 was shortened from 25 years to 10 years. Although an additional $344 was saved because of differences in loan balances, it did not offset the reduction in monthly savings that will have occurred from the 10th through the 25th year. In analyzing refinancing decisions, then, not only must costs and benefits (savings) be compared but the time period one expects to hold a property must also enter into the decision.[1]

Mortgage loan assumptions—financial implications

The final topic to be covered in this appendix deals with the possible advantage of purchasing a property by assuming the seller's mortgage loan. Mortgage loan assumptions are possible in some cases, depending on original borrowing terms.[2] The real advantage to selling under an assumption is for the buyer to retain the seller's mortgage terms, particularly if interest rates have risen significantly since the seller's mortgage was made.[3] For example, if an individual bought a $40,000 property and made a mortgage loan 5 years ago for $30,000 at 7 percent interest for a term of 25 years, the possibility of assuming such a loan might appear attractive if interest rates have risen. However, due to price appreciation and the fact that the

---

[1] Another point to be considered here is the probability the loan will be held for less than ten years. Obviously, if one expects to sell a property and to pay off the mortgage within ten years, the interest savings on the $1,201 will be even less. Hence, if a borrower expects to sell a property within a short time after refinancing, it will be difficult to justify refinancing to begin with.

[2] In many areas of the United States, properties are sold on assumption. However, in many other areas, the right to sell on assumption is precluded explicitly in the mortgage or by the lender not approving the new buyer. Lending practices vary widely depending on tradition and economic conditions in a given area.

[3] It should also be pointed out that when selling under an assumption, in the event a buyer defaults on an assumed loan, the seller becomes liable for payment. However, a release from liability may be obtained by the seller from the lender, making the new buyer the only party liable in the event of default.

loan has been amortized for five years, the amount of cash necessary for the buyer to assume the mortgage may be prohibitive for a buyer. For example, if the property has risen in value over the past five years to $50,000, the amount of cash equity required by the buyer to assume the seller's loan in our example would be $22,652, determined as follows:

```
Purchase price ............................  $50,000
Seller's mortgage balance
  ($30,000, 7%, 25 years, after 5 years) .........   27,348
Cash equity required to assume...............  $22,652
```

If the buyer does not have $22,652 in cash, even though he desires an assumption he may be unable to conclude the transaction.

Loan assumptions and second mortgages. One alternative open to the buyer who could not make the large cash outlay in the above example may be to obtain a second mortgage. However, using a second mortgage will be justified in this case only if the terms of the second mortgage, when combined with terms on the assumed mortgage, will make the borrower as well or better off than if the entire purchase had been financed with a new mortgage. If the entire purchase can be financed with a new 80 percent mortgage loan for $40,000 at 9 percent for 20 years, we must know how to combine a second mortgage with the assumed mortgage to determine whether or not the assumption would be as attractive as the new mortgage loan. If a second mortgage cannot be made on the required terms, a new mortgage loan should be made on current market terms. To analyze this problem we first compare monthly payments and amounts borrowed under a new loan, with monthly payments and amounts borrowed if an assumption is made:

	Amount borrowed	Monthly payments
New loan, 9%, 20 years...............	$40,000	$360.00
Assumed loan, 7%, 20 years...........	27,348*	212.10†
Difference	$12,652	$147.90

* Outstanding balance based on $30,000, 7 percent, 25 years, after 5 years.
† Payments based on $30,000, 7 percent, 25-year term.

From the above calculation if an assumption is made, the borrower will have to provide $12,652 more than will be borrowed if a new loan is made for $40,000.[4] By assuming the mortgage, $147.90 per month will be saved when compared to making a new loan. However, if the borrower does not have the extra $12,652 to assume the loan but can find a second mortgage for that

---

[4] It should be pointed out that under the assumption and the second mortgage, the buyer would pay the seller $10,000 down, assume the $27,348 mortgage balance, and find a second mortgage for $12,652, making the total purchase price of $50,000.

amount, up to what rate can he pay on the second mortgage and still remain as well off as if he financed with the $40,000 loan at 9 percent for 20 years?

The answer to this question is easily determined. If the second mortgage is to be fully amortized over a 20-year period, the solution can be obtained by finding the rate of interest that monthly payments of $147.90 would yield on a loan of $12,652. This is accomplished as:

$$\$147.90(MIFPVa, \ ?\%, \ 20 \ \text{yrs.}) = \$12,652$$
$$(MIFPVa, \ ?\%, \ 20 \ \text{yrs.}) = \$12,652 \div \$147.90$$
$$(MIFPVa, \ ?\%, \ 20 \ \text{yrs.}) = 85.54$$

By consulting the tables in the Appendix B for an *IF* in column 5 for 20 years, a search shows that the 13 percent table provides us with 85.36, or a solution very near 85.54. In other words, if a second mortgage bearing an interest rate of 13 percent for 20 years can be obtained, the combination of the assumed mortgage terms plus the second mortgage terms will be equivalent to financing the purchase with a new mortgage of $40,000 at 9 percent for 20 years.

The relationship can be seen more clearly by computing the combined mortgage payments on the assumed loan and a second mortgage loan made for 20 years at 13 percent.

Monthly payment assumed loan*	$212.10
Monthly payment second mortgage loan†	148.28
	$360.38 or
	$360.00 (rounded)

* Based on original $30,000 loan, at 7 percent, for 25 years.
† Based on second mortgage loan of $12,652 at 13 percent, for 20 years.

We can now see that the combined monthly payments equal $360, and a $40,000 loan at 9 percent interest for 20 years. *Obviously if a second mortgage can be found bearing an effective interest rate less than 13 percent for 20 years, the buyer will be much better off by assuming the existing loan, as the combined monthly payments will be lower than making a new loan at 9 percent.*[5]

Second mortgages and shorter maturities. In many cases second mortgages may not be available for a 20-year period. If a ten-year term were available on a second mortgage loan at 12 percent interest, would the borrower be better off by assuming the existing mortgage and making a second mortgage, or should the entire $40,000 loan be refinanced at 9 percent? To answer this question we must determine the combined interest cost on the assumed mortgage which carries a rate of 7 percent for 20 remaining years and the second mortgage which would carry a rate of 12 percent for 10 years. This combined rate can

---

[5] It should be apparent that such a high interest rate can be paid on the second mortgage because $27,348, or the amount assumed, carries a 7 percent rate and represents about two thirds of the $40,000 to be financed, while the second mortgage of $12,652 represents only one third. When weighted together by the respective interest rates, the total rate paid on the combined amounts is influenced more by the amount assumed at 7 percent.

then be compared to the current 9 percent rate for 20 years presently available, should the property be financed with an entirely new mortgage loan.

To combine terms on the assumable mortgage and second mortgage we add monthly payments together as follows:

	Monthly payments
Assumed loan*...............	$212.10
Second mortgage†	181.56
Total.................	$393.66

* Based on original terms: $30,000, 7 percent, 25 years.
†Based on $12,652, 12 percent, 10 years (loan constant, .01435).

The sum of the two monthly payments is equal to $393.66, which is far greater than the $360 payment required if a new loan for $40,000 is made at 9 percent interest for 20 years. However, the combined $393.66 monthly payments are made for only ten years. After ten years the second mortgage is completely repaid and only the $212.10 payments on the assumed loan will be made through the 20th year. This pattern compares to $360 under an entirely new loan made for 20 years at 9 percent interest.

Whether or not the combined mortgages should be used by the borrower can now be determined by solving for the combined cost of borrowing. This cost is based on the monthly payments under both the assumed loan and second mortgage, for the respective number of months payments must be made, in relation to the $40,000 amount being financed. This can be seen easily to be the monthly payments of $181.56 on the second mortgage for *10 years* and the $212.10 payments on the assumed mortgage for *20 years*, both discounted by an interest rate that results in the present value of $40,000.

$$\$181.56(MIFPVa, \ ?\%, \ 10 \ \text{yrs.})$$
$$+ \ 212.10(MIFPVa, \ ?\%, \ 20 \ \text{yrs.}) = \$40,000$$

By trial and error we search for the interest rate that gives the combinations of *IF*s that make the present value of the combined monthly mortgage payments equal to $40,000.

Discounting at 8 percent:
$181.56(82.42148)	= $14,965
$212.10(119.55429)	= 25,357
Present value	= $40,322

Discounting at 8.5 percent:
$181.56(80.654470)	= $14,644
$212.10(115.230840)	= 24,440
Present value	= $39,084

Interpolating:

Present value at 8%	= $40,322
− Desired present value	= 40,000
Difference	= $ 322

Present value at 8%	= $40,322
− Present value at 8.5%	= 39,084
Difference .5%	= $ 1,238

($322 ÷ 1,238) × .5% = .13%
Combined cost: 8% + .13% = 8.13%

By discounting at 8 percent and 8.5 percent and interpolating, the combined interest cost on both the existing mortgage if assumed for 20 years and the second mortgage made for 10 years is 8.13 percent. This combined package of financing still compares vary favorably to the 9 percent interest rate currently available on a $40,000 mortgage for 20 years.[6]

Loan assumptions and open-end mortgages.   The importance of an assumable open-end mortgage also becomes apparent when interest rates have risen since the seller of a property made his mortgage. Suppose the seller of the property is willing to increase the amount of the loan under an open-end mortgage provision that allows additional amounts, up to 80 percent of value, to be borrowed *at any time* on current lending terms. Returning to our example above, instead of the borrower having to find a second mortgage, the seller might merely exercise the open-end provision by borrowing an additional $12,652 which when coupled with the outstanding balance of $27,348 would provide the necessary $40,000 which would be assumed by the borrower.[7] The $27,348 loan balance would still bear an interest charge of 7 percent. But the incremental amount borrowed, or $12,652, would cost 9 percent for the

		Monthly payment
Existing loan	$27,348	$212.10*
Additional borrowing	12,652	113.87†
Total.	$40,000	$325.97

* Based on original loan $30,000, 7 percent, 25 years.
† Based on $12,652, 9 percent, 20 years.

---

[6] It should be noted, however, that the combined monthly payments of $393.65, should the assumption and second mortgage combination be made, is much higher than the $360 payments available under a new mortgage for the first ten years. Although this is offset by the much lower $212.10 payments after ten years, the borrower must decide which pattern of monthly loan payments best fits his income pattern, in addition to simply choosing the loan alternative with the lower interest cost.

[7] The seller would still realize the sales price $50,000, less the outstanding loan balance of $27,348, or $22,652. This is true because the buyer must pay $10,000 down to the seller and the seller keeps the additional $12,652 borrowed under the open-end borrowing. The buyer assumes the full debt owed by the seller of $40,000, or $27,348 plus $12,652.

remaining 20 years because it must be borrowed at current market interest rates. Combining the terms on the $27,348 balance with the $12,652 additional amount borrowed results in a total monthly payment of $325.97.

The main advantage in assuming the existing loan can be seen in the difference between monthly payments on a new loan for $40,000 at 9 percent for 20 years, which would be $360.00, and the combined payments if the loan is assumed *and* the seller exercises the open-end provision, which would be $325.97. By assuming the existing loan, the borrower will save $34.03 per month ($360 − $325.97).[8] Further, the combined effective interest cost on the assumed loan would be determined by finding the interest rate which would make the $325.97 combined payment on assumption equal to the $40,000 amount borrowed. This is done as follows:

$$\$325.97(MIFPVa\ ?\%,\ 20\ yrs.) = \$40,000$$
$$(MIFPVa\ ?\%,\ 20\ yrs.) = \$40,000/\$325.97$$
$$(MIFPVa\ ?\%,\ 20\ yrs.) = 122.71$$

Looking to the interest tables in Appendix B, we see that in column 5 in the 8 percent tables, the *IF* corresponding to 20 years is 119.554, which is close to 122.71. The combined payments of $325.97 on the mortgage assumption of $40,000 represent an effective cost of approximately 7.75 percent.[9] *Clearly the 7.75 percent effective interest cost on the mortgage assumption is far better than the 9 percent rate that would have to be paid if the new loan were made.*

Case problems (appendix)

A–1 Barry Borrower made a 30-year, 9.5 loan for $35,000 five years ago. Since then interest rates have fallen to 9 percent. He has contacted a lender who is willing to refinance the loan balance of $33,684 at 9 percent for 25 years. However, there will be $908 in loan origination and legal fees if the new loan is made.

a. Assuming the new loan is held to maturity, how should Borrower decide whether or not to refinance?

b. If Borrower's property is expected to be sold eight years from now, how should Borrower decide whether or not to refinance?

A–2 Ms. Mary Maeker has an opportunity to buy a property with a loan assumption. The price of the property is $50,000 and it has an outstanding loan balance of $30,000 for 25 years remaining at 7 percent interest. Monthly mortgage payments are $212.10.

---

[8] It should be pointed out that the seller will also recognize this saving and will probably raise his selling price to partially offset this advantage. It is clear that the $34.03 monthly saving is worth a considerable amount. If one looked at the $34.03 as an investment return, and if 9 percent represented a reasonable return on investment, the present value of those savings over 20 years would be $34.03 × (PV of $1 per mo., 9%, 20 yrs.) or $34.03 × (111.14) = $3,782. How much of this amount the buyer would be willing to pay over the $50,000 price would depend on competitive conditions and how much the buyer valued the interest savings.

[9] Interpolation between 7 percent and 8 percent results in a yield of approximately 7.75 percent.

a. How much equity would Ms. Maeker have to pay the seller to assume the loan if the property was purchased?

b. Assume Ms. Maeker could not provide the necessary equity in (*a*) but could finance an additional $10,000 with a second mortgage at 10 percent interest for 10 years or finance the entire purchase with a $40,000 loan at 9 percent interest for 25 years. Which alternative would be the least costly?

A–3 Ralph Brown has an opportunity to purchase a property with a loan assumption. The selling price is $40,000, and the owner has an open-end mortgage. The present mortgage balance is $25,000, carries an 8 percent interest rate, and has a remaining 20 years to maturity. Present monthly payments are $209.10. The owner of the property has agreed to exercise the open-end provision of the mortgage and to increase the loan amount to $35,000. However, this additional $10,000 amount would be financed at 12 percent interest over the remaining 20 years. Brown also has the option of financing the entire purchase with a $35,000 mortgage for 20 years at 9 percent.

a. What is the effective interest rate on the combined loans if the property is bought with the loan assumption?

Alternative mortgage instruments

9

For some time now, the fully amortized, constant payment mortgage has been the most widely used mortgage instrument in the United States. However, in more recent times, particularly during the decade of the 1970s, inflation and its effect on this "standard" mortgage instrument have caused problems for both lenders and borrowers. Because of these problems, a number of different mortgage instruments have been proposed as alternatives to the standard mortgage instrument. This chapter outlines the problems that inflation has brought for both borrowers and lenders who have relied on the standard mortgage instrument. Also included is a detailed description of some of the alternative mortgage instruments that are either being used in place of the standard mortgage instrument, or are currently being proposed for use.

Inflation and the mortgage interest rates

As illustrated in the chapter dealing with mortgage loans and effective interest costs, the fully amortized, constant payment mortgage loan (hereafter referred to as the standard mortgage instrument) is characterized by a series of *constant* periodic payments over a specified term that provides the lender with full repayment of the loan at the end of the term, plus some rate of interest earned on the outstanding loan balance. The impact of inflation on lenders and borrowers who have traditionally used the standard mortgages are many. We can begin with a discussion of interest rates and inflation.

In general, when lenders provide mortgage funds to borrowers for a given period of time, the interest rate that they offer is a function of *four* things. First, lenders expect to earn some annual *real* rate of return on the money they lend.

By real rate of return, we are referring to a rate of interest that would be generally available on productive investment in the economy, in the absence of any inflationary considerations. This real rate of interest is sometimes referred to in economics as the *marginal productivity of capital.* It represents a basic price determined by the supply and demand for funds that borrowers, which include individuals, corporations, or government, would pay for funds to undertake productive investment *in an inflationless economy.*

Second, when lenders make mortgage loans they expect to be compensated for taking risk. When mortgage loans are made, there is always some probability that the borrower will default. Because some probability of default loss exists, lenders expect to earn a *risk premium,* or an additional amount of interest over and above the real rate of interest.

Third, lenders expect to earn a rate of interest high enough to compensate them for the loss in purchasing power brought on by inflation during the period of time that the loan is outstanding. In other words, lenders attempt to "build" into current interest rates what they think inflation will be during the period that they expect the loan to be outstanding. In this way, they are compensated for the loss in purchasing power brought on by inflation.

Finally, the rate of interest lenders charge on mortgage loans is time dependent; that is, the rate of interest will be dependent on expected changes in the real rate of interest, the risk premium, and inflation over the period of time over which a loan is *expected* to be outstanding. As in our previous discussion regarding mortgages, this does not refer to the maturity of the loan but the expected repayment period. In general, we would expect higher interest rates to be associated with loans made for longer periods of time.[1]

In summary, when lenders compete in the marketplace and offer borrowers interest rates on mortgage loans, these interest rates in large part represent a consensus as to what lenders must earn during each year of the expected loan term to compensate them for risk and inflation, leaving some real rate of return on capital invested from which the lender must meet operating costs and earn a profit. Symbolically, if we let i_r equal the real rate of interest, i_p equal the premium expected for risk taking by mortgage lenders, i_f equal the inflation premium that lenders expect to earn to compensate them for inflation, and t represent the period of time that a loan to is to be outstanding, the nominal interest rate i_m that lenders offer in the marketplace at any given time can be expressed as follows:

$$(i_r + i_p + i_f)_t = i_m$$

or the nominal rate offered (i_m) on a mortgage loan with an expected term (t) is the sum of the real rate of interest plus premiums for risk and inflation over some expected time period. We should stress here that in practice, these

---

[1] This may not always be the case. In some periods, depending on the "term structure" of interest rates, short-term loans may carry higher interest rates than long-term loans.

components of the nominal interest rate (i_m) are really a consensus of expectations of *all lenders competing* in the marketplace as to what each of these components is likely to be in the future. Further, to the extent that borrowers are willing to pay the price, or nominal rate for mortgage funds, then it becomes the prevailing mortgage rate of interest.

Effects on lenders and borrowers

How does the above discussion relate to mortgage lending and difficulties faced by lenders and borrowers in an inflationary environment? The answer to this question can be easily illustrated. Let's initially assume that a $50,000 loan is being made at a time when *no* inflation exists. The loan is expected to be outstanding for a 30-year period. Because there is no inflation, an inflation premium (i_f) is not required; hence the lender will earn a return equivalent to the real interest rate (i_r) plus a premium for risk (i_p) over the period of the loan.[2] We assume that the interest rate charged under such assumptions would be 4 percent, representing a 3 percent real rate of interest and a risk premium of 1 percent over the period of the loan. Assuming this loan were made in an inflationless environment, the lender would collect constant payments of approximately $239 per month, based on the loan constant for 4 percent and 30 years. This amount is shown in Exhibit 9–1 as a straight line (RP) over the life of the loan and represents the series of constant real payments necessary to earn the lender the required 4 percent real return and risk premium each year that the loan is outstanding.

Now assume that the same loan is made in an *inflationary environment* where a 6 percent rate of inflation is expected to prevail during each year that the loan is outstanding. The interest rate on the mortgage loan would now increase to 10 percent. This includes the base rate of 4 percent earned when no inflation was expected, plus an inflation premium of 6 percent. Given that the standard mortgage instrument is to be used, the lender must now collect approximately $439 a month. This new payment pattern is shown in Exhibit 9–1 as the horizontal line labeled *NP*, representing a constant series of *nominal payments* received over the term of the loan. Hence, included in the series of nominal payments are amounts that will provide the lender with a 4 percent basic rate of interest representing a real return and risk premium, plus a 6 percent inflation premium over the 30-year loan term.

It should be noted that in our example the inflation rate of 6 percent caused an 85 percent rise in the monthly mortgage payments from $239 to $439, or by $200 per month. Why is there such a significant increase in these monthly

---

[2] Actually the interest rate charged will be related to the expected repayment period that may occur before maturity. However, this will not alter the concept being illustrated. The figures chosen here are arbitrary. Some studies indicate that the real rate of interest has historically been in the 3 percent range and risk premiums on mortgages in the 1–2 percent range. However, recent studies on productivity indicate that the real rate of interest has been in the range of 1 percent during the 1970s.

EXHIBIT 9–1
Real and nominal values of mortgage payments

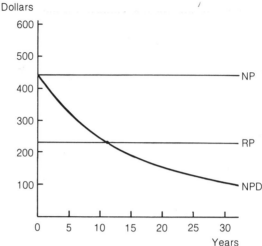

payments? The reason can be easily seen by examining Exhibit 9–1. Note the curve *NPD* in the exhibit. This curve represents the *real value* of the monthly payments that the lender will receive over the 30-year loan period. It is determined by "deflating" the $439 nominal monthly payments by the rate of inflation.[3] The importance of the *NPD* curve lies in the fact that because the lender realizes that inflation is going to occur, he also expects that the constant stream of $439 payments to be received over time will be worth *less and less* in future years because of lost purchasing power. Hence, in order to receive the full 10 percent interest necessary to leave enough for a 4 percent real return and risk premium over the life of the loan (*RP*), more *real dollars* must be collected in the *early years* of the loan. This is because payments collected toward the end of the life of the mortgage will be worth much less in purchasing power.

To illustrate, let's examine the real value of the $439 payments collected each month, as represented by the curve *NPD*. Note that for about the first ten years of the loan life, the real value of these payments is greater than the 4 percent required real return. However, after ten years, the real value of these payments fall below the required 4 percent return. Also, as shown in the exhibit, the real value of the nominal payments is equal to the required real payments at 4 percent, or *NPD = RP* as shown. This means that from the stream of nominal $439 monthly receipts, the lender will ultimately earn the

---

[3] This is done by computing the monthly inflation factor .06 ÷ 12, or .005, and multiplying $439 × (1 ÷ 1.005)¹ in the first month, $439 × (1 ÷ 1.005)² in the second month, and so on until year 30.

same real value as a stream of $239 payments, or 4 percent on investment after deflating the nominal payments by the inflation rate. However, in order to earn the same real interest rate, the real value of the payment stream (*NPD*) must be greater than *RP* in the early years, as it will fall below *RP* in the later years. This relationship is referred to as *tilting* the real payment stream in the early years to make up for the loss in purchasing power in later years.

This tilt effect also has a considerable impact on the borrower. Recall that before inflation, the borrower faced a $239 payment while after inflation a $439 monthly payment is necessary. When the loan is first originated, the difference in the two payments or about $200 per month, represents an additional amount of *real dollars* that the *borrower* must allocate from current *real income* to meet mortgage payments. This means that after the mortgage payment is made, the borrower will have less remaining real income available to spend, and will have to *cut back* or reduce current consumption of other goods and services by $200 per month. He must do this to provide the required inflation premium to the lender "up front," or in the beginning of the loan. Over time, this burden moderates. For example, by the end of the first year the real value of the $439 payments deflated by the 6 percent rate of inflation will be about $414 per month and the borrower's *real income* will have increased to $20,600 ($20,000 × 1.03, or by the real rate of growth in the economy). At that time, the borrower will have more real income to pay declining real mortgage payments. However, even during the second year the borrower will have to reduce the consumption of other real goods and services by $414 − $239, or by $175 per month, because of the tilt effect. Hence, even though the borrower's income is increasing both in real and nominal terms each year, it is not enough to offset the tilt effect in the early years of a loan. From this analysis, it becomes very apparent from Exhibit 9–1 why it is so financially difficult for first-time home buyers to qualify for loans during periods of rising inflation. This is because with the general rate of inflation and growth in the economy, income will grow *gradually*, or on a year-by-year basis. However, as expected inflation increases, lenders must build estimates of the *full increase* into current interest rates *when the loan is made*. This causes a dramatic increase in required real monthly payments relative to the borrower's current real income.

One final observation should be made concerning the tilt effect; that is, as the rate of inflation increases, the impact of the tilt effect on borrowers increases. This can be easily seen from Exhibit 9–2. In that case we show the effect of an increase in inflation from 6 *percent* in our previous example to 8 *percent* per year. Note that nominal monthly payments increase from $439 to $514 per month, the latter figure based on an increase in the mortgage interest rate to 12 percent. The impact of the tilt effect when inflation is expected to be 8 percent can be seen relative to the effect when inflation was expected to be 6 percent. Note that when the $514 monthly payments are deflated at 8 percent for inflation, the burden of the *real payments* to be made by the borrower

EXHIBIT 9–2
Relationship between real and nominal mortgage payments given an increase in inflation

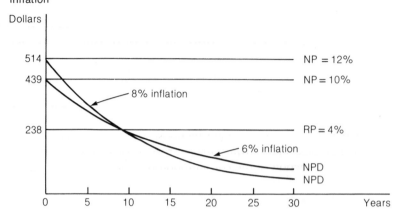

increase relative to the *real payments* required when inflation was 6 percent in the early years of the loan. This can be seen in Exhibit 9–2 as the curve corresponding to monthly payments deflated at 8 percent indicates that the real value of monthly payments on the 12 percent mortgage *exceeds* the real value of payments on the 10 percent mortgage for about the first ten years of the loan term. This is true *even though the lender will earn a 4 percent real return on both mortgages* after inflation. Further, because the borrower's *real income* will increase to $20,600, *regardless of the rate of inflation* (recall real growth is assumed to be 3 percent in our example), as inflation increases from 6 percent to 8 percent, it is clear that the borrower will have to allocate even more *current real income* to mortgage payments. This indicates that in the early years of the mortgage, the burden of the tilt effect on borrowers *increases* as the rate of inflation increases. Further, this makes it even more difficult for borrowers to qualify for loans and make payments from current income.

The impact of inflation on mortgage lending with the standard mortgage instrument can be summarized as follows:

1. Lenders must build inflation premiums into current mortgage interest rates in order to earn a basic or competitive real return on capital and for risk taking.
2. Because of the design of the standard mortgage instrument, as inflation occurs the nominal interest rate increases, thereby making the nominal stream of monthly mortgage payments increase sharply.
3. As inflation occurs, monthly mortgage payments rise sharply because the stream of monthly mortgage payments is constant over the life of the loan. The real value of those payments will decline over the life of the

mortgage due to inflation. Therefore, lenders must collect more *real* dollars in the earlier years of the loan to offset the loss in purchasing power in later years.

4. This tilting of the real value of the payment stream requires that more real dollars be paid by the borrower in the early years of the loan, thereby forcing a reduction in consumption of other goods and services. This burden moderates over time as the borrower's real income increases and the real value of mortgage payments declines.

5. The burden of the tilt effect increases as the rate of inflation increases. This is because the real payment stream must be tilted even more in the early years of the loan term, requiring households to make larger real payments on mortgage loans from current real income, thereby forcing an even greater reduction in the consumption of other goods and services.

Lender considerations. While much of the discussion has centered on the impact on the borrower, we should indicate at this point that lenders have also had much difficulty with the standard mortgage instrument and inflation. Recalling from our earlier discussion concerning interest rates and inflation, lenders must "build" inflationary expectations that they *expect* to occur over the time money is loaned into *fixed* interest rates that they charge borrowers at closing. With revenues collected from interest on these loans, they in turn must *pay savers interest on deposits.* Although most savings institutions and banks are highly regulated as to interest rates payable on deposits, those interest rates do tend to rise with inflation. Hence, if savings institutions do not correctly anticipate inflation when they make fixed interest rate mortgages in the marketplace, they will have difficulty in providing an adequate return to savers over time and may face a loss in savings deposits.

While we discuss the problem facing savings institutions in greater detail in a later chapter, we will say at this point that in more recent times, mortgage lenders have not anticipated inflation accurately. Lenders in the mortgage market have systematically underestimated inflation, making for mortgage interest rates that were lower than would be the case if inflation were fully anticipated and "built in" to those rates. This means that individuals who have borrowed heavily in recent years have been better off than savers who earned interest based on revenues earned on mortgage loans and other investments. This problem area is very complex and to some degree has been beyond the control of most deposit or thrift institutions that provide mortgage loans.

The point we wish to stress here is that not only has inflation caused problems for borrowers but it has also caused problems for *lenders* who have historically provided mortgage loans at *fixed* interest rates with constant monthly payments. Because these institutions have not been able to provide savers with an adequate rate of interest, partially due to regulation and because of the problem in accurately anticipating inflation in interest rates on loans that they have made, savers have begun to seek other investment opportunities. This has caused a shortage of funds (deposits) for mortgage loans in periods of rising interest rates. Lenders therefore are also seeking to modify the standard mortgage instrument in a way that will provide them with increased revenues *over time* as interest rates change. In this way they can pay more competitive rates on deposits to savers, thereby attracting savings and stabilizing the flow of funds to the mortgage market. This problem will be taken up in Chapter 18.

Alternative mortgage instruments

In an attempt to deal with the problems that both lenders and borrowers face with the standard mortgage instrument in periods of significant inflation, many alternatives have been proposed as potential solutions. Some of these alternatives have been adopted at both the federal and state level by regulatory agencies governing investment policies of lending institutions. Other instruments have been proposed and are being studied. In our discussion of alternative mortgage instruments, we will point out which of these new mortgage instruments are still in the proposal stage and which have been approved and are being used by lenders as of this writing.

The graduated payment mortgage

In an attempt to deal with the problem of inflation and its impact on mortgage interest rates and monthly payments, the FHA has instituted the graduated payment mortgage (*GPM*) plan under the Section 245 program.[4] The objective of the *GPM* is to provide for a series of mortgage payments that are lower in the initial years of the loan then would be the case with a standard mortgage loan. The *GPM* payments then gradually increase at a predetermined rate as the borrower's income is expected to rise over time. By designing such an instrument, the payment pattern offsets the tilt effect to some extent, hence reducing the burden faced by households on meeting progressively higher interest rates in an inflationary environment.

An example of the payment pattern for the graduated payment mortgage can be illustrated by looking to Exhibit 9–3. That exhibit contains information on how payments would be structured for the 30-year, $50,000 loan used in our previous examples at various interest rates and different annual rates of graduation. The present FHA Section 245 program has five separate plans allowing for differences in initial payment levels, rates of graduation, and graduation periods. Exhibit 9–3 contains information on *two* of the more popular payment plans. These plans allow for either a 5 percent or 7.5 percent rate of graduation in monthly payments over 5 years, after which time the

---

[4] For more detail the reader should obtain the *HUD Handbook, 4240.2 Rev.,* Graduated Payment Mortgage Program, Sect. 245. These handbooks are available from HUD regional insuring offices.

EXHIBIT 9–3
Comparison of *GPM* payment and standard level payment
mortgage—$50,000, 30-year maturity

	Interest rate		
	9%	10%	11%
Standard level payments.............	$402.30	$438.75	$476.15
GPM payments*: Rate of graduation = 7.5%			
Year			
1	303.94	333.50	364.13
2	326.74	358.51	391.44
3	351.25	385.40	420.80
4	377.58	414.31	452.36
5	405.90	445.38	486.29
6–30.............................	436.35	478.78	522.76
Rate of graduation = 5%			
Year			
1	333.55	365.29	398.07
2	350.23	383.56	417.97
3	367.74	402.74	438.87
4	386.13	422.87	460.81
5	405.44	444.02	483.85
6–30.............................	425.71	466.22	508.05

* Computed based on formula in appendix to this Chapter.

payments level off for the remaining 25 years. It should be pointed out that the computation of *initial* payments on a mortgage of this kind is a complex undertaking. The formula for determining *initial* payment levels is provided in the appendix to this chapter.

Looking at the information contained in Exhibit 9–3, we can see that for a standard mortgage loan of $50,000 originated at 10 percent for 30 years, the required constant monthly payments would be $438.75. A *GPM* loan made for the same amount and interest rate where the monthly payments are increased (graduated) at the end of each year at a predetermined rate of 7.5 percent begins with an initial payment of approximately $333.50. This initial payment will then increase by 7.5 percent per year, as shown in the exhibit, to an amount equal to $478.78 at the beginning of the sixth year and will remain constant from that point on. When compared to the standard mortgage payments, shown in Exhibit 9–3, *GPM* payments are initially lower by about $105 in the first year. This difference becomes smaller over time. The graduated payment level reaches approximately the same payment under the standard mortgage after about five years from origination (see Exhibit 9–3) and then *exceeds* the standard payment level by about $40 ($478.78 − $438.75) beginning in year 6. *GPM* payments remain at $478.78 level for the remaining 25 years of the loan term. *GPM* payments for mortgage loans with 5 percent rates of graduation can also be seen in Exhibit 9–3.

A graph comparing the payment patterns for a *GPM* and the standard mortgage is provided in Exhibit 9–4. These payments are based on the 7.5

EXHIBIT 9–4
Comparison of mortgage payment patterns (mortgage terms, 10 percent, 30 years, $50,000; *GPM* graduation rate, 7.5 percent for 5 years)

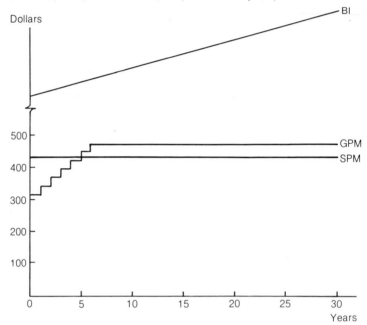

percent *GPM* plan and a standard mortgage, where both loans are originated for $50,000 at 10 percent interest for 30 years. Note that the *GPM* payment pattern is below that of the standard level payment mortgage (SPM) for approximately five years at which point the *GPM* payments begin to exceed (*SPM*) payments. The reason for this pattern should be obvious. Under either payment plan, the yield to the lender must be an annual rate of 10 percent compounded monthly (assuming no origination fees, etc.). Therefore, because the *GPM* payments are *below* that of the standard mortgage in the early years, *GPM* payments must eventually *exceed* the level payments on the standard mortgage loan to "make up" for the lower payments on the *GPM* in the early years. Hence, if the borrower chooses the *GPM* in our example, the payments will exceed those of a standard mortgage from years 6–30.

The advantages of the *GPM* program are very obvious from the borrower's standpoint. The initial payment level under either *GPM* plan shown in Exhibit 9–4 is significantly lower than is the case with the standard mortgage loan. Further, *GPM* payments correspond more closely to increases in borrower's income (see *BI* Exhibit 9–4). Hence the burden of the tilt effect requiring borrowers to allocate more current real dollars for mortgage payments from current real income in an inflationary environment is somewhat reduced, although not completely. Based on this analysis, it is easy to conclude that the *GPM* significantly reduces monthly payments for borrowers in the early years of the mortgage loan, corresponds more closely to increases in borrower income, and therefore increases the demand for mortgage credit.

   Outstanding loan balances—*GPM*.   Because the initial loan payments under all *GPM* plans are lower than payments under the standard mortgage plan, the outstanding loan balance under the *GPM* will increase during the initial years of the loan. It will remain higher than that of the standard mortgage until full repayment occurs at maturity. A comparison of loan balances for a *GPM* and a standard mortgage, based on the 10 percent, $50,000, 30-year terms used in our previous example are shown in Exhibit 9–5.

EXHIBIT 9–5
Comparison of loan balances—*GPM* and standard mortgage

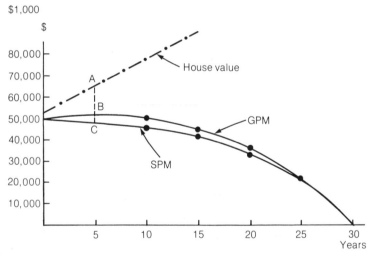

Based on Exhibit 9–5, we can see that the mortgage balance with the *GPM* increases until approximately year 4. It then begins to decline until it reaches zero in the 30th year. Hence, if a borrower sold this property during the first four years after making a *GPM* loan, *more* would be owed than originally borrowed. The reason why the loan balance increases during the first four years after origination is because the initial *GPM* payments are lower than the monthly interest requirements at 10 percent. Therefore, no amortization of principal occurs until payments increase in later periods. To illustrate, in our previous example, the interest requirements under a *GPM* after the first month of origination would be $50,000 × (.10 ÷ 12), or $416.67. The *GPM* payments during the first year of the loan are set at only $333.50, which are less than the monthly interest requirement of $416.67. The difference, or $83.17, must be *added* to the initial loan balance of $50,000 as if that difference represented an additional amount borrowed *each month*. This $83.17 monthly difference is referred to as "negative loan amortization" and must also accumulate interest at the rate of 10 percent compounded monthly. Hence, during the first year, $83.17 *per month* must be added to the $50,000 loan balance *plus accumulated interest*. This amounts to compounding a monthly annuity of $83.17 at 10 percent per month and adding that result to the initial loan balance to determine the balance at year-end. The procedure for determining the loan balance on a *GPM* is shown in Exhibit 9–6. Note that

EXHIBIT 9–6
Determining loan balance on a *GPM*

Year	Beginning balance	Required interest	GPM payment	Loan amortization	Increase in balance	Ending balance
1............	$50,000	$416.67	$333.50	$(83.17)	$1,045	$51,045
2............	51,045	425.38	358.51	(66.87)	840	51,885
3............	51,885	432.38	385.40	(46.98)	590	52,475
4............	52,475	437.29	414.31	(22.98)	289	52,768*
5............	52,768	439.70	445.38	5.68	—	52,688†

* Maximum balance.
† Present value of constant $478.78 monthly payments at 10 percent, compounded monthly for 25 years.

required interest in each period is computed based on the beginning loan balance and subtracted from the scheduled *GPM* payment. When negative amortization is indicated, each difference per period is then multiplied by the interest factor (*MIFCV*, 10%, 12 mos.), or 12.56558, to determine the total addition to the loan balance for the year. In our particular example, we note that the loan balance reaches a maximum at the end of the fourth year, or when negative amortization no longer occurs. At that point, a reduction in the loan balance begins, and it will eventually reach zero after 30 years.

The importance of the increasing *GPM* loan balance and negative amortization can be seen in relationship to the property value also shown in Exhibit 9–5. It should be noted that the margin of safety, or difference between property value and loan balance, is much lower when a *GPM* is compared to the standard mortgage. This makes a *GPM* loan more risky than a standard loan because more consideration must be given to the *future* market value of the real estate and *future* borrower income in the determination of granting the loan. For example, should the *GPM* borrower decide to sell a property after five years, when compared to the standard mortgage, the lender will have received relatively lower monthly payments up to that point. Hence the proceeds from sale of the property must be great enough to repay the loan balance that has *increased* relative to the original amount borrowed. In short with a *GPM*, the lender must now be more concerned about trends in real estate values because resale value will constitute a more important source of funds for loan repayment.

GPM mortgages and effective borrowing costs.   A closing note has to do with the question of effective yields and *GPMs*. In the absence of origination fees, the yield on *GPMs*, like yields on standard mortgage loans, are equal to the contract rate of interest as specified in the note. As was the case with the standard mortgage loan, this is true whether or not the loan is repaid before maturity. However, to the extent points or origination fees are charged, the effective yield will be greater than the contract rate of interest and it will increase the earlier the loan is repaid. In computing yields on *GPMs* originated with points, the same procedure should be followed as described with the standard mortgage; that is, the interest rate making the stream of *GPM* payments equal to the funds *disbursed* after deducting financing fees is the effective yield on the loan. Based on computations made by the authors in cases where origination fees are charged on *GPMs*, the effective yield is virtually identical with those computed for standard mortgage loans with the same terms and origination fees. This is true regardless of the loan amount or rate of graduation on the *GPM*.

Given the rather detailed discussion on *GPMs*, an obvious question in the mind of the reader is whether a borrower is better or worse off with a *GPM* when compared to a standard mortgage loan? Generally speaking, if a standard loan and a *GPM* are originated at the same rate of interest, with the same fees, then there will be little, if any, difference in the effective cost of each. However, because the graduated payment pattern reduces the tilt effect, the borrower is definitively better off with a *GPM* if it can be obtained at the same interest rate as the standard mortgage.

Would a *GPM* be generally available at the same interest rate as a standard mortgage? It would appear that because of the additional risk taken by the lender, in the form of an increasing loan balance due to "negative amortization" in the early years of the loan and lower cash flows received from reduced payments, the *GPM* lender may require a higher risk premium when the loan is originated. Hence a slightly higher interest rate may be required on a *GPM* relative to the standard mortgage loan. This would tend to neutralize some of the positive features of the *GPM* relative to the fixed interest rate mortgage. As to disclosure requirements to the borrower, because of the effective interest rate on a *GPM* computed using the same procedure as was discussed in the previous chapters on standard mortgage instruments, disclosure of the *APR* as part of the truth-in-lending documentation is essentially the same as described in the preceding chapters.

GPM and lender considerations.   What about the *GPM* from the lender's perspective? Does the *GPM* produce higher revenues to help the lender meet higher interest costs in savings deposits when interest rates generally increase? The answer to these questions is probably *not.* The reason why is that even though payments on a *GPM* increase, the *interest rate* remains *fixed* over time. Hence the lender is faced with the same problem of predicting inflation when interest rates on *GPM*s are determined as is the case with the standard, fixed interest rate mortgage. To the extent that lenders over- or underestimate inflation, they are in the same general position as they would be with a standard mortgage. Hence, it can be concluded that the *GPM* is really a mortgage primarily designed to help *borrowers* during periods of sharply rising interest rates. The match between loan payments and expected increases in borrower income is clearly beneficial to the borrower, or a stimulus to the demand side of the mortgage market. While lenders can expect to earn a slightly higher effective yield on *GPM*s, it is unlikely to help them meet rising interest costs on savings as interest rates increase.

Variable interest rate mortgages

These mortgage loans differ from both the standard mortgage and graduated payment mortgage in that the interest rate varies in accordance with an index agreed upon in advance by borrower and lender. Hence the term *variable rate mortgages (VRMs)*. Although these mortgages are not used as frequently as fixed rate mortgages, they are growing in importance in real estate financing.

The use of *VRMs* has come about because many lenders have grown reluctant to lend at fixed interest rates for relatively long periods of time. Because of unanticipated sharp rises in prices (inflation) and interest rates after loans are made, lenders have been looking more and more to *VRMs*. Rates on *VRMs* are tied to some market index of interest rates so that as prices and interest rates rise, income to the lender (cost to the borrower) increases automatically because the mortgage rate rises. This, in turn, provides increased revenues to pay on savings deposits and, therefore, additional funds to be loaned on new mortgages.

Variable rate mortgage loans have been permitted for some time from lending institutions regulated only by state agencies. These states include California, Ohio, and Florida to mention a few. However as of July 1, 1979, federally regulated savings and loan associations have been authorized to offer *VRMs* to borrowers. What follows is a general description of the more important requirements that lenders must adhere to if they want to offer *VRMs* to borrowers. These requirements are listed below:

1. The note must indicate that the interest rate is tied to an index and that future payments are not known at the time of origination.

2. The index used to adjust the interest rate is the Average Cost of Funds to FSLIC Insured Savings and Loan Associations in all Districts, published monthly in the *Federal Home Loan Bank Board Journal.*

3. Changes in the interest rate due to changes in the index may not be made more than once a year. However, lenders may make adjustments less frequently if they desire.

4. Adjustments (increases or decreases) in the interest rate may not exceed .5 percent per year, or 2.5 percent during the life of the loan. Adjustments cannot be made for less than .1 percent per year.

5. Adjustments which are not taken by the lender because they are too small *may* be accumulated for future *upward* adjustment. However, all downward adjustments less than .1 percent, *must* be accumulated and adjustments made in a future period.

6. The lender must notify the borrower at the same time each year whether or not an adjustment will occur. Given an *increase* in the index, the borrower has the following options:

    a. Payments will automatically increase unless the borrower notifies the lender that an *extension of the loan maturity* is preferred to the change in monthly payments.

    b. If the borrower prefers to extend the loan maturity, such an extension can never be for more than one third of the original mortgage term, provided that the monthly payment never falls below the original monthly payment.

7. All adjustments due to *decreases* in the index will be first applied to decreases in the loan maturity, limited to the original maturity period. Any subsequent adjustments due to decreases in the index will be applied toward lower monthly payments.

8. The lender must disclose to the borrower:

    a. A side-by-side "worst case" comparison with a fixed interest rate loan. The comparison must show differences in the *VRM* based on maximum payment adjustments for a period of six years and a total payment comparison over the life of both types of loans.

    b. The lender may elect to disclose a "best case" comparison based on maximum reductions possible on a *VRM;* however, such disclosure must be accompanied by a historical comparison showing actual adjustments based on the previous ten-year movement in the national index.

9. The lender must give the borrower the option to elect a standard, fixed rate mortgage.

10. The borrower has the right to prepay the mortgage, either in full or part, within 90 days after any increase in the interest rate, without penalty.

11. In addition to these requirements, truth-in-lending requirements provide that in addition to the *APR,* which is computed in the same manner as done on a fixed rate mortgage, the lender must disclose to the borrower what the payments on a *VRM* would be assuming a .25 percent increase in the interest rate, immediately after closing.

VRM loan mechanics. To illustrate the payment and yield characteristics of variable rate mortgages, we assume a borrower desires to purchase a property and finances it with a $40,000 variable rate mortgage loan at 8 percent interest for 25 years. The lender and borrower agree that the interest rate will be tied to the national cost of funds index and can be adjusted at the end of each year, either up or down as the index warrants. They further agree that in no event can the interest rate on the mortgage be increased by more than a total 2.5 percent from the original 8 percent rate. Generally, there will be no discount points or prepayment penalties associated with a variable rate mortgage, as there is little need for the lender to charge additional fees in light of the fact that the *VRM* will usually provide a current, competitive yield on the loan investment.[5]

To demonstrate what happens when the variable rate changes, we assume that the market index changes and the new variable rate at the end of the first year increases to 8.5 percent. What possibilities face the borrower at this point? The *VRM* agreement contains either one or both of the following options: (1) to increase the monthly mortgage payment or (2) to keep the mortgage payment constant and extend the maturity on the loan.

Increased payment option–VRMs. Looking to Exhibit 9–7, the procedure for determining new monthly loan payments is illustrated.

EXHIBIT 9–7
Determining new monthly payments on a variable interest rate mortgage loan

Option 1—increased monthly payments:
  Original mortgage, $40,000
  Interest rate, 8%
  Terms, 25 years
  Monthly payment: $40,000 × (loan constant, 8%, 25 yrs.)
                             = $40,000 × (.007718) = $308.72
  Change in *VRM* rate from 8% to 8.5% end of year 1
  a. Determine—loan balance end of year 1
    Loan bal. factor, 8%, 25-yr. loan, end of 1 yr. × loan = Mortgage balance
                   .9869 × $40,000 = $39,476
  b. Determine—new monthly payments—end of year 1
    Loan balance end of year 1 × (loan constant, 8.5%, 24 yrs.) = New monthly payment
               $39,476 × (.008151) = $321.77

---

[5] However, other loan origination fees representing fixed costs of origination by lenders may still be charged.

The first step requires the determination of the loan balance based on the original mortgage terms of 8 percent for 25 years after the first year when the adjustment occurs. Then the new monthly payment can be computed by finding the new loan constant corresponding to an 8.5 percent mortgage loan for 24 years, or .008151. When multiplied by the loan balance of $39,476, the new monthly payment of $321.77 is determined. This payment is $13.05 per month higher than the original payment of $308.72. The $321.77 will be paid monthly for 24 years or until the next adjustment occurs. If an adjustment is necessary at the end of the second year, the new monthly payments will be based on the loan balance at that time. That balance will be the balance after one year on a $39,476 loan at 8.5 percent interest made for 24 years. These were the relevant terms in force at the end of year 1. The new loan constant, based on the new variable rate, will be applied to that balance to compute the new monthly payment. This process will be repeated each time an adjustment in the interest rate is required until the loan is repaid.

Increased maturity option—VRMs.   Should the borrower choose the option to extend the loan maturity while keeping the monthly loan payment constant, the procedure for determining the new maturity period can be seen in Exhibit 9–8.

EXHIBIT 9–8
Determining the new maturity on a variable interest rate
mortgage loan

a. Loan balance end of year 1 (from Exhibit 9–7) $39,476
b. Original monthly payment (to be kept constant) $308.72
c. Determine new loan constant necessary to provide an 8.5% loan
    yield:

$$\frac{\$308.72}{\$39,476} = \underline{.00782}$$

d. Number of years and months corresponding to a loan yield of
    8.5% *and* a loan constant of .00782 (from column 6, Appendix
    B, 8.5% tables):

    Approximately 28 years

Since the borrower has the option to keep the $308.72 monthly payment the same while the mortgage rate has increased to 8.5 percent, it is clear that a greater number of monthly payments will be required for the lender to earn the increased yield. By dividing the loan balance at the end of the first year, $39,476, by the desired $308.72 constant monthly payments as shown in Exhibit 9–8, a new loan constant, .00782, is derived. The significance of this new loan constant is that since the new mortgage yield must be 8.5 percent and the payment remains at $308.72, the new term of the loan can be found by using the loan constant.

The new maturity period can be ascertained by looking to the 8.5 percent table in the Appendix B, locating column 6, and looking down the column until the loan constant closest to .00782 is found. The new maturity of the loan can then be determined by following the row in which the loan constant appears over to the column denoting years. Note that the loan constant closest to .00782 is the .007812 constant corresponding to 28 years. The new loan maturity will be slightly less than 28 years from the beginning of the second year.[6] Consequently, the borrower will pay $308.72 for approximately four additional years, from year 24 through year 28, if the variable rate increases to 8.5 percent. Note that in this example the four-year increase in maturity represents a 16.7 percent (4 ÷ 24) increase in the mortgage maturity, which is less than one-third of the original term of the mortgage; therefore the maturity extension option would be permissible under VRM regulations. Also, it should be pointed out that the relevant term for any future adjustments would be based on the new 28-year loan maturity and 8.5 percent interest. Hence, if the loan were to be repaid after one additional year, the relevant loan balance at that time would be computed for a 28-year loan at 8.5 percent interest, with 27 years remaining until maturity.

Disclosure requirements. As indicated in the list summary of regulations governing the use of VRMs listed above, the lender must provide the borrower with a "side-by-side" comparison of the worst case possible under a VRM and a standard fixed interest rate mortgage. The worst possible case for any VRM loan would be a series of .5 percent consecutive annual increases in the interest rate on the VRM until the rate reaches the maximum of 2.5 percent after five years, per the regulations, with all adjustments made assuming the increased monthly payment option. Such a comparison is provided in Exhibit 9–9.

Before discussing the comparison in Exhibit 9–9, some explanation of the loan balance column is necessary. The beginning balance in each year is determined by finding the present value of the remaining VRM payments at the end of the preceding year, at the VRM rate prevailing at that time, for the remaining term of the mortgage loan. For example, the loan balance at the beginning of year 4 is the present value of the remaining monthly payments at the end of year 3, discounted at the VRM rate prevailing in year 3, or 9.0 percent. The remaining number of years at the end of the third year would be 22 years. Hence the $38,420 balance is the product of $334.71 × (*MIFPVa*, 9%, 22 yrs.) or $334.71 × (114.787589) = $38,420.

Looking to the payment patterns described in Exhibit 9–9 it should be noted that the fixed interest rate chosen for comparison was 9 percent while the VRM rate was 8 percent. The reason for this difference is that the risk of future

---

[6] A more exact solution can be gained by interpolating, or with a more detailed set of mortgage tables. The new loan maturity is about 27 years and 11 months in this case.

EXHIBIT 9–9
Worst case comparison *VRM* versus fixed rate mortgage loan amount $40,000, 25 years; Original *VRM* rate = 8.0%; Original fixed rate = 9.0%

Beginning of year	VRM balance	Interest rate	Loan constant	VRM payment	Fixed rate (9%) mortgage payment
1	$40,000	8.0%	.007718	$308.72	$335.64
2	39,476	8.5	.008151	321.77	335.64
3	38,951	9.0	.008593	334.71	335.64
4	38,420	9.5	.009045	347.51	335.64
5	37,877	10.0	.009508	360.13	335.64
6	37,318*	10.5	.009983	372.55	335.64
.	.	.	—	.	.
.	.	.	—	.	.
.			—	.	
25	4,226	10.5	—	372.55	335.64

* Based on $372.55(*MIFPVa*, 10.5%, 20 yrs.) or $372.55 × (100.16910).

interest rate changes must be borne by the *borrower* with a *VRM*. With a fixed interest mortgage, the *lender* bears this risk. Hence, during periods when inflationary expectations persist, the risk of upward interest rate adjustments increase with the *VRM*. Because the lender no longer bears this risk, to induce a borrower to accept a *VRM*, it would have to be offered at a lower interest rate. Otherwise, the borrower would have no incentive to borrow at variable rates and would always choose the fixed rate mortgage. How much lower the initial interest rate on a *VRM* would be compared to the fixed rate alternative would depend on inflationary expectations at the time of origination and what inflation is expected to be while the loan is outstanding. In our example, we chose a 1 percent difference; however, depending on inflationary expectations that difference could actually be greater or less than 1 percent. In fact, in rare circumstances if inflation is expected to *decrease* sharply, the fixed interest rate could be lower than the rate offered on a *VRM*.

How would one go about evaluating a *VRM* in relation to a standard fixed interest rate, fixed payment mortgage? First of all, it should be stressed that the side-by-side comparison shown in Exhibit 9–9 is based on the worst possible case allowed under regulations governing *VRM*s. Hence, its effective cost represents the maximum that a borrower would pay should the *VRM* be selected. One question that could be answered, then, is after maximum adjustments does the *VRM* carry a higher effective interest cost than the 9 percent interest rate charged under the standard mortgage.[7] How do we determine the maximum effective cost of the *VRM*? This analysis is carried out in Exhibit 9–10.

---

[7] To the extent that the standard mortgage includes discount points and higher origination fees, the *APR* should be calculated and compared to the effective cost of the *VRM*.

EXHIBIT 9–10
Maximum effective interest cost—*VRM*

Year	VRM payment	MIFPVa, 8 percent	PV	MIFPVa, 10.5 percent	PV
1	$308.72	11.496	$ 3,549	11.344	$ 3,502
2	321.77	22.111–11.496	3,416	21.563–11.344	3,288
3	334.71	31.912–22.111	3,280	30.767–21.563	3,081
4	347.51	40.962–31.912	3,145	39.057–30.767	2,881
5	360.13	49.318–40.962	3,009	46.525–39.057	2,704
6–25	372.55	129.565–49.318	29,896	105.912–46.525	22,125
			$46,295		$37,581

In reviewing Exhibit 9–10, it should be noted that the interest rates chosen to discount the *VRM* monthly payments were 8 percent and 10.5 percent, which correspond to the original interest rate and maximum rate that would be allowed by regulation in the worst case example. Given the assumption that there are no origination fees, the effective rate in the *VRM* cannot be below 8 percent nor can it exceed 10.5 percent. Hence, we know it is between those two interest rates. The question is does it exceed the 9 percent rate available on the fixed rate mortgage? The reader should also note in Exhibit 9–10 that discounting of the monthly cash flows is done using the "netting out" procedure detailed in Chapter 7. This is necessary because although *VRM* payments change each year, they remain at a given level for 12 months between changes. We are dealing with a set of six separate annuities which must be discounted during the period in which they occur. Hence, we use the "netting" procedure described earlier in Chapter 7.

Based on the discounting procedure shown in Exhibit 9–10, we see that the present value of all cash payments discounted at 8 percent equals $46,295 and its payments discounted at 10.5 percent equals $37,581. The desired present value, or $40,000, falls between those two values. Interpolating we have:

PV at 8%	$46,295	PV at 8%	$46,295
PV at 10.5%	37,581	Desired PV	40,000
Difference	$ 8,714	Difference	$ 6,295

$$(\$6,295 \div 8,714) \times 2.5\% = 1.81\%$$
$$\text{add } 8\% + 1.81\% = 9.81\%$$

Hence, under the worst case assumption used in our example, the effective yield on the *VRM* would be about 9.81 percent which is greater than the 9 percent available on the fixed rate mortgage.

Is the *VRM* necessarily a bad choice? It should be stressed that in the above analysis the worst case for the *VRM* was analyzed relative to the fixed rate mortgage. This does *not* mean that the worst case will *in fact* happen. To the extent that the *actual* adjustments on a *VRM* are less than the worst possible case, its effective yield would be less. Also, the comparison that we made here is based on the assumption that the fixed rate mortgage would be made at 9 percent. If the fixed rate mortgage were offered at a rate higher than 9 percent, then the *VRM* alternative would be more attractive. Further, although we do not consider it here, the period during which the loan is expected to be outstanding will also affect the comparison.

What have actual adjustments in *VRMs* been in recent times? Based on the National Average Cost of Funds reported by all savings and loan associations in the United States, *VRM* adjustments have been compiled in Exhibit 9–11. Based on a *hypothetical* 8 percent *VRM* originated in 1973, we can trace the annual adjustments made in the interest rate based on the index of the average cost of funds by savings associations during that period. The index represents the annual change in savings cost which is multiplied by the *VRM* rate to get the adjusted *VRM* rate. However, because of restrictions allowing a maximum adjustment of .5 percent per year and a minimum adjustment of .1 percent, an overage column is used to accumulate amounts not used in adjustments and carried forward. From the data compiled in Exhibit 9–11 it would appear that

EXHIBIT 9–11
Estimates of *VRM* adjustments 1973–1980

Year	Cost of funds*	Index	Adjustment VRM	Maximum allowed	Overage
1973	5.60%	—	—	8.00	—
1974	6.14	1.10	8.80	8.50	.30
1975	6.32	1.03	9.06	9.00	.06
1976	6.38	1.01	9.15	9.21	—
1977	6.44	1.01	9.24	9.21	.03
1978	6.67	1.04	9.61	9.64	—
1979	7.23†	1.08	10.37	10.14	.23

* *Federal Home Loan Bank Board Journal,* January 1980.
† Through June 1979.

for any *VRM* originated in 1973, the maximum increase of 2.5 percent would have been almost reached by the end of 1979. Note that based on the estimate for the first half of 1979, the *VRM* interest rate would have reached 10.37 percent in our example, or almost the full 2.5 percent allowed. Hence, since 1973 at least, the worst case assumption may have been a reasonable estimate of future adjustments.

What does this mean for the borrower? Assuming that he faced an initial *VRM* rate of 8 percent in 1973, then based on the computation shown in Exhibit 9–10, he would have been as well off borrowing with a fixed interest rate mortgage at any rate up to approximately 9.86 percent, as previously computed in our worst case example. In other words, a loan originated in 1973, a *VRM* made at 8 percent or a fixed interest rate mortgage at 9.81 percent would have been roughly equivalent in terms of effective interest cost by the end of 1979.

While there is no assurance that this pattern is likely to repeat in the future, based on the above discussion of *VRMs* and fixed interest rate alternatives, the framework for analysis is set forth. *The borrower must make his best estimate of interest rate adjustments for the VRM based on inflationary expectations and compute the effective yield. The expected yield on the VRM should always be compared to whatever interest rate is offered on the fixed rate alternative, and a selection can then be made.*

The renegotiable rate mortgage

In addition to the *GPM* and *VRM*, a third alternative mortgage instrument is now available for use by lenders and borrowers. The proposed new instrument is called a *renegotiable rate mortgage (RRM)*. It is also known as a rollover mortgage. The rollover mortgage has been used for many years in Canada and is similar to the *VRM* in many respects. However, it contains several important features which differentiate it from the *VRM*.

Essentially, the rollover mortgage is a renegotiable loan secured by a mortgage. The amortization period of the loan, which determines the monthly payment, would generally be up to 30 years. However, the *term* of the loan would range from three to five years. Upon maturity of the note, the loan would become renegotiable; however, the mortgage terms would not. Interest rate determination at the time of renegotiation would be based on the current interest rate on existing homes being financed conventionally. As to the amortization period in the rollover, it too can be renegotiated, but can never exceed the initial 30-year amortization period. However, unlike the *VRM*, payments on the *RRM* are adjustable only after each renewal period.

Other important characteristics of the *RRM* are listed below:

1. No loan fees, points, or processing costs may be collected by the lender.
2. Regardless of the movement in the national index, the maximum increase in interest rates on a renegotiated loan is .5 percent per year. Interest rates cannot increase or decrease by more than 5 percent during the life of the loan.
3. Contrary to the *VRM*, any interest rate increases not allowed because of the maximum annual restriction of .5 percent *cannot* be accumulated and applied to future periods.
4. The lender *must* renew the mortgage loan at the time of renegotiation regardless of the mortgagor's past monthly payment record. There can be no prepayment penalty assessed at the time of renewal.

Unlike the *VRM,* the lender offering a rollover mortgage would not be required to offer the borrower a choice between an alternative fixed interest rate mortgage and a rollover mortgage. However, as part of disclosure requirements, the lender must disclose to the borrower a worst case comparison with the fixed interest rate mortgage during the first renewal period and indicate how the rollover mortgage is different. Finally, the regulations allow the borrower an option to prepay the rollover mortgage loan at periods *other* than renegotiation periods without penalty, after the first renewal period. For example, if a three-year rollover mortgage was originated and the borrower wanted to prepay the loan after two years or before the next renegotiation period, the lender could charge a prepayment penalty. Any prepayment beyond the first renewal (after three years) would be permissible with no penalty.

Lender and borrower considerations.   Based on regulations proposed for the rollover mortgage and the elements which differentiate it from fixed interest rate mortgages, *GPM*s and *VRM*s, both the borrower and lender are faced with a number of considerations when weighing the advantages and disadvantages of the rollover relative to other mortgage types. Although it is not exactly like a *VRM,* the rollover mortgage would more than likely be originated at interest rates below rates available on fixed interest rate mortgages and *GPM*s, and at an interest rate very close to that offered on a *VRM.* The reason for this pattern is that like the *VRM,* a borrower using the rollover mortgage will have to *bear the risk* of future changes in interest rates. Hence the initial rate available to a borrower using the rollover should be less than that on the standard fixed rate mortgage and the *GPM.*[8] However, because the adjustments to the interest rates are limited to .5 percent per year and increased payments are not *collected* by the lender until the renegotiation period occurs (from three to five years after origination), it may not be as attractive to the lender as a *VRM.* This could be true in spite of the fact that the maximum total increase in the interest rate on a rollover is proposed to be 5 percent while the maximum interest rate increase on *VRM*s is restricted to 2.5 percent. Assuming maximum increases occurred in each case, the *VRM* loan would be earning the lender the full 2.5 percent increase at the end of five years; however, the lender would also realize the .5 percent increase during each year until the maximum was reached. With a 3-year rollover, no increase would be realized until the end of the third year, and the maximum increase would not occur until 13 years after origination. Hence the cash outflow to the lender would occur sooner with a *VRM* when contrasted with the rollover, and even though the *VRM* has a lower maximum allowable interest rate, the opportunity to reinvest cash flows from the *VRM* could make it more attractive to the lender than a rollover type loan.

---

[8] Unless, of course, interest rates are generally expected to *fall* very sharply. In this event, it is possible that both the *VRM* and rollover could be originated at interest rates above those of the fixed rate and graduated payment mortgages.

Other considerations regarding the rollover loan that are favorable to the lender are: like the *VRM*, the risk of future interest rate changes are shifted to the borrower, hence the lender will not be as concerned about lending for relatively long periods of time and the loss of purchasing power as has historically been the case with the fixed interest rate mortgage. Also with a rollover loan the lender may earn more income with which to pay higher interest rates on savings deposits. Further, the lender may be able to match savings funds with mortgage loans that it makes by offering an attractive interest rate to savers willing to commit savings funds for three- to five-year periods. In this way lenders may be better able to match their sources (deposits) and uses (loans) of funds more efficiently, thereby making for more stability in the mortgage market (this aspect of the problem will be discussed in more detail in Chapter 18).

Reverse annuity mortgages

The final category of mortgage to be discussed in this chapter is the reverse annuity mortgage (*RAM*). This form of mortgage lending is presently authorized by regulation and is totally different from the other alternative mortgage instruments discussed in this chapter. It is intended for households who have owned houses for some time and have accumulated a considerable amount of equity because of (1) repayment of mortgages made during earlier years and (2) appreciation in the value of the dwelling over time. These households, because of their age and because they may not want to sell their houses, may prefer to borrow against the equity accumulated in their houses and use the proceeds from the loan to supplement retirement income. The amount borrowed is eventually repaid from proceeds as houses are eventually sold, or from the borrower's estate in the event of death.

To illustrate how a reverse mortgage, or *RAM*, could be used, consider a household with a house presently appraised at $100,000 which is free and clear of any debt. The head of the household is age 65 and wants to continue to occupy the dwelling for the foreseeable future. This household would like to utilize the $100,000 equity accumulated in the house by borrowing, thereby receiving a series of payments to supplement its retirement income. To illustrate, if a lender was willing to make a *RAM* for $50,000 on the $100,000 property at 12 percent for the household's remaining life expectancy of, say, ten years, a series of monthly payments could be determined which would result in a *total debt* of $50,000 *after ten years*. That monthly income would be found by dividing the loan amount by the appropriate sinking-fund factor as follows:

$$\text{Monthly annuity} = \$50,000(\textit{MSFF}, 12\% \text{ 10 yrs.})$$
$$\$217.35 = \$50,000(.004347)$$

Hence, if a lender was willing to made such a loan, the sum of $217.35 would be disbursed to the borrower each month for ten years, resulting in a total outstanding loan balance, including interest compounded monthly at 12 percent, of $50,000 at the end of ten years. Should the borrower sell the property at that time or should he die, the loan balance would be paid at that time. Should neither occur, the borrower would begin making monthly loan payments on the $50,000 loan balance.

The essential point here is that under this plan, the loan amount is being borrowed by the mortgagor in monthly installments, not as a lump sum when the loan is originated, hence the term *reverse annuity*. However, because of this reverse process, there are some complications that enter into the analysis. First, the lender may not be willing to extend a loan based on a high percentage of market value, or for relatively long maturities. This is because the property may be an older one; hence the probability of further price appreciation on the house could be lower than would be the case with a newer property. Further, because the *RAM* loan balance increases over time, the lender will not be willing to extend large loan amounts for long periods of time. This assures the lender that the property value will always exceed the loan balance which is increasing.

A second complication arises with the *RAM* in that the interest portion of the installments received by the borrower would not be deductible for income tax purposes each year. Based on present Internal Revenue Service regulations, interest would be deductible by the borrower in the year that the interest is actually repaid, or after ten years in our example. At that time a total of $50,000 would be due, of which $23,918 would be interest.[9] Because of this limitation, the *RAM* is not attractive from the standpoint of federal income tax treatment, as the homeowner's ability to use such a large deduction against income earned in one year is very unlikely.

A second *RAM* plan has been proposed which may have more potential for borrowers, than the one previously described. This plan involves borrowing against the accumulated equity in real estate whereby the borrower takes the full amount down at closing rather than borrowing in installments. The amount borrowed at closing would be used to purchase an investment annuity from a life insurance company. The investment annuity would provide the homeowner with a monthly income with which the homeowner would make interest-only payments on the *RAM*, keeping the remainder to supplement retirement income. For example, in the previous case, $50,000 was borrowed against an appraised value of $100,000 at 12 percent interest for ten years. Under this modified *RAM* plan, the borrower would obtain $50,000 at closing and be required to pay interest only or (12% ÷ 12) = 1% per month, or $500 per month for ten years, plus full repayment of $50,000 at that time.

---

[9] At that time a total of $26,082 or $217.35 × 120 months will have been paid to the borrower. Hence the amount repaid or $50,000 less the amount paid out by the lender or $26,082 leaves $23,918 as interest.

Obviously, the only way that the borrower would be any "better off" under such an arrangement would be if a return on the $50,000 in excess of 12 percent compounded monthly could be earned with an investment annuity. To the extent that the borrower earns in excess of 12 percent on the investment annuity in this case, that excess would represent the monthly increment to retirement income.

However as in the previous example, there exists a question of whether the interest paid on the mortgage loan would be deductible in each year. This problem arises from an IRS regulation which restricts the use of a loan to purchase a single premium annuity, such as the purchase of the investment annuity of $50,000 in our previous example. It carries out this restriction by disallowing interest deductions on the mortgage loan made to purchase the investment annuity. Further, the income from the investment annuity is taxable to the borrower as ordinary income. Hence, unless the interest on the *RAM* loan were allowed as a deduction against the income from the investment annuity, this approach would leave much to be desired.

RAM—other considerations.   The problems cited above notwithstanding, there are other problems with the *RAM* that make its immediate use doubtful.

1. A mechanism for making the *RAM* lender a beneficiary in the borrower's estate would have to become well established in law and practice to reduce the time required for *RAM* lender's interest to be satisfied from the borrower's estate in the event of death.
2. In light of (1), many lenders would require that term life insurance be carried by the borrower to pay the mortgage balance in the event of death before the *RAM* is paid off. This would tend to increase the cost of the *RAM* relative to other investment possibilities.
3. Many questions regarding the tax treatment of interest on *RAMs* would have to be clarified before significant numbers of borrowers would be interested in these loans.
4. The lender would most likely be required to recognize income from the *RAM* based on an accrual method accounting. Under the first category of *RAM* described above, this would require the lender to take the interest portion of each installment payment on the *RAM* into current income for tax purposes. This would be true even though the lender has not realized any cash income from the *RAM*.
5. Finally, in the current inflationary environment, lenders are concerned with structuring loans such that repayments by borrowers keep in line with inflationary pressures. The first type of *RAM* discussed above defers the receipt of cash far into the future, hence making it even more difficult for lenders to accomplish that goal. Payments under the second type of *RAM* would have to be indexed in a manner similar to the *VRM* or rollover mortgage in order to make it an attractive alternative to those types of mortgages.

Other alternative mortgage instruments

In addition to the alternative mortgage instruments just described, there are a number of other mortgage instruments presently being used where state and/ or federal regulations permit. One such instrument called the flexible payment mortgage (FPM), has been authorized for use by federally chartered savings and loan associations for some time. This mortgage is essentially an interest-only loan, where the borrower pays interest only each month on the principal borrowed for a period of five years. At the end of that time, amortization of principal begins. Because of the interest-only requirement, monthly payments during the first five years are lower than would be the case with a standard mortgage loan, thereby reducing to a slight degree the tilt problem discussed at the beginning of the chapter. This mortgage has not met with resounding success because of the very small reduction in monthly payments. As the reader is aware, the greatest portion of monthly payments in the early years of a mortgage is made up of interest, with a very minor portion going to reduction of principal (see Exhibit 7–3); hence, by not requiring amortization during the first five years of the loan, the reduction in payments is relatively small and unimportant to the potential home buyer. Also, the *FPM* is originated at a fixed interest rate which does not change over the life of the loan. Hence, from the lender's viewpoint, this mortgage is not as attractive as a *VRM* or *RRM*.

A second mortgage plan used in some states is referred to as a deferred interest mortgage (*DIM*). Essentially, payments are structured in relation to the borrower's income to meet the underwriting standards of the lender. If the monthly payments set by these standards are below monthly interest requirements, negative amortization occurs (see discussion under *GPM*), and the loan balance increases with time. The loan balance will be allowed to increase for a specified time, at which point a new amortization schedule will take effect and payments are adjusted to fully amortize the loan. Alternatively, if the property is sold, the outstanding loan balance would be met from proceeds from the sale. Another variation under this mortgage plan requires that a portion of the down payment made at closing be placed in an interest-bearing deposit account with a portion of the interest earned used to meet any monthly shortfall between payments and interest requirements.[10] The deposit balance with any remaining interest is eventually applied to principal at some point in the future (usually five years) at which time the new amortization schedule takes effect, which will fully amortize the loan over a specific term. This mortgage has met with some success because, like the *GPM*, payments are structured to rise with the income of the borrowers; hence, much of the tilt problem is reduced. However, like the *GPM*, these mortgages are usually originated at a fixed rate of interest and therefore do not help solve problems faced by lenders in an inflationary environment.

---

[10] This variation is sometime referred to as a "flip" mortgage.

The final type of mortgage presently in use on a limited basis is the "shared appreciation" mortgage. Essentially, under this plan, an agreement is reached between a lender which provides that the lender will contribute a significant portion of the required down payment on a property (usually 50 percent) and make a loan at a below market interest rate in exchange for a percentage participation (from 25 to 75 percent) in any amounts in excess of the loan balance, realized when the property is sold. This plan obviously aids first-time home buyers meet down payment requirements and monthly payments. However, the required participation in any appreciation is a significant disincentive to homeowners who purchase properties with an investment motive. Hence, it is difficult to predict how successful this relatively new plan will be.

Other proposed plans

Many additional proposals have been made to deal with mortgage problems faced by borrowers and lenders.[11] One such plan is referred to as the price level adjusted mortage (*PLAM*). This proposal is designed with the express purpose of completely removing the tilt effect problem from the standard mortgage instrument. Under this plan, the outstanding mortgage balance would be indexed to the price level. The contract rate of interest used to compute monthly payments and to amortize the loan would not require a premium (i_f) for inflation in the contract interest rate. In essence, the initial interest rate charged by lenders would be equivalent to the real interest rate plus a premium for default risk. The outstanding loan balance would increase or decrease with the price level and hence would always be valued at current prices. Monthly payments would rise and fall as computed based on the loan constant corresponding to the fixed contract rate of interest and term of the loan as applied to the variable loan balance.

The *PLAM* has much to commend it from both the borrower and lender perspective. The major problem with this plan, however, is that the initial monthly payments on a loan could be extremely low, and the loan balance could increase very rapidly in periods of inflation. For example, if a 12 percent mortgage was negotiated in a period when expected inflation was 10 percent, the contract rate used to compute initial mortgage payments over a specific term would be 2 percent. However, the loan balance would have to be increased 10 percent per period. The 2 percent interest rate would still be used to determine mortgage payments, and while those payments would increase as the loan balance increased with the price index, any reduction in the outstanding balance would be very small in the early years. Ulti-

---

[11] For an excellent discussion of many of these proposals, see *New Mortgage Designs for Stable Housing in an Inflationary Environment* (Boston: Federal Reserve Bank of Boston, 1975); and *Ways to Moderate Fluctuations in Housing Construction* (Washington, D.C.: Board of Governors of the Federal Reserve System, 1972).

mately, with continued inflation, the borrower would be faced with very large mortgage payments on a very large outstanding balance in the future. Lenders would undoubtedly be faced with greater uncertainty in predicting whether both borrower income and future property values would be high enough to support such a payment and loan balance pattern. For this reason, the likelihood of adopting the *PLAM* would appear remote.

Given the problems outlined with *PLAM*, other variations have been suggested. One representative alternative is the dual-rate variable rate mortgage. Under this plan two interest rates would be used, a short-term interest rate to adjust, or debit, the outstanding loan balance as price levels change, and a long-term interest rate to compute monthly payments over the amortization period. This pattern would be similar to the *PLAM* in the sense that the outstanding loan balance would be adjusted with changes in current economic conditions. However, the long-term rate chosen to compute monthly payments over a specific term would be lower than rates available on standard fixed interest rate mortgages, and would be either fixed or restricted in terms of maximum increases or decreases. By using a long-term rate to compute monthly payments, such payments would not rise as rapidly and would be somewhat more predictable for both lenders and borrowers than would be the case with a *PLAM*; however, payments in the early years would be lower than payments required under a standard mortgage instrument, thereby removing some of the tilt problem. From the lender's perspective, because the loan balance adjusts to economic conditions and payments also adjust, although more slowly than with a *PLAM*, more revenue would be available to meet rising costs on savings deposits during inflationary times.

Adjustable rate mortgages—international experience

The problems posed by inflation and the standard fixed interest rate–level payment mortgage are not unique to the U.S. economy. Indeed, many countries have adopted mortgage instruments similar to those presently in use or proposed for use in the United States. Canada, for example, has successfully used a rollover mortgage loan similar to the *RRM* discussed above for many years. A version of the variable rate mortgage (*VRM*) has been used in England since the 1930s. Although highly restricted by government regulation, these mortgages have reduced the problem of matching revenues and costs faced by lending institutions considerably and have become the mainstay of the British home finance industry. Variations of the price level adjusted mortgage (*PLAM*) have been tried in Brazil, Columbia, and Chile as well as in Finland and Israel with mixed results. In those South American countries and in Israel, all of which have been historically plagued with sharp increases in inflation, most loan agreements, bonds, and other financial instruments have indexed to the price level in order to facilitate borrowing and lending of any kind. On the other hand, these price-adjusted mortgage instruments have been phased out in

Israel, as that country has attempted to deal with the fundamental causes of inflation rather than continue to modify its financial system to accommodate price increases.

Will the trend toward these alternative instruments continue in the United States? Based on our preceding discussion, we have indicated that many alternatives to the present fixed interest rate–level payment pattern mortgage that we have grown accustomed to have already been approved by regulatory bodies and are being used. Many other proposed forms are presently being considered. The more fundamental question is will there be widespread use and acceptance of alternative mortgage instruments? The answer in large part depends on a more fundamental problem, that is, our ability to manage inflation in the U.S. economy. The alternative instruments described above are responses of lending institutions and regulatory bodies to the inadequacy of the standard mortgage instrument in an inflationary environment. If inflation is reduced, the need for these instruments will also be reduced. Indeed, some observers would argue that encouragement of the use of these instruments is implicit acknowledgment by regulatory bodies that continued inflation will persist and be tolerated. If continued inflation does persist, lenders will abandon their traditional role of bearing the risk of future price changes in current interest rates and pass this risk on to borrowers. We will address many of the strains placed on the mortgage market and housing industry by inflation in greater detail in Chapter 18.

The problem of inflation notwithstanding, other issues regarding consumer acceptance of such instruments and the ability of consumers and lenders to comprehend the rather complex mechanics associated with such mortgages will also affect the use of these instruments. In any event, this chapter has attempted to deal with the structure of many possible loan patterns that the reader may have to deal with at some point in the future. Also by exploring the relationship between inflation, interest rates, and the burdens placed on lenders and borrowers, the reader should be better equipped to examine many of the policies and reforms being offered as solutions to problems affecting the housing and mortgage finance industry.

Questions

1 What is meant by a real rate of return?

2 What is a risk premium in the context of mortgage lending?

3 When mortgage lenders establish interest rates through competition, an inflation premium is said to be part of the interest rate. What does this mean?

4 Why do monthly mortgage payments increase so sharply during periods of inflation? What does the tilt effect have to do with this?

5 As inflation increases, the impact of the tilt effect is said to become even more burdensome on borrowers. Why is this the case?

6   What is a graduated payment mortgage (*GPM*)?

7   A borrower makes a *GPM* mortgage loan. It is originated for $50,000 and carries a 10 percent rate of interest for 30 years. If the borrower decides to prepay the loan after ten years, would he be paying a higher, lower, or the same yield as the contract rate originally agreed on?

8   Would a borrower be likely to originate a *GPM* at the same *effective* interest cost as a standard mortgage loan?

9   What is meant by "negative amortization"? Why does it occur with a *GPM*? What happens to the mortgage balance of a *GPM* over time?

10 What is a variable rate mortgage (*VRM*)? How does it differ from both the standard and *GPM*? How would the *lender* view advantages and disadvantages of these three types of loans?

11 What options does the borrower have when the interest rate increases on a *VRM*?

12 What is the maximum annual increase permitted on a *VRM*? What is the minimum increase permitted? What is the accumulation feature in a *VRM*?

13 Who bears interest rate risk with a *VRM*? How should this risk affect the original interest rate negotiated with a *VRM* relative to a fixed rate mortgage?

14 How do lenders and savers benefit from the *VRM* compared to the *GPM*?

15 What is a renegotiable rate mortgage (*RRM*)? How does it work?

16 Would a *RRM* normally carry an initial interest rate higher than (1) a fixed interest rate mortgage, (2) a *GPM*, or (3) a *VRM*? Why?

17 How do *RRM*'s benefit lenders?

18 What is a reverse annuity mortgage (*RAM*)? Whom does it tend to benefit?

19 What are some of the problems with the *RAM*? Do lenders appear to benefit from *RAM*'s in an inflationary environment?

Case problems

1   Flirt Reynolds purchases a property for $80,000. He finances the purchase with a *GPM* carrying an 11 percent interest rate. The rate of graduation on the loan is 7.5 percent per year for five years and the initial payment is $509.78 per month. The initial loan amount is $70,000 for a term of 30 years. Reynolds expects to sell the property after seven years. If he can sell the property for $90,000, what will the net proceeds be from the sale?

2   Alfred Newman has made a *VRM* for $80,000 at 9 percent interest for 30 years. After two years, interest rates increase to 9.5 percent. What would the new monthly payments be for Newman? Assuming he chose to extend the maturity on the loan, what would the maturity be?

3   Ms. Doe Merrick makes a $90,000 *VRM* loan at 8.5 percent interest for 30 years. She expects the interest rate to increase at .5 percent for each of the next three years at which time she plans to sell the property. The lender offers her a 9 percent fixed interest rate mortgage as an alternative to the *VRM*. Which mortgage should she choose?

4 Mrs. Bette Middle is considering a renegotiable rate mortgage loan for $100,000 for 30 years at 9.5 percent interest. The renegotiation period will be three years at which time she expects the maximum increase in the interest rate will have to be paid. What will the payments be beginning in year 4? Assuming she could have made a fixed interest rate mortgage, what would be the maximum interest rate she could have paid on it and been as well off as with the renegotiable loan (assume a 6 year payoff period for both loans)?

5 Ronald Hegan is currently retired and owns a house appraised at $80,000 free and clear of debt. He would like to negotiate a *RAM* with his lender for 15 years at 11 percent. The lender advises that the amount borrowed cannot exceed $50,000 at the end of 15 years. What series of payments would Hegan receive during the 15 years? Assuming he sold the property after ten years, what would be the balance owed on the *RAM*?

APPENDIX: FORMULA FOR GRADUATED PAYMENT PATTERNS

The calculation of the initial loan constant for a graduated payment loan is based on a rather complex formula as shown below:

$$MLC = 1 \div (MIFPVa, i\%, 12 \text{ mos.}) (MSFF, u, T) +$$
$$\frac{(1 + g)^T (MIFPVa, i\%, N - T)}{(MIFCV, i\%, T)}$$

where:

MLC = monthly loan constant for a graduated payment loan

$MSFF$ = monthly sinking fund factor

u = sinking fund rate defined as $\dfrac{(1 + g)}{(MIFCV, i\%, 12 \text{ mos.})} - 1$

T = years that payments will be graduated

N = total term of the loan in years

g = rate of graduation in payments

i = mortgage interest rate

$MIFPVa$ = monthly interest factor, present value of an annuity (Appendix B, column 5)

$MIFCV$ = monthly interest factor, compound value of $1 (Appendix B, column 1)

To demonstrate the use of the formula, we compute the initial payment for the 30-year, 10 percent loan with a 5-year graduation period and a 7.5 percent rate of graduation shown in Exhibit 9–3. This is done as follows:

Step 1:   Compute value for u.

$$u = \frac{(1 + g)}{(MIFCV, i\%, 12 \text{ mos.})} - 1 = \frac{(1 + .075)}{(1.104713)} - 1 = -.0268966$$

The reader should take special note that the value computed for u is a *negative* or $-.0268996$.

Step 2:   Compute value for monthly sinking fund factor ($MSFF$) at a rate of u for a five-year period of graduation.

As the reader should recall, the sinking-fund factor is the reciprocal of the formula for the accumulation of 1 per period. The formula for the $MSFF$ at a rate of u is:

$$
\begin{aligned}
(MSFF, u, 5 \text{ yrs.}) &= \frac{(1 + u)^T - 1}{u} \\[2mm]
&= \frac{(1 - .0268966)^5 - 1}{-.0268966} \\[2mm]
&= \frac{.872559 - 1}{-.0268966} \\[2mm]
&= 4.738172
\end{aligned}
$$

Step 3:   Substituting values into the formula for MLC, we have the following:

$$MLC = 1 \div [(MIFPVa, 10\%, 12 \text{ mos.}) \, (MSFF, u, 5 \text{ yrs.}) +$$

$$\frac{(1 + g)^T (MIFPVa, 10\%, 25 \text{ yrs.})}{(MIFCV, 10\%, 5 \text{ yrs.})}$$

Values for each of the components in the formula are as follows:

$$
\begin{aligned}
(MIFPVa, 10\%, 12 \text{ mos.}) &= 11.374508 \text{ (Appendix B, column 5)} \\
(MSFF, u, 5 \text{ yrs.}) &= 4.738172 \text{ (computed)} \\
(1 + g)^T &= (1 + .075)^5 = 1.435629 \text{ (computed)} \\
(MIFPVa, 10\%, 25 \text{ yrs.}) &= 110.047230 \text{ (Appendix B, column 5)} \\
(MIFCV, 10\%, 5 \text{ yrs.}) &= 1.64309 \text{ (Appendix B, column 1)} \\
g &= 7.5\% \\
T &= 5 \text{ years} \\
N &= 30 \text{ years}
\end{aligned}
$$

Solving for *MLC*, we have:

$$MLC = 1 \div \left[(11.374508)(4.738172) + \frac{(1 + .075)^5 \times (110.047230)}{1.645309} \right]$$

$$= 1 \div \left[53.894375 + \frac{1.435620 \times 110.047230}{1.645309} \right]$$

$$= 1 \div [53.894375 + 96.022689]$$
$$= 1 \div 149.917064$$
$$= .006670$$

Step 4: Multiplying the *MLC* for a *GPM* made at 10 percent interest with a graduation rate of 7.5 percent per year for five years, we obtain the beginning monthly payment for a $50,000 loan as follows:

$$\$50,000 \times .006670 = \$333.50$$

Step 5: Monthly payments in each succeeding year will be determined as follows:

y = year	Initial payment	Rate of graduation	New payment
1	$333.50		$333.50
2	333.50	$(1 + .075)^1$	358.51
3	333.50	$(1 + .075)^2$	385.40
4	333.50	$(1 + .075)^3$	414.31
5	333.50	$(1 + .075)^4$	445.38
6–30	333.50	$(1 + .075)^5$	478.78

This formula, shown on a step-by-step basis, can be modified for any number of different mortgage terms, including changes in interest rates, maturity, rates of graduation, graduation periods, and so on. The reader need simply make the appropriate changes in the formula.[1]

Case problem (appendix)

Compute the initial payment for a *GPM* loan that is originated for $50,000 at 12 percent for 30 years. Payments are scheduled to graduate at the rate of 5 percent for the first five years of the loan. Then compute the payments required for the first six years of the loan term. Indicate what the outstanding loan balance would be at the end of the sixth year.

---

[1] For a more complete discussion and derivation, see J. S. Aronofsky, R. J. Frame, and E. B. Greynolds, Jr., *Financial Analysis Using Calculators: Time Value of Money* (New YorK: McGraw-Hill Book Co., 1980).

PART THREE

Analyzing income-producing properties

Valuation of income properties

10

A key consideration when financing or investing in income-producing properties is the determination of value. The value is the basis for lending decision since the property will be the security for the loan. In investment decisions, value, which corresponds to the price that an investor may pay for a property, will in large part determine the return on investment. In the context of real estate finance, appraisal reports on properties are a part of the documentation required by lenders when considering whether to make mortgage loans. Because lenders and borrowers/investors use appraisals in decision making, they should be familiar with the generally accepted approaches to appraisal or valuation. The purpose of this chapter is to explain the appraisal process and three approaches ordinarily used in valuation, giving special consideration to technique and methodology. At the same time, the foundation is laid for the financial and project analysis that follows in the next chapter.

Appraisal process

An appraisal is an *estimate* of value. In making this estimate, appraisers use a systematic approach. First, they ascertain the physical and legal identification of the property involved. Second, they identify the property rights. Although this discussion is concerned with the value of properties to be owned completely (or in fee simple), estimates of value can be made for long-term leases, partial ownership interests, and other rights in property, if necessary. Third, appraisers specify the purpose of the appraisal. Besides an estimate of market value, appraisals are also made in such situations as those involving condemnation of property, insurance losses, and property tax assessments.

Fourth, appraisers specify the effective date of the estimate of value. Since market conditions change from time to time, the estimate must be related to a given date. Fifth, appraisers must gather and analyze market data, then apply appropriate techniques to derive the estimate of value. This process is the main concern of this chapter.

In carrying out the appraisal process, a considerable amount of market data must be collected and analyzed. Market data on rents, costs, vacancies, supply and demand factors, expenses, and any other data considered to be an important influence on property values must be collected, summarized, and interpreted by the analyst when making in estimate of value. It is not the intent of this book to cover how to *conduct* market studies and to collect data for making appraisals. In real estate finance, it is more commonly the case that lenders, borrowers, and investors will *use* the appraisal report to make lending and investment decisions. Therefore, the user must understand the *approach* and *technique* used by the appraiser in estimating value and decide whether the market data used in that has been properly interpreted and supports the estimate of value.

In this chapter we are concerned with the *techniques* and *methods* used in estimating value. In the next chapter we provide a framework for analyzing the market data used in the appraisal, with emphasis given to the economic and financial risk of lending or investing in projects. As a result, we summarize only the methodology in this chapter and present a case study or project analysis based on market data in the next chapter.

Approaches to valuation

The role of appraisals cannot be overemphasized because appraised values are used as a basis for lending and investing. Methods and procedures used in establishing values are thoroughly reviewed and evaluated by lenders to prevent overborrowing on properties and by investors to avoid overpaying for properties. Lenders want to be assured that both the initial property value and the pattern of property value over time exceed the outstanding loan balance for any given property over the term of the loan.

In making income property appraisals at least two of three approaches are used. These approaches are the *cost approach,* the *market approach,* and the *income capitalization approach* to valuation. Although these three approaches to valuation are considered to be separate approaches, many would argue that each relies in part on market data and, therefore, the cost and income capitalization approaches are really derivatives of the market approach. The essentials of each of these approaches are reviewed here to provide insight into the process followed by appraisers in establishing the values considered as a basis for financing by lenders.

Cost approach. The rationale for using the cost approach to valuing (appraising) properties is that any informed buyer of real estate would not pay more for a property than what it would cost to buy the land and reproduce the structure. Hence the cost approach ordinarily involves determining the construction cost of building a given improvement, usually on a square footage basis, adding any amenities and extraordinary equipment requirements and the market value of the land. In the case of existing buildings, the reproduction cost is normally reduced by estimating any physical, functional or economic depreciation in arriving at final estimated value. This approach is procedurally identical to the cost approach detailed in the chapter on residential financing. In the case of income-producing property, however, the variations in structural design, equipment, and locational influences make the cost estimation process much more complex. Consequently, the cost approach may be at times difficult to apply, particularly if the property is not a new one.

There are many techniques that can be used in conjunction with the cost approach to value. The technique used in the appraisal will generally depend on (1) the age of the structure being valued, (2) whether or not the structure is highly specialized in design or function, and (3) the availability of data to be used for cost estimating. Generally if a project is in the proposal stage, cost data will be developed from plans and drawings by an appraiser or cost estimator.[1] If a project is in the proposal stage, specifications for material and equipment will have been set out in detail, usually making it possible to arrive at a relatively accurate cost estimate. Exhibit 10–1 contains a breakdown of direct and indirect costs for a hypothetical office-warehouse complex which is in the proposal stage of development. The cost breakdown shown in Exhibit 10–1 is based on categories that generally correspond to how various subcontractors would make bid estimates on improvements. This procedure is quite common for new, nontechnical construction.

In addition to the hard cost categories shown in Exhibit 10–1 for our hypothetical office-warehouse complex, we see two additional categories. One represents a soft cost category which includes estimated outlays for services and intangible costs necessary when designing and developing a project. The other category represents land cost. Estimates of land value are made from comparisons with other, recent land sales. These land sales should be as *comparable* to the land being appraised as possible.

In cases where the project to be financed includes an *existing* improvement, the detailed cost breakdown shown in Exhibit 10–1 is more difficult to use. This is because of the problem of physical and economic depreciation on the component parts that must be estimated by the appraiser. Generally when the cost approach to value is used for an existing improvement, the cost to reproduce the improvement is made and adjusted downward for depreciation caused by (1) physical deterioration, (2) functional or structural obsolescence due to the availability of more efficient layout designs and technological

---

[1] There are a number of cost estimation services available for use by appraisers. Companies providing such services are the Marshall and Swift Company and the Boeckh Division of the American Appraisal Company.

EXHIBIT 10–1
Cost breakdown—hypothetical office–warehouse complex, 73,530
square feet, (8,000, office, 65,500, warehouse), 3 land acres;
Projected economic life = 50 years

Component	Cost	PSF
Hard costs:		
Excavation—back fill.	$ 15,750	
Foundation	23,625	
Framing (steel).	80,250	
Corrugated steel exterior walls	133,875	
Brick facade (front)—glass	25,500	
Floor finishing—concrete	30,500	
Floor covering—offices	8,750	
Roof trusses, covering.	57,520	
Interior finish—offices	28,700	
Lighting fixtures—electrical work	41,500	
Plumbing.	57,250	
Heating—A/C	78,750	
Interior cranes, scales	69,530	
Loading docks, rail extension.	48,000	
Onsite parking, streets, gutters	88,000	
Subtotal	$ 787,500	$10.71
Soft costs:		
Architect, attorney, accounting	$ 100,000	
Construction interest.	62,500	
Builder profit	125,000	
Subtotal	$ 287,500	3.91
Land cost (by comparison)	$ 175,000	2.38
Value per cost approach.	$1,250,000	$17.00

changes that reduce operating costs (those changes that have come about since
the construction of the improvement), and (3) economic depreciation which
may result from style changes and external influences such as excessive traffic,
noise, pollution, and so on. These three categories of depreciation are very
difficult to determine, and in many cases require the judgment of appraisers
who specialize in such problems. This particularly applies to industrial
properties, special-use facilities such as public buildings, and properties that
are bought and sold very infrequently.

To illustrate how adjustments must be made to reflect physical, functional, and economic depreciation, we consider a different property, a 15-
year-old office-warehouse complex. The improvement if reproduced today
at *current prices,* using a costing procedure similar to that shown in Exhibit 10–1, would be $1,750,000. However, because the structure is 15
years old, certain adjustments must be made for necessary repairs, changes
in design technology, and depreciation, as shown in Exhibit 10–2.

The essence of the cost approach for existing properties is first to price the
improvement at its current reproduction costs. Then that amount is reduced by

EXHIBIT 10–2
Estimates of depreciation and obsolescence on improved property

Reproduction cost estimate.		$1,750,000
1. Physical deterioration:		
a. Repairable (curable):		
Interior finish.		25,500
Floor covering.		5,200
Lighting fixtures.		17,000
Total	$	47,700
b. Nonrepairable (incurable):		
15 years ÷ 50 years (age to economic life)		30%
2. Functional obsolescence:		
a. Layout design (inefficiency):		
Increasing operating costs (annually)	$	15,600
3. Location—economic obsolescene:		
a. Loss in rent.		$4,630
Site value by comparison.		$200,000

any costs that (*a*) can be expended to upgrade the improvement or to cure obvious deterioration due mainly to needed maintenance or (*b*) correspond to the economic loss associated with nonrepairable (or incurable) factors due to changes in design or layout efficiency that may make newer buildings less expensive to operate.

Hence, in our example, the appraiser estimates that a purchaser of the property would have to incur a cost of $47,700 simply to replace worn-out items, the result of deferred maintenance and replacement. However, because the structure is 15 years old and the economic life was 50 years when the building was constructed, the appraiser estimates that structual nonrepairable or incurable depreciation due to wear and tear would represent about 30 percent of current reproduction cost. This percentage was developed in the example by the ratio of age to economic life, or 15 ÷ 50. This estimate assumes that the building will wear out *evenly,* or the rate of 2 percent per year (100 ÷ 50 years), over its 50-year life. Because 15 years have passed, based on these assumptions, the building would be 30 percent depreciated. Estimates of physical depreciation are not always based on these simple assumptions. Many structures may wear out faster or slower over time. In this example, the appraisers chosen for such a task should be knowledgeable in industrial-commercial properties because the estimate of depreciation will critically affect the estimate of final value.

As for functional obsolescence in our example, it is estimated that operating costs will be $15,600 higher on the existing structure when compared to a completely new building. This could be caused by a number of factors, for example, the lack of suspended ceilings in an older structure that may contain posts and columns, thereby affecting traffic and storage patterns, or an older conveyor system designed into the initial structure, or other causes. This

$15,600 additional expense could represent added costs in manpower, machinery costs, and so on, due to functional inadequacies.

Finally, an estimate of $4,630 per year has been made for locational obsolescence. This cost comes about because of environmental changes, such as pollution, noise, neighborhood changes, and other external influences which result in lower rents when present. These characteristics are judged relative to comparable sites with none of these external influences present.

Adjustments to the reproduction cost estimate for the existing improvement in our example is shown in Exhibit 10–3. Note that any repairable or curable

EXHIBIT 10–3
Adjustment of reproduction cost estimate

Reproduced improvement costs at current prices............	$1,750,000
Less: Repairable physical depreciation....................	47,700
Subtotal......................................	$1,702,300
Nonrepairable (incurable) physical depreciation, 30%............................	510,690
Functional obsolescence (incurable): $15,600(*IFPVa*, 10%, 35 yrs.) $15,600(9.644159).............................	150,449
Economic/locational obsolescence: $4,630 ÷ .10	46,300
Add: Site value (by comparison)	200,000
Value per cost approach...............................	$1,194,861
Or (rounded).....................................	1,195,000

depreciation or obsolescence should be subtracted from the reproduction cost estimate before any reduction is made for nonrepairable or incurable costs (30 percent in our example). In other words, even with the curable items adjusted for, productivity loss due to functional obsolescence and structural depreciation would still exist. The estimate for those incurable items must be made based on the assumption that all curable items are repaired.

Another item of importance in the above procedure relates to the functional obsolescence estimate of $15,600 per year. It should be noted that the cost estimate is treated as a discounted annuity. This is because the increase in operating costs is expected to be $15,600 *per year* for the next *35 years*. Assuming the buyer could earn 10 percent annually on other investments, the adjustment for functional obsolesence would reduce the total operating costs to a present value of $150,449.[2]

---

[2] It is assumed that the owner could invest in a similar real estate venture or an investment of equal risk and earn 10 percent on total investment. This is discussed in more detail in the income capitalization approach later in the chapter.

The same rationale used to determine the cost of functional obsolescence applies to economic or locational obsolescence. If the subject property is located in an area with environmental problems, resulting in a decline in demand for the services, then account must be taken of this cost. The estimate for this cost is made in this case by comparing differences in rent obtainable on sites in areas not affected by the same economic obsolescence. This loss in rent is capitalized and used to reduce land value, to the extent comparable land sales do not reflect these negative factors. In our example, we assume this cost to be $4,630 per year. As was the case with functional obsolescence, this loss in income should also be discounted at 10 percent, representing the fact that the loss of $4,630 per year is not incurred all at once but deferred over the life of the site, which is considered to be infinite. Hence the discounted value of this loss, or $4,630 ÷ .10, represents $46,300 today.[3]

Finally, some comment must be made on the inclusion of land value at current market value. In practice, finding comparable land sales may be difficult. Land values may be difficult to obtain because the area may be completely developed and no vacant sites remain. Consequently, in cases where a significantly depreciated improvement located in a highly developed area is being valued, the cost approach may not be a desirable method to use. If data are available, estimating value using the remaining two approaches, namely the market and income capitalization approaches, may be preferable.

In summary, the cost approach is preferred in cases where the structure is relatively new and depreciation does not present serious complications. However, the adjustments that have to be made for depreciation, obsolescence, and the potential difficulty in finding comparable land sales make this cost approach less desirable in cases where older improved properties are being valued. Indeed, the more estimates that must be made, the greater the chance of error in determining any estimated value. Also, as can be seen in the preceding discussion, in cases where existing properties were valued, increasing reliance had to be placed on *market influences*. For example, when determining the cost of functional obsolescence, economic or locational obsolescence, and the rate at which the stream of expenses or lost income was discounted, land values, data from comparable sales, rents, and so on, data from the *market* were used. The more market data necessary to carry out the cost approach, the more likely the market approach (discussed next), and not the cost approach, is the appropriate method to use. However, in cases where there are very few sales and market data are scarce, the cost approach to valuing older, existing properties may be the only method available.

---

[3] In practice this estimate is extremely difficult to make. Further, some argue that the land/building value relationship for comparable properties should be used as a basis for splitting the cost of economic or locational obsolescence.

Market approach. The market approach to value is based on data provided from recent sales of properties *highly comparable* to the property being appraised. These sales must be "arms's length" transactions, or sales between unrelated individuals. They should represent normal market transactions with no unusual circumstances, such as foreclosure, or sales involving public entities, and so on.

To the extent that there are differences in size, scale, location, age, and quality of construction between the project being valued and recent sales of comparable properties, adjustments must be made to compensate for such differences. Obviously when this approach is used, the more differences that must be adjusted for, the more dissimilar are the properties being compared, and the less reliable the market comparison approach. The *rationale* for the market comparison approach lies in the principle that an informed investor would never pay more for a property than what other investors have recently paid for comparable properties. Selection of data on properties that are truly comparable along all important dimensions, and that require relatively minor adjustments because of differences in building characteristics or locational characteristics, is critical to the successful use of this approach.

In developing the market approach to valuation, data on comparable properties from the market area analysis is summarized and used in the development of expected rents and value for the property proposed for financing. An example of some of the data that could be used in the development of a market comparison approach is illustrated in Exhibit 10–4

EXHIBIT 10–4
Market area analysis and sales data—market approach, hypothetical office building

Item	Subject property	Comparable properties 1	2	3
Sale date	—	9/80	6/80	12/80
Price	—	$355,000	$375,000	$413,300
Gross annual rent	—	58,000	61,000	69,000
Gross square feet	13,200	14,500	13,750	15,390
Percent leaseable square feet	90%	91%	93%	86%
Price per square foot*	—	$24.48	$22.27	$26.86
Rent per square foot*	—	$4.00	$4.44	$4.48
Proximity to subject	—	2 mi.	2.5 mi.	.5 mi.
Frontage square feet	300	240	310	350
Parking spaces	130	140	130	155
Number floors	2	2	2	2
Number elevators	1	1	1	1
Age	—	3 yrs.	4 yrs.	2 yrs.
Exterior	Brick	Brick	Stucco	Brick
Construction†	Average	Average	Average	Average
Landscaping†	Average	Average	Average	Average

* Gross square footage (rounded)
† Quality.

for a hypothetical small office building and three comparable properties that have recently been sold.

Based on the data developed from the market area analysis shown in Exhibit 10–4, it can be seen that the subject property being appraised is very comparable to three small office buildings that have recently sold. A careful analysis of the data reveals relatively minor deviations in gross square footage, location, front footage on major streets, construction type and quality, parking space, and age of structures. The goal of the appraiser is now to adjust for the deviations between the property being appraised and the comparables. This adjustment can usually be accomplished in one of two ways. The price per square foot paid for each comparable can be adjusted to determine the market value for the subject, or the relationship between gross rental income and sale prices on the comparable can be applied to the subject with appropriate adjustment. Exhibit 10–5 shows how the price per square foot adjustment could be carried out.

EXHIBIT 10–5
Adjustments from comparables to subject property

	Comparable		
	1	2	3
Sale price per square foot...............	$24.48	$24.27	$26.86
Sale price	$355,000	$375,000	$413,300
Square footage........................	14,500	13,750	15,390
Adjustments:			
Sale date............................	—	+4%	—
Leasable square footage...............	−5%	−10%	+9%
Location.............................	+7%	+12%	+5%
Frontage	+10%	−8%	−10%
Age of structure.....................	+8%	+10%	+6%
Net difference	+20%	+8%	+10%
Adjusted price	$426,000	$405,000	$454,630
Adjusted price per square foot	$29.38	$29.45	$29.54
Appropriate price per square foot for subject			$29.50
Indicated market value, $29.50 × 13,300 square feet =			$392,350

In making such adjustments on a square footage basis, it should be noted that adjustments for any major physical locational deviations between the property being valued and the comparables recently sold must be made. Adjustments on the square footage cost should be made *relative to* the property being valued; that is, the comparable data must be adjusted as though one wants to make the comparables identical to the subject property. Positive features that comparables possess relative to the subject property require negative adjustments, and negative features require positive adjustments. All percentage adjustments are made by the appraiser based on knowledge of current market values and how various favorable and unfavorable attributes of comparable properties would affect the value of the subject. When adjusting for age differentials, front footage, or differences in the percentage of leasable square footage, the appraiser must be able to estimate the value of such attributes and how those attributes affect the value of properties. Needless to say, this is a subjective process and such adjustments should be justified with evidence based on recent experience with highly comparable properties; otherwise, serious errors can result.

A second technique used in conjunction with the market approach to valuation is to develop what are referred to as "gross income multipliers." These are relationships between gross income and sale prices for all comparable properties that are adjusted for physical, locational, and other influences, and then applied to the subject property. This technique also requires that an estimate of the gross income be made for the subject property. The gross income multiplier (GIM) is defined as:

$$GIM = \frac{\text{Sale price}}{\text{Gross income}}$$

or simply the ratio of sale price to gross income. Development of such multipliers are carried out for the properties comparable to the office building being valued.

From the data developed in Exhibit 10–6, we can see that the $GIMs$ range from 5.99 to 6.15 or it can be said that the comparable properties sold for

EXHIBIT 10–6
Development of GIM—comparable properties

	Comparable		
	1	2	3
Date of sale.	9/80	6/80	12/80
Sale price	$355,000	$375,000	$413,300
Current gross income	58,000	61,000	69,000
GIM	6.12 ×	6.15 ×	5.99 ×

approximately 5.99 to 6.15 *times* current gross income. If the subject property is comparable, it too should sell for roughly a price that bears the same relationship to its gross income.

In arriving at a value for the subject property, then, the appraiser must develop an estimate of gross income based on the market data on comparables shown in Exhibit 10–4. For example, in Exhibit 10–4 we see that annual rent per square foot ranged from $4.00 to $4.48 on the comparable properties; if based on current competitive conditions, the appraiser estimates that the subject office building can be rented for $4.70 per square foot, then its gross rent should be $4.70 \times 13,300$ square feet, or $62,510.[4] From the range of *GIMs* shown in Exhibit 10–6, the appraiser also must select an appropriate *GIM* for the subject property. This is done by observing the range in *GIMs* for the comparable properties as shown in Exhibit 10–6 and making adjustments based on all major physical, locational, and other economic differences with the subject property. Again, these advantages are made based on judgments of the appraiser and are subjectively carried out in much the same manner as the square footage adjustments shown in Exhibit 10–5. Assuming that the appraiser chooses a *GIM* of $6.25 \times$ as "appropriate" for the subject property, its indicated value would be $62,510 \times 6.25$, or $390,687 or $390,700 (rounded).

Income capitalization approach. The third approach used in income property appraising is the income capitalization approach. Many *techniques* are used in implementing the income capitalization approach to valuation. This chapter is limited to the more common techniques, but the reader should be aware of other methods.[5]

The rationale for the income capitalization approach to value is based on the premise that because improved real estate is capable of producing a flow of income over its economic life, investors will pay a present value for that flow of income that will provide them with a competitive return on capital invested in the property. A competitive return on investment means a return equivalent to what investors in comparable properties and other investments comparable in risk are receiving on their investment. Because the income capitalization approach does involve estimates of income, utilizing this approach relies heavily on the operating statement that must be developed for any property being appraised.

Development of the operating statement. In developing the operating statement, the economic studies discussed in the previous sections are heavily drawn upon by the appraiser. Data from the market area analysis and surveys on comparable projects, similar to the data utilized in establishing comparisons under the market approach (see Exhibit 10–5), must be used to establish what expected rents will be. Estimates must also be made for normal vacancy and collection losses based on economic conditions expected to exist at the time of the appraisal.

Income should be estimated for the time at which the property is scheduled for completion and normal occupancy is expected. Operating expenses are broken down into specific categories when possible, and a percentage relationship is established relative to effective income. Generally, data of this type are

---

[4] Care should be taken here to assure that significant changes in lease agreements are not expected to occur. For example, if a major increase in rent is expected on a comparable due to a lease expiration in the near future, this must be taken into account and adjusted for.

[5] For an example, see William N. Kinnard, Jr., *Income Property Valuation* (Lexington, Mass,: D. C. Heath and Co., 1971); and L. W. Ellwood, *Ellwood Tables for Real Estate Appraising and Financing* (Chicago: The American Institute of Real Estate Appraisers, 1977).

available through local property management firms, apartment owner associations, or from information collected on a national basis. In cases where an existing property is being valued, past operating statements serve as a point of departure for the appraiser. These statements can be used to project future operating statements based on expected economic conditions in the local economy and market area. The development of operating expense relationships will depend on the type of property being appraised. Exhibit 10–7 details

EXHIBIT 10–7
Data sources useful for income property research

Type of property

Apartment, condominium, cooperative	*Income and Expense Analysis: Apartments, Condominiums and Cooperatives* (Chicago, Ill.: Institute of Real Estate Management, annually).
Office buildings	*Office Building Experience Exchange Report* (Washington, D.C.: Building Owners and Managers Association International, annually).
Shopping centers	*The Dollars and Cents of Shopping Centers* (Washington, D.C., Urban Land Institute).
Industrial parks	*Site Selection Handbook* (Atlanta, Georgia, Conway Publications, Inc.).
Hotels/leisure and recreation property	No national statistics.

some sources of data available on a regional and national basis for many categories of property use that can be consulted in the development of such operating statements.

To develop and explain techniques used in the income capitalization approach, an operating statement for a hypothetical apartment project is shown in Exhibit 10–8. The operating statement is made with the assumption that the property will be efficiently managed. The use of data and averages for properties in the market area are reasonable. As will be seen in the analysis that follows, the estimate of net operating income is critical in the income capitalization approach. In general, holding all else equal, the higher the estimate of net operating income the higher will be the estimated property value. Hence, regardless of how much more "efficiently" optimistic investors believe that they will be able to manage properties in comparison to the competition, appraisers recognize that competitive forces in the local market for wages, materials, and so on should result in operating costs tending toward

EXHIBIT 10-8
Hypothetical apartment building, operating statement

Gross potential income...............	$600,000	
Vacancy and collection loss	30,000	5.0%
Effective gross income	$570,000	100.0%
Operating expenses:		
Personnel—wages	$39,900	
Utilities, common areas.............	22,800	
Management expense	28,500	
Paint and decorating...............	17,100	
Maintenance—repairs	45,000	
Miscellaneous.....................	5,700	
Insurance........................	7,000	
Real estate taxes	65,200	
Total operating expenses..........	$231,200	40.6%
Net operating income.............	$338,800	59.4%

the same percentage of effective gross income for most comparable properties.

In the development of the operating statement, it should be stressed that only items of income and expense expected to occur in annual operation of the property should be included. For example, capital expenditures, which are usually defined as expenditures expected to result in the production of income for a period greater than one year, should *not* be included in operating expenses. If an outlay is made for a new furnace that is expected to last ten years, it should not be treated as an expense but rather as an acquisition of an asset. Operating expenses should be viewed as outlays required for the operation of the project, excluding capital expenditures. Other items are also excluded in developing net operating income. Items of federal or state income tax, interest expense and mortgage payments are not considered to be operating expenses. These items are extremely important in investment analysis where investors are concerned with the aftertax return on equity invested. However, in valuation, appraisers typically estimate net operating income (NOI) and do not consider the effects of financing and depreciation on income.[6] Finally, estimates of expenses should be "stabilized" where necessary to reflect average annual expenditures. For example, if painting is expected to occur every five years, that expense should be averaged for a five-year period so that no one year will be overstated relative to others.

[6] Some critics of this procedure believe that items such as mortgage interest, depreciation, mortgage payments, and federal taxes should be included in the valuation process. Others argue that even though most appraisers utilize NOI when capitalization rates are chosen, financing and tax effects are implicit in those rates; hence it is unnecessary to adjust NOI.

Framework for income capitalization. As indicated previously, the rationale for the income capitalization approach is that when purchasing an income-producing property, an investor will pay an amount equivalent to the present value of all income produced by a property over its economic life. Symbolically, the present value of a stream of income produced by a property over its economic life is:

$$V = \frac{NOI_1}{(1 + r)^1} + \frac{NOI_2}{(1 + r)^2} + \cdots + \frac{NOI_n}{(1 + r)^n} + \frac{REV_n}{(1 + r)^n}$$

where *NOI* represents net operating income, per the development in Exhibit 10–8, and *r* represents the compounded rate of return on investment expected by investors should they pay *V*, or value, for the property.[7] *REV* represents the reversion value of land at the end of the economic life, *n*, of the improvement.

Although the present value approach formulated in the above expression is theoretically accurate, appraisers rarely attempt to estimate income over the entire economic life of a property and a reversion value for land. Instead, they attempt to simplify the capitalization procedure and the time periods over which estimates of income and reversion values can reasonably be made. Because the economic life of many real estate improvements could be 50–60 years or more, any estimate of income spanning such a time period is likely to be subject to significant error. In making modifications to the present value formulation shown above, two of the many techniques that could be used are (1) direct capitalization with an overall rate of return and (2) a discounted present value approach.

Direct capitalization with an overall rate. This technique is a very simple approach to the valuation of income-producing property. It is based on the idea that at any given point in time the current net operating income (*NOI*) produced by a property is related to its current market value. Symbolically:

$$\frac{NOI_1}{V} = R$$

where *NOI* is net operating income in the first year of normal operation, as developed from the operating statement, *V* is property value, and *R* represents a *current* return on *total investment V.* In other words, if an investor purchased a property for a price of *V*, the *current* return before any financing or income tax consideration would be *R*.

It should be noted that there is a significant difference between *r* in the present value formulation and *R* in the direct capitalization formulation. In the present value formulation, *r* represents a return on total investment value *over the entire economic life* of a property. It is based on the discounted value of

---

[7] This computation and meaning of this return (*r*) is the same as the yield computed on mortgage loans in earlier chapters. It is an internal rate of return on total investment.

NOI expected to occur each year over the economic life of the investment. In that sense, it represents the internal rate of return that would be earned on total investment, assuming that the property was owned for its entire economic life. On the other hand, *R* represents a *current return* on investment (before financing and taxes) based on only *one* year's net operating income relative to the market value of the property. For example, if a property were purchased for $10,000 and produced $1,000 in net operating income during the *first year*, *R* would be $1,000 ÷ $10,000, or 10 percent. However, if the property were held for its full economic life and if the land were sold at the end of that time, *r*, or the internal rate of return on investment, could be *considerably different* from 10 percent because of growth in *NOI*, appreciation in land value, or other influences that could occur over the economic life of the investment. Hence, in most cases, when determining property values, it will be generally true that *r* will not equal *R*. Stated another way, the *current* return on total investment does not necessarily equal the return earned over the entire life of the investment.[8]

However, estimating *R* can be useful in valuation. This is because in a competitive market if investors value properties (*V*), to earn a competitive return over the life of an investment, or *r*, then they must *also* value properties so that *R* represents a *competitive current return.* Hence, there is an economic relationship between *R*, or the current return, and *r*, the return over the life of the investment. If investors expect to earn some return (*r*) over the life of the investment, they must also expect to earn some series of current returns (*R*), based on annual amounts of *NOI*. Hence the overall rate can be used to "capitalize" *NOI* into a value (*V*) as follows:

$$\frac{NOI}{R} = V$$

This simply means that estimates of property value can be made with a current estimate of *NOI* and the current return on total investment (*R*) as long as (1) there are many comparable properties being bought and sold, (2) it can be shown that buyers of those properties are also earning the same competitive current return (*R*), and (3) the analyst believes that there is presently a *stable relationship* between current returns and long-term investment returns, or that current returns are not being affected by temporary speculative conditions that will not persist over the long term. If these conditions are met, then the use of *R* is a reasonable approach in determining value.

How should the analyst go about using *R* in determining value (*V*) in the relationship *V = NOI ÷ R*? Using our hypothetical apartment project example

---

[8] To illustrate further, assume you owned a share of stock worth $50 with a current dividend of $2. Because you expect more dividends in the future plus growth in stock value, the current dividend yield ($2 ÷ $50 = 4%) is not equal to the return that you expect based on future dividends *plus* growth in value. Given increasing dividends and growth in value, you would expect to earn a return greater than 4 percent.

to develop *NOI*, we have already seen from Exhibit 10–8 that when normal occupancy is reached, projected *NOI* is $339,500. How does the estimate of *R* come about? Based on Exhibit 10–9, we assume that the analyst has information on three comparable sales prices and information on the estimated

EXHIBIT 10–9
Comparable sales data used in the direct capitalization approach

	Comparable		
Item	*1*	*2*	*3*
Date of sale	10/80	8/80	12/80
Price	$3,500,000	$2,750,000	$3,625,000
NOI	343,000	239,250	333,500
NOI ÷ Price = *R*	9.8%	8.7%	9.2%

rents for each of these complexes. If the appraiser can also estimate operating expenses for each, an *NOI* figure can be developed. Or, if the appraiser has access to the operating statement for each project, the *NOI* can be estimated directly from these statements. If the complete statements are not available, estimated vacancy rates and operating expense ratios based on the same sources cited in the development of the operating statement for the subject property may be relied on. The *R* for each comparable project is developed as shown in Exhibit 10–9. In this case *R* is being used to convert income (*NOI*) into a value (*V*). This conversion process is referred to as *capitalization; R* in this context is referred to as the *overall rate of capitalization.*[9]

Based on data shown in Exhibit 10–9, the current returns on total investment (*V*) that were being earned when each of the projects was sold ranged from 8.7 percent to 9.8 percent. The appraiser will examine these current returns and make a judgment as to which is most appropriate for the subject, based on much the same criteria used when a gross income multiplier (*GIM*) was selected based on the market comparison approach (see Exhibit 10–6). Assuming that 9.5 percent is chosen as the "appropriate" overall capitalization rate for the subject, then the estimated value using this approach would be $339,500 ÷ .095, or $3,573,685.

Sensitivity of value estimate to overall rate. It should be stressed that estimates of value are highly sensitive to the overall rate chosen for capitalization. For example, in the above case, a capitalization rate that is .5 percent too low, or 9.0 percent, will result in an estimated value of approximately $3,772,200, or a difference of $198,515 from the estimate made at 9.5 percent. This represents a difference of over 5 percent in the estimate of value. Clearly,

---

[9] The distinction between a *current return on total investment* and an *overall rate of capitalization* with respect to *R* is largely definitional. When *R* is determined by investors as in *NOI* ÷ *V* = *R*, it is referred to as a current return on total asset investment before financing and taxes. When *R* is used to *determine value* as in *NOI* ÷ *R* = *V*, then *R* is referred to as a capitalization rate.

choice of an appropriate overall capitalization rate is extremely important in the determination of value and should be carefully analyzed and supported in an appraisal.

The weighted average approach to the overall rate. In the preceding example, R was determined because of the availability of data from comparable property sales. In many cases, there may be no directly comparable properties or no properties that have been recently sold. In that event the overall rate (R) must be estimated differently. This can be accomplished by developing a current estimate of anticipated annual payments on a mortgage loan expected to be obtained on the property being valued and a current estimate of the cash return on *equity* being earned by investors in comparable real estate, then "weighting" the two components together to estimate a current value for R. We refer to this process as the "weighted average" approach to developing an overall rate of capitalization.

To elaborate further, we recall that the development of R is partially based on some estimated *NOI*. Recall, also, that current *NOI* represents income *before* any account is taken of mortgage payments or cash return to investors. For example, if there is a high likelihood that debt financing will be used to acquire a property and we wanted to determine the current cash return to an investor, we would follow this format:

$$
\begin{array}{ll}
\text{Effective gross income} & (EGI) \\
-\ \underline{\text{Operating expenses}} & (OE) \\
\text{Net operating income} & (NOI) \\
-\ \underline{\text{Debt service}} & (DS) \\
\text{Before-tax cash flow} & (BTCF)
\end{array}
$$

Using this format, an investor who financed a property with mortgage debt would earn a current before-tax cash flow equal to $BTCF$, or NOI less the required debt service, or mortgage payment (DS). Similarly, we know that if a property is purchased, and it is likely to be financed with a mortgage (M), some downpayment or equity (E) is required of the investor. Both M and E also bear a relationship to V. For example, if it is likely that an investor could obtain a 70 percent loan when purchasing a specific type of property, then $M/V = 70\%$ and required equity must be 30 percent, $E/V = 30\%$, because $M/V + E/V$ must equal 100 percent. The required current mortgage payments made to the lender and the return on equity to the investor would be determined as follows:

$$\frac{DS}{M} = \text{Annual percent mortgage payments}$$

$$\frac{BTCF}{E} = \text{Percent cash return on invested equity } (ROE)$$

By weighting each component by the proportion of equity and debt expected to be used in acquiring the property, we can obtain an estimate of R. This can be seen as follows:

	Component	Weight	Weighted average
Mortgage	$\dfrac{DS}{M}$	$\times \quad \dfrac{M}{V}$	$=$ Debt component of R
Equity	$\dfrac{BTCF}{E}$	$\times \quad \dfrac{E}{V}$	$=$ Equity component of R Overall rate (R)

To illustrate the development of R, assume that a small shopping center is being appraised and there have been no recent comparable sales in the market area. The *NOI* at the time of appraisal is $250,000, and it is expected to remain relatively stable for the immediate future. Based on current mortgage market conditions, it is believed that a 70 percent mortgage could be obtained for 10 percent interest for 25 years. Based on this information, we can partially develop the estimate of R as follows:

$$.109044 \times .70 = .07633$$
$$ROE \times \underline{.30} = \underline{\text{Equity component of } R}$$
$$1.00 = R$$

It should be noted that even though we do not know the dollar amount of the mortgage (because we don't know value), the mortgage component of R can still be determined. This is done by taking the monthly mortgage constant for a 10 percent, 25-year loan, or .009087 from Appendix B, and multiplying by 12 months to get the appropriate *factor*, .109044, that corresponds to annual mortgage payments. Even though we do not know the dollar amount of the mortgage, we expect it will be 70 percent of value. Hence, by weighting the mortgage constant .109044 times 70 percent, the debt component of R or .07633 can be estimated.

The next step in the estimation of R is to estimate a value for the current cash return on *invested equity*, or ROE.[10] This is a more difficult problem. Data on cash returns presently being earned on equity by investors may be difficult to find because of a lack of comparable property sales. Required equity yields could be estimated by determining current yields on equity from recent sales of property that are less then comparable than the shopping center being valued in this case. Adjustments to the current yield would have to be made (either up or down) by (1) perceived differences in *risk* due to locational factors, (2) differences in business risks corresponding to property usage (e.g., manufacturing, warehousing, office building) that could affect rental income should business conditions expand or contract, and (3) differences due to current supply and demand conditions that could make for differences in current equity yields. Other benchmarks such as dividends on common and preferred stock may also be considered in making such adjustments.

---

[10] ROE is sometimes referred to as the equity-dividend yield.

Assuming it is determined from market data on other properties obtained by the analyst that a 6 percent current cash return on *equity (BTCF ÷ E)* invested is "appropriate" for the shopping center being valued, the estimate of *R* can be completed as follows:

	Component	Weight	Weighted average
Mortgage.............	.109044	× .70	= .07633
Equity	.06	× .30	= .01800
			.09433 = R

Based on expected *NOI* of $250,000, the shopping center value could be estimated at $250,000 ÷ .09433, or $2,650,270. Based on this value, we would expect that the mortgage amount would be $1,855,189, or 70 percent of value. Total debt service of $202,297 representing about 10.9044 percent would *represent total annual mortgage payments,* leaving *BTCF* of $47,703 (*NOI-DS*) as the current return to the investor. This would represent a 6 percent current cash yield on equity ($47,703 ÷ $795,081).

As pointed out earlier, the current equity yield (6 percent in the above case) does not represent the return that an investor would expect to earn on equity invested in such a project over the entire investment period. This is because no account is taken of potential appreciation or depreciation in property value, nor is any trend in *NOI* considered beyond the current year. The estimate of value under this approach is based on *current cash yields* prevailing in the marketplace, and as such are not intended to provide investors with estimates of long-term rates of return on equity investment. Rather, these current yields are intended to serve as market benchmarks that can be used in establishing property values. Since the purpose of this technique is to determine value, it should *not* be relied upon as an indication of what the potential yield could be from investing in a particular property for the entire investment period.

The present value method and income capitalization. In many instances the development of an overall rate of capitalization (*R*) is not possible because the appraiser may not be able to obtain data on current equity yields or there may simply be no comparable properties at all from which *R* can be developed. This situation frequently occurs when *special-purpose* properties, such as recreational property, large hotels, or properties involving agricultural or mineral production, are involved. In such cases, a present value approach to capitalization may have to be used in establishing value.

We have already seen that the discounted present value approach can be employed to determine value based on all income received over the economic life of a property. Recall the formulation:

$$V = \frac{NOI_1}{(1 + r)^1} + \frac{NOI_2}{(1 + r)^2} + \cdots + \frac{NOI_n}{(1 + r)^n} + \frac{REV_n}{(1 + r)^n}$$

However, as pointed out, because of the difficulty in making estimates of income over such long time periods, most appraisers do not attempt to estimate net operating income over the entire life of the investment. This is not done for three additional reasons: (1) properties are usually *sold* long before the end of their economic life; (2) under certain assumptions, the price that a property will sell for at any time is equivalent to the present value of the income stream remaining from the year it is sold until the end of its economic life; and (3) the property's sales price over some expected period of ownership is much easier to estimate and more accurate than estimating *NOI* over the entire economic life. These points must be elaborated upon before proceeding.

Because a property can be bought and sold many times before the end of its economic life, it can be argued that an estimate of its sale price at the end of an expected period of ownership is equal to the present value of *NOI* for the remaining economic life of the investment. This can be seen with a simple example: Assume a property is estimated to produce *NOI* of $100,000 per year for 25 years, the return, *r*, on total investment required by investors over the economic life of a property is 8 percent. What would be the present value of such a property? The solution would be simply:

$$V = \$100,000(IFPVa, 8\%, 25 \text{ yrs.})$$
$$= \$100,000(10.674776)$$
$$= \$1,067,478$$

or, the value of the property would be $1,067,478. However, if the property is sold after ten years *and* the *purchaser* requires the same 8 percent return on total investment that the seller required, then it follows that the value of the property to the second owner in year 10 will be equal to the present value of the remaining 15 years worth of income or:

$$REV = \$100,000(IFPVa, 8\%, 15 \text{ yrs.})$$
$$= \$100,000(8.559479)$$
$$= \$855,948$$

The point to be stressed here is that if the buyer and seller value the property in the same manner and desire the same internal rate of return (*r*), the present value of the income stream today, or *V*, also can be determined by taking the present value of *NOI* for ten years *plus* the reversion value of the property in the tenth year (*REV*). This can be seen as follows:

$$V = NOI(IFPVa, 8\%, 10 \text{ yrs.}) + REV(IFPV, 8\%, 10 \text{ yrs.})$$
$$= \$100,000(6.710081) + \$855,948(.463193)$$
$$= \$671,008 + \$396,469$$
$$= \$1,067,478$$

The estimate of value using a reversion value is $1,067,478, which is equivalent to the value (*V*) estimated for $100,000 annually received over the entire economic life of 25 years. The importance of the above analysis is that if the appraiser can estimate annual *NOI* over a typical period of ownership, *and a sale price at the end of that time, NOI* does not have to be estimated over the entire economic life. Again, this is true as long as buyers and sellers value properties consistently and require the same competitive return (r) on total investment. Hence, in our simplified example, if (1) *NOI* is estimated to be $100,000 annually for the next ten years, (2) a reversion value (REV) of $855,948 is also estimated at that time,[11] and (3) the required return on total investment by both buyer and seller is 8 percent, then the value of such a property today would be $1,067,500 (rounded).

Given that we have seen that the present value of an income stream can be determined by considering a combination of income and a reversion value, as opposed to estimating income over the entire life of a project, this enables us to modify the present value method of income capitalization when estimating value. However, even though we are able to modify the present value approach and consider shorter periods of ownership, other complications arise when using this technique. These complications have to do with the use of r in the discounting process. When r is used in discounting, it represents a return on total value (V). As was the case in the development of the overall rate (R), r is a composite of both debt and equity components. However, unlike R, r is more difficult to compile. This difficulty arises because r is a return spanning over more than one year, and therefore, current mortgage costs and current equity yields cannot be used in establishing r. Also, the simple weighting procedure used in developing the overall rate (R) cannot be used in estimating a yield on total investment (r) because weights based on mortgage and equity financing will change over the period of ownership. Hence the simple weighted average approach is more difficult to use.

To clarify why the simplistic approach used in developing R cannot be used, we first break down the expected cash flows from operation and sale of the property between the lender and the investor. Recall the development of *NOI* in the operating statement shown in Exhibit 10–8. The share of *NOI* that would be received by each of these suppliers of capital would be as follows:

Net operating income	(NOI)	
− Debt service	(DS)	(to be received by lender)
Before-tax cash flow	$(BTCF)$	(to be received by investor)

Similarly, the amount of the reversion value in the year of sale (n) to be received by each supplier of capital should be:

Reversion value	(REV)	(estimated sale price)
− Mortgage balance	(MB)	(to be received by lender)
Before-tax cash flow from sale	$(BTCF_s)$	(to be received by investor)

---

[11] We should point out that the reversion value (REV) does not always have to be less than the original value (V). *REV* is dependent on the expected pattern of *NOI* after the expected sale. Cases dealing with increasing and decreasing patterns of *NOI* are taken up in the appendix to this chapter.

Considering each component as an investment yield over an expected investment period, we would have:

$$\text{Mortgage loan} = \frac{DS_1}{(1 + i_m)^1} + \frac{DS_2}{(1 + i_m)^2} + \cdots + \frac{MB_s}{(1 + i_m)^s}$$

$$\text{Equity invested} = \frac{BTCF_1}{(1 + k)^1} + \frac{BTCF_2}{(1 + k)^2} + \cdots + \frac{BTCF_s}{(1 + k)^s}$$

In the above formulation, i_m is the effective yield (cost) on expected mortgage financing and k is the estimated return on equity over the total investment period. We should note that i_m is equivalent to the effective cost of mortgage credit, developed in an earlier chapter, and is the rate of interest necessary to make the stream of mortgage payments and payoff in years (s) equal to the initial mortgage loan. The estimate of k or the internal rate of return on equity (E), is based on the $BTCF$ received in each year from operating the property, plus the $BTCF_s$ realized in the year of sale (s). The latter value is a residual amount based on the estimated selling price less the mortgage balance remaining at that time.

Even though it is possible to develop estimates of i_m and k, these two components cannot simply be weighted by the initial proportions of mortgage debt and equity to obtain an estimate of r. The weights cannot be used in determining a value for r because of the effect of mortgage amortization (the difference between annual debt service and interest) which reduces the mortgage balance each year, thereby changing the weight that mortgage financing would have in any weighted average used to obtain r. Therefore the simple weighted average procedure used in the development of R based on current proportions of debt and equity would have to be modified to take account of these changing weights.[12]

To overcome these weighting problems, two techniques are provided here that do not rely on direct estimation of r, but provide an equivalent estimate of value as though r were used in the discounted present value approach. These two methods are (1) the mortgage-equity approach to value and (2) a modified approach to estimating an overall rate (R).[13]

---

[12] The simple weighted average approach could be used to weight i_m and k in determining r, if (1) the mortgage obtained did not require amortization, that is, if interest only were paid each year and the full mortgage balance was repaid in the year of sale; or (2) the loan was refinanced each year, at the same interest rate (i_m), such that the amount refinanced kept the mortgage balance equal to the original percentage of value when the property was first acquired. The weighted average formulation of r is frequently used in establishing required rates of return on investments by corporations that are "going concerns" and are considered to have indefinite economic lives. Improved real estate, however, is a wasting asset subject to many tax and other influences favorable to individual investors, and because of this, amortization will usually be required on mortgage loans. Hence a simple weighting process is not realistic in most real estate investment situations.

[13] This modified approach to estimating R is sometimes referred to as a modified "Ellwood Approach," named after L. W. Ellwood who first presented this approach. See *Ellwood Tables for Real Estate Appraising and Financing.*

Mortgage-equity approach. This method for estimating value is based on the concept that total value (V) must be equal to the present value of expected mortgage financing (M) and the present value of equity investment (E) made by investors. This technique relies on expressing all mortgage related components affecting M and E as a percentage of value, then solving for value algebraically. Although this technique has many steps in the process and appears somewhat complex, a close examination of the approach reveals its simplicity. In using the mortgage-equity approach to value, we begin with the following relationship:

$$V = M + E$$

This merely indicates that value must equal the sum of a mortgage (M) obtainable on a property plus the equity (E) required of an investor. However, because the amount of the mortgage is dependent on the value of a property, the exact dollar amount for (M) is unknown. But we can estimate the *percentage* of mortgage financing to be loaned and the other terms with a reasonable amount of confidence. This estimate can be made based on current mortgage interest rates and terms for comparable properties, discussions with lending institutions, and data published by lenders on properties recently financed.[14] Given that we can estimate an expected percentage of financing, also called the loan-to-value ratio, or L/V, we can modify our basic mortgage-equity equation to incorporate that estimate as follows:

$$V = M + E$$
$$V = L/V(V) + E$$

Hence, if we expect a 75 percent loan will be obtainable on a particular property, $L/V = 75\%$, then our equation would be:

$$V = .75V + E$$

Given this relationship, if we can now obtain an estimate for E, V can be easily solved.

How do we estimate E? Recalling the earlier analysis in this chapter, we know that one of the components of return to an investor making an equity investment on a property is before-tax cash flow. This annual return on equity was developed as follows:

Net operating income	(NOI)
− Debt service	(DS)
Before-tax cash flow	(BTCF)

We know that to estimate E we must include BTCF, or $NOI - DS$, for each year that the property is owned. Finally, we know that when the prop-

---

[14] For a summary of current financing data, see "Mortgage Commitments on Multi-Family and Non-residential Properties Reported by Life Insurance Companies," American Council of Life Insurance, Washington, D.C., current reports.

erty is sold, the investor will receive any excess of cash remaining after the outstanding mortgage balance is paid, or $BTCF_s$. In the year that the property is sold, REV or the price expected in the year of sale, must be reduced by any mortgage balance (MB) to get the net cash reversion to the investor at that time. Based on these modifications, we can rewrite our basic valuation relationship as:

$$V = M + E$$

or

$$V = (L/V)V + \frac{(NOI - DS)_1}{(1 + k)^1} + \frac{(NOI - DS)_2}{(1 + k)^2} + \cdots + \frac{(REV - MB)_s}{(1 + k)^s}$$

This new relationship merely says that value is equal to the mortgage amount (M) stated as $L/V(V)$, or the loan-to-value ratio times value, plus the present value of all proceeds to be realized by the equity investor. The latter amounts to all $BTCF$, which is equal to $NOI - DS$ in each year, plus any residual cash remaining from the sale of the property in year (s), after repayment of any mortgage balance ($REV - MB$).

It should be noted that in the above formulation, proceeds to be realized by the equity investor are discounted by k not r. This is because the equity that an investor is willing to invest in a project is equal to the discounted value of all cash returns to be realized on *equity* investment and not *total* investment. When attempting to estimate E, an estimate must be obtained for k, or the before-tax internal rate of return ($BTIRR$) investors expect to realize on their equity over the entire period of investment. In other words, because the estimate of E is "net" of debt financing and $BTCF$ is "net" of any debt service, the rate at which we discount must also be "net" of the influence of debt financing; therefore we must use k and not r when estimating E.

As indicated previously, determining the mortgage interest rate and other mortgage terms and what percentage of value lenders would be willing to loan on a particular property is relatively straightforward. However, estimating the internal rate of return on equity (k) that investors expect to earn over an expected period of ownership is more complex. Ideally appraisers would like to have data on ($BTCF$) sales prices and the original cost for all comparable properties that have been bought and sold during recent years. In this way, values for k could be computed. Unfortunately such information is not made public and is generally not available. Further, even if it did exist, estimates for k must be made with *expected* or *future* cash flows in mind. Estimates of k based on *historical* data may not be indicative of *future* trends. However, there are a few general guidelines that can be followed when estimating k.

1. As pointed out in Chapter 9 on alternative mortgage instruments, the interest rate on a mortgage (i_m) can be thought of as a composite of the

real rate of interest (i_r), a risk premium (i_p) and an inflation premium (i_f) over a specific time period (t) or:

$$(i_r + i_p + i_f)_t = i_m$$

When we deal with the question of k or the required investment yield on equity, it is comprised of the *same three variables*. However, the risk premium should be *greater* for an equity investor than it would be for the mortgage lender. Stated another way:

$$(k_r + k_p + k_f)_t = k$$

where $k_p > i_p$; hence, $k > i_m$.

2. The risk premium, k_p, earned by an equity investor should be *greater* than that earned by the lender because the equity investor takes more risk than the mortgage lender. This is because all debt-service (DS) requirements must be paid from NOI before the equity investor realizes any $BTCF$. Also because the property serves as security for the loan, the lender has first claim against proceeds from the sale of a property; that is, the mortgage balance must be paid from the proceeds from sales before any cash is received by the equity investor. Hence the equity investor is in a residual position, or one in which the claims of the lender must be met before the equity investor receives any return.

3. When estimating required yields on equity for a particular project, alternative yields on similar properties, to the extent information is available, or yields on other investments such as corporate bonds and stock can serve as a point of departure for estimation. However, justification must be made for differences in risk between the property being valued and any benchmark or average yields developed from other markets.

Now that the general framework for the present value technique has been established, we can illustrate the technique by attempting to estimate a value for a property that is expected to generate NOI of \$365,000 per year. It is anticipated that a 75 percent mortgage can be obtained at 10 percent interest for 25 years. Experience has shown that a property of this type is likely to be operated for about ten years before it is sold.[15] Further, appreciation in the property value over the next ten years is expected to total 10 percent. The appraiser believes that given the risk and other factors related to this investment, the investor should earn k of 13 percent return, or a risk premium of 3 percent over the mortgage rate, on equity (before taxes) over the ten-year period. How do we incorporate this data into an estimate of value?

---

[15] The factors involved in deciding when a property should be sold are explained in Chapter 14 on investment analysis.

Repeating the formulation of the problem we have:

$$V = M + E$$

$$V = (L/V)V + \frac{(NOI - DS)_1}{(1 + k)^1} + \frac{(NOI - DS)_2}{(1 + k)^2} + \cdots + \frac{(REV - MB)_s}{(1 + k)^s}$$

We must now incorporate known values into the discounting formula. First we expect that a 75 percent loan will be obtained. This means that $L/V = 75\%$. As for $NOI - DS$, although we know that this equals $BTCF$, a *dollar* value for DS cannot be obtained because the *dollar* amount of the mortgage is not known. Hence, we must use NOI which is known to be $365,000 annually and express DS as a *percentage* of V. This can be done because we do not know what the mortgage will be as a *percent* of value and we also know the expected interest rate and term of the loan. Because we expect the mortgage amount to be 75 percent of value, the annual debt service expressed as a percentage of value will be:

$$\begin{aligned} DS &= .75V(MLC, 10\%, 25 \text{ yrs.}) \times 12 \\ &= .75V(.009087) \times 12 \\ &= .081783V \end{aligned}$$

or expressed in relationship to value, DS would be based on a mortgage amount equal to 75 percent of value, times the monthly loan constant (MLC) for a 10 percent, 25-year loan (Appendix B). This loan constant, which is equal to .009087, is multiplied by 12 to obtain annual debt-service requirements as a percentage of V. As seen above, we ascertain that DS will be 8.1783 percent of value. This is true even though we do not know the dollar amount of the mortgage or the property value.

As for the dollar amount of mortgage balance in the year of sale, it too is unknown because it is based on the original mortgage amount which, in turn, is based on the unknown. However, like DS, the mortgage balance can also be expressed as a percentage of V. If it is expected that a 75 percent loan will be obtained when the property is purchased, the mortgage balance factor for a 10 percent, 25-year loan at the end of 10 years (Appendix C), which is equal to .8456, when multiplied by the original percentage of value borrowed, or 75 percent, represents the mortgage balance at the end of 10 years, expressed as a percentage of value. This is computed as follows:

$$\begin{aligned} MB &= .75V(MLB, 10\%, 10 \text{ yrs.}) \\ &= .75V(.8456) \\ &= .6342V \end{aligned}$$

Hence the mortgage balance after ten years should be 63.42 percent of the *initial* property value.

Finally an estimate of REV is required. Although we do not know V, it is estimated that whatever the present value of the property is today, it will appreciate in value by a *total* of 10 percent over the ten-year investment period. Hence, *REV* will be 1.10 times the current value (*V*), that is, the present value of the property plus 10 percent.

Now that we have values for *DS, MB, NOI, REV,* and *k,* we can estimate *V* as follows:

$$\text{Value} = M + E$$
$$\text{Value} = L/V(V) + (NOI - DS)(IFPVa, k\%, 10 \text{ yrs.}) +$$
$$(REV - MB)_s(IFPV, k\%, 10 \text{ yrs.})$$

where:

$$M = L/V(V) = .75\,V$$

and E is comprised of:

$$NOI = \$365,000$$
$$DS = .081783\,V$$
$$MB = .6342\,V$$
$$REV = 1.10\,V$$
$$k = 13\%$$

substituting these values we have:

$$V = .75\,V + [(\$365,000 - .081783\,V)(5.426243)] +$$
$$[(1.10\,V - .6342\,V)(.294588)]$$

$$= .75\,V + (\$1,980,579 - .443774\,V) + (.324047\,V - .186828\,V)$$
$$= .443445\,V + \$1,980,579$$
$$.55655\,V = \$1,980,579$$
$$V = \$3,558,640$$

Based on the estimates made for variables used in the present value approach, value is estimated to be $3,558,640 for the subject property. In examining this solution, many relationships must be considered. As indicated earlier, with the exception of *NOI,* all other variables have been expressed as a precentage of value (*V*). This is what makes the problem solvable, even though the amount of the mortgage is unknown, and even though appreciation in property value is included when the original property value is unknown. It should be noted that *NOI* is expected to remain constant[16] at $365,000 and the debt service, though unknown, will also be a constant outflow;[17] hence, both are, by definition, annuities. Because both variables are annuities, both can be discounted by the

---

[16] In an inflationary or deflationary environment, the probability of *NOI* remaining level over any significant period of ownership is not very high. If *NOI* is expected to increase or decline over the period of ownership, this should be incorporated into the analysis. This situation is considered in the appendix to this chapter.

[17] Even though the mortgage payments are made monthly, it is customary to assume they are grouped and paid annually. If this were not done, all other variables would have to be converted to monthly payments and discounted monthly. This would further complicate the analysis.

interest factor for the present value of an annuity at 13 percent. The final term in the discounting formula is the reversion value less the outstanding mortgage balance or $1.10V - MB$. Because it is a lump sum, it must be discounted by the interest factor for the present value of $1.

From the preceding analysis, it should be clear that the preceding approach to income capitalization can be modified for any combination of *NOI,* mortgage terms, mortgage amounts (as percent of value), expected investment period, required investment yield on equity, and reversion value. It is a valuable tool for estimating value for income-producing property. It should also be pointed out that rather than going through the extensive computational procedure shown here, a series of tables known as the Ellwood Tables have been developed to take account of the same variables used in the above formulation.[18] Based on the expected percentage of loan financing, terms of the loan, holding period, total appreciation or depreciation, and the required return on equity (k), various capitalization rates can be developed from those tables. Those capitalization rates when divided into *NOI* will yield the same estimates of value as the more extensive procedure outlined above.

A closer examination of the above procedure and an interpretation of the results would be useful at this point. Based on the preceding assumptions and the estimated value of $3,558,640, we can now demonstrate how *NOI* is split between (1) the mortgage lender so that a mortgage interest rate of 10 percent is earned and (2) the equity investor so that a 13 percent return on equity is earned. This exercise will verify the computational accuracy of the above procedure and help the reader to better understand the technique used here. A breakdown of the estimated value into its components is shown as follows:

	Investment	Years 1–10		Year 10	
Value, 100%.	$3,558,640	*NOI*	$365,000	*REV*†	$3,914,504
Mortgage, 75%.	− 2,668,980	*DS* −	291,036*	*MB* −	2,256,889
Equity, 25%.	$ 889,660	*BTCF*	$ 73,964	*BTCF*ₓ	$1,657,615

* $24,253 per month × 12 months.
† 1.10 × $3,558,640.

As can be seen below, the return to mortgage lender is equal to an annual rate of 10 percent compounded monthly. This is determined by discounting all monthly payments and the outstanding loan balance at 10 percent compounded monthly.

---

[18] See Ellwood, *Ellwood Tables for Real Estate Appraising and Financing.*

Present value = $24,254(*MIFPVa*, 10%, 10 yrs.) +
$2,256,889(*MIFPV*, 10%, 10 yrs.)

= $24,253(75.671163) + $2,256,889(.369407)
= $1,835,253 + $833,711
= $2,668,964

Because this present value solution comes very close to the initial mortgage amount of $2,668,980 (differences are due to rounding), this confirms that the yield to the lender is 10 percent compounded monthly as per our assumption.

With respect to the internal rate of return on equity, when the *BTCF* and the cash received upon sale of the property (*REV* − *MB*) are discounted by k = 13%, we obtain the following result:

Present value = $73,964(*IFPVa*, 13%, 10 yrs.) +
$1,657,615(*IFPV*, 13%, 10 yrs.)

= $73,964(5.426243) + $1,657,615(.294588)
= $401,347 + $488,313
= $889,660

Because the present value solution is $889,660, which is equal to the initial equity invested, this proves that the *BTCF* earned over ten years, plus the reversion value of $1,657,615 represents a before-tax internal rate of return (*BTIRR*), or k, of 13 percent annually on the initial equity invested. Hence, this component of the solution is consistent with our initial assumption concerning the value for k.

Sensitivity to assumptions. The reader should be aware that solutions obtained using the present value method of income capitalization are highly sensitive to the values assumed in the computation of value. For example, if in the above example the value selected for k were 12 percent instead of 13 percent, the estimated property value would be $3,668,879. This is $110,239 or 3.1 percent greater than the $3,558,640 estimated when k is 13 percent. Hence the increase in value is 3.1 percent, or over three times the 1 percent error in k. Similar differences in value result when small changes occur in other critical values such as *NOI*, the loan-to-value ratio, the interest rate, loan maturity, investment period, or reversion value. Even though many of these variables are difficult to forecast, it is important that care be taken to carefully estimate each because of the sensitivity of the solution to assumptions.

Mortgage-equity approach to estimation of R. The second method used in estimating value is equivalent to the mortgage-equity approach to estimating value, except that rather than using the present value of the mortgage plus equity, it modifies the weighted average process used in developing the overall rate (*R*) to take account of appreciation or depreciation in property value and mortgage amortization. By taking into account the impact of these two influences on the weights established in the first year of operation, this makes possible the development of an overall rate of capitalization (R), based on the monthly cost of mortgage funds, and k the internal rate of return on equity.

To accomplish this objective, we develop an estimate of value for the subject property as shown in Exhibit 10–10.

EXHIBIT 10–10
Modified mortgage-equity approach

(1) Component	(2) Initial weights	(3) Component	(4) Component value	(5) (2) × (4) Weighted average
Mortgage	.75	$MLC \times 12$	$.009087 \times 12$	.081783
Equity.	.25	k	.13	.032500
			Subtotal	.114283

Adjustment for changes in weighting:
Mortgage amortization:
$(1.00 - MLB) \times (L/V) \times (SFF, 13\%, 10$ yrs.$)$
$(1.00 - .8456) \times .75 \times .054290 =$ $- .006287$
Appreciation in REV:
(Total appreciation rate) $\times$ $(SFF, 13\%, 10$ yrs.$)$
$(.10) \times (.054290) =$ $-.005429$
Overall rate (R) .102567

Estimated value = $365,000 ÷ .102567 = $3,558,650

Essentially, this approach involves first, weighting the monthly cost of mortgage funds (not the mortgage interest rate), or the *monthly mortgage constant,* by the initial loan-to-value ratio, or 75 percent, then weighting the investment yield on equity k by the percentage of required equity (25 percent). That result is then adjusted for changes over time due to loan amortization and appreciation. These adjustments are made by first determining the percentage of loan that has been paid off during the ten-year investment period. This is done by finding the mortgage balance factor for the 10 percent, 25-year mortgage, or .8456, and subtracting from 1.00. This shows that 15.44 percent of the initial loan amount will be paid off over ten years due to amortization. This percentage amortization figure is then multiplied by the initial weight for the mortgage (75 percent) and the annual sinking-fund factor (SFF) at 13 percent for ten years. The latter sinking-fund factor is used to take account of the fact that part of the monthly mortgage payment is repayment of principal, which reduces the loan balance through time, thereby reducing the weight of the mortgage down from 75 percent. Holding all else constant, this amounts to a positive effect on E and is sometimes referred to as "equity buildup". The sinking-fund factor at the equity yield k is used to reflect that buildup. The second adjustment, necessary to reflect any appreciation in property value (a total of 10 percent), also has a positive effect on E because any positive appreciation in property value over the investment period will be realized by the equity investor with a higher $BTCF_s$. This equity appreciation or buildup is also reflected by using the sinking-fund factor SFF at k for the investment period. (If the property value declined over this period, the rate of depreciation would be entered as a positive in the construction of R.)

It should be noted that when equity buildup components are expected, they are *subtracted* in the weighted average process, and vice versa. This is because the desired result R will be *divided* into NOI to determine value. The effects of equity buildup and appreciation will increase property values; therefore, they are subtracted from R making R smaller and therefore V, or $NOI \div R$, larger. The effects of expected depreciation in property value would make R larger and therefore V smaller.

As can be seen in Exhibit 10–10, the value derived via the modified approach is $3,558,650 as compared to the value estimate of $3,558,640 via the discounted present value approach. The differences in the two values are due only to "rounding off." As shown in the previous section, that value can be broken down into mortgage and equity components; and it can be shown that the investment yield on the mortgage is 10 percent compounded monthly, and the investment yield on equity is 13 percent. Also, as was the case with the mortgage-equity approach in finding discounted present value, results using this approach to estimate the overall rate (R) are also highly sensitive to values chosen for NOI, k, and the appreciation rate as applied to REV. Significant changes in V will occur given only slight changes in any of the input values used in the analysis.

A note on residual values. It should be pointed out that in certain cases, a residual value is desired for land only or building only. This is particularly difficult to calculate if comparable land or building sales cannot be found. In that event, if the improvement assumed on the land is considered to be its highest and best use, an estimate of total property value can be made by using the market or income capitalization approach to estimate value. Then, if the cost of either the building or land is known, the other can be determined. For instance, in the previous example concerning the apartment complex valued at $3,558,640, should the cost of developing the improvement (building) be $3,100,000, then the land value should be $448,640. Conversely, if an estimate of building value is desired and the land value is known to be $448,640, then the building value would be $3,100,000.

A final note on appraisal methodology

Three approaches to valuation have been demonstrated here along with many of the techniques used in conjunction with each. Even though there are many combinations of approaches and techniques to valuation, such approaches and techniques are chosen when they best complement the data available for estimation. Stated another way, *the availability and quality of data should always dictate the method and approach chosen for valuation.* Regardless of the methods chosen, be it cost, market, or discounted present value, only one value exists in the marketplace, and any method chosen should not be chosen to influence estimates of value. There should be some correspondence between the three approaches to value, which is the reason appraisal reports will typically contain estimates of value based on at least *two* approaches to determining value. While this procedure helps to corroborate the opinion of value, in the final analysis, it is up to the *user* of the report to be able to interpret, understand, and critically analyze the estimates and methods used in valuation. Lenders and investors must be reasonably familiar with the techniques used and with the assumptions made in the development of the final estimate of value. As has been seen, market yields chosen by the appraiser are usually estimated and may either be current yields or yields over the entire investment period. As has been pointed out, results obtained using the income capitalization approach are highly sensitive to variables chosen for inputs in the techniques demonstrated in the chapter. Hence, it is very important that such estimates be justified by the appraiser based on sound economic principles.

Questions

1   Why is the appraisal so important to investors and lenders in real estate finance?

2   What are the five general steps in the appraisal process?

3   What are the three basic approaches to appraising? What are the rationales for each approach?

4   What does functional obsolescence mean?

5   Why is locational or economic obsolescence so difficult to measure?

6   How does the appraiser adjust for differences in comparable properties under the market approach?

7   What is a gross income multiplier (GIM)? When is such a relationship valid in valuing a property?

8   What is an overall rate of capitalization? What are the two ways that this rate can be estimated?

9   What is the weighted average approach to developing an overall rate of capitalization? What are the components and weights used in the process?

10   What is the mortgage-equity approach to valuation? Why is it difficult to use? What are the necessary data requirements to use this technique?

11   What two methods utilizing discounted present value are developed in the chapter under the mortgage-equity approach? Why can't a simple weighted average of the rates of return (i_m) and k, be used in these approaches?

Case problems

1   An investor is considering the purchase of an existing office complex approximately five years old. The building, when constructed, was estimated to have an economic life of 50 years, and the building-to-value ratio was 80 percent. Based on current cost estimates, the structure would cost $1,000,000 to reproduce today. The building is expected to continue to "wear out" evenly over the 50-year period of its economic life. Estimates of other economic costs associated with the improvement are:

a.	Repairable physical depreciation	$60,000
b.	Functional obsolescence (repairable)	20,000
c.	Functional obsolescence (nonrepairable)	7,500 per yr.
d.	Locational obsolescence	5,000 per yr.

The land value has been established at $300,000 by comparable sales in the area. The investor believes that an appropriate opportunity cost for any deferred outlays or costs should be 15 percent per year. What would be the estimated value for this property?

2   Barry Gladstone is considering the purchase of a 120-unit apartment complex in Steel City, Pennsylvania. A market study of the market area reveals that an average rental of $300,000 per month per unit could be realized in the appropriate market area. During the last six months, two very comparable apartment complexes have sold in the same market area.

Complex I, a 140-unit project sold for $4,704,000. Its rental schedule indicates that $280 per month per unit constitutes its average rent per unit. Briarwood, a 90-unit complex, is presently renting units at $310 per month, and its selling price was $3,214,080. The apartment mix for both complexes is very similar to that of the subject property and both appear to have normal vacancy rates of about 5 percent annually.

a.   Based on the data provided here, how would an appraiser establish an estimate of value for Gladstone?

b.   What other information would be desirable in reaching a conclusion as to the probable sale price that he could receive for his property?

3   LTD Corporation wants to buy a 320,000 square foot distribution facility on the northern edge of a large midwestern city. The subject facility is presently renting for $1.87 per square foot. Based on recent market activity, two properties have sold within a 2-mile distance from the subject facility and are very comparable in size, design, and age.

One facility is 350,000 square feet and is presently being leased for $1.85 per square foot annually. The second facility contains 300,000 square feet and is being leased for $1.90 per square foot. Market data indicates that current vacancies and operating expenses should run approximately 50 percent of gross income for these facilities. The first facility sold for $3,600,000 and the second sold for $3,000,000.

a.   Using an overall capitalization rate approach to value, how would an estimate of value be made for the subject distribution facility?

b.   What additional information would be desirable before selecting the final overall rate (R)?

4 Melissa Lancaster is considering the purchase of a commercial property containing five (5) units comprised of retail-commercial establishments. One of these units she plans to lease out as the Studio Minus 54 Disco. The commercial strip in question is presently 18,500 square feet. Current leases indicate the gross rents should be in the range of $2.25 per square foot annually, and operating expenses should be approximately 35 percent of gross income (including vacancy allowance).

Based on a market survey, it is established that no comparable properties have sold in recent years. Other relevant market indicators are that if purchased, lenders have indicated that an 11 percent mortgage would be obtainable with a 20-year term for approximately 70 percent of value. A survey of owners of small commercial strip centers reveals that they are earning a current cash return on equity in the range of 7 percent.

a. How would an estimate of value be made for this property?

b. How sensitive is this value to a 1 percent difference (up or down) from the current 7 percent yield equity reported by other owners?

5 Sportspectics Limited, a partnership, has recently been established with the intention of acquiring a multipurpose sports and entertainment facility. This facility will accommodate racketball, tennis, and squash, as well as provide for swimming and clubhouse activities.

The building is located in the heart of a suburban area of a large eastern city and has been operating for approximately five years. Based on financial records, current gross revenues are $650,000 annually and cash operating expenses have been normalized at about 30 percent per year. The present lender, who holds the mortgage on the property, is agreeable to refinancing the complex at 12 percent interest for a period of 25 years at 70 percent of value. Other lenders have indicated an interest in financing the project on essentially the same terms.

The appraiser believes in this case that an ownership period of about ten years is typical for this type of facility and has found that similar complexes in other cities, as well as large hotel/motel and recreational properties, have and will continue to appreciate in value at about 20 percent over the *total* ten-year period. A major risk in property of this type is that rental revenues are tied to the discretionary income of consumers, which tends to be highly sensitive to changes in business conditions. However, inclement weather throughout much of the winter provides a strong demand for such activities. These two factors have both a positive and negative effect on value from the perspective of risk. Based on a survey of past common stock performance in the recreational industries, and based on historical returns estimated from similar operations in similar sized cities growing at the same rate as the local economy, the appraiser assigns a 3 percent risk premium over and above the mortgage rate as a reasonable before-tax investment yield on equity for an investor in a property of this type over the term of the investment.

a. How would an estimate of value be made in this case?

b. Break down the returns to the mortgage lender and investor to verify that they earn 12 percent and 15 percent, respectively.

APPENDIX: INCOME CAPITALIZATION IN PERIODS OF EXPECTED INFLATION OR DEFLATION

As pointed out in the chapter, when the mortgage equity method of income capitalization is used, it is very possible that *both NOI* as well as property values may increase or decrease with time. This appendix is intended to show how the mortgage-equity method can be modified to take account of such increases and decreases, hence making this method very flexible and capable of handling virtually any situation in which it is desirable to use the income capitalization approach.

To illustrate, assume that a property could produce *NOI* of $200,000 today and that *NOI* is expected to grow at the rate of 5 percent per year over an investment period of ten years. Based on recent trends, property value should rise a total of 15 percent over the same ten-year period. The investor believes that a 70 percent mortgage can be obtained at 12 percent interest for 25 years. The investment yield on equity for such a project should be 15 percent for the ten-year investment period. How would an estimate of value be made?

The procedure for estimating value is similar to the one shown in Chapter 10 in the mortgage-equity analysis. Value can be estimated by using the following formulation:

$$V = (L/V)(V) + \sum_{t=1}^{s} \frac{NOI_t(1 + g)^t - (DS)_t}{(1 + k)^t} + \frac{(REV - MB)_s}{(1 + k)^s}$$

$$= (L/V)(V) + \sum_{t=1}^{s} \frac{NOI_t(1 + g)^t}{(1 + k)^t} - \sum_{t=1}^{s} \frac{DS_t}{(1 + k)^t} + \frac{(REV - MB)_s}{(1 + k)^s}$$

Summarizing the following information:

$L/V = 70\%$
$NOI = \$200,000$
$g = 5\%$
$t = \text{year of acquisition}$
$s = 10 \text{ years}$
$REV = 1.15\% \text{ of } V$
$k = 15\%$

The primary difference between this formulation and the example in the chapter is the fact that *NOI* is expected to *grow* at 5 percent per year.[1] Because of this fact, *NOI* is no longer an annuity and therefore, *NOI* for each year must be discounted separately by k. The symbol Σ, simply means "to sum" the discounted values of *NOI* for each year over the investment period beginning in year 1 and ending in year 10. From that sum the discounted value of all service *(DS)* must be subtracted so that the difference between the two

---

[1] The above formulation assumes that *NOI* also grows during the first year of ownership.

represents the present value of *BTCF.* Finally, the present value of the reversion less the mortgage balance is added to the present value of *BTCF* to obtain an estimate of *E* which is then added to the mortgage (*M*) or *L/V*(*V*), to obtain the estimate of *V.*

The first step in the computational procedure is carried out in Exhibit 10A–1. Note that *NOI* for each year is compounded by the expected rate of increase, or 5 percent, then discounted at the expected 15 percent equity yield. The present value of the increasing stream of *NOI* is $1,254,462. With this value, we can now proceed using a slightly modified approach to that used in the chapter.

Compiling values for the equation we have:

$$
\begin{aligned}
PVNOI &= \$1{,}254{,}462 \\
L/V(V) &= .70\,V \\
DS &= .70\,V(.010532 \times 12) = .0884688\,V \\
REV &= 1.15\,V \\
MB &= .8776(.70\,V) = .61432\,V
\end{aligned}
$$

Substituting, we have:

$$
\begin{aligned}
V &= M + E \\
&= L/V(V) + PVNOI - DS(IFPVa,\ 15\%,\ 10\ \text{yrs.}) + \\
&\quad (REV - MB)(IFPV,\ 15\%,\ 10\ \text{yrs.}) \\
&= .70\,V + \$1{,}254{,}462 - .0884688\,V(5.018769) + \\
&\quad (1.15\,V - .61432\,V)(.247185) \\
&= .70\,V + \$1{,}254{,}462 - .4440\,V + .1324\,V \\
&= \$1{,}254{,}462 + .3884(V) \\
&= \$2{,}051{,}115
\end{aligned}
$$

When comparing this procedure to the approach used in the chapter, special note should be taken of the fact that *PVNOI* is used in place of *NOI.* This is because when *NOI* increases, it must be discounted each year as was carried out in Exhibit 10A–1. Hence it must be entered separately; otherwise it would be discounted twice, as would be the case if it were included in the formulation shown in the chapter.

The modified mortgage-equity approach to find value is not widely used in the practice of real estate valuation, although tables have been developed for possible use by appraisers.[2] This is somewhat puzzling because, as we have shown, when the mortgage-equity or discounted present value approach is used to value property, the mortgage interest rate (i_m) and the internal rate of return on equity, *k,* are components in the analysis. These components include expected premiums for a real return, risk, and inflation. Also, these approaches

---

[2] See L. W. Ellwood, *Ellwood Tables for Real Estate Appraising and Financing* (Chicago: The American Institute of Real Estate Appraisers, 1977). In the Ellwood book, set of "J" factors are available for use in cases where *NOI* is expected to increase.

EXHIBIT 10A–1
Present value of increasing NOI

Year	NOI	× IFCV, 5%	× IFPV, 15%	= Present value
1	$200,000	1.050000	.869565	$ 182,609
2	200,000	1.102500	.756144	166,730
3	200,000	1.157625	.657516	152,231
4	200,000	1.215506	.571753	138,994
5	200,000	1.276282	.497177	126,908
6	200,000	1.340096	.432328	115,872
7	200,000	1.407100	.375937	105,796
8	200,000	1.477455	.326902	96,597
9	200,000	1.551328	.284262	88,197
10	200,000	1.628895	.247185	80,528
Total.				$1,254,462

allow for property values to increase through the reversion feature (REV). Hence, if nominal interest rates (i_m) and nominal yields (k) are used in estimating value, then nominal increases or decreases in (NOI) should also be included. Further, it seems only reasonable that if property values (REV) are expected to rise (or fall) over the investment period, the NOI must also rise or fall. This follows because, as we have seen, property value is directly related to the present value of NOI. We suspect that in practice, when property values and NOI are expected to rise due to inflation, an average of NOI over the investment period is being used in lieu of NOI for the first operating period. This average is then used in the mortgage-equity formulation developed in the chapter. The estimate of value obtained using an average NOI will *not* be equal to the value developed according to the procedure used in this appendix. However, the difference may not be material.

Finally, because both NOI and property value can go down as well as up, should NOI be expected to fall, then NOI for each year would be computed as $NOI_1(1-g)^1 + NOI_2(1-g)^2$ . . ., and so on. Similarly, if property values were expected to fall, then REV would be computed as $1 -$ (the total rate of decline in value) $\times (V)$. In other words, if a property were expected to decline a *total* of 20 percent over any given investment period, REV would equal $(1 - .20)(V)$.

Case problem (appendix)

A–1 A property is presently generating NOI of $45,000 per year and is expected to grow by 8 percent this year and each year thereafter. The property value is expected to increase a *total* of 8 percent over an expected investment period of eight years. Mortgage terms presently available are 12 percent interest for 75 percent of value for 25 years. The required before-tax investment yield on equity (k) is 14 percent.

How would an estimate of value be made for this property?

Financial analysis of income-producing properties

11

This chapter deals with the *permanent, or* long-term, mortgage financing of income-producing properties such as apartment complexes, office buildings, warehouses, and shopping centers. Financing these types of real estate differs considerably from residential financing. Risks associated with the economic condition of the national and local economy, competitive pressures from other businesses, and locational considerations all influence the profitability of a given income-producing property. Consequently, the ability of an investor to repay a mortgage loan is affected by all of these forces in combination.

Considering the many types of risks to consider, the lender and borrower are faced with complex decisions when evaluating income-producing properties and the amount of financing that may be provided for a given venture. Modern techniques are available for use in financial analysis, which help in the assessment of risk and profitability of a particular investment. These techniques form the basis of this chapter. Knowledge of these techniques and their application will create an understanding of the economic requirements of a project that must be met to obtain long-term financing.

Financial analysis of income-producing properties

Developers and investors in income-producing properties must provide appropriate documentation to financial institutions when seeking *long-term,* or *permanent* funding for projects. This documentation is usually referred to as a *loan submission package.* Generally included in such a package are items on the following list:

I. Loan application.
   a. Amount of request.
   b. Interest rate requested.
   c. Term of the loan (years).
   d. Borrower identification.
   e. Commitment terms—expiration dates.
II. Property characteristics.
   a. Plot plan of site or survey.
   b. Topographical or contour map.
   c. Aerial maps, photos.
   d. Building plans, renderings, specifications.
   e. Soil tests—drainage.
   f. Utility hookups available.
III. Legal documentation.
   a. Legal description of property.
   b. Easements, property taxes, assessments, deed restrictions.
   c. Title opinion or insurance binder.
   d. Zoning, land use restrictions, relevant building codes.
   e. Environmental controls, potential hazards.
IV. Borrower data.
   a. Experience, development history.
   b. Credit reports, financial statement.
V. Appraisal report.
   a. Data from economic studies.
   b. Data from feasibility studies—site selection studies.
   c. Survey data, vacancy surveys.
   d. Site analysis—market analysis.
   e. Cost approach (if appropriate).
   f. Market approach (if appropriate).
   g. Income approach (if appropriate).
   h. Correlation and opinion of value.
   i. Operating statement.

Loan application

Loan submission packages usually include a request for the amount of funds desired to finance the property in question. Generally borrowers will indicate an amount related to the appraised value (Section V) of projects being proposed for financing. Included with the request for funds will be request for a specific rate of interest and a maturity period desired.

Commitment terms include a time limit for the lender to act on the loan application and any other conditions that a borrower deems essential to the financing of a project. For *proposed* developments, permanent or long-term financing commitments must usually be obtained *before a* commitment is arranged for the construction, or interim, loan. Because permanent lenders fund projects *after* construction is completed, they must be certain that borrowers carry out certain responsibilities during the proposed development period. Common *contingencies* found in loan commitments from permanent lenders are listed below:

a. Time allowed for acquisition of a construction loan or interim financing by the borrower.
b. Completion date for construction phase of project.
c. Minimum rent-up requirements for permanent financing to become effective.
d. Provisions for gap financing, should the rent-up requirement not be met.
e. Expiration date for loan commitment and gap extensions.
f. Provisions for design changes and approval.

Essentially these items represent *contingencies* that must be negotiated before loan applications are approved. When financing is being sought on *proposed projects,* these contingencies are especially important because they establish that the loan, if approved, will be made *subject to* specific conditions. Should those specific conditions not be met, the permanent commitment can expire, thereby releasing the lender from any obligation to make the long-term loan.

These contingencies are indispensable to lenders because they require that developers carry out certain responsibilities should the permanent loan be approved. For example, provisions (*a*) and (*b*) require that the borrower have a specified time to find an interim lender willing to make a loan to cover construction and development costs, and that the project be completed by a specific date. In some cases, the permanent lender also may be providing construction funds; however, because large permanent lenders are usually life insurance companies, pension funds, and so on, they are not likely to be located in the city where the project is to be developed. The permanent lender will usually prefer to rely on a local lender to provide construction, or interim, funds and to monitor construction. The completion date contingency acts as an incentive to developers to work as efficiently as possible toward a pre-agreed completion date, or face the possibility of losing the loan commitment.

As for minimum rent-up requirements, this contingency is used to help assure permanent lenders that local economic conditions, which were used to justify the appraised value and feasibility of the project, are favorable. The permanent lender will usually require a provision such as this to shift some project and economic risk to the interim lender who should be very familiar with the local market and who specializes in construction lending in that market. Should the project not rent up to a specified percentage of occupancy, or a pre-agreed break-even point, within a reasonable period of time after completion, the rent-up contingency results in the expiration of, or a modification in, the long-term commitment. Expiration would force the construction lender to extend its interim loan beyond the term originally intended. At that time, another long-term lender would have to be found, or the construction lender would have to assume the risk of long-term financing. This is, of course, unless the interim, or a third party, lender is willing to agree to some type of "gap" financing. In that event, should the occupancy requirement not be met, long-term funds are usually advanced by the long-term lender *in proportion* to the occupancy achieved by the expiration date, with allowances for full funding made as occupancy increases. The difference, or gap financing, is provided by the interim, or a third party lender, usually at a higher interest rate.

The last item in the above list of contingencies, that is, approval of construction and design changes, is placed in the loan terms to guarantee permanent lenders that proposed projects are developed substantially as agreed when loans are originally negotiated. This helps to insure against substitution of substandard materials and shortcuts to save costs that may jeopardize project quality. This, in turn, would affect the collateral value for the permanent loan. We should again note that this list of contingencies are more relevant in situations where a proposed project is being considered for financing. Where *existing properties* are being financed, or refinanced, most of these contingencies are not as generally applicable. In these cases, the terms of financing and the expiration date on the commitment are generally most important to lenders and borrowers.

The loan application and the detail cited above serve as a focal point around which lenders and borrowers negotiate. Although offers and counteroffers by borrowers and lenders are likely, unless a formal request for funds is initially made and specific terms requested, lenders have no way of gauging the seriousness of financing requests. By requiring formal loan applications and a submission package, investors, or their representatives, must disclose all relevant facts involving projects, thereby incurring cost, time, and effort. Based on this effort, lenders are, in turn, willing to spend the necessary time and effort in seriously analyzing loan proposals.

Property characteristics

Because sites and proposed improvements serve as collateral for mortgage loans, lenders require documentation on property characteristics as part of loan submission packages. Lenders want to know the physical attributes of the real estate being financed: its topography, drainage characteristics, size, and its shape and location relative to other improvements. In addition, its proximity to public right of ways as well as certification that electric, water, gas, and telephone utilities are available to the site must be included.

With regard to building plans and specifications for proposed projects, when amounts requested for financing are large, lenders will have staff or consulting engineers inspect the plans for engineering feasibility within the cost range indicated in the loan proposal. Lenders will be as concerned as developers with design esthetics and conformity with sound construction practices. A detailed breakdown of all materials specified to be used in construction is also reviewed as to quality and cost estimates.

Legal documentation

This section of loan requests generally includes a legal description of a property; a title opinion or commitment for title insurance including a description of any easements, assessments, liens, land use controls, deed restrictions, relevant building code or zoning regulations; and variances that may affect the value or future marketability.

Considerations external to the property, such as any environmental impact and adjacent hazards, should also be included in the proposal. These considerations are important for financing projects being proposed for development as well as for existing properties.

The primary legal concerns of lenders are that the nature of the lien created by the permanent financing be made absolutely clear, and what, if any, *potential* liens or other influences could possibly develop in relation to the property being financed. Further, lenders want assurance that in the event of default, the property can be readily sold, if necessary, after foreclosure and that the lender's position in the distribution of proceeds in the event of foreclosure and sale is clearly defined.

Borrower data

As indicated in an earlier chapter, when a borrower signs a note for a loan on mortgaged real estate, he generally becomes personally liable in the event of default. Hence, lenders will require personal financial statements and credit reports from borrowers to determine credit history and involvement in present and past transactions.

One recent development, however, in the field of real estate finance has been a trend of limiting the liability of borrowers when very high-quality, secure properties are financed. This is done by including a nonrecourse clause in the mortgage. Essentially this clause limits the liability of borrowers by restricting the claim of lenders to proceeds from the sale of the *real estate* in the event of default. Because this is a limitation of the borrower's liability and potentially reduces the lender's ability to recover losses in the event of default and foreclosure, it is a point that is negotiated by lenders and borrowers. This provision also places more emphasis on the quality of the property from the lender's perspective, as income produced from the property must repay the loan, and the property value must always be sufficiently high to repay the loan balance should a property become financially troubled.

Lenders also consider the experience of borrowers in the field of real estate development and financing before extending loans. Generally, a resumé of the borrower's development activities and projects will be included in the loan submission package in addition to credit reports and personal financial statements. Because real estate financing involves lending large sums of money to many individual borrowers and relatively small development companies, the success or failure of a particular development hinges largely on the performance ability of relatively few "key" individuals. Hence a history of past successes and failures coupled with credit reports gives lenders more information on which to base the decision to lend.

It should also be pointed out that borrowers may be general partners in a partnership formed to develop proposed projects or to buy existing real estate. In this event, lenders will want to examine partnership agreements to determine the identity of other partners, how and when equity capital will be raised, and whether liability for the partnership is clearly placed with the general partners. (Partnerships and equity investment in real estate are discussed in more detail in Chapter 17.) Any partnership agreements will usually be reviewed by the lender's legal staff to assure the lender's lien position and to make certain that proper provisions for management of the project and provisions for selling or transferring general and limited partner interests are clearly set out in the agreement. In cases where loans are made to partnerships, lenders want assurance that the general partners, be they individuals, corporations, or other partnerships, are effectively the management that will be responsible for developing and managing the real estate being financed. Provisions that allow for ownership to change through the transfer or sale of partnership interests to other general partners may effectively bring about a major change in management or ownership. Further, if no restrictions on the transfer of partnership interests are made by the lender, the character and management capability of new partners may be substantially different from the partners who originated the loan. Hence, lenders usually require some minimum net worth requirement and some experience requirement of any subsequent general partners as a condition of obtaining the loan. Otherwise any transfer or sale of partnership interests may be viewed as a material change in partnership ownership, and lenders may choose to treat the situation as if a sale of the property occurred. Therefore, lenders may choose to incorporate a "due on transfer" clause in the mortgage, making the mortgage loan balance due should any new general partners not meet the criteria set out in the loan agreement.

Appraisal reports and project analysis

Also included as a part of loan requests submitted from borrowers to lenders on income-producing properties are appraisal reports. Appraisals are usually done by independent fee appraisers who are commissioned by borrowers. These appraisals are then reviewed by a lender's staff appraisers or lending officers, knowledgeable in appraising at the lending institution. As discussed in the previous chapter, when developing an appraisal, the appraiser is charged with the responsibility of making an independent estimate of value for a property being financed. This estimate of value and the operating statement that is also developed in the appraisal are then used by investors, lenders, and other parties who must perform a financial analysis and make lending and investment decisions.

In most cases involving real estate, lenders and borrowers have the same objective in mind, that is, a successful, economically viable project. The appraisal and the economic studies utilized in its development are the foundation for decision making by all parties to the transaction. Even though the appraisal and economic data gathered in its support are developed by an independent appraiser, who works for a fee not contingent on the loan being approved and who has no ownership interest in the development, the estimate of value is based on a considerable amount of estimation and judgment. As we discussed in the previous chapter, the availability and quality of data usually dictate which of the three approaches to value will be used. Further, the use of economic data from market studies and a market area analysis must be used to generate rental schedules, expenses, vacancy rates, and estimates of market yields that directly affect value. Because the opinion of value is *estimated,* based on projections made from data, there can be variation in accuracy of the estimate. It is the objective of lenders and investors to carefully review the appraisal data and determine whether the development of the estimate of value is based on sound economic principles.

Appraisal reports. To illustrate how the appraisal section of a loan submission package may be viewed by lenders and investors, a hypothetical example involving the Sandalwood apartment complex has been chosen for analysis.

The Sandalwood proposal provides for 108 units of mixed one-, two-, and three-bedroom apartments in the northern section of the city, where most development of rental property in the higher rental range has been occurring during the past five years. The property is well located, being near the intersection of two major interstate highways and within 5 miles of the largest regional shopping center in the city.

The site is 5.5 acres with gently sloping terrain, excellent drainage, and no apparent hazards. The area is presently zoned for apartment development and has no unusual easements or land use restrictions. All utilities are available at the site, and no off-site development is required. The development is to be undertaken by D. C. Hall, Inc., a real estate firm with 20 years of development experience in the Southwest. Financial statements for the firm have been included, and a favorable credit report has been obtained on the firm from Dun and Bradstreet.

Economic information provided in the appraisal reveals that the Sandalwood project is located in a large city in the southwestern part of the United States. Economic base data provided in the appraisal report indicate the existence of a growing local economy with petroleum, electronics, banking, and computer processing comprising the base industries. Information developed and recently updated from a market study of housing needs in the area indicate that the area population is growing at the rate of about 1,000 persons per month from in-migration plus natural increase. Housing demand appears to be very strong as measured by very high rates of absorption in the market area of single-family and apartment units and a vacancy rate in rental property in a range of from 2 to 3 percent.

In addition to the generally favorable background report, information from the market area analysis on Sandalwood and three comparable apartment projects is shown in Exhibit 11–1. Detailed information has been compiled on apartment mix, square footage, amenities (pool, tennis, sauna, clubhouse), parking, laundry facilities, utilities, acreage, and age of the projects in the area. Rental schedules for each comparable project have been gathered from a field survey of the market area. It should also be noted that the three comparable units selected for use in the analysis have been sold within the last six months.

Analysis of the cost approach. Estimates of market value were made using all three approaches to valuation. Data relevant to the cost approach to valuation is provided in Exhibit 11–2. In examining the cost breakdown in Exhibit 11–2 it can be seen that the final cost estimate including land for our hypothetical project is $2,585,350. This represents about $26.60 per square foot of improvement and an average cost of about $23,938 per rental unit. Component parts of the structure as a percentage of total cost are broken down as follows:

	Per-cent of total	Cost per square foot
Base cost	60.7%	$16.14
Other on-site costs	7.5	2.01
Amenities	7.7	2.06
Indirect costs	10.6	2.83
Land cost	13.4	3.56
Total	100.0%	$26.60

The preceding breakdown should be carefully considered to determine (1) if the Sandalwood project can be constructed within the cost estimate and (2) whether the percentage breakdown of construction cost components (e.g.,

EXHIBIT 11–1
Summary of market area analysis—comparable properties

	Turkey Creek	Moss Point	Oakwood	Sandalwood
Number of units/ square feet (average)	120/825	135/875	90/850	108/844
Number of one bedrooms	75	75	60	68
Number of two bedrooms . . . . :	30	45	30	26
Number of three bedrooms	15	15	0	14
Total square feet improvement	107,000	126,000	80,500	97,200
Total rentable square feet	99,000	118,125	76,500	91,200
Pools	2	2	1	2
Tennis courts	2	4	No	4
Sauna	No	Yes	No	Yes
Clubhouse	3,000 sq. ft.	3,500 sq. ft.	2,500 sq. ft.	3,000 sq. ft.
Covered parking	No	No	No	No
Parking per unit	1.75	1.75	1.75	1.75
Laundry hookups.	Common facility	Yes	Common facility	Yes
A/C	Yes	Yes	Yes	Yes
Individual metering	Yes	Yes	Yes	Yes
Land (acres)	5.75	7.25	4.0	5.5
Age	2 yrs.	6 yrs.	3 yrs.	—

	Rent schedule as of –			
	1/81	*1/81*	*1/81*	*Est.*
One bedroom	$ 288	$ 306	$ 270	$ 295
Two bedrooms	338	356	320	345
Three bedrooms	388	406	–0–	395
Average rent	313	333	287	320
Gross income	450,000	540,000	309,600	414,800
Sale price	2,700,000	3,348,00	1,795,680	—

	Sale date			
	9/80	*7/80*	*12/80*	
Sale price per unit	$22,500	$24,800	$19,952	—
Sale price per square foot	$25.23	$26.57	$22.30	—

land, amenities, etc.) are similar, or whether they deviate from cost breakdowns on comparable apartment projects constructed in similar locations. This latter aspect is crucial because if one or more of Sandalwood's component costs are above or below component costs for competitive projects in the same market area, such differences will affect rents. For example, if the proportion of land cost and the cost of amenities included in the Sandalwood project are

EXHIBIT 11–2
Cost estimate—hypothetical Sandalwood apartment project

Description:
    108 units, 97,200 square feet, two-story (garden) walk-up, swimming
    pool, sauna, 189 parking spaces, 4 tennis courts, 5.5 acres.

Item:

Excavation.	$ 53,320	
Foundation and backfill.	81,090	
Basement/storage facilities	80,210	
Framing	276,965	
Flooring	80,650	
Carpeting.	72,400	
Plumbing.	152,275	
Heating—A/C.	205,455	
Electrical—lighting fixtures.	82,180	
Masonry/outside walls	147,680	
Interior walls—finish and trim.	121,045	
Painting and wall covering	76,640	
Roof structure.	81,090	
Roof sheeting/covering	57,650	
Base cost.	$1,568,650	60.7%
Other on-site costs:		
Parking lot.	$ 80,000	
Streets, gutters	115,000	
Total	$ 195,000	7.5%
Amenities:		
Swimming pool.	$ 85,750	
Tennis courts—clubhouse	100,200	
Landscape.	15,000	
Total	$ 200,250	7.7%
Indirect costs:		
Construction interest and fees	$ 175,000	
Legal, architect, accounting		
fees, overhead	100,000	
Total	$ 275,000	10.6%
Total improvement costs.	$2,238,900	
Land (by comparison)	346,450	13.4%
Total cost	$2,585,350	100.0%
Total cost per square foot.	$26.60	

greater than those costs in competing projects, there should be justification for these differences and additional support for higher rents which will be necessary to cover the higher costs.

Such justification could be that Sandalwood is in a better location than the competition (hence the higher land cost) or that the amenity package is more attractive. In any event, in addition to carefully reviewing the accuracy of estimates when looking at the cost breakdown for any project, comparisons, when possible, between the project proposed for financing and the competition in the *same market area* should be made. Any deviations in size, cost, design, and amenities should be considered carefully, and justification must be provided indicating how such deviations will be received in the marketplace.

In many cases, a detailed breakdown of cost is not available on existing properties that have been recently constructed in the market area. However, lenders do have experience with projects that have been constructed in the past in similar locations which can be helpful in making comparisons. Even though construction costs may have increased rapidly, the *proportional* relationships between land costs, indirect costs, amenities, and other site costs may still be used for comparison purposes. Also, building cost manuals are available to estimate current building costs that can, in turn, be used to verify the accuracy of proposed construction costs.

Analysis of the market approach. In making an analysis of the data used in the market approach, information from the market analysis provided in Exhibit 11–1 will be used by the lender to review the development of the rent schedule for Sandalwood. It should be noted from the exhibit that much of the data that is presented with the appraisal report deals with the size of the improvement, the number and type of rental units, parking space, amenities, and current information on rents that are being collected as well as current vacancy experience. From the data presented, the rental schedule was developed based on a careful comparison of Sandalwood with its competition. This was done by weighing the pros and cons of each major aspect of Sandalwood with comparable properties and attempting to "price" those advantages and disadvantages accordingly. This market data should be reviewed to decide whether or not the rental schedule is justified from the data.

As can be seen in Exhibit 11–1, the rental schedule developed for Sandalwood is $295 per month for one-bedroom apartments, $345 per month for two-bedroom apartments, and $395 per month for three-bedroom apartments. This rental schedule is justified with the following analysis. Note that the rental figures for Sandalwood are higher than those presently established at Oakwood and Turkey Creek, but lower than rents at Moss Point. An inspection of the data in Exhibit 11–1 reveals that Sandalwood units are slightly larger and more amenities (pool, sauna, etc.) are offered when compared to Turkey Creek. The opposite relationship exists in the same comparison with Moss Point. Compared with Oakwood, Sandalwood units are slightly smaller on the average, but offer much more in amenities (individual laundry hookups, tennis, and sauna facilities).

In addition to the general observations that have been made relative to Sandalwood and the three comparables, several other relationships should be weighed. A sample of these comparisons are listed in Exhibit 11–3. An examination of the comparative ratios in Exhibit 11–3 coupled with the data in Exhibit 11–1 provides insight into whether a project *conforms* to competing

EXHIBIT 11–3
Comparative ratio analysis—market area—property characteristics

		Turkey Creek	Moss Point	Oakwood	Sandalwood
a.	Cost/price per square foot........	$25.23	$26.57	$22.30	$26.60
b.	Rent per square foot	$ 4.21	$ 4.29	$ 3.85	$ 4.27
c.	Ratio rent to cost	16.7%	16.1%	17.3%	16.1%
d.	Rentable to total square feet	92.5%	93.8%	95.9%	93.8%
e.	Units per amenities (tennis).......	60	33.75	—	27
f.	Units per acre of land	21.0	18.6	22.5	19.6
g.	Parking spaces/unit	1.75	1.75	1.75	1.75

properties in a market area, or whether a proposed project *differs* in the quantity of space and services offered to consumers. To the extent a proposed project conforms to what the competition offers, the rents and costs must also conform with the competition. On the other hand, to the extent the combination of space and service differs from the competition, then any differences in rents and costs must be justified in the analysis as being a favorable difference, or one that fills a need in the marketplace.

Such a comparative analysis is shown in Exhibit 11–3. The ratios labeled (*a*) and (*b*) in the exhibit summarize cost and rent per square foot and the ratio between the two. The ratio developed in (*c*), or how much rent is expected per dollar of cost, is extremely significant relative to what the competition is offering. The ratio of rentable square footage to total square footage (*d*) reveals how *intensively* the improvements have been designed and how much space has been allotted to common use areas such as clubhouses, lobbies, hallways, and so on. Excessive space allocated to common areas may be viewed as too luxurious and nonproductive. This measure is vital in the analysis of shopping centers, office buildings, and hotel/motel developments than in apartment development. However, it should always be carefully considered in all developments.

The amenities package offered by the developer (if any) should be gauged in relation to the number of potential users. Item (*e*) in Exhibit 11–3 gives some idea of how extensively amenities will be used in the development. Other ratios could be developed for swimming pools, clubhouses, golf facilities, and so on, on the basis of dollars spent on amenities per unit, if available. If such facilities are not provided in the proper amount or quality, this must be eventually reflected in rents charged per unit, as the market responds to the amenity package offered. Significant deviations from what the competition offers must be justified on the basis of whether or not a need exists in the market area being served.

Land use ratios as in (*f*) and (*g*) show how dense occupancy will be relative to the land area. Generally if a low-density development is proposed (holding all else constant), higher rents must be charged. Support must be given as to whether there is sufficient demand for such intensity of development. Of course the opposite holds true if a high-density development (relative to competing properties) is being proposed; it may be possible to offer lower rents. But whether tenants will like high-density living must be carefully analyzed. These ratios are meant to illustrate only a few of the comparative ratios that help to describe the service-cost package being offered in a development. Depending on the kind of project, the types of ratios that will be developed will differ somewhat, although the goal of the analysis is the same.

Based on these summary ratios, the "gap" in the market that Sandalwood is attempting to reach becomes apparent. Relative to Turkey Creek and Oakwood, Sandalwood offers more amenities per unit and slightly lower building to land density of development, leaving more open space. The rental units are slightly smaller; however, the efficiency in design could be favorable, as indicated by the ratio of rentable square feet to total square feet of improvements. From this analysis, the trade-off facing the renter becomes clear, a slightly smaller, more efficiently designed unit in a less intensely developed (units per acre) project with more amenities, for a slightly higher rental. When viewed in this way, Sandalwood could fill a gap between Turkey Creek and Mosspoint. The costs of achieving this design for Sandalwood also appear to be in line with the suggested rent schedule. If market demand is strong, this combination of attributes could be very successful.

Based on the justification of the rent schedule developed for Sandalwood through the market area analysis, and by virtue of the fact that the three comparable properties used in the market area analysis have recently sold, gross income multipliers for each of the comparable properties were used in the market approach to value and are provided in Exhibit 11–4.

EXHIBIT 11–4
Development of gross income multipliers for comparable properties

	Comparable property		
	Turkey Creek	Moss Point	Oakwood
Date of sale	10/80	11/80	5/80
Sale price	$2,700,000	$3,348,000	$1,795,680
Gross income	$ 450,000	$ 540,000	$ 309,600
GIM	6.0	6.2	5.8

Given these *GIM*s for the comparable properties and the gap in the market that Sandalwood appears to fill between Turkey Creek and Moss Point (per Exhibit 11–3), coupled with the detailed market area analysis, a *GIM* of 6.2 was selected for use for Sandalwood, via the market approach. With

Sandalwood's gross income estimated at $414,800, when multiplied by 6.2, this resulted in an estimated value of $2,571,750 (rounded).

Based on the analysis provided in the example, this estimate of value may be reasonable. However, in many cases when there are not as many properties directly comparable to the subject property, such judgments are not as easily made. In these cases, it may be necessary to place more reliance on the cost approach or the income capitalization approach. As pointed out previously, under the market approach the fewer comparable properties available, the greater the likelihood of error in the *GIM* chosen for valuation. As we have pointed out, the estimate of value is also highly sensitive to the *GIM* chosen.

Analysis of the income capitalization approach. This third approach to valuation was also used in the estimation of value for Sandalwood. In developing this approach to value, an estimated operating statement was included based on market data and a survey of competing properties. This operating statement for Sandalwood is shown in Exhibit 11–5. As can be seen

EXHIBIT 11–5
Projected operating statement—Sandalwood project

Annual rent schedule:		
One bedroom	68 @ $295	
Two bedrooms	26 @ $345	
Three bedrooms	14 @ $395	
Gross potential income	$414,800	—
Less: Normal vacancy and collections loss @ 5%	20,740	—
Effective gross income	$394,060	100%
Operating expenses:		
Personnel—wages/expenses	$ 25,080	6.4%
Utilities common areas	15,650	3.9
Management expense	20,420	5.2
Painting and decorating	22,067	5.6
Maintenance—repairs	16,400	4.2
Miscellaneous	3,010	.7
Insurance	6,125	1.6
Real estate taxes	48,050	12.2
Total operating expenses	$156,836	39.8%
Net operating income	$237,224	60.2%

from the statement, net operating income from the project is expected to be $237,224, or approximately 60 percent of gross potential income from the rental schedule considered appropriate for Sandalwood.

Because three comparable properties were available for use for the market approach to value, that data would obviously be very useful for developing the income capitalization approach, and more specifically for developing an over-all rate (*R*) of capitalization. However, if the market approach was not used in the estimate of value because of a lack of quality data, then the cost approach and income capitalization approach would have to be used. More specifically, developing an overall rate (R) would have to be estimated based on current mortgage terms and current equity yields. Otherwise the mortgage-equity approach, or the modified mortgage-equity approach would be used.

Through the market area analysis the prevailing rent schedules and vacancy rates considered to be normal for each of the comparables has been obtained as shown in Exhibit 11–6. Based on prevailing operating expense ratios collected

EXHIBIT 11–6
Determining overall rates of capitalization

	Comparable		
	Turkey Creek	Moss Point	Oakwood
Gross income	$ 450,000	$ 540,000	$ 309,600
Percent vacancy and collection loss	5%	5%	5%
Effective gross income....................	$ 427,500	$ 513,000	$ 294,120
Percent operating expenses	40%	40%	40%
NOI....................................	$ 256,500	$ 307,800	$ 176,472
Sale price.............................	$2,700,000	$3,348,000	$1,795,680
NOI ÷ Sale price	9.5%	9.2%	9.8%

from a local apartment management association, an expense ratio very close to 40 percent of effective gross income has been estimated for Sandalwood. This same ratio is considered to be applicable to the comparable properties, hence estimates of NOI are developed as shown in the exhibit. Ratios of NOI to recent sales prices or the overall rate (R) have been developed for each property as also shown in the exhibit. The indicated range in R for Sandalwood should fall between 9.2 and 9.8 percent. Relying on much the same analysis that was presented in the analysis of the market approach, an overall rate (R) of 9.3 percent was considered appropriate for Sandalwood. The estimated value per that approach would be $237,224 ÷ .093 or $2,550,796.

Final correlation. Based on individual estimates made under all three valuation approaches, that is, cost, market, and income capitalization, the appraiser will make a final judgment by choosing a value believed to be most indicative of market value. It may be equal to the value obtained under any of the three approaches, or it may be somewhere between the three estimated values. Exhibit 11–7 summarizes values derived under the approaches used for Sandalwood.

The appraiser makes the final judgment, giving weight to the method for which the best qualitative information was available and based on experience in appraising similar properties. In our illustration we assume the final appraised value chosen was $2.55 million.

EXHIBIT 11-7
Summary of appraised values under various
appraisal methods

Method	Dollar value
Cost	$2,585,350
Market comparison (GIM)	2,571,750
Income capitalization	2,550,796

The appraisal and operating statements—lender considerations. A primary function of the estimate of value and the operating statement from the lender's point of view is to determine the ability of a borrower to repay a loan, should one be granted. In order to make such a determination, the lender will perform a *financial ratio analysis.* The results of this analysis will then be compared with financial data from comparable properties to judge the accuracy of the operating statement. Results from the analysis will also aid the lender in determining the income potential of the property and its ability to cover loan payments.

To illustrate the use of financial ratio analysis, the reader should again refer to Exhibit 11-5 which provides a breakdown of the income and expenses for Sandalwood apartments for which the borrower is seeking a permanent mortgage loan commitment.

Initially, the borrower is seeking a permanent 25-year loan for 70 percent of value, or $1,785,000 based on the project's appraised value of $2,550,000. How would the lender make a financial analysis of the project?

Debt-service coverage. One of the primary considerations of the lender is the project's ability to generate sufficient income to cover mortgage payments. To help make this determination, the debt-service coverage ratio is widely used by lenders. Using data from the operating statement, this ratio is simply defined as net operating income (NOI) divided by the mortgage payments made during the year for a given loan amount and terms.

Assuming that current lending terms available at the time the borrower is seeking financing are 10 percent interest for 25 years, the debt-service coverage ratio is calculated as:

$$\text{Mortgage payment: } \$1,785,000 \times .009087^* = \$16,220$$
$$\text{Total mortgage payment per year: } \$16,220 \times 12 = \$194,644$$

* Monthly loan constant, 10 percent, 25 years.

$$\text{Debt-service coverage} = \frac{NOI}{\text{Total mortgage payment}} = \frac{\$237,224}{\$194,644} = 1.22 \times$$

Based on the computation of debt-service coverage, it can be seen that income after operating expenses, or NOI, covers the annual mortgage payments 1.22 times. In other words, if the 70 percent loan is granted, there is a cushion or margin of safety for the lender of ($237,224 − $194,644) $42,580. This means that net operating income can fall by $42,580 before the lender will be in any danger of not receiving mortgage payments.

Generally the coverage ratio acceptable to the lender is determined by policy established by the particular lending institution based on *past loan experience* on comparable properties. In cases where loans have gone into default, coverage ratios used when these loans were originated may tend to represent a minimum acceptable or cutoff point for a given lender. A cutoff rate historically used in the real estate industry for debt coverage ratios on residential income property is between 1.20 to 1.25. In other words, most lenders set this range in coverage ratios as the *minimum* amount of coverage they require for any prospective loan in that category. If that industry yardstick is applied in the preceding example, the 70 percent loan, if granted, should result in a debt-service coverage ratio that will just meet the acceptable minimum.

Operating expense ratio. It must be stressed that no one ratio computation made by the lender is sufficient to indicate whether a loan should be made or how much should be loaned. The lender must rely on a series of ratios and review all of them together as part of an overall financial analysis. Another equally important ratio, which is computed by most lenders, is the operating expense ratio. This is simply the ratio of total expenses to effective gross income. In our illustration it is computed as:

$$\text{Operating expense ratio} = \frac{\text{Operating expenses}}{\text{Effective gross income}} = \frac{\$156,836}{\$394,060} = 39.8\%$$

This ratio can then be compared to operating ratios compiled from comparable properties or from published industry data.[1] If there is a significant deviation from operating expense ratios reported from comparable properties, the lender will then make an item-by-item percentage comparison from data in the operating statement. In this way it can be determined what expense category caused the difference. An industry standard used by lenders for the operating expense ratio on new residential income properties ranges from 35 percent to 40 percent of gross potential income. This means that the ratio computed in our example, or 39.8 percent, generally falls within the range of operating expenses reported on a national basis by apartment managers.

It is clear that a higher operating ratio, say, significantly above 40 percent, will leave very little net operating income to cover debt service and will probably make lenders reluctant to finance a project. Does it also follow that a significantly lower operating expense ratio, say, less than 35 percent, will make a lender more eager to finance a project? Not necessarily, as many developer/

---

[1] A commonly used source of industry data for apartment complexes is National Association of Realtors, Institute of Real Estate Management, *Apartment Building Expense Analysis* (Chicago: National Association of Realtors, annual issues).

borrowers have been known to "dress up" operating statements by reducing expenses in order to show a higher net operating income. They then argue that with the higher net operating income, more can be borrowed since the debt-service coverage will be acceptable, even with greater amounts borrowed. Lenders are usually aware of such possibilities and will closely question any operating expense ratio that is considerably lower than the industry average. The borrower then has to prove how the project might be managed more efficiently and at a lower cost than comparable properties.

Vacancy and collection loss ratio.   Another part of the operating statement that will be given careful attention by the lender is the adequacy of the vacancy and collection loss estimate. Obviously, this ratio must bear a close relationship with vacancy rates reported by managers of other apartment complexes in locations similar to the subject property. This ratio is highly sensitive to local economic conditions and signals when housing or other investment property has reached a saturation point, or a point of oversupply that may be critical to the market absorption of any new units. Lenders are aware of vacancy rates in their lending areas and constantly monitor and update this information.

Although no hard-and-fast industry ratios exist for vacancy rates, it is generally believed that when residential income properties consistently run vacancies in excess of 5 to 7 percent of potential revenue, they may be risky ventures and have difficulty in meeting debt service.[2] Similarly, any attempt on an investor's part to use a ratio below 5 percent will also be questioned closely by a lender. As was the case with the operating expense ratio, this may simply be an attempt by the investor to "dress up" the operating statement, and the lender will challenge any attempt to do so. Therefore, the ratio used in this case should be a reflection of the current rate experienced in the local apartment market, unless the borrower has a compelling reason to do otherwise.[3]

Break-even ratio.   Another commonly used ratio indicates the amount of occupancy required before a project can meet all cash outlays associated with operation and debt service. This ratio is called the break-even ratio and is computed as:

$$\text{Break-even ratio} = \frac{\text{Operating expenses} + \text{Debt service}}{\text{Gross potential income}}$$

In our example, based on the 70 percent loan being considered by the lender, the break-even ratio is:

$$\frac{\$156,836 + \$194,644}{\$414,800} = 84.7\%$$

---

[2] For commercial properties such as shopping centers and office buildings, less than a 5 percent vacancy factor could be normal because of the long-term leases usually applicable in those situations.

[3] Such a reason may be that the subject property has a distinct locational or design advantage over other complexes, or perhaps has a better amenity package than its competition. However, a lender would still have to be convinced of such an advantage.

This ratio indicates that should the 70 percent loan be granted, the complex must be rented up to 84.7 percent of its potential revenue before all cash outlays for operations and debt service can be met. At that point the owner is earning a zero operating profit, or is "breaking even."[4]

Another way of looking at the same ratio is to consider the maximum vacancy rate tolerable, if the loan is granted, that will still enable the owner to break even. This vacancy rate in our example is simply 100 percent, representing gross potential income, less the break-even ratio, or 84.7 percent, leaving 15.3 percent as the maximum reduction in revenue from vacancies that can occur before the owner incurs losses.[5]

Standard break-even occupancy ratios used in underwriting income producing residential property range from 80 to 85 percent of gross potential income. As has been pointed out, when properties are to be developed, permanent lenders *require a minimum occupancy* ratio before the lending commitment becomes effective.[6] Obviously, a lower break-even occupancy ratio is desirable for both lender and borrower, given an accurate operating statement, as both are better off after the break-even point is reached. In our example, the break-even point of 84.7 percent estimated for the property in question, falls within the 80–85 percent suggested as an underwriting standard.

Return on total investment. Another ratio used widely by lenders in underwriting decisions involving income-producing properties is return on total investment. This ratio indicates how much income before debt service is being earned on total invested capital and is also a measure of current profitability to the investor. In our example, this ratio is computed as:

$$\text{Return on investment} = \frac{NOI}{\text{Total assets}} = \frac{\$237,224}{\$2,550,000} = 9.3\%$$

The importance of this ratio lies in the fact that lenders desire some indication of a property's total return. Unless an owner is earning a reasonable profit, property management and maintenance may suffer. As has been shown previously, this ratio has also been used for R, or the overall capitalization rate when the income capitalization approach was used in valuation. From the perspective of *investors* and *lenders,* however, this ratio is viewed as an indication of *profitability* and should be judged relative to the return on total investment on comparable properties, which ranged from 9.2 to 9.8

---

[4] It should be pointed out that when the break-even ratio is calculated in this case, all operating expenses were assumed to be fixed. In other words, the ratio was computed assuming that operating expenses would be the same regardless of the occupancy rate.

[5] When these ratios are used, it is assumed that all operating expenses tend to be fixed, that is, not dependent on occupancy. To the extent some of the expenses are variable, they may be lower as occupancy declines and should be reflected in the computation. Another assumption made here is that actual occupancy is proportional to gross potential income.

[6] In these cases a permanent commitment is made that involves the sale of a construction loan to the permanent lender. When an occupancy standard is used as a contingency in the permanent commitment, the lender is not required to purchase the construction loan until that standard is reached.

percent. Consequently, the property being analyzed in our example is expected to return a yield that is roughly competitive with yields on total investment earned by other investors in similar properties. However, this yield will fluctuate over time on all properties depending on the changes in inflation, interest rates, the supply and demand for housing, and many other factors affecting the national as well as local economy. Hence, unlike the break-even and debt coverage ratios, this ratio cannot be interpreted as a standard for comparison over time. In order to interpret this ratio properly, comparable ratios must be compiled on comparable properties covering the same time interval for which the comparison is desired.

Return on equity (ROE). This ratio is simply defined as:

$$ROE = \frac{BTCF}{Equity} = \frac{\$42,580}{\$765,000} = 5.6\%$$

It measures the current cash dividend earned by investors on the equity invested in a project. This yield is sometimes referred to as the "cash on cash" return. While lenders are generally more concerned with the ability of a property to generate sufficient revenue to cover debt service, it is also recognized that if investors do not receive some reasonable return on equity there is potential for deferral of maintenance and repair on the improvement that could jeopardize the security for a loan. Therefore, the extent of a current yield to investors can be used as an indication of the incentive for investors to maintain the property.

As was the case with the return on total investment (R), the current return on equity (ROE), will vary with economic conditions. There is no fixed standard against which this relationship may be compared. It should be comparable to current yields being realized by investors who own similar properties. It could also correspond to dividend yields earned on some common stocks, depending on the type of property being analyzed. Based on the selling prices for each of the three comparables in Exhibit 11–1, if they were currently mortgaged on the same terms as requested by Sandalwood, that is, a 70 percent, 25-year, 10 percent interest loan, the respective current equity yields would range from 5.2 percent to 7.3 percent. This range would serve as an appropriate standard for judging Sandalwood.

Summary—financial analysis

The financial ratios computed for Sandalwood and the standards against which it is being compared are summarized in Exhibit 11–8. Based on a comparison of these *financial characteristics* and the ratios computed on *property characteristics* in Exhibit 11–3, it appears that if the borrower is financially sound and has satisfactory experience in developing similar projects in recent years, the Sandalwood project seems to be both *economically feasible,*

EXHIBIT 11–8
Summary financial ratio analysis

Ratio	Sandalwood	Standard
Debt-service coverage	1.22×	1.20–1.25×
Operating expense ratio	39.8%	35–40%
Vacancy—collection loss	5.0	5–7
Break-even occupancy rate	84.7	80–85
Return on total investment (R)	9.3	9.2–9.8
Return on equity (ROE)	5.6	5.2–7.3

based on the comparative analysis of cost and service to be provided, and *financially feasible,* based on its expected ability to produce income, meet expenses, repay debt, and provide investors with a satisfactory return. The loan in all probability would be granted in this instance.

Rating loan terms

As seen from the preceding analysis, if a 70 percent loan were requested for financing Sandalwood, it would more than likely be granted. However, there are many instances when properties proposed for financing seem to be *economically* viable, but because of the amount of the loan request, they appear not to be *financially* feasible. To illustrate, assume that the Sandalwood project was proposed for *80 percent financing* instead of *70 percent financing.* What would have been the reaction of the lender? With the interest rate of 10 percent for 25 years, the annual payments on an 80 percent loan based on a value of $2,550,000 would be a mortgage loan amount of $2,040,000 with monthly payments of $18,537 shown as follows:

$$\$2,040,000 \times .009087^* = \$18,537$$
$$\$18,537 \times 12 = \$222,444$$

* Monthly loan constant, 10 percent, 25 years.

Annual payments based on this level of financing would cause deterioration in three key ratios shown in Exhibit 11–8. These three key ratios are recomputed as follows:

$$\frac{NOI}{DS} = \frac{\$237,224}{\$222,444} = 1.07 \times \text{ (debt-service coverage)}$$

$$\frac{DS + \text{Operating expense}}{\text{Effective gross income}} = \frac{\$222,444 + \$156,836}{\$394,060} = 96.2\% \text{ (break even)}$$

$$\frac{NOI - DS}{\text{Equity}} = \frac{\$237,224 - \$222,444}{\$510,000} = 2.9\% \ (ROE)$$

Obviously when compared to the standards shown in Exhibit 11–8, these ratios fall short of the normal underwriting guidelines. Hence a loan at 80 percent of value would undoubtedly not be granted.

When viewed from the lender's perspective, how can a loan amount be established such that the debt-service requirements based on the amount loaned fall into an acceptable underwriting range? In the present case, for example, we know that a loan in the range of 70 percent of value was acceptable for Sandalwood. That was the amount initially applied for, and from the ratio analysis, it appeared financially acceptable. But what if the original application had been for some other percent of value? How would the lender determine an acceptable range for financing?

Such a range is usually determined from the debt-service coverage ratio. Generally it is established by lending policy; then given loan terms, a maximum loan amount can be ascertained so that an acceptable underwriting range is met. In the example at hand, let us assume that the lender will require a minimum debt-service coverage ratio of 1.25 × net operating income. This information can be used to establish the maximum loan amount by beginning with the familiar debt-service coverage ratio:

$$\frac{NOI}{DS} = 1.25 \text{ (desired coverage ratio)}$$

The debt-service ratio also indicates that (NOI) must be 1.25 × debt service as follows:

$$NOI = 1.25 \ (DS)$$

Substituting NOI of \$237,224 from the Sandalwood operating statement, we have:

$$\$237,224 = 1.25 \ (DS)$$
$$\$189,779 = (DS)$$

and $(DS) \div 12 = \$15,815$ per month

or, monthly debt service (MDS) cannot be greater than \$15,815, given that the lender insists on 1.25 × debt-service coverage. Assuming that current loan terms are 10 percent for 25 years for this type of property, then the maximum loan amount will be determined as:

$$\begin{aligned} \text{Maximum loan amount} &= MDS(MIFPVa, 10\%, 25 \text{ yrs.}) \\ &= \$15,815(110.047230) \\ &= \$1,740,397 \end{aligned}$$

Because the stream of monthly payments must provide an annual yield of 10 percent compounded monthly to the lender, by discounting the \$15,815 monthly payments by the required mortgage interest rate, the \$1,740,397 maximum loan amount is determined. This represents a loan of approximately 68 percent of value.[7] Obviously, the solution to this type of problem will vary by type of property, risk, loan terms, and the desired debt-service coverage ratio.

Inflation, valuation, and rating loan terms

Much of the preceding analysis involving financial ratio analysis was based on the assumption that the economic environment at the time the project was proposed was relatively stable. In recent years, because of increasing inflationary pressures, traditional ratio analysis and some underwriting standards have been modified. Further, the problems associated with the fixed interest rate mortgage (discussed in Chapter 9 on alternative mortgage instruments) are also shared by lenders on income-producing properties, and the traditional mortgage payment pattern has also been modified from time to time in response to inflation.

The problems faced by lenders and borrowers on income-producing properties are much the same as those faced by lenders and borrowers financing single-family residential properties. As expected inflation rises, NOI produced by properties is also expected to increase. However, as we have already seen, when anticipated inflation increases, monthly payments on fixed rate mortgages increase sharply. This is because lenders incorporate anticipated inflation over the expected loan term into mortgage interest rates in order to provide them with the same real return that prevailed before the increased inflation. This results in the "tilt effect" previously discussed. In the case of income-producing properties, this economic scenario is shown in Exhibit 11–9. In that exhibit, note the distance between the debt service (DS) for a given loan, given inflation rates A and B, and net operating income (NOI) under the same two rates of inflation. The difference between NOI and DS represents the amount of "cushion" or excess of NOI over required debt service. Given a sharp increase in the rate of inflation from A to B, debt-service requirements for a given loan amount will increase sharply from $(DS - A)$ to $(DS - B)$. NOI will increase from $(NOI - A)$ to $(NOI - B)$ as anticipated inflation is actually realized each year. However, the cushion or difference between NOI and DS in the early years of the loan is reduced from RK to RM as the inflation rate increases from A to B. This means that even though an increase in the rate of inflation will *eventually* result in an increase in NOI, the change in debt-service requirements occur *immediately*. Hence the debt-service coverage ratio will fall. Also, as a result of the increased debt-service requirements, the break-even ratio will increase and ROE will decline.

The ultimate effects of an increase in the rate of inflation from the lender's perspective are many: (1) traditional debt coverage ratios may have to be

---

[7] Recall in the Sandalwood example the debt-service coverage was 1.22 ×, and the loan was 70 percent of value.

EXHIBIT 11-9
Inflation, net operating income, and debt service

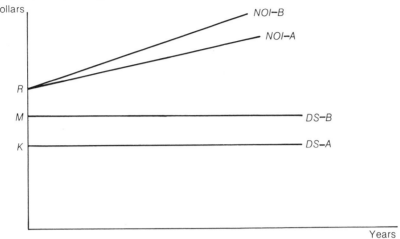

modified to reflect such sharp rises in inflation, (2) smaller loans may have to be made to reduce debt service, thereby keeping the traditional debt-service coverage; or (3) a modification must be made to the fixed interest rate mortgage which results in a better balance between the net operating income produced by a property and required debt service.

Modification in underwriting standards

To illustrate the problems and alternatives faced by lenders, we assume that early in the year a property with a projected value of $1,000,000 is being proposed for development, expected inflation is running at 6 percent annually, and market interest rates are 10 percent for 25 years for a $750,000 loan, or 75 percent of value. Market studies reveal that NOI is projected to be $103,000 at the time that the project is completed.[8] Based on these conditions, monthly payments would be ($750,000 × .009087) $6,815, or $81,780 per year, making the debt-service coverage ratio 1.26×, which is in the acceptable range for underwriting purposes. Before permanent funding can be obtained on the above project, assume that the expected inflation rate increases to 8 percent. If this occurred, mortgage interest rates would suddenly increase to 12 percent. Debt-service requirements would increase from $81,780 to $94,788 per year. Traditional underwriting standards would not be met. Even allowing NOI to increase at an inflation rate of 8 percent, making it approximately equal to $104,900 by year-end, would not support debt service

---

[8] This includes a 6 percent increase in income by year-end because of inflation. NOI at the beginning of the year would be about $97,130.

based on the $750,000 level of proposed financing. This sharp increase in mortgage payments means that service coverage would fall from 1.26× to 1.11×, which would be unacceptable considering traditional underwriting standards. Similarly, the break-even ratio would rise and the current equity yield would fall relative to previous standards.

However, because inflation in rents is expected to increase at the rate of 8 percent annually, and assuming that the project is economically sound, *NOI* would be expected to increase relative to debt service in each year as follows:

	Year				
	1	2	3	4	5
NOI	$104,900	$113,292	$122,355	$132,444	$142,716
DS	94,788	94,788	94,788	94,788	94,788
Ratio	1.11	1.20	1.29	1.39	1.51

Although the debt-service coverage is "below normal" in the first year, it improves considerably with time. Based on this projection, the lender may be willing to modify underwriting standards by accepting below standard debt-service coverage and other ratios, in the initial phase of operation, with the expectation that such ratios will improve in a short period of time.

This underwriting problem is brought on due to the design of the level payment, standard mortgage to which lenders are accustomed, and increased inflation. This instrument tends to work well in periods of stable prices. When inflation occurs, however, sharp increases in mortgage payments result because the tilt effect and traditional underwriting standards may have to be modified. Otherwise, lenders may turn away profitable lending opportunities and economically viable projects may go unfunded. Relaxation of underwriting standards does increase the risk of default to the lender because of the smaller cushion above debt-service requirements. The lender must carefully consider the liquidation value of the property, the personal assets of the borrower, and the possibility of charging a slightly higher rate of interest as compensation for the added risk.

Reduction in amount loaned

Assuming the project is economically viable but the lender is not satisfied that underwriting standards should be modified, a reduction in the amount borrowed, thereby maintaining some desired coverage ratio, could be considered. The procedure established in the preceding section would be followed. In our example, maintaining 1.25 coverage, given an *NOI* equal to $104,900 and a 12 percent mortgage rate for 25 years, would require that the lender limit financing to $663,992 or 66.4 percent of value.[9] By reducing the loan-to-value ratio to 66.4 percent, the desired coverage ratio would be maintained. However, the equity requirement would be 33.6 percent as opposed to 25 percent, had the initial proposal been funded. This increased equity requirement may be unacceptable to the investor because of the unavailability of equity funds, and because he may be forced to earn a lower current and investment yield on equity.[10] So this alternative may be unacceptable to the investor.

Use of equity participations or "kickers." In an attempt to provide investors with sufficiently large mortgage loans, when because of sharp increases in inflation such loans do not meet lenders' underwriting standards, there has been an increase in the use of equity participation loans. The term *equity participation* is somewhat of a misnomer because generally the lender does not acquire an ownership interest in the project. Rather, the lender usually makes a loan, structuring payments to meet the minimum acceptable debt coverage standards, and then requires a participation in gross income, net operating income, or in any income in excess of a predetermined *break-even point.* Such a participation provision or "equity kicker" is required to be paid to the lender over a specific number of years, called the lock-in period. The lender earns this "kicker," which really amounts to a risk premium for taking additional risk, by modifying underwriting standards. A substantial penalty is usually required should the loan be prepaid during the lock-in period. The penalty is either specified at the time of origination or is negotiated with the lender at the time of prepayment. A prepayment penalty is usually required because the inital payments on the mortgage are set below market levels, and should the prepayment occur shortly after the loan is originated, the lender would want to be assured that enough compensation for risk taking up until that time would be received.

To give an illustration of how such an arrangement could work, in our previous example, the $750,000 loan being considered could not be made at a market interest rate of 12 percent because of an inadequate debt-service coverage ratio (recall that at 12 percent interest annual mortgage payments were $94,788 and the debt-service coverage ratio was 1.11×). Assuming that the lender decides that a minimum ratio of 1.25× would be acceptable, the maximum monthly payments that the borrower could ordinarily meet from *NOI* would be:

$$NOI \div \text{Debt service} = 1.25$$
$$\$104,900 \div \text{Debt service} = 1.25$$
$$\text{Debt service} = \$83,920 \text{ (or } \$6,993 \text{ per month)}$$

---

[9] Recall the formula $NOI \div DS = 1.25$ and $DS \times 1.25 = NOI$, then $DS \times 1.25 = \$104,900$ and $DS = \$83,920$, or $6,993 per month. Finding the present value of $6,993 at 12 percent compounded monthly at 12 percent results in a loan of $663,992, or 66.4 percent of value.

[10] The effect of debt financing on equity yields is considered in the next chapter.

Based on payments of $6,993 per month, the debt-service coverage would be in the desired range. For a $750,000 loan, the loan constant corresponding to that level of monthly payments would be $6,993 ÷ $750,000, or .009324, which is close to the loan constant for a 10 percent, 25-year loan. Hence the mortgage payments could be initially structured on the basis of a 10 percent, 25-year loan in order to satisfy the debt-service coverage requirement. The initial mortgage payment would be:

$$\$750,000(MLC, 10\%, 25 \text{ yrs.}) = \text{Base mortgage payment}$$
$$\$750,000(.009087) = \$6,815$$

or annual payments based on the 10 percent mortgage constant would be equal to $81,780 per year. However, the lender must earn a yield equal to or *higher* than the current 12 percent market interest rate on this loan. This is because of the added risk undertaken because of the reduction in debt service being made to accommodate the investor and the added risk taken by the lender. To earn a higher return, we assume that a participation of 25 percent in any excess of *NOI* over the base level of debt service (defined at the break-even point) will be required by the lender. Assuming that *NOI* increases at 8 percent annually, total mortgage payments would be determined as shown in Exhibit 11–10.

EXHIBIT 11–10
Equity participation loan payment pattern

	Year				
	1	*2*	*3*	*4*	*5*
NOI	$104,900	$113,292	$122,355	$132,144	$142,716
− Base payment	81,780	81,780	81,780	81,780	81,780
Cash flow over "breakeven"	$ 23,120	$ 31,512	$ 40,575	$ 50,364	$ 60,936
× 25% participation	$ 5,780	$ 7,878	$ 10,144	$ 12,591	$ 15,234
+ Base payment	81,780	81,780	81,780	81,780	81,780
Debt service	$ 87,560	$ 89,658	$ 91,924	$ 94,371	$ 97,014

Looking at Exhibit 11–10, it can be seen that the payments under the equity participation agreement range from $87,560 to $97,014 over the five years shown. Should the investor desire to refinance or prepay the loan balance after five years, a penalty would have to be negotiated with the lender at that time. That is, of course, unless the penalty was specified at the time of loan origination.

Obviously, the investor would prefer knowing in advance what the penalty for refinancing or selling the property during the lock-in period will be. There are many ways such a penalty could be spelled out. One way would be to specify that the penalty be high enough to compensate the lender for the yield that would have been earned if the loan had been originated at the market rate (12 percent) plus an additional risk premium. A risk premium would be added for the risk taken by the lender by originating the loan at below market rates, and for placing a heavier reliance on the property to produce income in the future. Assuming such an additional premium to be 2 percent, the sum of all mortgage payments received each year, plus the prepayment penalty would have to be great enough to yield the lender a total of 14 percent in that case.[11] Hence the penalty would be written in such a way as to guarantee the lender an annual 14 percent yield regardless of when the loan is repaid. The prepayment penalty in our example is $182,179 and would be determined by discounting the total of all mortgage payments received each year plus the mortgage balance by 14 percent as follows:

Annual payments	×	IFPV, 14%	=	PV
$87,560		.877193		$ 76,807
89,658		.769468		68,989
91,924		.674972		62,046
94,371		.592080		55,875
97,014		.519369		50,386

Present value payments = $314,103

Mortgage balance $\times$ IFPV, 14% = PV
$750,000 × .9416* = $706,200 × .519369 = $366,778

* 10 percent, 25-year loan prepaid after 5 years.

Solving for the penalty, we would have:

$750,000 = PV of payments + PV of mortgage balance + PV of penalty
$750,000 = $314,103 + $366,778 + Penalty(.519369)
$750,000 = $680,881 + Penalty(.519369)
$ 69,119 = Penalty(.519369)
$133,083 = Penalty

Note that the loan balance ($706,200) plus the penalty ($133,083) or $839,283 exceeds the initial amount borrowed. Hence the lender will receive a sizable share of any appreciation in property value.

It should also be noted that the lender's participation rate could be based on gross income, net operating income, or some other measure. Some lenders prefer to tie the participation rate to gross income rather than to net operating income because gross income is more easily determined. In cases where net operating income is used, disagreement could arise concerning the appropriateness of some items deducted by the owner as operating

---

[11] This yield is expressed as an annual rate of compound interest.

expenses. However, investors would argue that net operating income should be used for participation rates because if lenders are to participate in the potential growth in income on a project, they should also be expected to share in expenses. Hence, in some instances, a participation rate in *both* gross and net operating income may be negotiated.

The equity participation example just described is but one of many alternatives that lenders and borrowers could agree on in designing an alternative to the fixed payment mortgage during periods of increasing inflation. Obviously, the main points to be considered in such an arrangement are (1) the initial payment level, (2) the participation rate during the lock-in period, and (3) a prepayment penalty which is either specified or must be negotiated if prepayment occurs during the lock-in period. It should be noted here that there are great similarities in the equity participation mortgage, the variable rate mortgage, and graduated payment mortgages that were previously discussed in relation to single-family residences. While these mortgages are not yet prevalent for income-producing properties, there is every reason to believe that such mortgages could be used more in the future. Also, while the example used for illustrating equity participation was based on an apartment complex, similar mortgages are also used when funding commercial properties such as office buildings, shopping centers, and other properties, the discussion of which follows next.

Financing commercial properties

Shopping centers.   Another important area of real estate lending involving income-producing properties is the financing of shopping centers. Shopping centers have developed widely since World War II with the advent of modern highways, automobile transportation, and the consequent suburban relocation of households. Generally, three categories can be used to classify shopping centers. The *neighborhood center* is primarily comprised of businesses providing essential goods and services as well as some convenience goods. This category will average approximately 50,000 square feet of leasable area. The *community center* contains businesses which, in addition to essentials and convenience goods, provide some consumer durables such as furniture and appliances as well as clothing apparel. These centers average about 175,000 square feet of leasable floor area. The third category is the *regional center* which is fully diversified, including a larger number of the business activities contained in neighborhood and community centers, and also recreation, eating establishments, and banking. These centers contain about 500,000 square feet, or more, of leasable floor space.

Approaches to development and financing.   Generally, there are three approaches to developing and financing shopping centers and other commercial properties. Each approach affects the risk of financing as viewed by a lender. One approach is referred to as the *primary tenant-owner* approach. This approach is used when a large, well-established retail department store, for example, takes it upon itself to develop and finance a shopping center, making itself the primary tenant. The idea behind this approach is that since its retail business will be the primary economic attraction for most consumers in the trading area, by developing the center itself, the store can exert control over its competition as well as complementary business lines. In addition, the store can earn investment returns from leasing space to other firms. If the firm is a financially sound enterprise and if the locational and market analyses are favorable, most lenders find financing of this kind of center very desirable. The primary tenant-owner approach is not frequently used, however, as many large retailers do not have the expertise or desire to become involved in real estate development and management.

The second approach to financing and developing shopping centers is the *preleased* approach. This approach commonly involves the developer contacting prospective tenants during the design and planning stages. Lease commitments are obtained from them in advance of actual development. Often a developer can prelease space to prospective tenants if a major retailer has signed a long-term lease. Indeed, a developer may offer a major tenant a below-market rental inducement to obtain a lease. If the market analysis is sound, this "anchor" tenant will help draw customers for other business establishments, thereby making additional preleasing much easier. With preleasing, terms established at the time the lease agreement is made are binding commitments. Consequently, the revenue to be generated from the center after completion is viewed with more certainty by lenders. This in turn implies that debt service will be covered with more certainty, making the loan more attractive to lenders. The preleased approach to shopping center development is the method most widely used by developers.

The last approach is referred to as *speculative* development. In this approach, a developer has a market study and site analysis made. If development proceeds immediately, before competitors see the opportunity, space can be leased easily and quickly. In other words, little preleasing takes place under this method; financing occurs on the strength of the location, market study, and background of the developer. The developer must be established and financially sound to obtain mortgage financing for such an endeavor. The risks are greater under this approach, compared to the other two approaches. Lenders are extremely reluctant to finance such projects unless convinced otherwise. This technique is used least in the development of large shopping centers because of the great risk involved. However, for smaller centers, it is more frequently used.

Market and location analysis.   A market study and location analysis are vital in obtaining financing for shopping centers. These studies must be as technically correct as possible when used as a basis for financing. Items which must be considered in the market analysis, and which will be analyzed closely by lenders, include the following:

a. Establishment of a trading area for the center.
b. Projection of population and income within the trade area.
c. Breakdowns of retail expenditure patterns of households in the trade area.
d. Attitude surveys of nearby residents who may use the shopping facilities.
e. Traffic count of vehicles on main traffic arteries adjacent to the center.
f. Competition from other shopping centers.
g. The supply of available space in other shopping centers.
h. Rent levels on available space in other centers.
i. Appropriateness of the business mix planned in the center.
j. Adequacy of parking space.

Financial analysis—shopping centers.   When a developer leases space to a prospective tenant, there are three basic methods used in determining the lease payments. These lease payment patterns are referred to as *straight, net,* and *percentage.* Any one of these lease patterns may be used in a given situation, but in many cases facets of all three patterns are combined when a lease agreement is written.

Straight lease.   Under a straight lease agreement, rent is generally negotiated at a fixed price based on the square footage in the area to be leased. The price per square foot generally will vary somewhat with the location within the center and with the total quantity of space leased by a particular tenant. The lease will be made for a specific time period and will usually contain provisions for escalation in the event insurance costs, taxes, or other specific costs increase during the term of the lease.

Smaller businesses in shopping centers generally contract under a straight lease agreement. This is because their sales volume is not enough to induce them to enter into a percentage lease agreement. Sometimes a major tenant also may be able to negotiate a fixed straight lease agreement on favorable terms, especially if the lease is somewhat vital to preleasing and development of the entire project.

Net lease.   The net lease usually contains the same provisions as the fixed or straight lease with additional provisions that all operating expenses, maintenance, utilities, insurance, and taxes are to be paid by the tenant. The rent negotiated in this case represents a net return to the owner of the shopping center. With proceeds under the net lease, the owner pays only debt service and perhaps costs associated with maintaining common areas in the shopping center.

The net lease relieves the owner of the shopping center from managerial burdens which are shifted to the tenant. In many cases, this form of lease comes into being when tenants have personnel requirements that are essential to the business, such as food stores that are maintained continuously or department stores with changing display areas and redecorating done by store personnel.

In recent years the so-called *net-net* lease has developed whereby the tenant pays operating expenses, plus a prorata share in property taxes and insurance. This technique is used to protect the owner from sharp increases in these expenses.

Percentage lease. The percentage lease gets its name from the fact that rents are partially determined by the sales volume of the business that is leasing space. Generally, rents in this situation are determined in two parts. A fixed, or flat, charge per square foot is made, which is the minimum rental requirement regardless of the sales volume. Then a percentage is negotiated which is applied to all sales volume above a specific sales level. For example, a store may pay $1.75 a square foot annually, payable in monthly installments, plus 2 percent on annual sales volume over $1 million. In this event, the $1.75 per square foot represents the minimum rental that a tenant can expect to pay. The additional 2 percent over the $1 million sales volume is applicable only if sales exceed $1 million. The amount of rent received over and above the minimum price per square foot is called *overage.*

Under a percentage lease, the minimum price per square foot available to a tenant is lower than the rent under a straight lease. This is because the owner of the shopping center is actually in somewhat of an equity position in each of the businesses in the shopping center, as part of the lease payments may come from overage. Since a potentially higher rental income can be earned with higher levels of sales, the owner must also share in the risk of decline in sales. This will be reflected in a lower minimum price per square foot compared to what would be paid under a straight lease.

In some cases percentage leases are also net leases in the sense that all taxes, insurance, maintenance, and so on, are paid for by the tenant. The cost of this service, when paid for by the tenant, is reflected in the rental determination as negotiated between the owner and tenant.

Lenders analyze provisions in all leases executed between developers and tenants very carefully. The credit standing of the businesses and their ability to make the lease payment are scrutinized closely by lenders. This is necessary because lease payments from tenants ultimately provide the income that the owner of the shopping center will use for debt service. Special consideration is given to situations in which many of the leases executed in a given shopping center are of the percentage-lease type. This is true because, contrary to the fixed or straight lease, the rental income to the developer will change with sales from establishments in the center. Consequently the ability of the borrower to repay debt will also change depending on business activity.

Additional items that the lender will closely evaluate when approached by a developer for financing include:

a.   The length or time of executed leases—if obtained from high-quality tenants, longer leases reduce risk to the borrower and lender.

b. Lease restrictions regarding changes in tenants. To what extent are existing tenants protected from competing businesses?

c. Are tenants required to join a merchant's association for promoting business of the entire shopping center?

d. How are common areas to be maintained? If the management of the shopping center is expected to maintain these areas, is there sufficient income for leases to cover it?

e. What conditions exist in leases for increases in taxes, insurance, and so on, which may face the owner of the center?

f. What is the minimum income from leases? How much overage is expected? What have been trends in the sales of tenants in comparable locations?

As was the case with the residential income property analysis, a financial ratio analysis and a ratio analysis of property characteristics would be carried out for shopping centers based on data provided in a loan submission package and from other sources available to the lender. Ratios that take on particular importance in shopping center analysis are (1) the ratio of leaseable area to total area contained in the improvement, (2) the ratio of leaseable area to total land area, and (3) expected sales revenue per leaseable square foot. The first ratio indicates the percentage of total improvement area that can actually be leased and used for business activity. Common areas in shopping centers, such as mallways, rest areas, and escalators, are obviously not used directly for business activity, but costs associated with construction and maintenance of these areas must be recovered in lease revenue. Hence, excessive or elaborate mallways with fountains will result in higher lease costs, which may not be covered by revenues. These design characteristics have serious financial implications and must be judged relative to the retail market area being served. In higher income markets, households may prefer more elaborate design and be willing to pay slightly more for products and goods to shop in such an environment. On the other hand, lower income households may be more price conscious of goods that are being purchased. They may consider design characteristics of a shopping environment to be secondary in importance.

The second ratio, leaseable area to total land area represents the proportion of land on which lease income will be earned relative to the total land requirements necessary for the project. It is an important ratio because if too much land is used for nonleasable area such as parking, and so on, lease income may never be high enough relative to total project investment to provide an adequate return. On the other hand, if too little space is provided for parking and adequate common areas of movement into and around the shopping center, the resulting inconvenience may hurt the sales volume of individual business establishments.

Finally, the revenue projected per square foot of leaseable area should be based on the percentage of income of households in the area that is spent on consumer goods, and on the relative mix of businesses within the center. Such projections should be based on a planned layout of businesses within the center and the potential revenues to be generated by each. Rents and any overage can then be assessed by considering all combinations of mix and location so that total rental revenue per leaseable square foot is maximized.

Office buildings. Financing office buildings, another form of commercial property, is similar to financing shopping centers. Ordinarily, development and financing consist of the primary owner-tenant, preleased, and speculative approaches—the same approaches discussed in connection with shopping centers. As to the types of lease executed between owner and tenant, the straight lease, net lease, and net-net lease are used most often. Should the straight or net lease be used, both usually include an escalator provision for possible increases in insurance and taxes. In the case of special-purpose, preleased office space (such as in medical buildings), the unit is generally unfinished with the tenant taking responsibility for equipment installations. Long-term leases are normally executed in these cases with escalator provisions for general price increases between lease renewal periods.

Market study. A major area of departure between shopping center and office building development lies in the market study. The general office building market has traditionally been in central-city areas. Suburban locations have developed more slowly because of the necessity of a central workplace in urban areas which is generally accessible to the urban labor market. For firms utilizing relatively large amounts of labor, the central city areas have been the most feasible location for most types of office buildings.

The first category of office complex to move into suburban areas has been special-purpose types, such as small professional buildings. The reason for this arises because of the services provided and the need for proximity to the households served. The advent of interstate highways with inner-belt and outer-belt connections has modified the traditional journey to work pattern in central cities. Locations on outer-belt perimeters are now as accessible as downtown locations for much of the labor force. As a result, many general office building complexes that would formerly have located in central city areas are locating in suburban areas. Increased accessibility, coupled with rising center city property taxes and income taxes on employees, also has made suburban locations more attractive to both businesses and employees. This changing pattern of development has made the market study for office buildings increasingly more complicated because of the even greater importance attributable to location.

In market studies for office buildings, many factors are closely evaluated by lenders:

a. Population growth in the market study area.
b. The historical ratio of office space to population.

c. A market survey of all available market space in the market area.
d. A breakdown of vacancies at the time of the market study by:
  1. Location.
  2. Size of building.
  3. Age and condition of structure.
  4. Rent range per square foot.
e. An historical analysis of the *absorption rate* of office building space, or how rapidly new office space developed in recent years has been absorbed by market demand.
f. An accounting of all proposed office building construction slated to occur in the market area, by location and rent range.

Essentially what the market study must provide is enough data to support the fact that population increases warrant the development of additional office space. Coupled with a current inventory of available space by location and rent range, the lender wants assurance that a loan is not being made on an office complex in a market that is already, or will soon be, overbuilt. Particular attention, therefore, is given to the historical ratio of population to office space and present *absorption rates* on new, recently developed office space.

To the extent that the proposed complex is preleased or is to be an owner-occupied situation, the lender will be more disposed to make a loan commit-ment. In this event, the lender is able to perform a financial analysis on the prospective tenants and to determine their ability to make the expected lease payments. This does not relieve the investor of performing an adequate market study because leases are not permanent. A poor location or an inadequate analysis of the structure of market demand may result in future problems for the investor when leases are to be renewed.

Questions

1 What are the general categories of data that are usually included in a loan submission package?

2 What are some common contingencies included in permanent lending commitments?

3 What is a nonrecourse clause in a mortgage? Why is it used?

4 Why should a mortgage lender be concerned if a permanent loan is being sought by a partnership?

5 When comparing a project against comparable properties in the same market area, deviations in size, rents, design, location, and amenities are said to be important. Why is this true? Explain.

6 What does "final correlation of value" mean?

7 Why should a lender be concerned with profitability ratios? Shouldn't this be a concern only of investors?

8 When rating loan terms, why are traditional underwriting standards sometimes difficult to apply?

9 In periods when expected inflation increases significantly, what modifications in rating loan terms do lenders consider? Why does inflation cause problems in relying on traditional underwriting standards?

10 Why is the term *equity participation* a misnomer? What does the term *lock-in* period mean?

11 When lenders use equity participation loans, why do they usually insist on a prepayment penalty?

12 What parallels do you see between equity participation loans and graduated payment loans or variable rate loans discussed in earlier chapters?

13 When financing shopping centers, what is an "anchor" tenant? How are lease payments structured for such a tenant?

14 Why is preleasing so important in shopping center and office building financing? What is meant by developing on "speculation"?

15 What are the three main categories of lease agreements? What is meant by overage on a lease?

Case problems

1 Equity Life Insurance Company is considering a permanent funding commitment for One Main Place, a three-story suburban office building proposed for financing. An extensive market study has been conducted by Jackson and Rogers, a real estate consulting firm, and a portion of that study has been included in the appraisal report section of the loan submission package. Additional data provided in the submission package is based on two comparable projects that have recently been sold in the market area. The data provided below are considered to be the most significant areas of difference. You have been assigned the responsibility of organizing the data for One Main Place and the two comparable properties in a form that can be used for comparison purposes.

	One Main Place	Comparison I	Comparison II
Location......................	1900 Elm Pkwy.	2050 Elm Pkwy.	Smith at Oak (SE)
Proximity to subject..............	—	1 mile	2 miles
Square footage..................	40,000	37,500	39,000
Leaseable footage...............	30,000	28,000	27,000
Lease price (per square foot).......	$5.50	$5.20	$5.30
Land area......................	1.5 acres	1.75 acres	1.9 acres
Cost*/price....................	$1,130,000*	$1,050,000	$1,100,000
Parking.......................	100	120	150
Land cost (estimate).............	$106,000	$57,000	$42,750
Age..........................	—	2 yrs.	3 yrs.
Stories	2	2	2
Vacancy rate (estimate)	5%	5%	4%
Months since sold...............	Present	1 yr.	6 mos.

Operating data on the two comparable properties was available only in summary form and is presented as follows:

Operating data

Location	One Main Place	Comparison I	Comparison II
Gross income...........................	$165,000	—	—
Vacancy and collection loss.............	8,250	—	—
Effective gross income	$156,750	$145,600*	$153,700*
Operating expenses.....................	47,025	50,960	53,795
Net operating income	$109,725	$ 94,700	$ 99,905

* Actual data.

Based on current market conditions, financing in a range of 70 percent of value for 25 years at 12 percent interest is expected. The cost estimate for One Main Place is $1,130,000. All three projects are of similar structural design, layout, and quality. One Main Place is located in a slightly more advantageous area, since it has better accessibility to the largest freeway.

a. You have just joined Equity Life Insurance Company's real estate division. How would you begin to compile comparative data on this financing proposal (consider ratios based on *market data and financial ratios* in your answer)?

b. Are there any *major* areas of inquiry that would lead you to request more detailed information from the borrower?

Note: Use standards in Exhibit 11–8 in your financial analysis.

2 Exchange Savings Association is considering a loan application from Peachtree Limited, a real estate partnership, for a 100-unit apartment building. Exchange believes that the project is a sound investment and would like to make a loan on it. However, current interest rates have moved upward from 10 percent, when the feasibility study and appraisal were done on the apartment project, to 13 percent at present.

Rents are presently estimated at $240,000 annually, and based on local economic conditions, demand is strong. Exchange believes rents will keep up with expected increases in the price level, which has been forecast to rise at the rate of 9 percent per year. Vacancy and collection allowances are estimated at 5 percent, and operating expenses at 40 percent of effective gross income. The property has been valued at $1,400,000.

Peachtree has applied for 75 percent financing on this project for a period of 25 years. Exchange normally requires debt service coverage ratio of 1.20 on very good quality proposals ranging upward to 1.25 on more risky proposals.

a. Would it be feasible for Exchange to consider the loan as proposed, given that it expects rents to rise at 9 percent annually (consider a five-year time horizon)?

b. If Exchange requires a minimum debt coverage of 1.20, what would be a reasonable counterproposal?

c. What current return on equity would Peachtree earn if it accepted the counterproposal?

3   Rock of Hartford Insurance Company is presently analyzing a loan proposal from Alkon, a large hotel developer, for $12,000,000 to develop Plaza Center, a high-rise hotel complex in the downtown area of a large midwestern city.

Because of the present high interest rates, Rock of Hartford knows that it cannot make the loan on the property at the requested 70 percent of value. Interest rates have risen sharply from 9 percent to 11 percent in recent months and are expected to hold at that level for the near term.

Alkon had presented a strong case for developing the property even at present high interest rates, as the market is strong and expected to continue to be strong in the future. Rock of Hartford agrees with Alkon's market analysis and would like to make a good counteroffer because it believes that a profitable loan can be made.

Hartford makes a proposal to finance the $16,000,000 project with a $12,000,000 loan and an equity participation. Mortgage payments and loan amortization would be based on a 9 percent interest rate for 25 years. However, Hartford would collect 3 percent of effective gross income annually. It would also receive 15 percent of net operating income (less the sum of the base mortgage payment and the 3 percent of gross income) for a lock-in period of 15 years. Should the loan be repaid within the lock-in period, the agreement stipulates that Hartford will earn a minimum yield of 13 percent annually based on all income received to that point.

Currently, Alkon expects rents on the structure to be approximately $2,500,000 with a 5 percent vacancy and collection loss, plus 35 percent in operating expenses (based on effective gross income). Rents and property value are expected to increase at 6 percent annually for the near future.

a.   Develop a 5 year schedule of cash flow for Hartford and Alkon based on the terms of the equity participation.

b.   Assuming Alkon wanted to pay off the loan after five years, what penalty, if any, would have to be paid to Hartford? What percentage of the outstanding loan balance would this penalty be?

Investment in income-producing properties

─ 12 ──────────────────────────

Thus far this section of the book has dealt with the valuation and financial analysis of income-producing properties. In this chapter income-producing properties are considered from the perspective of the investor. Many variables must be considered by the investor when acquiring income properties. Tax influences, how to assess risk when comparing investment proposals, as well as the proper procedures to use when measuring return on investment, all constitute major questions that must be considered by investors.

In this chapter, many of these issues will be addressed. An appropriate framework for analyzing decisions relating to the acquisition, financing, operation, and disposal of properties will be presented in some detail. Particular attention should be given to this framework as it is a valuable tool for investors, and it will be used to consider many other issues addressed in this and later chapters.

The reader should be aware that the chapter material assumes knowledge of the more important federal income tax provisions affecting the acquisition, operation, and sale of real estate. These provisions as well as considerations affecting the selection of depreciation methods, the minimum tax, and investment related tax strategies are described in the appendix to this chapter. Readers not familiar with federal tax rules affecting real estate are urged to read this appendix *before* reading this chapter.

Measuring returns on investment

One of the criteria that must be met in any investment on income-producing property is that it must provide a competitive return on investment. By competitive return, we mean a return that is equal to returns being realized by investors who own properties equivalent in risk. There are basically two components in measuring return on investment from the investor's perspective. Funds invested during the acquisition phase must be related to funds earned from the *operation* of the property, or from *operation and sale* of the property, if it is sold before the end of its economic life. Funds earned from the operations and/or disposition phase of the investment also can be measured on a *before-tax or aftertax basis*.

To illustrate various measures of return on investment, let us begin with the example of an investor considering the acquisition of a new apartment complex, called Phase I apartments, for a purchase price of $1,000,000. We initially assume that the investor can obtain a loan for 70 percent of value, or $700,000, at 10 percent interest for 25 years. The apartment project, based on market studies, is expected to generate $161,943 in rents during the first year, vacancy and collection losses are estimated to be 5 percent per year, and operating expenses are estimated at 35 percent annually. Based on estimated trends in the market, rents are expected to grow at about 4 percent per year for the next four years. The initial question facing the investor is if the property were purchased for $1,000,000, what would the investor earn on investment?

Determination of cash flow. Exhibit 12–1 contains a summary of all expected *cash* inflows and *cash* outflows associated with the *operation* of the property for five years on a *before-tax* and *aftertax* basis. In looking at the development of before-tax cash flow (*BTCF*), it should be recalled from the previous two chapters, that the operating expense component of cash outflow is composed of all *cash expenses* associated with operating the property for the year. No capital outlays should be included in operating expenses, nor should any noncash items of cost (such as amortization or depreciation) be included. The objective of preparing an estimated statement of cash flow is to provide the investor with a summary of the cash inflows and outflows for the year. This is important because in any type of investment analysis, only cash paid, cash received, and the timing of those cash flows are relevant for investment decision making.

Based on the assumption that the investor can obtain a mortgage of $700,000 at 10 percent interest for 25 years, the amount of debt service that must be paid annually in cash is shown in Exhibit 12–1 to be $77,118. In computing debt service, we have assumed that mortgage payments will be made *annually;* hence the debt service is based on the annual loan constant of .110168 taken from column 6 in Appendix A at the end of this textbook. This assumption was made to simplify the computations throughout this chapter. In practice, mortgage payments would be made monthly; however, this simplification will not alter materially the conclusions drawn from the analysis that is presented in the chapter. Based on the *NOI* expected to be produced from Phase I in years 1–5, the debt service of $77,118, when subtracted from *NOI*, leaves *BTCF*, which is cash available for distribution to the investor from operating the property each year. This is the estimated cash return that the investor would receive from rents less all operating expenses and required debt service.

Aftertax cash flow

The determination of aftertax cash flow (*ATCF*) from operations is also shown in Exhibit 12–1. The fact that the investor has acquired Phase I as an

EXHIBIT 12–1
Estimates of before-tax and aftertax cash flow—Phase I project

	Year				
	1	*2*	*3*	*4*	*5*
A. Statement of before-tax cash flow					
Rents	$161,943	$168,421	$175,158	$182,163	$189,451
Less: Vacancy and collection loss	8,098	8,421	8,758	9,108	9,473
Effective gross income	$153,845	$160,000	$166,400	$173,055	$179,978
Less: Operating expenses	53,845	56,000	58,240	60,569	62,992
Net operating income (*NOI*)	$100,000	$104,000	$108,160	$122,486	$116,986
Less: Debt service (*DS*)	77,118	77,118	77,118	77,118	77,118
Before-tax cash flow (*BTCF*)	$ 22,882	$ 26,882	$ 31,042	$ 35,368	$ 39,868
B. Statement of taxable income or loss					
Net operating income (*NOI*)	$100,000	$104,000	$108,160	$112,486	$116,986
Less: Depreciation	40,000	38,000	36,100	34,295	32,580
Interest.	70,000	69,288	68,505	67,644	66,697
Taxable income (loss)	$ (10,000)	$ (3,288)	$ 3,555	$ 10,547	$ 17,709
(Tax) or savings at 50%	$ 5,000	$ 1,644	$ (1,778)	$ (5,274)	$ (8,855)
C. Statement of aftertax cash flow					
Before-tax cash flow (*BTCF*). . . .	$ 22,882	$ 26,882	$ 31,042	$ 35,368	$ 39,868
Less (tax) or add savings.	5,000	1,644	(1,778)	(5,274)	(8,855)
Aftertax cash flow (*ATCF*)	$ 27,882	$ 28,526	$ 29,264	$ 30,094	$ 31,013

investment has considerable federal income tax consequences. Because the investment is expected to produce income and may be eventually sold at a gain, the taxes payable on such income and gain must be included in the investment analysis framework if accurate estimates of return on investment are to be made.

In Section B of Exhibit 12–1, we have included a statement of taxable income or loss, the results of which must be integrated with *BTCF* in order to estimate an aftertax return on investment. In this example, because we are assuming that the investor is purchasing a new apartment complex from a developer, our discussion of tax influences is limited to deductions for depreciation and interest expense. There are many other tax considerations that may affect a real estate investment depending on the circumstances. A summary of some of these tax influences is contained in the appendix to this chapter.

As can be seen in Exhibit 12–1, depreciation in the amount of $40,000 and interest in the amount of $70,000 were deducted from net operating income in the first year in the determination of taxable income. We begin with *NOI* in this statement because we assume that all operating expenses also will be deductible from realized rents for tax purposes. Because interest on the mortgage loan represents an expense associated with the use of capital, it is tax deductible. However, it should be stressed that only the interest portion of the debt-service requirement on the mortgage is tax deductible, as the difference between the mortgage payment and interest, or amortization, represents repayment of the loan which is *not* tax deductible.

The depreciation charge of $40,000 is based on the cost of the improvement only. Of the $1,000,000 purchase price, it is assumed that $800,000 represents the building cost and $200,000 represents land value. Because this is a *new residential income-producing property,* depreciation expense may be computed under any of the depreciation methods recognized by the Internal Revenue Service. In this case, the double-declining-balance method was selected, based on a 40-year tax life. It is assumed that there will be no salvage value at the end of 40 years. Thus, the depreciation charge was computed by first determining the straight-line rate of depreciation or 100% ÷ 40 years = 2.5%, then doubling the rate to 5 percent.[1] The building cost of $800,000 is then multiplied by the allowable rate of 5 percent in arriving at the charge of $40,000. The charge in the second year is determined by reducing the building cost by the first year's charge of $40,000 and again applying the 5 percent rate in the declining balance. Hence, in the second year we have ($800,000 − $40,000) × 5%, or $38,000, and so on. In choosing the double-declining-balance method, we assume that we are dealing with noncorporate investors, who are sharing profits and losses from this investment equally, and who are *not* affected by tax provisions that apply to items of tax preference.[2] (We will discuss the problem in the context of a single

---

[1] If the reader is not familiar with depreciation methods, establishing depreciable lives, and the tax basis for improvements, the appendix to this chapter should be carefully reviewed.

[2] For a discussion, see the appendix to this chapter.

investor; however, the outcome will be the same for a group of partners in the same tax bracket who own and share equally in the investment.)

Based on deductions for interest and depreciation, taxable income or loss is determined in Section B of Exhibit 12–1. It should be noted that in years 1 and 2 of operation, there are net losses of $10,000 and $3,288, respectively. However, as has been already determined, before-tax cash flow in those two years is positive; that is, if the estimates are accurate, the investor will receive $22,882 and $26,882 in cash flow from operations and yet report losses of $10,000 and $3,288 in each year for tax purposes. This loss occurs because of the depreciation deduction, which is a noncash expense, yet is allowable as a deduction for tax purposes. Reportable tax losses in cases where *BTCF* is positive are sometimes referred to as *artificial accounting losses*. All losses from investments in real estate may be deducted from other income earned by taxpayers who own real estate individually, or through ownership interests in partnerships.[3] These investors are said to be able to "shelter" income earned from other sources by the amount of the loss.[4] Thus, a taxpayer earning ordinary income and in a 50 percent tax bracket would save taxes at the rate of 50 percent on any losses that could be offset against ordinary income. In this case, losses shown in years 1 and 2 would be worth the amount of the loss times the effective rate on ordinary income, or 50 percent of such amounts. In the determination of aftertax cash flow (*ATCF*), the value of these losses is then *added to BTCF*. (This is a very important aspect of real estate investment and should be understood by the reader before continuing.)

Looking again at the *ATCF* pattern in Exhibit 12–1, it is important to see that both the depreciation deduction and interest deduction decline each year due to the declining depreciable basis of the improvement and the declining mortgage balance. These declines, coupled with growth in rents, eventually result in taxable income (year 3) on which taxes must be paid at the investor's marginal tax rate.

Cash flow from sale of property.   Based on the assumption that the investor expects to own the property for a period of five years and then sell it, there will be an additional amount of cash inflow at that time. That amount will be equal to the estimated sale price of the property less the mortgage balance at the end of the fifth year. A schedule of annual mortgage payments, interest and principal, on the $700,000 loan made at 10 percent interest for 25 years is presented as follows:

---

[3] Individuals with interests in corporations or trusts may not use operating losses to shelter other earned income. Such losses cannot be distributed by these entities to investors but must be carried back or forward and offset against net income earned in those years. The ability of individual investors to offset operating losses against current taxable income is a distinct advantage over corporations and trusts investing in real estate. Also individual investors in real estate are not subject to "double taxation" on income, as are investors in corporations. See the appendix to this chapter for a more in-depth discussion.

[4] Hence, investments in real estate are known as tax-sheltered investments.

Year	Beginning balance	Payment	Interest*	Principal	Ending balance
1	$700,000	$77,118	$70,000	$ 7,118	$692,882
2	692,882	77,118	69,288	7,830	685,052
3	685,052	77,118	68,505	8,613	676,439
4	676,439	77,118	67,644	9,474	666,965
5	666,965	77,118	66,697	10,421	656,544

* Interest is simply 10 percent times the outstanding loan balance.

Assuming that the investor estimates that the property will increase in value to $1,134,000 at the end of five years, the before-tax cash flow in the year of sale ($BTCF_s$) would be:

Sale price.........................	$1,134,000
Less: Mortgage balance	656,544
$BTCF_s$	$ 477,456

Aftertax cash flow—sale year. To complete the rate of return computation in the investment analysis shown here, the *aftertax cash proceeds must be included when the property is sold* at the end of the fifth year of operation. To determine aftertax cash flow from sale, taxes due in the sale year must be computed.

Determining taxes payable in the sale year requires a slightly more complicated procedure. To begin, the book value, or adjusted basis, for the property must be established. Book value is defined as the asset cost less total depreciation expense charged during the five-year investment period (see Exhibit 12–1).

Cost basis*.........................	$1,000,000
Accumulated depreciation.............	180,975
Book value (adjusted basis)............	$ 819,025

* This is defined as cost of the property plus any additions made during the ownership period.

Once book value is determined, the total taxable gain on the sale of the asset is arrived at by subtracting book value from the sale price of the asset (less any commissions) at the end of the fifth year.

Sale price.........................	$1,134,000
Book value (adjusted basis)	819,025
Taxable gain	$ 314,975

Since the property in our illustration was held for five years, a portion of the taxable gain is subject to long-term capital gains tax with the remainder subject to ordinary tax rates. To determine what portion of the gain is subject to ordinary tax rates requires that the recapture of depreciation rule be considered.[5] This rule requires that all depreciation taken by accelerated methods in *excess* of straight-line depreciation during the investment period must be taxed at ordinary rates to the extent of total taxable gain. The remainder of any gain, after deduction of ordinary income, is subject to long-term capital gains tax rates. To illustrate:

Accumulated depreciation	$180,975
Less: Straight-line depreciation	100,000
Ordinary income	$ 80,975
Total taxable gain	$314,975
Less: Ordinary income	80,975
Long-term capital gain	$234,000
Total taxes:	
Ordinary income tax: $80,975 × .50	$ 40,488
Long-term capital gain tax: $234,000 × .20*	46,800
Total taxes at sale	$ 87,288

*Based on 50 percent times 40 percent of the capital gain.

Note that in computing ordinary income, an annual straight-line depreciation charge is computed as 2.5% × 800,000 × 5 years, or $100,000, and is subtracted from accumulated depreciation actually taken. This computation is based on the recapture of excess depreciation regulation, which requires that any excess of accelerated depreciation over what would have been taken had straight-line depreciation been used, be taxed at ordinary rates.[6] The amount recaptured, to the extent of any capital gain, is subject to the investor's ordinary income tax rates. Any excess gain is subject to the investor's capital gains tax rate. Total taxes payable in the year of sale can then be subtracted from $BTCF_s$ as shown in Exhibit 12–2 in determining $ATCF_s$.

EXHIBIT 12–2
Aftertax cash flow at sale, Phase I apartment complex, five-year investment period

Cash flow after mortgage repayment:	
Sale price	$1,134,000
Less: Mortgage balance	656,544
Cash flow before tax ($BTCF_s$)	$ 477,456
Less: Taxes at sale	
Taxes on ordinary income	40,488
Taxes on capital gain	46,800
Cash flow after tax at sale ($ATCF_s$)	$ 390,168

---

[5] For a more detailed explanation of recapture of depreciation, see the tax appendix to this chapter.

[6] See the appendix to this chapter for more discussion of this requirement.

Developing measures of investment return

Although the statement of expected before-tax and aftertax cash flow has been developed for Phase I in Exhibit 12–1, there is really no way an investor can judge whether the property will prove to be a profitable investment unless some attempt is made to relate the cash inflows to required investment outflows. By developing measures of return on investment, investors can make decisions regarding expected profitability by comparing such measures against alternative investments.

Exhibit 12–3 contains five measures of return on investment developed for the Phase I investment that may be used by the investor when deciding whether the investment should be undertaken. The first measure of return, called the overall rate of return (R), has been introduced in the two previous chapters. It is defined as $NOI \div$ total investment, where the value of the project is assumed to equal the total investment cost or purchase price.[7] It is equivalent to the overall rate of capitalization (R), used in valuing income properties. However, this measure of return is estimated each year in Exhibit 12–3, as opposed to only the first full year of operation, as would be the case when R is being used only for valuation purposes. Hence, by estimating R annually, some idea of the expected *trend* in net operating income relative to the initial cost of the property can be judged, as well as the ability of the property to produce income over time.

The second measure of return, return on equity (ROE), has also been introduced in the previous two chapters. This measure is now developed on a before-tax *and* aftertax basis and is computed as $BTCF \div$ Equity and $ATCF \div$ Equity. The before-tax ROE, or ROE (BT), is the "cash on cash" return on equity, or cash expected to be received by the investor $BTCF$ in relation to the *original cash equity investment*. The aftertax ROE, or ROE (AT), simply relates increases in $BTCF$ because of tax savings due to artificial losses, or

EXHIBIT 12–3
Selected measures of return on initial investment—Phase I project

Measure	| Year					
	0	1	2	3	4	5
Overall (R)............		10.0%	10.4%	10.8%	11.2%	11.7%
ROE (BT).............		7.6	9.0	10.3	11.8	13.2
ROE (AT).............		9.3	9.5	9.8	10.0	10.3
BTIRR................	18.3%					
ATIRR................	14.3					

---

[7] We use total investment instead of value in the denominator because value is an estimate and total investment represents the actual cost paid by the investor. Also, the investor may have to put additional capital investment into the property after acquisition, making return on total investment a more relevant measure of return.

decreases in *BTCF* because of taxes expected to be paid in years when net income is reported for tax purposes, to initial equity.

Two patterns should be noted from the annual before-tax and aftertax return on equity estimates shown in Exhibit 12–3. First, both series increase each year, with before-tax *ROE* eventually exceeding the rate of return on total investment in years 4 and 5. This is a result of financial leverage, or the use of debt financing in the purchase of the property. Note that the debt service remains constant while the net operating income increases, causing annual return in equity before and after taxes to rise. The issue of financial leverage will be explored in more detail in the next chapter. The second pattern that should be noted is that *ROE* aftertax *exceeds ROE* before tax in years 1 and 2. This occurs primarily because of the artificial tax loss which benefits the investor in those years. These "losses" were discussed in conjunction with the statement of cash flow. By using these measures of return based on initial investment, the investor obtains some estimate of what returns may be both before and after tax, based on original investment or cost.

Current yields on real estate—subsequent years

In Exhibit 12–3 the measures of return developed for total investment (overall R) and on equity (ROE) were based on the *initial* cost of the property and the *initial equity* invested, respectively. While these measures of return on investment are used very frequently in analyzing real estate investments when they are being *considered* for acquisition, it is also meaningful to develop such measures based on current market values *after* a property has been acquired and is being operated. This is especially true if real estate returns are going to be compared with current yields on other investments, such as stocks or bonds, which are based on current market values.

To accomplish measures of *current yields* on real estate (as opposed to returns on initial investment or cost), the market value of the property should be determined each year. Then current yields can be computed on both current property value and on the current value of the investor's equity in a property. In our example, the initial cost of Phase I was $1,000,000, and it is expected to increase in value to $1,134,000 over five years, or at a rate of about 2.5 percent per year. If the property increased in value according to the pattern shown in Exhibit 12–4, our estimates of *NOI, BTCF, ATCF,* and mortgage balances, which were computed earlier, can be used to develop measures of current yields on total investment and on equity.[8] This has been done in the exhibit. Based on the current yields shown in Exhibit 12–4, the investor would be in a position to make comparisons with yields on other investments, which would be computed using current market prices.

---

[8] Instead of using estimates of market value, some promoters of real estate investments add the annual mortgage amortization to original equity to obtain an estimate of current equity. This approach is usually more conservative than what is being shown here. Others may add amortization to *BTCF,* treating it as part of the investment return. Such treatment is improper.

EXHIBIT 12–4
Current yields on investment and on equity

	End of year				
	1	2	3	4	5
Actual property value	$1,025,000	$1,050,625	$1,076,890	$1,103,815	$1,134,000
Less: Mortgage balance ...	692,882	685,052	676,439	666,965	656,544
Current equity	$ 332,118	$ 365,573	$ 400,451	$ 436,850	$ 477,456
NOI	$ 100,000	$ 104,000	$ 108,160	$ 112,486	$ 116,986
BTCF..................	22,882	26,882	31,042	35,368	39,868
ATCF	27,882	28,526	29,264	30,094	31,013
Current yield on total investment: NOI ÷ Current property value	9.8%	9.9%	10.0%	10.2%	10.3%
Current yield on equity: a. Before tax: *BTCF* ÷ Current equity......	6.9	7.4	7.8	8.1	8.4
b. After tax: *ATCF* ÷ Current equity......	8.4	7.8	7.3	6.9	6.5

When making comparisons with yields on other investments, it is imperative that such yields be computed both on a before-tax and aftertax basis, as was done for our Phase I illustration. This is because most alternative investments being considered by investors relative to real estate will usually be either fully taxable or tax exempt. To illustrate, assume one year from acquisition of Phase I that an investor was comparing current yields on common stock, corporate bonds, tax-exempt bonds, and Phase I. Hypothetical current yields on common stock (defined as current dividend per share divided by market price), corporate bonds and tax-exempt state and municipal bonds (defined as the annual interest payment divided by market price), and the current yields on equity at the end of the first year of operation of Phase I are illustrated as shown here:

	Current yield before tax	Current yield after tax*
Common stock...............	12 %	6 %
Corporate bonds	10	5
Municipal bonds.............	7	7
Phase I	6.9	8.4

* Assuming a 50 percent tax bracket investor.

Limiting the comparison to only a current before-tax yield on equity would be very misleading as Phase I would appear to provide a relatively low return before-tax. However, the current aftertax yield on Phase I is considerably higher than the other yields because of the tax shelter aspect of real estate. This does *not* necessarily mean that Phase I should be chosen over the other alternatives because (1) there could be a considerable difference in risk between Phase I and the other alternatives and (2) only one year out of the entire investment period is being considered.[9] Nonetheless, it is important to point out that such comparisons should be made both on a before-tax and aftertax basis because real estate investments do have the unusual tax shelter property brought about because of artificial accounting losses.[10]

In summary, when developing or using reports containing measures of return on investment or current yields, the investor should be certain as to whether or not such measures are based on original investment or current market values, and whether they are before or after taxes. This is particularly important when making comparisons with investment opportunities in real estate or with other investment securities. In all instances, however, no attempt has been made to incorporate an important element of return to the real estate investor into the analysis, that is, the capital gain element. Also, no attempt has been made to consider the importance of timing of the receipt of cash flow. Because return on investment and current yields do not incorporate these extremely important elements, we must rely on the internal rate of return. This is the subject of the next section of this chapter.

Measuring internal rates of return on equity

Referring again to Exhibit 12–3, two additional measures of return on investment are shown. These measures, abbreviated as *BTIRR* and *ATIRR*, mean before-tax internal rate of return and after-tax internal rate of return, respectively. The internal rate of return concept has been used throughout the preceding chapters of this textbook. In this case, it represents the annual rate of compound interest earned on the equity over the entire period the investor expects to own the Phase I complex. In our example, we compute those rates of return both before and after tax, under the assumption that the property is acquired, then operated for five years and sold at that time. Illustrating the computation on a *before-tax* basis, it would be computed as follows:

$$E = \frac{BTCF_1}{(1+k)^1} + \frac{BTCF_2}{(1+k)^2} + \frac{BTCF_3}{(1+k)^3} + \frac{BTCF_4}{(1+k)^4} + \frac{BTCF_5 + BTCF_s}{(1+k)^5}$$

---

[9] The subject of risk and investments is briefly discussed in the next chapter and in the appendix to that chapter.

[10] The reader may wonder why real estate is subject to such preferential tax treatment. Historically, real estate has been a "favored" industry, or one in which Congress has thought that tax incentives should be provided to induce investment in residential and other types of real estate.

Using the values for $BTCF$ and $BTCF_s$ for Phase I developed in Exhibits 12–1 and 12–2 in the preceding section we have:

$$\$300,000 = \frac{\$22,882}{(1 + k)^1} + \frac{\$26,882}{(1 + k)^2} + \frac{\$31,042}{(1 + k)^3} + \frac{\$35,368}{(1 + k)^4} + \frac{\$39,868 + \$477,456}{(1 + k)^5}$$

The *before-tax* internal rate of return on the $300,000 equity invested in the property for the entire life of the investment is represented by k. This value represents the annual rate of compound interest from before-tax cash inflow that the investor earns on the $30,000 equity invested. This has been discussed previously in Chapter 10.

Because of the uneven pattern of cash flow expected to be generated from this property, it is somewhat difficult to compute k. However, we can first *approximate* k by using an average rate of return on investment formula (ARR), long used to compute bond yields and other yields before the widespread acceptance and understanding of compounding and discounting procedures.[11] An ARR is computed as follows:

$$ARR = \frac{\text{Average } BTCF + \dfrac{BTCF_x - E}{s}}{\dfrac{BTCF_x + E}{2}}$$

where:

Average $BTCF$ = the average of all before-tax cash flows received during the investment period

$BTCF_x$ = before-tax cash flow received in year of sale

E = equity investment

s = period of investment

Including the information for the investment under consideration, we have:

Average $BTCF$ = ($22,882 + $26,882 + $31,042 + $35,368 + $39,868) ÷ 5 = $31,208

$BTCF_x$ = $477,456

s = 5

E = $300,000

---

[11] This formula is also referred to as the approximate yield to maturity and also can be applied to bonds, mortgages, stock, and so on, when approximating yields.

Substituting:

$$ARR = \frac{\$31{,}208 + \dfrac{\$477{,}456 - \$300{,}000}{5}}{\dfrac{\$477{,}456 + \$300{,}000}{2}}$$

$$= \frac{\$31{,}208 + \$35{,}491}{\$388{,}728}$$

$$= 17.2\%$$

Essentially, this "approximation" approach to solving for k involves adding the average appreciation in property value, or the difference between ($BTCF_s$) and the initial equity invested (E), with the average before-tax cash flow from operations ($BTCF$), to arrive at an overall average cash inflow. This average inflow is then divided by average investment, or the amount initially invested, plus the investment value at the end of five years divided by two. This latter average is used to arrive at an *average* value for the equity investment *during* the five-year investment period. The result, or ARR, is 17.2 percent, which represents an *average return* on equity investment.

The above formulation is an extremely useful procedure for approximating internal rates of return.[12] However, it is only an *approximation* to the actual rate of compound interest (k) that we are seeking, and its accuracy will vary considerably depending on the stability of the annual cash flows and the size of cash proceeds realized upon sale of the asset.

To find the true $BTIRR$, which is equal to k, we must use a "trial and error" discounting procedure. Generally the interest rates used to discount the cash flows should be chosen from rates above and below the ARR, which in this case was 17.2 percent. Therefore, we chose interest factors for the present value reversion of $1 in the 15 percent and 20 percent tables from Appendix A and discount as shown on the top of page 337.

Based on the above computations and interpolation, we find that the $BTIRR$ or k is equal to 18.3 percent. This means that if the investor purchases Phase I and estimates of $BTCF$ and $BTCF_s$ are accurate, an investment of $300,000 will earn the equivalent of 18.3 percent compounded annually. Because this rate of return is measured as of the day the $300,000 equity commitment is made, the 18.3 percent $BTIRR$ is listed above as year 0 which represents the time of the outlay. All subsequent cash inflows are assumed to occur at the *end* of each successive year.

We should point out that while the ARR of 17.2 percent closely approximates the $BTIRR$ of 18.3 percent, this will not always necessarily be the case. Hence, it is always advisable to compute the actual internal rate of return to be assured of accuracy.

---

[12] This approximation has many other applications in the field of finance and can be modified to fit any situation in which the cash outflows and inflows can be identified.

Year	BTCF	IFPV, 15 percent	PV	IFPV, 20 percent	PV
1	$ 22,882	.869565	$ 19,897	.833333	$ 19,068
2	26,882	.756144	20,327	.694444	18,668
3	31,042	.657516	20,411	.578704	17,964
4	35,368	.571753	20,222	.482253	17,056
5	39,868	.497177	19,821	.401878	16,022
6	477,456	.497177	237,380	.401878	191,879
Total			$338,058		$280,657

Interpolating:

PV at 15%	$338,058	PV at 15%	$338,058
Desired PV	300,000	PV at 20%	280,657
Difference	$ 38,058	Difference	$ 57,401

($38,058 ÷ $57,401) × 5% = 3.3%, add 15% + 3.3% = 18.3%

Looking at the measures of rates of return again at the bottom of Exhibit 12–3 we can see that there is a significant difference between the *BTIRR* and the other measures shown in the exhibit. This comparison points out a number of deficiencies in using annual measures of return on investment such as *R*, *ROE(BT)* and *ROE(AT)* for decision making. The problems with using annual return on investment are that these measures do *not*:

1. Take account of reversion values of property when sold.
2. Take account of the timing in the receipt of cash flow. Cash flows are not discounted to take account of the "time value of money," or the fact that an investor must wait to receive cash flows produced by an investment. Because of this, an opportunity cost is incurred and should be reflected in the return on investment.
3. Provide a single result that can be interpreted as a return on investment. Annual measures of return on investment change from year to year and results are difficult to interpret. The *IRR* can be interpreted as an annual rate of compound interest.

The internal rate of return methodology solves many of these problems and serves as a superior method for evaluating an investment over the *entire investment period.* However, there is also an advantage in computing annual measures of return on investment that *complement* the discounted cash flow approach; that is, it is valuable to know what annual cash flow received each year is in relation to the original investment. It can be shown that a project can have a very high *BTIRR* and have little, or even a negative, *BTCF* from operations each year.[13] This can occur when the value of the asset appreciates rapidly due to inflation or speculation and the investor receives

---

[13] This subject is treated in conjunction with risk analysis in the appendix to this chapter.

a very large cash inflow when it is sold. Hence, if an investor is concerned about receiving an annual cash return, which may be viewed as a dividend, in addition to the compounded rate of interest earned on equity, annual measures of return on investment are useful.

Measuring internal rates of return after tax. The preceding discussion concerning the internal rate of return on equity *before* tax also applies *after* tax. The *ARR* can also be used to approximate the *ATIRR* for Phase I. An *ARR* can be computed with *ATCF* and *ATCF$_s$* as follows:

$$\text{Average } ATCF = (\$27,882 + \$28,526 + \$29,264 + \$30,094 + \$31,013) \div 5 = \$29,356$$

$$ATCF_x = \$390,168$$
$$s = 5$$
$$E = \$300,000$$

$$ARR = \frac{\$29,356 + \dfrac{\$390,168 - \$300,000}{5}}{\dfrac{\$390,168 + \$300,000}{2}}$$

$$= 13.7\%$$

The resulting approximation again aids us in selecting discount rates for trial and error discounting. To solve for the more accurate *ATIRR*, we select 12 percent and 15 percent from Appendix A and discount to find the present values as shown below:

Year	ATCF	IFPV, 12 percent	PV	IFPV, 15 percent	PV
1...........	$ 27,882	.892857	$ 24,895	.869565	$ 24,245
2...........	28,526	.797194	22,741	.756144	21,570
3..........	29,264	.711780	20,830	.657516	19,242
4..........	30,094	.635518	19,125	.571753	17,206
5..........	31,013	.567427	17,598	.497177	15,419
5..........	390,168	.567427	221,392	.497177	193,983
Total			$326,581		$291,665

Interpolating:
PV at 12%	$326,581		PV at 12%	$326,581
Desired PV........	300,000		PV at 15%	291,665
Difference	$ 26,581		Difference	$ 34,665

($26,581 ÷ $34,916) × 3% = 2.3%   Add: 12% + 2.3% = 14.3%

Based on the above computation, the *ATIRR* is 14.3 percent. This result is extremely close to the approximation arrived at with the average return on investment. However, as pointed out, the accuracy of that estimate will vary from case to case; hence the *ATIRR* should be computed.

Looking back again to Exhibit 12–3, we note that when compared to the *BTIRR* of 18.3 percent, the *ATIRR* is lower because of the influence of federal income tax during each year of operation, the ordinary income tax on recapture of excess depreciation, and the long-term capital gain tax in the year Phase I is expected to be sold. However, the important relationship to notice between the *BTIRR* and *ATIRR* for Phase I is that although the investor is in the 50 percent tax bracket, the *ATIRR* is *not* simply one half of the *BTIRR*, or *BTIRR* × (1 − tax rate), or 9.2 percent. Rather, the *ATIRR* is 14.3 percent, or some 5 percent higher than 9.2 percent. This is because of the combination of artificial accounting losses that give rise to a tax-sheltered cash flow and capital gains tax rate that is far below 50 percent. As previously pointed out, when measuring current returns on investment, comparisons of rates of return on real estate, stocks, bonds, and so on, using the internal rate of return, should also be carried out *before tax and after tax.* Many alternative investments *do not* have similar tax characteristics, so comparing only before-tax returns can be seriously misleading.

Additional tax considerations in investment analysis

From the preceding analysis, it should be obvious that tax considerations are very important in real estate investments. In the preceding example, we have pointed out that for proper decision making, the internal rate of return should be computed both on a before-tax and aftertax basis. The *ATIRR* was computed for Phase I for an investor in a 50 percent tax bracket. It should be apparent to the reader that the aftertax return on investment is highly sensitive to the marginal tax rate of the investor who is considering such an investment.

To illustrate, if we assumed that investors in a 40, 60, and 70 percent marginal tax bracket were also considering Phase I as an investment, it is clear that the *ATIRR* computed for each of these investors will be different.[14] This is because of "artificial accounting losses" that shelter other income and taxes that are paid in the year of sale. The value of these artificial losses to the investor differ in relation to tax rates. Exhibit 12–5 contains a breakdown of the *ATCF* and *ATCF_s* that would be relevant for investors in various tax brackets and the *ATIRR* for each.

An extremely important aspect of the relationship between federal income tax and real estate investment can be seen at the bottom of Exhibit 12–5. At the bottom of the exhibit, the *BTIRR* and *ATIRR* for Phase I have been recomputed under the various tax rates considered. It should be noted that as investor tax rates increase, the *ATIRR* for Phase I will decrease. However, the *ATIRR* will never reach a fully taxable situation, or one in which the *BTIRR*

---

[14] Marginal here means the rate at which the next dollar of income will be taxed.

EXHIBIT 12–5
Influence of investor tax brackets on *ATIRR*—Phase I

			Year			Sale	
	1	*2*	*3*	*4*	*5*		
40% marginal tax rate:							
BTCF	$22,882	$26,882	$31,042	$35,368	$39,868	*BTCF*ₛ..........	$477,456
Tax savings or (tax)	4,000	1,315	(1,422)	(4,219)	(7,084)	Tax ...	(69,830)
ATCF	$ 26,882	$28,197	$29,620	$31,149	$32,784	*ATCF*ₛ..........	$407,626
60% marginal tax rate:							
BTCF	$ 22,882	$26,882	$31,042	$35,368	$39,868	*BTCF*ₛ..........	$477,456
Tax savings or (tax)	6,000	1,973	(2,133)	(6,328)	(10,625)	Tax ...	(104,745)
ATCF	$ 28,882	$28,855	$28,909	$29,040	$29,243	*ATCF*ₛ..........	$372,711
70% marginal tax rate:							
BTCF	$ 22,882	$26,882	$31,042	$35,368	$39,868	*BTCF*ₛ..........	$477,456
Tax savings or (tax)	7,000	2,302	(2,489)	(7,383)	(12,396)	Tax ...	(122,203)
ATCF	$ 29,882	$29,184	$28,553	$27,985	$27,472	*ATCF*ₛ..........	$355,253

	(1) *BTIRR*	(2) *ATIRR*	÷	(3) (1 − Tax rate)	=	(4) *BTIRR**
Equity = $300,000						
40% tax rate	18.3%	15.1%		60%		25.2%
50% tax rate	18.3	14.3		50		28.6
60% tax rate	18.3	13.4		40		33.5
70% tax rate	18.3	12.5		30		41.7

* Equivalent before-tax internal rate of return.

would be subject to the tax rate applicable to ordinary income, that is, *BTIRR* × (1 − tax rate). However, in column 4 of the exhibit, we have computed what we refer to as "a fully taxable equivalent *BTIRR*." This simply means we have taken the *ATIRR* and computed what the *BTIRR* *would have to be* for an alternative investment that is *fully taxable* at the investor's marginal tax bracket. For example, for an investor in the 60 percent tax bracket to find a *fully taxable* investment that would give the same 13.4 percent *ATIRR* as Phase I, that other investment would have to provide a 33.5 percent *BTIRR* to yield the same *ATIRR* as Phase I.

Using before-tax equivalent returns is an important concept because it explains why high tax bracket investors prefer to invest in real estate. An investor in the 60 percent tax bracket, for example, would have to find a fully taxable investment, equivalent in risk, that would provide a *BTIRR* equal to 33.5 percent to earn an *ATIRR* of 13.4 percent, whereas Phase I must only generate a *BTIRR* of 18.3 percent to provide the same 13.4 percent *ATIRR*. Hence, it is clear how the tax shelter status works to the advantage of high tax bracket investors and why there is considerable demand for tax-sheltered investments such as real estate.[15]

Questions

1   What is an artificial loss and how is it beneficial to individual investors in real estate?

2   What is the difference between return on initial investment and current return on investment in real estate, as defined in the chapter? What is the "cash on cash" return?

3   Why are measures of return on investment in real estate such as *ROE (BT)* and *ROE (AT)* usually not representative of the return on investment over the entire period of investment?

4   For many alternative investments, such as newly issued corporate bonds, the *ATIRR* can be computed by multiplying the *BTIRR* by 1-ordinary tax rate. Why is this inappropriate in real estate? Why is there a significant difference in the relationship between *BTIRR* and *ATIRR* in real estate when compared to many other alternatives?

Case problems

1   You are an employee of Multiplex Properties, Ltd., and have been given the following assignment. You are to present an investment analysis of a new small residential income-producing property for sale to a potential investor. The asking price for the property is $1,100,000; rents are estimated at $185,000 during the first year and are expected to

---

[15] We should point out that some investments such as common stocks and bonds also could have substantial capital gain and tax elements to consider. Profits earned from such investments may provide an *ATIRR* which, like real estate, could be high in relation to the *BTIRR*. However, this possibility would have to be considered on a case-by-case basis.

grow at 4 percent per year. Vacancies and collection losses are expected to be 5 percent of rents. Operating expenses, will be 35 percent of effective gross income.

Mortgage financing of $770,000 can be obtained at 11 percent interest for 25 years. The building represents 90 percent of value, it has a useful life of 40 years, and double-declining-balance depreciation will be used (no salvage value). The property is expected to appreciate in value at 3 percent per year and is expected to be owned for five years and then sold. You are expected to prepare the following analysis for the investor who is in the 40 percent tax bracket:

a. A statement of before-tax and aftertax cash flows each year (assume annual mortgage payments).

b. Measures of annual return on initial investment and current return on investment (before and after tax). Compute these measures on total investment and on equity.

c. Measures of the internal rate of return before and after tax for the entire investment period.

d. What would be the required before-tax equivalent yield on a fully taxable alternative investment that would give the same *ATIRR* as the property being analyzed?

APPENDIX: TAXATION AND INCOME-PRODUCING PROPERTIES

As seen in the preceding chapter, federal income taxation seriously affects real estate investment and financing in a number of ways. The material presented in the chapter was based on tax considerations that one could normally expect to affect a real estate investment decision for a typical individual investor. However, there are numerous rules and regulations that affect income-producing property when the investor elects various options available under the federal tax code. The tax material included in this appendix contains a selection of subjects from existing tax regulations deemed most relevant for many typical problems encountered when individuals invest in income-producing property. It is not intended to be an exhaustive treatment of the subject, but rather a collection of the more important aspects of federal taxation that could likely be encountered by the individual investor.

It should be stressed that federal tax treatment of real estate changes frequently as Congress passes additional legislation. Because this textbook is not revised each year, it is incumbent on the reader to remain abreast of changes in federal taxation that have occurred beyond the date of this publication.

Individual and corporate tax rates

In the preceding chapter we undertook numerous examples of investment analysis for an investor in the "50 percent tax bracket." To explain more fully

EXHIBIT 12A-1
Personal income tax schedule, married—joint return or surviving spouse, 1979 income

Taxable income			Marginal rate applied to income in excess of column (a) up to column (b)
(a) Over	(b) Not over	Tax on amount in column (a)	
$ 3,400	$ 5,500	$ 0	14%
5,500	7,600	294	16
7,600	11,900	630	18
11,900	16,000	1,404	21
16,000	20,200	2,265	24
20,200	24,600	3,273	28
24,600	29,900	4,505	32
29,900	35,200	6,201	37
35,200	45,800	8,162	43
45,800	60,000	12,720	49
60,000	85,600	19,678	54
85,600	109,400	33,502	59
109,400	162,400	47,544	64
162,400	215,400	81,464	68
215,400		117,504+	70

what this means, Exhibit 12A–1 shows the tax rates applicable to the taxpayers filing joint returns in 1979.[1] We should first point out that the tax rates increase as income increases. The term *tax bracket* or *marginal tax rate* used in this text refers to the tax rate on income earned above a break in income in the tax schedule. For example, an investor with taxable income of $33,000 (see column [a]) would be in the 37 percent tax bracket, or have a marginal tax rate of 37 percent. This simply means that the *next dollar* of income earned from any source will be taxed at 37 percent. If that taxpayer were to undertake a real estate investment, net income from that investment when added to the investor's taxable income would be subject to a 37 percent tax.[2] This is the tax bracket that should be used by the investor when analyzing alternative investments.

While the primary focus of the preceding chapter is based on the individual taxpayer who invests in real estate directly or through a partnership, corporations also must consider real estate acquisitions based on marginal tax rates. The tax rates that corporations are subject to are shown in Exhibit 12A–2.

---

[1] There are other tax schedules for single heads of households and married individuals filing separate returns.

[2] In the case of the artificial losses discussed in the chapter, when written off against taxable income of $33,000 they result in a "tax savings" at the rate of 37 percent.

EXHIBIT 12A–2
Tax rates on net income of
corporations—1979

Taxable income	Rate (percent)
$ 0–$ 25,000..............	17
25,001– 50,000..............	20
50,001– 75,000..............	30
75,001– 100,000..............	40
100,001–over	46

Classification of real estate ownership

From the perspective of federal taxation, real estate ownership can be categorized as follows:

a.   Personal residences.
b.   Held for resale to others.
c.   Held for the production of income or investment (capital asset).
d.   Held for use in trade or business (Section 1231 asset).

Property held for resale to customers is viewed as inventory and profit from the sale of the inventory is treated as ordinary income. Individuals holding property for resale to others in the ordinary course of business are referred to as *dealers, not investors.* All income produced from operations and sales in that activity is subject to taxation as *ordinary income* and not subject to lower long-term capital gain tax rates. Examples of individuals or firms with *dealer status* would be developers who develop lots for resale or other activities in which real estate is not intended to be held as an investment; rather it is held for immediate resale.

Under federal tax provisions, when depreciable real estate is held only for income or investment (item [c] above) and is not *operated* by its owner in a trade or business, it is classified as a *capital asset* for tax purposes. This could be a situation in which an investor will receive income from the investment but will *not* be actively engaged in *operating* the property for a profit. This is much like owning stocks or bonds. For example, an investor may own raw, unimproved land with an intent to sell it at a later time. Or he may purchase a warehouse and lease it to another individual or business, on a "net" lease basis. In the latter case, the investor would receive some specific return, "net" of operating expenses over some specified period. This would be similar to receiving a dividend payment on stock or interest on a bond, as the investor is purchasing the warehouse with the intention of *investing* and not for the purpose of operating it in trade or business to *produce income.*

In contrast to real estate categorized as a capital asset, we now consider classification (*d*), or property held for use in trade or business. *Most real estate investments are in this category.* In this case, the investor acquires real estate with the intent to operate, modify, or do whatever necessary to produce income in a trade or business. This can be done either individually or as a partnership, corporation, or trust. The classification (Section 1231 assets) also applies to capital equipment (such as machinery, etc.) purchased by businesses who use such assets in the production of income. In addition to producing income, owners of property in this classification may deduct expenses for operating, maintaining, and repairing such property; they may deduct property taxes and interest and in addition they are allowed a deduction for depreciation. When sold, capital gain and loss provisions (to be discussed) apply to these assets.

The Section 1231 classification, or an asset held for use in trade or business, is an important one and is generally desired by most investors in real estate. This is because if the property is not classified as being used in a trade or business, then (1) the deductibility of interest on mortgage loans and other indebtedness is limited to $10,000 annually plus net income produced from the investment and (2) an asset categorized as being held for use in trade or business receives potentially more favorable capital gain or loss treatment when sold. In this appendix, and throughout the remainder of this textbook, we assume that all real estate investments qualify as Section 1231 assets, or property held for use in a trade or business.

Acquisition or development of a property

An item of initial concern when a property is acquired is the establishing of its *basis*. The basis of a real estate investment is generally equal to its cost (unless inherited or acquired by gift). Cost generally includes the acquisition price plus any installation costs associated with placing it into service. The cost of any capital improvements to the property made during the ownership period are also included in the basis when such outlays are made.

In the case of a property *that is to be developed,* cost generally includes (*a*) purchase price of the land; (*b*) outlays for constructing building improvements; (*c*) outlays for site improvements (parking lots, curbing, sidewalks, etc.); (*d*) outlays for off-site costs (sewer connections, utilities) when necessary for property development; and (*e*) outlays for architects fees, legal fees, engineering fees, and other "soft costs" incurred in the design and development of property improvements.

Other capitalized costs. In addition to the acquisition and development costs, certain other costs must be capitalized, then written off (amortized) over specific periods of time. These items include:

a. Construction period interest and property taxes—all interest and property taxes paid during the construction period must be capitalized and written off in accordance with the following schedule:

Year paid	Residential income property amortization period	Year paid	Other income-producing property/amortization period
1976	—	1976	4* yrs.
1977	—	1977	5
1978	4 yrs.	1978	6
1979	5	1979	7
1980	6	1980	8
1981	7	1981	9
1982	8	Thereafter	10
1983	9		
Thereafter	10		

* Fifty percent allowed in year 1 and 50 percent over years 2 through 4, only in 1976.

b. Loan fees (such as fees paid for attorneys, appraisers, title costs, transfers and loan commitments) and discount points must be capitalized and written off over the term of the loan. Two amortization periods may apply when a construction loan and a permanent loan are obtained separately.

c. Organization fees incurred when a business entity such as a partnership, corporation, or trust is established to acquire and manage a real estate investment must be capitalized and written off over at least a five-year period.

Operation of income-producing property

Tax considerations in the operating phase of real estate are centered around the treatment of income and operating expenses. Recognition of income and expenses may be based on a cash or accrual method, at the taxpayer's option. When the cash method of accounting is chosen, the general rule is to recognize income when it is *received* and expense when it is *paid*. When the accrual method is used, income is recognized when *earned* and expenses are recognized when *incurred*. In general, income from rents are recognized as income when received or earned. All items of income from ancillary services (wash facilities, parking, etc.) are recognized in the year that they are received or earned.

Operating expenses.   Operating expenses associated with the production of income and maintaining property are deductible in the year incurred or paid (depending on the method of accounting). Care must be exercised in establishing whether certain outlays for repair and maintenance are *expenses* or *capital outlays.* Any expenditure made to extend the economic life of an asset, improve it or materially increase the production of income over the economic life of the property cannot be deducted as an expense in the current period. Examples of such expenditure could include conversion from gas to electric appliances, additions to and partitions of floor space, replacement of roof, and so on. In each of the latter examples, the cost of such improvements must be added to the basis of the improvement and must be depreciated over its remaining life.

Items of expense that are usually currently deductible are those that are required to maintain a constant flow of service. Such items generally include outlays for wages, supplies, painting-decorating, management fees, utilities, advertising, insurance, property taxes, and so on. Other nonoperating items deductible in the current period are losses from nonpayment of rents and some commissions paid for obtaining rentals or leases.

Interest deductions. Mortgage or other interest on debt is deductible in the year paid or accrued. Generally prepaid interest is deductible on the current period, but only to the extent that it represents the equivalent of one year's interest. The remainder must be capitalized and deducted (amortized) over the term of the loan. As previously pointed out, the interest deduction on real estate acquisitions classified by the Internal Revenue Service as investment property is limited to the extent that the investment produces income plus an additional $10,000. However, because most real estate investments are classified as being held for use in trade or business (Section 1231 assets), the IRS has ruled that this limitation *does not apply* to properties in that classification.

Depreciation

Depreciation expense is one of the most important charges affecting taxes paid by real estate investors. Generally all assets decrease in value due to physical wasting or wear and tear and are subject to depreciation. Investors are allowed to recover capital costs invested in real estate improvements by charging depreciation against current income. Such improvements usually include buildings, sidewalks, parking areas, and other land betterments. Land itself, however, is not depreciable.

Establishment of value and economic life. Generally, the purchase price paid for a property, or costs expended in the development of improvements plus any acquisition expenses, serve as the *depreciable basis* for depreciation calculations. Acquisition expenses typically include title fees, broker's commissions, attorney's fees, appraisal costs, and surveys. When an *existing* property is purchased, it is possible that the depreciable basis established by the buyer may not be related to either the *original* price paid for the property by the seller or the amount of depreciation taken by the seller. Each time a property is purchased the buyer establishes a depreciable basis which is determined by the purchase price plus acquisition fees, less the estimated value of the land at that time.

The economic life of an improvement is an *estimate,* made by the taxpayer, of the number of years over which the asset in question will be useful. This estimate is extremely important as it serves as a major component in all depreciation methods allowable under tax regulations. Economic lives established by independent appraisals made on a property are also permissible for tax purposes. The Internal Revenue Service (IRS) has also established guidelines suggesting economic lives under some 75 categories of assets. Taxpayers are not required to use these guidelines, however, if they can provide justification for using a different economic life.

A sample of some of the useful lives suggested by the IRS are as follows:

Asset depreciation ranges (*ADR*)

Type of structure or improvement	Guideline life (years)
Apartments	40
Banks	50
Dwellings	45
Factories	45
Garages	45
Hotels	40
Office buildings	45
Retail stores	50
Theaters	40
Warehouses	60
Farm buildings	25
Land improvements (curbs, sidewalks, sewers)	20
Trees and landscaping	*

* Depends on geographic area and climate.

Generally, taxpayers are encouraged to use the suggested guideline life established for the asset being depreciated; however, the IRS will allow a 20 percent variance in the guideline life (higher or lower) without contesting its use. It is important to understand that the above guidelines apply to specific categories of assets without any reference to the age of an existing property. Hence, if an improvement is already 20 years old when purchased, the guideline life may not be appropriate and the taxpayer would be justified in establishing an estimate of useful life, independent of the guidelines. Also, the useful life established by a taxpayer is *not* dependent on the useful life established by previous owners. For example, if a buyer is considering the purchase of a 10-year-old apartment building from an owner who had established a 40-year useful life, the buyer is *not* required to use a 30-year useful life (40 years − 10 years) for depreciation purposes. The useful life of the property should be established independently, taking into account changes in the neighborhood and other economic conditions that may have occurred in the intervening ten years.

Salvage value. In addition to establishing a useful life for improvements, the taxpayer must estimate the value, if any, of the improvement at the end of its useful life. No asset can be depreciated below its salvage value, which is defined as any estimated proceeds upon sale or other disposition, less any costs of removal. As a practical matter, many real estate investors estimate salvage value to be zero, assuming that the estimated cost of demolition will equal sale proceeds from scrap value at the end of the asset's useful life.

Establishing land values—used properties. When an existing property is purchased, it may be difficult to establish a current land value which must be subtracted from total value (price) in establishing the depreciable basis on the improvement portion of the asset. Generally, the investor can make an estimate, use an estimate made by an independent appraiser, or an estimate made by the local property taxing authority, as justification for establishing the depreciable basis.

Allowable methods of computation. There are generally three basic methods used to compute depreciation on improvements made on real property. The first approach is referred to as the *straight-line method.* Under this approach the basis of the property, less any salvage value, is divided by the economic life of the asset, resulting in an annual depreciation charge.

Example. A new property is purchased for $100,000. The land is valued at $20,000 with improvements valued at $80,000. The improvement is estimated to have an economic life of 40 years at the end of which time the building shell is estimated to have $10,000 salvage value. The annual depreciation charge would be:

$$\frac{\text{Improvement value} - \text{Salvage value}}{\text{Economic life}} = \text{Straight-line depreciation charge}$$

$$\frac{\$80,000 - \$10,000}{40} = \$1,750$$

Accelerated depreciation methods. These methods of depreciation are allowable for certain categories of property to be discussed below. The first methods demonstrated here are called the *declining-balance methods* of depreciation. The technique for computing the depreciation charges under all declining-balance methods is based on the *depreciation rate* obtained under the straight-line method. For example, in the example above, $1,750 is the amount chargeable under the straight-line method. The straight-line depreciation *rate* is computed as:

$$\frac{\text{Annual straight-line charge}}{\text{Cost-salvage value}} = \frac{\$1,750}{\$80,000 - \$10,000} = 2.5\%$$

a. Double-declining-balance method. Under this method, up to twice the straight-line depreciation rate may be taken on an improvement over its economic life. The depreciation charge is computed by doubling the straight-line rate ($2 \times 2.5\% = 5\%$) and applying the rate obtained to the basis of the improvement (ignoring salvage value). In each succeeding year, the depreciable basis of the asset is reduced by the amount of depreciation taken in the preceding year; hence the term *declining balance.*

To illustrate this method using the same example as above, a partial depreciation schedule is shown in Exhibit 12A–3.

EXHIBIT 12A–3
Depreciation schedule—double-declining balance method

Year	Depreciable basis	Rate	Depreciation charge
1	$80,000	× 5% =	$4,000
2	76,000	× 5% =	3,800
3	72,200	× 5% =	3,610
4	68,590	× 5% =	3,430
5	65,160	× 5% =	3,258

Note in the exhibit that under this method, the depreciation rate remains the same and the depreciable basis of the asset declines with each year. The schedule seen above can be carried out for 40 years or the economic life of the asset.

b. 150 percent declining-balance method. This technique is allowable on certain categories of real estate. The computation process is the same as under the double-declining-balance method except that the depreciation rate differs. The rate is computed simply as $1.50 \times 2.5\% = 3.75\%$ or one and one-half times the straight-line rate. The 3.75 percent rate obtained would be substituted in the rate column in Exhibit 12A–3, and the annual depreciation charge determined accordingly.

c. 125 percent declining-balance method. Under this technique the depreciation rate would be $1.25 \times 2.5\% = 3.125\%$. This rate would be used in place of the 5 percent rate in Exhibit 12A–3 in completing the depreciation schedule, should this method be used.

The second major method allowable under accelerated depreciation methods is referred to as the *sum-of-the-years'-digits* method. Under this technique, the depreciation rate used on each year changes while the depreciable basis remains the same. Its computation is carried out by first summing cumulatively over the number of years contained in the asset's economic life. In our example, this would be done as follows: $1 + 2 + 3 + \cdots + 40 = 820$. However, a shortcut solution is also obtained with the following formula:

$$N \left(\frac{N + 1}{2}\right) = \text{sum-of-the-years' digits}$$

where N equals the economic life of the improvement. In our example:

$$40 \left(\frac{40 + 1}{2}\right) = 820$$

The depreciation charge under this method is then determined by taking the last year in the sequence of digits (40 in our example) and dividing it by the sum-of-the-years' digits (820) to obtain the depreciation rate in the first year. In each succeeding year, the numerator changes by the next year in the reverse sequence. To demonstrate this technique a partial depreciation schedule is completed in Exhibit 12A–4. Note in the exhibit that the depreciable basis of

EXHIBIT 12A–4
Depreciation schedule—sum-of-the-years'-digits method

Year	Depreciable basis	Rate	Depreciation charge
1.............	$70,000 ×	40/820 =	$3,415
2.............	70,000 ×	39/820 =	3,329
3.............	70,000 ×	38/820 =	3,244
4.............	70,000 ×	37/820 =	3,159
5.............	70,000 ×	36/820 =	3,073

the asset remains the same while the rate changes in each year. The initial depreciable basis under this method is cost *minus salvage value,* when salvage value is estimated. This differs from the declining-balance techniques which *ignore* salvage value altogether in determining the depreciable charge.

Component versus composite depreciation.   The same economic life does not have to be used for the entire improvement. It is possible to establish *different* economic lives for different components within the same project or development. For example, one economic life can be chosen for the building shell, another for the roof, and still another for sidewalks. This approach is referred to as *component* depreciation. It may be valuable for a particular investor if the depreciation charge derived by assigning different economic lives to components exceeds the charge computed under an overall *composite* depreciation rate selected for the entire improvement. However, use of component depreciation must be justified by the taxpayer.

Ordinarily, the component method is justifiable when a property is new and evidence can be presented to the effect that some parts of an improvement will wear faster than others. However, when an existing property is purchased, it is more difficult to justify assigning different economic lives to different components. This is particularly true if the property in question has been in existence for some time.

Choice of depreciation methods—specific types of real estate. The choice of depreciation methods allowed under tax regulations is very rigid and depends on specific categories of real estate being depreciated. The four major criteria for classification of real estate on *property acquired after July 25, 1969,* can be best seen in Exhibit 12A–5. The major criteria used to categorize

EXHIBIT 12A–5
Depreciation methods allowed on specific types of income-producing real estate

	Residential	*All Others*
New	Sum-of-the-years' digits Double-declining balance 150% declining balance 125% declining balance Straight line	150% declining balance Straight line
Existing	125% declining balance* Straight line	Straight line

* When useful life is at least 20 years; otherwise straight line.

property are whether a property is *residential* or *other* and whether a property is *new* or *existing.*

Residential real estate generally refers to income-producing (rental) residential property. At least 80 percent of rental revenue must be derived from residential use for a property to be categorized as residential real estate. This rule is sometimes important for mixed use properties, or properties which have a commercial and residential mix within the same improvement. All *other* real estate generally refers to commercial properties such as shopping centers, office buildings, and industrial properties.

Changing depreciation methods. Once a depreciation method has been chosen by the taxpayer, it can be changed only once during an asset's economic life. The taxpayer may elect to change from any method to straight-line depreciation only. Once the election to switch to straight line is made, the taxpayer may not change depreciation methods for that asset again. If an investor uses one of the declining-balance methods, it will be advantageous to switch to straight-line depreciation during the economic life of the investment. This is true because at some point the depreciation charge based on the straight-line method will exceed the charge computed under the declining-balance method. The reader should recall that charges under the declining-balance method decline each year; hence the investor is interested in knowing the year when the straight-line charge will exceed the charge available under the declining-balance method.

A formula has been compiled for determining the last year in which a declining-balance method should be used or when the switchover from any of the declining-balance methods to straight line should occur. It is:

$$\text{Useful life} - \frac{\text{Useful life}}{\text{Percent of (S/L)}} + 1 = \text{last year to use declining-balance method}$$

Hence, if one owned a property with a useful life of 20 years and was using double-declining-balance depreciation, the year that it would be advantageous to switch to straight line would be:

$$20 - \frac{20}{2.0} + 1 = 11\text{th year}$$

After the 11th year the investor should switch to straight line. The straight-line depreciation charge would then be computed based on the book value of the improvement (cost − accumulated depreciation) remaining in the 11th year divided by the 9 years of useful tax life remaining.

The above formula can be modified for all declining-balance methods by substituting the appropriate percentage of straight line allowed under each method. Hence, in the case of 150 percent declining balance and 125 percent declining balance, 1.50 and 1.25, respectively, would be substituted. When sum-of-the-years' digits (SYD) is used, there will never be a switchover point to straight line. The SYD method always provides a greater annual depreciation charge than straight line, regardless of the useful life of the asset.

In certain circumstances, the IRS may allow a taxpayer to switch from straight line to an accelerated depreciation method during the period that an asset is owned. However, the taxpayer must justify that straight-line depreciation does not adequately reflect the declining usefulness of the improvement over time. The same justification must be made in the event a taxpayer wants to increase depreciation charges or shorten a property's useful life because of obsolescence. While it is possible to accomplish a reduction in useful life due to obsolescence, or to change depreciation to an accelerated method, the case would have to be well documented when presented to the IRS for approval.

The minimum tax—excess depreciation. In an attempt to reduce the advantages of using accelerated depreciation on real estate and other forms of tax sheltered income, Congress passed legislation that could affect the choice of depreciation for some investors in high tax brackets. Based on regulations in existence as of 1978, the *minimum tax* is a provision which effectively identifies certain items of income as receiving preferential tax treatment (these are called *preference tax items*). These items of income are subject to a minimum tax to the extent that such items exceed a statutory exclusion.

One item of tax preference affecting real estate is the annual deduction of any accelerated depreciation minus straight-line depreciation. This excess, to the extent that it exceeds the statutory exclusion of the greater of $10,000 or the taxpayer's regular income tax, is subject to a minimum tax of 15 percent. For taxpayers with substantial amounts of other income earned in real estate, oil production, and from other preferred items, the minimum tax provision may cause them to limit their choice of depreciation methods to straight line.[3] This is because they may want to avoid any excess depreciation, and hence the minimum tax.

The maximum tax. This provision was passed with the intent of limiting the maximum marginal tax rate to 50 percent for taxpayers who earn most of their income through salaries and wages (called personal service income), as opposed to income from investments and items of tax preference. It is important to note, however, that as such taxpayers make investments in tax preferred items, a smaller proportion of their total income becomes subject to the maximum tax, and hence the taxpayer's marginal tax rate could increase. In other words, as an investor subject to the maximum tax rate of 50 percent makes investments designated as being tax preferred, such as in real estate where accelerated depreciation may be taken, a greater amount of ordinary income will no longer be subject to the maximum tax limitation of 50 percent. This results in more personal service income being subject to higher tax rates. This aspect of tax regulations must be considered by taxpayers who earn most of their income through salaries and wages and are considering making tax-sheltered investments.

Treatment of operating income or loss

After deducting all allowable operating expenses, interest, and depreciation allowances from gross income from operation of the property, either operating income or an operating loss will result. As pointed out in great detail in the chapter, for individual owners or owners of partnership interest in real estate assets, such losses may reduce other earned income in the determination of federal income taxes. This latter attribute is extremely important as it *reduces federal tax liability in the year of loss.*

In the case of corporations and trusts, such operating losses can be combined with income produced from other assets to reduce federal taxes. However, if there is no other income to combine losses with (that is, if a corporation owns a single property or properties which all show an operating

---

[3] Other tax preferred items include accelerated depreciation on personal property, intangible drilling costs, depletion allowances, stock options, and other items. These items must be taken into account with real estate investments in establishing whether or not the exclusion on items of tax preference has been exceeded.

tax loss), then *corporations and trusts cannot distribute or pass through such losses to stockholders.* In this event, such losses are subject to certain carryback and carryforward rules set forth in the federal tax code.

The importance of these characteristics cannot be stressed enough. Individuals, or individuals owning partnership interests in entities operating Section 1231 assets (assets used in trade or business), have a *distinct* advantage over other forms of business organizations, such as corporations and trusts, in that operating losses may be combined with other personal income in the year of occurrence, thereby reducing personal income taxes. This stands in contrast to the possibility of having to carry such losses back or forward as corporations and trusts must do.

Another advantage of individual versus corporate ownership of real estate occurs in years when operating *income* is earned from the operation of Section 1231 assets. Individual taxpayers and individuals owning partnership interests in such entities retain an advantage over corporations in that such income is only taxed *once,* at the individual level. Should such assets be owned and operated by a corporation, operating income is taxed at the *corporate level* (see tax rates in Exhibit 12A–4), *and* then at the *individual level* if dividends are paid to stockholders. Hence the advantages of corporate ownership and operation of real estate are very limited. Corporations are clearly at a relative disadvantage when compared to individual or partnership ownership. This is why in the chapter on real estate investment analysis, the tax circumstances of the individual owner-investor are stressed. Because of the advantages over corporations and trusts, the individual owner-investor and partnership ownership of real estate assets are very important forms of ownership of income-producing real estate.

Disposal of property

When property is sold, it will generally be sold at a taxable gain or loss. If the property has been held for more than one year before sale, the transaction qualifies for long-term capital gain or capital loss treatment; otherwise, any gains or losses are treated as short-term gains or losses.

In establishing whether or not a capital gain or loss has occurred when a property is sold, the gross sales price must be established. The gross sales price is equal to any cash or other property received in payment for the property sold, plus any liabilities against the property assumed by the buyer. From the gross sales price, the *adjusted basis* of the property and any fees and expenses associated with the sale are subtracted. The adjusted basis of a property is its *original basis* (cost plus acquisition fees), plus the cost of any alterations or additions made during the period of ownership, less accumulated depreciation taken to date. For property owned longer than one year, any excess of gross sales price over adjusted basis is a long-term capital gain; any deficit is a long-term capital loss. To illustrate: An office building was acquired five years ago at a total cost of $500,000. To date a total of $100,000 in depreciation has been taken and it has just sold for $900,000. In this case:

Gross sale price		$900,000
Adjusted basis:		
Cost	$500,000	
Accumulated depreciation...........	−100,000	400,000
Long-term capital gain...............		$500,000

Had the gross sale price been $300,000, a long-term capital loss of $100,000 would have resulted ($300,000 − $400,000).

Recapture of excess depreciation. For properties acquired after July 25, 1969, when a gain is realized on the sale of an asset, the *recapture of depreciation* provision must be applied. This regulation requires that if a property is sold for more than its adjusted basis, all depreciation charged in excess of what would have been charged had the straight-line method of depreciation been used, is treated as ordinary income to the extent of total gain, and must be taxed at ordinary tax rates. The total gain on sale is then reduced by the amount of depreciation recaptured and the remainder is subject to capital gains tax.

To illustrate, assume a property was purchased new five years ago for $100,000 ($80,000 building and $20,000 land). The property's useful tax life was 40 years with $10,000 salvage value. We assume that it was acquired after July 25, 1969, held for five years and sold for $120,000. It was depreciated using double-declining-balance method depreciation. Assuming the investor is in the 50 percent tax bracket, what would be the taxes at sale?

Step 1. Computing gain:		
Sale price................................		$120,000
Adjusted basis, 5th year:		
Cost	$100,000	
Less: Accumulated depreciation	18,098	81,902
Total gain.............................		$ 38,098
Step 2. Recapture of depreciation:		
Accumulated depreciation, DDB.............	$ 18,098	
Less: Straight line ($1,750 × 5)	8,750	
Ordinary income		9,348
Capital gain		$ 28,750

Based on the above computation, taxes would be paid at ordinary income tax rates on $9,348, which is the excess depreciation subject to the recapture provision and becomes *ordinary income* in the year of sale. The difference between the taxable gain and ordinary income, or $28,750, is subject to capital gain tax rates. Of course, in the above example, if straight-line depreciation had been used, there would be no recapture of excess depreciation.

In the event that the total gain is *less* than the amount subject to recapture, then the amount of excess depreciation subject to ordinary income is limited to the amount of the gain. For example, in our example above, if the property would have been sold for $85,000, the total gain would have been $85,000 less $81,902 (adjusted basis), or $3,098. Even though excess depreciation is $9,348, the amount subject to ordinary tax rates would be limited to $3,098. There would be no long-term capital gain tax paid.

When a long-term capital gain is realized by a noncorporate taxpayer, taxes payable on those gains are determined by (1) excluding 60 percent of the gain and (2) applying the ordinary tax rate to the excess. Returning to our $100,000 property owned for five years sold for $120,000 in the previous section, and assuming an individual taxpayer in the 50 percent tax bracket, we have

Long-term capital gain.	$28,750
Less: 60% exclusion.	−17,250
Capital gain subject to tax.	$11,500
Ordinary tax rate.	×.50
Capital gain tax	$ 5,750

(It should be noted that in the chapter the same result was obtained by multiplying the percentage of gain subject to tax [40%], times the ordinary tax rate [50%], obtaining 20% × $28,750 = $5,750.)

Given ordinary income of $9,348 in the above example, total taxes in the year of sale would be:[4]

Ordinary income	$ 9,348
Ordinary tax rate	×.50
Ordinary tax	4,674
Add: Capital gain tax.	5,750
Total taxes	$10,424

"Offsetting" capital gains and capital losses. If there are other capital gains or losses incurred by the taxpayer in the year of sale, those gains and losses must be netted together before computing capital gains taxes. For example, if the taxpayer had capital gains or losses shown below, the net gain or loss must be computed as follows:

Long-term capital gains	$100,000	
Long-term capital losses.	60,000	
Net long-term capital gain		$40,000
Short-term capital losses	$ 50,000	
Short-term capital gain.	25,000	
Net short-term capital loss		25,000
Excess of net long-term gains over short-term losses		$15,000

[4] For certain investors with considerable tax preference income, additional tax may be required. This possibility is discussed below.

In this example the *net* long-term gain of $15,000 would be subject to the long-term capital gain treatment explained above. Any recapture of excess depreciation would be computed *separately* for each asset sold and treated as ordinary income (it is not "netted").

In the event that the "netting out" procedure required above yields a net short-term capital gain, it is taxed as ordinary income. Should net short-term losses or net long-term losses result, such losses would result in a reduction of other ordinary income.[5]

The alternative minimum tax—capital gains.   As was the case with excess depreciation, the minimum tax provision may also affect the investor upon disposal of a property. The reader should recall that when the long-term capital gain is determined in the year of sale, it was subject to 60 percent exclusion in determining the capital gains tax. This exclusion is considered to be a tax preference item.

In 1978 Congress passed an Alternative Minimum Tax provision under which certain investors must pay the greater of the 15 percent minimum tax or the alternative minimum tax on the excluded portion of the capital gains. The alternative minimum tax is determined by first adding the 60 percent exclusion on long-term capital gains to excess personal itemized deductions that the taxpayer had in the year a property is sold, plus the taxpayer's taxable income. This amount is then subject to a $20,000 statutory exclusion with the remainder subject to a progressive minimum tax of (*a*) 10 percent on the first $40,000, (*b*) 20 percent on the next $40,000, and (*c*) 25 percent of the excess. The taxpayer then pays a minimum tax based on the greater of the 15 percent minimum tax or the alternative minimum tax.

Other methods of disposing of property

In addition to selling a property, there are other methods of disposition that have important tax consequences. Such methods include installment sales, exchanges for like-kind property, and gift, to mention but a few. An in-depth treatment of these subjects is beyond the scope of this book.

Questions (appendix)

A–1   What is meant by marginal tax rate?

A–2   What is the difference between (*a*) property held for resale to others, (*b*) property classified as an investment or capital asset, and (*c*) property used in a trade or business? Which category usually applies to the acquisition of income property made by individuals? Why is the latter category so important?

---

[5] This assumes that the assets in question are Section 1231 assets. If classified as an *investment* held for income or gain (see our earlier discussion at the beginning of this appendix), then special rules apply to the treatment of short- and long-term capital losses.

A–3   What is the difference between basis, adjusted basis, and depreciable basis?

A–4   Differentiate between a capital expenditure and a maintenance expenditure?

A–5   How can land value be established for an existing property for federal tax purposes? Why is the allocation of value between land and building important to the owner-investor?

A–6   What methods of depreciation are allowable on (*a*) residential income-producing property (new or used), and (*b*) commercial property (new or used)?

A–7   What is the minimum tax? The maximum tax?

A–8   Regarding operating losses, why do individual investors have a tax advantage over corporations and trusts in the treatment of such losses?

A–9   What is the recapture of excess depreciation provision? How are such excesses taxed?

A–10 Why do investors switch over from accelerated to straight-line depreciation during the useful life of an asset? If an asset has a useful life of 50 years, and the investor uses the 125 percent declining-balance method of depreciation, when would it be best to switch over?

A–11 It is said that the same amount of depreciation is taken under all depreciation methods over an asset's useful life. If this is true, how can one method be superior to another?

A–12 What is composite depreciation? How is it used?

A–13 How may the minimum tax affect the choice of depreciation methods?

Financial leverage, investment risk and return

13

This chapter contains two parts. In Part 1 we consider the effects of financing on real estate investment. The term *financial leverage* is now part of standard terminology in many investments, including real estate, and in this chapter we extensively explore the effects of financial leverage and return on investment in real estate. To accomplish this, we reconsider and extend the Phase I investment that was analyzed in the previous chapter.

In Part 2 of this chapter we discuss some of the basic elements in risk analysis. Discussion is centered around risk differences that must be considered when comparing returns on different real estate projects and between real estate and other investments. The discussion of risk in the chapter is kept at a rather intuitive level. For readers interested in the quantification of risk, some basic concepts on that subject may be found in the appendix to this chapter.

PART 1: FINANCIAL LEVERAGE

In this section we are concerned with the effect of financing on return on investment. In the previous chapter we considered an investment in the Phase I project and assumed that it would be financed with a 70 percent mortgage. Our goal in that chapter was to introduce the reader to various measures of return on investment. Our goal here is to examine the impact of different levels of financing on before-tax and aftertax return on equity. It will be seen that return on equity, measured on initial investment or as an internal rate of return, is *very sensitive* to the amount of mortgage financing and its cost.

The effects of mortgage financing on investment returns

To begin the analysis, we reconsider the Phase I project which will cost $1,000,000. By way of summary, we show again in Exhibit 13–1 computation of *BTCF* and *ATCF*, assuming 70 percent financing at 10 percent interest for 25 years. We also show the *ATCF$_s$* for Phase I which serves as a point of departure for the discussion that follows.

EXHIBIT 13–1
Estimates of before-tax and aftertax cash flow—Phase I project

	Year				
	1	*2*	*3*	*4*	*5*
A. Statement of before-tax cash flow					
Rents	$161,943	$168,421	$175,158	$182,163	$189,451
Less: Vacancy and collection loss	8,098	8,421	8,758	9,108	9,473
Effective gross income...........	$153,845	$160,000	$166,400	$173,055	$179,978
Less: Operating expenses	53,845	56,000	58,240	60,569	62,992
Net operating income (*NOI*)	$100,000	$104,000	$108,160	$112,486	$116,986
Less: Debt service (*DS*)	77,118	77,118	77,118	77,118	77,118
Before-tax cash flow (*BTCF*)......	$ 22,882	$ 26,882	$ 31,042	$ 35,368	$ 39,868
B. Statement of taxable income or loss					
Net operating income (*NOI*)	$100,000	$104,000	$108,160	$112,486	$116,986
Less: Depreciation	40,000	38,000	36,100	34,295	32,580
Interest	70,000	69,288	68,505	67,644	66,697
Taxable income (loss)............	$ (10,000)	$ (3,288)	$ 3,555	$ 10,547	$ 17,709
(Tax) or savings at 50%	$ 5,000	$ 1,644	(1,778)	$ (5,274)	$ (8,855)
C. Statement of aftertax cash flow					
Before-tax cash flow (*BTCF*)......	$ 22,882	$ 26,882	$ 31,042	$ 35,368	$ 39,868
Less (tax) or add savings	5,000	1,644	(1,778)	(5,274)	(8,855)
Aftertax cash flow (*ATCF*)	$ 27,882	$ 28,526	$ 29,264	$ 30,094	$ 31,013

Aftertax cash flow at sale, Phase I apartment complex, five-year investment period

Cash flow after mortgage repayment:	
Sale price.....................................	$1,134,000
Less: Mortgage balance....................	656,544
Cash flow before tax (*BTCF$_s$*)	$ 477,456
Less: Taxes at sale	
Taxes on ordinary income	40,488
Taxes on capital gain	46,800
Cash flow aftertax at sale (*ATCF$_s$*)	$ 390,168

One very important question that investors must deal with when purchasing real estate is how much should be borrowed? What effect does the cost of borrowing have on return on investment both currently and over the entire investment period? How does an investor go about deciding how much to borrow? These are obviously very important questions that must be answered prior to undertaking the acquisition of a real estate investment.

To help answer these questions, we compare the previous results for Phase I, where we assumed that 70 percent financing was obtained at 10 percent interest for 25 years, with results assuming that Phase I is acquired for $1,000,000 *cash*. In the latter case, then, no debt financing is used. We begin with a comparison for the first year of operation for Phase I as shown in Exhibit 13–2.

EXHIBIT 13–2
Effect of debt financing on first year operating results—Phase I

	0 percent debt	70 percent debt
Before-tax cash flow:		
NOI	$100,000	$100,000
DS	–0–	77,118
BTCF	$100,000	$ 22,882
Taxable income or loss:		
NOI	$100,000	$100,000
Depreciation	40,000	40,000
Interest	–0–	70,000
Taxable income or (loss)	$ 60,000	$(10,000)
(Tax) or savings at 50%	$ (30,000)	$ 5,000
Aftertax cash flow:		
BTCF	$100,000	$ 22,882
(Tax) or savings	(30,000)	5,000
ATCF	$ 70,000	$ 27,882
ROE (BT)	10.0%	7.6%
ROE (AT)	7.0%	9.3%
Equity	$1,000,000	$300,000

Looking to Exhibit 13–2, two important patterns emerge from our comparison of the two debt levels that could be used to acquire Phase I. First, on a before-tax basis we see that *ROE (BT)* is *lower* when 70 percent debt financing is used than when no debt financing is used. On the other hand, when federal income taxes are taken into account, we see that the aftertax return on equity in the first year of operation *ROE (AT)* is *greater* when debt financing is used when compared to the case when no debt financing is used. From this analysis, we seem to be confronted with conflicting results in trying to answer the question whether or not debt financing should be used. That is, if we limit the analysis to a before-tax comparison, it would appear that no debt financing would be the preferred alternative. On the other hand, based on the aftertax comparison, and assuming the investor is in a 50 percent tax bracket, it would appear that 70 percent financing is more desirable. Which comparison should be relied on by the investor? The answer is, the *aftertax* comparison. This is because investors should always be concerned about the aftertax consequences of financing and investment decisions. After all, it is the aftertax cash flow that is ultimately realized by investors and given the nature of real estate, with its artificial losses and attendant tax shelters, to ignore the aftertax consequences of any decision would not be giving recognition to one of the most important features of the investment.

Does the analysis in Exhibit 13–2 mean that any amount of debt financing should be used to purchase Phase I at any cost? This question *cannot* be answered based on a simple *single period analysis*. In order to fully understand the effect of financing on real estate investment, account must be taken of trends in net operating income, trends in property value, and tax effects over the *entire investment period*. A simple one period analysis, used in many textbooks in real estate finance, is inadequate when analyzing the impact of debt financing on return on equity investment.

To illustrate the impact of debt financing, *ROE* for each year during an expected investment period of five years, both before and after tax, have been compiled in Exhibit 13–3 for Phase I. These computations have been made again assuming no debt financing and assuming 70 percent debt financing. Based on the annual aftertax returns in each period *ROE (AT)*, the investor would consistently earn a higher return on equity with debt financing than without it. Furthermore, even the annual measures of before-tax return on

EXHIBIT 13–3

Effects of debt financing on rate of return—Phase I

			Year			
	0	*1*	*2*	*3*	*4*	*5*
0% debt:						
ROE (BT)		10.0%	10.4%	10.8%	11.2%	11.7%
ROE (AT)		7.0	7.1	7.2	7.3	7.5
BTIRR	12.8%					
ATIRR*	8.0					
70% debt:						
ROE (BT)		7.6	9.0	10.3	11.8	13.2
ROE (AT)		9.3	9.5	9.8	10.0	10.3
BTIRR	18.6					
ATIRR*	14.3					

* Assuming 50 percent tax rate.

equity *ROE* (*BT*) are greater when 70 percent debt financing is considered in years 4 and 5 as compared to the no debt financing situation.

While the period-by-period comparison shown in Exhibit 13–3 is useful for measuring the impact of financing on annual operating results, it is still somewhat incomplete in that the appreciation or depreciation in the property over the investment period is not considered. Also, there is no *single* measure of return that can be relied on by the investor to indicate whether debt financing is beneficial when he is confronted with a series of annual measures of return on equity. To remedy these problems, the internal rate of return can be used because it incorporates annual cash flows from operation, taxes, appreciation or depreciation, and capital gains and losses into a rate of compound interest that is useful for financial decision making. Thus, the internal rate of return on equity has been computed for Phase I, again assuming the zero and 70 percent debt levels, and it appears in Exhibit 13–3. Based on these computations (not shown), it becomes clear that both the before-tax and aftertax internal rate of return *increase* for Phase I as debt financing is increased from 0 to 70 percent of value. Note that *BTIRR* increases from 12.8 percent to 18.3 percent, and, more importantly, the *ATIRR* increases from 8.0 percent to 14.3 percent at the respective debt levels. Hence, based solely on the internal rate of return, it is clear that the investor is better off *with* debt financing than without it.

The relationship we have just described, that is, the effect of debt financing on the rate of return earned by equity investors, has been traditionally described as *financial leverage.* More specifically, *financial leverage is defined as the use of debt financing by investors with the expectation that returns* on *equity invested will increase.* In the previous example for Phase I, we can see from Exhibit 13–3 that when 70 percent debt financing is used, the *ATIRR*, in fact, increases. When return on equity investment *increases* as a result of using debt financing, this is usually referred to as *positive* financial leverage. However, financial leverage is not always positive in its effect on equity investment. Indeed, depending on the actual trend in *NOI*, property value, and tax effects during the investment period, the use of financial leverage can have a *negative* effect on return on equity. We now turn to an analysis of positive and negative financial leverage and the influence of various levels of debt financing on return on equity investment.

Positive and negative financial leverage

To illustrate both positive and negative financial leverage, the effect of various combinations of mortgage financing on the *ATIRR* on equity invested in Phase I has been computed, and results are shown in Exhibit 13–4. These computations were made under *two* assumptions concerning growth in net operating income and property value. The first condition (Case A) is the same condition that was assumed in our initial example shown in Exhibit 13–1. That is, *NOI* for Phase I is expected to *increase* at the rate of 4 percent per year, and the property value is assumed to *increase* from the original value of $1,000,000

EXHIBIT 13–4
Relationship between *ATIRR* and financial leverage—Phase I project

Recap of assumptions

Initial *NOI*.	$100,000	Initial property value	$1,000,000
Tax bracket	50%	Capital gains tax rate.	20%
Depreciation	*DDB*	Mortgage interest rate	10%
Investment period	5 yrs.	Mortgage term	25 yrs.

A. *NOI growth* at 4% per year, property value *growth* at 2.5% per year

	Debt level			
	0%	50%	70%	80%
ATIRR	8.0%	10.8%	14.3%	18.2%

B. *NOI decline* at 4%, property value *decline* at 2.5% per year

	Debt level			
	0%	50%	70%	80%
ATIRR	3.6%	2.0%	.07%	−3.9%

to $1,134,000 or approximately 2.5 percent per year during the five-year investment period. Results are presented in Exhibit 13–4 based on debt levels of 0 percent, 50 percent, 70 percent, and 80 percent of value. In Case B, *NOI* is assumed to *decline* at the rate of 4 percent per year and property value is assumed to *decline* from $1,000,000 at the rate of 2.5 percent per year to a value of $881,096 at the end of five years. Results are shown for the same debt levels as used in Case A. Looking to Exhibit 13–4, we can see that in Case A, when *NOI* and property values are *increasing* as in our original example, if we initially assume no borrowing or a loan-to-value ratio of zero, the *ATIRR* on equity will be 8 percent if Phase I is operated for five years and then sold. If we assume that a mortgage loan with a 10 percent interest rate can be made for 50 percent of value, the *ATIRR* on equity *increases* to 10.8 percent and continues to *increase* as a greater percentage of value is borrowed (or as more "leverage" is used). This is *clearly a case of positive financial leverage.* This case is diagrammed as *PFL* in Exhibit 13–5. Essentially, what happens in this case is that as more and more is borrowed, the amount of equity investment required decreases faster than the reduction in *ATCF* brought on by the increase in debt service and interest charges. Hence the *ATIRR increases* as leverage is *increased.*

On the other hand, when *NOI* and property value are assumed to *decline* over the five-year investment period as in Case B, we see that when no borrowing occurs, the *ATIRR* is be 3.6 percent. If mortgage financing based on the same terms as in Case A are used, *ATIRR declines* further as the amount of debt financing increases. This is clearly a case of *negative* financial leverage, and it is diagrammed as *NFL* in Exhibit 13–5. Clearly, in Case B, no debt financing would be the preferred alternative, that is, no leverage should be

EXHIBIT 13–5
Positive and negative leverage illustrated

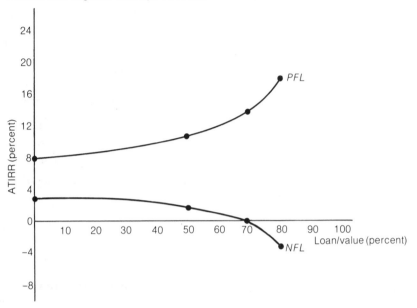

used. From this analysis we should conclude that the use of financial leverage will be dependent on estimates of *NOI* and property value *over the investment period.* We can also conclude that if positive financial leverage exists, aftertax returns on equity investment (*ATIRR*) will *increase* as more debt financing is used. Conversely, if negative financial leverage exists, *ATIRR* will *decrease* as more debt financing is used. Hence the effect of debt financing on aftertax return on equity is *magnified* in both cases as the *degree of financial leverage* used is increased.

This relationship regarding the degree or extent of financial leverage can be more clearly seen in Exhibit 13–5. Note that the curve labeled *PFL* increases as the amount of financial leverage used increases, and, conversely, the curve labeled *NFL* decreases as the amount of financial leverage used increases. The point to be made here is that financial leverage is a two-edged sword. If estimates of *NOI,* property values, and tax effects are accurate, and positive financial leverage results, *ATIRR* earned by investors will *increase* (*PFL*) as the degree of financial leverage is *increased.* On the other hand, if estimates of *NOI,* property values, and tax effects indicate the existence of negative financial leverage, then the *ATIRR* earned by investors will *decrease* (NFL) as the degree of financial leverage is *increased.*

In concluding this section, we reiterate that to properly analyze financial leverage in real estate, its effect must be considered over some expected period of investment. As has been pointed out in previous chapters, mortgage interest rates (i_m), contain premiums for expected inflation and risk, and include a real return to lenders. Investors want to earn an expected return (k) on equity. However, unless the effects of inflation and the other elements of return are considered by examining *NOI* and property value in relation to mortgage debt over an expected period of ownership, it is not possible to determine the extent to which financial leverage can be used favorably.

The "break-even" interest rate—financial leverage. While it is instructive to consider the "sensitivity" of the *ATIRR* on equity to various levels of debt financing as was done in Exhibit 13–4 and 13–5, it is somewhat cumbersome to have to estimate *ATIRR* on equity for many combinations of debt levels to ascertain whether or not positive financial leverage exists. Furthermore, the estimates of *ATIRR* for Phase I, shown in Exhibit 13–4 and diagrammed in Exhibit 13–5, were based on the assumption that all debt amounts, that is, 50 percent, 70 percent, and 80 percent, could be obtained with the *same mortgage interest rate* of 10 percent for 25 years. Given that lenders are aware that as the amount of mortgage financing increases, the interest rate should also increase due to added risk, it will be more likely the case that interest rates will be *changing* as debt levels change. These changes in the cost of borrowing definitely complicate the analysis of financial leverage. Therefore, an important question faced by the investor is whether there is a way to determine the conditions that must exist to make financial leverage positive or negative *in advance* of considering many levels of debt financing. Clearly, this would be preferable to computing many estimates of *ATIRR* for various combinations of debt levels and mortgage terms.

What follows is a rather straightforward approach to the questions raised above. The concept to be illustrated is the break-even interest rate for using financial leverage. *This break-even interest rate represents the maximum interest rate that an investor can pay for borrowed funds if financial leverage is to be positive in its effect on return on equity.* To illustrate, we reconsider our Phase I project under the assumption in Case A, that is, when *NOI* is expected to grow at 4 percent annually and the property value is expected to grow at about 2½ percent per year. First, using data already compiled in Exhibit 13–1, we compute the *ATIRR* for Phase I *assuming no debt financing.* The statement of aftertax cash flow under those assumptions is shown in Exhibit 13–6. Assuming that the property is sold after five years for a price of $1,134,000, the $ATCF_x$ computation for Phase I would be the sale price less total taxes at sale shown previously in Exhibit 13–1, or:[1]

Sale price..........................		$1,134,000
Less: Ordinary income tax	$40,488	
Capital gains tax	46,800	
Total tax................		87,288
$ATCF_x$.............................		$1,046,712

---

[1] The reader should note that federal taxes paid *in the year of sale* are not affected by the amount of mortgage financing.

EXHIBIT 13–6
Statement of aftertax cash flow—Phase I—no debt financing

	Year				
	1	2	3	4	5
Before-tax cash flow:					
NOI	$100,000	$104,000	$108,160	$112,486	$116,986
Less: Debt service	–0–	–0–	–0–	–0–	–0–
BTCF	$100,000	$104,000	$108,160	$112,486	$116,986
Taxable income or loss:					
NOI	$100,000	$104,000	$108,160	$112,486	$116,986
Less: Interest	–0–	–0–	–0–	–0–	–0–
Depreciation..........	40,000	38,000	36,100	34,295	32,580
Taxable income (loss)	$ 60,000	$ 66,000	$ 72,060	$ 78,191	$ 84,406
(Tax) or savings at 50%	$ (30,000)	$ (33,000)	$ (36,030)	$ (39,095)	$ (42,203)
Aftertax cash flow:					
BTCF	$100,000	$104,000	$108,160	$112,486	$116,986
Less (tax) or add savings	(30,000)	(33,000)	(36,030)	(39,095)	(42,203)
ATCF	$ 70,000	$ 71,000	$ 72,130	$ 73,391	$ 74,783

Solving for the $ATIRR$ on equity, which is $1,000,000 assuming no debt, we discount the $ATCF$ in each year plus the $ATCF_s$ in the year of sale. An ARR is computed to estimate the $ATIRR$ on equity, a step we do not show here, and it yields a solution close to 8 percent. Using 8 percent as the discount rate, we solve for the present value of the annual $ATCF$ and $ATCF_s$ as follows:

Year	ATCF	IFPV, 8 percent	PV
1............	$ 70,000	.925926	$ 64,815
2............	71,000	.857339	60,871
3............	72,130	.793832	57,259
4............	73,391	.735030	53,945
5............	74,783	.680583	50,896
6............	1,046,712	.680583	712,374
Present value......................			$1,000,160

From the above computation, we see that the $1,000,160 is very close to the $1,000,000 in equity that would be required if no debt financing were used to purchase Phase I. Hence, we can say that if our investor purchased Phase I for $1,000,000 in equity, the $ATIRR$ on equity that would be earned would be 8 percent.

What does going through this exercise mean? It is very important because the 8 percent *ATIRR*, assuming no debt financing, gives us the essential ingredient to determine the break-even interest rate for using financial leverage. The break-even interest rate (*BEIR*) for financial leverage is computed as follows:

$$\frac{ATIRR \text{ (no debt)}}{1 - \text{Ordinary tax rate}} = BEIR$$

Hence, in our example, *BEIR* would be computed as:

$$\frac{.08}{1 - .50} = .16, \text{ or } \underline{\underline{16\%}}$$

This rate of interest represents the maximum cost that an investor can pay for any amount of debt financing and still be certain that positive financial leverage will occur. *If the investor pays more than the BEIR (16 percent) for any quantity of debt, negative financial leverage will occur. If the investor can acquire mortgage financing at a rate less than BEIR (16 percent), financial leverage will always be positive.* This will be true regardless of the amount borrowed. If we wanted to repeat the computation for Case B when *NOI* and property values were expected to decline, the *BEIR* would be based on the 3.6 percent *ATIRR* computed based on no debt (see Exhibit 13–4), divided by (1 − .50) resulting in a *BEIR* of 7.2 percent. Therefore, if declining income and property values are expected as in Case *B*, the investor cannot borrow any amount at an interest cost in excess of 7.2 percent if positive financial leverage is to occur.

To illustrate the *BEIR* concept and financial leverage for Case A, we recompute the *ATCF* for Phase I under the assumption that a mortgage loan for $700,000 or 70 percent of value is obtained at 16 percent interest for 25 years with annual amortization. The property is again assumed to be sold for $1,134,000 after five years. The statement of aftertax cash flow is shown in Exhibit 13–7. Again assuming the project is sold after five years for $1,134,000, $ATCF_s$ would be computed as:

Sale price.......................		$1,134,000
Mortgage balance................		680,684
$BTCF_s$.....................		$ 453,316
Less:		
Ordinary income tax	$40,488	
Capital gain tax	46,800	
Total tax		87,288
$ATCF_s$.....................		$ 366,028

Finding the present value of *ATCF* and $ATCF_s$ at 8 percent, which was the *ATIRR* in the previous example, we have:

Year	ATCF	IFPV, 8 percent	PV
1	$ 11,191	.925926	$ 10,362
2	11,967	.857339	10,260
3	12,886	.793832	10,229
4	13,794	.735030	10,139
5	14,836	.680583	10,097
5	366,028	.680583	249,112
			$300,199

From the discounted value of all cash inflows and outflows, we see that the computed present value, $300,199, is approximately equal to the $300,000 equity required with 70 percent financing. This means that if we borrowed 70 percent of value at 16 percent interest in Case A, its *ATIRR* in equity would be 8 percent, *or the same ATIRR that was shown in the previous case when no debt financing was assumed.* This proves that the 16 percent *BEIR* represents an indifference point, or the maximum rate of interest at which it makes no difference whether financial leverage is used.

We should also stress the point that the *BEIR* holds true *regardless of the amount borrowed.* However, if the investor can borrow any amount at interest rates *below* the *BEIR,* financial leverage will always be positive. By the same

EXHIBIT 13–7
ATCF for Phase I; mortgage rate, 16 percent

	Year				
	1	*2*	*3*	*4*	*5*
Before-tax cash flow:					
NOI.	$100,000	$104,000	$108,160	$112,486	$116,986
Less: Debt service*	114,809	114,809	114,809	114,809	114,809
BTCF	$ (14,809)	$ (10,809)	$ (6,649)	$ (2,323)	$ 2,177
Taxable income or loss:					
NOI.	$100,000	$104,000	$108,160	$112,486	$116,986
Less: Interest	112,000	111,551	111,029	110,424	109,723
Depreciation	40,000	38,000	36,100	34,295	32,580
Taxable income (loss).	$ (52,000)	$ (45,551)	$ (39,069)	$ (32,233)	$ (25,317)
(Tax) or savings.	$ 26,000	$ 22,776	$ 19,535	$ 16,117	$ 12,659
Aftertax cash flow:					
BTCF	$ (14,809)	$ (10,809)	$ (6,649)	$ (2,323)	$ 2,177
Less (tax) or add savings . . .	26,000	22,776	19,535	16,177	12,659
ATCF.	$ 11,191	$ 11,967	$ 12,886	$ 13,794	$ 14,836

* Annual payments and amortization at 16 percent.

token, any amounts borrowed at interest rates above the *BEIR* will always result in negative financial leverage.

To illustrate the relationship between *BEIR* and positive and negative financial leverage, Exhibit 13–8 has been constructed for Case A to show the

EXHIBIT 13–8
Relationship between *BEIR* and financial leverage

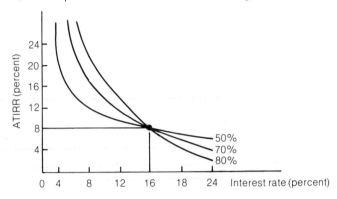

relationship between *ATIRR* on equity, computed for *different amounts borrowed at different interest rates,* and the *BEIR*. In other words, looking at Exhibit 13–8, we can read off the resulting *ATIRR* for Phase I (vertical axis) under conditions in Case A where *NOI* and property values increase over the five-year investment period, for either 50 percent, 70 percent, or 80 percent financing at various interest rates (horizontal axis). The important concepts to note in the exhibit are that (1) regardless of the amount borrowed, when the interest rate on borrowed funds equals 16 percent, the *ATIRR* on equity will always be equal to 8 percent, and (2) when the interest rate on borrowed funds is below 16 percent, the *ATIRR* on equity will increase due to favorable financial leverage. Furthermore, when borrowed funds cost less than 16 percent, the *ATIRR* will increase as the amount borrowed increases. Hence, one can conclude that when the investor is in the favorable financial leverage range, the *ATIRR* on equity increases as the amount borrowed increases. Conversely, when mortgage interest rates are above 16 percent, negative financial leverage exists, and the *ATIRR* will decline as more funds are borrowed. This is a very important relationship, and the reader should carefully consider the results in Exhibit 13–8.

Financial leverage and borrowing

The preceding analysis is a useful concept in that given the estimates of cash flow from operation and estimates of property value over the investment period, it helps to define the range where positive and negative financial leverage will occur. Does this mean that investors should always borrow until the interest rate charged by lenders equals the *BEIR?* A little reflection on this question will yield a logical answer. Recall that in our previous example, the *BEIR* was 16 percent. At that point the investor's *ATIRR* on equity was 8 percent, or equal to the *ATIRR* in our base case when no debt financing was used. Clearly, at this point, there would be no incentive for the investor to borrow further. This is because the *ATIRR* without borrowing would be equivalent to the *ATIRR* with borrowing. Therefore, to earn an adequate return on equity, the investor must always borrow funds at an interest rate *below* the *BEIR,* or below 16 percent. This would make the *ATIRR* on equity increase as the amount borrowed increases.

How much below the 16 percent interest rate should the investor restrict borrowing? This is a more difficult question to answer. As we have pointed out earlier, when funds are borrowed, the investor takes an added risk of loss by virtue of the fact that (1) the mortgage lender has a prior claim on cash flow produced by the property which must go to pay debt service, and (2) the lender does have a prior claim on any proceeds from the sale of the property which must first be applied to any outstanding mortgage balance before the investor receives any residual.

Recall in Chapter 10 on the valuation of income properties, we formulated the following relationships:

$$(i_r + i_p + i_f)_t = i_m$$

and

$$(k_r + k_p + k_f)_t = k$$

where i_m was equal to the mortgage interest rate and k was equal to the *BTIRR* on equity invested. The subscripts were identified as follows: r represented the real rate of return, p represented a risk premium, and f represented an inflation premium. We went on to say that k_p, or the risk premium associated with equity investment, had to be greater than i_p, or the risk premium on mortgage debt, because of the added financial risk associated with equity ownership. Hence, we would also expect that k, or the *BTIRR* on equity, would always be greater than i_m, or the interest rate on mortgage funds. Also, on an aftertax basis, the *ATIRR* on equity should be greater than the aftertax interest rate on mortgage funds, or $i_m (1 - \text{tax rate})$.[2] Hence the *investor* must always expect to earn a higher aftertax return on investment than the *lender* earns due to the added financial risk; otherwise the investor would be better off by becoming a lender.

---

[2] Recall from Chapter 12 that we cannot define *ATIRR* on equity as $k (1 - \text{tax rate})$ because of the "tax-shelter" characteristics of real estate. Because of this, it may be possible that in some extreme cases, an investor could be satisfied with k being equal to i_m because the *ATIRR* on equity could still be greater than $i_m (1 - \text{tax rate})$ due to the real estate tax shelter.

The extent to which equity investors are willing to borrow then is dependent on the "premium" they earn for taking additional financial risk as the amount borrowed increases. Similarly, the amount that lenders are willing to lend is dependent on the interest rate that they can charge as more funds are loaned.

Financial leverage—other considerations.   There are other considerations in addition to the $BEIR$ and risk premiums earned on equity that enter into the decision to lend and borrow on real estate. First, there are underwriting standards that lenders impose on borrowers, such as debt-service coverage requirements which were discussed in the previous chapter. Second, state and federal regulations restrict the loan-to-value ratios that may be used by many lenders in underwriting real estate loans. Finally, for all incremental amounts borrowed by investors, there exists a marginal cost of borrowing that must be considered. To illustrate, if the amount borrowed on Phase I increased from 70 to 80 percent and the interest rate increased from 10 percent to 12 percent, this would represent a 20 percent increase in borrowing costs (i.e., $2\% \div 10\%$), or 10 percent after tax.[3] This marginal cost to the investor of acquiring additional funds would have to be offset by earning an equal or greater amount on some other alternative investment. Hence the $ATIRR$ which *additional* borrowed funds will earn must also be considered by the investor as incremental amounts of borrowing are evaluated.

Financial leverage and inflationary expectations.   One further aspect of financial leverage deserves some consideration here; that is, its relationship to inflationary expectations. Based on our formulation of mortgage interest rates (i_m) and before-tax returns on equity investment (k), we have indicated that both returns include premiums for expected inflation $(i_f$ and k_f, respectively). If lenders and investors are *accurate* in their predictions of inflation, *both* will earn expected inflation premiums in their expected returns. In that event, the use of financial leverage will result in $k > i_m$, or investors earning a higher return than lenders only because of added risk. However, one additional element that must be discussed has to do with the issue of *unanticipated inflation*.

When inflation is unanticipated, this means that the rate of *expected* inflation premium (i_f) included in the lending rate is *less* than the premium that should be actually earned by the lender. Because inflation affects investment in real estate through rising rents and ultimately NOI, if *actual* inflation is greater than *expected* inflation, then debt service will be too low, and the equity investor will realize greater $BTCF$ on equity, or $k_f > i_f$. Hence, if a property is highly leveraged and lenders underestimate inflation, equity investors will earn returns on investment that are *greater* than the risk premium for using financial leverage. In other words, k will be greater than i_m by more than the risk premium brought about by financial leverage. If this occurs, property

---

[3] This also represents a risk premium earned by lenders for loaning additional funds in the 70–80 percent range.

values will adjust by appreciating through time, as returns to lenders (i_m) and investors (k) adjust back into a more normal spread relationship. However, in the interim, equity investors holding mortgages made at fixed interest rates will be better off because of the rise in their property values.

Many observers in real estate have argued that because of an overexpansion in the supply of money in the economy, interest rates are reduced and inflation is not completely reflected in those rates for a long period of time.[4] As a result, we have seen opportunities for abnormally high returns on equity investment in real estate and rapidly rising property prices.[5]

In summary, while the maximum interest rate $(BEIR)$ at which positive financial leverage will occur can be estimated for a given project, the actual interest rate that investors and borrowers will ultimately agree upon is dependent on many considerations. While considerable research has been done on this subject, it is far from conclusive. However, it is reasonable to believe that competitive forces in the market for mortgage credit and among investors in real estate would cause a tendency for an "equilibrium," or competitive, risk premium to be earned by investors over interest rates earned by lenders in various categories of real estate.

Rate of return analysis and equity participation loans

In the preceding sections we have assumed throughout that the investor is able to acquire the traditional, level payment mortgage loan. We have also pointed out that in periods when inflation is expected to increase, interest rates and debt-service requirements increase sharply and traditional underwriting standards used by lenders (such as debt-service coverage requirements, break-even points, etc.) when analyzing income properties may indicate that a project is not financially feasible. While such feasibility standards may not be met with the traditional level payment mortgage loan, equity participations are frequently used in place of such loans when projects are otherwise economically feasible.

To illustrate how an investor would analyze the effects of an equity participation mortgage on investment returns, we reconsider the example of the equity participation mortgage used in Chapter 11. In that example, we considered a property with a $1,000,000 value ($800,000 building, $200,000 land). The requested loan amount was $750,000 for 25 years, with a 10 percent base interest rate. In addition, the lender required 25 percent of the cash flow over the "break-even point." The break-even point was defined as any cash flow remaining after deducting the base mortgage payment from *NOI*. We also determined that should the mortgage be repaid after five years, the prepayment penalty would be $133,083.

---

[4] We discuss the causes of this problem in Chapter 18 on the mortgage market.

[5] This same pattern has existed in the market for single-family houses.

To compute investment returns with equity participation financing, we further assume that (1) *NOI* at the end of year 1 is expected to be $104,900, and will increase at 8 percent per year; (2) the property value will increase at 4 percent per year over the 5-year expected period of ownership; (3) the taxpayer elects to use straight-line depreciation over a 40-year expected useful life; and (4) the investor's ordinary income is taxed at a marginal rate of 50 percent. To simplify the computations, we assume that the mortgage payments are made *annually;* hence the *annual* mortgage payments based on the 10 percent base mortgage rate are $82,626 ($750,000 × .110168 from Appendix A, column 6), and the loan balance at the end of the fifth year is $703,443. These mortgage payments differ slightly from the figures used in Chapter 11, which were based on monthly payments.

Looking to Exhibit 13–9, the reader should note very carefully that in the computation of taxable income *both* the annual interest charge *and* the lender's participation in *NOI* are *tax deductible.* The participation in *NOI*

EXHIBIT 13–9
Investment returns with an equity participation mortgage

	Year				
	1	2	3	4	5
A. Debt service					
NOI	$104,900	$113,292	$122,355	$132,144	$142,716
− Base mortgage payment	82,626	82,626	82,626	82,626	82,626
Cash flow over "break-even"	$ 22,274	$ 30,666	$ 39,729	$ 49,518	$ 60,090
25% participation	$ 5,569	$ 7,667	$ 9,932	$ 12,380	$148,106*
+ Base mortgage payment	82,626	82,626	82,626	82,626	82,626
Total debt service	$ 88,195	$ 90,293	$ 92,558	$ 95,005	$230,732
B. Cash flow					
NOI	$104,900	$113,292	$122,355	$132,144	$142,716
− Debt service	88,195	90,293	92,558	95,005	230,732
BTCF	$ 16,705	$ 22,999	$ 29,797	$ 37,139	$ (88,016)
C. Taxable income					
NOI	$104,900	$113,292	$122,355	$132,144	$142,716
− Interest	75,000	74,237	73,399	72,476	71,461
− Participation	5,569	7,667	9,932	12,380	148,106*
− Depreciation	20,000	20,000	20,000	20,000	20,000
Taxable income (loss)	$ 4,331	$ 11,388	$ 19,024	$ 27,288	$ (96,851)
(Tax) savings at 50%	$ (2,166)	$ (5,694)	$ (9,512)	$ (13,644)	$ 48,426
D. After-tax cash flow					
BTCF	$ 16,705	$ 22,999	$ 29,797	$ 37,139	$ (88,016)
(Tax) or savings	(2,166)	(5,694)	(9,512)	(13,644)	48,426
ATCF	$ 14,539	$ 17,305	$ 20,285	$ 23,495	$ (39,590)

* Includes $15,023 participation and $133,083 penalty.

is considered as interest for tax purposes and hence must be included in the determination of taxes. It should be noted that the prepayment penalty of $133,083, in addition to reducing cash flow, is also tax deductible as *interest* in the year of sale. This effectively reduces the taxpayer's tax liability in determining *ATCF*.

In the year the property is sold, the selling price is determined as $1,000,000 × (1.04)⁵ = $1,216,653. Based on this price and assuming that a 6 percent sales commission is paid in the year of sale, we compute the $ATCF_s$ as shown in Exhibit 13–10. Based on the computation shown in Exhibit 13–

EXHIBIT 13–10
Computation of $BTCF_s$ and $ATCF_s$—equity participation financing

Computation of $BTCF_s$:

Sale price	$1,216,653
Less: Commission at 6%	73,000
Mortgage balance	703,443
$BTCF_s$	$ 440,210

Computation of taxes:

Sale price	$1,216,653
Less: Commission at 6%	73,000
Adjusted basis (book value)	900,000
Total gain	$ 243,653
Recapture of excess depreciation	–0–
Long-term capital gain	$ 243,653
Long-term capital gain tax at 20%	$ 48,731

Computation of $ATCF_s$:

$BTCF_s$	$ 440,210
Less: Long-term capital gain tax	– 48,731
$ATCF_s$	$ 391,479

10, the $ATCF_s$ is seen to be $391,479. With an initial equity investment of $250,000 and given the annual *ATCF* shown in Exhibit 13–9 and $ATCF_s$ shown in Exhibit 13–10, the *ATIRR* in this case is approximately 12.6 percent (calculation not shown, reader should verify).

In summary, the computation of the aftertax internal rate of return on equity investment is somewhat more complex with an equity participation mortgage. The essential differences between the computation of return with an equity participation and with the standard mortgage payment pattern lie in the tax treatment of the lender's participation in income and the prepayment penalty in the year of sale. While this type of financing is still somewhat unusual in mortgage markets it is gaining in importance. The above illustration serves as framework for considering equity participation financing in an investment context.

PART 2: INVESTMENT RISK AND RETURN

Comparing investment returns

To this point in the chapter we have illustrated the role of financial leverage on returns on real estate investment. At this point, we wish to briefly explore considerations that investors should take into account when comparing measures of return on investment on a specific real estate investment with *other* real estate investments, and *other* investments generally.

After having gone through a reasonably detailed illustration of an investment analysis of an income-producing property, and after having developed measures of return on investment, an investor must decide whether or not an investment in such a project will provide an "adequate" or "competitive" return. The answer to this question will depend on (1) the nature of alternative real estate investments, (2) other investments which are available to the investor, (3) the respective returns that those alternatives will yield, and (4) the differences in *risk* between the investment being considered relative to those alternative investments available to the investor.

In Exhibit 13–11, we have constructed a hypothetical relationship between rates of return and risk for various classes of alternative investments. The vertical axis represents the *ATIRR* on equity on real estate and before-tax yields presently available on U.S. Treasury Bills, municipal bonds (exempt from federal income taxes), corporate bonds, corporate preferred stock and common stock.[6] The horizontal axis represents the degree of risk inherent in each category of investment. No attempt has been made to measure or to quantify risk in the diagram, although much research has been done on the subject.[7] Risk, as presented in Exhibit 13–11, is considered only in relative terms; that is, as one moves to the right on the axis, an investment is considered more risky and to the left less risky. Hence, investments with higher risks should yield investors higher returns and vice versa.

Based on the risk-return "ranking" indicated in Exhibit 13–11, the reader should note that the security with the lowest return, U.S. Treasury bills, also has the lowest risk (zero on the horizontal axis). As we move out on the risk-return line in the exhibit, we see that expected aftertax returns on investments in real estate (such as Phase I in our previous illustrations) offer a considerably higher expected return but are also much riskier than investing in U.S. Treasury bills. What are the investment characteristics peculiar to real estate that make it more risky than investing in government securities? Similarly, what risk characteristics differentiate real estate investment from the other alternatives such as common and preferred stock, corporate bonds, and

---

[6] For a complete discussion of these securities and the yield computations for each, see William F. Sharpe, *Investments* (Englewood Cliffs, N.J.: Prentice-Hall, Inc., 1978).

[7] See appendix to this chapter for a basic discussion of the quantification of risk.

EXHIBIT 13–11
Relationship between risk and return-alternative investments

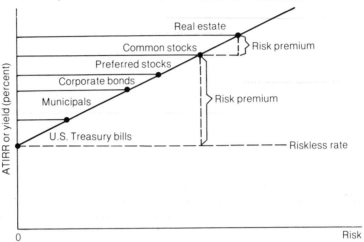

municipal bonds also shown in Exhibit 13–11? To answer this question we must consider some of the characteristics that are the source of risk differences among various categories of investments. What follows is a brief summary of major investment risk characteristics that must be considered by investors when deciding among alternative investments.

Business risk—the risk of loss due to fluctuations in economic activity and its effect on the variability of income produced by the business or economic entity being invested in. For example, changes in economic conditions such as a recession may affect some business or activity more than others. Those affected to a greater degree than others would be riskier.

Financial risk—the risk of loss due to financial leverage. The extent of risk will depend on the extent of prior claims of lenders on income and proceeds upon liquidation of the business or economic unit being invested in.

Liquidity risk—this risk occurs to the extent of the lack of a continuous market with many buyers and sellers and frequent transactions. The more difficult an investment is to liquidate, the greater the risk that a price concession may have to be given to a buyer should the seller have to dispose of the investment quickly.

Purchasing power risk—This risk occurs to the extent income from a security does not adjust to inflation, thereby reducing the real value of the underlying security. Also, it may be that certain types of business activity are more favorably or adversely affected by inflation than others. Hence, this is a source of risk that must be considered in an investment analysis.

Management risks—This risk will be based on the capability of management and its ability to innovate, respond to competitive conditions, and operate the business activity efficiently.

Interest rate risk—Changes in interest rates will affect the price of all securities and investments. However, depending on the relative maturity (short-term versus long-term investments), some investment prices will respond more than others thereby increasing the potential for loss or gain.

Legislative risk—This risk comes about in the form of tax law changes, rent control, zoning, and other restrictions imposed by government that could adversely affect the profitability of investments.

Essentially, these risk characteristics are, in large part, the reasons for differences in returns between the alternative investments shown in Exhibit 13–11. For example, U.S. Treasury bills are a very short-term investment (90 or 180 days). They are free from business risk, management risk, and financial risk because they are guaranteed by the U.S. government. Because the government has the potentially unlimited ability to tax, it is not likely to default on its obligations. Further, because of the vast, continuous market in government securities, the risk of loss due to the inability to sell a government security when a sale is desired or necessary is very low. As to inflation and interest rate risk, because of the extremely short-term nature of these investments, these risks are thought to be minimal. Consequently, Treasury bills, with extremely short maturities, are thought to be the closest thing to a riskless investment available in the economy. Hence, as shown in the exhibit, this investment is shown to have essentially zero risk and a very low return relative to other securities. In theory, then, a Treasury bill with a given maturity should carry an interest rate that provides the investor with a real rate of interest, plus a premium for expected inflation at the time of purchase, with *no* risk premium for any of the categories of risk discussed above.

In considering each of the investment categories in Exhibit 13–11, in conjunction with the list of risk characteristics just discussed, it is slightly more easy to place real estate investment into an overall, risk-return context with alternative investments. For example, when considering a real estate investment, it is clear that many of the risks included in the above list are very important for an investor to consider. Business risk is a very important influence to consider because a sudden downward turn in the economy could cause unemployment, a slowdown in business expansion, and perhaps reduced demand for rental space. Financial risk is present in real estate because of financial leverage. Should default occur, mortgage lenders have prior claim over any equity investors thereby increasing the risk of loss. There is considerable liquidity risk present should an equity investor desire to suddenly sell an interest in a real estate project. It could take a considerable period of time to sell, or the investor may have to sell at a below-market price should funds be needed quickly. As to purchasing power risk, because the income stream should change with inflation, this risk may be somewhat lower when compared to other investments paying a fixed income to investors. Also, management risks in real estate are present and would have to be carefully considered when making an investment choice.

Looking to Exhibit 13–11, then, we can now understand why the return on real estate should be considerably higher than the return on U.S. Treasury bills. Should real estate be selected for investment, the *risk premium,* or differential shown in the exhibit, is the "price" that investors must earn for the additional risks taken relative to alternative investments, in this case, U.S. Treasury bills.

The risk premium concept shown for real estate relative to Treasury bills also applies to all other investments shown in Exhibit 13–11. The risk premium concept also applies *among* individual investment categories shown in the exhibit (see the risk premium as represented by the difference in return on real estate relative to common stock in the exhibit). Each investment type differs in the extent to which the sources of risk described above influence each investment's expected return.

Contrasting the above investment types and assessing the risk of each, we should note that municipal bonds are issued by municipalities that have limited powers to tax (such power is limited by voter approval or limited to specific projects or districts). Although some of the business risk is eliminated by this power of taxation, financial risk is present to the extent a municipality overissues debt and defaults (New York City bonds, for example). Further, there is not as continuous a market for these securities when compared to U.S. obligations; hence, there must be a risk premium for the lack of liquidity.

Looking to common stock, preferred stock, and corporate bonds, each of these security types usually have good marketability. However, they are significantly affected by business risk, management risk, financial risk, and all of the remaining categories of risk previously discussed. Hence, they should also command a premium over both treasury obligations and municipal bonds, but not as high a premium as an equity investor would earn on real estate, which is riskier in many ways.

We should stress at this point that we have been discussing investment alternatives in very broad *categories.* It may be very possible to find *individual* investments *within* a category where expected returns are below those expected in another category (an individual real estate investment may provide a lower return on investment than *some* common stocks, for example). These categories were chosen in order to facilitate a discussion of major risk characteristics affecting each investment type. In the final analysis, a prospective investor in a specific real estate project must estimate and compute an expected return on that project and compare that return with expected returns on other *specific* investments. Any risk differentials must then be carefully considered relative to any risk premium, or difference in expected returns, in all such comparisons. Investors must then make the final judgment as to whether an investment is justified.

There are also many characteristics in real estate *markets,* however, that differentiate it from markets for other investments shown in Exhibit 13–11. Many of these market characteristcs make investment decisions in real estate more difficult and therefore more risky relative to other investments. Some of these market characteristics are:

A. Highly technical product—many categories of real estate include improvements that are of a technical nature in design, construction, or use. Generally, the more complex a real estate investment is the more difficult it is to value. Hence, in these cases, there will be greater differences in prices investors are willing to pay. On the other hand, for more homogeneous properties (houses, apartment buildings, etc.) with fewer complexities, there will be greater agreement on property value.

B. Continuous information—volume of buying and selling—contrary to many other markets such as the market for wheat, other commodities, and common stock, the real estate market does not present a continuous flow of investment opportunities. Real estate investments of all types are not always available at all times. Purchases and sales in a local market occur less frequently than in many other markets. Hence, prices and market conditions may change between sales of property, and the investor does not have access to a more continuous flow of information as to how changes in those market conditions are changing prices.

C. Changes in local and regional growth patterns—many regions of the country and locations within cities experience differences in the rate of growth due to changes in demand, population changes, and so on. Because of the lack of continuous price and other market data, such changes are not easily determined.

While other characteristics tend to differentiate real estate markets from other markets, it is reasonable to believe that even though the real estate market can be characterized as competitive, there are enough of these features that may make possible opportunities for higher real returns from buying and selling real estate. How much higher these returns may be and how long such returns are likely to persist in a given market are more difficult to answer.

Questions

1 What is financial leverage? Why is a one-year measure of return on investment inadequate in determining whether positive or negative financial leverage exists?

2 What is the break-even mortgage interest rate (*BEIR*) when viewed in the context of financial leverage? Would you ever expect an investor to pay a "break even" interest rate when financing a property? Why or why not?

3 What is meant by *positive* and *negative* financial leverage? How are returns or losses "magnified" as the degree of leverage is increased?

4   What is meant by unanticipated inflation? How does it affect returns on equity in real estate?

5   What is a risk premium? Why does such a premium exist between interest rates on mortgages and rates of return earned on equity invested in real estate?

6   What are some of the types of risk that should be considered when analyzing real estate and other categories of investment? Why is real estate investment generally more risky than other investments discussed in the chapter?

7   What are some of the market characteristics that make real estate investment more risky than other investments?

Case problems

1   K. C. Sunshine is concerned over a financing problem he is currently facing. He would like to purchase a new warehouse-office property for $2,000,000. However, he is faced with the decision as to whether he should use 65 percent or 75 percent financing. The 65 percent loan can be obtained at 10 percent interest for 25 years. The 75 percent loan can be obtained at 11 percent interest for 25 years.

Other important information is, *NOI* is expected to be $190,000 per year and increase at 3 percent annually, the same rate at which the building is expected to increase in value. The building and improvements represent 80 percent of value and have an expected economic life of 40 years (no salvage value). Depreciation will be taken on a 150 percent declining-balance basis (see appendix to Chapter 12). The project is expected to be sold after five years. Sunshine's tax bracket is 50 percent.

a.   What would the *BTIRR* and *ATIRR* be at each level of financing (assume annual mortgage amortization)?

b.   What is the break-even interest rate (*BEIR*) for this project?

c.   What is the marginal cost of the 75 percent loan? What does this mean?

2   Bette Fidler is considering the purchase of a shopping center complex. However, interest rates have just risen very sharply in a matter of months, and she is concerned as to whether the project is financially feasible.

Mutual of Bigrock Insurance Company has made a 75 percent loan proposal to Fidler. The proposal calls for a base interest rate of 10 percent for 25 years and an equity participation of 40 percent in cash flow over "break even" (or the excess of cash flow remaining after the base debt service is subtracted from *NOI*) for a period of 10 years. In the event the loan is repaid before that time, a prepayment penalty of 10 percent of the outstanding loan balance (based on 10 percent amortization) will be required.

The property is expected to cost $5,500,000. *NOI* is estimated to be $475,000 including overages during the first year and increase at the rate of 10 percent per year for the next five years. Fidler estimates she will be able to realize $6,000,000 at that time. The improvement represents 80 percent of cost and depreciation will be restricted to straight line because it is an existing shopping center. The useful life is estimated to be 33.3 years (3 percent depreciation rate), and no salvage value is estimated. Fidler has approached you for advice on this project. She plans to hold the project for five years and sell, and she is in a 50 percent tax bracket.

a. Compute the before and aftertax cash flow each year on the project, taking into account the equity participation (use annual amortization).

b. Compute the *BTIRR* and *ATIRR* after five years taking into account the equity participation.

c. What would the *BEIR* be on such a project? What is the projected cost of the equity participation financing, including the prepayment penalty?

APPENDIX: RISK CONSIDERATIONS IN REAL ESTATE INVESTMENT—SOME EXTENSIONS

This appendix is intended for the reader interested in some further considerations in analyzing the risk associated with investing in income-producing real estate. Two additional aspects of risk analysis are considered here. One has to do with a more in-depth analysis of a specific real estate investment, and the other has to do with comparing risk and return between real estate projects.

Partitioning internal rates of return

In this and the previous chapter, a considerable amount of attention was given to the development of the aftertax internal rate of return on equity invested in real estate projects. While this measure of return is useful in helping the investor to decide whether or not to invest in a project, or in deciding how long to retain ownership, it is helpful to "break down" or "partition" that rate of return into some meaningful components. This partitioning allows the investor to obtain some idea as to the relative weights of components of the return and some idea as to the timing of the receipt of the largest portion of that return.

To illustrate what is meant by partitioning the return, it should be recalled that the aftertax internal rate of return on equity investment in real estate is comprised of two sources of cash flow: (1) aftertax cash flow from operations and (2) aftertax proceeds from the sale of the investment. In Exhibit 13A–1, we present the *ATCF* and *ATCF_s* for a real estate project requiring an equity investment of $72,170. The internal rate of return for the next five years is computed to be 11 percent. Because both of the above-mentioned components make up the 11 percent internal rate of return, we have no way of knowing what proportion *each component bears to the total return.* A breakdown of each component would be useful to an investor concerned with how much of the return is made up of *aftertax cash flow* from operations realized from the project and how much is due to aftertax proceeds from *appreciation* in value of the property.

To consider these questions, it is a simple matter to reconsider the present value of the *ATCF* and *ATCF_s* in a slightly different manner as shown in

EXHIBIT 13A–1
Partitioning the internal rate of return—Project 1

Year	ATCF	IFPV, 11 percent	PV
1.............	$ 4,852	.900901	$ 4,371
2.............	5,205	.811622	4,224
3.............	5,563	.731191	4,068
4.............	5,926	.658731	3,904
5.............	6,294	.593451	3,735
	ATCF$_x$		
5.............	$87,403	.593451	51,869

PV of ATCF............... $20,302
PV of ATCF$_s$............... 51,869
Total PV............ $72,171

Ratio of:
PV, ATCF ÷ Total PV = 28%
PV, ATCF$_s$ ÷ Total PV = 72%

Exhibit 13A–1. We should note that all cash flow components expected to be received from the project are discounted to find the aftertax internal rate of return of 11 percent. Then the PV of $ATCF$ and $ATCF_x$ are summed to get the total PV of $72,171. The ratio of the PV of $ATCF$ and PV of $ATCF_x$ can now be taken to the total present value. These ratios now represent the respective proportion of the internal rate of return made up by aftertax cash flow (28 percent) and aftertax cash flow from appreciation in property value and sale after five years (72 percent).

Why is partitioning an internal rate of return important? Because it helps the investor to determine how much of the return is dependent on annual operating cash flow and how much is dependent on expected appreciation in the value of the property.[1] It would seem that to the extent a greater proportion of the internal rate of return is made up of *expected appreciation in the future,* this *could* be indicative of greater risk facing the investor. For example, assume that this project with its 11 percent $ATIRR$, made up of 28 percent annual $ATCF$ and 72 percent $ATCF_s$, is being compared with another project requiring the same investment of $72,170 with estimated $ATCF$ and $ATCF_x$ as shown on the top of page 385.

This second project, with its estimated $ATCF$ and $ATCF_s$ and $72,170 equity investment, also provides the investor with the same $ATIRR$ of 11

---

[1] It should also be pointed out that other components of $ATIRR$ could be partitioned in addition to $ATCF$ and $ATCF_x$. For example, tax-shelter effects could be partitioned separately, and so on.

Year	ATCF	PV at 11 percent
1	$ 500	$ 450
2	600	487
3	700	512
4	800	527
5	900	534
	$ATCF_s$	
5	$117,381	69,660

PV of ATCF	$ 2,510
PV of $ATCF_s$	69,660
Total PV	$72,170

Ratio of:
  PV, ATCF ÷ Total PV = 3%
  PV, $ATCF_s$ ÷ Total PV = 97%

percent. However, when the *ATIRR* is partitioned, we can see that the proportions of the return are 3 percent for annual *ATCF* and 97 percent for the estimated appreciation in value of the project in five years on an aftertax basis. Hence, it can be seen that even though *both* investments have an 11 percent *ATIRR,* a much higher proportion of the return in the second case is dependent on future appreciation in property value.[2] Given this outcome, the investor may want to compare any differences in risk between projects more carefully because even though the two projects are estimated to yield the same *ATIRR*, there is a strong likelihood that there are significant risk differences between the two.

Variation in returns and risk

Many of the sources of risk discussed in the chapter, such as business risk, financial risk, and so on, affect returns on real estate investment by making such returns more *variable*. Generally speaking, the higher the variability in returns, the higher the risk in a project. For example, assume that we have two properties being considered for investment. The first is an office building located in a part of town that is rapidly growing, rents are steadily increasing, and vacancies are low. If the office building is purchased, it is expected that good quality leases will be executed with triple A corporate tenants, who are looking for branch office space, and vacancies will be minimal. The second property is a special-purpose recreational property that includes a building for amusements, outdoor facilities for mechanical baseball batting cages, a driving

---

[2] The reader should be aware that it is possible to have negative *ATCF* and still have a *positive ATIRR.* Hence the operating cash flows are an important consideration that must be taken into account in addition to the *ATIRR.*

range for golf, and related activities. The latter facility is located near a growing middle income residential development. In the event of an unsuccessful venture in the latter case, the recreational property can be converted to some other commercial use, but not without significant expense for redeveloping the land.

A close examination of these alternatives would indicate that the office building would probably be less risky than the recreational property. The office building would be less influenced by business risk than the recreational property because consumer spending on recreational activity is more sensitive to economic trends and personal income. The income produced by the recreational property will be highly dependent on the state of the national and local economy. On the other hand, the office building is located in a growing area and will be secured by leases with strong tenants. While there may be some losses in the latter case, the likelihood of such losses, when compared to the recreational property, would be lower. Given this characterization, we could say that the income stream expected from the recreational property could be more *variable* over time than the office building, given changes in the economic environment.

To illustrate, Exhibit 13A–2 contains an estimate of the aftertax internal rate of return over a ten-year investment period for the office building and the

EXHIBIT 13A–2
Payoff matrix two investment alternatives

(1) State of Economy	(2) Probability of economic state (1) occurring	(3) Estimated ATIRR given state in (1) occurs	(4) Expected rate of return (2) × (3)
A. Commercial office building			
Rapid growth..................	.20	.17	.034
Slow growth	.60	.12	.072
Decline......................	.20	.07	.014
	1.00	Expected return........	.120
B. Recreational property			
Rapid growth..................	.20	.35	.070
Slow growth	.60	.15	.090
Decline......................	.20	−.05	−.010
	1.00	Expected return	.150

recreational property under three different economic senarios. Essentially, what Exhibit 13A–2 contains is estimates of the *ATIRR* made for both investments, under three general economic senarios that could occur over the investment period. That is, estimate of rents and expenses would be made for both investment alternatives under three assumptions regarding economic conditions. Then, given the debt-service and tax effects appropriate for each investment, the *ATCF* would be compiled as well as an estimate of the property value at the end of the investment period.

After compiling the *ATIRR* under each case, the investor could then make an estimate of the probability that each of the economic senarios that affect the income-producing potential for both alternatives will occur. The estimated *ATIRR*, when multiplied by the probability that a given economic senario will occur, produces an expected or "most likely" return for each investment.

Based on results in Exhibit 13A–2, we see that the recreational property produces the highest expected return, of 15 percent, compared to the 12 percent expected return for the office building. Does this mean that the recreational property should be selected over the office building? Not necessarily. At this point the reader should recall our discussion of risk characteristics in the chapter and how each investment may be affected by those considerations. A property that provides a high expected return may also be more risky relative to investments with somewhat lower returns.

In dealing with the problem of comparing risk and return among investments, there are some techniques that can be used to complement the qualitative considerations discussed at the end of the chapter. We now turn to a discussion of a more quantitative approach to the treatment of project risk.

In trying to deal with all risk characteristics particular to an investment, some researchers and market analysts argue that in combination these risks (e.g., business risk, financial risk, etc., discussed in the chapter) serve to induce *variability in a project's rate of return.* In our above example, the recreational project is clearly more risky than the commercial property, and in fact if one closely examines the estimates of *ATIRR* under each economic senario, a much *wider range* in possible *ATIRR*s is encountered with the recreational property when compared to the office building. In fact, if we diagrammed the relationship between the probability of the possible economic states of nature and the expected *ATIRR* for that state of economic nature, we would have a pattern such as that shown in Exhibit 13A–3. In that exhibit, we have plotted the probability of the state of the economy and expected *ATIRR* on each investment, given the state of the economy. We have "smoothed" the curves in the diagram between each probability point to show what the *ATIRR* would most likely be at points in between those specifically estimated. The key concept one should grasp from the exhibit is that even though the expected return for the recreational property is higher than that computed for the office building, the range of expected returns for the recreational property is from −5 percent to 35 percent. This represents a far wider range than that for the office building which has a range of outcomes estimated from 7 percent to 17 percent. The "narrowness" in the range of outcomes for the office building relative to the outcomes for the recreational property indicates that there is

EXHIBIT 13A–3
Probability distribution of *ATIRR*—office building and recreational property

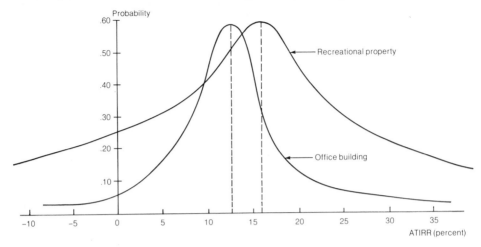

lower variability in the possible returns for the office building than is the case with the recreation property. *Lower variability* in returns is considered by many analysts to be associated with *lower risk,* and vice versa. Therefore, if a statistical measure of *variance* in returns is developed, one has an indication of the extent risk is present in an investment.

Measures of variance and risk. Computing the statistical variance in returns is a very simple procedure and is done for the recreational property and for the office building as shown in Exhibit 13A–4. Taking the square root of

EXHIBIT 13A–4
Expected return and variance, two real estate investments

(1) Estimated returns	(2) Expected return	(3) Deviation (1) − (2)	(4) Squared deviation	(5) Probability	(6) Product (4) × (5)
A. Office building				
17.0	12.0	5.0	25.0	.20	5.0
12.0	12.0	.0	.0	.60	.0
7.0	12.0	−5.0	25.0	.20	5.0
				Variance	10.0
B. Recreational property				
35.0	15.0	20.0	400.0	.20	80.0
15.0	15.0	.0	.0	.60	.0
−5.0	15.0	20.0	400.0	.20	80.0
				Variance	160.0

the variance, 160.0, we have the standard deviation (σ, called sigma) of 12.65 for the recreational property and 3.16 for the office project. What does the variance, or σ^2, mean? What does the standard deviation, or σ, mean? Looking first to the measure of variance, we find that the *variation about the mean return* for the recreational property of 160.0 is *far greater* than that for the office building which is only 10.0. This measure of *dispersion* tells us that the actual return for the office building is *more likely* to be *closer* to its expected return of 12.0 percent when compared to the recreational property. Since the measures for the recreational property were $\sigma^2 = 160.0$ and $\sigma = 12.65$, this tells us that the actual return for the recreational property is *less likely* to be closer to its expected return of 15 percent, when compared to the office building. Hence, if variation in returns is a good indicator of risk, then the recreational property is clearly the more risky of the two investments.

If the probability distribution of *ATIRR*s for the two investments being considered is normal, the standard deviation of returns for each investment also gives us valuable information.[3] The standard deviation gives us a specific range over which we can expect the actual return for each investment to fall in relation to its expected return. For example, for the recreational property, we can expect its *actual* return to fall within $\pm 1\sigma$ of its expected return of 15 percent, 68 percent of the time. This means that we can expect the return on the recreational property to fall between 15% + 12.65%, or 27.65 percent, and 15% − 12.65%, or 2.35 percent, 68 percent of the time. We can expect its actual return to fall within $\pm 2\sigma$ from its expected return approximately 95.5 percent of the time and $\pm 3\sigma$ from its expected return approximately 99.7 percent of the time.[4] In contrast, the actual return on the office building will fall in a much more narrow range of $\pm 1\sigma$ from its expected return, or 12% + 3.16% = 15.16% and 12% − 3.16% = 8.84%, 68 percent of the time, and so on.

Risk and return. The relevance of these statistical measures, in addition to giving the investor a more quantitative perspective on dispersion and variance as proxies for risk, can also be related to the *ATIRR* in developing a measure of *risk per unit of expected return*. This is done for both investments by dividing the standard deviation of the *ATIRR* by the expected *ATIRR*. For the office building this computation would be 3.16 ÷ 12.0, or .263, and for the recreational property it would be 12.65 ÷ 15.0, or .843. This statistic, called the *coefficient of variation*, is a measure of relative variation; that is, it measures *risk per unit of expected return*. In the case of the recreational property, the coefficient of variation is much higher than that of the office building. This simply means that although the expected return for the

---

[3] For normal distributions and skewed distributions in investment analysis, see William F. Sharpe, *Investments* (Englewood Cliffs, N.J.: Prentice-Hall, Inc., 1978).

[4] The percentages associated with the standard deviations which set out the intervals in which the actual returns are likely to fall are *fixed,* if the distribution of returns is normal.

recreational property is higher than that of the office building, when the *variation* in returns, or risk, is taken into account, the *reward* per unit of risk is not as high as it is for the office building.

Risk, reward, and project selection.   Based on the preceding analysis, we have concluded that the recreational property, when compared to the office building, does not provide the same return *per unit of risk taken.* Does this mean that the office building should be chosen over the recreational property? For many investors, the answer would be yes. Unless the coefficient of variation for the recreational property were at least *equal* to the coefficient computed for the office building, there would be a tendency for many investors to select the investment with the *lower* coefficient of variation.

However, we should stress that not all investors view risk the same way. For some investors, the incremental risk taken should the recreational property be purchased may not appear to be that significant relative to the higher expected return. These investors would be those who could be characterized as more aggressive, or risk takers. On the other hand, many investors who fear the probability of failure or loss would never choose the recreational property over the office building. These investors are sometimes characterized as being more conservative, or risk averse. Hence, even though we have developed a way to quantify risk, we are still unable to state with complete confidence that one investment should always be chosen over another, based on its risk-return relationship. Nonetheless, this treatment of risk is useful in gauging the relative risk among investments and does aid in decision making.

Other extensions and considerations.   While the above discussion of risk has been limited to investment analysis, there are other applications that would be useful to lenders, such as those interested in assessing the extent to which the degree of financial leverage may affect the variability in returns and related issues.

We should also point out that certain problems are encountered in the above analysis when, unlike the assumption made in our illustration, possible returns on investment in a project are not normally distributed. When this condition occurs, problems in interpreting the coefficient of variation arise and information provided by the risk-return analysis is not as helpful in decision making.[5]

Finally, we have not considered here the possibility of reducing risk by combining investments into a *portfolio.* By developing a portfolio of *different* investment properties, and also including stocks and bonds, a significant reduction in risk can come about due to *diversification.* By diversifying among investment types, much of the nonbusiness risk discussed in the chapter can be eliminated by combining returns from many investments in a portfolio. Diversification usually serves to lower the variance of total returns from all

---

[5] When possible returns are not normally distributed, they are said to be "skewed" to the right or left of the expected return. For treatment of these and other complications, see Sharpe, *Investments.*

investments in a portfolio because high and low expected returns tend to offset one another when combined. This results in less variation about an expected mean return for the entire investment portfolio. While this type of analysis is an interesting aspect of real estate finance, it is too vast a subject to be explored here.[6]

Questions (appendix)

A–1   What is meant by partitioning the internal rate of return? Why is this procedure meaningful?

A–2   If a greater portion of the *ATIRR* on an investment is received later in its economic life, would that investment generally be more risky or less risky than an investment paying a greater portion of the return earlier in its economic life? Why?

A–3   Why could the measure of variance in expected returns for an investment be a proxy measure for risk?

A–4   What is the coefficient of variation? How is it measured? Why is it useful for comparative purposes?

A–5   The coefficient of variation is sometimes referred to as a ratio of reward to risk. What does this mean?

Case problems (appendix)

A–1   Two investments have the following pattern of expected returns:

ATCF—year	1	2	3	4	Year 4 ATCF$_s$
Investment A	$ 5,000	$10,000	$12,000	$15,000	$120,000
Investment B	2,000	4,000	-0-	5,000	182,700

Investment A requires an outlay of $110,000 and B requires an outlay of $120,000.

a.   What is the *ATIRR* on each investment? (Hint: Try using the *ARR* method first.)

b.   If the *ATIRR* were partitioned based on *ATCF* and *ATCF$_s$*, what proportions of the *ATIRR* would be represented by each?

c.   What do these proportions mean?

A–2   Mike Riskless is considering one of two projects. He has estimated the *ATIRR* under three possible economic scenarios and assigned probabilities of occurrence to each scenario.

---

[6] For a good introduction to portfolio analysis, see Sharpe, *Investments*.

State of economy	Probability	Estimated ATIRR Investment I	Estimated ATIRR Investment II
Growth...............	.10	.15	.25
Stability	.80	.10	.15
Decline..............	.10	.05	.05
	1.00		

Riskless is aware that the pattern of returns for Investment II looks very attractive relative to Investment I; however, he believes that Investment II could be more risky than Investment I. He would like to know how he can compare the two investments considering both the risk and return on each. What do you suggest?

Financing and investment strategies

14

In the preceding chapters in Part Three of this textbook, much attention has been given to how return on investment in real estate should be measured, to what extent financial leverage should be used, federal income tax treatment of real estate investment, and real estate investment risk as compared with risk on other investment securities. In this chapter we consider other important questions that confront borrowers and lenders. Special attention is given to how one should analyze whether or not a property should be sold, refinanced, or converted to an alternate use.

Alternatively, if the investor has decided to sell a property, problems associated with reinvestment of funds from a sale in other real estate arise and risks associated with that course of action must be considered. The questions of installment sales, tax implications, and wraparound financing also become relevant should the decision to sell be made.

The material in this chapter is analytic and decision making in orientation. Although the material is somewhat complex, it should be understood by all professionals embarking on a career in real estate finance. Several frameworks are presented to properly analyze courses of action open to the investor or developer involving property already owned or to be acquired.

The decision to sell a property

In the preceding chapters, much attention was given to questions dealing with determining the rate of return on real estate investments that were acquired, operated, and sold over a specific time period (usually five years). However, in practice, it is difficult to decide when a property should be sold once it has been purchased and operated for a number of years. What follows is a procedure that should be used by the investor to determine whether a property should be sold or whether ownership should be retained. It is based on an incremental, or marginal, return criteria that should be utilized by investors when faced with such decision making.

To illustrate the criteria that should be applied when making a decision to keep a property or to sell it, we assume that an investor with a 50 percent tax rate acquired a very small, retail property five years ago at a cost of $200,000. The Apex Center was 15 years old at the time of purchase and was financed with a 75 percent mortgage made at 11 percent interest for 25 years. Depreciation is being taken on a straight-line basis with 90 percent of the original cost ($180,000) allocated to the building and 10 percent allocated to land. A tax life of 30 years was established for depreciation with no estimated salvage value. Results during the past five years of operation are shown in Exhibit 14–1.

The essential question facing the investor at this time is whether or not Apex should be sold and funds from the sale invested in another property. The answer to this question will be based on a number of considerations; however, the first task facing the investor is to determine what the *ATIRR* would be on

EXHIBIT 14–1

Past operating results, Apex Center

			Year		
	1	2	3	4	5
A. Statement of cash flow					
Rents	$39,000	$40,560	$42,182	$43,870	$45,624
Less: Operating expenses	19,500	20,280	21,091	21,935	22,812
NOI	$19,500	$20,280	$21,091	$21,935	$22,812
Less: DS*	17,811	17,811	17,811	17,811	17,811
BTCF	$ 1,689	$ 2,469	$ 3,280	$ 4,124	$ 5,001
B. Taxable income (loss)					
NOI	$19,500	$20,280	$21,091	$21,935	$22,812
Less: Depreciation†	6,000	6,000	6,000	6,000	6,000
Interest*	16,500	16,356	16,196	16,018	15,820
Income (loss)	$ (3,000)	$ (2,076)	$ (1,105)	$ (83)	$ 992
(Taxes) savings, 50%	$ 1,500	$ 1,038	$ 553	$ 42	$ (496)
C. Aftertax cash flow					
BTCF	$ 1,689	$ 2,469	$ 3,280	$ 4,124	$ 5,001
(Taxes) savings	1,500	1,038	553	42	(496)
ATCF	$ 3,189	$ 3,507	$ 3,833	$ 4,166	$ 4,505

* Assumes annual amortization (loan constant .118740).
† Depreciation rate = .0333 (straight line).

equity investment in Apex assuming *no* action were taken, that is, if the property were not sold. In this way a gauge or guide is established that will indicate what the investor is giving up if the property is sold.

Because Apex has been owned and operated for the past five years, we must first establish what the investor's equity position is at this time. The investor believes that the *present* market value for Apex is $215,000. The original mortgage on Apex was for $150,000; however that has been amortized down to $141,835 during the past five years. The difference between market value, $215,000, and the outstanding mortgage balance of $141,835 is the present value of the investor's equity, or $73,165 (made up of $15,000 appreciation, $8,165 in mortgage amortization, and the original $50,000 equity invested).

The next task is to determine what the *ATIRR* on present equity of $73,165 will be, assuming that the investor continues to own Apex. To establish what the *ATIRR* would be, we must remember that the investor has owned Apex for five years; hence, we are concerned with what the *future ATCF* will be from Apex beginning with the sixth year.

Assuming that the investor believes that a reliable forecast for Apex can be made for the next five years, estimates of *ATCF* are made for years 6–10 and are presented in Exhibit 14–2. The investor believes that past trends in rents and expenses will continue to grow at about 4 percent per year for the next five years. Note in the exhibit that in addition to *NOI* growing at 4 percent,

EXHIBIT 14–2
Estimated future operating results, Apex Center

	Year				
	6	7	8	9	10
A. Statement of cash flow					
Rents	$47,448	$49,346	$51,320	$53,372	$55,508
Less: Operating expenses	23,724	24,673	25,660	26,686	27,754
NOI	$23,724	$24,673	$25,660	$26,686	$27,754
Less: *DS*	17,811	17,811	17,811	17,811	17,811
BTCF	$ 5,913	$ 6,862	$ 7,849	$ 8,875	$ 9,943
B. Taxable income (loss)					
NOI	$23,724	$24,673	$25,660	$26,686	$27,754
Less: Depreciation	6,000	6,000	6,000	6,000	6,000
Interest	15,602	15,359	15,089	14,789	14,457
Income (loss)	$ 2,122	$ 3,314	$ 4,571	$ 5,879	$ 7,297
(Taxes) savings, 50%	$ (1,061)	$ (1,657)	$ (2,286)	$ (2,949)	$ (3,649)
C. Aftertax cash flow					
BTCF	$ 5,913	$ 6,862	$ 7,849	$ 8,875	$ 9,943
(Taxes) savings	(1,061)	(1,657)	(2,286)	(2,949)	(3,649)
ATCF	$ 4,852	$ 5,205	$ 5,563	$ 5,926	$ 6,294

depreciation charges remain at $6,000 based on original cost, and that mortgage payments and interest charges are still based on original financing.

If the forecast period is considered to be five years (ten years from the date of purchase), $ATCF_s$ must also be computed. The owner estimates that Apex should increase in value to $240,000 by then, and based on that estimated price, an estimate of what $ATCF_s$ will be is computed as follows:

A. $BTCF_x$

Apex selling price..........................		$240,000
Less:	Mortgage balance (year 10)...........	128,076
	Selling expenses (6%)...............	14,400
$BTCF_x$.....................................		$ 97,524

B.   Long-term capital gain tax

Apex selling price..........................		$240,000
Less:	Selling expenses..................	14,400
	Adjusted basis....................	140,000
Total gain (long term)......................		$ 85,600
Taxes (50% × 40%)		$ 17,120

C. $ATCF_x$

$BTCF_x$.....................................	$ 97,524
Less: Taxes	17,120
$ATCF_x$.....................................	$ 80,404

Now that estimates of $ATCF$ and $ATCF_s$ have been made for the next five years, it is possible to compute the $ATIRR$ for the investor based on *present equity* of $73,165. This is done by first establishing a range using the average rate of return approach demonstrated in Chapter 12 (not shown again here), then computing the $ATIRR$. We find the $ATIRR$ to be 9.2 percent as follows:

Year	ATCF	IFPV, 10 percent	PV	IFPV, 8 percent	PV
1	$ 4,852	.909091	$ 4,411	.925926	$ 4,493
2	5,205	.826446	4,301	.857339	4,462
3	5,563	.751315	4,180	.793832	4,416
4	5,926	.683013	4,048	.735030	4,356
5	6,294	.620921	3,908	.680583	4,284
	$ATCF_x$				
5	$80,404	.620921	49,925	.680583	54,722
Totals........................			$70,772		$76,733

Interpolating: [($76,733 − $73,165) ÷ $76,733 − 70,772)] × 2% = 1.2%
Adding: 8% + 1.2% = 9.2%
$ATIRR$ = 9.2%

From the above computations, based on the estimates made by the investor, if the property is not sold but operated for a period of five additional years, an

ATIRR of 9.2 percent would be earned on the present value of his equity in Apex.[1]

Selling a property

Alternative investments.   To fully analyze whether or not a property should be sold also requires investigation into (1) the alternative investments available in which cash realized from a sale may be reinvested and (2) the tax consequences of selling one property and acquiring another. We have just seen from the Apex example that if the investor does nothing, or continues to operate the property, an *ATIRR* of 9.2 percent will be earned. Clearly, if Apex is sold and an alternative investment is made, that investment will have to provide the investor with a high enough return to make up for the return given up if Apex is sold. The question is how much of an *ATIRR* must the alternative investment provide if Apex is sold?

At first glance, the answer that may occur to the reader is 9.2 percent, or the return that the investor would earn if Apex were operated for five additional years. However, if Apex is sold to acquire another property, capital gain taxes and selling expenses (if any) must be paid before funds are available for reinvestment. Hence, when considering the sale of one property and the acquisition of another, the first task facing the investor is to ascertain how much cash would be available for reinvestment should the Apex Center be sold. The estimated sale price for the Apex Center at this time is $215,000. However, the relevant data for the investor to consider is how much cash will be available for reinvestment after payment of the mortgage balance, taxes, and selling expenses. This is found by computing $ATCF_s$ as if the property were sold immediately. This is done as follows:

A. $BTCF_s$

Apex selling price.	$215,000
Less: Mortgage balance	141,835
Selling expenses (6%)	12,900
$BTCF_s$.	$ 60,265

B.   Long-term capital gain tax

Apex selling price.	$215,000
Less: Selling expenses.	12,900
Adjusted basis	170,000
Total gain	$ 32,100
Taxes (50% of 40%) × gain.	$ 6,420

C. $ATCF_s$

$BTCF$	$ 60,265
Less: Taxes	6,420
$ATCF$	$ 53,845

---

[1] This analysis can be carried out for any property for any expected period of ownership or its economic life. Computer programs are available for this purpose.

From the preceding computations, it can be seen that $53,845, and not the present equity value of $73,165, would be available for reinvestment should the investor decide to sell Apex at this time (it should be noted that no recapture of depreciation computation is required because straight-line depreciation was used on Apex).

The owner must now consider whether or not the $53,845 can be reinvested at a greater rate of return (*ATIRR*) than the return that would be earned *if Apex was not sold*. In other words, we want to know what the *minimum ATIRR* would have to be on an alternative investment (equivalent in risk to Apex) to make the investor indifferent between continuing to own Apex and purchasing the alternative property.

The answer is relatively straightforward. We know that the cash available to reinvest is $53,845 if Apex is sold. Also, we know that if Apex is sold, the investor gives up ATCF from years 6–10 (Exhibit 14–2) and also gives up the $ATCF_s$ of $80,404 at the end of the year 10. Hence the $53,845 must generate a high enough ATIRR to offset the loss of the ATCF from years 6–10 plus the $ATCF_s$ at the end of year 10. The ATIRR required to offset the cash flows lost by selling Apex is computed as follows:

Year	ATCF	IFPV, 15 percent	PV	IFPV, 20 percent	PV
1	$ 4,852	.869565	$ 4,219	.833333	$ 4,043
2	5,205	.756144	3,936	.694444	3,615
3	5,563	.657516	3,658	.578704	3,219
4	5,926	.571753	3,388	.482253	2,858
5	6,294	.497177	3,129	.401878	2,529
	$ATCF_s$				
5	$80,404	.497177	39,975	.401878	32,313
Totals			$58,305		$48,577

Desired PV = $53,845   ATIRR = 17.3% (by interpolation)

Stated alternatively, the investor would have to earn an ATIRR greater than 17.3 percent on the funds obtained from the sale of the Apex Center. These funds must be used to purchase some alternative investment, equal in risk, to justify selling Apex. In this case, if an alternative investment is equal in risk to Apex and the investor estimates that the ATIRR from that alternative would *exceed* 17.3 percent, then the sale of Apex and the acquisition of the alternative would be justified. If the ATIRR on the alternative is expected to be less than 17.3 percent, then Apex should be retained.

Why is there such a large difference between the ATIRR that the investor would earn by continuing to own and operate Apex (9.2 percent) and the return that would have to be earned on an alternative (17.3 percent)? The answer lies in the fact that capital gains tax and selling expenses must be paid immediately if Apex is sold. In that event, the amount available to reinvest ($53,845) is far less than the value of equity presently invested in Apex ($73,165). Hence, more must be earned on the $53,845 to compensate for the $19,320 cash outflow for taxes and selling costs. Obviously, results in problems such as these are highly dependent on taxes and selling costs and will vary depending on assumptions made in the analysis. Nonetheless, this is the appropriate framework to analyze this type of problem.

Alternatives to disposal of property—improvement or alteration

Rather than selling one property to acquire another, an additional option that may be available to the investor would be to consider improving a property or altering it by changing its economic use. For example, depending on economic trends in the local market and in the location where the property is located, one may consider improving a property by enlarging it or by making major capital improvements to upgrade quality and reduce operating costs. Alternatively, one may consider converting the improvement to accommodate a different economic use, such as converting a small multi-family residence to a small professional office building in an urban neighborhood (assuming zoning allows such a conversion).

The issue that we want to address here is how to properly analyze such an option. To illustrate, we reconsider modernizing Apex Center which is presently 20 years old and has been owned by an investor in the 50 percent tax bracket for 5 years. A summary of relevant facts concerning Apex at present are listed as follows:

a.	Present market value	$215,000
b.	Present mortgage balance	141,835, 11%, 20 years remaining
c.	Present adjusted basis	170,000
d.	Present depreciable basis	150,000, straight line, 25 years remaining

The owner is considering a modernization project that would cost $50,000. Because of the risk involved in the project, the bank will agree to refinancing the present loan balance ($141,835) plus 70 percent of the $50,000 cost of modernizing, or $35,000, for a total loan of $176,835.[2] The new mortgage would carry an interest rate of 12 percent for 25 years.[3] If the owner

[2] If the bank would not consider making a loan based on the present market value plus the cost of improvement, this may be a sign that it does not believe the project to be economically viable and that the market value of the property will not be equal to $215,000 plus the added cost of $50,000 after improvement.

[3] Other alternatives could include a second mortgage for $50,000, or, if the present mortgage has an open-end provision, increasing the loan balance back to the original loan amount of $150,000. In any event, the procedure provided here would still be applicable to the problem.

undertakes the modernization project and wants to conduct an aftertax analysis of the investment proposal, the equity that the owner will have in the property must be reestablished. Equity will be equal to the present market value ($215,000), plus modernization cost ($50,000), or $265,000, less the new mortgage of $176,835, or $88,165. We should note that this equity requirement is more than the equity in the property of $73,165 ($215,000 − $141,835) before renovation.

Given the estimated cost of modernization and refinancing to be accurate, the critical elements now facing the investor are the estimates of rents, expenses, property value, and expected period of ownership. Obviously the results of this plan are dependent on such estimates, which require a careful market analysis and planning, as we have previously discussed in Chapter 10. Assuming such a plan is carried out, a five-year projection made by the owner/investor for the modernized Apex Center is shown in Exhibit 14–3.

EXHIBIT 14–3
Projections for Apex Center—after modification

	Year				
	6	7	8	9	10
A. Statement of cash flow					
Rents.........................	$51,357	$53,411	$55,548	$57,770	$60,080
Less: Operating expenses.......	20,543	21,364	22,219	23,108	24,032
NOI	$30,814	$32,047	$33,329	$34,662	$36,048
Less DS*	22,546	22,546	22,546	22,546	22,546
BTCF	$ 8,268	$ 9,501	$10,783	$12,116	$13,502
B. Taxable income (loss)					
NOI	$30,814	$32,047	$33,329	$34,662	$36,048
Less: Interest	21,220	21,061	20,883	20,683	20,460
Depreciation†	6,900	6,900	6,900	6,900	6,900
Income (loss)	$ 2,694	$ 4,086	$ 5,546	$ 7,079	$ 8,688
(Taxes) savings, 50%............	$ (1,347)	$ (2,043)	$ (2,773)	$ (3,540)	$ (4,344)
C. Aftertax cash flow					
BTCF	$ 8,268	$ 9,501	$10,783	$12,116	$13,502
(Taxes) savings................	(1,347)	(2,043)	(2,773)	(3,540)	(4,344)
ATCF	$ 6,921	$ 7,458	$ 8,010	$ 8,576	$ 9,158

* Annual amortization, 12 percent, 25 years (.1275 loan constant).
† Economic life 29 years (straight-line rate .0345 or 1.00 ÷ 29 years rounded).

Looking to Exhibit 14–3, we should note that based on the modernization plan, rents in year 6 are estimated to increase from $47,448 without renovation (see Exhibit 14–2) to $51,357 with modernization. Operating expenses will fall from 50 percent of rents to 40 percent of rents, making NOI increase from

$23,724 to $30,814, or by almost 30 percent. As before, rents are expected to continue to increase at 4 percent per year. Debt service is based on the new $176,835 mortgage loan made at 12 percent for 25 years. The depreciation charge of $6,900 is computed by first adding the cost of modernization of $50,000 to the depreciable basis of $150,000 (recall original cost was $200,000, building represented $180,000 and at the end of the fifth year $30,000 in depreciation had been taken; hence the present depreciable basis is $180,000 $-$ $30,000 $=$ $150,000), making the new depreciable basis $200,000. The straight-line depreciation rate is .0345 (rounded) based on a *new estimated useful life* of 29 years after modernization, which is expected to add 4 additional years of useful life to the remaining 25-year life being used for depreciation.[4] The increase in rents, reduction in operating expenses, increased interest charges, and depreciation charges result in a higher *ATCF* throughout years 6–10 when compared to what Apex would have produced had no modernization been undertaken (shown in Exhibit 14–2).

A five-year expected investment period has been selected for analysis, and the investor believes that $310,000 will be a likely selling price for Apex at the end of that period. Based on this estimate, $ATCF_s$ is computed as follows:

A. $BTCF_s$

Apex selling price		$310,000
Less:	Mortgage balance	168,412
	Selling expenses (6%)	18,600
$BTCF_s$		$122,988

B. Long-term capital gain tax

Apex selling price	$310,000
Less: Selling expenses	18,600
Adjusted basis	185,500
Total gain	$105,900
Taxes (50% × 40%) × gain	$ 21,180

C. $ATCF_s$

$BTCF_s$	$122,988
Less: Taxes	21,180
$ATCF_s$	$101,808

In examining the computation of $ATCF_s$, the adjusted basis should be elaborated on. It is computed as original cost ($200,000), plus the cost of modernization ($50,000), less total depreciation taken during the first five years of ownership ($6,000 × 5), or $30,000, less total depreciation taken during the second five years ($6,900 × 5), or $34,500, leaving $185,500 as the adjusted basis. Again, because straight-line depreciation was used, no computation of recapture of depreciation is required.

---

[4] Tax regulations require that the useful life be reestimated because of the capital improvement made to the property.

In computing the *ATIRR* on the modernized Apex Center, we relate the equity after renovation of $88,165 to the *ATCF* and *ATCF$_s$* for Apex and solve for the solution, as shown many times before.

Year	ATCF	IFPV, 15 percent	PV	IFPV, 10 percent	PV
6	$ 6,921	.869565	$ 6,018	.909091	$ 6,292
7	7,458	.756144	5,639	.826446	6,164
8	8,010	.657516	5,267	.751315	6,018
9	8,576	.571753	4,903	.683013	5,858
10	9,158	.497177	4,553	.620921	5,686
	ATCF$_x$				
10	$101,808	.497177	50,617	.620921	63,215
Totals			$76,997		$93,233

Interpolating: [($93,233 − $88,165) ÷ ($93,233 − $76,997)] × 5% = 1.6%
Adding: 10% + 1.6% = 11.6%
$$ATIRR = 11.6\%$$

The estimated *ATIRR* on total equity of $88,165 if Apex is modernized is 11.6 percent for the next five years. This return is *greater* than the 9.2 percent *ATIRR* estimated on Apex if nothing is done and it is operated with no modernization. Hence the proposal appears to be profitable. However, before the investor can judge whether or not the modernization project is worthwhile, the *incremental* or *marginal return* on the additional equity investment must be computed. Recall that if no modernization occurs and the owner chooses to operate Apex over the next five years, the expected *ATIRR* would be 9.2 percent based on present equity of $73,165. Should the modernization work be done, equity will increase to $88,165, or by $15,000. The marginal return would be:

	Equity	ATIRR	ATCF
Modernize Apex	$88,165 ×	.116	$10,227
Take no action	73,165 ×	.092	6,731
Difference	$15,000		$ 3,496

Marginal return..... $3,496 ÷ $15,000 = 23.3%

This computation shows that by modernizing, the investor will earn 23.3 percent on the $15,000 in additional equity required for the project, *plus* the 9.2 percent earned if no action is taken. This is important to know because now the investor can consider other options in addition to modernization. For example, if another alternative that is equal in risk to modernizing presents itself and requires $15,000 in equity, unless it provides an *ATIRR* in excess of

23.3 percent, it should not be considered and Apex should be modernized. If, however, that alternative provides an *ATIRR greater than* 23.3 percent, then Apex should not be modernized. The owner should operate Apex as is and make the $15,000 investment in the alternative.

Disposal of properties—installment sales and wraparounds

To this point in the chapter, we have considered various options that an investor-owner of real estate may consider relative to the sale of property. In this section we assume that *the investor has made the decision to sell* and consider some alternative methods of disposing of the property besides selling for cash and immediately reinvesting the proceeds. These options will generally fall under the discussion of installment sales; however, there are some financing variations that can be considered within the context of installment sales.

Essentially, an installment sale is a sale of a property where the buyer agrees to pay the seller in a *series of installment payments* rather than all at once. In return, the seller may agree to give title to the property immediately or agree to a transfer of title at some future date under a land contract (previously discussed in Chapter 4). This situation usually arises when (1) the property cannot be easily financed by the buyer due to unavailability of credit, (2) because the buyer may be a significant credit risk, (3) because the property may be too risky for financing, (4) seller is faced with a large capital gain tax bill should the property be sold and payment received immediately, or (5) any combination of the first four conditions occur. *Installment sales can be applied to the sale of a personal residence as well as income-producing properties.*

Because the seller of a property will receive payments over time according to an installment sale agreement, the transaction may qualify for special federal tax treatment. This treatment allows the investor to recognize any long-term capital gain over the period during which installment payments will be received. The rationale for this special treatment is that because the seller does not receive the full selling price all at once, then the capital gain tax should also not have to be paid all at once, but paid over time when matched by the receipt of funds. The portion of installment payments recognized as capital gains will be dependent on the sale price of the property, whether any debt is assumed by the buyer, the adjusted basis of the property, selling expenses, the portion of each payment determined to be interest on amounts financed by the seller's installment note, and whether the seller is an investor or dealer in real estate.

A significant change in the taxation of installment sales has recently come about with the passage of the Installment Sales Revision Act of 1980.[5] This act will undoubtedly make installment sales more widely used.

---

[5] For a good discussion see: *Installment Sales Revision Act of 1980: Law and Explanation,* (Chicago: Commerce Clearing House, Inc.)

The essential question faced by a seller considering the use of an installment sale is whether the present value of installment payments received over time exceeds the value of aftertax cash flow that would be immediately received if the property were sold outright. This analysis is very straightforward; however, defining the relationships that go into the recognition of deferred capital gains tax and interest from installments received by the seller are sometimes difficult to establish. Attendant problems, including consequences of the buyer defaulting on the installment note, sale of the note by the seller of the property before the end of the installment period, sales of property among individuals in the same family, and other complications, make this a very technical subject. The reader should seek counsel or do considerable research on the subject before attempting its use.

A note on wraparound loans

Another alternative to selling a property outright or an installment sale could be wraparound financing. Here a lender assumes responsibility for payments on a loan previously made by a borrower and extends an amount to the borrower equal to the additional funds requested by the borrower. The primary goal under this method of financing is to keep the original mortgage "alive" instead of originating a new loan to acquire additional funds. This is because the original loan may carry a very low interest rate, a benefit that the borrower would have to give up if complete refinancing was necessary.

To illustrate, Ace Development Company owns a property with a mortgage with an outstanding loan balance of $50,000 at 8 percent interest with ten years remaining until maturity. Ace would like to raise an additional $40,000 for 25 years and does not want to sell the property to do so. Ace would also like to retain the advantage of the very low 8 percent interest rate on the outstanding loan. To do so, Ace can refinance the entire $90,000 amount with a wraparound loan at 11 percent interest for 25 years with Pension Fund Limited, a nonprofit, nontaxable entity. The cost of the wraparound loan should be analyzed as follows:

The outstanding mortgage requires monthly payments of $606.65 for 10 years, and a new wraparound mortgage would require monthly payments of $882.09 for 25 years *if it was made* at a rate of *11 percent interest*. The net cash outflow for Ace would be the following:

	Years 1–10	Years 11–25
Cash flow (wraparound)	$882.09	$882.09
Less: Cash flow (existing)	606.65	–0–
Net cash outflow	$275.44	$882.09

Ace would receive $90,000 - $50,000, or $40,000, and the internal rate of return would be:

$$\$40,000 = \$275.44(MIFPVa, \ ?\%, \ 10 \ \text{yrs.}) +$$
$$\$882.09(MIFPVa, \ ?\%, \ 25\text{--}10 \ \text{yrs.})$$

Discounting until the present value of the net cash flow is equal to $40,000 shows that an *IRR* of approximately 12.4 percent (before taxes) would be the cost of the wraparound.[6] Given the cost of wraparound financing in this case is 12.4 percent, Ace can now consider the cost of other financing alternatives. For example, if a second mortgage for $40,000 is available at less than 12.4 percent interest, it may be a better choice. On the other hand, if a second mortgage loan would cost more than 12.4 percent, then the wraparound would be the preferred alternative.

It should be noted that the wraparound loan is similar to a second mortgage. Indeed, in terms of its legal status, it is subordinate to the original mortgage and is equivalent to a junior or second lien. Hence the cost of additional funds raised by wraparound financing and second mortgages should be similar. The major difference here is that the wraparound lender has more control over protecting his interest than would be the case with a second mortgage, as he collects on the total indebtedness monthly payments from the borrower and in turn remits to the first lien holder. In the event the borrower becomes delinquent, the wraparound lender may continue to make payments on the original mortgage to prevent foreclosure if it is in his best interest to do so. While a second mortgage holder also has this privilege (see Chapter 2), delinquency on the first mortgage may not be discovered until foreclosure proceedings are instituted.

Questions

1   If an investor estimates the *ATIRR* on one property to be higher than the *ATIRR* on another, should the property with the higher *ATIRR* always be chosen? What other differences should enter the analysis?

2   What is meant by an incremental or marginal return on investment? Why is it important?

3   What is an installment sale? Why may it be desirable to use an installment sale?

4   What is a wraparound loan? How could it be used as a refinancing tool?

Case problems

1   Royal Oaks Apartments have been owned by Pritchard Burton for six years. Burton is presently thinking about selling Royal Oaks and purchasing the Royal Palms, an apartment complex in what Burton believes is a more lucrative location.

---

[6] This computation ignores the effect of any point or prepayment penalties.

Burton paid $2,000,000 for Royal Oaks six years ago with the land representing approximately $200,000 of that value. He believes the property is worth about $2,200,000 today. When purchased, Burton financed the property with a 75 percent mortgage at 10 percent interest for 25 years (assume annual payments for simplicity). Since the date of purchase, he has been using straight-line depreciation over a 40-year tax life with no salvage value. During the past year, effective gross income from Royal Oaks was $295,000 and the operating expense ratio was 40 percent. Burton presently estimates his marginal tax rate at 50 percent and will not be subject to a minimum tax on any preference income because of substantial income earned from theater interests. If he sells Royal Oaks, selling expenses will be 6 percent of the present market value.

Mr. Burton estimates that if he continues to own Royal Oaks, rents will probably increase at about 6 percent per year, and that he could sell the property for approximately $2,600,000 five years from now. He has also analyzed the Royal Palms deal, and although it appears to be sound, he doesn't know how much he should earn on it over the five years to justify selling Royal Oaks. Burton has turned to you for advice. He would like to know:

a. What *ATIRR* can he presently expect to earn if he continues to own and operate Royal Oaks over the next five years?

b. What is the minimum *ATIRR* that he must earn on Royal Palms to make it worthwhile to sell Royal Oaks?

c. Is there any advice that you can give him regarding risk considerations?

2 Henry Kissingher presently owns the Marine Tower Building that is 20 years old and which he is considering renovating. He purchased the property two years ago for $800,000 and financed it with a 20-year, 70 percent loan at 10 percent interest. Of the $800,000, he established that the land was worth $200,000 and the building $600,000. Since the date of purchase, he has been using straight-line depreciation (no salvage value) over a tax life of 25 years.

At the present time Marine Towers is producing $178,000 in effective gross income with an operating expense ratio of 60 percent. Rents are expected to increase at 4 percent per year over the next six years, and the property value is estimated to be $850,000 at that time. The current market value of the structure is $820,000.

If renovation occurs, Kissingher believes that the cost will be $200,000 and its useful life will increase by five years. However, effective gross income should increase 10 percent from current levels, and it should grow at 5 percent per year. The property value should be worth at least $1,100,000 after six years, and operating expenses should be reduced to 50 percent of effective gross income. The renovation can be financed with a 70 percent mortgage on the current value ($820,000) and renovation cost ($200,000) at 12 percent interest for 20 years (assume annual mortgage payments). Kissingher has a 40 percent tax rate.

a. If Kissingher did nothing but continue to operate Marine Tower as is, what would be his *ATIRR* on equity from the present until sale in six years? (Assume a 6 percent selling expense).

b. Should Kissingher renovate Marine Tower? What will be the *ATIRR* on equity if Marine Tower is renovated and sold after six years?

c. If Kissingher has to invest more equity in Marine Tower to upgrade, what is the marginal return on his investment (after taxes)? What advice would you give him concerning this additional investment?

3 Steve McKing, the owner of Disco Roller Skates, Inc., presently owns a manufacturing facility and land worth $2,000,000. He wants to expand his facility to accommodate the demand he sees from the senior citizen centers springing up around the United States. The property presently has a mortgage balance on it in the amount of $900,000 at 8 percent interest with ten years remaining.

American Accident and Casualty Company is presently negotiating with McKing to assume the $900,000 mortgage and wrap around it a subordinated purchase money mortgage for 75 percent of value for a term of 20 years at 10 percent interest. Payments on both mortgages are made monthly.

What is the effective yield (cost) to the lender (borrower) in this transaction?

Sale-and-leaseback financing and subordinated ground leases

— 15 —————————————————————————————

This chapter deals with sale-and-leaseback analysis, or the decision to lease or buy. Both the sale-and-leaseback approach to financing, and the decision to lease or to buy, require a reasonably sophisticated framework for analysis that will be new for many readers. Because lease agreements span many years, and because changing amounts of depreciation and interest are included in the analysis each year, modification of the discounted present value approach used in previous chapters is required. In addition to the straight sale-and-leaseback, or lease versus buy decision, the subordinated ground lease is also considered. The chapter concludes with some helpful modifications that can be used for step-lease and indexed lease payments.

Meaning

A sale-and-leaseback financing arrangement involves an investor who acquires a property, sells it to another party, and then leases it back from that party based on some agreed schedule of lease payments. When this type of transaction occurs, the lessee is usually comparing the sale-and-leaseback approach to some conventional mortgage financing alternative. Sale-and-leaseback consists of two steps which are taken simultaneously, although they appear to be separate and distinct. First, an institution with funds to invest, such as a life insurance company, a college or university, a religious body, or a charitable institution, purchases the real estate owned and used by a well-established business corporation—usually a retailer or a manufacturer. Second, the property is leased back to the seller by the purchaser. From these two steps we obtain the name *sale-and-leaseback*. Other names used to designate this practice are *purchase-and-leaseback* and *liquidating lease.*

While sale-and-leaseback financing can be applied to existing properties, it can also be frequently applied to properties yet to be developed. Some developers agree to purchase a site to be selected by the lessee, construct a building according to plans and specifications, turn the complete product over to the lessee, and arrange sale-and-leaseback financing with a lender, all without any capital outlay by the lessee.

Lease terms

The risk in such an arrangement depends primarily upon the financial stability of the lessee. The customary term of such a lease ranges from 20 to 40 years. Leases on retail property are customarily for longer terms than on industrial real estate. The lease may provide for a renewal or even for a repurchase at or before the expiration date. The rental payment is usually "net" to the lessor. The lessee pays all taxes and assessments, insurance, maintenance and repair costs, utility charges, and so on. The net rent is fixed at such a level that it is expected that within the original term of the lease, the lessor will have recovered the purchase price of the building and earned an adequate return. In some such leases the lease payments are not constant for the entire life of the lease but may be graded, with highest payments in the early years, followed by declining payments for successive periods. This practice permits the lessor to expense the lease payments for tax purposes more rapidly.

In the event that the lessee fails to meet any of the charges assumed by him, the lessor is empowered to make any payments required and subsequently collect from the lessee. This follows the usual pattern of long-term leases. Defaults—whether due to nonpayment of rent, assignment for the benefit of creditors, or any other action of the lessee that may jeopardize the position of the lessor—usually give the latter the right to terminate the lease. Condemnation clauses are usually well defined. Total destruction of structures is dealt with both in leases and in state laws governing them.

Character of lease contract

The sale-and-leaseback contract results in an actual sale of a property with delivery of both legal and equitable title to the purchaser. Upon attaining the status of ownership, the purchaser then executes a valid lease upon terms agreed upon at the time the two-step agreement was made. Since the sale follows traditional real estate transfers, there is nothing peculiar about it.

There are some very important aspects of the lease agreement that must be considered prior to entering into a sale-and-leaseback transaction. Three of these considerations have to do with (1) repurchase options by the lesser; (2)

the price at which the repurchase will occur, should the option be exercised; and (3) cancellation privileges. In the case of the repurchase option, the lease agreement will usually specify that the lessee may purchase the property at stated intervals. This option is usually exercised when the lessee believes that it is financially worthwhile to do so, or when a material modification of the improvement is desired to expand production, floor space, and so on. In the latter event, if the lessor does not want to become a party to financing such an expansion (particularly if the structure will be altered as opposed to the lessee constructing a separate, identifiable building), the lessee may purchase the property, then refinance any existing and additional debt required for expansion, with another lender.

With regard to the price that the lessee pays should the option to repurchase be exercised, there is a danger here that unless the option price *is subject to market conditions at the time* of repurchase, the lease may be construed to be, in fact, a mortgage. In this event, the lessor would be acting as a lender and no repurchase would be allowed because the lessee would, in fact, be the owner. If this occurred, it would destroy any benefits from the sale-and-leaseback arrangement, as both parties would have to amend previous statements of income and taxes to reflect this change. To illustrate, if a lease is executed on a property worth $1,000,000 with payments based on an amortization schedule at 10 percent interest for 30 years, and the repurchase option specifies that the lessee can purchase the property without refusal by the lessor, for what amounts to the unamortized balance of the $1,000,000 cost after specified intervals, then the transaction appears to be nothing more than a mortgage loan. Why is this so important? For two reasons, if the lease is considered to be a mortgage (1) the lessee will be able to deduct interest only instead of the full lease payment for tax purposes, and (2) the lessee will also have to carry the property as an asset and the lease as a mortgage liability on its balance sheet; this could cause some concern to the lessee.

To increase assurance that a lease will not be found to be a mortgage by the IRS, or in a court of equity, one of two provisions is usually included in the lease. First, the repurchase option will usually be based on the *higher* of either the appraised value of the property or the unamortized balance of future lease payments. In this way market conditions influence the purchase price, which ostensibly means that the lessee would have to pay the same price as any other buyer. This eliminates the possibility of the lessee having the advantages of deducting all lease payments for tax purposes *and* eventually realizing capital gains based on a below-market purchase price. The second provision in the lease agreement is the *lease cancellation privilege* whereby at given intervals the lessee may request cancellation of lease, subject to the lessee purchasing the property at a price equal to the unamortized value of the property plus some premium. However, it should be noted that this cancellation clause is a *privilege* not an *option*, hence the lessor may refuse the cancellation request. Further, the lease may require that if the cancellation request is *refused*, the lease agreement terminates, thereby enabling other parties to enter into a new lease with the owner-lessor. Hence the lessor is not guaranteed that repurchase of the property will be possible in the future. This increases assurance that the arrangement is a lease and not a substitute for mortgage financing.

Advantages claimed for lessee

The advantages usually claimed for business corporations which sell their real estate and lease it back include the following: (1) This plan may provide funds for expansion of business and for working capital at lower cost and for a longer period of time than will be available from any source. (2) The funds released from the sale of real estate can be invested to better advantage and at a higher rate of return when used to expand business operations. (3) This device may simplify the financial plan of the business corporation, makes possible a smaller debt structure, and avoids the hazards of refunding bonds or other forms of debt. (4) It enables business corporations not skilled in the management of real estate problems to pass them along to the purchaser of the property. (5) It is a flexible form of financing the business, resulting in a minimum of investment in fixed assets. (6) Where cancellation clauses are included, they enable the lessee to select a new location for his business, should he see fit to do so. (7) The tax advantage will be discussed in the next section.

Advantages to lessor

The advantages of the sale-and-leaseback device to the purchaser who becomes the lessor center around the following: (1) The term of the investment is relatively long, and there is little concern with prepayments. (2) The amounts invested are relatively large, thereby reducing management costs. (3) Only well-seasoned, well-managed corporations are accepted as lessees. (4) The rate of return after amortization of the principal of the investment is relatively high. (5) The lessor has more control over real estate which it owns than over that on which it merely holds a mortgage. (6) There may be a substantial remainder of value after the lease expires which will serve as a hidden reserve for the lessor. (7) There may be possible income tax advantages in this method of financing real estate.

Tax exemption of lessor. Prior to 1950, certain classes of investors enjoyed a sweeping federal income tax immunity which provided a direct stimulus to purchase-and-leaseback programs. Had it not been that nonprofit enterprises were totally exempt from corporate income taxes, it is not likely that this plan would have developed to its present proportions. By specific provision of the Internal Revenue Code, educational, charitable, and religious institutions were exempt from the payment of income taxes. In practice, life insurance companies were also given virtual exemption because of the formula permitted by the Treasury Department for the computation of their taxable income.

Hence, institutions in these classes that became lessors under the sale-and-leaseback program had little concern about the tax consequences of their receipt of one type of income as compared with receipt of another type.

Nonexempt investors can no longer be as free in their choices of investment outlets. If a financial institution lends money on an amortized real estate mortgage as security, it need report for income tax purposes only that part of the payments which represents interest on its investment. Amortization of principal is not considered to be taxable income. But if it purchases the real estate and leases it back, it must report as taxable income all rents received, minus only such amounts as are properly deductible for allowed depreciation.

An amendment to the Internal Revenue Code in 1950 made tax-exempt organizations subject to income tax on their "unrelated business net income." Included in unrelated business income are rentals received from property leased to others for a period exceeding five years, where the lessor with the tax exemption borrowed funds to effect the purchase or acquisition of the property and such indebtedness is still outstanding. The purchase-and-leaseback situation commonly fits this pattern.

The taxable business lease income of exempt organizations is determined by application of the following formula:

$$\frac{\text{Business lease indebtedness at end of tax year}}{\substack{\text{Adjusted basis of premises} \\ \text{covered by business lease at} \\ \text{end of tax year}}} \times \substack{\text{Annual business lease} \\ \text{rental (less allocable} \\ \text{expenses)}} = \substack{\text{Unrelated business} \\ \text{taxable income}}$$

The current tax law has moved in the direction of limiting the flexibility of a tax-exempt lessor in dealing with a taxable lessee. Note, however, that the annual business lease income equal to the proportion of the actual capital investment of the tax-exempt investor is still excluded from taxable income. Thus, the leasehold rental income of a tax-exempt investor who does not borrow to finance his acquisition of property is still tax exempt.

There has also been a reduction in the tax advantages afforded life insurance companies. Whereas their taxes through the mid-1950s were negligible, these companies now find an increasing percentage of their income subject to federal tax. The amended tax formula results in a substantial increase in the proportion of life insurance company investment income subject to tax. The new formula, however, still leaves these companies with a decisive advantage over the ordinary corporate investor, whose income from interest on mortgage loans or from leasehold rentals is fully taxable.

The sale-and-leaseback decision or the decision to lease or buy

At the outset it should be pointed out that the framework to be presented below can be used in a number of situations. It can be used to examine the situation described to this point, that is, the case where property is owned then sold to another party and leased back from that party. This analysis not only applies to new properties to be developed. Companies that have owned facilities for many years may choose to enter into a sale-and-leaseback agreement to raise capital for operations and expansion. The analysis used here can *also* be applied to the decision to finance the *use* of a property by leasing it rather than purchasing it. In other words, the decision to lease or purchase a property can be analyzed in the same way as a sale-and-leaseback.

It should be stressed that sale-and-leaseback financing is a *financing technique* that should be considered as an alternative to conventional and other forms of financing. The decision as to whether or not an investment in a property will be profitable should be made *first* using the criteria described in the previous chapters; that is, the decision to invest in a property should be based on the *ATIRR* an investor earns on equity investment *given conventional mortgage financing*. If the *ATIRR* with conventional financing is acceptable to the investor, the property should then be considered for investment. If it is not acceptable, it should not be considered.

Sale-and-leaseback financing is simply an alternative *method of financing the investment in a property*. Hence the analysis should be carried out relative to conventional and other financing arrangements to determine the *cost of financing* under each approach. It should *not* be used to establish profitability. This is true because with sale-and-leaseback financing, the equity requirements will almost always be different from those required to finance an investment conventionally. When sale-and-leaseback financing is proposed, it will generally reduce, or eliminate, equity funds (or the down payment) required to undertake the real estate investment. This amounts to raising additional capital, which carries a cost, just as mortgage funds do. It is our goal in this chapter to establish the cost of funds raised under various sale-and-leaseback techniques. We determine what the cost of funds is when considering a sale-and-leaseback. The investor can then compare that cost with other financing alternatives as well as establish what the minimum *ATIRR* must be on those additional funds when reinvested to make the sale-and-leaseback profitable. If a property first meets the profitability test under conventional mortgage financing conditions, and it *then* can be determined that funds made available by selling and leasing a property back can also be invested at high returns, the investor will be that much better off.

Trade-offs in the sale-and-leaseback decision

The decision to enter into a sale-and-leaseback decision involves many trade-offs that the lessee must carefully consider. To illustrate the analysis, we consider the following problem. Good Discount Company, a corporation, is in the process of a very rapid expansion of its discount stores and its fast-food franchises. It is attempting to conserve as much cash as possible for growth and it wants to consider the feasibility of using sale-and-leaseback financing instead of conventional mortgage financing for expanding its outlets. A prototype of the typical discount outlet is as follows: total cost, $2 million; land, $200,000; and building, $1,800,000. Because the building is new, depreciation is to be based on the 150 percent declining-balance method for 40 years with no estimated salvage value. If conventional financing is used, terms would be based on 75 percent of value (cost), 10 percent interest for 25 years. An interested lender is willing to enter into a sale-and-leaseback agreement with Good based on a 40-year lease agreement which calls for monthly lease payments of $16,982, or a total of $203,784 per year. These lease payments are equivalent to the property cost of $2 million being amortized monthly at an annual rate of 10 percent over a 40-year period. The lease effectively represents 100 percent financing for Good when compared with the 75 percent conventional financing arrangement which would require $500,000 down. Good has the option to buy the property every five years during the life of the lease at the *higher* of *fair market value* or the *unamortized cost of the lease.*[1] Good has decided that the project would be profitable if it were purchased and financed conventionally, and it is committed to undertake the venture. Good now wants to know whether the sale-and-leaseback approach to financing is more beneficial than conventional financing and also what that approach will cost.

Exhibit 15–1 contains an estimate of Good's income statement and statement of cash flow for the coming year for each method of financing. First, looking to the conventional financing alternative, we should note that depreciation during the first year is $67,500 based on 150 percent of the straight-line rate of 2.5 percent, or 3.75 percent of the building value of $1,800,000. Of course, the depreciation expense will decline each year beyond the first year. Debt service is based on *monthly payments* of $13,631 (computed as $1,500,000 × .009087) multiplied by 12 months, arriving at $163,572 for the year. We are using monthly payments rather than annual payments in this case because of some special tables which will be introduced into the analysis. The interest charges for the year, based on monthly mortgage payments, can be easily calculated by using the loan balance factors in Appendix C at the end of this textbook.[2]

An important aspect of the results shown in Exhibit 15–1 is that under the sale-and-leaseback alternative, *ATCF* will be some $48,897 *lower* than would be the case with conventional debt financing. However, we should also point

---

[1] Because the lease payments are based on an amortized schedule, the unamortized lease balance is determined in the same way that a mortgage balance is determined.

[2] Subtracting the loan balance factor for a 25-year loan made at 10 percent at the end of year 1 from 100 percent, and multiplying by the original loan amount gives amortization for the year. This can be subtracted from total debt service to obtain interest for the year. During the second year the loan balance factor for year 2 should be subtracted from the loan balance factor for year 1, then multiplied by the original amount of the loan to determine amortization in the second year. That amount can be subtracted from total mortgage payments in the second year to establish interest in the second year, and so on.

EXHIBIT 15–1
Operating data—Good Discount chain

	Conventional	Sale-and-leaseback	(Difference) if sale-and-leaseback used
Income statement–summary			
Sales	$950,000	$950,000	—
Cost of goods sold	425,000	425,000	—
Gross income	$425,000	$425,000	—
Operating expenses	75,000	75,000	—
Net operating income	$350,000	$350,000	—
Depreciation	67,500	—	$ 67,500
Interest	155,166	—	155,166
Lease payment	—	203,784	(203,784)
Net income	$127,334	$146,216	$ 18,882
Taxes (46%)	$ 58,574	67,259	$ 8,685
Net income after taxes	$ 68,760	$ 78,957	$ 10,197
Cash flow—summary			
Net operating income	$350,000	$350,000	—
Less: Debt service	163,572		$ 163,572
Lease payment		203,784	(203,784)
Before-tax cash flow (*BTCF*)	$186,428	$146,216	$ (40,212)
Taxes	58,574	67,259	(8,685)
Aftertax cash flow (*ATCF*)	$127,854	$ 78,957	$ (48,897)

out that Good does not have to put $500,000 down should it lease rather than own the property and finance conventionally. Hence the $48,897 represents the first year's "cost" of saving $500,000 in equity with lease financing, and it must be related to the $500,000 that Good can use for other business purposes. The question now facing Good is whether acquiring the $500,000 in additional funds should be acquired at a cost of "giving up" *ATCF* of $48,897 in the first year of operation, plus additional cash flow in later years.

Before we consider the question of cost, however, we must consider what the "loss" in *ATCF* will be in *each succeeding year* that the property is leased, as it will differ from the first year's reduction. First, looking to Exhibit 15–1, we must consider what the differences in *ATCF* are attributable to, then consider changes in those variables over the time period of analysis. One thing that becomes immediately obvious from the exhibit is that operating revenues and expenses are *unaffected* by the method of financing. Hence, as far as *ATCF* is concerned, attention need only be focused on five influences: depreciation, mortgage debt service, mortgage interest, lease payments, and the tax effects of each. In essence, Good "gives up" depreciation when it chooses to lease rather than own, and must make a series of lease payments in place of mortgage payments. Depreciation and interest are tax deductible, should the property be owned, but the entire lease payment is tax deductible should the property be leased. Hence, these influences must be "netted out" over all years that the alternatives are considered to determine the net cost of leasing. In the first year then, we can summarize as follows:

$$\text{Lease costs} - \text{ownership costs} = ATCF^*$$
$$LP(1 - t) - [DS - I(t) - D(t)] = ATCF^*$$

where:

$$LP = \text{lease payments}$$
$$DS = \text{debt service}$$
$$D = \text{depreciation}$$
$$I = \text{interest}$$
$$t = \text{ordinary tax rate}$$
$$ATCF^* = \text{difference in } ATCF \text{ caused by leasing}$$

Substituting information from Exhibit 15–1, we have:

		Amount	ATCF
A.	Lease costs:		
	$LP(1 - t)$.	$203,784(1 − .46)	$110,043
B.	Less ownership costs:		
	DS.	163,572	$163,572
	$-I(t)$	155,166(.46)	(71,376)
	$-D(t)$.	67,500(.46)	(31,050)
	Net ownership costs.		$ 61,146
	$ATCF^*(A)-(B)$.		$ 48,897

Looking to this formulation, we have the aftertax cost of leasing, or $LP(1 - t)$, which should be reduced by aftertax cost of conventional financing and depreciation $DS - I(t) - D(t)$, resulting in the difference in $ATCF$ (which we designate by using an asterisk or "star," $ATCF^*$) *due to lease financing.* Note that the value for $ATCF^*$ is $48,897, which means that the aftertax cost of leasing is *greater* than that of owning.[3] This computation is simply a shortened version of what was done in Exhibit 15–1.

Reversion value in year of sale.   The formulation developed above recognizes the *difference* in $ATCF$, or $ATCF^*$, when the property is either owned or leased; however, there is an additional cost of leasing that must be considered. This cost is the loss of any $ATCF_s$ brought on by the decision to lease. In our example, if Good chooses not to buy the property, it gives up the property value at that time. In either case the reversion value represents a *cost of leasing,*

---

[3] If $ATCF^*$ is negative, then the cost of owning would be greater than leasing.

either as a cost of buying the property at the expiration of the lease, or as the value given up at that time because Good chose to lease rather than own. Given that Good is considering a 40-year lease period and the useful life of the building is estimated to be 40 years, if the building has completely depreciated at that time, then only land value will remain after 40 years.[4] If the land is originally valued at $200,000, and it is estimated to increase in value at an average annual rate of 6 percent, then its estimated value after 40 years would be $400,000(1 + .06)^{40}, or $200,000(10.285718) = $2,057,144. The aftertax value of the property at that time would be as follows:

A. $BTCF_s$

Market value	$2,057,144
Mortgage balance	–0–
$BTCF_s$	$2,057,144

B. Tax

Selling price	$2,057,144
Adjusted basis	200,000
Gain	1,857,144
Capital gain tax (46% × 40%)	$ 341,714

C. $ATCF_s$

Selling price	$2,057,144
Less: Taxes	341,714
$ATCF_s$	$1,715,430

Therefore, if the property is leased rather than owned, Good *gives up* the value after the lease period of $1,715,430. This is an additional *cost of leasing* relative to owning and must be included in the cost of leasing in determining the cost of leasing relative to owning.

Interest and depreciation—special considerations. In the above discussion, we have pointed out that $ATCF^*$ will not be the same from year to year. This is because interest and depreciation *change* each year. Essentially, we would like to formulate our problem as follows:

$$PV \text{ of } ATCF^* + PV \text{ of } ATCF_s = \text{Funds acquired by leasing}$$

We would like to find the interest rate, or internal rate of return that will make the costs associated with leasing, or PV of $ATCF^*$ and PV of $ATCF_s$, equal to the funds acquired by leasing. The internal rate of return tells us the cost of obtaining additional funds by leasing. The problem with this approach, however, is that $ATCF^*$ *changes* each year due to changes in I and D. Over a 40-year lease period this would mean that $ATCF^*$ would have to be computed 40 times, then discounted 40 times to determine if the present value of lease

---

[4] If the lease is terminated before the end of 40 years, the higher of market value of the property or the unamortized balance of the lease payments would represent the cost to Good. $ATCF_s$ would be computed based on the higher of those two amounts.

costs were equal to funds acquired by leasing. If somehow *ATCF** could be *converted* to a level annuity, this would reduce required computations considerably.

To accomplish this goal, a series of factors have been established which *convert* the interest and depreciation streams into what are referred to as an *equivalent ordinary annuity.* This concept can be very easily explained as follows: Assume that we have the following cash flows, which change each year:

	Returns—year		
Cost	1	2	3
$786	$400	$300	$200

Estimating the internal rate of return, we have:

Cash flow	IFPV, 8 percent	PV
$400	.925926	$370
300	.857339	257
200	.793832	159
	Present value	$786

Because the present value computed equals the cost of $786, we know that the 8 percent discount rate reflected for discounting equals the *IRR.* By referring to the 8 percent tables (Appendix A) and selecting the ($IFPV_a$) for three years (2.577097) and dividing that factor into $786, we obtain $305 per year, which is a level annuity for three years. When this amount of $305 is set equal to the $786, it can be seen that the *IRR* obtained from the level annuity is *equivalent* to the *IRR* obtained from the uneven cash flow. This is shown as follows:

Year	IFPV, 8 percent	Uneven flow	PV	Annuity	PV
1	.925926	$400	$370	$305	$282
2	.857339	300	257	305	261
3	.793832	200	159	305	242
			$786		$786*

* Rounded.

From this exercise, it has been demonstrated that given an outlay of $786, the $305 annuity and the declining cash flows of $400, $300, and $200 in consecutive years *are equivalent* in that both result in an *IRR* of 8 percent.

Hence the $305 can be said to be an *equivalent annuity* based on an *IRR* of 8 percent for three years.

The problem of interest and depreciation declining each year in our *ATCF** formulation above can now be resolved by *creating equivalent ordinary annuities* for various mortgage terms and depreciation methods over various time periods. Exhibit 15–2 contains what we will refer to as *EOA* (equivalent

EXHIBIT 15–2
EOA factors for mortgage interest*

Discount rate	Interest rate						
	8%	10%	11%	12%	13%	14%	15%
	Twenty-year mortgage						
5%	.0563	.0730	.0817	.0905	.0996	.1087	.1180
10%	.0613	.0790	.0881	.0974	.1068	.1163	.1260
12%	.0630	.0810	.0902	.0996	.1092	.1188	.1286
15%	.0651	.0836	.0930	.1026	.1123	.1220	.1319
20%	.0680	.0870	.0966	.1064	.1162	.1262	.1362
25%	.0702	.0894	.0992	.1091	.1191	.1291	.1392
	Twenty-five year mortgage						
5%	.0598	.0776	.0868	.0962	.1057	.1153	.1251
10%	.0653	.0841	.0937	.1035	.1135	.1233	.1333
12%	.0670	.0861	.0958	.1057	.1157	.1257	.1358
15%	.0691	.0885	.0984	.1084	.1185	.1286	.1388
20%	.0717	.0915	.1015	.1116	.1218	.1319	.1422
25%	.0735	.0934	.1035	.1137	.1238	.1341	.1433
	Thirty-year mortgage						
5%	.0629	.0816	.0912	.1009	.1108	.1207	.1307
10%	.0686	.0882	.0982	.1082	.1183	.1285	.1387
12%	.0703	.0901	.1001	.1102	.1204	.1306	.1409
15%	.0722	.0922	.1023	.1125	.1228	.1330	.1433
20%	.0740	.0942	.1044	.1146	.1248	.1351	.1454
25%	.0757	.0960	.1062	.1164	.1266	.1369	.1471

* These tables were made available by Professor Jeffrey Fisher of Indiana University.

ordinary annuity) factors for 20-, 25-, and 30-year mortgage loan terms, and discount rates which convert the interest streams for each set of terms into an equivalent ordinary annuity, using the procedure described above. *EOA* factors have also been included for the 150 percent declining-balance method of depreciation in Exhibit 15–3 for various discount rates and years of useful tax life.[5] There are other *EOA* factors for other methods of depreciation;

---

[5] These *EOA* factors are based on monthly mortgage payments which are accumulated annually and then discounted by annual interest factors. This is the reason why we chose to use monthly lease and mortgage payments in our Good Discount store example. Depreciation factors are based on annual deductions and do *not* assume a switch over to straight line.

EXHIBIT 15–3
EOA factors for 150 percent declining-balance
depreciation*

Discount rate	Useful life (years)			
	20	*25*	*30*	*40†*
5%	.0443	.0363	.0309	.0272
10%	.0488	.0405	.0349	.0307
12%	.0504	.0420	.0363	.0319
15%	.0526	.0439	.0380	.0334
20%	.0557	.0465	.0401	.0353
25%	.0582	.0485	.0417	.0367

* This table was made available by Professor Jeffrey Fisher
of Indiana University.
† Estimated by authors.

however, sale-and-leaseback financing most frequently occurs in conjunction with commercial property, where the investor will be limited to either 150 percent declining-balance or straight-line depreciation. Because straight-line depreciation is, by definition an annuity, no *EOA* factors are necessary when that method is used.

Computing the effective cost of sale-and-leaseback financing

Now that the idea of the equivalent ordinary annuity has been developed, it will be extremely helpful in determining the effective cost of sale-and-leaseback financing. Recapitulating our problem to this point, we have the following formulation to deal with:

$$PV \text{ of } ATCF^* + PV \text{ of } ATCF_x = \text{Funds acquired by leasing}$$

In other words, if we can convert $ATCF^*$ to an annuity, we need only to find a rate of discount that will make $ATCF^*$ and $ATCF_x$ *equal* to funds raised by Good because of sale-and-leaseback financing. We should recall that $ATCF^*$ is equal to:

$$LP(1 - t) - [DS - I(t) - D(t)] = ATCF^*$$

We have values for *DS, t,* and *LP* given in the problem, and we now need to develop values for *D* and *I* before finding the *PV* of *ATCF**. For these values we consult the *EOA* tables for factors corresponding to a 10 percent, 25-year mortgage which are the terms available if conventional financing is chosen. However, we must also *preselect* the discount rate which will be used in determining the *PV* of *ATCF**.[6] When we choose an *EOA* factor that

---

[6] This is done as a part of a trial and error process in trying to find a discount rate that will make the present value of *ATCF** and *ATCF_x* equal to equity saved by leasing.

corresponds to that preselected discount rate, *all values* used in determining the effective cost of sale-and-leaseback financing also *must* be discounted by that rate. To illustrate, we preselect an *EOA* of .0861 from Exhibit 15–2, for a *discount rate* of 12 percent to determine the equivalent ordinary annuity for *interest* on a 10 percent, 25-year mortgage. We now multiply .0861 by the conventional mortgage amount ($1,500,000) that would be used if the property were owned rather than leased; and we obtain $129,150, which is the equivalent ordinary annuity for all interest that would be expensed on a 10 percent, 25-year mortgage, *assuming* that those payments will be discounted by 12 percent when the present value of ATCF* is found. We also obtain an *EOA* factor for depreciation D for a 40-year useful life. This factor is .0319 and when multiplied by $1,800,000 (cost of building), we have a value for D, or $57,420. These values may now be substituted for D and I in determining PV of ATCF*. All other values (*LP, DS, ATCF_s*) *must* also be discounted by 12 *percent* when we solve for present value. To illustrate, we now have the following information:

		Amount	Years	*IFPVa, 12 percent*	*PV*
A.	Lease costs:				
	LP(1 − t).................	$ 203,784(1 − .46)	40	8.243777	$ 907,173
B.	Less ownership costs:				
	DS......................	163,572	25	7.843139	$1,282,918
	− I(t)	129,150(.46)	25	7.843139	(465,953)
	− D(t)..................	57,420(.46)	40	8.243777	(217,745)
	Net ownership costs..........				$ 599,222
	ATCF* (A) − (B)............				$ 307,951
C.	Add: Land value (reversion)			*IFPV, 12 percent*	
	ATCF_s......................	1,715,430	40	.010747	18,436
	Present value (ATCF* + ATCF_s)...............................				$ 326,387

After discounting all values in our formulation by 12 percent, we find that the present value obtained, or $326,387, is *not* equal to the $500,000 in equity saved. Hence, our discount rate (12 percent) is too high. In other words, we have chosen a discount rate to find the effective cost of the $500,000 saved by sale-and-leaseback financing that is too high. The effective cost of the sale-and-leaseback alternative is lower than 12 percent.

Continuing to solve for the effective cost by trial and error, we decrease the discount rate to 5 percent (by estimation). We must now select *new EOA* factors for interest and depreciation based on this 5 percent discount rate and discount all values in the formula by 5 percent. The *EOA* factor for interest is

.0776, and for depreciation, the *EOA* factor is .0272. Multiplying .0776 by the $1,500,000 mortgage loan, we have a new value for *I*, $116,400, and multiplying .0272 by the $1,800,000 building cost, we have a new value for *D* or $48,960. We now find the present value for *all values* again discounting everything at 5 percent as follows:

	Amount	Years	IFPVa, 5 percent	PV
A. Lease costs:				
$LP(1 - t)$..................	$ 203,784(1 − .46)	40	17.159086	$1,888,243
B. Less ownership costs:				
DS......................	163,572	25	14.093945	$2,305,375
− *I(t)*....................	116,400(.46)	25	14.093945	(754,646)
− *D(t)*...................	48,960(.46)	40	17.159086	(386,450)
Net ownership costs..........				$1,164,279
ATCF* (A) − (B)............				$ 723,964
C. Add: Land value (reversion)			IFPV, 5 percent	
$ATCF_s$......................	$1,715,430		.142046	243,670
Present value (*ATCF** + $ATCF_s$)..				$ 967,634

Based on the above computations, when $ATCF^*$ and $ATCF_s$ are discounted at 5 percent, we find the present value to be equal to $958,634, which is far greater than the $500,000 we are seeking. This means the 5 percent discount rate selected is too *low*. We can now find the solution to our problem by interpolating as follows:

PV at 5%...........	$967,634	PV at 5%	$967,634
PV at 12%.........	326,387	Desired PV..........	500,000
Difference.........	$641,247	Difference	$467,634

$$(467,634 \div 641,247) \times 7\% = 5.1\%$$
$$\text{Adding } 5\% + 5.1\% = \underline{10.1\%}$$

Based on the computations shown above, we find that using the sale-and-leaseback approach to financing, in this case, will have cost the equivalent of 10.1 percent *after taxes* for Good to raise an incremental $500,000 with the sale-and-leaseback approach. If it can use the additional $500,000 to expand its discount chain by acquiring additional facilities, and so on, that will provide an internal rate of return *aftertax* that is greater than 10.1 percent, it should do so. This is because the "cost" of sale-and-leaseback financing is 10.1 percent after taxes. We should stress that the 10.1 percent determined here is an *aftertax cost.*

In summary, when sale-and-leaseback financing is considered as an alternative to conventional financing, the cost associated with the lease alternative will be dependent on the difference between lease payments and debt service, less aftertax values for interest and depreciation, plus any reversion value given up by leasing. The solution obtained in a sale-and-leaseback analysis will depend on the size of the debt service, lease payments, depreciation, interest, and the appreciation rate in land value over the term of the lease. The solution obtained under this approach gives the owner of a property the cost of funds acquired by leasing, which must be judged relative to other financing alternatives and be reinvested at an aftertax rate of return at least equal to its cost.

Land sale-and-leaseback only

In the preceding case involving a full sale-and-leaseback agreement, we found that Good had to give up depreciation expenses on the building when the real estate was sold and leased back. Many investors are very reluctant to do this because of the tax benefits from depreciation that would be given up when the *improvement* is sold. Hence, many investor-developers have used a land sale-and-leaseback to achieve many of the advantages of sale-and-leaseback financing, while retaining the ownership of the improvement for tax purposes.

To illustrate the essentials of this financing technique, we reconsider the Good Discount store example. In this example we assume that Good sells *only the land* and leases it back from the buyer for a 40-year period with options to buy it back at stated intervals. Good retains ownership of the improvement.

If we assume that Good sells the land and leases it back, and can acquire 75 percent financing on the *building cost* of $1,800,000, then we can see that Good's investment in this project would be $50,000 less than it would be if the store was owned and financed conventionally. To summarize the effect of the land sale-and-leaseback versus Good owning both the building and land with conventional financing, we have:

	Conventional financing	Land sale-and-leaseback
Costs to be financed:		
Building...................	$1,800,000	$1,800,000
Land......................	200,000	200,000
Total value...............	$2,000,000	$2,000,000
Mortgage (75%)...............	1,500,000	1,350,000*
Equity before land sale...........	$ 500,000	$ 650,000
Less: Land sale	—	200,000
Equity	$ 500,000	$ 450,000

* Mortgage on building only.

In other words, if Good can sell the land and lease it back, it will have at its disposal $50,000 extra dollars for reinvestment, while still retaining ownership of the building and realizing benefits of tax deductions for mortgage interest and depreciation. However, Good would still give up the value of any land residual after the term of the lease. How much will this arrangement cost Good?

The analysis for this alternative is very similar to the framework used in the previous analysis involving the full sale-and-leaseback. If we assume that the *lease* payments on the $200,000 land value are based on a 12 percent amortization schedule for 40 years, monthly payments would be $2,017, or a total of $24,204 annually. To compute the effective cost of Good acquiring the additional $50,000 in cash, we first summarize the required information as follows:

LP (land only)..........................	$ 24,204 ($2,017 per month)
DS (building only)	147,204 ($12,267 per month)
DS (conventional financing)	163,572 ($13,631 per month)
ATCF$_x$ (land reversion)................	1,715,430

In developing our analysis of the land sale-and-leaseback, we recall our formulation for the full sale-and-leaseback:

$$PV \text{ of } ATCF^* + PV \text{ of } ATCF_x = \text{Funds raised by leasing}$$

We should also recall that PV of $ATCF^*$ was comprised of $LP(1 - t) - [DS - I(t) - D(t)]$. Because we are dealing with a land sale-and-leaseback only, (D) depreciation is retained by the owner; hence, it will not affect $ATCF^*$. As for debt service (DS) and interest (I), we should note that the amount of mortgage financing *changes* if the land sale-and-leaseback is chosen over conventional financing. If conventional financing is chosen, the mortgage debt will be $1,500,000, whereas debt will be $1,350,000 should the land be sold and leased back. In other words, under the sale-and-leaseback, Good will be making mortgage payments on the building based on a loan of $1,350,000 and will also deduct interest on those payments for tax purposes.

To solve for the present value of costs under the lease alternative, we must again determine what the value for (I) will be for *both* mortgage amounts using *EOA* factors from Exhibit 15–2. As we did with the full sale-and-leaseback, we must "preselect" a discount rate for finding the present value of lease costs, when taking an *EOA* factor from the exhibit. Beginning our trial and error process, we choose 10 percent as the discount rate. We then select an *EOA* factor for a 10 percent mortgage with a 25-year term. That *EOA* factor is .0841 which we can apply to both mortgage amounts to find I. Hence, the appropriate value for I under the land sale-and-leaseback will be $1,350,000(.0841), or $113,535, and under conventional financing it would be equal to $1,500,000(.0841), or $126,150.

Based on the data assembled to this point, we can now determine the present value of the lease costs by discounting at 10 percent as follows:

		Amount	Years	IFPVa, 10 percent	PV
A.	Lease costs:				
	$LP(1 - t)$................	$ 24,204(1 − .46)	40	9.779051	$ 127,814
	+ DS(building).............	147,204	25	9.077040	1,336,177
	−$I(t)$.....................	113,535(.46)	25	9.077040	(474,058)
	Net lease costs				$ 989,933
B.	Less ownership costs:				
	DS(entire property)..........	163,572	25	9.077040	$1,484,750
	−$I(t)$.....................	126,150(.46)	25	9.077040	(526,732)
	Net ownership costs...........				$ 958,018
	$ATCF^*$ (A − B)				$ 31,915
C.	Add: Land value (reversion)			IFPV, 10 percent	
	$ATCF_x$.....................	$1,715,430	40	.022095	37,902
	Present value ($ATCF^* + ATCF_x$)				$ 69,817

Based on the desired present value of $50,000, which is the amount of equity made available to Good by the land sale-and-leaseback, we can see that the 10 percent rate chosen for discounting is too low. Hence, by trial and error we increase the discount rate to 15 percent and select new values for *I* based on the appropriate *EOA* factor from Exhibit 15–2 which is .0885. We can then solve for the present value as follows:

		Amount	Years	IFPVa, 15 percent	PV
A.	Lease costs:				
	$LP(1 - t)$..................	$ 24,204(1 − .46)	40	6.641778	$ 86,809
	+ DS(building)..............	147,204	25	6.464149	951,549
	− $I(t)$.....................	119,475(.46)	25	6.464149	(355,260)
	Net lease costs				$ 683,098
B.	Less ownership costs:				
	DS (entire property)	163,572	25	6.464149	$1,057,354
	− $I(t)$.....................	132,750(.46)	25	6.464149	(394,733)
	Net ownership costs...........				$ 662,621
	$ATCF^*$ (A) − (B)				$ 20,477
C.	Plus: Land value (reversion)			IFPV, 15 percent	
	$ATCF_g$.....................	1,715,430	40	.003733	6,404
	Present value ($ATCF^* + ATCF_g$)				$ 26,881

Based on this result which is less than $50,000, we can see that the solution falls between 10 percent and 15 percent. Interpolation shows that the cost of acquiring the additional $50,000 with the land sale-and-leaseback is 12.3 percent.

Interpolating:

PV at 10%	$69,817		PV at 10%	$69,817
PV at 15%	26,881		Desired PV..........	50,000
Difference	$42,936		Difference	$19,817

$$($19,817 \div $42,936) \times 5\% = 2.3\%$$
$$\text{Adding } 2.3\% + 10\% = 12.3\% \; ATIRR$$

Hence, if Good decides to (1) sell-and-leaseback the land in this case, (2) retain ownership of the building, and (3) pay the equivalent of 12 percent on the lease for 40 years, the $50,000 obtained by financing in this manner will cost an equivalent of 12.3 percent after taxes and, therefore, must be reinvested at a rate in excess of 12.3 percent after taxes.

Subordinated ground leases

In addition to the land sale-and-leaseback financing technique, there is a variation that is sometimes used that not only involves the sale-and-leaseback of land but also mortgage financing on the land lease. This form of financing is frequently used in shopping center development and in other situations where the owner of the land not only leases it back to an investor-developer but also agrees to subordinate his ownership interest to a lender willing to make a loan against the land lease. Obviously, in this case, a lender would have to be convinced that the lease payments were very secure as evidenced by long-term lease commitments from financially sound tenants. However, if an investor-developer can convince the landowner to subordinate, this will usually "free up" more equity capital for the developer than would be the case with the land sale-and-leaseback.[7]

To illustrate the subordinated ground lease method, we assume the same facts as in the previous case except that, in addition to selling and leasing back the land, the Good Discount chain can obtain 75 percent mortgage financing on the lease.

It can be seen that if the subordinated ground lease approach is used, $200,000 more in funds become available for use than would be the case with conventional financing. The investor would still retain depreciation on the building and finance it with a 75 percent mortgage. If the cost of the *mortgage on the land lease* is 12 percent over 25 years, and land lease

---

[7] Usually when the landowner agrees to subordinate, the opportunity to mortgage the land is also given up as the lender on the lease will have a first lien on the land.

	Conventional financing	Subordinated ground lease
Costs:		
Building	$1,800,000	$1,800,000
Land	200,000	200,000
Total.....................	$2,000,000	$2,000,000
Less funds from:		
Mortgage—building	—	1,350,000
Mortgage—land lease...........	—	150,000
Conventional mortgage..........	1,500,000	—
Less funds from:		
Sale of land	—	200,000
Equity.......................	$ 500,000	$ 300,000

payments remain the same as previously assumed, we have the following comparison to consider:

LP (land)...........................	$ 24,204 ($2,017 per month) for 40 years
DS (building only)	147,204 ($12,267 per month) at 10%, 25 years
DS (land lease)	18,960 ($1,580 per month) at 12%, 25 years
DS (conventional financing)...........	163,572 ($13,631 per month) at 10%, 25 years
$ATCF_x$ (land reversion)................	1,715,430

As was the case with the land sale-and-leaseback problem, we must first compare the difference in debt service and interest between the alternatives. To take account of the difference in interest payments in our comparison, we must determine EOA factors for each layer of debt. This is done by preselecting a 12 percent discount rate to be used in estimating the present value of $ATCF^*$ and $ATCF_x$ and selecting EOA factors for interest (I) from Exhibit 15–2. These factors are as follows:

	Term	Interest rate	EOA at 12 percent	(I)
$ 150,000 debt (land lease)	25	12%	.1057	$ 15,855
1,350,000 debt (building only)............	25	10	.0861	116,235
1,500,000 debt (conventional)............	25	10	.0861	129,150

Based on an estimated discount rate of 12 percent, we have developed values for (I) for each of the mortgages listed above. We can now discount all relevant values by 12 percent as follows:

		Amount	Years	IFPVa, 12 percent	PV
A.	Lease costs:				
	LP(1 − t).................	$ 24,204(1 − .46)	40	8.243777	$ 107,747
	+ DS (building)............	147,204	25	7.843139	1,154,541
	− I(t).....................	116,235(.46)	25	7.843139	(419,358)
	+ DS (land lease)	18,960	25	7.843139	148,706
	− I(t)....................	15,855(.46)	25	7.843139	(57,202)
	Net lease costs				$ 934,434
B.	Less ownership costs:				
	DS (conventional)	163,572	25	7.843139	$1,282,918
	− I(t)....................	129,150(.46)	25	7.843139	(465,953)
	Net ownership costs..........				$ 816,965
	ATCF* (A) − (B)............				$ 117,469
C.	Add: Lease cost (reversion)			IFPV, 12 percent	
	ATCF$_s$.....................	1,715,430	40	.010747	18,435
	Present value (ATCF* + ATCF$_s$)				$ 135,904

Based on the present value of $135,905 computed above, the 12 percent discount rate is too high, as the desired present value is $200,000, or the amount of additional funds available under this technique. Hence, we try a very low discount rate of 5 percent for a new present value. Using a discount rate of 5 percent, the *EOA* for interest to be applied to 25-year mortgages carrying interest rates of 10 percent will be .0776, and .0962 for debt carrying an interest rate of 12 percent (Exhibit 15–2). We recompute the appropriate values for (*I*) and incorporate them in our formulation on page 429.

From these computations, we can see that the present value of $486,384 is greater than the $200,000 value we were seeking. Hence, we know that the internal rate of return falls between 5 percent and 12 percent. Interpolation (not shown) provides a solution of 10.7 percent. Hence, based on these results, the $200,000 in equity saved would cost Good 10.7 percent after taxes. These funds would have to be reinvested in excess of that rate for subordinated ground lease financing to be acceptable.

The reader may wonder why the owner of the land (the lessor) would be willing to give a land lease and subordinate his interest to enable the lessee to find a mortgage lender willing to lend on a leasehold interest. One reason is because, as we have seen, if the lessor is a tax-exempt foundation, it is somewhat limited in the extent to which it can borrow, or leverage against lease income due to special tax treatment; hence, it may be willing to also give back a subordinated ground lease. Or, if the lessor originally owned the land, this may be the only option available to provide a developer with enough incentive to develop the land. This arrangement is used frequently in shopping

	Amount	Years	IFPVa, 5 percent	PV
A. Lease costs:				
$LP(1-t)$	$ 24,204(1 − .46)	40	17.159086	$ 224,272
+ DS (building)	147,204	25	14.093945	2,074,685
− I(t)	104,760(.46)	25	14.093945	(679,182)
+ DS (land lease)	18,960	25	14.093945	267,221
− I(t)	14,430(.46)	25	14.093945	(95,553)
Net lease costs				$1,793,443
B. Less ownership costs:				
DS (conventional)	163,572	25	14.093945	$2,305,375
− I(t)	116,400(.46)	25	14.093945	(757,646)
Net ownership costs				$1,550,729
ATCF* (A) − (B)				$ 242,714
C. Add: Lease costs (reversion)			IFPV, 5 percent	
$ATCF_s$	1,715,430	40	.142046	243,670
Present value (ATCF* + $ATCF_s$)				$ 486,384

center development, where much acreage is involved. In this event, the lessor may also receive some overage, or equity participation, in addition to receiving monthly lease payments.[8]

Sale-and-leaseback financing—a summary

Based on the analysis presented to this point, we have approached the cost of sale-and-leaseback financing from the perspective of the investor-developer and determined the required *ATIRR* that must be earned on reinvested funds to justify use of the technique. One question that is frequently raised in connection with this approach is how should this analysis be used when the investor-developer cannot finance conventionally and *must* use some form of sale-and-leaseback, or other financing, to supplement conventional financing to undertake a project. Under each of the cases considered thus far, the amount of equity required by the developer varies considerably. A summary of these amounts is as follows:

	Equity required	Equity saved	Required ATIRR	Before tax cost of funds
Full sale-and-leaseback	–0–	$500,000	10.1%	18.7%
Subordinated ground lease	$300,000	200,000	10.7	19.8
Land sale-and-leaseback	450,000	50,000	12.3	22.8

[8] If the lessor originally owns the land, the analysis remains the same as if the developer buys the land then sells it and leases it back.

Obviously, if Good Discount stores used the full sale-and-leaseback method, our approach indicates that $500,000 would be saved and available for other use. However, what if Good did not have the $500,000 to begin with for conventional financing? The answer is that if this was the case, if it could have brought in additional equity investors, made a second mortgage, or sought other ways to raise $500,000 in equity at *less* than an aftertax cost of 10.1 percent (or 18.7 percent before taxes) it would still be better off than financing with a sale-and-leaseback. Given an aftertax cost of 10.1 percent, the equivalent before-tax cost of those funds, if Good were to borrow them, would be 10.1% ÷ (1 − .46), or 18.7 percent. This is equivalent, then, to borrowing $500,000 at 18.7 percent interest. Good may not have the $500,000 to finance conventionally, however, when it uses a sale-and-leaseback method, it is, in effect, *borrowing funds*. The cost of those funds is made up of lease payments and tax deductions on depreciation and interest plus appreciation in property value which are given up. Hence the acquisition of this additional equity is clearly not "costless." Before-tax and aftertax costs that can be compared to other forms of financing are also shown for the land sale-and-leaseback and subordinated ground lease alternatives. Although the developer retains ownership of the building in these cases, the before and aftertax cost of acquiring funds under each is considerable.

An equally important point to make is that under sale-and-leaseback financing, the investor-developer's equity is lower than would be the case if the property was financed conventionally; hence, in effect, more financial leverage is being used. Indeed, sale-and-leaseback financing can be viewed as using more financial leverage. In many cases, if one were to use sale-and-leaseback financing, the *ATIRR* on equity invested would increase. However, even though this may be the case, the analysis is incomplete unless the comparisons detailed here are made. Even though return on equity may increase with sale-and-leaseback, it still may be in an investor's best interest to finance conventionally when the full cost of additional funds obtained under sale-and-leaseback financing is taken into account.

Step and indexed lease payments—a final note

In the preceding examples, we have assumed that all lease payments were constant over time. In many cases this may not be the case. Some lease agreements are based on "step-lease" payments. Some payments are tied to a price index which may change with time, or the rate of increase may be specified by the parties in advance. Also, some payments may include "overage" based on sales revenue. How would such variations be included in our analysis?

For step leases, this involves "netting out" discount factors at the discount rate chosen for the appropriate time intervals. If lease payments were made annually for ten years at $5,000 and increased to $7,000 for the next ten years, and we wanted to discount at 12 percent, we would have:

$5,000(*IFPVa*, 12%, 10 yrs.) + $7,000(*IFPVa*, 12%, 20–10 yrs.)

or

$5,000(5.650223) + $7,000(7.469444 − 5.650223) = $40,986

The present value of the step-lease payments would then be reduced by $(1 - t)$ and substituted as the aftertax present value of lease payments in all of our above formulations when all other values are discounted at 12 percent.

To illustrate the use of indexed lease payments and lease payments that are to increase at a specific rate, assume that a series of *annual* lease payments are to be paid at the *end* of each year. The first annual payment is scheduled to be $5,000; however, it has been estimated that these payments will increase at 6 percent per year thereafter over the term of the lease, which is 40 years. The required rate of return or preselected discount rate to be used in the analysis (k) is 10 percent. What would be the present value of these escalating series of lease payments? The formula for such an increasing series is as follows:

$$LP \times \frac{1 - \dfrac{(1 + g)^s}{(1 + k)^s}}{k - g} = PV \text{ of } LP$$

where LP = lease payments, g = the rate of increase in payments, k = the required rate of discount, and s = the number of years in the sale-and-leaseback agreement. Substituting, we have:

$$\$5,000 \times \frac{1 - \dfrac{10.285718}{45.259256}}{.10 - .06} = PV \text{ of } LP$$

Simplifying, we have:

$$\$5,000 \times \frac{1 - .227262}{.04} = PV \text{ of } LP$$

Simplifying further, we have:

$$\$5,000 \times 19.318445 = \$96,592$$

Hence, in this case, we have determined that the present value of a series of $5,000 annual lease payments increasing at 6 percent and received at the end of each year would be $96,592. This would then be reduced by $(1 - t)$ to arrive at an aftertax present value and used in the sale-and-leaseback analysis described above.[9]

---

[9] It should be noted that the values for $(1 + g)^{40}$ and $(1 + k_e)^{40}$ come from the amount of $1 at compound interest (column 1) in Appendix A, or they can be computed with an electronic calculator.

We should also note that if the first $5,000 payment is required in advance, or at the beginning of the year, which is the case in many lease agreements, the formula is changed as follows:

$$PV \text{ of } LP(1 + k)^1 = PV \text{ of } LP \text{ (beginning of period)}$$

Where PV of LP, obtained when payments are received at the end of the period, is simply compounded by the required return on equity (k) to obtain the present value of lease payments assuming beginning of period payment.

These formulas can also be converted to find the present value of monthly lease payments. When payments are to be received at the *end* of each month, the terms LP, g, k, and s in the end of year formula detailed above must be divided by 12.[10] When payments are received in *advance*, or at the beginning of the period, the present value of all monthly payments is simply compounded by $(1 + k/12)^{12}$.

Finally, in the unusual circumstance where lease payments are expected to *decline* at a specific *rate* (g) each year, the above formulas can be easily altered by simply changing the sign on the growth term g as follows:

$$LP \times \frac{1 - \dfrac{(1 - g)^s}{1 + k)^s}}{k + g} = PV \text{ of } LP$$

This revised term can be inserted in any of the above discussed formulas where a declining stream of lease payments is expected.

These formulas are very useful in finding the present value of any series of income payments that are expected to (1) increase or decrease at an estimated rate (g), (2) be received either annually or monthly, and (3) be received at the beginning or end of a period. Other applications can be used in establishing property and lease values and in situations other than lease payments as warranted.

One final note of caution, however, in all cases dealing with increasing payments, the above formulas can only be used when g, which is the rate of growth, is less than k. The reason for this restriction can be seen by looking at the denominator $k - g$ in the formula. If $g > k$, then the solution for PV of LP becomes negative, implying negative lease payments, which would be incorrect.

Questions

1   Briefly describe the parties involved in a sale-and-leaseback financing transaction. Why may such a method be superior to conventional financing?

---

[10] When indexed leases require monthly payments, these payments are usually adjusted at the end of each year. The modification suggested here for monthly payments, that is, dividing LP, g, k, and s by 12 assumes that lease payments are adjusted *monthly* at a rate equal to $(g \div 12)$. While this is not equivalent to the case in which monthly payments are adjusted annually, the results will be very close, and this method can be used to approximate.

2   What categories of properties are frequently used in sale-and-leaseback situations?

3   What are repurchase options and lease cancellation privileges? Why are these important in sale-and-leaseback financing?

4   Why should sale-and-leaseback financing be considered relative to conventional financing and not be used to establish whether a project will be profitable or not?

5   What "trade-offs" are generally made when sale-and-leaseback financing is considered relative to conventional financing?

6   What is an equivalent ordinary annuity? Why is it useful in analysis?

7   What is a subordinated ground lease? How is it different from sale-and-leaseback financing? Why would a landowner agree to such a transaction?

8   Why is a sale-and-leaseback considered to be another form of financial leverage? If less equity is required with sale-and-leaseback financing, why should this be viewed as borrowing? How can the cost of this borrowing be established on an aftertax and a before-tax basis?

Case problems

1   LTD Trucking Company has decided that it would be profitable to locate a new terminal in a growing region of the United States. It is considering the use of a sale-and-leaseback arrangement with an investor syndication. LTD has been rapidly expanding in this market and would like to consider sale-and-leaseback financing on the land and buildings because it thinks funds can be used for investment in a truck fleet and complementary equipment. However, LTD realizes that certain benefits of property ownership will be given up with the sale-and-leaseback, and it is wondering what the "cost" of undertaking this form of financing would be.

If LTD finances the project conventionally, it can obtain a mortgage loan at 75 percent of value at 12 percent interest for 25 years. The value of the building is estimated at $2,000,000, and land is valued at $200,000. Should it decide to enter into a sale-and-leaseback agreement, it would be for 40 years with options to buy at various intervals at the higher of market value or the unamortized balance of the $2,200,000 value of the property based on a 12 percent schedule for 40 years.

Under the lease agreement, payments would be $266,244 annually, beginning at the end of the first year. If the property were financed conventionally and purchased, declining-balance depreciation would be taken at 150 percent of straight line over 40 years. Land value is estimated to increase at 6 percent per year over the life of the lease. LTD is a corporation subject to a 46 percent marginal tax rate.

a.   What would be the aftertax cost of the $550,000 in equity saved under the sale-and-leaseback proposal (compute debt service monthly and multiply by 12 to obtain annual debt service)? What would be the before tax cost of this proposal?

b.   If lease payments were scheduled to increase by 150 percent or to $399,366 after 20 years, how would this affect the analysis? What if lease payments are indexed and are expected to increase at 4 percent annually (use approximation)?

c.   Given the same terms used in (*a*) above, what if the land value was expected to increase at 10 percent per year? How would the cost be affected?

d. Assume that LTD could enter into a lease agreement whereby it would sell the land only for $200,000 and lease it back for $26,150 per year for 40 years. LTD would still acquire 75 percent financing on the building at 12 percent interest for 25 years. Given all other terms in (*a*), how would this affect the analysis?

2 Dracon Development Corporation is about to acquire the land to develop a shopping center. It has studied the possibility of 70 percent conventional financing for 25 years at 10 percent interest based on the current project value of $3,000,000 and believes the project to be profitable. However, the company believes that it can sell the land for $300,000 and also arrange subordinated ground lease financing with Tower of Light Foundation. Dracon would sell the land to Tower of Light, then obtain a subordinated lease on the land for 40 years amortized at 12 percent. Based on the subordinated lease agreement, Dracon has negotiated with the Life Assurance Society and obtained a commitment for a 60 percent mortgage on the lease for 20 years at 15 percent interest (value of the lease is $300,000). If the subordinated lease agreement can be worked out, Dracon would still finance the building with a 70 percent conventional mortgage at 10 percent interest.

a. How much equity does Dracon* require with subordinated ground lease financing?

b. How would you analyze the cost of financing for Dracon*? (Compute all payments monthly to determine total annual payments; assume the land value will increase at 8 percent per year).

c. If the subordinated ground lease agreement requires overages or an equity participation "kicker" to be paid to the owner of the land, and the overage, or kicker, is expected to increase lease payments by an average of 6 percent per year (beginning in the second year), how would this change the result in (*b*)?

   * Dracon is a corporation with a 46 percent tax rate.

3 Ajax Investment Corporation has executed a sale-and-leaseback agreement with Zerox Corporation. Zerox sold land to Ajax who leased it back to Zerox. The lease that Ajax holds calls for payments of $115,025 per year for 30 years. Ajax now wants to borrow against the lease, given that Zerox is an excellent credit risk. Nexxon Corporation is willing to lend 75 percent of the lease value; however, Nexxon must earn a *before-tax return (BTIRR)* of 15 percent on the mortgaged lease. Assuming that the required return (*k*) is the rate at which Nexxon will value the entire stream of lease payments, what is the value under each of the following conditions:

a. Lease payments are made annually at the end of each year?

b. Same as (*a*), but lease payments are scheduled to increase at 6 percent per year?

c. Same as (*a*), lease payments are made annually but at the beginning of the year?

d. Assume that lease payments are made monthly ($9,585 per month) at the end of each month?

e. Same as (*d*), but lease payments are expected to grow at 6 percent (assume monthly approximation)?

f. Same as (*d*), but lease payments are made at the beginning of each month?

4 Schmaltz holds a lease on a building that is 40 years old and scheduled for demolition in 10 years. He would like to sell the lease to Schmidt. A "net" lease has been negotiated with the tenant, who is financially sound. However, because the operating expenses,

which must be absorbed by the tenant, are expected to rise sharply during the next ten years because of the age of the property, a *declining* series of net lease payments have been negotiated. The lease payments will begin at $1,000 at the end of the first year and *decline* at the rate of 8 percent for the next ten years. Schmidt has indicated that he must earn at least a before-tax return (*BTIRR*) of 12 percent on the stream of lease payments. What is the value of the lease to Schmidt?

Construction and land development loans

16

Perhaps two of the most complex areas of lending in real estate finance, both from the standpoint of lenders and investors, are construction loans and land development loans. This chapter contains a description of the basic characteristics of each type of financing, as well as illustrations designed to provide the reader with some insight as to how these loans are negotiated by lenders and borrowers, and how terms for disbursement and repayment are determined. In addition to financial characteristics, considerable emphasis is also given to procedural matters ranging from obtaining loan commitments to the closing of each type of loan and control over the disbursement and repayment of funds. This emphasis is necessary in understanding these particular methods of financing because of the technical characteristics of the construction and development process.

Construction lending and permanent financing commitments

Before construction loans on income-producing properties are negotiated between developers and lenders, the developer first makes contact with a lender who might be willing to make the long-term or *permanent loan* on a proposed project. This procedure is followed because most construction lenders are short-term lenders who do not want to make long-term loans. Rather, they specialize in construction lending which is usually short term in nature. Because the construction lender is only interested in the short-term financing of a project, assurance must usually be provided by the developer that a long-term lender has been found who is willing to finance the project when it is completed. In this way, since another lender will provide funds when the project is completed, the construction lender's involvement in financing usually ceases with completion of the project.

In order to gain insight into how most construction loans are made, it is necessary to understand how long-term loan commitments are negotiated between developers and permanent lenders. This section of the chapter provides a brief overview of how *permanent financing* is arranged in *advance* of construction loans.

Takeout commitment. It should be stressed that any long-term or permanent lender will first evaluate a proposed project, whether it is an apartment complex, shopping center, or office building, by using the financial analysis provided in the preceding chapter. The market study, building plans and costs, as well as the operating statement, are analyzed carefully by the lender who determines whether a loan should be made and, if so, on what terms. Should the loan be approved and the borrower and lender agree on the terms, the lender issues what is known as a takeout commitment. This represents a commitment to *become* the permanent lender. In other words, since the project has not yet been developed, the borrower must find a construction lender to finance development. However, construction lenders are usually unwilling to make loans unless they are certain that a developer has found a permanent mortgage lender who will provide funds that will be used to pay off the construction loan when the project is complete. If a lender is making both the construction loan and the permanent mortgage loan, such an arrangement is unnecessary. However, in practice it is more common to find different lenders making the construction loan and the permanent loan.[1] Consequently, the takeout commitment for the permanent mortgage usually must be found by the developer *before* the construction loan will be granted by a local lender.[2]

As previously discussed in Chapter 11, takeout commitments issued by most long-term lenders contain *contingencies* that must be met by the borrower before the lender's commitment becomes legally binding. If these contingencies are not met, the lender does not have to release funds upon completion.

Commitment fees—takeout commitments. The long-term lender normally charges a nonrefundable fee for making a takeout loan commitment. This fee must be paid by the borrower at the time of commitment. The fee is usually comprised of two parts: (1) the out-of-pocket costs and overhead incurred by the lender when the financial and credit analyses of the loan application and

---

[1] Usually, construction loans are made by short-term lenders with an excellent knowledge of the local real estate market, such as commercial banks and some savings and loan associations. The permanent lenders on income-producing properties tend to be large life insurance companies who rely on the local lender to make construction loans and to control the disbursement of funds. For a good review of construction lending practices, see Peter A. Schulkin, *Commercial Bank Construction Lending* (Research Report No. 47, Federal Reserve Bank of Boston, 1970).

[2] Some lenders may be willing to lend without a takeout commitment, speculating that the permanent loan will be found before completion of the project. However, in light of the disastrous results experienced by real estate lenders in the mid-1970s, this practice has practically ceased.

loan applicant are performed, and (2) an indirect charge for the loss of investment opportunities associated with funds that have been committed to the borrower for delivery at a future date and that cannot be invested at maximum advantage during the interim period.[3] Should the developer not meet the completion date or fail to fulfill contingency provisions in the takeout commitment, the commitment fee is usually forfeited.

Takeout commitments—buy and sell agreements.   In past years many borrowers may have obtained a takeout commitment from a lender and intentionally forfeited the commitment fee by not closing the permanent loan. This may have been profitable if mortgage interest rates fell significantly during the time development was being completed or if the borrower found another permanent lender willing to offer better loan terms. In more recent years, permanent lenders have required what is called a *buy and sell agreement.* This agreement is signed by the borrower, the permanent lender, and the construction lender and essentially provides that the construction loan mortgage will be delivered to the permanent lender on the completion date. In essence, the permanent lender *buys* the construction loan mortgage from the construction lender. In this way, the construction loan is repaid and the permanent loan is closed simultaneously. Under this approach, the permanent lender has more assurance that the permanent loan will be made and that both the borrower and construction lender will endeavor to complete the project on time and to fulfill all contingency requirements.

Standby commitments.   Standby commitments also arise in cases where the borrower is seeking a permanent commitment in order to obtain a construction loan from another lender. Standby commitments differ from takeouts in that neither the borrower nor the lender expects the standby commitment to become binding. The borrower generally expects to find more favorable terms on the permanent loan elsewhere. However, the borrower wants to begin development and needs a commitment to obtain the construction loan, but believes that better terms will be found during the development period. The borrower will continue to search for more favorable terms until the completion date becomes effective under the standby commitment. If more favorable terms are found elsewhere, the borrower will complete the requirements for the permanent mortgage with another lender. If more favorable terms are not found by the completion date, then the standby commitment will be used and the permanent loan will be closed with the lender who issued the standby commitment.

Even though permanent lenders who offer standby commitments charge a commitment fee and are legally bound to deliver mortgage funds on the completion date (if the borrower decides to use the commitment), many banks are unwilling to make construction loans when a borrower has only a

---

[3] Some short-term investments may be available, but returns on these would more than likely be less than returns on loans normally made by the lender.

standby commitment. Neither the borrower nor the permanent lender really expects to complete the transaction. Should the borrower decide to use the commitment, the permanent lender may balk at his responsibility. For example, if a period of tight credit occurs in the economy after the commitment is made, the permanent lender may not have the full amount of funds necessary to make good on the commitment. In situations such as these, lenders who have issued standbys may look for "technical violations" of contingencies in the commitment (for example, minor changes in construction plans not approved by the permanent lender, and so on). For this reason, very few construction lenders are willing to make loans when the borrower has only a standby commitment. Indeed, a study of commercial bank lending practices showed that 45 percent of banks surveyed would under no circumstances make a construction loan when the borrower had only a standby commitment. In *only special instances* would the remaining 55 percent of banks surveyed make a construction loan when the borrower had only a standby commitment, or no takeout commitment at all.[4]

The construction loan

Generally a construction loan is secured by a mortgage for future advances, or an open-end mortgage. Under this type of mortgage, the lender has first lien on the land and all subsequent improvements as funds are disbursed for labor and materials used in the development of the improvements. With the exception of loans made for single-family properties, most construction loans are made by commercial banks. This is because these banks are local in orientation and are very familiar with local lending conditions. They are also usually in a good position to control disbursement of funds and to monitor construction progress.[5] As indicated previously, most construction lenders require evidence from the borrower that a permanent takeout commitment has been obtained from a long-term lender as a precondition of obtaining a construction loan. This is not always true for developers of single-family properties who, based on their own financial strength as well as the local demand for housing, may be able to obtain construction loans for a number of houses to be built on speculation. However, when a loan for a home to be custom built is negotiated, usually the buyer has already obtained a permanent mortgage commitment, which may be used as the basis for a builder to obtain a construction loan.

Special risks in construction lending.   Even though most construction loans are made with relative assurance of permanent financing, special risks must be recognized in conjunction with this type of lending. Many sources of risk in

---

[4] See Schulkin, *Commercial Bank Construction Lending,* pp. 32–53.

[5] A sizable number of construction loans on residential income properties are also made by savings and loan associations.

construction lending can result in project failure or other difficulties for both the construction lender and borrower. First, there are the possibilities of strikes, inclement weather, or unforeseen problems with building design or geologic structure which may slow down construction and consequently increase costs. If a slowdown occurs, interest charges, overhead, inflation in material costs, and real estate taxes accumulate. This may eventually require that the borrower invest additional equity funds or that the bank increase the loan over the initial amount of the construction loan commitment. A second area of risk that may cause problems in construction lending lies in the possibility of poor management in the development firm or a firm's inexperience in a particular field of construction. These conditions can lead to cost overruns and delays that can threaten the solvency of the developer and the economic feasibility of a project.

Finally, although most construction loans are made to borrowers with takeout commitments, contingencies in the takeout commitment, if not met, can cause the permanent lender to retract the commitment. It may be recalled that most takeout commitments require a completion date for construction, the right of the permanent lender to approve all construction change orders, a specific lease rental achievement, and other possible conditions before the commitment becomes binding. Unforeseen problems with construction can delay the project beyond the completion date, result in structural design changes unsuitable to the permanent lender, or cause the developer not to meet the necessary rental achievement. If any or all of these events should occur, the permanent lender can retract the commitment and the construction lender may have to carry the completed project until a new permanent lender can be found.

Construction loan analysis. Even though a takeout commitment may be obtained by a given borrower, construction lenders must perform their own underwriting function. Based on the special categories of risk just discussed, it is apparent that the construction lender faces the possibility of loss even when a takeout commitment exists.

First to be considered in the construction lending underwriting process is the financial adequacy and past construction experience of the developer. In making construction lending decisions, the lender must be assured that the builder has had successful building experience in the type of project for which financing is being sought. Lenders are reluctant to extend credit to inexperienced developers or to developers who have not demonstrated ability within specialized areas of construction. A developer's financial adequacy is equally important. In the event that slowdowns in construction are encountered, the developer must have adequate working capital to see a project through to completion without reliance on additional borrowing from the bank. Consequently, the bank normally will require as part of the loan application documentation, a complete set of financial statements from the developer along with a record of past construction experience, which may be thoroughly investigated by the lender. Assuming that the lender finds the data obtained on the developer satisfactory, personal guarantees may be required of the developer as a condition for obtaining the loan. These guarantees generally allow the lender to look to the developer's personal financial assets for satisfaction in the event a project goes into default.

Project review.   If a developer has a takeout commitment for a project from a permanent lender, this usually means that a market study and an appraisal report have been compiled and extensively studied by the long-term lender. The construction lender generally reviews the market study and appraisal to determine how much should be loaned based on economic value. Should the market study or appraisal not be adequate in the eyes of the construction lender, new studies may be conducted by the construction lender, ordinarily by staff appraisers. In any event, the construction lender seldom, if ever, agrees to lend an amount greater than the amount of the takeout commitment, regardless of the appraised value. Further, some construction lenders will not lend any more than the cost of the improvement being constructed, exclusive of the land value.

Risk analysis.   In addition to reviewing the appraisal and market reports, the construction lender normally performs a detailed ratio analysis of projected operating statements submitted by the developer. These statements accompany loan documentation given to the permanent lender and already have been analyzed in the manner shown in the preceding chapter. Nevertheless, the construction lender, who is very familiar with local market conditions in real estate, reviews these statements to see if assumptions made in the estimates are realistic. Then, after computing key financial ratios and comparing them to industry standards and present local market conditions, the construction lender makes a judgment as to whether the project should be underwritten. In addition to the appraisal review, other requirements are imposed on the developer by the construction lender. These items are outlined below.

Detailed cost breakdown.   The developer usually must submit detailed cost estimates and plans for constructing the improvement. The cost breakdown generally must be certified by an architect chosen by the lender, usually at the expense of the developer, for accuracy in accordance with building plans and specifications. Then the lender usually requires the developer to contract with the architect, again at the developer's expense, to verify on a monthly basis all costs as construction work progresses and as the lender disburses funds.

Building contracts and subcontracts.   Normally, lenders require developers to obtain fixed-price contracts for specified amounts of construction from subcontractors. The lender may require these contracts as a means of protecting against cost overruns that may occur if material or labor prices rise during construction.

Labor and material payment bonds/completion bonds.   Many lenders require that developers purchase labor and material payment bonds and completion bonds. The first type of bond assures the lender that any unpaid bills for labor and material will be paid by the bonding company should a developer default. The completion bond assures the lender that the construction will be completed by the bonding company in the event that the developer defaults during construction.

Title insurance. As a condition for obtaining a construction loan, title insurance generally must be purchased by the developer. This is to assure the lender that no liens superior to its lien exist on the property when construction commences. In addition, as funds are disbursed and construction progresses, the lender usually requires that the title company continually update the title abstract in order to verify that no liens have been filed before each disbursement is made by the lender. In fact, many lenders disburse construction funds directly to a title company which makes payment to the developer, or directly to subcontractors, *after* verifying the absence of any liens. This practice is used to assure the lender that no mechanics' liens have been filed during construction. Should a lien exist, and if the title company makes disbursement, the title company becomes liable for any loss to the owner, and ultimately to the lender.

Assignment of lease rents. In cases where long-term leases have been obtained by the developer, the lender may require assignment of these leases until the construction loan is liquidated. This assures the lender of receiving all rental payments should the project be completed and occupied with the developer in default.

Assignment of commitment letter. The construction lender usually requires the borrower to assign the takeout commitment letter obtained from a permanent lender to the construction lender. In this way, if the project is finished by the completion date and all contingencies are met, the permanent mortgage funds can be collected directly from the permanent lender by the construction lender, bypassing the developer.

Tri-party buy-sell agreement. In lieu of assignment of the commitment letter, the borrower, developer, and long-term lender may enter into an agreement whereby the permanent lender agrees to buy the construction mortgage loan directly from the construction lender on the completion date, assuming all contingencies are met. As previously indicated, this agreement gives the construction lender greater assurance that funds will be delivered when the construction project is completed and all contingencies honored.

Other requirements prior to closing. In addition to the foregoing, other requirements must be fulfilled by the developer prior to closing. These include boundary surveys, soil samples and tests, verification of payment of all outstanding property taxes, checking zoning status and building permits, determination of the availability of necessary public utilities, a binder evidencing the purchase of hazard insurance coverage during the construction period, environmental impact statements, and establishment of the date on which construction is to commence and to end.

Rating loan terms and fees. For large-scale construction projects, construction lenders may also charge nonrefundable loan commitment fees. These fees are forfeited in the event that a loan commitment is not accepted by the borrower within a specified time period. As with fees charged for takeout commitments, these fees range upward from amounts necessary to cover out-of-pocket underwriting costs, depending on market conditions. In addition, loan origination fees, intended to increase the loan yield to the lender, are charged at closing. Origination fees usually range from 1 to 3 percent of the loan commitment.

Interest rates on construction loans generally reflect short-term borrowing rates. Since the term of a construction loan is almost always less than three years, the rates charged on new loans vary considerably from period to period in response to current lending conditions. Many lenders, particularly commercial banks, have begun to rely on a system of *floating interest rates* on construction loans. A system of floating rates is based on the bank's *prime lending rate,* or short-term interest rate charged on commercial loans to the bank's most creditworthy customers. A construction loan normally is evaluated as to risk during the underwriting process, and the interest rate quoted on the loan is made in conjunction with the prime rate. For example, an interest rate on a construction loan may be quoted as "two points over prime." This means that if the prime lending rate is 12 percent at closing, the interest rate charged on the construction loan will be 14 percent. More importantly, however, if the prime lending rate increases during the construction period, the interest rate on the construction loan also increases, maintaining the 2 percent difference over the prime lending rate. In addition, some lenders have used a *floor,* or lower limit, on declines in interest rates permissible on construction loans with floating rates. Usually this floor is equivalent to the initial rate at which the construction loan was originated. Hence, in our example, the rate on the construction loan would be two points over prime with a floor of 12 percent.

Disbursement of funds.   As indicated in an earlier chapter, a cardinal rule followed by real estate lenders is never to loan more than the economic value of the property that serves as security for the loan. This rule applies equally well in construction lending. Generally, as construction progresses, disbursements are made by the lender in one of three ways. In the *stage method,* funds are disbursed as stages of construction are completed. For example, when a building is under roof and work has been verified by the lender, the first disbursement is made. As construction progresses and the building is plastered, the second disbursement is released. Completion of the project qualifies the builder for the final disbursement. This technique, used primarily in single-family construction, assures that the economic value being created in construction is in place and subject to a lien by the lender as disbursements are made. Consequently, the security for the loan is being improved continuously with the disbursement of funds.

The second way to disburse funds is the *monthly draw method.* This method is used extensively in the construction of larger scale projects requiring sizable loans. The developer requests a draw each month based on the work completed in the preceding month. If an architect verifies that such work is in place, the lender disburses the funds. Again, the collateral value for the loan increases simultaneously with the disbursement of funds.

The final method of disbursement is a *voucher system.* The developer submits invoices from subcontractors for actual work completed to date. These invoices are submitted to the lender or to a title insurance company, depending on whether the lender is using the services of a title company for updating the title abstract, and then they are paid. With all these methods of disbursement, as payments are made, contractors and subcontractors sign an agreement that they have been paid for work done to date. This precludes their filing mechanics' liens.

Holdbacks.   In many cases, construction lenders "hold back" a proportion of each disbursement payable to a developer. This occurs when a developer is using a number of subcontractors and is holding back a portion of the funds due under subcontracts. The developer holds back to be sure that subcontractors perform all work completely prior to receiving final payment. Consequently, the construction lender holds back from the developer so that no excess funds are made available to the developer during the period the developer is holding back from subcontractors.

Construction lending illustrated.   Global Development Company has approached State City Bank for a construction loan for an apartment complex. Global has already obtained a takeout commitment from Acme Life Insurance Company for up to $1.1 million on a total appraisal value of $1.5 million. Major contingencies in the takeout commitment specify that the project must be completed within 12 months and that 70 percent of all units must be leased before the commitment is binding.

State City Bank has reviewed the appraisal report and analyzed the cost estimates based on the market study. It believes the project to be economically feasible. If State City makes the loan, financing is available at a floating rate of 9 percent interest, or 2 percent over prime, with a 3 percent loan origination fee. The bank will not make a construction loan commitment for more than the take-out commitment. The appraised value of the project is $1.5 million. Of that amount, land value constitutes $400,000. Global owns the land free and clear and is willing to give State City first lien on the land as a condition of obtaining the construction loan.

A summary of detailed cost estimates submitted by Global is shown in Exhibit 16–1. The total estimated cost of building the improvement excluding land, is $1,084,000, which is slightly less than the takeout commitment of $1.1 million. This cost must be certified by an architect who judges conformance with building plans and specifications before the construction lender will make a loan commitment. It should also be noted that as part of the "soft costs" anticipated by the developer an estimate for construction interest cost has been included. This is customary in many construction lending situations, as no cash

EXHIBIT 16–1
Summary of cost estimates, Global Development Company

Hard costs:		
On site:		
Building ($17.00 per square foot)	$810,000	
Fixtures	60,000	
Landscaping	5,000	
Parking area	42,000	$ 917,000
Off site:		
Water and sewer extension	50,000	50,000
Soft costs:		
Closing fees and taxes.	10,000	
Loan origination fees	33,000	
Construction interest	61,000	
Architect—Engineering	8,000	
Architect inspections	5,000	117,000
Total costs		$1,084,000

flow will begin from the project until it is completed. Consequently, unless the developer chooses to pay interest from internal sources, it is effectively carried forward in the construction loan balance, which is then purchased by the permanent lender. This point will be developed more fully as the illustration is completed.

Assuming State City Bank agrees to make the loan, all bonding requirements, surveys, title and hazard insurance policies, the tri-party or buy-sell agreement, payment of property taxes, and other requirements of the construction lender must be completed by the developer prior to closing. At closing, soft costs, including closing costs and taxes, origination fees, and layout costs will be advanced.[6] A summary of closing costs and soft costs approved for disbursement is provided in Exhibit 16–2.

Based on the rate at which construction progresses, Global will be requesting draws against the construction loan commitment extended by State City Bank. Exhibit 16–3 shows a hypothetical schedule of monthly draws that might occur as Global completes the project and as construction is verified by an independent architect. Looking closely at the exhibit, it should be noted that as actual monthly draws are taken down by Global, *interest* is included as part of the draw on each month. This means that the developer is borrowing, as part of the draw, current interest charges each month. Since a construction loan is an "interest-only" loan, only interest is paid by the developer each

---

[6] In some cases, lenders may be willing to make an additional advance for materials at closing. This depends on the financial condition of the developer and whether bonding is in effect. Conservative lenders prefer the developer to use internal funds for initially acquiring materials. Reimbursement is then made after the materials are in place.

EXHIBIT 16–2
Summary of closing costs and soft costs, construction loan—Global
Development Company

Legal, layout costs	$ 5,000
Engineering fees-survey.	8,000
Title abstract	500
Title insurance.	2,000
Taxes and recording fees.	2,500
Origination fee-State City Bank (3%)	33,000
Amount authorized for disbursement	$51,000

EXHIBIT 16–3
Draw schedule-loan statement, construction loan—Global Development Company

Month	Actual draws Construction costs	Interest*	Total monthly draw†	Cumulative loan balance	Interest payments	Net cash to developer
Close.	$ 18,000	$33,000‡	$ 51,000	$ 51,000	$ —	$ 18,000
1	—	383	383	$ 51,383	383	—
2	175,000	385	175,385	226,768	385	175,000
3	175,000	1,701	176,701	403,469	1,701	175,000
4	150,000	3,026	153,026	556,495	3,026	150,000
5	125,000	4,174	129,174	685,669	4,174	125,000
6	100,000	5,143	105,143	790,812	5,143	100,000
7	90,000	6,564	96,564	887,376	6,564	90,000
8	50,000	7,365	57,365	944,741	7,365	50,000
9	30,000	7,841	37,841	982,582	7,841	30,000
10	20,000	8,155	28,155	1,010,737	8,155	20,000
11	20,000	8,389	28,389	1,039,126	8,389	20,000
12	10,000	8,625	18,625	1,057,751	8,625	10,000

* Computed on previous month's ending balance at .75% for months 1–6, and .83% for months 7–12.
† End of month.
‡ Loan fee.

month and no reduction in loan principal occurs.[7] Therefore, the balance due to the bank will increase each month by the full amount of *construction cost plus interest* that is borrowed by the developer. The *net cash* amounts taken down by the developer are shown in the last column of Exhibit 16–3. They reflect the proceeds the developer has for use each month after the draw is made and interest charges are paid.[8] Also at closing, the amount drawn is

[7] This is true unless the developer chooses to make payments in excess of interest due for the month from internal funds. This amounts to the developer paying down the loan balance or loan principal.

[8] We assume that the developer makes the draw and immediately pays interest from the draw each month.

$51,000; however, the loan origination fee of $33,000 charged by State City Bank actually leaves $18,000 in cash for the developer to pay closing and soft costs.

Recalling that this loan was made with a floating interest rate initially at 9 percent, we assume that the prime lending rate increases 1 percent at the beginning of the seventh month, making the interest rate on this loan 10 percent. Based on the draw schedule in Exhibit 16–3 and taking into account the interest rate change, the total amount owed State City Bank at the end of 12 months is $1,057,751. This is slightly less than the construction loan commitment of $1.1 million and the take-out commitment which was also $1.1 million.

The draw schedule and corresponding interest and loan balance computations serve as the construction lender's *financial control* on the project. Should the loan balance as a percentage of the total commitment become higher than the percentage of construction completed, this would signal a possible cost overrun due perhaps to rising material or labor prices. Similarly, if the developer and the architect, who is verifying the construction in place, differ on the amount of draw necessary to pay for materials and labor used in the preceding month, this may signal a potential problem both for the developer and the lender.

Project completion and sale of the construction mortgage. Assuming that the project is ready to begin leasing space by the end of 10 months[9] and that the 70 percent occupancy contingency and all other contingencies in the take-out commitment are met at the end of 12 months, the construction mortgage is ready for sale to the permanent lender. Since the $1,057,751 mortgage amount shown in Exhibit 16–3 is slightly below the $1.1 million commitment made by the permanent lender, that lender will issue payment for $1,057,751 to the construction lender in exchange for the construction mortgage and note.[10]

Effective interest cost and construction loans. An interesting question for the developer now arises concerning the actual cost of this construction loan. What would State City Bank's yield, or internal rate of return, be on this loan? Since the original interest rate on the loan was 9 percent, and since the prime rate went up by 1 percent at the beginning of the seventh month, making the monthly interest charge 10 percent, and a loan origination fee of $33,000 was charged by State City Bank, it is not clear precisely what the effective cost (yield) to the developer (lender) is in this case. The solution to this problem can be determined by again reviewing the data in Exhibit 16–3. The last column in

---

[9] Rentals usually begin before the last draws are made by the developer. By obtaining leases as soon as possible, the 70 percent rental achievement, which is a contingency in the take-out commitment, has a better chance of being met.

[10] If the construction mortgage balance should exceed $1.1 million, the permanent lender would be committed to only $1.1 million if the project were finished on the completion date and all other contingencies were satisfied. The construction lender would then be forced to hold a second mortgage for the difference between the construction loan balance and $1.1 million, if the construction lender approved the additional draws.

the exhibit shows the actual net cash outflow to Global. This outflow represents State City's net *investment* in the construction loan made to Global. Since the construction loan is sold to Acme Life Insurance Company for $1,057,751, this represents the *net cash return* to State City Bank. Hence the yield on this construction loan can be determined by *finding the interest rate which makes the present value of the return equal to the present value of the investment outlays*. This unknown interest rate is the internal rate of return or true yield on the construction loan.

The procedure used to find the interest rate which will make the present value of inflows and outflows equal is detailed in Exhibit 16–4. The series of cash flows is unusual in this case because the net cash outflows from the bank go out over different time intervals, and the single cash return comes in at the end of the loan period. By discounting *all cash inflows and outflows* during the period in which the flows occur, we take into account the very important fact that interest is earned *on loan amounts, only as those amounts are actually disbursed*.

In computing the present values we do not know what interest rate to use. (This is what we are searching for.) We must use a trial and error approach.[11] Note in Exhibit 16–4 that the first interest rate used for discounting, 16 percent, results in a present value of outflows equal to $905,189 and a present value of inflows of $902,314. If 16 percent were the correct internal rate of return, the present value of inflows and outflows would be equal. Since they are not equal, we know that 16 percent is not the correct rate. However, we do know that the present value of inflows is less than the present value of outflows when 16 percent is used; hence, we know that 16 percent is too large. By trying 15 percent, we see that the present value of inflows, $911,263, is now greater than the present value of outflows, $908,650.[12] We know now that the true yield on this loan falls between 15 and 16 percent. This yield is obviously much higher than either the original interest rate on the loan of 9 percent or the increase to 10 percent that occurred after six months. This higher yield is primarily caused by the $33,000 origination fee charged at closing, which the borrower has paid back with loan funds obtained from the take-out commitment.[13]

---

[11] The rate is found as a part of the trial and error process. However, we do know from Exhibit 16–3 that total net cash flow to the developer is $963,000 and the loan balance totaled $1,057,751 after 12 months. The difference, or $94,751, is the net cash return received by the bank over the undiscounted outlays ($963,000). If we assume for the moment that the $1,057,751 loan balance occurred evenly over 12 months, the *average* loan balance would be one half, or $528,876. The cash return of $94,751 divided by $528,826 is about 18%. This rough average percentage gives us a starting point.

[12] Note that both the present values of inflows *and* outflows change when the discount rate is charged.

[13] This result would not change even if the origination fee was paid in cash by the borrower at closing.

EXHIBIT 16–4
Determining the effective interest cost of construction loans

Month	Net cash outflows	IF, PV of $1 (16 percent)	PV	IF, PV of $1 (15 percent)	PV
Outflows:					
Close	$ 18,000	—	$ 18,000	—	$ 18,000
1	—	—	—	—	—
2	175,000	.97386	170,426	.97546	170,706
3	175,000	.96104	168,182	.96342	168,599
4	150,000	.94840	142,260	.95152	142,728
5	125,000	.93592	116,990	.93978	117,473
6	100,000	.92360	92,360	.92817	92,817
7	90,000	.91145	82,031	.91672	82,505
8	50,000	.89946	44,973	.90540	45,270
9	30,000	.88762	26,629	.89442	26,827
10	20,000	.87549	17,519	.88318	17,664
11	20,000	.86442	17,288	.87228	17,446
12	10,000	.85305	8,531	.86151	8,615
Present value total outflows			$905,189		$908,650

Month	Net cash inflow	IF, PV of $1 (16 percent)	PV	IF, PV of $1 (15 percent)	PV
Inflows:					
12	$1,057,751	.85305	$902,314	.86151	$911,263

Interpolation–construction loans. Should the solution of between 15 and 16 percent not be precise enough for the lender or borrower, interpolation will result in a closer approximation to the actual yield. Interpolation is slightly more complicated in this situation than in examples shown in earlier chapters because we do not have a desired present value. However, we can proceed according to the following formula:

$$PV \text{ of inflows} - PV \text{ of outflows} = \text{Difference}$$

Discounting at 16 percent:	$902,314	–	$905,189	=	–$2,875
Discounting at 15 percent:	$911,263	–	$908,650	=	$2,613

We would like to know the interest rate which when used for discounting will make the difference in present values of all inflows and outflows equal to zero. By looking at the relative size of differences in present values obtained after discounting, we can see that the difference obtained when 15 percent is used, or $2,613, is closer to zero. This indicates that the solution is closer to 15 percent. To estimate the actual yield, we first determine the total difference from zero that results when both 15 and 16 percent are used for discounting. This total difference is $2,613 + $2,875 or $5,488. Note that when finding this total difference we ignore the fact that $2,875 is negative. This is because when interpolating we are interested only in how far each difference is from zero without regard to whether the difference is positive or negative. To solve for the yield we proceed as follows:

Difference in interest rate (16% − 15%)	= 1%
Sum of differences in present values	= $5,488
Difference in present value for *lowest* interest rate (15%)	= $2,613
Ratio of ($2,613 ÷ $5,488) × 1%	= 0.48%
Adding 15% + 0.48%	= 15.48%

This interpolation procedure shows that a better estimate of the true yield (cost) of this loan to the lender (developer) is 15.48 percent.

Land development loans

To raise the capital necessary to acquire undeveloped land, make on-site and off-site improvements, and then subdivide and sell parcels for homesites or for mixed uses, developers rely on land development loans. As with construction loans, funds are borrowed or "taken down" in stages, usually monthly, based on the percentage of development work completed and verified. An open-end mortgage is used as security for the loan. It usually gives the lender first lien on the land being developed and first lien on all improvements when completed and as funds are disbursed. As in the case of a construction loan, the lender normally requires bonding and personal guarantees by the developer as a condition for obtaining the loan.

Unlike the construction loan, however, repayment of the land development loan is dependent on the sale of building sites to other developers. In other words, in the case of a construction loan, a takeout commitment generally is obtained by a builder, assuring the construction lender that the loan will be purchased by a long-term lender. This is usually *not* the case in land development situations, as loan repayments are made when parcels are sold to *individual builders*. As a result, land development loans are usually *more risky* than most construction loans. The lender must accurately assess the risk of the project and the rate at which parcels will be sold in order to determine whether the loan can be repaid.

Much of the analysis and many requirements used in construction lending are also utilized in land development lending. Financial statements, appraisal reports, and market studies are analyzed closely by the lender. In addition, detailed plans and costs are reviewed by an architect or engineer. As development progresses, monthly inspections must be made to verify all work done before a draw can be made against the loan commitment. All preclosing requirements relating to bonding, subcontracts, title insurance, hazard insurance, zoning verification, building permits, and so on, discussed in connection with construction loans, also commonly apply to land development loans. However, since usually no takeout commitment exists in land development situations the lender making the development loan assumes the full financial risk associated with the success or failure of the project.

Funds for repaying the loan come from the sale of individual parcels by the developer; therefore, a portion of the proceeds from each parcel sale must be paid to the lender. This amount, negotiated by the lender and developer, is referred to as the *release price.* When a parcel is sold and the developer pays the release price to the lender, the lender in turn signs a release statement waiving all liens against the parcel sold. Clear title may then pass to the buyer of the parcel. The lender uses this release clause in the mortgage as a control on the development loan to assure repayment as parcels are sold.

Land development loans illustrated. Landco Development Company has approached Mid City Mortgage Company concerning a 50-acre tract of land which it would like to improve and subdivide into 120 building sites. The land is available at $8,000 per acre, or $400,000, and has been zoned R-1 for residential development. Each parcel should sell in a price range of $8,000 to $12,000, depending on location within the subdivision. An appraisal has been made on the project based on comparable building sites available in the market. At an average value of $10,000 per parcel, it is estimted that the project will have an appraised value of $1.2 million when completed. Landco figures that direct costs on the project will total $733,000, as shown in detail in Exhibit 16–5.

EXHIBIT 16–5
Project cost estimates, Landco Development Company

Land...	$320,000
Other direct costs:	
$30 per lineal foot................................	300,000
1. Grading.	
2. Streets.	
3. Subsurface improvements.	
Engineering and other fieldwork.......................	23,000
General and administrative expenses directly	
associated with development......................	80,000
Miscellaneous......................................	10,000
Total...	$733,000

Landco wants to borrow this amount from Mid City. Landco has made a $100,000 down payment on the land.

Mid City will make a careful analysis of Landco's appraisal report, cost estimates, and market study. Then it will conduct its own appraisal, based on comparable land sales, to confirm whether the $1.2 million value estimated for the completed project is reasonable. If granted, the loan will represent approximately 61 percent of value ($733,000 ÷ $1,200,000). This loan-to-value ratio falls within the range acceptable by most lenders.[14] Based on current financial market conditions, if Mid City agrees to make the loan, it will be made at 12 percent interest and, in addition, a loan origination fee of $15,000 will be charged.

Mid City has agreed to disburse the $320,000 balance required to purchase the land and to fund the $15,000 origination fee from the loan commitment at closing. A monthly schedule of the draws estimated by Landco as necessary to complete the project on time is detailed in Exhibit 16–6.

EXHIBIT 16–6
Schedule of estimated monthly cash draws for development costs, Landco Development Company

Month	Amount	Month	Amount
Closing	$320,000	7.	$ 33,333
1.	50,000	8.	33,333
2.	50,000	9.	33,333
3.	50,000	10.	18,833
4.	35,500	11.	18,833
5.	35,500	12.	18,333
6.	35,500	Total	$733,000

Landco believes that sales of parcels should start seven months after development begins and that sales will progress according to the following schedule:

Months	Sales per month	Cumulative sales
7–12	4	24
13–24	5	60
25–36	3	36
		120

Based on this estimate, all the parcels should be sold three years from the beginnning of the development.

Repayment pattern—land development loans.   The first item to be negotiated between the developer and lender is the *release price* for each parcel, that

---

[14] Most lenders will not allow the loan-to-value ratio on land development loans to exceed a range of 60 to 70 percent of value, or the actual cost of improvements.

is, the amount that must be repaid by the developer to the lender from the proceeds of each parcel sale. To accomplish this, the lender will first estimate the *average loan and interest per parcel* available for sale. This is computed by taking from Exhibit 16–6 (1) the monthly estimates of draws necessary for Landco to complete the project and (2) the estimated rate at which parcels will be sold, and then combining these estimates in a schedule such as the one in Exhibit 16–7. Recalling that the first draw of $320,000 will be taken down at

EXHIBIT 16–7
Schedule of monthly draws and loan repayments, Landco Development Company

(a)	(b)	(c)	(d)	(e) Present value	
			IFPV of $1 per month	(b) × (d)	(c) × (d)
Month	Repayment	Draws	12 percent	Repayment	Draws
Close	-0-	$335,000	—	-0-	$335,000
1–3	-0-	50,000	2.941	-0-	147,050
4–6	-0-	35,500	5.795– 2.941	-0-	101,317
7–9	4(x)	33,333	8.566– 5.795	11.084(x)	92,366
10–12	4(x)	18,833	11.255– 8.566	10.576(x)	50,642
13–24	5(x)	-0-	21.243–11.255	49.940(x)	-0-
25–36	3(x)	-0-	30.108–21.243	26.595(x)	-0-
				98.195(x)	$726,375

closing, and that a $15,000 loan origination fee will be charged, the loan balance payable as of the closing date is $335,000. Exhibit 16–7 summarizes the way in which the cash inflows and outflows must occur from the closing date for Landco to repay the initial $335,000 loan balance and all subsequent draws at the end of three years.

Looking at Exhibit 16–7 more closely, column (a) represents the months during which future inflows and outflows are expected to occur. Column (b) represents the loan and interest per lot that must be paid to the lender by the developer to assure that the loan is repaid during the 36-month period in which sales are to occur. Since we do not know yet how much must be paid to the lender from parcel sales, we designate those dollar payments as x, or the unknown we are trying to determine. We do know, however, that these unknown amounts x will be repaid at the rate of four payments per month during months 7–12. Five payments per month during months 13–24, and three payments per month during months 25–36. Column (c), represents loan draws that are expected during the period of development and parcel sales.

Column (d) in Exhibit 16–7 contains interest factors for the PV of $1 per month at 12 percent. As was done in the previous section on construction lending, these factors are applied against the amounts in both columns (b) and (c). This assures that when x is determined, it will be great enough to earn the lender 12 percent on all net loan amounts outstanding over the 36-month period. Discounting all outflows by 12 percent assures that interest will be earned on loan amounts only when they are drawn down. By discounting the inflows at 12 percent, account is taken of the fact that the repayments do not occur all at once but rather over time. Hence the return being earned by the lender is occurring over time.[15] It should be noted that the *IFs* used in column (d) must also be netted out so that only the *portion* of the IF applicable to a given time period is used. For example, in months 7–9, the *IF* for nine months, 8.566, must be reduced by the *IF* for six months, 5.795, so that the difference, 2.771, representing the specific 7–9 month interval, is used in the computation. This netting of *IFs* must be done each time the cash inflow or outflow changes during a specified time interval, such as three months, a year, and so on.[16] Column (e) represents the present value of all inflows and outflows occuring over the 36-month period. Since the original loan balance of $335,000 must be repaid from the net repayments, it should now be clear that x, the unknown amount of loan repayment, must be large enough to repay the initial $335,000 loan balance and all subsequent draws, plus 12 percent interest.

With all of the information assembled in Exhibit 16–7, the estimated loan and interest per parcel can be determined. Since the present value of all loan draws, $726,375, must equal the present value of x payments, x can be solved as follows:

$$726,375 = 98.195(x)$$
$$726,375 \div 98.195 = (x)$$
$$7,397 = (x)$$

From this analysis it can be seen that from the average parcel sale price of $10,000, if the lender wanted the loan fully repaid after 36 months when all parcels are sold, the amount of loan repayment would be $7,397 per parcel, or effectively 74 percent of the average parcel price.[17]

Determination of the release price. Based on the estimated loan and interest per parcel of $7,397, if sales of building sites proceed as scheduled, the

---

[15] This procedure is exactly the same as that used earlier in determining the internal rate of return on the construction loan. Only now we know the rate of return on which repayments are to be based is 12 percent and we are trying to determine the loan repayments. This situation also differs from construction lending in that like the draws, the returns also occur over time. In the construciton lending case, only one return was realized by the lender when the loan was sold to the permanent lender.

[16] It should be recalled from the problems at the end of Chapter 6 that what is being done here is netting out *IFs* to correspond to annuities received during specified time intervals.

[17] At this point, the reader can return to Exhibit 16–7 and substitute $7,397, for all of the x's in column (b). When discounted by 12 percent (column [d]), carried over to column (e), and totaled, it can be seen that the present value of repayments would equal $726,375, or the present value of all draws. This proves that the loan is fully repaid and that the lender has earned 12 percent on th. monthly outstanding loan balance.

borrower will have the development loan repaid when all 120 parcels are sold, or after 36 months. When most land development loans are made, however, the lender will demand a release price *greater* than the estimated loan and interest per parcel. This is because the lender usually does not want to take the risk associated with a possible slowdown in sales in the later stages of the project. In many land developments, choice parcels are sold early and less desirable ones remain unsold over time. Since some parcels are difficult to sell, the lender wants assurance that the developer takes this added risk. Consequently, the lender will bargain for a high release price, hoping that the loan will be repaid before all 120 parcels are sold.

Another reason for negotiating a higher release price is that since Mid City puts most of the "front-end" money into the development during the first 12 months (see the draws in column [c] of Exhibit 16–7), it wants assurance that the loan repayment is given preference as sales proceeds are realized. In addition, since the average sales price is estimated to be $10,000, if the loan repayment is set at $7,397, the developer will share in proceeds in the amount of $10,000 − $7,397, or $2,603 for each parcel sold. Since the lender wants the loan repaid more rapidly, there is still room to negotiate for a higher release price, such that the developer retains a smaller portion of the $2,603 available from each sale.

In many land development loans, the release price per parcel ranges from 110 to 120 percent of the estimated loan and interest per parcel. The exact price is negotiated based on how soon the lender wants the loan repaid, how much cash the developer must retain from each parcel sale to cover other expenses and profit, and conditions in the loan market. For example, if a 110 percent release price is chosen, the developer retains about $1,863 per sale ($10,000 less $7,397 × 1.10); and if 120 percent is used, the developer will retain only $1,124. Most lenders prefer to have the loan fully repaid when approximately 80 percent of all parcels are sold. They try to negotiate a release price to accomplish this end. In our illustration this would mean that after 96 parcels are sold the lender would like to have the loan repaid.

Obviously the release price chosen will affect the cash flow of both the lender and developer and will be determined by competition among lenders desiring to make the loan. The developer usually prefers the loan offer with the *lowest* release price to increase cash flow in the early stages of development. In practice, the effects of any particular release price must be projected to determine (1) when the loan can be repaid and (2) whether the cash position of the developer is strong enough to maintain cash solvency over the development and marketing period.

Loan repayment schedule—land development loans.   To estimate when the land development loan will be repaid by Landco under a negotiated release price, we assume that the release price is set at 120 percent of the $7,397 loan and interest per parcel. This results in a $8,875 (rounded) release price per parcel. Based on an average appraised value of $10,000 per parcel, the release price represents 88.75 percent of the value of individual parcels.[18] With the schedule of draws, the forecasted sales schedule, and the release price known, a repayment schedule like the one shown in Exhibit 16–8 can be developed to ascertain when, and after how many parcels are sold, the loan will be repaid.

Looking at Exhibit 16–8, the first column contains the beginning loan balance in each month the loan is outstanding. The second column shows the monthly draws required by the developer to complete construction (Exhibit 16–6). Interest is computed at an annual rate of 12 percent compounded monthly, or at a monthly rate of 1 percent (12% ÷ 12 months). No payments are made for six months until parcel sales begin. Interest is accrued during that time period and carried in the loan balance. The loan payments, based on the $8,875 release price times the number of monthly parcel sales, are shown in the third column. If development proceeds as scheduled, draws are taken down as estimated, and parcel sales are made as projected, the developer will repay the loan during the 29th month. In terms of parcel sales, as of the 28th month, 96 parcels would be sold. Since a $9,924 loan balance remains going into the 29th month and the release price is $8,875, this means that the loan will be repaid with the sale of two additional parcels in the 29th month, or after a total of 98 parcels are sold. With the sale of 98 parcels required to repay the loan, this represents about 82 percent of the 120 parcels available. This percentage is close to the 80 percent requirement specified by most lenders on land development projects.[19]

Developer—cash flow, profitability. From the loan repayment schedule just detailed, with a negotiated $8,875 release price based on an average sale price of $10,000, the developer will retain an average of $1,125 ($10,000 − $8,875) from each parcel sale until the 29th month, or until the 98th parcel is sold. After that point is reached, the developer will retain the full $10,000 average sale price through the sale of the 120th parcel. Clearly, this is when the greatest profit will be earned by the developer. However, during the development period and until the sale of the 98th parcel, a question arises concerning the developer's ability to meet operating expenses and other requirements. The amount loaned to the developer is to cover only the *direct costs* associated with development. Other obligations, such as sales commissions, property taxes, and general and administrative expenses after actual development is complete, must be covered from the cash retained by the developer from each parcel sale or from internal working capital.

---

[18] In practice, the developer will provide the lender with a schedule of lot prices for each parcel within the development. The lender will in turn apply approximately 88.75 percent to each parcel price to obtain the schedule of release prices for all parcels in the project. When each parcel is sold and the scheduled release price is paid, the lender then signs the release form giving clear title to the buyer.

[19] This percentage can also be estimated by subtracting the release premium of 20 percent from 100 percent, thereby obtaining 80 percent of the parcels. The loan payoff period can then be established by consulting the estimated rate of absorption.

EXHIBIT 16–8

Loan repayment schedule, Landco Development Company

Month	(1) Beginning balance	(2) Draws*	(3) Payments*	(4) Interest†	(5) Ending balance
Close..................	$ 15,000‡	$320,000		—	$335,000
1.....................	335,000	50,000		$ 3,350	388,350
2.....................	388,350	50,000		3,884	442,234
3.....................	442,234	50,000		4,422	496,656
4.....................	496,656	35,500		4,967	537,123
5.....................	537,123	35,500		5,371	577,994
6.....................	577,994	35,500		5,780	619,274
7.....................	619,274	33,333	$ 35,500	6,193	623,300
8.....................	623,300	33,333	35,500	6,233	627,366
9.....................	627,366	33,333	35,500	6,274	631,473
10....................	631,473	18,833	35,500	6,315	621,121
11....................	621,121	18,833	35,500	6,211	610,665
12....................	610,665	18,833	35,500	6,107	600,105
13....................	600,105		44,375	6,001	561,731
14....................	561,731		44,375	5,617	522,973
15....................	522,973		44,375	5,230	483,828
16....................	483,828		44,375	4,838	444,291
17....................	444,291		44,375	4,443	404,359
18....................	404,359		44,375	4,044	364,028
19....................	364,028		44,375	3,640	323,293
20....................	323,293		44,375	3,233	282,151
21....................	282,151		44,375	2,822	240,598
22....................	240,598		44,375	2,406	198,629
23....................	198,629		44,375	1,986	156,240
24....................	156,240		44,375	1,562	113,427
25....................	113,427		26,625	1,134	87,936
26....................	87,936		26,625	879	62,190
27....................	62,190		26,625	622	36,187
28....................	36,187		26,625	362	9,924
29....................	9,924		10,023	99	—
		$733,000	$862,025	$144,025	—

* Draws and payments occur at the end of the month; columns do not total because of rounding.
† Computed at 1 percent per month on the beginning monthly loan balance.
‡ Loan origination fee funded from commitment.

To investigate the developer's ability to carry this project until the loan is repaid, a schedule of cash flows for the developer must be constructed that contains not only the direct cost elements but also additional day-to-day operating expenses. In this way, the developer's cash position can be projected and the risk of loan default better analyzed. Exhibit 16–9 contains a quarterly summary of all cash inflows and outflows for Landco over the entire life of the project. The outflows for direct costs in the cash flow schedule are taken from the schedule of monthly draws (Exhibit 16–6). Loan repayments are taken from the schedule of loan repayments (Exhibit 16–8). Other operating

EXHIBIT 16–8

Schedule of cash flow, Landco Development Company

Quarter	Close	(1)	(2)	(3)	(4)	(5)	(6)	(7)	(8)	(9)	(10)	(11)	(12)
Inflow:													
Sales	$335,000			$120,000	$120,000	$150,000	$150,000	$150,000	$150,000	$90,000	$90,000	$90,000	$90,000
Loan draws		$150,000	$106,500	100,000	56,500								
Total inflow	$335,000	$150,000	$106,500	$220,000	$176,500	$150,000	$150,000	$150,000	$150,000	$90,000	$90,000	$90,000	$90,000
Outflow:													
Land purchase	$300,000												
Closing fees	35,000												
Loan repayment		$150,000	$106,500	$106,500	$106,500	$133,125	$133,125	$133,125	$133,125	$79,875			
Direct costs				100,000	56,500						$36,648		
Other expenses:													
General and administrative					3,000	3,000	3,000	3,000	3,000	3,000	2,000	2,000	2,000
Property tax					3,000		2,500		2,500		2,000		1,500
Sales expense				6,000	6,000	7,500	7,500	7,500	7,500	4,500	4,500	4,500	4,500
Total outflow	$335,000	$150,000	$106,500	$212,500	$175,000	$143,625	$146,125	$143,625	$146,125	$87,375	$45,148	$6,500	$8,000
Net cash in (out)	-0-	-0-	-0-	$7,500	$1,500	$6,375	$3,875	$6,375	$3,875	$2,625	$44,852	$83,500	$82,000

expenses, including general and administrative expenses, sales commissions, and property taxes, have been estimated on a quarterly basis and included in the exhibit.

An analysis of Exhibit 16–9 provides insight into Landco's ability to carry the cash needs of the entire project. It should be noted that in the first two quarters there is no net cash flow available to Landco, and from the third through ninth quarters, cash flow is positive but a very small amount. It is during such periods that estimates concerning costs, sales, rates, and repayment conditions become crucial to both Landco and Mid City. If the time needed for development exceeds initial estimates, if development costs exceed estimates, or if sales do not materialize as projected, it is clear that Landco's cash flow position will change dramatically. Similarly, if Mid City requires a release price that is too high, this may also serve to reduce the cash flow to Landco, which may jeopardize Landco's ability to carry out the project and to repay the loan. For this reason, Landco's own financial resources must be considered by Mid City in the event that any of these adverse factors materializes. Clearly, if Landco's cash position in this project becomes questionable, Mid City will be reluctant to advance funds for operating expenses in addition to direct costs. In this event, Landco will be expected to share in some of the risk by contributing working capital from its own resources to complete sale of the project successfully. To analyze Landco's ability to advance working capital, should it be necessary, Mid City will thoroughly review the company's income statement and balance sheet as well as possibly requiring additional loan security or guarantees from Landco beyond this particular project.

Finally it should be noted that based on Exhibit 16–9, Landco's profitability does not materialize significantly until the last three quarters of the project. This is in keeping with the way in which risk is taken during the project. Because the lender puts in "front-end" capital, it wants assurance of a high priority in the sales proceeds as the development matures. Consequently, Landco must wait until the lender's prior claim is satisfied before it realizes a return. However, from Landco's viewpoint, since its equity in the project increases with the market value of the project as actual development occurs, and since its front-end investment is virtually zero, all returns are appropriately deferred to the later stages of the project.

Extension agreements. In the land development case just illustrated, the date that Mid City anticipates that the loan will be repaid is during the 29th month. Since it is possible that the loan will not be paid at that time due to development problems or the slow sale of parcels, the lender will usually require an extension clause in the initial loan contract. This clause specifies that an additional charge will be made for any extra time needed to repay the loan. This amounts to gap financing, or additional interim financing, and the lender will usually charge an extension fee in addition to interest on the outstanding loan balance, if an extension is needed.

Questions

1   For undeveloped properties on which borrowers seek permanent financing, what are the two major types of loan commitments? Which category do construction lenders prefer and why?

2   What is a buy and sell agreement? Why have these agreements been used with increasing frequency?

3   What is gap financing? Why is it necessary? Is its use desirable by both borrowers and lenders?

4   "The fact that takeout commitments are commonly required as a condition for obtaining a construction loan takes a lot of the risk out of the situation for the construction lender." Evaluate this statement.

5   What does bonding mean? When is it used?

6   What does a floating interest rate loan mean? How does it work?

7   What controls are usually employed by the construction lender when disbursement of loan funds is made? How does the lender attempt to control risks of cost overruns?

8   When a construction loan is made, interest charges are often built into cost estimates by the developer. Why is this done? How does this affect the monthly cash position of both the lender and borrower? Since the interest is effectively borrowed, how and when does the bank earn its return?

9   What is usually the maximum loan amount that a construction lender will make a commitment for?

10   If a construction loan totals more than the takeout commitment due to a cost overrun or other cause, what are the obligations of the construction lender and the permanent lender who made the takeout commitment?

11   How do land development loans and construction loans differ with respect to lending risks?

12   What is a release price? How is it determined? Why is it used?

13   How does use of a release price in a land development loan tend to even out the risks to the borrower and developer in land development situations? Why do lenders usually insist that land development loans be repaid when approximately 80 percent of parcels are sold?

14   How can the lender and developer be assured that the release price in a land development loan is reasonable and that the developer will be able to carry the projects until all parcels are sold?

Case problems

1   ABC Development Company has approached National County Bank concerning a construction loan for a shopping center on land owned by ABC. ABC has a takeout commitment for up to $1,000,000 from Rock of Gibraltar Insurance Company. National County Bank has reviewed the project costs, ABC's financial statements, the appraisal, and the takeout commitment and has decided to make the construction loan.

The loan commitment will be for up to the same amount as the takeout commitment and will carry a 12 percent interest rate plus a 2 percent loan origination fee ($20,000).

ABC has provided the estimates of monthly construction costs which National City agrees are realistic. Closing costs are included in this schedule and the $20,000 loan origination fee is included in closing costs.

Monthly construction cost estimate
ABC Development Company

Month		Month	
Close	$ 40,000		
1.	—	7.	$50,000
2.	200,000	8.	50,000
3.	200,000	9.	40,000
4.	100,000	10.	40,000
5.	75,000	11.	30,000
6.	75,000	12.	10,000

Based on the estimated completion schedule, the permanent lender is scheduled to buy the construction loan from National County Bank 12 months after closing the construction loan.

a. Complete a draw schedule and loan statement like the one in Exhibit 16–2 (assume the estimated monthly construction costs are accurate).

b. Assuming the permanent lender buys the construction loan for the balance outstanding after 12 months, what is the yield (cost) to the lender (developer)?

2 Community Development Corporation (CDC) is seeking financing for acquisition and development of 90 home sites. The land acquisition will cost $350,000 and direct development costs are estimated to be an additional $350,000. City Federal Bank has indicated that it is interested in making the loan at 12 percent interest with additional closing costs of $10,000 and a loan origination fee of $20,000 to be funded from the loan commitment. The appraised value of the project, based on an average parcel price of $10,500, is $945,000. After making a down payment of $100,000, CDC believes that it will have to take down $250,000 of the land cost, the closing fee of $10,000, and the $20,000 origination fee when the loan is actually closed. The remaining direct cost of $350,000 will be taken down in ten equal installments of $35,000 beginning the first month after closing. Parcel sales are expected to begin during the seventh month after closing at the rate of five parcels per month. The company and the bank have also agreed to a release price of 120 percent of the estimated loan and interest per parcel.

a. Based on the above information, compute an estimate of the loan and interest per parcel for sale by CDC.

b. From your answer in (*a*), what will be the release price?

c. Based on (*b*) and the pattern of loan draws, when will CDC have the loan fully repaid?

d. Besides the computations above, what other factors will the lender consider in evaluating CDC's loan proposal?

Real estate syndication

17

Meaning

The concept of real estate syndication extends generally to any group of investors who have contributed funds for the common purpose of carrying out a real estate project requiring a concentration of capital. It may take the business form of:

1. Corporation.
2. Joint ownership.
3. Joint venture.
4. Partnership.

The corporate form.   Incorporation of the business generally provides such advantages as continuity of life, marketability of ownership shares, and ease of estate planning, since security values are more ascertainable. It also limits the liability of the shareholders to the amount of the cost of their shares. A major disadvantage of this form, however, is the exposure of the investor to double taxation. The corporation pays income tax on the project earnings and the investor-shareholder pays income tax on the residual earnings at his marginal tax rate, as they are paid to him as dividends by the corporation. For this reason, the corporate form has been less attractive than others in providing less vulnerability to taxation.

Joint ownership.   There are also difficulties attendant upon the use of joint ownership, usually tenancy-in-common. Death of a syndicate investor brings problems of estate administration into the project. The refusal of one member to cooperate may under some conditions create a general stalemate.

Joint venture.   This form has been used extensively for private real estate syndicates. Groups may acquire a succession of properties calling for differing arrangements with investors and for financing with each separate property. The precise tailoring required for each venture limits the usefulness of this form for public syndication.

Partnership.   The partnership, usually modified to a limited partnership, has become the *most popular* syndicate form. The partnership is not treated as a separate entity for tax purposes, and therefore, the profits are flowed directly to each member of the firm in proportion to his participation. When the limited partnership form is used, the investor may become a limited partner and thereby limit his liability of loss to his capital contribution. Only the general partner carries unlimited liability for creditor obligations of the firm. Properly established, the limited partnership form provides most of the advantages, without the tax disadvantages, of the corporate form. This explains its attraction for public syndication.

Types of syndicates

There are two important types of syndicates: private and public. A private syndication is so limited in the number of participants in the offering as to render compliance with securities laws a minimal task. A public offering, on the other hand, is characterized by rigorous compliance requirements of the federal and state securities divisions governing the sale of securities to the public. Numerous reports, brochures, prospectuses, and the like are required to qualify an issue for sale to the public.

Private real estate syndicates.   Private real estate syndicates are usually made up of a few local friends and business associates who think they see a speculative opportunity in real estate operations. They operate informally, sometimes to their disadvantage, and the public seldom knows of their existence. They pool their resources to establish a fund, either for the purpose of purchasing an equity in a property already encumbered by a mortgage or upon which a mortgage is placed as a part of the deal, or for the purpose of paying for a property so that they may own it free from encumbrances. Different circumstances may dictate one or the other of these methods of financing the property.

Each separate transaction is set up as a joint venture, even though the same individuals may participate in successive deals of this kind. Title to the property purchased may be taken in the name of one member of the syndicate who serves as its manager or in the name of some corporate trustee. In either event, the terms of the syndicate agreement should be set forth with greater particularity than is usually followed. Misunderstandings and miscalculations may be better avoided by more explicit written agreements. Even though an elaborate agreement is drawn up, it is usually known only to participants in the syndicate. No representation is made to outsiders that would lead them to consider this type of syndicate as a general partnership.

As in any other business venture, numerous questions may arise in the future that should be anticipated at the time the deal is made. Among them are the following: (1) responsibility, compensation, and authority of manager or trustee, if one is used; (2) method of voting upon issues to be settled by members—one vote per man or votes distributed according to amount of financial contribution to the resources of the syndicate; (3) improvement policies—modernization of old buildings or even replacement as the best means of realizing greatest profits from the venture; (4) assessments of members and methods of collecting them; (5) methods of dealing with members who refuse or are unable to meet assessments; (6) methods of disposal of syndicate interests of members wishing or forced to dispose of them; and (7) names of syndicate members, the amounts of their individual contributions, and the manner of sharing profits or losses.

This type of syndicate is normally used to finance a real estate speculative venture. It can, however, be used for investment purposes as well. The kinds of properties dealt in include vacant land thought to be about ready for subdividing; apartment or office buildings, or even factories; or any kind of property whose present owners may be in need of immediate financial rescue. In other words, real estate syndicates may be associated with financial distress.

The qualifications of members of real estate syndicates of this type should include the following: (1) They should have available resources that could be devoted to such a venture for whatever period of time is necessary without embarrassment. (2) They should have the courage required to embark upon a type of business operation that may involve considerable risk. (3) They should have the patience needed to stay with the program which they undertake until they test their best opportunities for profit from it. In some cases this may take several years with annual expenses and taxes to pay but no income to offset them. (4) They should be well enough acquainted with each other to be able to act in harmony, come what may. Ventures of this kind require a high degree of mutual confidence, both among the members and in the syndicate manager.

Various practices are followed with respect to the determination of issues to be settled involving the interests of syndicate members. Under one method of operation, the chief contribution made by the members is financial. They pay their money over to the manager and let him make all decisions concerning its use. This has the advantage of avoiding conflicts of opinions but places a considerable burden of choice upon one man. Under other methods, all major decisions are made by syndicate members. This is the more democratic approach, but may result in differences that are not easily resolved. If a trustee holds title to the property in trust for the members, it is not expected that he will be required or permitted to make major decisions affecting their interests. The agreement should make this clear, to avoid future complications.

Public real estate syndicates. Particularly since the mid-1950s, a number of large syndicators have spearheaded a new trend involving the public in real estate syndication. Certificates of participation have been sold in units as low as $500, $1,000, or $5,000—amounts which were previously considered too small. The result has been that instead of a few participants of substantial means and risk-taking ability, the syndicate membership may be composed of thousands of small investors who have been intrigued by promises of a tax-sheltered high return per year. An early example of the operation finds the syndicator and his chosen associates advancing $100,000 for the general partnership interest. Limited partnership interests were then offered to the public in $1,000 or $5,000 units for a total of $4.4 million. With the $4.5 million of equity funds, the syndicate bought a real estate complex costing $10 million, mortgaging the property for the difference. The promised high return to limited partners was to a great extent conditional on the income potential of the property. Furthermore, at least a portion of the return was considered for tax purposes to be a recovery of capital for depreciation of the property. Many investors in such cases assume a permanently rising price level which will offset actual dollar depreciation in real estate. If this condition does not hold, however, the investor finds that his depreciation deduction is a true cost as well as a tax item, and that his return is lower by that amount.

In an operation of this kind the syndicate general partners share few of the risks. They may have originally bought through another business entity and sold it to the syndicate at a profit. Through another company which they own they may receive substantial remuneration for management services. Above all, as the general partners, all earnings and capital gains not contracted away to the limited partners accrue to their benefit. They stand to gain all residual benefits. This has been a matter of increasingly grave concern to state and federal securities sales regulators.

Use of the limited partnership in private and public syndicates.   The limited partnership is the most widely used legal form of organization for syndications. The limited partnership has the major advantage of a corporation—liability for firm business obligations limited to a specific capital contribution—and does not incur the disadvantage of the corporate form of not being able to pass business operating losses through to the firm owners. The limited partnership is not treated as a separate taxable entity like the corporation. The partnership losses, therefore, are distributable directly to the partners in accordance with their loss-sharing ratio, whereas in a corporation such losses can only be offset against corporate income of other periods.

In establishing the limited partnership, great care must be taken that the contractual terms identify it in effect as a partnership and not as an "association" as understood by the Internal Revenue Service. An association is taxed like a corporation. The six criteria for treatment like a corporation are the presence of:

1. Business associates.
2. An objective to carry on the business and divide the gains therefrom.
3. Continuity of life.

4. Centralization of management.
5. Limited liability.
6. Free transferability of interest.

A corporation must have more corporate than noncorporate characteristics to be classified as a corporation for tax purposes. Criteria 1 and 2 above are common to both corporations and partnerships. It is, therefore, commonly understood that a business firm will receive treatment as a partnership if two of the criteria 3 through 6 are absent.

Most limited partnerships have a centralization of management similar to corporations, so differentiation normally will take place in 3, 5, and 6. Under the Uniform Partnership Act, after which most state statutes are patterned, the general partner has the power to dissolve the partnership at any time, thus denying it continuity of life. Otherwise, a terminal date may be provided for in the partnership articles. The criterion of limited liability is negated by the very fact that one partner is a general partner with unlimited liability. Finally, free transferability of interests can be limited by requiring permission of the general or other limited partners to effect a change of ownership. This restriction has been deemed by the Treasury regulations such an impingement as to constitute a legal curtailment of transferability of interests. By proper combination of these provisions, tax treatment as a partnership can be achieved.

The sole general partner of a limited partnership is often a corporation. The advantage of this arrangement lies in the limited personal liability the builder-sponsor of a project can achieve by holding his interest in the limited partnership in his corporation. An incorporated general partner can also provide better continuity of management. To avoid "dummy" characteristics in the sole corporate general partner, the Internal Revenue Service follows internal guidelines (called safe harbor rules) imposing certain ownership and minimum capital requirements. In regard to ownership, limited partners may not own, individually or in the aggregate, more than 20 percent of the corporate stock. The tax rules of attribution of ownership relating to members of the partners' families also apply. The net worth requirement of the corporate general partner depends upon the total contributed capital of the partnership. If the contributed capital is less than $2.5 million, the corporate general partner must have a net worth at least equal to 15 pecent of the total partnership capital, but not to exceed $250,000. Where the contributed partnership capital is $2.5 million or more, the corporate general partner must maintain at all times a net worth of at least 10 percent of the partnership capital.

It is a uniform rule that property can be depreciated only to the extent of its tax basis, usually cost. In a general partnership, where all partners have unlimited liability, the tax basis, or cost, includes both equity contributions and debts for which all partners are responsible. Thus, the full cost, whether financed by equity or debt, can be claimed as a depreciation deduction over time for income tax purposes. A consistent application of this rule to limited partners would seem to limit their depreciation deduction to their equity interest, since they assume no liability beyond that amount. In this instance, however, there is an exception where none of the partners has any liability in connection with the property acquisition.[1] This is true in regard to a mortgage on real estate acquired by a partnership on a "subject to" basis without assumption by the partnership or any of the partners of any liability on the mortgage. Under such conditions, the full cost of the property, whether acquired by funds provided by equity or debt, may be taken as a depreciation deduction by the partners, whether general or limited. Thus, where a depreciable property was financed by $9 of debt for each $1 of equity, the partner has leveraged his depreciation deduction to 10 to 1. Over time, the taxpayer partner may claim $10 of depreciation deductions against taxable income for each $1 of equity invested. In a 50 percent tax bracket, his cumulative tax savings could amount to $5, or five times his equity investment.

Regulation of public real estate syndicates

From substantial beginnings during the 1950s and early 1960s, there was a veritable stampede into real estate investment through syndicates during the late 1960s and early 1970s. Investors were aggressively seeking a hedge against high rates of inflation, highly predictable returns, and tax shelters. The most respected Wall Streeet underwriters began to bring out SEC-registered limited partnerships to invest in properties and less distinguished promoters were active across the country.

The great flexibility of the limited partnership led to abuses, particularly in investment policies, promoters' and managers' compensation, and investor suitability standards. It is in these areas that federal and state regulatory authorities have expressed the greatest concern.

Investment policies. In the early experience with limited partnerships and until the late 1960s, capital was normally raised to finance identifiable parcels, which were described in the prospectus or offering circular in detail. Such specific definition of the investment assets set the standards of securities commissioners in a fairly rigid pattern.

In 1969, however, Goodbody & Company underwrote Burnham Properties, a $20 million public limited partnership with an undefined portfolio. Approval of the sale was obtained in California on the principle that there should be no greater objection to public investing in an undescribed portfolio for real estate than to mutual funds investing in stocks and bonds on a discretionary basis. In a short time, several similar issues were permitted in other states. Although such offerings are not looked upon with favor, state securities commissioners have generally come to accept them. They are known

---

[1] Treas. Regs. § 1.752–1(e); see also Sheldon Schwartz, "How to Find Tax Shelter as a Limited Partner," *Real Estate Review*, vol. 1, no. 2 (Summer 1971), pp. 54–59.

as "blind pool" syndications and should be recognized as pure venture capital funds, since there can be no property descriptions or relevant economic or financial data available for the investor's guidance. After a review of abuses invited by blind pool offerings, a real estate advisory committee established by the SEC recommended that if such offerings are to be permitted at all, specific investment criteria should be disclosed in the prospectus as well as the sponsor's background, experience, and previous results.[2] In addition, the committee recommended that the issuer be required to file annual reports on its operations with the SEC and to send them as well to its investors. These reports should show investment results in detail and demonstrate how the use of the funds conformed with the standards enunciated in the prospectus.

Promoters' and managers' compensation.   A second major area creating problems for syndicate investors arises in connection with promotional and management fees. Keeping these fees to reasonable levels becomes especially difficult because of the many ways in which compensation can be paid. It may be in the form of a brokerage fee, portfolio management fee, a promotional interest as a general partner, or an insurance commission, to name a few.

Management fees have been based on gross assets, net assets, gross rentals, net income, and cash flow. Each method will yield its own unique results dependent upon the fortunes of the syndicate operation. Unfortunately, projections of results are often based on hypotheticals without valid underlying assumptions. Bad projections will distort judgments regarding what is appropriate compensation, or, for that matter, what is a proper method for determining it. In all instances, full disclosure of conflicts of interest of principals, as well as all direct and indirect compensation payable by the partners to promoters, general partners, underwriters, and affiliates, should be made. This disclosure should describe the compensation as to time of payment and amount and it should detail the service rendered to earn it.

Investor suitability standards.   An outstanding weakness of a limited partnership interest as an investment is its lack of liquidity or marketability. By virtue of the restrictions on the assignability of the capital interest, a new partner must have the consent of the existing partners to acquire and enjoy the full interest of a selling partner. Furthermore, state-imposed requirements of financial responsibility of potential investors have complicated the problem of developing a secondary market for such interests. Even an issue of certificates of beneficial interest in a limited partnership is complicated by the fact that the limited partner becomes a securities issuer and subject to separate registration requirements.

Another weakness of the syndicate lies in the fact that it often has limited appeal to any but the investor in the high tax brackets. Yields on other than a

---

[2] These results were published by the Real Estate Committee, established May 3, 1973, by the SEC. See also the article titled "What Lies Ahead for Real Estate Regulation?" by the Committee chairman Raymond R. Dickey, in *Real Estate Review,* vol. 3, no. 1 (Spring 1973), pp. 13–19.

tax shelter basis may be negligible. The low-income investor may acquire a syndicate interest with too little appreciation of the weak economic viability of the venture. The nature of the investor's expected return in the traditional sense, as well as the hypothetical tax savings, should be clearly delineated in all cases.

Federal and state securities authorities. The federal and state securities laws and regulations are relevant to any real estate syndication. Disclosure requirements under the Securities Act of 1933 and the Securities Exchange Act of 1934 set the federal basis for civil liability to investors and criminal fraud liability of principals and their professional counsels for failure to disclose full information about a public issue. State blue-sky laws require securities salespersons to be registered in the local jurisdiction. These laws often go beyond the federal requirements in permitting the state commissioner to disqualify a security on its merits, in addition to determining the required degree of disclosure of specific facts about the issue. Neglect of the issuer to qualify the issue may permit the investor to rescind the whole transaction and demand his money back. Beyond these laws are the safe antifraud statutes to deal with fraudulent practices in connection with security registration. Although the degree of applicability of federal or state laws and regulations differs with the characteristics of each issue, full and active compliance will yield the best results for both the syndicator and his investors.

Private syndication problem illustrated

When embarking on a syndication with other investors, it is essential for all parties, be they investors or lenders, to understand the framework in which the venture will operate. What follows is a rather detailed analysis of a *private* real estate syndication that is being formed to undertake the development of the Plaza Office Building. In this syndication, six individuals have been approached by Dallac Investment Corporation which has agreed to act as the sole general partner in a *limited partnership*. Dallac is trying to raise sufficient equity capital to undertake the project and has decided to use the *limited partnership* form of organization, which will limit the liability of all other partners to capital contributed to the venture. The partnership would be organized effective immediately and construction would take one year.

The venture to be undertaken and relevant cost and financial data are summarized in Exhibit 17–1. Dallac has obtained an option on the land and has a permanent financing commitment from Prudent Life Insurance Company. An interim construction loan commitment has been obtained from the Fifth National Bank. Both loans are contingent on lender approval of the partners selected for investment in the project and require prior approval of any change in the general partner at any time in the future. Dallac has obtained prelease commitments for 50 percent of the space in the office building effective immediately after construction; and based on these commitments, Prudent is

EXHIBIT 17–1
Plaza Office Building development cost and financing summary

Construction period.........	1 year	Financing data:	
Appraised value.............	$4,000,000	Construction loan.........	$3,000,000
Cost breakdown:		Interest rate............	11%
Land....................	625,000	Loan fee..............	$60,000 (2%)
Hard costs...............	2,835,000	Term..................	1 year
Construction interest.......	165,000	Permanent loan	$3,000,000
Construction loan fee	60,000	Interest rate...........	11%
Other capital costs		Term..................	25 yrs.
(architect, engineering,		Loan fee*	$120,000
etc.)	275,000	Annual debt service	$356,220
Property taxes during			
construction	40,000	To be funded upon completion of	
Total cost............	$4,000,000	project.	

* Payable in 1982 after completion of construction.

willing to fund the permanent loan at that time, with the expectation that Dallac will obtain more firm lease agreements during construction. In addition to interest, the interim loan and permanent loan require a 2 percent and a 4 percent origination fee, respectively, payable at closing. The construction loan would be closed January 2, 1981, and the permanent loan on January 2, 1982.

a. **Financial considerations—partnership agreement.**   The financial aspects of the partnership agreement and the equity requirements of the general and limited partners for this example are summarized in Exhibit 17–2. At a minimum, partnership agreements should specify how and what proportion equity will be initially contributed, whether assessments will be made should the project experience a cash shortfall during construction or operation, or should the improvement need substantial repair in the future. In this example, Dallac has agreed as general partner to contribute 10 percent of required equity with the limited partners investing 90 percent or a total of $153,000 each.[3] Future assessments due to cash shortfalls will be made on the same proportions.

The partnership agreement should also specify how profits, losses, and cash flow will be distributed during operation and from the sale of the property in the future. In our example, profits and losses will be distributed 10 percent to Dallac and 90 percent to the limited partners. However, the limited partners will receive a preferential 8 percent *cash* return on all equity plus assessments invested, to the extent annual operating cash flow is available (noncumulative).

[3] In this case, we assume each limited partner invests equally or 15 percent of the cash required from each partner. Obviously, in practice this may not be the case as different proportional interests could be purchased by each partner. Also, in many syndications, the general partner may invest as little as 1 percent of the equity.

EXHIBIT 17–2
Partnership facts and equity requirements—Plaza Office Building syndication

a. Organization—December, 1980.
b. Number of partners: 1 general partner; and 6 limited partners.
c. Equity capital contribution: general partner, 10 percent; and limited partners, 90 percent (15 percent each).
d. Cash assessments: to be funded in same proportion as equity contribution.
e. Cash distributions from operations: limited partners to receive a noncumulative, preferential 8 percent return on all equity and assessments paid to date. Any excess cash flow to be distributed 50 percent to limited partners and 50 percent to general partner.
f. Profits and losses: to be distributed 90 percent to limited partners; and 10 percent to general partner without regard to cash flow distributions.
g. Sale and liquidation of partnership assets: after payment of mortgage and selling expenses, each partner (general and limited) is to receive all equity invested plus any assessments. Any excess is to be distributed 75 percent to limited partners and 25 percent to the general partner.
h. Partnership organization fees: to be paid in same proportion as equity requirements.

Initial equity requirements:
Total project costs $4,000,000
  Add: Organization fees.   20,000
  Total cash requirements. $4,020,000
  Less: Mortgage financing.   3,000,000
Equity requirements. $1,020,000
General partner (10%)   102,000
Limited partners (90%)   918,000
  Investment per limited partner ÷ 6.   153,000
Equity payable to partnership December 31, 1980.

Any excess cash flow over this 8 percent return will be split 50-50 between the general partner and the limited partners. The preferential distribution of cash, or a similar provision, is fairly common in such ventures as an additional incentive for limited partners to invest. Dallac, on the other hand, will receive the management contract for 5 percent of effective gross income and will receive a cash distribution in the year of sale equal to 25 percent of any cash available after debt and selling expenses are repaid, and after all partners recover their initial equity investment plus any assessments made up until that time. Hence, in this example, Dallac is willing to "trade off" or give the limited partners a greater preference for operating cash flow while hoping to receive a significant share of capital appreciation, should it occur. In this case, Dallac is taking more risk while anticipating a greater return. This, or a similar pattern, is common in syndication agreements.

b. **Operating and tax projections.** Projections made by Dallac regarding operations and tax-related matters are summarized in Exhibit 17–3. It should be stressed that all projections made in connection with a syndication offering must be carefully and prudently made, as any misrepresentation may result

EXHIBIT 17–3
Plaza operating and tax projections

Potential gross income.................	$775,000
Vacancy and collection expense.........	5%
Operating expenses	40% (includes property taxes)
Depreciation method	Straight line—40 years
Salvage value.......................	None
Annual depreciation expense	
(straight-line method)	Hard costs ($2,835,000), other capital
	costs ($275,000) over 40 years, or $77,750
Management fee	5% of effective gross income
Amortization periods:	
Construction period interest	
and property taxes	$205,000 (9 years), $22,777 annually
Organization fees...................	$20,000 (5 years), $4,000 annually
Construction loan fee	$60,000 (1 year)
Permanent loan fee	$120,000 (25 years), $4,800 annually
Rent-up period......................	One year, 75% average occupancy 1st year
Projected growth in income............	5% annually
Projected increase in property value......	$5,000,000 at end of 5th year of operation

in legal action by the limited partners. In the case of *public* offerings (discussed below), most states require that a prospectus be filed with the state securities and exchange commission and such projections are carefully scrutinized before approval to offer is granted. Interstate offerings must be filed with the U.S. Securities and Exchange Commission and also undergo a similar examination. Because of this scrutiny by public agencies and the potential for legal action by limited partners, many general partner-syndicators make very general projections regarding future results, or provide only a description of the projects that will be invested in, and only give detail into the business background of the general partner or partners (much like the "blank-check" trust to be described in connection with real estate investment trusts in Chapter 21). In some states such as California, however, such syndicators choose to make detailed financial projections, they must also make known to potential investors the financial results of previous syndications undertaken in past years.

In addition to projections for rental income, operating expenses, management fees, and the like, Dallac has also disclosed the method of depreciation to be used on improvements. It has detailed the period over which loan fees, organization fees, and construction period interest and property taxes will be amortized for federal income tax purposes. These latter expenses cannot be deducted in the year in which payment occurs. Each of these items must be amortized over a prescribed time period established by tax regulations.[4] These expenses are important from the investor's perspec-

---

[4] Beginning in 1982, all construction period interest and property taxes must be written off over a ten-year period for most types of construction (see the appendix to Chapter 12).

tive because the cash flow requirement occurs when the expenses are paid; however, the tax influence of these items occurs over the period of years during which amortization occurs.

c. **Statements of net income or loss.** To illustrate the effect of the projections made in Exhibit 17–3, a statement of taxable income or loss has been constructed for the syndication—partnership investment in the development of the Plaza Office Building, and it is shown in Exhibit 17–4. Special note should be made of items in the statement which differentiate it from statements constructed for *existing* properties. First, it should be noted that during the year of constuction, the partnership will report a taxable loss even though the project has not as yet produced any revenue. This loss comes about from a deduction of the construction loan origination fee, which must be amortized over the term of the loan (one year in our example), a deduction for construction period interest and property taxes which are paid during 1981 but which must be amortized over nine years, and amortization of organization fees which are paid in 1981 but which must be amortized over five years.[5] Hence a limited partner making a $153,000 investment at the end of December 1980 would have a $13,017 taxable loss to report during 1981 while the project is under development. Other important items of note occur during 1982. In that year gross income is expected to be 75 percent of gross potential income of $775,000 due to the vacancy during the remaining rent-up period expected during the first full year of operation. This normal "lag" in rent-up, coupled with interest and depreciation deductions, plus an additional deduction due to the payment of the permanent loan fee at the beginning of 1982 which will be written off over 25 years, gives rise to an extraordinarily large operating loss during 1982 of $20,344 per limited partner. The pattern of losses shown in the exhibit eventually change to net income in 1984 as rental income increases. Beginning in 1984, therefore, investors would have to report taxable income, which would be subject to ordinary rates of taxation at that time.

d. **Statement of before-tax cash flow (*BTCF*).** While the pattern of net income and losses projected for tax purposes is described in Exhibit 17–4, an equally important projection to be considered is the statement of cash flow. In addition to the $153,000 investment made per limited partner in 1980 which is expected to cover cash needs during development, the statement shown in Exhibit 17–5 summarizes the before-tax cash inflow (*BTCF*) or cash shortfalls expected from Plaza after completion of the development phase of the project. Important aspects of the cash flow summary in the exhibit show up in 1982 or the first year of operation when, due to the lag in lease-up, a negative BTCF, or cash shortfall, of $172,517 is expected. At that point, a cash *assessment* will be made in the same 10 percent and 90 percent ratios used for initial equity

---

[5] There may be other expenses that are charged by either the general partner and/or syndicator which are usually paid when the partnership is formed or in the early years of operation. Some of these items will be discussed later in the chapter.

EXHIBIT 17-4

Pro forma statements of income (loss), Plaza Office Building syndication

	1981	1982	1983	1984	1985	1986
Gross income	—	$ 581,250*	$813,750†	$854,438	$897,159	$942,017
Less: Vacancy and collection expenses	—	29,063	40,688	42,722	44,858	47,101
Effective gross income	—	$ 552,187	$773,062	$811,716	$852,301	$894,916
Less: Operating expenses	—	220,875	309,225	324,686	340,920	357,966
Management expenses	—	27,609	38,653	40,586	42,615	44,745
Net operating income	—	$ 303,703	$ 425,184	$446,444	$468,766	$492,205
Less: Interest expense	—	330,000	327,116	323,914	320,360	316,416
Depreciation expense	—	77,750	77,750	77,750	77,750	77,750
Less: Amortization						
Construction loan fee	$ 60,000					
Construction interest and property tax	22,777	22,777	22,777	22,777	22,777	22,777
Permanent loan fee	—	4,800	4,800	4,800	4,800	100,800‡
Organization fee	4,000	4,000	4,000	4,000	4,000	—
Taxable income (loss)	$(86,777)	$(135,624)	$ (11,259)	$ 13,203	$ 39,079	$ (25,538)
Distribution:						
General partner (10%)	$ (8,678)	$ (13,562)	$ (1,126)	$ 1,320	$ 3,908	$ (2,554)
Limited partner (90%)	(78,099)	(122,062)	(10,133)	11,883	35,171	(22,984)
Per limited partner (÷ 6)	(13,017)	(20,344)	(1,689)	1,980	5,862	(3,831)

* Seventy-five percent of potential gross income, based on average occupancy during year.
† Potential income of $775,000 increased by 5 percent annually.
‡ Unamortized loan origination fees expensed in year of sale.

EXHIBIT 17-5
Pro forma statement of before-tax cash flow, Plaza Office Building

	1982	1983	1984	1985	1986
Net operating income	$ 303,703	$425,184	$446,444	$468,766	$492,205
Less: Permanent loan fee	120,000	—	—	—	—
Debt service	356,220	356,220	356,220	356,220	356,220
BTCF	$(172,517)	$ 68,964	$ 90,224	$112,546	$135,985
Assessment:					
General partner (10%)	$ (17,252)				
Limited partners (90%)	(155,265)				
Per limited partner (÷ 6)	(25,878)				
Distribution:					
8% to limited partners*	—	$ 68,964	$ 85,861	$ 85,861	$ 85,861
Remainder:					
50% to general partner.	—	—	2,181	13,343	25,062
50% to limited partners	—	—	2,182	13,342	25,062
Total general distribution . .	—	–0–	$ 2,181	$ 13,343	$ 25,062
Total limited distribution. . .	—	$ 68,964	88,043	99,204	110,923
Per limited partner (÷ 6). . .	—	11,494	14,674	16,534	18,487

* Eight percent of initial equity $918,000 (Exhibit 17-2) plus the assessment of $155,265 during first operating year, to the extent of available cash.

investment by the general and limited partners. Hence a limited partner in this example would have to contribute an estimated $25,878 in cash during 1982. The question of future assessment of investors is an important aspect of a syndication-partnership agreement. Because the financial status of the partners can change drastically from the year of organization into the future, in some cases partners may not have the funds to meet a future assessment. In that event, the agreement should spell out any penalties for deficient partners, requirements of other partners to meet such shortfalls, admission of new partners, sale of partnership interests in arrears, and so forth. In some cases, reserves, escrows, or other plans may be set up in advance to eliminate some of these difficulties. The three most common assessment problems arising in ventures of this sort are due to (1) actual development costs exceeding estimated development costs requiring additional assessment from partners during the development period, (2) working capital deficiencies due to costs exceeding revenues during operation, and (3) extraordinary repair costs during later years of ownership.

Another aspect of the statement of cash flow that is important deals with the distribution of cash to partners. It should be noted that in 1983 the project is expected to generate $68,964 for distribution. The limited partners have a preferential claim on cash flow equal to 8 percent of all equity plus the assessment in 1982. The agreement also specifies that this prior claim on cash is noncumulative, or the deficiency does *not* have to be made up from cash flow in future years.[6] Consequently, in each successive year the limited partners are expected to realize the 8 percent plus 50 percent of the excess of *BTCF* generated in each year.

   e. **Distribution of cash from sale of asset.** As to the sharing from the cash proceeds from the sale of the property, Dallac estimates a holding period of five years after completion of the project at which time it is expected to bring $5,000,000. Exhibit 17–6 shows a breakdown of the

EXHIBIT 17–6
Distribution of cash flow from sale of asset and dissolution of partnership

Sale price		$5,000,000
Selling expenses		30,000
Mortgage balance		2,836,707
Available for distribution		$2,133,293
Less recovery of equity and assessments:		
Limited partners:		
Original equity	$918,000	
Assessments	155,265	
General partner:		
Original equity	102,000	
Assessments	17,252	
Total		1,192,517
Excess available for distribution		$ 940,776
25% to general partner		$ 235,194
75% to limited partners		705,582
Total cash distributed from sale:		
General partner		$ 354,446
Limited partners		1,778,847
Distribution per limited partner (÷ 6)		296,475

cash distribution from the sale of the property and simultaneous dissolution of the partnership venture. As indicated in the agreement, after paying selling expenses and the outstanding mortgage, each partner is to receive an amount equal to the original equity contributed, plus all cash assessments made prior to sale. Any excess is then split with 25 percent going to the general partner and 75 percent to the limited partners. Based on these provisions, should the property bring $5,000,000, each limited partner would receive $296,475.

   f. **Determining long-term capital gain tax.** While the computation of the cash distribution from sale of the Plaza Office Building is a relatively straightforward procedure, determining the capital gains tax on such an investment is somewhat more complicated. For an individual investor-taxpayer to compute the capital gains tax in such a venture, the adjusted basis

---

[6] In practice both cumulative and noncumulative provisions are used in syndications.

of his interest in the asset in the year of sale must be ascertained. This is done in Exhibit 17–7 in which the adjusted basis is seen to be the original equity contributed, plus assessments, plus the partner's interest in net income earned each year, less any share in net losses and less any share in cash distributions made during each year of ownership. The summary of all of these influences would determine the adjusted basis for capital gains purposes should the partnership asset be sold, or should the partner decide to sell his partnership interest to another partner.[7]

From the adjusted basis determined in Exhibit 17–7, the capital gain tax can be computed as shown in Exhibit 17–8. We have assumed that the limited partners in this case are in the 50 percent tax bracket and are not subject to any minimum tax provisions. Also, no ordinary tax is required on recapture of

EXHIBIT 17–7
Summary of limited partner adjusted basis (per partner)

| | Year | | | | | | | |
	1980	1981	1982	1983	1984	1985	1986	Total
Partner's share in:								
Equity	$153,000							$153,000
Assessments			$ 25,878					25,878
Net income					$ 1,980	$ 5,862		7,842
Net losses		$(13,017)	$(20,344)	$ (1,689)			$ (3,831)	(38,881)
Cash distributions ..				(11,494)	(14,674)	(16,534)	(18,487)	(61,189)
							Adjusted basis.....	$ 86,650

EXHIBIT 17–8
Determination of capital gain tax—limited partner

Cash distribution from sale (Exhibit 17–6)....	$296,475
Adjusted basis (Exhibit 17–7)...............	86,650
Total gain.........................	$209,825
Recapture of excess depreciation...........	–0–
Gain subject to capital gain tax............	$209,825
Tax (50% of 40%) or 20%.................	$ 41,965
$ATCF_s$ per partner:	
Cash distribution from sale...............	$296,475
Less: Taxes..........................	41,965
$ATCF_s$.................................	$254,510

---

[7] We should stress that this procedure must be followed in our example because while profits and losses are shared 90 percent and 10 percent for limited partners and the general partner, respectively, the cash flow is not distributed in those proportions. Hence, one cannot merely compute total assets, subtract total liabilities, and divide the resulting net worth among partners for tax purposes.

excess depreciation, as straight-line depreciation was used. Based on the cash distribution and capital gains tax computed in Exhibit 17–8, we can see that if the project is sold for $5,000,000, our limited partner could expect $ATCF_x$ of $254,510.

g. **Determining *ATIRR* on equity.** Based on all of the preceding exhibits, the limited partner is in a position to estimate an *ATIRR* on equity invested in the Plaza development. This is done by combining data from Exhibits 17–5 and 17–4 which provide information on *BTCF* and the data on net income or losses necessary to determine federal income tax each year. This information is combined at the top of Exhibit 17–9 and *ATCF* is established each year. Given the *ATCF* each year and $ATCF_x$ from Exhibit 17–6, the *ATIRR* on the initial $153,000 in equity invested by a limited power partner in a 50 percent tax bracket can be computed. As shown at the bottom of the Exhibit, the estimated *ATIRR* is 12.6 percent for a limited partner investing in the syndicate formed to develop the Plaza Office Building. In computing the *ATIRR,* special note should be taken of the negative *ATCF* realized in 1982. That amount is discounted in the same manner as other positive cash flows shown in the exhibit. It should be pointed out that this negative cash flow amounts to an *additional investment* that is made two years after the original equity was invested. As shown at the bottom of the Exhibit, the estimated will yield them an aftertax return which is less than 12.6 percent. If this is so, some would argue that the true *ATIRR* on the Plaza syndication is less than 12.6 percent because those additional funds committed at a later time would not earn the same return as the Plaza investment.

h. **Other observations.** Based on the Plaza Office Building example, the reader should have a general framework in mind with which potential investments involving limited partnerships may be considered. We should stress that the Plaza problem is meant to be illustrative of one possible way in which an investment can be structured. Indeed, many consider the field of real estate syndication financing and partnerships one of the most complex areas of federal tax law, subject to great variation in structuring of terms among partners. Hence, much study in the law and federal taxation beyond what is presented here is required to gain expertise in the area.

However, there are a few underlying generalizations to keep in mind when evaluating such investments. One generalization is that syndication arrangements are subject to the same economic influences that all investments are subject to, that is, risk and return. Any one real estate investment is capable of producing only so much income, regardless of whether it is syndicated or not. When syndicated under a limited partnership, cash flows from operating and the eventual sale of assets are simply split among different parties. The promoter of the syndicate, who in many cases becomes the general partner, will offer limited partners only what is necessary under current competitive conditions to induce them to invest in the project. Such a return must be commensurate with the risk and return available to investors from comparable syndication offerings or other investment oppor-

EXHIBIT 17–9
Determination of *ATCF* and *ATIRR* for limited partner in 50 percent tax bracket

	1980	1981	1982	1983	1984	1985	1986
BTCF (Exhibit 17–5).........	—	—	$(25,878)	$11,494	$14,674	$16,534	$18,487
Taxes: Net income (Exhibit 17–4)					$ 1,980	$ 5,862	
Or net (loss) (Exhibit 17–4)		$(13,017)	$(20,344)	$ (1,689)			(3,831)
(Tax) or saving at 50 percent......		6,509	10,172	845	(990)	(2,931)	1,916
ATCF: BTCF	—	—	$(25,878)	$11,494	$14,674	$16,534	$ 18,487
(Tax) savings........		$ 6,509	10,172	845	(990)	(2,931)	1,916
ATCF		$ 6,509	$(15,706)	$12,339	$13,684	$13,603	$ 20,403

Computation of *ATIRR* on original equity invested 12/80: $153,000

ATIRR:

Year	ATCF	IFPV, 12 percent	PV	IFPV, 15 percent	PV
1981	$ 6,509	.892857	$ 5,812	.869565	$ 5,660
1982	(15,706)	.797194	(12,521)	.756144	(11,876)
1983	12,339	.711780	8,783	.657516	8,113
1984	13,684	.635518	8,696	.571753	7,824
1985	13,603	.567427	7,719	.497177	6,763
1986	20,403	.506631	10,337	.432328	8,821
	ATCF$_s$				
1986	$254,510	.506631	128,943	.432328	110,032
	Present value		$157,769		$135,337

Interpolation:			
PV at 12%...................	$157,769	PV at 12%	$157,769
PV at 15%...................	110,032	Desired PV..................	153,000
Difference..................	$ 22,432	Difference	$ 4,769

(4,769 ÷ 22,432) × 3% = .6%   Adding: 12% + .6% = 12.6% = *ATIRR*

tunities. Hence the *ratios* used to establish contribution of equity assessments, splitting of cash flows, and so on, should be structured in such a way that given reasonable projections of income and property value, investors will earn a competitive return, as measured by the procedure described in this section of the chapter.

Investors should be in a position to compare terms offered by competing syndicators, given the risk and required equity investment, and to judge whether expected returns are adequate. However, it should be kept in mind that the general partner must also earn a competitive return in order to profitably perform the economic function of syndicating. Essentially, syndicators view their role in the investment process as more of an agent who seeks and finds properties for acquisition or development, finds equity investors, operates and manages properties during ownership by the syndication, and eventually disposes of properties. Because syndicators perform these services, they must also be reasonably assured of being compensated. Hence, they attempt to charge *fees* for all services such as finding properties for purchase, renting up facilities, promoting the sale of partnership interests, managing and accounting for the partnership investment, in addition to legal and accounting costs of organizing the partnership. Limited partners must consider the reasonableness of these fees, plus the general partner's share in cash flows and appreciation in property value, when comparing among syndication alternatives. The primary concern of the limited partner is whether the general partner is "carving out" too much in fees and participation in future cash flows which would make the return on investment unattractive to limited partners. On the other hand, the general partner must be assured of earning a reasonable return on the risk and time involved in promoting the investment. Further, if the syndicator is attempting to earn all compensation from fees and is not taking some equity risk in the project, it may appear to a limited partner that the syndicator-general partner really has no "stake" in the project and is acting more as a broker earning only a fee with little concern over the long-run performance of the investment. If *expertise* in the operation and management of the investment is part of the syndication that is appealing to the limited partner, then a "stake" in the profits in lieu of fees paid to the general partner may be more satisfactory to the limited partner. Clearly, there are many facets to be considered here, and some balance must be reached between partners to make for a satisfactory agreement.

One further note on syndications and limited partnerships has to do with tax considerations when structuring partnership agreements. Because limited partners will generally be in high tax brackets, in order for them to take full advantage of tax losses produced from developing and operating real estate projects, there may be a tendency for the partnership agreement to provide a greater share of losses to limited partners. This is particularly true if their tax brackets are greater than that of the general partner. This may be an added inducement for such individuals to invest in the limited partnership. It is even possible for ratios used to share profits and losses, as well as other terms of the partnership agreement, to be amended at any time. This latter provision may tempt individuals to allocate even more losses to limited partner investors who may be willing to accept a lesser amount of cash flow in return. While partnership agreements are usually recognized by the IRS as a valid mechanism for distributing profit and loss, it should be stressed that such distributions and subsequent amendments must have a business purpose and substantive economic reasoning behind them. Attempts to create distributions in a partnership agreement *essentially to avoid taxation* will generally be challenged by the IRS. Hence, limited partners should be aware of overzealous promoters and syndicators with such objectives in mind. In fact, it may be wise for the limited partnership agreement to be submitted to the IRS for a "prior approval" review before embarking on such an arrangement. While not binding on the IRS, such approval does lend some credibility to the structure of the agreement from the viewpoint of a limited partner, who is usually not an expert in tax law.

Questions

1 Why is the limited partnership such a popular form for real estate syndication?

2 What are the principal governmental regulatory problems in connection with public real estate syndications?

3 How does the general partner-syndicator usually structure the partnership to offer incentives to limited partners? What is meant by an excessive "carve out" in such an arrangement?

4 Why is the Internal Revenue Service concerned with how partnership agreements in real estate are structured?

Case problems

1 Venture Capital Ltd., a corporation specializing in syndicating, developing, and managing properties for limited partner investors, has approached five limited partners to invest in the Tall Towers office building project to be developed next year. Essentially, the proposal provides that Venture contribute 10 percent of the equity and the five limited partners will invest equally (18 percent) in all equity requirements and any future assessments. A schedule of important data is detailed below:

TALL TOWERS PROJECT
Offered by Venture Capital Ltd.
Cost and Financial Data

Construction period	1 year	Construction loan	$6,000,000
Appraised value	$8,000,000	Interest rate	12%
Cost breakdown:		Loan fee	3% or ($180,000)
Land	1,000,000	Term	1 yr. (Acme
Direct development cost	5,670,000		National Bank)
Construction interest	400,000		
Construction loan fee	180,000	Permanent loan:	
Other indirect costs	560,000	Interest rate	12%
Property taxes during		Term	25 yrs.
construction	190,000	Loan fee	4% ($240,000)
Organization expenses	150,000	Annual debt service	$765,000
Total costs	$8,150,000	To be funded upon completion of	
Less: Financing	6,000,000	construction (Adams State Life Co.)	
Equity required	$2,150,000		
General partner	215,000		
Limited partners	1,935,000		
Per limited partner (÷ 5)	387,000		

Venture has also included a schedule of how it expects to amortize expenses and depreciate the cost of the project as follows:

Item	Amortization period
Construction period interest and property taxes	10 yrs.
Construction loan fee	1 yr.
Permanent loan fee	25 yrs.
Depreciation	40 yrs.—straight-line depreciation
Salvage value	None
Organization expenses	5 yrs.

Venture has obtained firm lease commitments for 60 percent of the space to be developed, and the permanent loan should be closed after one year of construction with the loan fee payable at that time. It estimates gross potential rent at $1,570,000; however, it expects an 80 percent *average* occupancy during the *first* year of operations. Rents should increase at 6 percent of potential income per year thereafter. Vacancies should average about 5 percent each year. Operating expenses should be 40 percent of effective gross income. Venture will collect an additional 5 percent of effective gross income as an annual management fee. Venture also estimates that it could sell the property for $9,700,000 after five years of operation.

Terms of the partnership agreement have the general partner receiving 10 percent of all profits and losses with limited partners receiving 90 percent of the same. Cash flow will be distributed to limited partners based on 6 percent of all equity and assessments made to date, with any excess being split equally between the general and limited partners. The preferential 6 percent return to limited partners is cumulative; that is, any current deficiency must be made up in future years, beginning in the second year after completion of construction. Cash flow in the year of sale will first go to retire mortgage debt with any excess going first to recovery of all equity and assessments contributed by all partners. The excess is to be split 30 percent to the general partner and 70 percent to limited partners.

Ralph Blunt has been approached by Venture to make an investment in the project. He has asked you to advise him in this matter. You may assume that his tax rate is 50 percent.

a. Make projections of all cash investment requirements, distributions of cash flow, income and losses, and assessments for Blunt.

b. Determine Blunt's position regarding cash distribution and capital gains tax if the property is sold as projected (assume no minimum tax).

c. What is Blunt's *ATIRR?*

PART FOUR

The mortgage market and sources of real estate credit

Introduction to the mortgage market

18

This chapter serves as an introduction to the mortgage market. It includes a discussion of the sources of funds available for mortgage lending and the major institutional participants in the market for mortgage loans. These institutions are identified as to specialization by type of mortgage lending. In addition, the major causes of instability in the availability of mortgage credit from period to period are investigated. The intent herein is not to furnish an exhaustive analysis of the mortgage market. The objective is to provide a basic understanding of funds flows, as subsequent chapters deal with each institutional source in more detail.

Flow of funds and the financial system

To understand the nature of the mortgage market, it is helpful to place it in context with other financial markets in our economy. Generally, when referring to financial markets, a distinction is made between money markets and capital markets. Money markets are usually defined as markets for financial claims with maturities of less than one year. Examples of claims with maturities of less than one year include U.S. government Treasury bills, some securities of U.S. government agencies, and commercial paper issued by corporations, to mention a few. Capital markets generally refer to markets in which obligations with maturities greater than one year are bought and sold. Examples of these obligations include corporate bonds and stocks, mortgages, long-term bonds issued by the federal government, and long-term bonds issued by state and local governments. The stock market, bond market, and mortgage market can be thought of as component parts of capital markets.

While it is sometimes useful to analyze money and capital markets separately, a greater understanding of our financial system can be obtained through flow of funds analysis. Flow of funds analysis integrates money and capital markets into a framework that enables one to trace the primary flows between economic sectors in the economy. Exhibit 18–1 contains a simplified

EXHIBIT 18–1
Simplified flow of funds diagram

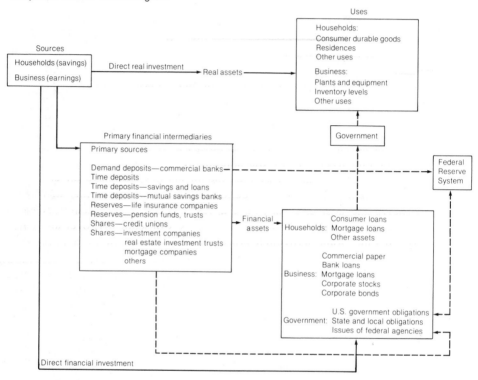

flow of funds diagram that enables tracing of money and capital flows from sources that supply funds to economic units that use or demand funds.

Sources and uses of funds. Over any given time period sources of funds available for investment include primarily savings of households and earnings from business.[1] In the case of households, determinants of savings include the amount of income earned over the period and the amount of current consumption of that income. The amount consumed partially depends on interest rates that can be earned for not consuming, or saving, and expected price levels. Determinants of business earnings are generally governed by competitive forces governing sales, cost of output, and ex-

---

[1] More specifically, this includes retained earnings plus capital consumption allowances.

pected capital investment less necessary dividend payments to investors. What remains after dividend payments is the amount business has for future investment.

Primary uses of funds are shown in the upper right-hand corner of Exhibit 18–1. Part of the demand for funds comes from households desiring to acquire consumer durable goods, such as automobiles and appliances, and to construct new residences. In addition, businesses requiring expansion in production facilities, including new plants and machinery, as well as increases in inventory levels, provide additional demand for funds. Therefore, a considerable amount of funds generated by businesses and households as sources is invested directly in *real assets*[2] as shown at the top of the figure.

Channels of funds flows. One of the main purposes of the diagram in Exhibit 18–1 is to show how funds provided by individual households and businesses are channeled to other individual households and businesses, and perhaps government, which demand funds in excess of their current levels of savings and earnings. Many individual households and businesses that provide funds may not invest exactly the amount of funds at their disposal in real assets. Those individual households and businesses will have an excess or surplus of funds during any one period of time. However, other individual households and businesses will have a need for funds in excess of amounts which they can derive from their own sources. Consequently, over any given period of time, some individual households and businesses will be seeking funds to use for investment in real assets, while others will have excess funds the use of which they are willing to sell. Government at the federal, state, and local levels may also enter the market for funds depending on their respective budgetary-expenditure patterns over a given period in time.[3]

To raise the necessary funds, households, business, and government create financial claims and obligations. For households these claims usually take the form of consumer and mortgage loans. Businesses generally make business and mortgage loans and issue stock, commercial paper, and bonds; while government agencies usually issue bonds, bills, and notes.[4] These financial claims become *financial assets* for lenders who will supply funds for some specified period and earn either interest or dividends in return for the use of funds.[5] A summary listing of financial assets used by households, business, and govern-

---

[2] Real assets are meant here to include stocks of physical goods which are expected to yield productive service over time.

[3] Whether government enters the market for funds depends in large part on tax revenues and expenditures. If a governmental unit runs a budgetary deficit over a given period, it must raise funds. On the other hand, if a unit runs a budgetary surplus, it will enter the market to retire outstanding obligations from preceding periods.

[4] Depending on the maturity of these financial claims, they may be classified as money market instruments or capital market instruments.

[5] We refer here to new issues or additional amounts of financial assets only. It should be recalled that existing issues of stocks, bonds, and so on, that are traded among individuals provide no net increase in funds to households and businesses seeking to expand or invest in real assets.

ment to raise funds in money and capital markets is shown in the lower right-hand corner of Exhibit 18–1.

Financial assets can be sold to suppliers of funds directly through the various bond or stock markets (see direct financial investment arrow at the bottom of Exhibit 18–1).[6] However, most funds available for investment in financial assets are channeled through financial intermediaries.

Financial intermediaries and funds flow. Because direct financial investment of savings by households (shown at the bottom of Exhibit 18–1) requires (1) knowledge concerning financial assets (how to buy securities and other financial assets), (2) a willingness to take certain risks (price fluctuation on securities or bankruptcy by the issuer), (3) some minimum amount of funds to buy certain financial assets (mortgages, for example), and (4) the necessary underwriting knowledge to make large business loans, mortgage loans, and so on, it is usually not practical for most households to invest in financial assets directly.[7] Most individuals do not meet one or more of the four criteria listed above because of the specialization required to underwrite or purchase assets, or because they have small savings balances which they do not want to risk the possibility of losing. Consequently, financial intermediaries have developed that specialize in (1) consolidating many small amounts of savings from individuals and making large loans (mortgages, business loans, etc.); (2) diversifying funds over many different types of financial assets so as not to risk all funds in one investment; and (3) underwriting and studying characteristics associated with investments, which requires managerial expertise. Clearly these functions could not be performed by individual households.

In the middle of Exhibit 18–1 an abbreviated list of major financial intermediaries and their primary methods of attracting savings from households is provided. Basically each institution, either by design or by government regulation, offers a certain inducement such as interest, dividends, or a service in return for savings flows. These flows are then aggregated and invested in a diversified portfolio of financial assets (loans, mortgages, bonds, etc.) on which a return is earned by the intermediary.[8] The intermediary in turn pays individual households in the form of interest, service, and so forth, for the use of savings flows and earns a profit for performing this intermediation function. As will be seen later in this chapter, the degree to which households choose to

---

[6] A direct purchase will generally require the services of a broker or investment banking firm. Nonetheless, in our discussion, it still constitutes a direct purchase.

[7] Businesses with surplus funds also face some of these problems. However, these surpluses tend to be very short term in nature. Because of the dynamic nature of the economy, individual firms with surpluses in one period may be large borrowers in the next. Hence, most firms keep surplus funds in short-term investments. Since our focus here is on the mortgage market, which is a long-term capital market, we are more interested in long-term sources of savings. Hence, our discussion centers more on households.

[8] It must be pointed out here that most intermediaries are highly regulated by either state or federal government as to the types of financial assets they may invest in. This discussion must be interpreted by the reader in general terms at this point.

use financial intermediaries or purchase financial assets directly can drastically affect funds available for mortgage lending.

Government debt and financial markets.   Government influence is felt in financial markets when that sector (particularly the federal government) increases a budgetary deficit or surplus. Deficits occur when tax receipts fall short of expenditures (see the government sector in Exhibit 18–1). To finance a deficit, government, like households and business, must borrow by creating financial claims, as it is a net *user* of funds. When such deficits occur at the federal level, debt obligations are issued consisting of short-term U.S. Treasury bills, notes, and bonds which are bought by individuals and intermediaries. When budgetary receipts exceed expenditures, a surplus occurs. In this event, government usually repurchases obligations issued in previous periods or adds to the flow of funds.[9]

The impact of government deficits on financial markets partially depends on the magnitude of the deficit and on the timing. If a large governmental deficit occurs simultaneously with rapid business expansion, for example, there is a tendency for interest rates on financial assets to increase in the short run as households and business compete with government for funds. On the other hand, in periods of declining economic activity, such deficits are used to stimulate investment in the business sector through increased government spending. In the latter case, the impact on interest rates tends to be slight due to low levels of demand for funds.

The Federal Reserve System and financial markets.   Another significant way in which government can influence financial markets is through actions taken by the Federal Reserve System (see Federal Reserve System at the extreme right of Exhibit 18–1). This public agency is charged with management of the nation's monetary system while promoting the attainment of maximum economic income, minimum unemployment, and stable prices. The supply of money is defined as currency in circulation and demand deposits at commercial banks. Only about one half of the commercial banks belong to the Federal Reserve System; however, they account for about 80 percent of deposits in all banks in the United States. All banks are required to keep a specific percentage of demand and time deposits on reserve in district Federal Reserve banks. This is referred to as the reserve requirement for member banks. The Federal Reserve System, in turn, provides them with check-clearing services, transfer of funds services, and currency. It will also lend money to member banks and will supervise and audit their performance.

Reserve requirements.   One way in which the Federal Reserve influences financial markets and the supply of money is through changes in the reserve requirements. By requiring more reserves, the Federal Reserve System reduces the amount of funds available for investment. This occurs because commercial

---

[9] Since World War II, government, particularly at the federal level, has been in the position of financing deficits.

banks have to increase their reserves at district banks. These funds are withheld by district banks from financial markets, thereby reducing funds available for investment (see relationship between commercial banks and the Federal Reserve System in Exhibit 18–1).

Changes in reserve requirements may be used when the economy is expanding too rapidly and inflationary pressure develops. To reduce the rate of expansion, the Federal Reserve may choose to increase reserve requirements and to reduce the supply of money and hence funds available for investment. Interest rates are driven up as business, households, and perhaps government agencies compete for a smaller supply of funds. Eventually, as interest rates rise high enough, some investment outlays are postponed or eliminated and the economy begins to return to stability. During this period, however, mortgage interest rates, as well as rates on all financial assets, rise rapidly and credit is extremely difficult to obtain. While changing reserve requirements is certainly an effective way to reduce the availability of funds, it is considered a somewhat drastic step and is not used frequently by the Federal Reserve.[10]

Open-market operations.   Another, more commonly used method of monetary management by the Federal Reserve is open-market operations. With this technique, the Federal Open-Market Committee of the Federal Reserve System decides whether to buy or sell U.S. Treasury obligations in an attempt to increase or decrease the supply of money. The Federal Reserve System maintains a portfolio of U.S. Treasury securities which it adds to by buying additional securities or which it reduces by selling securities. Sales of securities tend to *reduce* the money supply and funds available for investment, while purchases of securities tend to *increase* the money supply. Sales of securities by the Federal Reserve reduce the money supply because as they are sold, checks are drawn against demand deposits (checking accounts) at commercial banks by individuals and businesses making purchases. Hence, demand deposits are reduced, and the amount of loanable funds is reduced because the Federal Reserve does not allow these funds to reenter the banking system (see relationship between government securities and the Federal Reserve system in Exhibit 18–1).[11]

Open-market sales of securities by the Federal Reserve System cause a contraction in the supply of money and hence in loanable funds. It serves to drive interest rates upward as competition by households and business for a smaller quantity of funds increases. Open-market operations, like reserve requirements, can be used in an attempt to reduce the rate of expansion and inflationary pressure in the economy or to stimulate activity in the economy.

---

[10] The reverse process can also occur during a period of economic recession. By reducing reserve requirements, more funds become available for investment at lower interest rates. With lower interest costs, the Federal Reserve hopes to stimulate investment.

[11] Purchases of treasury securities by the Federal Reserve has the opposite effect. In this case sellers of securities receive checks from the Federal Reserve which are deposited at banks. This would increase demand deposits and loanable funds.

However, these operations are used much more frequently than changes in reserve requirements. This is the case because changing reserve requirements can have a more sudden and drastic effect on the money supply and hence the flow of funds. Open-market operations, however, are used as part of a continuous system of monitoring and management of the money supply by the Federal Reserve. Through gradual increases and decreases in holdings of securities, the desired effects on financial markets can be achieved with an element of timing that may be more desirable by monetary authorities.

Changing the discount rate and credit restrictions. The final tool at the disposal of the Federal Reserve System for altering the money supply, and hence the funds flow in the economy, is changing the discount rate. The discount rate measures charges made to member banks for borrowing from the Federal Reserve System. Changing the discount rate affects the flow of funds because if commercial banks desire to borrow from their district Federal Reserve bank to make additional loans to business and individuals, the price or interest rate charged on loans made by the Federal Reserve System will partially determine whether the commercial bank borrows and how much. Obviously if the Federal Reserve chooses to raise the rate on loans made to commercial banks, fewer loans will be made, and vice versa.

Experience has shown that changing the discount rate has a much less important direct effect on the supply of money than either open-market operations or changing reserve requirements. In practice, changing the discount rate has generally served as a signal given by the Federal Reserve System as to the policy it plans to implement concerning the money supply in the near future. Raising the discount rate is usually a signal that a reduction in the money supply, or a period of "tighter money," is desired by the Federal Reserve, and generally open-market operations will reflect that policy objective. Lowering the discount rate usually signals that an increase in the money supply, or a period of "easy money," may be in the offing. The Federal Reserve is also empowered to impose credit restrictions on various kinds of loans made to businesses and households should the economic situation warrant it. This power, however, is seldom used, as emergency conditions would have to exist in the economy before the Federal Reserve would enact credit restrictions on any broad scale.

Flow of funds—illustrated. To familiarize the reader with the flow of funds concept, a summarized segment of a flow of funds statement for the period 1969–1979 is presented in Exhibit 18–2. The segment presented deals with (1) the portion of the flow of funds diagram relating to the flow between financial intermediaries and users of capital (middle of Exhibit 18–1) and (2) the portion of the diagram dealing with direct financial investment by households (bottom of Exhibit 18–1). In other words, we are focusing on how individual firms, households, and government obtained funds in financial markets either (1) from financial intermediaries or (2) directly from households and businesses buying financial assets.

EXHIBIT 18–2
Funds raised and advanced in credit markets, 1969–1979 ($ billion)

	1970	1971	1972	1973	1974	1975	1976	1977	1978	1979
Funds raised by instrument:										
Mortgages	29.9	52.5	76.8	79.9	60.5	57.2	87.1	134.0	149.0	158.1
Corporate bonds	23.3	23.5	18.4	13.6	23.9	36.4	37.2	36.1	31.6	32.2
Corporate stock and investment company shares	10.5	15.0	13.3	9.2	4.1	10.7	11.9	4.0	3.7	5.2
U.S. government securities	21.7	30.9	23.6	28.3	34.3	98.2	88.1	84.3	95.2	89.9
State and local obligations	11.2	17.4	14.7	14.7	16.5	16.1	15.7	23.7	28.3	21.4
Consumer credit	5.4	14.7	19.8	26.0	9.9	9.7	25.6	40.6	50.6	42.3
Bank loans	7.3	11.0	26.1	48.8	41.3	−12.2	7.0	29.8	58.4	52.5
Commercial paper	2.1	−.1	1.6	8.3	17.7	−1.2	8.1	15.0	26.4	40.5
Other loans	7.5	3.5	8.4	19.1	22.7	8.7	15.3	25.2	38.6	39.5
Total (rounded)	119.0	168.4	202.6	248.0	230.8	223.5	296.0	392.5	481.7	481.4
Funds advanced by:										
Financial institutions	77.0	109.4	148.3	161.3	125.7	122.5	190.1	257.0	296.9	293.0
Commercial banks	35.7	50.4	70.3	84.6	66.8	29.4	59.6	87.6	128.7	121.1
Savings institutions	17.4	39.4	47.3	35.1	24.2	53.5	70.8	82.0	75.9	54.6
Insurance and pension funds	17.0	13.6	16.9	23.7	29.8	40.6	49.9	67.9	73.5	72.9
Redemption of mutual funds/equities	10.5	15.0	13.3	9.2	4.1	10.7	11.9	4.0	3.7	5.2
Other finance	6.9	6.1	13.9	17.9	4.8	−1.0	9.8	19.6	18.7	44.3
Government and related institutions	28.6	44.0	19.4	31.8	53.7	44.6	54.3	85.1	109.7	80.3
Sponsored credit agencies and pools	10.4	5.9	8.8	19.1	26.5	14.8	20.3	26.8	44.6	57.7
Federal Reserve System	5.0	8.9	.3	9.2	6.2	8.5	9.8	7.1	7.0	7.7
U.S. government	2.8	2.8	1.8	2.8	9.8	15.1	8.9	11.8	20.4	22.6
Foreign sources	10.5	26.4	8.4	.6	11.2	6.1	15.2	39.4	37.7	−7.7
Total	119.0	168.4	202.6	248.0	230.8	223.5	296.0	392.5	481.7	481.4

Source: *Flow of Funds Accounts* (Washington, D.C.: Federal Reserve System, May 1980).

The top half of Exhibit 18–2 concentrates on the types of financial claims created by households, business, and government to raise funds. These claims, also listed in Exhibit 18–1, include mortgages used by households and business for real estate improvements and bonds and stocks issued by corporations for plant expansions and equipment outlays, as well as securities and obligations used by government at all levels to raise capital. Note the increases and decreases in funds invested in mortgages during each of the years from 1969 to 1979. This fluctuation is very important as it shows that funds flowing into the mortgage market were more available in some periods than others. The availability of mortgage funds has a direct bearing on housing construction and other real estate development, a point to be explored further later in this chapter. It should also be pointed out that funds flowing into each of the sectors detailed in the top half of the exhibit are also a reflection of the competition for funds. Each claim created by business, households, and government has either an interest or dividend rate, which reflects the price each borrower is willing to pay to raise funds. Hence the relative share of total funds available for borrowing from each sector will be determined by competition.

The bottom half of Exhibit 18–2 lists financial intermediaries that advanced funds by buying financial assets or claims created by households, business, and government with funds flowing through such intermediaries. It also provides categories for federally related institutions and government as well as for households and businesses that invested or advanced funds into the financial system by buying financial assets directly. Special note should be taken of funds advanced by financial institutions that fluctuated significantly from 1970 to 1979. As will be developed later, funds advanced by intermediaries are especially critical to the mortgage market since deposit-type intermediaries are the most significant mortgage lenders in our economy. When funds advanced by these intermediaries decline in a particular year, it is likely to be a result of a reduction in savings deposits from households which choose to make more direct investments in financial assets such as stocks and bonds.

The mortgage market

From the discussion to this point, we have seen that the flow of funds from sectors of the economy with a surplus of funds to sectors with a net demand for funds depends, in part, on a complex system of financial intermediaries. In addition, the flow of funds can be altered by actions taken by government financing debt and policies of the Federal Reserve System. Since the mortgage market is only one component of the financial system just described, it is definitely affected by changes that occur in the overall flow of funds. Although we discuss the mortgage market in isolation here, it must be kept in mind that it is a part of the overall financial system and is responsive to changes affecting that system.

In this section we separate the mortgage market from the rest of the financial system and provide more detail on mortgage market participants. A simplified diagram of the mortgage market is presented in Exhibit 18–3. The intent of the diagram is to identify the major participants in the mortgage markets and to

EXHIBIT 18–3
The mortgage market

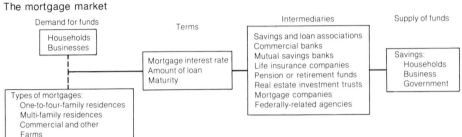

depict how the interaction of the supply and demand for mortgage funds sets the terms for mortgage lending and borrowing.

The demand for mortgage funds. The demand for mortgage funds emanates from business and households desiring to make investments in real assets, such as single-family residential housing, multifamily housing, apartment complexes, and commercial developments (shopping centers, hotels, and office buildings) which require financing. This group is depicted in the left portion of Exhibit 18–3. There are many determinants of demand for housing and other real assets requiring mortgage financing. Many of these factors were discussed in Chapter 10 when market studies for income-producing properties were discussed. A general list of these demand factors is provided below. While many of these demand characteristics are more relevant in determining the demand for housing and residential mortgage loans, most of these characteristics are also important in the demand for commercial structures and commercial mortgage financing.

1. Changes in population.
   a. Changes in the number of household formations.
   b. Changes in the structure of households.
      (1) Age of head of household.
      (2) Size of household.
      (3) Age distribution of members of household.
   c. Changes in geographical distribution of households.
      (1) Rural-urban shifts.
      (2) Urban-suburban shifts.
2. Changes in income and employment.
   a. Current levels of income.

  b. Changes in the distribution of income.
    (*1*) By size and age distribution of households.
  c. Changes in industrial and business location.
    (*1*) Skilled and unskilled employment demand.
    (*2*) Wage structure.
3. Changes in construction costs.
  a. Price of construction materials, land, and labor.
  b. Price of financing and credit costs.
  c. Changes in consumer tastes, style preferences.
  d. Changes in environmental conditions.
    (*1*) Changes in relative price of fuel used for power and heat.
    (*2*) Environmental restrictions of air and water pollution.
4. Changes in housing-related services.
  a. Property tax structure.
  b. Quantity and quality of public services provided.
  c. Federal tax structure.
    (*1*) Treatment of homeowners-renters.
  d. Changes in maintenance costs.
  e. Changes in utility costs.
5. Stock of existing supply of structures.
  a. Vacancies.
  b. Distribution of rents and prices by type of structure.
  c. Distribution of stock by type of structure and location.
  d. Demolitions, conversions.

Based on the flow diagram in Exhibit 18–3, it can be seen that the interaction of the demand for mortgage funds with the supply of available funds determines the mortgage interest rate and market terms on which funds are available. However, it should also be kept in mind that there are risk differentials among individual loan transactions, based on the relative financial strength of borrowers, geographical differences in project location, and other factors. These differences result in a distribution of mortgage interest rates and terms. Hence, when reference is made to the interest rate on mortgages, these differentials must be kept in mind. In addition, although the mortgage market diagram in Exhibit 18–3 excludes other sectors of the financial system, it must be kept in mind that the mortgage market is a part of the larger system. Further, the demand for mortgage funds is a part of the demand for all funds in the economy, and competition among all sectors influences mortgage interest rates.

  The supply of mortgage funds. Referring again to Exhibit 18–3, suppliers of mortgage funds are listed on the right-hand side of the diagram. The institutions through which the supply of funds are channeled listed in Exhibit 18–3 are the most important participants in the mortgage market. While other institutions listed in Exhibit 18–1 may make some mortgage loans, they are not significant in dollar amount. Hence, our discussion will focus on only the most important intermediaries in the mortgage market, though it must be kept in mind that there are other intermediaries competing for savings flows.

The institutions listed in Exhibit 18–3 may be classified into one of three categories. Depository-type institutions include savings and loan associations, commercial banks, and mutual savings banks, as these intermediaries offer a variety of deposit accounts to savers. Contractual-type institutions include life insurance companies and pension and retirement funds as these intermediaries usually provide a service to individuals that involves a contractual commitment of savings over a long period of time. The third category, including mortgage companies, real estate investment trusts, and federally related agencies, might be called specialized mortgage market intermediaries. These intermediaries restrict their investment activity to the mortgage market primarily, and most of the funds that they use for making investments in mortgages do not come directly from savers. The following section briefly describes some of the overall functions of each institution.[12]

Mortgage lenders in the mortgage market. Insight into the operation of the mortgage market can be gained by becoming familiar with the major financial institutions involved in mortgage lending and the type of lending in which each tends to specialize. There are four major private institutions that are significantly involved in the mortgage market: savings and loan associations, mutual savings banks, commercial banks, and life insurance companies. Exhibit 18–4 provides a breakdown of total real estate mortgage loans held by each of the major private lenders, plus a breakdown of loans held by federally related agencies and other lenders, by category of loan.

Looking to the last column in Exhibit 18–4 it is clear that savings and loan associations are the largest real estate lenders in the United States. Of the four largest private real estate lenders, savings and loan associations held approximately 39 percent of total mortgage loans outstanding at the end of 1975. They were followed by commercial banks (19.1 percent), life insurance companies (9.4 percent), and mutual savings banks (8.2 percent). These institutions accounted for about 75.7 percent of total mortgage loans outstanding at the end of 1979 and are by far the most important institutions in the mortgage market. Federal agencies and state and local credit agencies have increased their holdings dramatically in the postwar period. At the end of 1979, they held 17.8 percent of all mortgage loans. Included among the federal agencies are the Federal Home Loan Mortgage Corporation (FHLMC), the Farmers Home Administration, and the Federal Land Bank System. Other categories of lenders detailed in Exhibit 18–4 including pension funds, mortgage companies, real estate investment trusts, and mortgage-backed pools, together accounted for about 6.4 percent of total mortgage debt.

---

[12] A more complete discussion of each institution is contained in subsequent chapters.

EXHIBIT 18–4
Total mortgage debt held by type of lender—1979*

Institution	One- to four-family (percent)	Multi-family (percent)	Commercial land, and other (percent)	Farm (percent)	Total (percent)
Savings and loan associations	$397,444 (47.6)	$ 37,516 (31.5)	$ 36,752 (18.5)	$ 444 (.1)	$ 472,156 (39.0)
Commercial banks.	148,911 (17.8)	10,765 (9.0)	63,393 (31.9)	8,519 (14.8)	231,588 (19.1)
Life insurance companies.	15,512 (1.9)	18,458 (15.5)	67,943 (34.2)	12,158 (21.1)	114,071 (9.4)
Mutual savings banks	67,874 (8.1)	15,829 (13.3)	15,518 (7.8)	14 —	99,235 (8.2)
Real estate trusts.	459 (.1)	1,379 (1.2)	2,390 (1.2)	3 —	4,231 (.3)
Mortgage companies.	12,536 (1.5)	1,568 (1.3)	1,529 (.1)	—	15,633 (1.3)
Federal—state—local credit agencies	154,403 (18.5)	23,473 (19.7)	6,540 (3.3)	31,148 (54.1)	215,564 (17.8)
Mortgage pools	33,813 (4.0)	6,496 (5.4)	90 —	5,284 (9.2)	45,683 (3.8)
Pension and retirement funds	4,268 (.5)	3,755 (3.1)	4,425 (2.2)	23 —	12,471 (1.0)
Totals	$835,220	$119,239	$198,480	$57,593	$1,210,632

* Includes construction, land development, and permanent loans ($ millions).
   Source: *The Supply of Mortgage Credit 1970–1979* (Washington, D.C.: Office of Financial Management, U.S. Department of Housing and Urban Development, 1980).

Specialization in real estate lending: An overview. In addition to total mortgage lending activity, data in Exhibit 18–4 show areas of lending specialization by category of loan and lender. For example, data in the first column show that savings and loan associations are by far the largest holder of one- to four-family mortgage loans. Of the $835.2 billion in single-family loans (one- to four-family category) outstanding in 1979, savings and loan associations held over 47 percent of the total. They were followed by commercial banks (17.8 percent), federally related agencies (18.5 percent), mutual savings banks (8.1 percent), and life insurance companies (1.9 percent). In the multifamily loan category, detailed in the second column, savings and loan associations accounted for about 31.5 percent of the $119.2 billion in loans outstanding, followed by life insurance companies (15.5 percent), mutual savings banks (13.3 percent), federally related agencies (19.7 percent), and commercial banks (9.0 percent). The pattern of commercial mortgages held by major financial institutions is completely different from both the one- to four-family and multifamily categories, with life insurance companies accounting for the largest percentage (34.2 percent) of the $198.5 billion in total loans outstanding in that category, followed by commercial banks (31.9 percent), savings and loan associations (18.5 percent), and mutual savings banks (7.8 percent). These patterns of mortgage investment indicate clearly that lenders specialize in certain areas of real estate lending. Exhibit 18–5 contains a summary of selected characteristics of the major participants in the mortgage market. This summary provides an overview of the role that each intermediary plays in the mortgage market and is a convenient reference for the discussion in this and subsequent chapters.

Savings and loan associations.   As the summary in Exhibit 18–5 shows, these institutions are specialists in underwriting residential mortgage loans, both in the one- to four-family and multifamily categories. This specialized lending pattern follows from the fact that government regulations have historically allowed savings and loan associations to offer higher interest rates on savings deposits than commercial banks. These regulations have generally provided savings and loan associations with a relatively stable source of funds for lending purposes; consequently, they are in a good position to make long-term loans. Government regulations have also restricted the investment policy of savings and loan associations by requiring the origination of primarily residential loans in their local lending area. Consequently, these institutions have developed expertise in underwriting both construction loans and permanent loans on single-family and multifamily residential real estate and have evolved into the most important lending institution in those categories.

During the period 1970–79, of all loans made by savings and loan associations, 80 to 85 percent were made on single-family (one- to four-family category) properties. Although loans on single-family properties have been the mainstay of savings and loan associations, the share of loans made on multifamily and commercial mortgage loans has been increasing in recent years with the two categories accounting for about 20 percent of total loans by the end of 1979. Most residential loans made are conventional; that is, loans underwritten by individual institutions with no FHA insurance or VA guarantee, although private mortgage insurance is required on many loans.

Savings and loan associations have kept about 100 percent of time deposits invested in real estate loans with cash and other liquid investments accounting for only a relatively small percentage of total assets.[13] Since savings and loan associations are the second largest group of financial institutions in the United States, their role in the mortgage market is clearly a dominant one. Conse-

---

[13] Cash and liquid assets have been roughly equivalent to equity and reserves for most associations in recent years.

quently, changes in economic conditions and government policies affecting these intermediaries clearly have a tremendous effect on the mortgage market.

Commercial banks. In contrast to savings and loan associations, commercial banks, the largest group of financial institutions in the United States, have relatively low stability in their sources of funds. Since about 40–45 percent of their funds come primarily in the form of demand deposits, the availability of funds for mortgage lending on a long-term basis is considerably lessened because of the short-term and fluctuating nature of demand deposit balances. Hence, as Exhibit 18–5 indicates, commercial banks invest only 15–20 percent of total demand and time deposits in mortgage loans. In keeping with the relatively unstable nature of deposit flows, commercial banks have developed expertise in short-term lending in primarily business and consumer loans, while keeping reserves in highly marketable government obligations.

In addition to being the second largest holder of single-family mortgage loans among private lenders, commercial banks tend to specialize in commercial mortgage loans and in all phases of construction lending. Specialization in commercial mortgages follows from their relationship with business customers who make short-term business loans and rely on these banks for mortgage loans when new plants and office buildings are needed. Since banks are familiar with business organizations from continuing short-term lending relationships, development of commercial mortgage lending is a natural outgrowth of that activity.

Many of the mortgages made by banks are construction and land development loans which will ultimately be held by another lender, such as a life insurance company, upon completion of construction. Banks also make short-term loans and extend lines of credit to mortgage companies and real estate investment trusts (REITs) which are not reported as mortgage loans in Exhibit 18–4 but are nonetheless related to the real estate industry.

Life insurance companies. These contractual-type intermediaries enjoy a relatively high degree of stability in the availability of funds for investment when compared with both commercial banks and savings and loan associations. This stability follows from the contractual nature of premiums on insurance policies and the amount of benefit payouts required at any point in time. As a consequence, investments in long-term assets are more desirable for these intermediaries.

As shown in Exhibit 18–4, life insurance companies, like commercial banks, make substantial investments in commercial mortgage loans and loans on multifamily properties. Their commercial lending activity lies more in large shopping center developments, motels, and larger scale office buildings throughout the entire United States, as contrasted with more local, smaller scale loans made by commercial banks. Life insurance companies tend not to be interested in underwriting smaller scale projects but specialize in larger scale projects that involve large outlays of funds. They rely on mortgage bankers and commercial banks to make construction loans and to monitor

EXHIBIT 18–5
Participants in the mortgage market—selected characteristics

Characteristics	Source of funds	Stability of funds flow	Percent of funds invested in mortgages*	Preferred mortgage loans and recent lending trends	
				Long-term mortgage loans*	Short-term loans
Savings and loan associations	Time deposits	Low	97–100% of deposits	Largest of all lenders on single-family properties (80–85% of loans made). Most single-family loans conventional. FHA/VA loans account for only 12–15% of single-family loans made. Multifamily and commercial mortgages growing relative to single-family mortgages in recent years.	Largest single-family construction lenders. Also make considerable amounts of construction and land development loans for multifamily residences.
Commercial banks...........	Time and demand deposits	Low	15–20% of deposits	Make primarily single-family loans (55–65% of all loans made). FHA and VA mortgages range 11–30% of single-family loans. Largest of all lenders on commercial properties (28–35% of all loans made). Share of multifamily and commercial mortgages growing in recent years.	Largest construction lenders in multifamily and commercial categories. Extend large short-term loans to mortgage companies and REITs.
Mutual savings banks...........	Time deposits	Moderate	73–85% of deposits	Make primarily single-family loans (50–65% of all loans made). Second largest holder of FHA/VA mortgages (50–70% of single-family loans made). Make significant numbers of multifamily loans. Mortgage loans as a percent of deposits declining in recent years.	Very little construction lending due to geographic separation from developers. Make long-term commitments to mortgage companies and REITs that make construction loans.
Life insurance companies........	Reserves	High	30–38% of assets	Make primarily commercial and multifamily mortgage loans. Commercial and multifamily loans increasing in recent years.	Very little construction lending due to geographic separation from developers.

				Loans on single-family properties declining in recent years. Total mortgage loans as a percentage of assets declining in recent years.	Make long-term commitments to mortgage companies and REITs.
Mortgage companies.........	Equity and short-term loans	Low	Nearly 100% of assets	Long-term mortgages not a preferred investment. Although a high percentage of assets held in mortgages, this represents principally year-end balances of unsold mortgages. Largest originator of FHA/VA mortgage loans. Primary function-loan origination and servicing.	Significant number of loans for construction and land development.
REITs.............	Equity and short-term loans	Low	Nearly 100% of assets	Long-term multifamily and commercial mortgages preferred by some trusts.	Significant number of loans for construction and land development for specialized projects—primary function of many trusts.
Pension funds........	Payroll deductions/contributions	High	10% of assets	Increased activity in multifamily and commercial mortgages. Rely on other institutions for originations.	Very little activity due to inexperience in underwriting mortgage loans.
Federally related agencies..	Notes and bonds	Moderate	90–100% of assets	Largest holder of FHA/VA mortgage loans. Significant holder of multifamily mortgage loans. Purchase mortgage loans from lenders in secondary market. Share of mortgage holdings growing significantly.	Very little activity in direct lending for construction and land development.

* All statistics in table are high and low percentages applicable to the period 1969–79.
Source: Board of Governors, Federal Reserve System.

construction at the local level. Local lenders, because of their geographic proximity to the construction and development, are more efficient in performing that function. As a result, life insurance companies are more interested in only the permanent financing on large projects.

Mutual savings banks.   Like savings and loan associations, mutual savings tend to specialize in single-family lending. However, as shown in Exhibit 18–4, a larger portion of lending by mutual savings banks occurs in multifamily and commercial lending when compared to savings and loan associations. This is the case because mutual savings banks are located primarily in the northeastern section of the United States and must seek out loans in other areas of the country when savings inflows exceed the level of loan demand in their respective local lending markets. When this occurs, like life insurance companies, they prefer larger scale projects on which they issue commitments for permanent financing, with commercial banks, mortgage companies, or perhaps savings and loan associations making the construction loan and overseeing the project at the local level.

Also because of their geographical location, mutual savings banks purchase FHA-insured and VA-guaranteed mortgages from other parts of the United States. The FHA insurance and VA guarantee make mortgages on one- to four-family properties (usually originated by mortgage bankers in other areas) marketable investments for mutual savings banks. Hence, next to federally related agencies, they are the largest holders of FHA and VA mortgages in the United States.

Federally related agencies.   These agencies have become a very important force in the markets for single-family loans, multifamily loans, and farm lending. The development of the Federal National Mortgage Association, Federal Home Loan Mortgage Corporation, and various other agencies[14] has occurred primarily in response to recurrent problems[15] faced by private lenders during periods of rapidly rising interest rates. Essentially, these institutions provide a secondary market for existing single-family and multifamily loans for lenders who seek an outlet for mortgages made during periods of rising interest rates, when funds for originating new loans become scarce. By raising capital with various types of obligations and notes, these federally related institutions then purchase loans from private lenders during periods of capital shortages, thereby providing funds with which lenders may originate new loans. Because of recurrent problems in financial markets, these institutions have continuously increased their holdings of mortgage loans in recent years.

Mortgage companies.   These lenders held $15.6 billion in mortgage debt at the end of 1979. However, most of this debt was held in the form of construction loans and loans on newly completed properties, many of which were originated as construction loans by mortgage companies. This character-

---

[14] Farm credit programs are discussed in Chapter 25.

[15] These problems are discussed later in the chapter.

izes much of the mortgage banker's role in the mortgage market, that is, an originator and seller of mortgages to other financial institutions.

Mortgage companies are ordinarily privately owned concerns with limited funds for outright mortgage lending. They usually operate on the basis of commitments which they obtain from other financial institutions to buy loans to be closed by mortgage companies at a future date. With these commitments, mortgage companies can usually obtain short-term loans from commercial banks to originate loans that are to be delivered to other lenders in the future, at which time they repay the short-term loans. They may repeat this activity many times during one year, and as a result, the year-end figures shown in Exhibit 18–4 do not reflect total originations made during the year.

Mortgage companies tend to be very active in the one- to four-family market, obtaining commitments primarily from federal agencies and then originating FHA-insured and VA-guaranteed loans. In the market for multifamily and commercial mortgages, mortgage companies also act as middlemen by seeking permanent loan commitments for developers and investors and then making the construction loan themselves or arranging construction financing with another lender. In most cases, after construction is completed, mortgage companies retain the loan servicing function for the permanent lender.

Real estate investment trusts. Although they accounted for $4.2 billion in loans outstanding at the end of 1979, real estate investment trusts have been declining in the total amount of mortgage funds supplied in the mortgage market particularly during the past five years. These trusts are usually categorized as mortgage trusts or equity trusts, depending on whether they specialize in making mortgage loans or in purchasing property. Mortgage trusts, however, dominate as the major type of real estate investment trust.

Mortgage trusts generally raise capital from equity investors and make short-term loans from commercial banks. These funds are used primarily to originate construction loans and land development loans in the multifamily and commercial loan category. Some of these loans are held as investments by the trusts; however, many are sold to other financial institutions. Consequently, like mortgage companies, total loan originations made during a year may far exceed mortgage loans held by these institutions at year-end. Although real estate investment trusts had been rapidly expanding during the first part of the 1970s, the industry faced a severe downturn in lending activity in 1974–75. Problems faced by these trusts are taken up in Chapter 21.

Pension–retirement funds. Another group of institutions that are increasing in importance in the mortgage market are insured and noninsured pension and retirement funds. As shown in Exhibit 18–4, mortgage holdings by these institutions totaled approximately $12.5 billion at the end of 1979. Stringently regulated by state law, these institutions have traditionally made investments in high-quality stocks and bonds. However, with a growing realization of the relatively high yields available on high-quality mortgage loans and the acquisition of underwriting expertise by administrators of these funds, they have slowly increased their commitments to purchase mortgages made in the multifamily and commercial loan categories.

Growth and instability in the supply of mortgage funds

Growth in mortgage lending.   Mortgage loans constitute the largest type of credit outstanding in the United States. Further, residential mortgage loans constitute the largest category of loans among the various types of mortgages made in the United States. To show the importance of mortgage credit relative to many other forms of credit, Exhibit 18–6 provides a summary of growth in selected types of credit in the United States from 1950 to 1979.

EXHIBIT 18–6
Growth in selected types of credit, 1950–1979* ($ billion)

	1950		1979	
	Dollars	Percent	Dollars	Percent
Real estate mortgage loans:				
One- to four-family..........................	45.2	(15.2)	835.2	(29.2)
Multifamily	10.1	(3.4)	119.2	(4.2)
Commercial properties	11.5	(3.9)	198.6	(6.9)
Farm properties	6.1	(2.0)	57.5	(2.0)
Total	72.9	(24.4)	1,210.5	(42.3)
Corporate bonds	35.6	(11.9)	337.7	(11.9)
State and local bonds.....................	24.4	(8.2)	313.4	(11.0)
Consumer debt	21.5	(7.2)	354.6	(12.4)
Federal debt............................	216.5	(72.7)	664.5	(22.5)
Totals	298.0	(100.0)	2,860.7	(100.0)

* Estimated from data obtained from the U.S. League of Savings Associations, the Federal Reserve System, and from *Credit and Capital Markets, 1980,* Bankers Trust Co., New York.

From Exhibit 18–6, it can be seen that at the end of 1979 total mortgage credit outstanding totaled approximately $1,210.5 billion. Compared to the other major categories of credit use, mortgage credit is by far the single largest use of credit in our economy. At the end of 1979, mortgage credit accounted for 42.3 percent of many of the long-term uses of credit in our economy. This far exceeds credit usage by corporations, state and local government, consumers, and even the federal government.

Not only is mortgage debt the single most important use of credit in the United States, but its role has increased in importance in the post–World War II period. As shown in Exhibit 18–6, mortgage credit accounted for about 24 percent of long-term debt outstanding in 1950, but increased to 42 percent by 1979. Indeed, total mortgage credit increased well over 16 times during the

1950–79 period. These facts give some indication of the relative importance of mortgage credit as well as its growth as the major use of credit in the economy.

Changes in interest rates and housing starts

While the growth in mortgage credit during 1950–79 might be character-ized as phenomenal by some, it must be stressed that during this same time period, the availability of mortgage credit in *individual years* changed dramati-cally. Exhibit 18–7 provides some basic information concerning mortgage

EXHIBIT 18–7
Patterns in interest rates and housing starts, 1965–1980

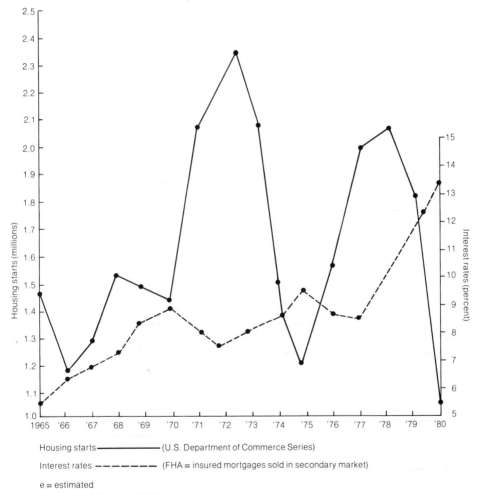

Housing starts ——————— (U.S. Department of Commerce Series)

Interest rates — — — — — — (FHA = insured mortgages sold in secondary market)

e = estimated

Source: *Federal Reserve Bulletins.*

interest rates and housing starts during the ten-year period 1965–75. Data in the exhibit reveal that sharp declines in housing starts occurred during the years 1966, 1969, 1973–74, and in 1979–80. During the same three periods, mortgage interest rates increased sharply. These years, particularly 1966, 1973–74, and 1979–80, have been characterized as the most severe downturns in housing starts and real estate development in the post–World War II period. In other years, notably 1967, 1971, 1972, 1976, 1977, and 1978, data in Exhibit 18–7 show sharp reversals in mortgage interest rates and increases in housing starts. Indeed, from the plot of data in the exhibit, it can be easily concluded that housing starts are *inversely,* or negatively, related to interest rates. This pattern is very evident in 1972, 1975, 1977, and 1980 when the extremes between housing starts and interest rates is most apparent.

Instability in the mortgage market

Interest rate volatility in the mortgage market is influenced by many of the same influences that generally affect interest rate levels in our economy. A complete discussion of the problems experienced in the U.S. economy during the last 10–15 years is obviously beyond the scope of this text. However, we will provide a summary of some of the more important trends affecting savings flows and financial institutions which are important in the mortgage market, and also discuss some of the proposed remedies for problems faced by these lenders.

Rate of savings and the price level. One fundamental change in the economy in recent times has been a reduction in the savings as a percentage of disposable personal income earned by households. Exhibit 18–8 shows this relationship between 1972 and 1980, and also shows the change in the

EXHIBIT 18–8

Year	(A) Savings as percent of disposable personal income	(B) Change in consumer price index*	(C) Deposits interest rates S&L's†	(C) − (B) Difference
1972	6.2%	3.3%	5.4%	2.1%
1973	8.1	6.2	5.6	(.6)
1974	7.3	11.0	6.0	(5.0)
1975	7.4	9.1	6.2	(2.9)
1976	5.6	5.8	6.3	(.5)
1977	5.0	6.5	6.4	(.1)
1978	4.9	7.7	6.6	(1.1)
1979	4.5	11.3	7.3	(4.0)
1980ᵉ	3.7	11.5	—	—

ᵉ Estimated.
* Base year 1967 = 100, U.S. Department of Labor Series.
† Average interest paid on average deposits at savings and loan associations.
Source: *Federal Reserve Bulletin* (various issues).

consumer price index, and average interest rates available at savings and loan associations during the same period. Based on data shown in the exhibit, it becomes apparent that Americans are consuming more out of disposable income than they are saving. Two influences not shown in the exhibit that have contributed to this pattern have been increases in personal income taxes at the state and local level and increases in social security withholding. However, the increase in the consumer price index in relation to the rate of interest paid on average deposit balances at savings and loan associations (which generally pay higher rates than those available at other financial institutions) also indicates that in addition to a decreasing relative supply of savings, the interest rate offered by financial intermediaries has not been high enough to induce savings from income earned by households. Indeed, in some years, most notably 1974–75 and 1979, potential losses in real purchasing power (based on the difference between the rate paid on savings and the change in the consumer price index) on amounts saved increased to a level that caused a significant change in the proportions of funds saved at intermediaries. In those years, increasing amounts of savings were invested directly in other investments, such as stocks, bonds, and in real assets, which offered yields that were expected to keep pace with rising price levels. When substantial shifts in the flow of funds away from financial intermediaries directly into the market for securities and other assets occurs, this process is called *financial disintermediation.*

Thrift and depository institutions have not been able to deal effectively with the problem of financial disintermediation because of deposit interest rate regulation and because of problems in "gap management" by intermediaries in the face of rising interest rates and inflation. The first problem is due to the regulatory lag between current market interest rates and what government regulation will allow intermediaries to pay on time deposits. These regulations restricted what institutions could pay on deposits as interest rates on other investments increased. However, significant changes occurred in 1978 when regulators allowed savings institutions to offer money market certificates at yields that changed with market conditions. Also, landmark legislation was passed in 1980 providing for eventual de-control of interest rate ceilings and liberalization of lending powers by deposit-type intermediaries.[16]

The problem of gap management comes about because of the maturity imbalance between assets and liabilities of most thrift institutions making mortgage loans. In periods of rising interest rates when rates paid on *all deposits* increase, the cost of those funds, which must be paid by intermediates, increases sharply. However, intermediaries that have significant numbers of mortgage loans made at historically low interest rates can only recover the increased cost of funds from revenues earned based on interest rates charged on new mortgages. Because new mortgages made in any one year may only

---

[16] This legislation is discussed more thoroughly in Chapter 20.

represent from 10 to 12 percent of total mortgages owned, revenues from *all* mortgages do not keep pace with the rising cost of funds. Hence, interest rates offered to borrowers must increase sharply to avert losses, and the "gap" between yields earned from mortgages and other assets, and costs paid for the use of funds, *narrows.* Lenders can no longer compete as effectively in the marketplace for savings. At that point, savers divert funds to assets in other markets that are expected to keep pace with interest rate changes.

One further aspect to be considered in conjunction with the imbalance between revenues and costs of financial intermediaries has to do with a more fundamental problem of why intermediaries cannot properly *anticipate* what their cost of funds will be when they originate loans. As was discussed at the beginning of Chapter 9 on alternative mortgage instruments, mortgage interest rates are based on expectations of lenders concerning the real rate of interest, plus premiums for risk and inflation over the period during which loans are expected to be outstanding. If this is true, why isn't enough revenue earned on assets to pay for the cost of funds (deposits) over the same period? One possible answer to this problem has to do with differences in *expected inflation* and *actual inflation.* Because interest rates on mortgages are based on expected inflation over the period of the loan, if actual inflation is greater than what was expected, the cost of deposits will rise relative to revenue generated from mortgages. At that point a profit squeeze develops. What causes actual inflation to be different from expected inflation? Many observers argue that this is due to an excessive supply of money caused by overexpansion by the Federal Reserve System. If the growth in the supply of money is too high in relation to the growth of real output and productivity in the economy, nominal prices will eventually rise because of inflation. As inflation rises, so will interest rates. Unfortunately, it is difficult for lenders to predict what monetary policy will be when they originate loans with long maturities. Historically, there is some evidence showing that lenders have underestimated inflation in interest rates. This has made borrowers better off than savers over the decade of the 1970s and accounts in large part for the reduction in savings relative to income shown in Exhibit 18–8. It has also been argued that this inflationary effect has been capitalized into house prices, accounting in large part for the rapid increase in new house prices during the 1970s.

Instability in the mortgage market and proposed remedies. Based on material presented to this point, it is apparent that the relative instability in availability of mortgage funds has brought many problems to the real estate industry. One remedy that is presently being phased in is the elimination of government-regulated ceilings on interest rates paid on deposits made at financial institutions. As has been pointed out, because of the regulatory lag in adjusting interest rates payable on deposits, the spread between yields on direct investments and deposits increases and provides incentives for financial disintermediation. With deregulation of ceiling rates, institutions could better compete for savings by offering higher interest rates on deposits and the flow of funds to the mortgage market might be maintained.

Adjustable interest rate mortgage. Another possible suggested solution to the problem of instability in the mortgage market is to institute a system of mortgages with adjustable interest rates. These mortgages, previously discussed in Chapter 9, have provisions allowing the interest rate originally negotiated on the loan to change with market conditions. This would allow interest rates to change on *all mortgages* made with such a provision, as interest rates are changing. Consequently, with income rising from changes in the interest rate on all mortgage loans, savings institutions could raise interest rates on deposits to compete for additional savings. It is argued that this in turn would result in a more stable flow of funds to the mortgage market and would eliminate much of the boom-bust cycle in real estate lending.

Other alternatives. To help cushion the blow on real estate lending and housing starts, the federal government has chosen to create a system of federally related, private institutions in the secondary mortgage market. These institutions, including primarily the FNMA, GNMA, and FHLMC, have been created to act as a buffer during periods of rising interest rates. By issuing government-backed securities during periods of high interest rates, these institutions raise capital to buy mortgages from mortgage lenders and thus provide funds to the lenders for additional loans. This technique, along with various subsidy schemes used in conjunction with these federally related institutions, provides some funds for mortgage lending even during periods of financial disintermediation. These institutions, their functions, and the operation of private mortgage lenders are taken up in detail in the chapters that follow.

Questions

1 From data provided in this chapter, describe the areas of mortgage lending in which the four major private financial institutions specialize.

2 Rank the four major financial institutions in the mortgage market in terms of total mortgage investment.

3 Based on the discussion in this chapter, what are the fundamental determinants of savings by households? What determines how savings are allocated among depositary institutions and investments in our economy?

4 What is financial disintermediation? How does this process come about? What is its effect on the housing and mortgage markets?

5 What is meant by gap management? How do differences between expected and actual inflation come about? What problems does this cause among lenders, savers and borrowers?

6 What remedies have been proposed as a solution to the problem of financial disintermediation as it affects the housing and mortgage markets?

Financing of real estate by savings and loan associations

19

Early associations

The foundation stones of modern savings and loan associations are two in number: thrift and homeownership. Neither is currently placed ahead of the other in importance. In the day-to-day operation of an institution of this character, if the savings and investment funds pile up because of lack of mortgage demand, the progressive manager tries to stimulate loan applications. If the latter exceed the capacity of the institution to supply funds, efforts are made to increase savings. Within reasonable limits, liquidity requirements taken into consideration, an attempt is made to maintain a balance between receipts and disbursements. As a matter of fact, until quite recently the statement that interested savings and loan managers most was neither the balance sheet nor the income statement based upon accruals, but the statement showing cash receipts and disbursements.

In the early days there was a definite difference in emphasis. Homeownership by its members was the goal of the early "building societies" organized by our forefathers of English origin and of the "Bauvereine" organized by their German neighbors. The end was homeownership; the means was a kind of forced savings which were no longer considered essential once the home was paid for. The emphasis upon homeownership was so great that our usual concept of saving for a purpose was definitely reversed. Today we are accustomed to think that those who save accumulate funds against their use for a specific purpose which involves their expenditure at a later date. In other words, saving precedes spending. The basic idea in building associations was to encourage the borrower to borrow, with his home as security, funds which he would then repay from future savings. In this case, spending precedes saving.

510

The ambition for homeownership was not an indigenous American plan. Neither was the plan for cooperative financing of homes. Both were imported from Europe. Except among the German settlers, early American building societies followed the Anglo-Saxon model. Without benefit of parliamentary sanction, the English had made considerable progress with voluntary associations before the first American counterpart was started in Frankford, Pennsylvania, in 1831. The avowed purpose of this first American cooperative home-financing institution, known as the Oxford Provident Building Association, was to "enable the contributors thereof to build or purchase dwelling houses."

This first association could not even qualify as a mortgage finance institution as we know this term today. It gave no heed to the financial needs of those who owned homes already; its purpose was to help its nonhomeowning members to acquire homes for themselves by purchase or construction. Neither was it concerned with thrift as a desirable objective by itself, since it had nothing to offer to the person who wished to save for some purpose other than homeownership.

Share-accumulation sinking-fund loan plan.   The early American associations used a loan plan that few members of the associations ever understood; and not even the elected nonsalaried managers could forecast its full meaning. It operated in this manner: Suppose that A subscribes for five shares of stock and later borrows $1,000 from the association. He gives a mortgage on his home for this amount. In effect this is an unamortized term loan without any definite term stated. Each month he pays the interest, which is credited to the income of the association. In addition, he continues to make his regular payments on his shares.

More often than not, the interest rate was 6 percent. The borrower would pay each month to the association $5 for interest and an additional $5 dues to be credited on his share account. This was the beginning of requiring the borrower to pay 1 percent of his original loan principal per month, regardless of the percentage of loan to property value, and so forth. While most modern lending practices have adjusted monthly payments to a variety of factors, savings and loan associations have remained with a monthly reduction formula.

High percentage loans were common in the early building associations. While the borrower was expected to have some capital to put into his home, the amount required was likely to be a token amount only as a gesture of good faith on the part of the borrower. Even this rule was relaxed when the board of directors felt that the property was being acquired at a bargain, if the borrower enjoyed a reputation for honesty, sobriety, and industry. In any event both the real estate acquired and the member's stock were put up as collateral to protect the loan.

Since funds were limited to the amount paid in on stock subscriptions and earnings on loans, the money available had to be allocated. Often the loan was made to the member willing to pay the highest premium, commonly determined by auction. Some associations had a fixed premium rate; others gave the loans to borrowing members in the order of filing applications or by lot.

At the end of the year the earnings of the association, minus any expenses, which were small, and any losses, which had to be calculated annually, were credited to the share accounts on a pro rata basis. The credits to the share account thus cumulated from dues and from credited income. Charged against this account were unpaid fees, fines, and forfeitures of stock or dividend credits for failure to make required payments or premature withdrawals. Whenever these net credits were equal to the amount of the original mortgage, the shares were declared to be matured and were used to offset and cancel the loan. In the beginning, this terminated the member's need for the association. He had reached the goal for which he had set out. Other members would continue paying their dues and borrowing funds needed to finance the purchase or construction of their homes. The "last man" would in effect borrow his own savings and hence have no obligation to pay interest. As his obligations were met, the association terminated.

Serial associations. In order not to put a premium upon late joiners in a terminating association, anyone joining after the date of organization was forced to make an initial contribution equal to the existing credits per share. Lack of accumulated capital foreclosed this possibility after the credits were of substantial size. This denied participation to many who would have liked to join the association. With the machinery all set up and in operation, an American idea was added that had not been commonly used in England. Why not start a new series with new members? Thus was the serial association born. In effect it amounted to a succession of terminating associations. Whenever it appeared that there was sufficient demand, a new series was started. This meant increasing the number of meetings, perhaps to one a week instead of one each month.

Managerial duties increased, and the secretary and attorney began to receive compensation in the form of fees. Directors, who supplanted the trustees of early voluntary associations when the corporate form of organization was introduced, still served without compensation. The mere introduction of the use of serial associations did not change the methods of operating these associations. The same methods of lending their money on mortgages were continued.

Savings members. Gradually the need for more attention to the desires of savings members began to be felt in the operation of building associations. In some cases the member who started with full expectations of acquiring a home by this means changed his plans or had them changed for him. Perhaps the lady of his choice said "No" instead of "Yes." There were other members who were not ready to buy or build a home even when the credits to their shares accumulated to a point where they reached their face value. Other thrifty people wanted an opportunity to accumulate savings but had no interest in homeownership. Even the member who had secured a debt-free home through the aid of his building association wished to continue as a member of the association because he had acquired thrifty habits and liked them.

While homeownership was the major objective of these building associations, there was nothing to prevent a member from taking out cash by the maturity of his shares instead of through the process of giving back a mortgage as evidence of a loan. Hence the practice of maturing shares in cash gradually developed. Even in such event some members, well satisfied with the returns they had received from their investment, were loath to withdraw the cash due them. They preferred to leave their investment intact or even to add to it as before.

Modern associations

With the emergence of the savings member who did not borrow from the association, the whole character of the association underwent a radical change. From a purely local community association of friends, anxious to help one another acquire homes, it was on the verge of becoming a financial institution equipped to serve two distinct groups of people, many of whom had no direct interest in the others. On the one hand, there were the thrifty people who needed the assistance of a financial institution equipped to care for their savings against the time when they would be needed for any purpose. On the other hand, another group of people needed assistance in financing the homes of their choice. Some might save systematically until they accumulated enough to make the down payment on a home. Thereafter they preferred to make payments on a mortgage debt instead of on share accounts to be later offset against the mortgage. Others might continue to build savings accounts after the mortgage was paid off. Still others preferred to borrow the amount needed over and above the funds accumulated by other means to buy a home.

This change in character broadened the scope of operations and brought other changes in thrift and home-financing institution operations. Among these was a gradual change in name to recognize the new position of savings members. The word *savings* began to be used in some combination with *building* and *loan.* Gradually the modern standard pattern of the savings and loan association began to take shape. This is the one most commonly used today, except in Louisiana where those operating under a state charter are still called homestead associations, and in Massachusetts where the corresponding name is cooperative bank. This latter name has become so well established that even federal savings and loan associations are commonly spoken of in that state as banks.

With the change in the character of these associations, the older emphasis upon forced savings gradually disappeared. With its disappearance went most of the use of fees, fines, and forfeitures. Investing members were encouraged to bring in their savings in either regular or irregular amounts and at regular or irregular intervals, and to withdraw them as they needed them. Penalties took the form of loss or reduction of income. Borrowers were put on their own responsibility without reference to the performance of other borrowers. Delinquencies were dealt with in terms of those responsible, but losses were not charged against those who met their obligations promptly.

Types of accounts.   With the new emphasis upon savings accounts came a classification of shares into groups that undertook to represent the needs of various types of investors. For the investor whose shares had matured but who nevertheless wished to retain his investment, *full-paid shares* (sometimes called income shares) were provided. These came to have a face value of $100. Dividends were paid in cash. *Prepaid shares* set a pattern that has since been followed by E bonds issued by the government. Purchased at $75, they matured at $100 through the credit of dividends over a series of years. There is no magic in these amounts: $700 could be left to grow into $1,000; or $360 to grow into $500; and so on. The prepaid share is simply the plan arranged for the lump-sum investor who does not need his dividends in the form of cash as they accrue. Many of these then became full-paid shares. *Installment thrift shares* encouraged the small investor dependent upon earnings to set aside a definite amount each month to add to his account in his savings and loan association. This type of share emphasized the advantages of regular savings habits. To clinch the argument in their favor, some associations either penalized failure to make all payments on time by the assessment of fines for late payments or rewarded the shareholder who met all payments as scheduled by giving him an extra bonus in the form of an increased dividend payment.

In contrast to the emphasis upon regularity of payments under installment thrift shares, the Dayton plan (originated in Dayton, Ohio) encouraged thrifty people to make additions to their investments when and as their resources permitted. Each account holder established his own pattern of savings, and his contributions were rewarded in proportion to his individual accomplishments. In keeping with the removal of pressure to save, these shares were given the name *optional savings shares.* While some associations still favor the practice of encouraging regular savings, most savings and loan associations have long since adopted the practice of accepting savings at the option of their owners.

Savings and loan associations started out as mutual institutions with no distinction among the claims of those who contributed capital. Later, some were organized with a permanent capital in the form of nonwithdrawable "guarantee stock," so-called because it was supposed to serve as a cushion to absorb possible losses which might otherwise have been assessed against ordinary shares. Where guarantee stock was used, its ownership was concentrated in the management. Other investors received as evidence of their commitments a variety of certificates—full-paid, prepaid, installment, accumulative, and so forth. These corresponded to the types of shares already discussed. The accumulative certificate was similar to the Dayton plan share.

Deposits were sometimes protected by nonwithdrawable stock. In other cases no cushion of investment was provided, since shares as well as deposits were freely withdrawable. In fact, in many instances shares and deposits were so similar in character that great confusion resulted. Some investors never were sure whether they owned shares or deposits.

In recent years there has been a distinct movement in the direction of simplifying the capital structure of savings and loan associations. The pattern followed by mutual associations—the predominant type—calls for only two types of accounts: savings accounts and investment accounts. The former are optional as to amounts and times of deposit, although systematic saving is still encouraged in some quarters. Earnings are credited to these accounts. Investment accounts serve the needs of lump-sum investors who prefer to receive their earnings distributions in cash.

With the passage of the Housing and Urban Development Act of 1968, savings and loan associations were permitted to use the terms *deposit* and *interest* in place of *share accounts* and *dividends*. They were also allowed to issue notes, bonds, debentures, and long-term certificates of deposit for the first time. The Depository Institutions Deregulation and Monetary Control Act of 1980 authorized issuance of *mutual capital certificates*. Such certificates pay dividends subject to net worth requirements.

Need for a central system

Out of the Great Depression of the 1930s several weaknesses of home mortgage financing became starkly apparent. Under the heading of causes of financial distress, the following stood out:

1. The instability of real estate values in this country—due to a combination of factors which we need not stop to discuss here—resulted in low-percentage loans in relation to values. Even normally low percentages were further reduced in periods of economic distress so that refinancing became very much restricted when most needed.

2. Low-percentage first mortgages required supplementary financing for many real estate owners. This took the form of short-term second and third mortgages. Refunding of these short-term obligations was costly under the best of circumstances because of the prevalence of heavy discounts. Under circumstances which represented less than the best, mortgagees, fearing the future, pressed for liquidation of their claims, precipitating numerous foreclosure actions.

3. The prevalence of short-term primary financing in some sections of the country resulted in increases in demands for repayment when the mortgagor had least opportunity for refinancing with other lenders on mortgage security. Because these short-term mortgages made no provision for amortization, the mortgagees lacked this source of liquidity with which mortgagors could have been assisted. Unsatisfied demands for repayment of matured mortgages invited increased foreclosures.

4.   Short-term funds invested in long-term mortgages became frozen at a time when the demand for the withdrawal of these funds was greatest. In general, whether a real estate mortgage is written for a long or a short term, it is to be considered a frozen asset unless the debt secured by it is actually amortized. If you list the cities where commercial banks were in greatest difficulties during the early 1930s and then make another list of localities where banks were heavy lenders on real estate mortgages, you will find a striking coincidence.

5.   Inefficient and unsystematic appraisal practices resulted in the virtual purchases of many real estate parcels at the time mortgages were placed against them. Many lenders had only vague ideas on the subject of appraisal techniques. They let some of their borrowers make their appraisals for them by shopping around for loans until they found the highest bidder for their business. If what is said in this paragraph seems to be in conflict with what is said under 1, keep this in mind. Some loans were actually 40 or 50 percent loans. Others, labeled 40 or 50 percent loans, were actually 110 percent loans because of excessive appraisals. Frequently the amount of the loan was agreed upon, and the appraisal was adjusted to make the loan fit the announced lending policy of the mortgagee.

6.   The dependence of real estate lenders upon purely local sources of loanable funds created an uneven flow of mortgage money in different parts of the country at the same time. Under normal economic conditions, one city might have a plethora of funds and a dearth of loan demand; another city might have a great backlog of loan demand and insufficient funds with which to meet it. In the absence of any kind of mechanism to shift funds from one section of the country to another for this purpose, real estate lenders were shut off from access to national capital markets.

7.   There was a lack of standards for quality of construction. Lenders did not ordinarily undertake to tell contractors and owners what type of structures to build. Indeed, some of them had no yardstick by which to measure construction quality. They merely responded favorably or unfavorably to applications for loans. Since the nature of the response to such applications was conditioned, in part at least, by their anxiety to put to work the surpluses of cash that they might have on hand, in times of surplus jerry-builders undoubtedly received more encouragement and support than in times of shortages.

8.   Too many real estate parcels were held by weak holders who lacked the capacity to meet their obligations when their economic circumstances were disturbed ever so little. Like some of their more fortunate friends and acquaintances, they, too, made an emotional response to the sentimental appeal for homeownership. But lacking the financial resources with which to back up their emotions, they fell easy prey to foreclosure action as soon as the economic road became rough. These foreclosures flooded a market already glutted with unwanted properties, caused wider fluctuations in all real estate values, and

raised doubts in the minds of even strong holders about the desirability of investment in real estate.

The Federal Home Loan Bank System

To deal with these and other shortcomings of the thrift and home financing institutions, largely the savings and loan associations, the Federal Home Loan Bank System was created by authority of the Federal Home Loan Bank Act which was approved on July 22, 1932. Operating in 12 districts, encompassing the United States, Puerto Rico, the Virgin Islands, and Guam, the Federal Home Loan Banks function as a central credit facility for all federally chartered savings and loan associations, and on a voluntary basis to qualified state-chartered savings and loan associations, mutual savings banks, and life insurance companies.

Objectives of the Home Loan Bank System. By its design, the Home Loan Bank System, except through the Federal Home Loan Mortgage Corporation as discussed in Chapter 24, does not and cannot inject liquidity into individual mortgages. What it does is to provide liquidity for the institution that holds the mortgage. As a credit reserve system, it is not necessary for it to undertake the difficult task of making mortgages marketable. It merely accepts them as security for advances to members of the Home Loan Bank System. In some cases, unsecured advances are also made.

In providing this service it gives its members an alternative source of funds. Before the Home Loan Bank System was organized, savings and loan associations were accustomed to obtain cash on occasion from the commercial banks of their locality. Usually such loans were collateralized with mortgages held by the borrower. In this manner local banks aided the plans of mortgage lenders materially. One difficulty with such a plan was the limitation of availability of funds at a time when such funds were most urgently needed.

Of necessity, commercial bank loans were made for short periods of time only. They were extended with care in such manner as to protect the lending institution. When the borrower most needed new advances, the lender was least likely to look with favor upon granting them. In addition, such advances as had already been made were likely to be called at most embarrassing times for the borrower.

The Home Loan Bank System was not intended to take business away from local commercial banks. Instead, it was developed for the purpose of providing more dependable liquidity for its members, for a longer period of time, if necessary, than that for which commercial banks could commit their funds. Some members of the Home Loan Bank System still depend upon their local commercial banks for at least a part of their short-term needs for cash. The reasons for this practice are several. In some cases the close relationship between the savings and loan association manager and his banker is so cordial that friendship dictates the use of local bank credit. On other occasions, the local bank may be so anxious to get loans that it will lend money at lower rates of interest than those currently charged by the Home Loan Bank of the district. Even when local banks are used as sources of cash, the member-borrower enjoys the feeling of security that membership in the Home Loan Bank System affords it.

As a precaution against excessive demands by members upon the regional banks, the system regulates interest rate ceilings at liquidity. The interest rate ceilings have done much to stabilize the competitive climate for savers' funds, both among associations and with respect to other types of thrift institutions or investment vehicles. Under the terms of the new Depository Institutions Deregulation and Monetary Control Act of 1980, these interest rate ceilings are being phased out and new competitive conditions will be brought into play. New liquidity reserve requirements are also being installed to take into account institutional changes. Factors bringing about the legislative change are discussed in the next chapter (Appendix).

Sources of Home Loan Bank funds. Since July 2, 1951, all of the stock of Home Loan Banks has been owned by the membership. Subscription requirements are based on the amount of home mortgage loans held by the institution.

In addition to the capital of the Home Loan Banks, other sources of funds consist of:

1. Consolidated bonds and notes which are sold in the open market by the Home Loan Bank Board as they are needed, with the proceeds distributed among the various regional banks on the basis of their probable loan demands. These bonds and notes carry such maturity as best seems to meet the needs of the system. Interest rates reflect the cost of money for that type of paper at the time the bonds and notes are issued. By the sale of these bonds and notes, the member institutions have access to the capital markets of the country.

2. Deposits of members who have excess funds. Demand deposits pay no return to their owners. Interest rates on time deposits vary with the length of time and with the needs of the banks. Recently a new pattern using a definite maturity certificate of deposit has been introduced into the system. By combining operations, excess deposits in one bank can be borrowed by another bank in the system.

Provision for federal savings and loan associations. Federal chartering of savings and loan associations was originally authorized in the Home Owners Loan Act of 1933. In brief, the act set up a plan for chartering and supervising federal savings and loan associations under the Home Loan Bank Board, which is the senior governing body of the Federal Home Loan Bank System. In addition to newly chartered federal associations, the Board was authorized to set up rules and regulations for converting state-chartered associations into federal associations. At the present time, over 98 percent of the assets of all savings and loan associations are held by members of the Federal Home Loan Bank System. The fact of this broad-encompassing acceptance testifies to the need for this leadership and stabilizing influence.

Nature of federal associations. Whereas each state savings and loan association operates under its own local laws, the federal associations are governed by a uniform law. State-chartered associations that have sought membership in the Federal Home Loan Bank System qualify for that membership by meeting standards comparable to those set for the federal associations.

This type of association is intended to be primarily a local thrift and home-financing institution, mutually owned by its investors. Borrowers are given the right to attend shareholders' meetings and to cast one vote each. Every federal association is required to be a member of the Home Loan Bank System and is expected to make use of its facilities if and when it can use them to advantage. Borrowing from other sources is much more definitely restricted. In addition, the federal association must have its accounts insured by the Federal Savings and Loan Insurance Corporation.

Lending or investment authority. The lending or investment authority of federal savings and loan associations is set forth in the Home Owners Loan Act of 1933, as amended to 1980, generally as follows:

I. Loans or investments without a percentage of assets limitation.
   A. Loans secured by savers' accounts.
   B. Single-family and multifamily mortgage loans.
      1. Up to 66.67 percent of the appraised value of unimproved real estate.
      2. Up to 75 percent of the appraised value if the real estate already has off-site improvements, such as street, water, sewer, and other utilities.
      3. Up to 75 percent of the appraised value if the real estate is in the process of being improved by a building to be constructed or in the process of construction.
      4. Up to 90 percent of the appraised value if the real estate is improved by a building.
      Notwithstanding the foregoing loan-to-value limitations, the Federal Home Loan Bank Board may permit loans exceeding the 90 percent limit where a building is on site and that portion of the unpaid balance of the loan exceeding 90 percent of appraised value is guaranteed or insured by a qualified public or private insuror or in the case of any loan to provide low-income housing.
   C. U.S. government securities.
   D. Investments in the stock or bonds of a Federal Home Loan Bank or of the Federal National Mortgage Association.

    E. Investments in mortgages, obligations, or other securities which are or ever have been sold by the Federal Home Loan Mortgage Corporation.

    F. Investments in obligations, participations, or other instruments of, issued by, or fully guaranteed as to principal and interest by, the Federal National Mortgage Association, the Student Loan Marketing Association, or the Government National Mortgage Association, or any other agency of the United States.

    G. Bank deposits.

    H. State securities.

    I. Purchase of insured loans on improved real estate.

    J. Home improvement and manufactured home loans.

    K. Insured loans to finance the purchase of a fee simple.

    L. Loans to financial institutions subject to federal supervision and brokers and dealers registered with the Securities and Exchange Commission.

    M. Investments eligible to satisfy the institutional liquidity requirements.

    N. Equity investments in the national housing partnership corporation and qualified partnerships, limited partnerships, or joint ventures in furtherance of Housing and Urban Development programs.

    O. Loans guaranteed under various sections of Housing and Urban Development Act programs.

    P. State housing corporation investments.

    Q. Investment companies registered with the Securities and Exchange Commission under the Investment Company Act of 1940.

 II. Loans or investments limited to 20 percent of institution assets.

    A. First-mortgage liens on improved commercial real estate.

    B. Consumer loans and investments in commercial paper and corporate debt securities as defined and approved by the Federal Home Loan Bank Board.

III. Loans or investments limited to 5 percent of institution assets.

    A. Education loans.

    B. Community development investments.

    C. Nonconforming loans, primarily for residential or farm purposes.

    D. Construction loans without security.

IV. Other loans or investments.

    A. Business development credit corporations.

    B. Savings and loan association service corporations.

    C. Certain guaranteed loans for foreign assistance.

    The effect of the enactment of the Depository Institutions Deregulation and Monetary Control Act of 1980 has been generally to expand savings and loan lending authority. Former geographical lending restrictions have been removed. First-lien restrictions on residential loans are no longer imposed. Second trust loans may now be made. There is broader authority to make acquisition, development, and construction loans. In all cases, the dollar limit (most recently $75,000) has been removed in favor of a 90 percent loan-to-value ratio limitation on residental real estate loans.

Loan policies and underwriting standards.   Within the rules for compliance with federal statutes and regulations, federal savings and loan associations make their own determination of institutional obligations and guidelines which become their statement of underwriting standards. An abbreviated, but fairly typical, example of such a statement might run as follows:

Star Federal Savings and Loan Association, Any Town, U.S.A.
Underwriting Standards for One- to Four-Family Properties

The primary business of Star Federal is to encourage thrift and promote homeownership. Savings accounts are attracted through payment of competitive interest rates, and provide the funds to make long-term loans principally for buying, building, renovating, or refinancing homes. Because borrowers should have the opportunity to consider the factors affecting their loan applications, these underwriting standards are being made available.

The loan process starts by the applicant completing a standard loan application form which requests information about the borrower's income, employment, assets, debts, credit references, what the loan proceeds will be used for and what property will secure the loan. The application form must be completed, in writing, before Star Federal can act upon any request. *Every person is entitled to make a written mortgage loan application.* We may also require your authorization to verify your employment, income, or checking or savings balances, in addition to obtaining a credit report. If the property is being purchased, a sales contract will also be required.

Underwriting is the process that lenders go through in evaluating a loan request from an applicant and arriving at their lending decision. Underwriting usually boils down to (1) an applicant's *ability* to repay the requested loan, (2) an applicant's *attitude* toward financial obligations, and (3) the market *value* of the real estate offered to secure the loan.

Star Federal does not consider an applicant's race, color, religion, sex, or national origin in judging the merits of any loan request. Neither will the age or location of a property by themselves cause a loan application to be denied.

Applicant's ability to repay the loan

The applicant's source of income, the amount, and the dependability that it will continue are all vitally important in the underwriting decision. In other words, is the income sufficient and is it stable? The various types of income normally considered are:

1. Regular full-time employment.
   a. Self-employment (average of last two years, supported by IRS returns or profit and loss statements).

2. Part-time employment or second jobs (average of last two years).
3. Commissions, bonuses, and tips (on the basis of average earnings as shown by IRS return copies for past two years).
4. Rental property—net income after deducting various expenses including mortgage payments of principal, interest, taxes, and insurance (PITI).
5. Public assistance programs.
6. Alimony or child support if the applicant chooses to include it but, if so, the applicant will be required to give information about the payer of the income (consider whether received according to written agreement or court decree, length of time received and regularity of receipt).
7. Any other lawful income.

Star Federal employs certain calculations to determine if the applicant's income appears sufficient to carry the expense of homeownership and other installment obligations that the applicant might have. These calculations (called screening ratios) are almost universally used by credit grantors, but not necessarily set at the same limits. Star Federal's guidelines are that no more than 25 percent of applicant's gross income should be required for Housing Expense and that no more than 35 percent of gross income should be required for total expense obligations (housing expense and installment debts). These ratios are developed as follows:

1. Income used is the gross allowable income of the applicant; allowable income is after income taxes.
2. Housing expense is the estimated payment of principal and interest, taxes and insurance (PITI) on the mortgage applied for (condo fee is added for condominium). Insurance may include one or more of the following:
    a. Hazard insurance.
    b. FHA insurance.
    c. Flood insurance.
    d. Risk insurance.
3. The ratio of housing expense divided by income equals the housing expense ratio and should not exceed 25 percent.
4. Total expense includes housing expense plus all installment payments (excluding those with six months or less to run) and any child support, alimony, or separate maintenance payable.
5. Total expense divided by income equals the total expense ratio which should not exceed 35 percent.

These screening ratios may be exceeded in some cases where the applicant can demonstrate the ability and history of carrying a heavier debt load; has been able to accumulate substantial assets while carrying a normal debt load; has tax-free income, automobile furnished or other reason to have lower than average expenses; where the loan-to-value ratio of the loan requested is lower than normal. These ratios also take into consideration the need for food, clothing, health care, education, and a number of other essential factors affecting the average family.

Applicant's attitude toward financial obligations

This aspect is often expressed as the borrower's "willingness to repay." It is probably best exemplified by the applicant's past record of handling credit. Prompt, conscientious repayment of previous or current obligations is a good indicator of a borrower's sense of responsibility. A lender will normally assume that this attitude will continue. Limited credit use will not be an adverse factor in the underwriting decision.

Problems in the past may not necessarily prevent an applicant from securing a loan from Star Federal. Extenuating circumstances such as illness, divorce or separation, and loss of employment through layoffs or shutdowns will be considered. In most cases, the more current credit history is given the most weight. Bankruptcy, mortgage foreclosure, repossession, or judgments against the applicant will be considered reason for rejection unless sufficient evidence can be shown that the credit failure was beyond the applicant's control.

The value of the secured property

Almost all of Star Federal's lending involves real estate being mortgaged as security for a loan. Therefore, it is essential that we obtain an estimate of value of the real estate from a qualified, approved appraiser. As a federally chartered savings and loan association, our loan amount is restricted to a percentage of property value (or in some instances, a sales price, if lower than the value) and therefore all of our home loans must be supported by a current appraisal. Often, this appraised value is obtained by comparing the security property with like properties in the immediate vicinity for such things as type of construction. In addition, the availability of government services, zoning requirements, utilities, presence of hazards to health and safety, ingress and egress, overimprovements, excess land and adherence to building codes are some of the other factors that could have a bearing on the collateral property's value. Star Federal does not lend on personal property such as furniture or furnishings with the exception that we do make loans on mobile homes.

Types of loans and relevant terms (One- to four-family properties)

Star Federal will not make a conventional real estate loan for more than 30 years. This term is generally reduced on older properties as a result of the remaining economic life of the property. Star Federal may lend up to 95 percent of the value (or sales price, if smaller), on an owner-occupied single family dwelling. For a loan over 80 percent up to 90 percent, the maximum is $75,000; over 90 percent up to 95 percent, the maximum is $60,000. Any loan over 80 percent must have an escrow account for payment of taxes and insurance, and Star Federal policy requires mortgage risk insurance.

Loan requests of up to 80 percent of all other owner-occupied real estate properties will be considered; however, loans in excess of $150,000 will be made at less than an 80 percent level. Loans on investor-owned properties will not exceed 75 percent of either the purchase price or value.

The above terms apply to our conventional residential real estate lending programs. While Star Federal makes home loans under the FHA-insured or VA-guaranteed programs, the terms do not vary nationwide and are in accordance with the regulations established by those governmental agencies.

Financing of mobile homes which are permanently affixed to the underlying land and treated as real estate under state law will be considered under terms similar to those applicable to site-built homes. Lending on such homes is limited to those located in condominiums, planned unit developments, or subdivisions designed and zoned for use as sites for modular/mobile home units. Loan repayment terms are generally for a shorter period of time than for site built homes and rates may differ depending on market conditions.

Conventional home improvement. For purposes of this program, a home improvement loan is defined to be "A loan for which the total proceeds will be used for the addition of permanent improvements, to one- to four-family real property residence." In addition, proceeds may be used to refinance an existing loan which is proven to have been exclusively for a property improvement on the subject property and to cover closing costs or other expenses associated with the new loan. These loans are assumable in accordance with the Association's prequalified/rate adjusted assumption procedure. FHA Title I Property Improvement Loans are made available in conjunction with Community Development Agencies.

Equity loan. The equity loan program is designed to provide homeowners, who have achieved a substantial equity position in their residences, the ability to use a portion of that equity as collateral for second (2nd) mortgages. The proceeds from these loans may be used for any purpose the homeowner desires, that is, vacations, investments, auto purchase, and so on.

Developed lot loans are available for individuals wishing to buy a lot in advance of constructing their permanent home on the site. The loan must not exceed 75 percent of value or sales price, and the site not more than one acre in size. These loans are repaid on a monthly basis with a balloon payment of the loan balance, approximately 60 percent of the original loan amount, coming due at the end of five years.

Mortgage interest rates change from time to time and are a reflection of market conditions. There are loan fees and other costs for obtaining a mortgage loan; an estimate of these charges will be provided to a prospective borrower *at time of application.*

Loan applications are considered on a case basis; this means that all relevant factors concerning the applicant and the property are taken into account. If Star Federal is unable to grant a loan in the amount or terms requested, it will attempt, if possible, to offer an alternative even though the terms might be considered more stringent by the applicant. If a loan application is turned down, Star Federal will provide the applicant with a Notice of Adverse Action, which will identify the reasons.

Applications will be acted upon within 30 days after receipt of the completed application, application fee, contract (if applicable), and any other data requested. If you feel that you have not been treated fairly and in accordance with these standards and the various nondiscrimination laws and regulations, please contact the Star Federal compliance officer.

Importance of mortgage lending.   At the beginning of 1980, savings and loan associations held real estate mortgages of about $475.8 billion. This represented 39.4 percent of the total real estate mortgages outstanding. The extreme importance of these institutions to *residential* home financing is apparent from the outstanding savings and loan mortgage balance of $382.5 billion on one- to four-family homes, equal to 48.8 percent of the total outstanding mortgage financing ($784 billion) in this category.

Savings and loan service corporations

Savings and loan associations in recent years have been permitted to spin off service corporations. Such corporations may engage in many areas of business activity denied the parent corporation. A mere listing of allowable areas suggests the great potential in this direction. Of particular interest in real estate finance are:

1. Originating and servicing real estate loans, even under less restrictive conditions than those imposed upon the association.
2. Purchasing, servicing, and brokering mobile home loans.
3. Making combined loans on property improvement and household furnishings.
4. Investing in National Housing Corporation loans.[1]
5. Providing consulting and allied professional services, including appraisal, maintenance and management, construction loan inspection, bulk purchasing, and advertising.
6. Acting as agent or broker in areas of hazard and title insurance.

Although the service corporations are fairly new to the savings and loan industry, they have shown a significant degree of success in generating new loans and participations which are, in turn, often passed on to their parent corporations.

Private mortgage insurance companies

Of increasing importance to savings and loan associations has been a capability to make higher percentage loans with safety. A welcome response to this need has been the emergence of private mortgage insurance. Where buyers have been reluctant to seek FHA/VA government assistance, if in fact they were eligible, and both borrowers and lenders have sought to avoid delays and paperwork, private mortgage insurors have offered attractive alternatives. So

---

[1] See discussion of the National Corporation for Housing Partnerships in Chapter 23.

rapid has been the growth that since 1971, private mortgage insurance has been covering more new one- to four-family mortgage loans each year than the FHA/VA programs.

History.   Prior to the provision of mortgage insurance by the federal government during the 1930s, the field was exclusively occupied by private companies. These companies sold insurance coverage principally on mortgage loans on large commercial and high-rise apartment buildings with little or no emphasis on insurance on loans for single-family dwellings. Further, their operations were for the most part on a regional basis with inadequate regulation, and the insured loans were not regularly amortized. Under the impact of the Great Depression, these firms either failed or ceased operations as a matter of good judgment.

From the depression period until 1957, the mortgage insurance and guarantee field was left to the federal government with its Federal Housing Administration and Veterans Administration programs. In 1957, however, the Mortgage Guaranty Insurance Corporation was organized and licensed by the Wisconsin Insurance Commissioner. It is now authorized to do business nationwide. From the time of its organization to December 31, 1974, its insurance in force has increased sharply. The business is generated about equally from new housing and from sale of existing homes. The bulk of the company's business has been with savings and loan associations. Recently, however, a growing number of banks, credit unions, and insurance companies have been using this protection. There are several private insurance companies from which private and federal institutions accept insurance in their conventional loan programs. The Mortgage Guaranty Insurance Corporation is the most important, however, by a wide margin. It accounts for over half of the loans insured by private companies.

Method of operation.   These companies offer insurance to approved mortgage lenders against financial loss on first mortgage loans where mortgagors fail to make required payments. This insurance is ordinarily not utilized unless the loan exceeds 80 percent of appraised value. Mortgage Guaranty Insurance Corporation coverage, for instance, insures the top 20 percent of the mortgage loan regardless of balance, to a maximum limit of 95 percent of appraisal value. Such protection makes it possible for lenders to increase the volume of conventional loans by lending at loan-to-value ratios that would be excluded under their normal lending policies.

An institution becomes an approved lender by applying to an insurer and having a master policy issued in its favor. Factors considered by the insurance company as part of its approval process include size, supervisory history with regulatory agencies, appraisal experience and qualifications, operating policy, and membership in the Federal Savings and Loan Insurance Corporation or (for commercial banks) the Federal Deposit Insurance Corporation. Most applicants have been savings and loan associations, although commercial banks, mutual savings banks, and mortgage bankers are also extensive users of the service.

By the terms of the master policy, a *default* is declared when payments have not been made for four months. The insured institution must give notice to the insurer within ten days after the insured loan has become in default. The insurer may then direct the insured institution to initiate appropriate legal proceedings. In any event, the proceedings must be instituted within nine months of the time the loan first went into arrears. Within 60 days after completion of the legal proceedings, the insured institution files notice of loss and conveys its title to the insured. The amount of loss payable to the insured institution includes the principal balance due under the mortgage, back interest, real estate taxes, hazard insurance premiums, all expenses incurred in preservation of the property, and all legal expenses, including court costs and reasonable attorney's fees. In the determination of the loss payable, the insurer may exercise an option not to acquire the property but to leave it with the insured institution, and thereby limit liability to 20 percent of the allowable claim. The effect of this option is to shift the risk of 80 percent of the allowable claim to the institutional lender, which for satisfaction of its claim must look to the value of the property it has as security.

These insurance companies approve only loans that meet their underwriting standards. When approved, one of two types of loan policies will normally be issued. The policy most frequently used provides for a year term with annual renewals, called the annual plan. The premium for the first year is 1 percent of the amount of the loan; and for succeeding years it is .25 percent of the declining balance of the loan. Under the second plan, a single premium is paid in the amount of 2.5 percent of the initial amount of the loan to cover a ten-year term. The premium under all plans is paid by the borrower. The policies are subject to cancellation by the insured institution, and it may then receive a partial refund of premium. The insurance companies also require that the borrower pay an appraisal fee of $20 to accompany each application for insurance where the loan exceeds 80 percent of appraised value. This fee provides a fund to finance additional appraisals by agents of the insuror to verify the quality of the lender's appraisals.

Extension of coverage.   Private insurance companies now cover over 14 percent of the total home mortgage debt outstanding. It is also interesting to note that they are now extending this type of insurance to multifamily, commercial, and industrial properties. Commercial Loan Insurance Corporation, a subsidiary of MGIC Investment Corporation, for example, extends loans to every type of commercial and industrial real estate, including shopping centers, factories, nursing homes, retail stores, and warehouses. As in insurance of home mortgages, the protection extends to the top 20 percent of the outstanding loan balance. A five-year noncancelable policy may be purchased for a single premium of 2.9 percent of the loan, or for an annual premium of

1.2 percent of the loan for the first year and .5 percent of the outstanding principal balance at the beginning of each year thereafter. The renewal premium is .5 percent of the outstanding principal balance at the beginning of each renewal term.

Lease guarantee insurance has been assuming importance in recent years. It has been typical in the financing of shopping centers and other commercial or industrial developments that the bulk of the mortgage payments be covered by prime tenants. These tenants, occupying a major part of the space, therefore command lower rental rates because of the developer's reliance upon their credit. Since many mortgage lenders will accept minor lessees whose leases are insured in lieu of a prime tenant, there is often an advantage in increasing the occupancy percentage for insured minor tenants and cutting back the space alloted to major tenants. The insurance premium is usually only a fraction of the differential gain from the higher rents obtained through the shift in space allocation.

The possible advantage of lease guarantee insurance may be illustrated by assuming alternative uses of a 100,000 square foot warehouse costing $1 million. This space may be rented to:

1.   An AAA-1 tenant for $95,000 annually, or 9.5 percent; or
2.   Two minor tenants at a combined rental of $120,000, or 12 percent. To qualify with the lender on the warehouse mortgage, however, these tenants must be covered by lease guarantee insurance.

Over a 15-year span, at $25,000 per year higher rentals, the lesser tenants would pay the developer/owner $375,000 more in rentals than would be received from the AAA-1 tenant. The cost of the insurance for the two minor tenants might run $50,000. Deducting this amount from the rental advantage of $375,000 still leaves a net cumulative overage of $325,000 in favor of the second alternative.

Risk.   The character of the risk inherent in private mortgage insurance is well-stated in a prospectus filed in 1961 with the United States Securities and Exchange Commission by Mortgage Guaranty Insurance Corporation:

> In common with insurers of other types of risk, the mortgage loan insurer proceeds on the assumption that past experience, adjusted for applicable changes in conditions, will prevail on average in the future.
>
> Application of this basic assumption to the field of mortgage loan insurance is believed to involve substantially greater dependence on broad estimates, and consequently less likelihood of accuracy, than most other forms of insurance. Losses on first mortgage loans do not necessarily follow a generally steady and reasonably predictable pattern from year to year. Under favorable economic conditions, losses are likely to be small. The great risk in the residential mortgage loan insurance field would appear to be a period of adverse general economic conditions of substantial duration. However, a localized depression affecting an area in which a significant amount of loans has been insured might also affect its

operations materially. . . . Whether and when a period of adverse economic conditions will occur and the extent of the losses which may be suffered by first mortgage residential lenders and insurers are all unpredictable.[2]

How the inherent risk is being dealt with in Wisconsin is described in a 1963 prospectus of the Mortgage Guaranty Insurance Corporation:

> Regulations of the Wisconsin Insurance Department require MGIC to maintain two separate reserves for losses, a case basis reserve and a contingency reserve. . . . The contingency reserve is designed to protect against the effect of adverse economic cycles. MGIC is required to credit to this reserve (by charges of surplus and not to income) an amount equal to 50% of all premiums earned. Subject to the approval of the Wisconsin Commissioner of Insurance, this reserve is available for payment of losses to the extent losses in a given year exceed 30% of the premiums earned in that year. Funds credited to the contingency reserve, to the extent not used in payment of losses, must remain in the reserve for fifteen years.[3]

Questions

1   What were the origins of the savings and loan association?

2   What were terminating associations and how did they differ from serial associations?

3   Describe the share-accumulation sinking-fund loan plan.

4   Under the practices of early associations, what penalties were assessed against a member who withdrew from the organization before completion of the project for which the association was organized?

5   What were Dayton plan associations, and how did they expand the scope of savings and loan activities?

6   What weaknesses existed in the home mortgage financing structure in the early 1930s?

7   What are the objectives of the Federal Home Loan Bank System and how does it accomplish these objectives?

8   In addition to equity capital, what other sources of funds do the Federal Home Loan Banks have?

9   What are the chief factors affecting lending policies of savings and loan associations?

10   Why do savings and loan associations prefer to make loans on single-family dwellings over other forms of residential or commercial real estate?

11   Why do these institutions make loans on nonresidential properties, and under what restrictions do they operate?

12   What has been the trend of the percentage of loan to appraised value in recent years, and what conditions have influenced this trend?

13   What justification can you give for granting savings and loan associations broader powers? See further in appendix to next chapter.

---

[2] "Prospectus," Mortgage Guaranty Insurance Corporation, October 17, 1961, p. 5.

[3] "Prospectus," Mortgage Guaranty Insurance Corporation, May 14, 1963, pp. 17–18.

Case problems

1   A developer is planning a 400,000 square foot shopping center. He is considering two plans of tenant recruitment:

Plan 1:   Lease 70 percent of the space to major tenants at $3.50 per square foot and the remaining 30 percent to local tenants at $6.00 per square foot.

Plan 2:   Lease 60 percent of the space to major tenants at $3.50 per square foot and the remaining 40 percent to local tenants at $6.00 per square foot. To obtain the credit equivalent of Plan 1 from the mortgage lender, lease guarantee insurance would have to be taken out costing $100,000.

Evaluate the alternative plans for tenant allocation.

2   Mr. and Mrs. Arthur Green are applying to Star Federal Savings and Loan Association to borrow $50,000 at 11.5 percent for 30 years. They are buying a property for a residence costing $60,000, with $10,000 cash payment down. Real estate taxes and hazard insurance are $1,200 annually. Their gross allowable income (after income taxes) is $28,000. Installment payments for personal debt with more than six months to run are $205 monthly.

a.   Compute (1) the housing expense ratio and (2) the total expense ratio.

b.   List what other information you would need to make a good lending decision in this case.

Financing of real estate by banks

20

Current real estate lending by banks

In this chapter are discussed real estate lending practices of three kinds of banks: mutual savings banks, state-chartered commercial banks, and national banks. Since the policies of all commercial banks have much in common, they will be discussed as one class, except for the differences noted below. Real estate mortgages are expected to involve long-term commitment of funds, regardless of the specific terms for which mortgages are written. Therefore, it is to be expected that both experience and regulations should dictate that only capital, surplus, and time deposits be used by commercial banks for making real estate loans. Since mutual savings banks are not looked upon in the same light as commercial banks, most deposits in the former are considered to be time deposits.

As of December 31, 1979, the total savings and time deposits of all banks in this country were $820 billion. Of this total, commercial banks held $676 billion and mutual savings banks $144 billion. The relatively small number of saving banks, scattered throughout the country, that are owned by stockholders are classed as commercial banks for our purposes, since their operations more nearly parallel those of state-chartered commercial banks than of mutual savings banks.

The real estate mortgage holdings of all banks as of December 31, 1979, are set forth in Exhibit 20–1. It is interesting to note the concentration of real estate mortgages on residential property as security, with commercial loans in second position and farm real estate in third.

EXHIBIT 20-1
Mortgage holdings of all banks as of December 31, 1979 ($ billions)

	Nonfarm residential	Farm	Commercial	Total
Commercial banks.....................	$158.7	$10.4	$77.7	$246.8
Mutual savings banks	81.9	.1	16.9	98.9
Total	$240.6	$10.5	$94.6	$345.7

Source: *Federal Reserve Bulletin,* April 1980, p. A41.

MUTUAL SAVINGS BANKS

Origin of mutual savings banks[1]

The origin of mutual savings banks in this country has much in common with the origin of savings and loan associations. Both had their impetus outside of the group to be served. Like their predecessors in England and on the continent of Europe, the clergy, philanthropically minded people, and others interested wished to encourage thrifty habits and frugality among the growing numbers of working people. The sponsors of these "frugality banks" recognized the need for institutions which could care for the savings of those dependent upon wages for a living against the time when incomes might be reduced for one reason or another. Even the names of some of the early savings banks attempt to describe their purposes. The first to start business in this country was the Philadelphia Savings Fund Society, which opened for business in the fall of 1816. It is fitting that the first institution of this kind should have been started in the city made famous by the thrift teachings of Poor Richard. This was soon followed by the Provident Institute for Savings, started in Boston in the spring of 1817. The idea of such banks soon spread to other cities. All contemporary accounts of their operation lay emphasis upon the services rendered to humble people of small means who would probably squander their earnings except for the exhortations of savings banks to save something against the time of need.

Concentration of mutual savings banks[2]

Today mutual savings banks are found in only 17 states. Most of them are concentrated in three states—Massachusetts, New York, and Connecticut. In

[1] See also the monograph prepared for the Commission of Money and Credit titled *Mutual Savings Banking* (Englewood Cliffs, N.J.: Prentice-Hall, Inc., 1962).

[2] Important data for this discussion were derived from the 1979 *National Fact Book of Mutual Savings Banking,* National Association of Mutual Savings Banks, 200 Park Avenue, New York, N.Y. 10017. Updating may be accomplished by reference to later annual publications of this fact book.

these three states, savings banks have attracted much more savings funds than have all other types of banks and savings and loan associations combined. Outside New England, New York, New Jersey, Delaware, Pennsylvania, and Maryland, there are only a few mutual savings banks—8 in the Middle West and 13 in the far West, including Alaska.

Management of mutual savings banks

Savings banks have no stockholders. By a broad use of language, their owners are called depositors. The return they receive upon their investments is called interest. There is no backstop of stock to protect deposits against the shocks of losses. As a mutual institution only, the deposits, plus whatever reserves have been retained in the business to absorb losses, may be looked to for the purpose of meeting the effects of unusual losses.

Since the depositors are not considered to be stockholders, they have no voice in the management of their own funds. This task is entrusted to a self-perpetuating board of trustees. The original board was selected by the organizers of the bank. Vacancies resulting from resignations, deaths, or other causes are filled by the remaining board members. This system has worked quite satisfactorily over the years. In actual practice it differs only in form from the manner of selecting the boards of directors of many American corporations whose stockholders enjoy voting rights that are seldom or never exercised. In such corporations, boards of directors are virtually self-perpetuating bodies.

Growth of savings banks

There can be no question about the need for savings banks, the quality of the services rendered, or the nature of the responses by the people who took advantage of these services. The number of such banks increased steadily for a time, both in total assets and in number of depositors. The number of banks grew steadily until it reached a maximum about 100 years ago. Since then the number of banks has shown a considerable decline which is especially marked in recent years.

In 1820 there were ten mutual savings banks in the United States with total assets of $1 million. The number increased to a peak of 674 in 1875, when total assets amounted to $850 million. Since that date the number has declined to a low of 465 in 1978. By the end of 1978, total assets amounted to about $158 billion.

Undoubtedly the growth of savings and loan associations and savings departments of commercial banks played their part in other sections of the country, leaving the bulk of savings business in the above-described "savings bank" area to the mutual savings banks. The recent rapid growth of federal savings and loan associations in New York and New England suggests that there may be other reasons for the failure of savings banks to expand into new areas in recent years.

Savings banks and their investors

Since the owners of deposits in mutual savings banks expect to withdraw their savings on demand, the banks must operate in such a manner as to meet these requirements. The laws under which they operate permit them to "go on notice" for 30 to 90 days before paying withdrawal demands. Except in times of emergency, they make no use of this protection. To make common use of it would discourage patronage. While some banks have suffered more than others, in general, withdrawal demands have not frequently been unduly burdensome to most savings banks. Since withdrawals are closely associated with confidence of the investors, the strong reputation of savings banks has helped to keep down "fear" withdrawals.

For the protection of safety of deposits, the states in which savings banks operate have enacted laws restricting the investments of such institutions to "legals" which are supposed to be of high quality. Within statutory limits that set forth the categories of investment opportunities available to savings banks, the management has wide latitude of choice in selecting what seems to it to serve best its requirements for safety, liquidity, and return.

Restrictions upon real estate lending

All mutual savings banks receive their charters from states. The laws regulating their operation represent quite a wide range of patterns in their mortgage-lending programs. The ratio of maximum loan to value varies from 50 to 90 percent (except for FHA and GI loans).

Savings banks are also subject to state restrictions on the percentage of assets or deposits that may be placed in mortgages. These limitations, depending on the state, typically establish the maximum amount of conventional mortgage loans at 65 to 70 percent of the assets, or deposits, of the bank. FHA and VA loans are excepted from these limitations; however, in some states the availability of funds for federally underwritten mortgages is limited to an additional 15 percent of assets, or deposits, whichever is used as the standard.

State laws regulate maximum terms for loans, as well as other characteristics. New York provides the terms on its "90 percent" loans shall not exceed three fourths of the useful life of the property or 30 years, whichever is less. Massachusetts and Connecticut have a 25-year maximum term for their "80 percent" loans.

Because trustees of mutual savings banks are traditionally conservative, self-imposed restrictions may be even more rigid than those imposed by law. In general they prefer loans on single-family dwellings. Only the largest institutions, whose investment funds present constant pressure for investment, get into the fields of investment in apartment-house, commercial, and industrial mortgages.

Lending territories are usually determined by their short distance from the home office so that the problems of servicing will not be so difficult as they are when property securing mortgage loans is located at great distances. In recent years the pressure of investment funds has recommended removal of distance restrictions when mortgage loans are insured by the FHA or are guaranteed by the VA. In New York state, where more than half of all assets of mutual savings banks are located, recent changes in legislation governing lending territory have been expanded to permit such banks to make even conventional loans in the neighboring states of Connecticut, Massachusetts, New Jersey, Pennsylvania, Rhode Island, and Vermont. Similarly, Massachusetts and Connecticut may make loans in their own and adjoining states. In the case of the latter states, however, the loans must be located in a city or town situated within a specified distance of the bank. By way of contrast, there are no state territorial limitations for savings banks located in some other states such as Delaware, Maryland, Pennsylvania, Rhode Island, Vermont, and Washington. In all cases, geographic limitations do not apply to FHA and VA loans.

It was particularly significant that under the Financial Institutions Regulatory and Interest Control Act of 1978 state savings banks were granted the option to convert to federally chartered savings banks in the states where they now operate. Such a conversion would broaden their powers. Under the terms of the Depository Institutions Deregulation and Monetary Control Act of 1980, federal mutual savings banks are permitted to hold up to 5 percent of their assets in commercial, corporate, or business loans provided such loans are made within the state in which the bank is located or within 75 miles of its home office.

Mortgage experience of savings banks

Before the depression of the 1930s, savings banks had long been the major source of mortgage money in the areas in which they operated. From the time that savings banks became significant caretakers of savings funds until the 1930 depression, real estate mortgages had been looked upon with favor as satisfactory investment outlets for funds deposited with them. During the last quarter of the last century and the first three decades of this one, mortgages always absorbed at least a third and frequently as much as half of the total resources of savings banks. After 1932 the mortgages held by all savings banks in the United States decreased year by year. While there was some recovery in the decade of the 1940s, by the middle of that decade the total amount of mortgages in their portfolios was still less than in the previous decade. Meantime, corresponding figures for savings and loan associations on a national basis showed an increase of approximately two thirds. The percentage increase in residential mortgages held by insurance companies from the middle 1930s to the middle 1940s was even greater.

Changes in policy. The factors that accounted for this change in policy concerning real estate mortgages as investments are not too clearly defined in the record. Patriotic desire to help finance the needs of the government during

World War II undoubtedly played some part. The decline in the demand for real estate financial assistance was also a factor. The supply of real estate buyers had undoubtedly declined for a part of this period, while the supply of government bonds for most of it was ample to meet all requirements. During this period, interest rates on mortgage loans declined somewhat, but government bond interest rates declined relatively more.

The above evidence leads to the conclusion that for reasons best known to their managements, the savings banks definitely decided to restrict their holdings of real estate mortgages. This of course was their right. The only purpose of emphasizing it here is to show that borrowers had that much of their opportunities contracted. They were required to look elsewhere for real estate financial assistance.

Since about 1947, however, savings banks have generally experienced another change in attitude toward mortgage investments, particularly those insured by the FHA or guaranteed by the VA. This change was due in part to a desire to decrease their holdings of U.S. government bonds. When they liquidated sizable quantities of governments, they again turned to corporate bonds and to real estate mortgages as outlets for their funds.

Several factors have combined to make mortgages especially attractive to savings banks. Regular amortization, improved marketability, better yields than were otherwise available, and federal underwriting have provided liquidity and earning power in the same investment, together with security of principal. Their investment program was given nationwide significance by legislative changes in most savings bank states permitting out-of-state lending both conventionally and through the purchase of FHA and VA mortgages derived in other sections of the country.

Volume of mortgage holdings.   At the end of 1979, the mutual savings banks of the United States held a total of $98.9 billion in real estate mortgages. The distribution of these mortgages was approximately two thirds within and one third outside the state. The distribution of the types of loans of these banks at the end of 1979 showed them to be about three fourths conventional and one fourth federally underwritten. Savings banks as a financial institution held slightly over 8 percent of the dollar volume of all real estate mortgages in the United States. Residential loans represented about five sixths of this total and commercial loans the balance.

COMMERCIAL BANKS

Nature of commercial banks

As the name implies, commercial banks—whether national or state chartered—are the reservoirs of credit for the commerce of the country. Unlike savings and loan associations and savings banks, they are not mutual in character. Their financial plan is based upon stockownership, frequently quite closely held; the investors look upon their commitment as a source of profit through the dividends they receive. The people who supply most of the funds of commercial banks, the depositors, have no voice in management and do not share in the dividends distributed to the shareholders.

Bank depositors are divided into two groups. Demand depositors consist of individuals, corporations, and other groups of people, who place their working capital in their local banks for safekeeping, to be drawn out as needed by the owner. Such funds are not looked upon as investment money. They are simply placed where they are more secure than if they were left in the home or the office. Because they are withdrawable on demand, the bank's use of them is necessarily greatly restricted. In contrast, those who place time deposits in commercial banks look upon such an operation as an investment on which they expect an interest return. Because such funds are expected to remain in the bank longer than are demand deposits, they can be invested in long-term commitments, including real estate mortgages. While commercial banks reserve the right to require 30 days' notice before time deposits can be withdrawn, this right is seldom exercised.

Savings growth in commercial banks

Up to the turn of the century, savings accounts in commercial banks were incidental to the major operations of these banks in other financial fields. The law which created national banks made no mention of savings accounts. In 1903 a significant ruling of the Comptroller of the Currency gave the green light to the opening of savings accounts by national banks. The effect of this ruling was that since the legislation establishing these banks failed either to authorize or to prohibit savings accounts, each bank was free to make its own choice on this question. Nearly half of the national banks chose to open savings departments within the next decade. Then the Federal Reserve Act of 1913 specifically sanctioned such departments by encouraging their operation.

The development of savings departments in state-chartered commercial banks more or less paralleled that of savings departments in national banks. In general, state banks gave favorable consideration to savings accounts somewhat ahead of national banks. Even then it was not until 1917 that the savings deposits of all commercial banks in the country equaled the deposits of all mutual savings banks. Thereafter the commercial banks forged ahead rapidly until the depression years of the 1930s. In 1932 the commercial banks fell behind for the first time in a decade and a half. Taking the lead again in 1935, the commercial banks never lost it. At the present time, their savings and time deposits are about four times those of savings banks.

There are, however, many who question the propriety of commercial banks taking advantage of the total increased mortgage lending potential created by their present time deposits, because of the increased need for liquidity in connection with their commercial banking function. They point out that a great part of the increase in savings and time deposits is represented by certificates of deposit (CDs), which the banks first began issuing in 1961. Two types of certificates are issued. One type is the large-unit (probably $100,000 or more), negotiable certificate issued to the larger business firms; the other is the small-unit, nonnegotiable certificate issued to smaller businesses and individuals. A corporation, which was previously carrying funds in a commercial account at no interest, can now place the same money at interest with the bank and receive a certificate therefor which is as negotiable as a stock or bond. If it needs the funds again, all it has to do is sell the certificate in the market. Savings and loan associations as well as other corporations have extensive holdings of CDs for funds deposited in commercial banks.

These funds tend to be temporarily placed and may be withdrawn in large amounts when the certificates mature and more attractive interest rates can be found elsewhere.

Trusteed funds.   In addition to the resources in savings accounts that may be used for mortgage lending, commercial banks may have trusteed funds in their trust departments which must be invested. In general, such funds have been left with the bank by individuals who may have very definite ideas about their investment. As a consequence, one trust may be so set up as to prevent the investment of its funds in real estate mortgages. Another may set limits upon the amounts that may be so invested. It might even specify the types of real estate security acceptable for real estate loans. Still another may leave wider discretion to the trustee. Since trusts are enjoying substantial growth, it is likely that an increasing amount of money for real estate lending will be available from this source.

History of real estate lending by commercial banks

As originally passed in 1863, the national bank law permitted national banks to make loans on both real and personal property as security. A year later the law was amended in such manner that the term *real property* was taken out. Thereafter and until the second decade of this century, national banks were not permitted to make loans on real estate directly. However, they were permitted to accept real estate mortgages as secondary collateral to prevent losses on loans previously made in good faith on legal types of collateral.

Until state banks and trust companies used their authority to grant real estate loans in a manner to place competing national banks at a distinct disadvantage, the latter kept out of the field of real estate mortgage lending. But when the competitive advantage possessed by state banks began to embarrass the operating plans of national banks, supervision of the latter was relaxed in a manner to give more leeway in making mortgage loans, even though the laws under which they operated failed to sanction such practices.

It is fortunate that commercial banks—both state and national—did find it advantageous to grant real estate loans. In many sections of the country there have been neither savings banks nor savings and loan associations to assist in the financing of real estate purchases. Even today there are areas where mortgage money is restricted to that made available by commercial banks. While this is less true than formerly, it still describes some real estate markets.

Lending authority

As originally enacted in 1913, the Federal Reserve Act opened the door to real estate loans by national banks by providing that they could make loans on improved and unencumbered farms for periods up to five years and for amounts not in excess of 50 percent of their value. No national bank could invest for this purpose more than one fourth of its capital and surplus or one third of its time deposits.

In 1916 this law was amended to permit national banks to make loans on improved and unencumbered real estate other than farms. The same limitations were imposed as stated above for farm loans, with the further restriction that on real estate other than farms, the maturity of the loans was limited to one year instead of five. It is significant to note that one-year loans on urban real estate was the common pattern at that time for many of the competitors of national banks in some areas. Consequently, the one-year limitation placed national banks in a competitive framework in such markets. Not all of the state banks limited real estate loans to one year as a matter of practice. Because of this, a demand arose almost immediately for further liberalization of the lending powers of national banks in the real estate field. This demand presently received the active support of the Comptroller of the Currency. No changes were made, however, until the passage of the McFadden Act of 1927. This law permitted five-year, 50 percent loans on urban real estate. For unamortized loans, this law has remained intact to date.

Beginning in 1935 the Federal Reserve Act was further amended to permit national banks to make loans at progressively higher loan-to-value ratios where the loan was amortized. In 1970 the authority was increased to permit home loans up to 90 percent of appraised value with an amortization not to exceed 30 years. The Federal Reserve Act was further amended in 1974.

Current provisions of the law governing real estate loans by national banks include the following:

1. National banks may not make real estate loans in excess of the greater of unimpaired capital and surplus or time and savings deposits, except that real estate loans secured by other than first liens, when added to unpaid prior liens, are to be limited to 30 percent of unimpaired capital and unimpaired surplus combined. Furthermore, they are authorized to make real estate loans in excess of 70 percent of time and savings deposits only if the total unpaid amount loaned does not exceed 10 percent of the maximum amount that may be invested in real estate loans.

2.   Under present law, national banks are authorized to make various loan-to-value ratio loans secured by other than first liens where the lien, when added to prior liens, does not exceed the applicable loan-to-value ratio for the particular type of loan.

3.   National banks are not required to classify as real estate loans various loans insured, guaranteed, or backed by the full faith and credit of the federal government or a state.

4.   Loans with maturities of less than 60 months are classified as commercial loans when made for construction of buildings and secured by a commitment to advance the full amount of the loan upon completion.

5.   Loans made for the construction of residential or farm buildings with maturities of not more than nine months are eligible for discount as commercial paper if accompanied by an agreement for firm takeout upon completion of the building.

6.   National banks are permitted to make loans on leaseholds that have at least ten years to run beyond the terminal date of the loan.

7.   Loans made to manufacturing or industrial businesses are exempt from real estate loan limitations even though the bank takes a mortgage on real estate as security where the bank relies primarily on the general credit standing and earning power of the business as the source of repayment.

Volume of mortgage loans held by banks

For all commercial banks of the country, real estate mortgage loans constitute about one seventh of total assets and about one third of the amount of time deposits. Loans on residential properties, including apartments, account for approximately two thirds of the dollar volume of all mortgages, with all other types of real estate security making up the other one third. In number of mortgages held, residential loans represent an even higher percentage than is true for dollar volume. Approximately nine tenths of the total number of loans on real estate as security are residential loans. Grouped as a single type of financial institution, commercial banks at the end of 1979 held about 20 percent of the dollar volume of all real estate mortgages in the United States.

The distribution of mortgage holdings among different sizes of commercial banks varies somewhat, although the differences are not too significant. In general, the largest banks have a smaller percentage of assets invested in real estate mortgages. The greatest concentration is recorded for banks in the smaller asset categories, though not in the very smallest groups.

Fluctuations in mortgage holdings

Unlike savings and loan associations whose major outlet for funds is real estate mortgages, commercial banks vary greatly in the dollar volume of mortgages held. Two conditions account for these fluctuations. In the first place, many commercial banks—particularly the larger ones—would prefer to invest their funds elsewhere. Consequently, whenever the demand for money for commercial loans is great, they show less interest in real estate mortgage commitments. In the absence of a commercial loan demand of sufficient magnitude to absorb their available funds, some of them become more interested in loans against real estate as security.

In the second place, commercial banks have in the past approached the business of making loans on real estate with considerable caution. In general, they have followed smaller loan-to-value ratios than have savings and loan associations. Also, in periods of smaller demand for real estate mortgage credit, commercial banks are generally content to let their competitors make most of the available loans. In the middle 1930s commercial banks were not active bidders for mortgage loans. Their proportion of total mortgage debt dropped considerably from its level at the beginning of the depression. By contrast, in the post–World War II period the proportion of total real estate mortgage debt held by commercial banks rose to a point approximately double the ratio of the middle 1930s. It must be remembered that insurance of loans by the FHA and the guarantee of loans by the VA entered into the picture in the postwar period. Commercial banks made more generous use of both insurance and guarantee of mortgages than did some of their competitors. The use of insurance and guarantee is reflected also in loans made by the larger banks. In general, the larger the commercial bank which holds mortgages, the more generous the use of insurance and guarantee of mortgage loans.

During the late 1960s and early 1970s, many commercial banks sponsored real estate mortgage investment trusts. As described in Chapter 21, their adverse experience in this type of venture has added a new tinge of conservatism to their real estate lending practices.

Methods of acquiring mortgages

Commercial banks follow either of two practices in acquiring mortgages on real estate. Some have mortgage loan departments that are so well organized that they are active competitors within their markets for real estate loans. Indeed, their advertising for mortgages may be pitched on a very aggressive plane. If their time deposits are large and dependable over a period of years, they are likely to be more active bidders for real estate mortgages. As will be pointed out in Chapter 21, they may even have become sponsors of mortgage investment trusts. In the process, many banks have developed or acquired their own mortgage banking business. They not only originate the loans which they carry in their portfolios but they service them as well. In some communities that lack specialized real estate financial institutions, commercial banks may be the most reliable agencies for making loans on real estate.

Other commercial banks, which place less emphasis upon real estate mortgages as sources of income, may not even have a mortgage department worthy of the name. Such mortgages as they may acquire from time to time are purchased from mortgage bankers or dealers. As pointed out in Chapter 22, commercial banks that purchase their real estate mortgages are likely to be "in-and-outers" so far as their mortgage acquisitions are concerned. Some of them may even let their mortgages be serviced by their loan correspondents, particularly if the security is located in a city other than the one in which the bank is located. Finally, some commercial banks prefer not to engage in mortgage lending under any circumstances.

Interim financing

Even banks without particular expertise in real estate lending may engage in mortgage loan "warehousing" with mortgage bankers as the principal originators. In this type of lending, commercial bankers' loans are secured by institutional takeout commitments held by mortgage bankers who seek interim development and construction loans from the commercial banks until final placement with the permanent lenders at completion of the project.

Institutional commitments in mortgage lending. In many respects the mortgage banker stands in about the same relationship to the institutions and other investors to whom he sells his mortgages as the investment banker stands to the investing public which buys his corporate securities. He must originate a satisfactory obligation, and he must finance it until such time as it is sold to the ultimate investor. Prior to the time that a real estate mortgage is ready for sale, however, there has often been a long gestation period, and many arrangements for interim credits have had to be made—often more complicated and of longer duration than the investment banker must undertake. These interim financing problems arise because of the basic conditions out of which a new mortgage is derived. Often a new property or a new development is being constructed. The builder is ill equipped to provide his own financing, and the mortgage banker with a thin capital equity is not able to give him much help from his own funds. To accomplish their objectives, both need a construction loan. To support the construction loan credit, a commercial bank or other lender which might make such a loan often requires a firm commitment from an institutional investor to take over the mortgage on the property once the building has been completed. In fact, such commitments have proved to be increasingly important to the mortgage-lending operation in recent years. The commitments have been principally of two types: (1) advance or forward commitments and (2) standby commitments.

The first type of commitment, called an *advance* commitment by the Federal Housing Administration and termed a *forward* commitment by the Life Insurance Association of America, is virtually a purchase order for a mortgage on property to be constructed. A firm obligation is undertaken for the period of the commitment to purchase the federally underwritten mortgage on property to be constructed in accordance with acceptable plans and specifications. On the strength of the knowledge that the mortgage has a market once the property is completed, other institutions are willing to provide the necessary interim financing to bring the property to such a state of completion that the mortgage is eligible for sale under the commitment.

The *standby* commitment is an arrangement, usually worked out with a commercial bank, whereby the latter will buy mortgages, generally from a mortgage banker, at a substantial discount in event they cannot be sold more favorably to an institutional or other investor by the end of the commitment period.

The advance, or forward, commitment has been used in greatest volume at those times when credit conditions have eased, and the institutions with large volumes of funds to place have taken this means of providing for ready investment of their cash inflow. As money rates tighten, the institutional lenders find alternative uses for their funds equally attractive, and they are less inclined to enter into such commitments, as they feel overcommitted at lower rates on the obligations that they have already undertaken. Furthermore, rising interest rates with declining bond prices tend to make the sale of bonds for the purpose of obtaining funds for an alternative use an unattractive prospect.

A correlative of a restriction in advance commitments is an increased need for the standby commitment. In the absence of a certain market for the mortgage once construction is complete, the mortgage banker or the builder will accept an alternative avenue for disposition at a substantial discount, on the chance that a more desirable buyer can be found after origination of the permanent mortgage and before expiration of the commitment period. The use of this device tends to exert a stabilizing influence upon the availability of funds at times when a tight money market tends to dry up the supply. The effect is limited, however, by the fact that as the volume of standby commitments increases, the bank issuing the commitments will lower its forfeiture price until the potential financing costs become prohibitive and the plans for more construction are dropped.

Mortgage inventory loans, or mortgage warehousing. Interim loans by commercial banks to nonbank lenders are often specifically designated as *mortgage inventory* loans. Bankers commonly identify as inventory loans those made on securities being underwritten by an investment banker while the issues are being prepared for sale and distribution to individuals and financial institutions who buy them for their investment portfolios. Mortgage inventory loans serve exactly the same purpose for the mortgage banker, as he requires financing to expedite the origination, sale, and distribution of his mortgages to permanent investors. The practice of granting such loans has been called mortgage warehousing. The notion of warehousing arises from the temporary nature of the advance as the mortgage passes from its originator to the ultimate lender.

There are three general types of warehouse loans. Two of these commonly involve mortgage bankers directly. The most common is the committed-technical warehousing loan, which has been made for many years. Under this arrangement, the commercial bank simply lends to the mortgage banker to provide financing between the time of payment for construction and the time when he can deliver perfected mortgages to the permanent investor. This loan is supported by a prior commitment of the investor to purchase the mortgages when completed. Numerous details must be handled before the mortgage is ready for purchase. The loan must be closed; the credit of the owner of the property must be checked; the FHA insurance or the VA guarantee must be obtained; title insurance or a counsel's opinion must afford adequate title protection; other appropriate insurance must be bound; and delivery and recordation of necessary documents must be effected. All of these processes, together with assembling mortgages in the proper amounts, usually take five to six months. The amount of the warehousing loan is usually based upon the commitment of the permanent investor. The lending bank will be limited to the amount of the commitment or to a figure slightly less than that amount.

A second type of warehousing loan is called the uncommitted-technical loan. It differs from the first only in that there is no prior commitment of a permanent investor to take up the loan from the mortgage banker. When a commercial bank lends under this arrangement, it may lend either with or without recourse. If the loan is with recourse and a permanent investor has not been found by the end of the interim lending period, the mortgage banker must take up the loan from the commercial bank. He must then either carry the financing himself or arrange it elsewhere until he manages to sell the mortgage. If the warehousing loan from the bank is without recourse, there is a different result. In case the mortgage banker has not placed the mortgage with a permanent investor before the maturity date of the interim loan, the commercial bank retires the loan by purchasing the mortgage given as security at its prearranged forfeiture price, which is normally at a discount. The obligation of the commercial bank in this situation is the previously mentioned standby commitment for which it is paid a fee irrespective of whether a forfeiture is declared.

Still a third type of warehousing loan has come into prominence since the mid-1950s. It has been designated as committed-institutional warehousing. This type of loan is made directly to large institutional investors rather than to mortgage bankers, and the credit is designed to give investors more flexibility in arranging for mortgage investments by providing for their unusual requirements for investable funds which will later be met permanently out of the receipts of funds in the ordinary course of business. These loans by the commercial bank are usually of longer duration, ranging from a year to 18 months, with the borrower having a prepayment option. The use of this financing method is largely the result of the decline in the bond markets in recent years, rendering these securities relatively unavailable for sale by institutional investors to provide funds to meet advance commitments to mortgage bankers. As bond prices rise again, so that capital gains instead of capital losses may result from bond sales, it may be presumed that committed-institutional warehousing tends to become less important for this purpose. The method is available, however, to deal with any situation in which the cash inflow of an institution does not meet its expectations.

Questions

1 How do mutual savings banks and commercial banks differ in their general purposes?

2 How have the differences in the purposes of mutual savings banks and commercial banks affected their lending policies with respect to mortgage loans on real estate?

3 Where are most of the mutual savings banks located? Why are they not found in other parts of the country?

4 How has recent legislation liberalized the lending practices of mutual savings banks?

5 Why have commercial banks been so slow in entering the real estate lending field?

6 How important statistically are commercial banks and mutual savings banks as sources of mortgage money to finance real estate purchases?

7 How do commercial banks and mutual savings banks acquire their mortgages?

8 Do you expect the commercial banks to be relatively more important or less important as a source of real estate financing in the future? What considerations have influenced your opinion?

9 Distinguish between advance or forward commitments and standby commitments and define each.

10 What is mortgage warehousing?

11 What are the three general types of mortgage warehouse loans? Describe each.

APPENDIX: TRENDS IN FINANCIAL STRUCTURE AND REGULATION

In 1971 a presidential commission, commonly called the Hunt Commission, after extensive study issued a report setting forth 89 recommendations designed to improve the health and stability of the nation's financial institutions, housing industry, and general economy.[1] In essence, the report contained a series of recommendations that would change savings and loan associations, mutual savings banks, and even credit unions into near-commercial banks; and commercial banks would be induced to expand the proportion of their activities in areas of real estate finance. All of the institutions would handle their assets and liabilities in similar fashion and be uniformly regulated and taxed. Further, permission of all institutions to convert their charters to commercial banks was recommended.

---

[1] *The Report of the President's Commission on Financial Structure and Regulation* (Washington, D.C.: U.S. Government Printing Office, 1971).

In 1975 the House Committee on Banking, Currency, and Housing, published a study titled *Financial Institutions and the Nation's Economy: Discussion Principles.*[2] This became known as the FINE report. This report corroborated the Hunt Commission work by recommending equal treatment for savings and loan associations, savings banks, commercial banks, and credit unions.

As a result of continuing consideration, the Congress has recently passed a piece of landmark legislation titled *The Depository Institutions Deregulation and Monetary Control Act of 1980,* effective March 31, 1980. Although the new legislation did not precisely confirm the Hunt Commission and FINE studies, it took many directions to soften the impacts of competitive differences between the major financial institutions. A number of previous recommendations were incorporated into the law.

The primary goals of the new act are to:

1.   Broaden payment powers of banks and thrift institutions.
2.   Extend reserve requirements to all depository institutions with transaction (check-type) accounts and nonpersonal time deposits.
3.   Phaseout of interest rate ceilings.
4.   Improve the asset mix of thrift institutions.

Broadened payment powers

As of December 31, 1980, the new law permits federally insured savings and loan associations, savings banks, and commercial banks to offer Negotiable Order of Withdrawal (NOW) accounts nationwide. A NOW account is an interest-bearing checking account. Until this law, such accounts were legal on a limited basis in only eight states. By additional provisions, commercial bank automatic transfer accounts (from savings), thrift institution remote service units, and credit union shares drafts were all legally accredited on an unrestricted basis effective March 31, 1980.

Expanded reserve requirements

The effect of this legislation has been to recognize that thrift institutions have already been offering checking-type services. The next step was to create similar reserve requirements in the interest of equity and monetary control. Accounts were classified as transaction and nonpersonal time accounts. "Transaction" accounts include all checking-type accounts, involving a transfer of funds to a payee. All depository institutions with such accounts that are federally insured or insurable must maintain reserves.

Under the law, new reserve requirements are being put into place over an

---

[2] 94B Congress, 1st sess., November 1975, pp. 1–21.

eight-year period for institutions that are not members of the Federal Reserve System and over four years for member banks. For any new types of deposits, there is no phase-in period. This rule applies to NOW accounts in states where they have not previously been authorized, but not in the eight states where they are currently permitted by law.

For institutions with transaction accounts over $25 million the range of reserve requirements is from 8 to 14 percent, and initially the rate is 12 percent. The range of required reserves on nonpersonal time deposits is from 0 to 9 percent, and the initial rate is 3 percent.

All depository institutions holding transactions accounts now have access to the Federal Reserve discount window under the same conditions as member banks. Furthermore, for a reasonable price, they have available to them all services of the Federal Reserve Banks performed for member banks.

Over 17,000 financial institutions will be immediately affected by the new law. They include about 5,400 member banks, 9,000 nonmember banks, and 3,400 savings and loan associations and mutual savings banks.[3] There is a leveling effect of money costs from general reserve requirements. Further, this step should go a long way toward stemming the attrition of the Federal Reserve System, as member banks have recently been relinquishing their memberships to avoid the requirement of holding sterile assets in reserve accounts.

Phaseout of interest rate ceilings (Regulation Q)

Since the beginning of the Federal Deposit Insurance Corporation in the 1930s, interest rate ceilings have been imposed on savings and time deposits of insured commercial and savings banks and savings and loan association members of the Federal Home Loan Bank System. The terms were set by Regulation Q. As of May 31, 1980, for example, these rates were as shown in Exhibit 20A–1. Very apparent is the high degree of differentiation in interest rate ceilings.

It will be noted from the exhibit that mutual savings banks and savings and loan associations have been allowed to pay, typically, .25 percent higher interest rates than commercial banks. This advantage rests on the premise that commercial banks are full-service institutions and some premium should be available to the other thrift institutions to induce the saver to go out of his way to place his money with them. Since all institutions are taking on more and more the complexion of commercial banks, there is less reason to maintain this differential. Even more to the point, the whole system of rate ceilings is subject to challenge.

---

[3] The authors wish to acknowledge especial assistance from the article titled "Historic Legislation," by Verle Johnston, in the *Federal Reserve Bank of San Francisco Weekly Letter,* April 4, 1980. For an excellent summary of the new legislation, see Charles R. McNeill and Denise M. Rechter, "The Depository Institutions Deregulation and Monetary Control Act of 1980," *The Federal Reserve Bulletin,* June 1980, pp. 444–53.

EXHIBIT 20A-1

1.16 MAXIMUM INTEREST RATES PAYABLE on Time and Savings Deposits at Federally Insured Institutions

Percent per annum

Type and maturity of deposit	Commercial banks				Savings and loan associations and mutual savings banks			
	In effect May 31, 1980		Previous maximum		In effect May 31, 1980		Previous maximum	
	Percent	Effective date	Percent	Effective date	Percent	Effective date	Percent	Effective date
1 Savings	5¼	7/1/79	5	7/1/73	5½	7/1/79	5¼	(1)
2 Negotiable order of withdrawal accounts [2]	5	1/1/74	(3)	....	5	1/1/74	(3)	....
Time accounts [4]								
Fixed ceiling rates by maturity								
3 30–89 days	5¼	8/1/79	5	7/1/73	(3)	....	(3)	....
4 90 days to 1 year	5¾	1/1/80	5½	7/1/73	6	1/1/80	5¾	(1)
5 1 to 2 years [5]	6	7/1/73	5½	1/21/70	6½	(1)	5¾	1/21/70
6 2 to 2½ years [5]			5¾	1/21/70			6	1/21/70
7 2½ to 4 years [5]	6½	7/1/73	5¾	1/21/70	6¾	(1)	6	1/21/70
8 4 to 6 years [6]	7¼	11/1/73	(7)	....	7½	11/1/73	(7)	....
9 6 to 8 years [6]	7½	12/23/74	7¼	11/1/73	7¾	12/23/74	7½	11/1/73
10 8 years or more [6]	7¾	6/1/78	(3)	....	8	6/1/78	(3)	....
11 Issued to governmental units (all maturities)[8]	8	6/1/78	7¾	12/23/74	8	6/1/78	7¾	12/23/74
12 Individual retirement accounts and Keogh (H.R. 10) plans (3 years or more)[8,9]	8	6/1/78	7¾	7/6/77	8	6/1/78	7¾	7/6/77
Special variable ceiling rates by maturity								
13 6-month money market time deposits[10]	(11)	(11)	(11)	(11)	(11)	(11)	(11)	(11)
14 2½ years or more	(12)	(12)	(13)	(13)	(12)	(12)	(13)	(13)

1. July 1, 1973, for mutual savings banks; July 6, 1973, for savings and loan associations.

2. For authorized states only, federally insured commercial banks, savings and loan associations, cooperative banks, and mutual savings banks in Massachusetts and New Hampshire were first permitted to offer negotiable order of withdrawal (NOW) accounts on Jan. 1, 1974. Authorization to issue NOW accounts was extended to similar institutions throughout New England on Feb. 27, 1976, and in New York State on Nov. 10, 1978, and in New Jersey on Dec. 28, 1979.

3. No separate account category.

4. For exceptions with respect to certain foreign time deposits see the FEDERAL RESERVE BULLETIN for October 1962 (p. 1279), August 1965 (p. 1084), and February 1968 (p. 167).

5. No minimum denomination. Until July 1, 1979, a minimum of $1,000 was required for savings and loan associations, except in areas where mutual savings banks permitted lower minimum denominations. This restriction was removed for deposits maturing in less than 1 year, effective Nov. 1, 1973.

6. No minimum denomination. Until July 1, 1979, minimum denomination was $1,000 except for deposits representing funds contributed to an Individual Retirement Account (IRA) or a Keogh (H.R. 10) plan established pursuant to the Internal Revenue Code. The $1,000 minimum requirement was removed for such accounts in December 1975 and November 1976 respectively.

7. Between July 1, 1973, and Oct. 31, 1973, there was no ceiling for certificates maturing in 4 years or more with minimum denominations of $1,000; however, the amount of such certificates that an institution could issue was limited to 5 percent of its total time and savings deposits. Sales in excess of that amount, as well as certificates of less than $1,000, were limited to the 6½ percent ceiling on time deposits maturing in 2½ years or more.

Effective Nov. 1, 1973, ceilings were reimposed on certificates maturing in 4 years or more with minimum denomination of $1,000. There is no limitation on the amount of these certificates that banks can issue.

8. Accounts subject to fixed rate ceilings. See footnote 6 for minimum denomination requirements.

9. Effective January 1, 1980, commercial banks are permitted to pay the same rate as thrifts on IRA and Keogh accounts and accounts of governmental units when such deposits are placed in the new 2½ year or more variable ceiling certificates or in 26-week money market certificates regardless of the level of the Treasury bill rate.

10. Must have a maturity of exactly 26 weeks and a minimum denomination of $10,000, and must be nonnegotiable.

11. Commercial banks, savings and loan associations, and mutual savings banks were authorized to offer money market time deposits effective June 1, 1978. The ceiling rate for commercial banks on money market time deposits entered into before June 5, 1980, is the discount rate (auction average) on most recently issued six-month U.S. Treasury bills. Until Mar. 15, 1979, the ceiling rate for savings and loan associations and mutual savings banks was ¼ percentage point higher than the rate for commercial banks. Beginning March 15, 1979, the ¼-percentage-point interest differential is removed when the six-month Treasury bill rate is 9 percent or more. The full differential is in effect when the six-month bill rate is 8¾ per cent or less. Thrift institutions may pay a maximum 9 percent when the six-month bill rate is between 8¾ and 9 percent. Also effective March 15, 1979, interest compounding was prohibited on six-month money market time deposits at all offering institutions. The maximum allowable rates in May for commercial banks were as follows: May 1, 10.790; May 8, 9.495; May 15, 8.782; May 22, 8.923; and May 29, 7.753. The maximum allowable rates in May for thrift institutions were as follows: May 1, 10.790; May 8, 9.495; May 15, 9.000; May 22, 9.000; and May 29, 8.003. [NOTE. Effective for all six-month money market certificates issued beginning June 5, 1980, the interest rate ceilings will be determined by the discount rate (auction average) of most recently issued six-month U.S. Treasury bills as follows:

Bill rate	*Commercial bank ceiling*	*Thrift ceiling*
8.75 and above	bill rate + ¼ percent	bill rate + ¼ percent
8.50 to 8.75	bill rate + ¼ percent	9.00
7.50 to 8.50	bill rate + ¼ percent	bill rate + ½ percent
7.25 to 7.50	7.75	bill rate + ½ percent
Below 7.25	7.75	7.75

The prohibition against compounding interest in these certificates continues. In addition, during the period May 29, 1980, through Nov. 1, 1980, commercial banks may renew maturing six-month money market time deposits for the same depositor at the thrift institution ceiling interest rate.]

12. Effective Jan. 1, 1980, commercial banks, savings and loan associations, and mutual savings banks were authorized to offer variable-ceiling nonnegotiable time deposits with no required minimum denomination and with maturities of 2½ years or more. The maximum rate for commercial banks is ¾ percentage point below the yield on 2½ year U.S. Treasury securities; the ceiling rate for thrift institutions is ¼ percentage point higher than that for commercial banks. Effective Mar. 1, 1980, a temporary ceiling of 11¾ per cent was placed on these accounts at commercial banks; the temporary ceiling is 12 percent at savings and loan associations and mutual savings banks. [NOTE. Effective for all variable ceiling nonnegotiable time deposits with maturities of 2½ years or more issued beginning June 2, 1980, the ceiling rates of interest will be determined as follows:

Treasury yield	*Commercial bank ceiling*	*Thrift ceiling*
12.00 and above	11.75	12.00
9.50 to 12.00	Treasury yield − ¼ percent	Treasury yield
Below 9.50	9.25	9.50

Interest may be compounded on these time deposits. The ceiling rates of interest at which these accounts may be offered will vary biweekly.]

13. Between July 1, 1979, and Dec. 31, 1979, commercial banks, savings and loan associations, and mutual savings banks were authorized to offer variable ceiling accounts with no required minimum denomination and with maturities of 4 years or more. The maximum rate for commercial banks was 1¼ percentage points below the yield on 4-year U.S. Treasury securities; the ceiling rate for thrift institutions was ¼ percentage point higher than that for commercial banks.

NOTE. Before Mar. 31, 1980, the maximum rates that could be paid by federally insured commercial banks, mutual savings banks, and savings and loan associations were established by the Board of Governors of the Federal Reserve System, the Board of Directors of the Federal Deposit Insurance Corporation, and the Federal Home Loan Bank Board under the provisions of 12 CFR 217, 329, and 526, respectively. Title II of the Depository Institutions Deregulation and Monetary Control Act of 1980 (P.L. 96–221) transferred the authority of the agencies to establish maximum rates of interest payable on deposits to the Depository Institutions Deregulation Committee. The maximum rates on time deposits in denominations of $100,000 or more with maturities of 30–89 days were suspended in June 1970; such deposits maturing in 90 days or more were suspended in May 1973. For information regarding previous interest rate ceilings on all types of accounts, see earlier issues of the FEDERAL RESERVE BULLETIN, the Federal Home Loan Bank Board *Journal*, and the *Annual Report* of the Federal Deposit Insurance Corporation.

Source: Federal Reserve Bulletin, June 1980, p. A9.

In 1973–74, and again in 1979–80, interest rates in the money markets were such that savers' funds in the financial institutions were attracted directly into money market instruments and were withdrawn on a massive scale from financial institutions. This disintermediation nullified the real estate lending potential of the institutions. The interest rate ceilings thwarted an ability to compete to retain the savings within the institution.

Beginning June 1, 1978, a flexible rate tied to Treasury bills was introduced on six-month deposits to enable the institutions to compete to retain their accounts; but the money market rates rose so fast that, had they chosen to do so, the institutions could not have placed the funds from such deposits in the mortgage market on a profitable basis. More crucially, to place short-term funds in a long-term investment without adequate protection for future rate changes would be courting disaster. Thus, the real estate mortgage market suffered much as though the funds had, in fact, been withdrawn.

Under the new law, there will be a slow phaseout of rate ceilings, ultimately allowing market forces to determine deposit interest rates. The federal regulatory authorities are to complete the phaseout over a period of up to six years. Meanwhile, during the transition period, the rate differential in favor of mutual savings banks and savings and loan associations over commercial banks has been retained.

The phaseout period is justified by the long-term mortgage rates on loans made prior to the recent interest rate increases in that market. It is estimated, for example, that possibly one half of the $475 billion in savings and loan association mortgages are at 7.5 percent interest or less. As of April 1980, only about one fifteenth of their mortgages carried yields equal to the money market certificate rates accounting for about one third of savings and loan deposits. The profit squeeze thus becomes apparent.

This law also preempted state usury ceilings on mortgage and other loans. On mortgage loans the preemption is permanent, but it may be overridden by state legislative action.

Asset mix of thrift institutions

The new law permits an asset mix for federal savings and loan associations more consistent with their performing certain commercial banking functions. They are now permitted to invest up to an aggregate limit of 20 percent of assets in unsecured or secured consumer loans, commercial paper, and corporate debt securities. They are also allowed to invest in, redeem, or hold shares or certificates of open-end investment companies. They may also exercise trust and fiduciary powers and offer credit card services.

In regard to real estate, savings and loan geographical lending restrictions, formerly an important part of the Home Owners Loan Act, were removed. Residential real estate loans are no longer restricted to first liens; second trust loans are authorized; and a 90 percent loan-to-value ratio requirement has been substituted in place of a dollar value upper limit for residential real estate loans.

Case problem (appendix)

The 1980 legislation created a Depository Institutions Deregulation Committee, comprising the Secretary of the Treasury, the Chairman of the Board of Governors of the Federal Reserve System, the Chairman of the Board of Directors of the Federal Deposit Insurance Corporation, the Chairman of the Federal Home Loan Bank Board, and the Chairman of the National Credit Union Administration Board. Each member is to make an annual report to the Congress on the economic viability of depository institutions that is to include the following:

1 An assessment as to whether the removal of any differential between the rates paid by banks and those paid by thrift institutions will adversely affect housing finance or the viability of the thrift industry.

2 Recommendations for measures to encourage saving, provide for the equitable treatment of small savers, and ensure a steady and adequate flow of funds to thrift institutions and housing.

3 Findings concerning disintermediation of savings deposits from insured institutions to uninsured money market innovators paying market rates to savers.

4 Recommendations for legislative and administrative actions necessary to maintain the economic viability of depository institutions.

Assume you are a member of this committee. Develop a framework for study of each of the four areas indicated above; and offer any tentative recommendations that you may consider to have merit.

Financing of real estate by life insurance companies and real estate investment trusts

21

PART 1: LIFE INSURANCE COMPANIES

Life insurance companies as lenders on real estate security

Like some other types of financial institutions, life insurance companies have followed a pattern in lending on real estate as security that has adjusted itself to changing economic conditions. At one time farm loans were popular outlets for investable resources of insurance companies. Later, enthusiasm for this type of investment cooled materially. From time to time mortgages on urban real estate have been favored. Since life insurance companies, unlike savings and loan associations, for example, were not organized primarily for the purpose of financing homes, it is to be expected that they will seek the outlets for their investment funds which will best meet the requirements of the investor at the time the investment is made.

Great differences appear in the mortgage-lending operations of life insurance companies. These differences are accounted for by variations in size, investment experience, and mental attitudes of those who manage the companies. As may be expected, smaller companies are less well equipped to handle mortgage lending than are their larger competitors. Some companies limit their mortgage holdings to residential properties as security, while others lend on commercial, financial, and even industrial property as well.

In spite of the pressure of funds for investment and for reinvestment, life insurance companies occasionally experience something akin to the "in-and-out" policies of commercial banks in their mortgage investment programs. This is particularly true of advance commitments. At times they will gladly indicate to their correspondents their willingness to purchase agreed-upon quantities of mortgages for future delivery. On other occasions they become more cautious and prefer to consider purchases only as mortgages are offered to them. In unusual situations—where money rates appear quite uncertain—they may even withdraw from the market temporarily.

Life insurance assets.   According to the *Life Insurance Fact Book,*[1] total assets of life insurance companies in 1890 were $771 million. They doubled in each decade until in 1960 they totaled about $120 billion. As of December 1978, they were estimated at $390 billion, indicating continued rapid growth. In recent years insurance companies have experienced quite a change in their investments in real estate mortgages. In 1947, about 16.8 percent of all assets were so invested. The holdings amounted to a grand total of about $8.7 billion. From that year to 1966, there was a constant increase in the proportion of assets invested in mortgages to a high of 38.6 percent, amounting to $64.6 billion. From 1966 through 1978, the proportion of mortgage holdings declined to 27.1 percent. Because of extremely rapid growth of company assets, however, the dollar volume increased to nearly $105.8 billion. This amounted to nearly one tenth of all the mortgage debt in the country. The magnitude of the stake of life insurance companies in the mortgage market is thus apparent in spite of the increasing competition of alternative investments for the use of their funds.

Mortgage experience

On the whole, the distribution of real estate loans in recent years has shown a distinct trend toward apartment complexes and commercial and industrial properties. Mortgage holdings of one- to four-family residential properties represented over half of all mortgage holdings from 1950 through 1964, reaching a high of 61 percent in 1956. Since 1964 this proportion has steadily declined. At the 1978 year-end, it was about 18 percent. At that time, over 77 percent of total mortgage holdings were on apartment developments and commercial properties, with the balance on farms.

Restrictions upon real estate loans by insurance companies

Most of the states have passed laws governing the operations of insurance companies. These fall into two classes: law governing the operations of companies domiciled within the state; and those controlling activities of companies domiciled elsewhere, but doing business within the state that passed the law. Since the major purpose of both types of laws is the protection of the

---

[1] A considerable part of the statistical material contained in this chapter has been adapted from the *Life Insurance Fact Book.* Updating may be accomplished by reference to the most current issue.

policyholders, the features of the legislation dealing with investments are more or less incidental to this major purpose. For this reason, a brief discussion of legislation of the latter type must be presented.

While most laws dealing with insurance companies domiciled within the state permit investments in real estate mortgages, such permission is usually hedged about with various types of restrictions. Only the most common restrictions will be discussed here. Those interested in the less common types are referred to the laws of the various states for such information. In general, the permission to make loans on real estate is limited, for example, to "improved land," including farms. While such improved land is supposed to be unencumbered, such encumbrances as taxes, assessments, easements, and building restrictions are excepted.

One common type of restriction that impinges heavily upon real estate finance, and that will probably be subject to review from time to time, is the upper limit of individual loans and the limit of assets which may be devoted to this type of investment. For example, in New York an insurance company may not invest more than a modest dollar limit or 2 percent of its total assets (whichever is greater) in a mortgage on a single property. If the company's assets are less than $1 or $2 million, it is effectively restricted to loans on residential or small business properties, including farms. If its assets exceed $100 million, this 2 percent limitation becomes less important. In New York, also, not more than 50 percent of the total assets of a life insurance company may be invested in all real estate mortgages held by it at one time. Again the size of the company has an important bearing upon its competitive position in the field of real estate finance.

Where legislation governing the operation of life insurance companies makes specific mention of such subjects as leaseholds and land contracts, they too are subject to the restrictions defined in the law. For example, no loan may be made by an insurance company domiciled in the state of New York on a leasehold whose unexpired term is not at least equal to the lesser of 40 years or a sufficient term that normal amortization will have been completed within four fifths of the remaining leasehold period. In Minnesota the corresponding term is 40 years; in Ohio 99 years, renewable forever; and in Texas for a period at least 10 years beyond the term of the loan.

Where restrictions of the kind mentioned above are included in the law which governs the operation of insurance companies domiciled in another state but doing business in the state that passes the law, the purpose is to protect the domestic companies against unfair competition as well as to protect the policyholders.

Restrictions setting the upper limits of loans in relation to the value of the security therefor are considered to be quite conservative in today's markets. Such loan-to-value ratios usually range between 66.67 and 75 percent for conventional mortgages. FHA and VA loans are usually exempted from these as well as from most of the other restrictions discussed herein.

In respect to one type of restriction, not mentioned above, insurance companies usually enjoy greater freedom than their competitors. They are not usually required to amortize their real estate loans nor to limit them to any maximum maturity. Recent changes in policy on such questions have been dictated more by competition than by law. For example, insurance companies are making freer use of amortized loans on residential properties than was their earlier practice.

Geographical limitations. Here is an area in which laws governing insurance companies operate quite differently from those governing the operations of other types of lending institutions. For example, until recently savings and loan associations have been discouraged from making loans outside of a restricted lending area defined in the regulatory laws. As discussed in Chapters 19 and 20, the 1980 legislation affecting depository institutions has removed territorial lending restrictions for institutions governed by the Home Owners Loan Act. Savings banks have been subjected to geographical limitations somewhat more liberal than those for savings and loan associations, but nevertheless restrictive.

Geographical limitations for insurance companies have been much more liberal. For the most part the lending area for them is considered to be the United States. In some state laws even Canada is added. One potent reason for this difference is that insurance companies are commonly national in their markets for writing insurance policies. It has been thought fair to allow them to invest their funds in areas from which they have been obtained in the usual course of conducting their insurance business. Indeed, some states have been so insistent that this be done that their legislation is slanted in this direction.

Preference for larger loans. Although life insurance companies make loans on single-family residences, many of them prefer the larger loans in this category. Seldom will they compete actively for smaller residential loans except when they are buying them in bulk. To an even more marked degree, they prefer loans on multifamily dwellings and on commercial properties such as hotels and office and loft buildings. Even in the field of industrial real estate, they are an important financial influence.

Another development in the mortgage market affecting life companies is the rapidly growing importance of local lenders, especially savings and loan associations and commercial banks. Insurance companies are experiencing increasing difficulty in competing for conventional residential loans. For this reason, also, these companies are seeking loans on income property occupied by tenants with superior credit ratings. The advantages of purchase-and-leaseback arrangements have been sharply curtailed during the past few years by changes in the federal income tax law. Out of the leaseback experience, however, life companies have learned that they can accomplish an approximate equivalent by 100 percent loans. Since the definite approval of such loans in New York state, insurance companies have been looking with increasing favor on 100 percent loans on income property when the tenants are of unquestioned financial responsibility and the net rent will support the loan.

Relative freedom from maximum loan limitations and territorial restrictions gives the life companies an advantage over their competitors in regard to this type of property.

Lending with equity participation.   The stronger inflationary forces of the past decade have caused institutional lenders, and particularly life insurance companies, to become increasingly interested in equity participations in projects in which they have a lending interest. Tight money markets have pressured hopeful borrowers into conceding some degree of equity participation as an inducement for a mortgage loan. Since equity-participation loans usually have a high loan-to-value ratio, mortgage loan officers are not reluctant to accept (or insist upon) the equity participation in return for the assumption of the equity-type risk. In addition to a favorable loan limit, the borrower may be accorded lower interest rates and slower repayment terms as well.

The most commonly used participation arrangements have been previously discussed in Chapters 12 and 13. They include the loan pattern in which the lender receives a percentage of gross or net income generated by the mortgaged property or where the lender is granted a participation in income over a defined break-even point.

Certain other, more complex, arrangements are in sufficiently common usage to merit consideration. They include:

1. Sale and buy-back agreement.
2. Joint venture with "front money" partner.

Sale and buy-back agreement.   A related type of financing is the *sale and buy-back* of installment sales contract. Under this arrangement, the investor buys the property from the developer and simultaneously sells it back to him under a long-term installment agreement whereby the investor retains legal title. The developer-buyer obtains an equitable interest in the title and may claim depreciation. His payments are set approximately equal to the current mortgage constant for the purchase price, plus a contingent payment related to property performance. The buyer normally has prepayment privileges in the form of contract termination options which when exercised will also result in a profit windfall to the investor.

To visualize the fact pattern for sale and buy-back financing, assume that Brown has just completed for $2.5 million a 170-unit garden apartment complex on land that he has owned for several years. The current land value is $400,000. The economic value of the land and buildings is $3.5 million, based on the following projection of income and expenses (10 percent capitalization rate):

Effective gross income	$500,000
Fixed and operating expenses	150,000
Net income	$350,000

Brown now sells this project to an insurance company for $2.9 million, his total investment value, and at the same time agrees to buy back the property over a 30-year period. At $300,000 paid annually, the installment payments will amortize the total cost over approximately a 27-year term at 9.5 percent interest annually. Under this arrangement, the insurance company will receive its special participation by virtue of the last three annual payments as a bonus.

Joint venture with front money partner. Recently, there has been a decided emergence of *front money* transactions. Quite commonly, experienced developers team up with partners who have no development experience but who can provide cash outlays necessary to carry a development through its initial stages. These often are institutional investors. The split on net income and relative positions in regard to control of the venture are negotiated. Terms of a joint venture of this kind might follow the general outlines of this example: Brown, a developer, enters into a joint venture agreement with a *money partner* to acquire and develop land and build a condominium on it. With the land to cost $500,000 and the improvements to cost an additional $4,000,000, the venture might be projected to gross $5,500,000 on sale of the units. The money partner lends $500,000 to the venture to buy the land. A construction loan is arranged for $3,700,000. To make up the deficiency between building costs and the construction loan and to provide working capital, each partner contributes $300,000. As sales of the condominium units are made, the proceeds are distributed according to the agreement as follows:

1. The construction loan is repaid.
2. The money partner receives back the $500,000 advanced for land purchase.
3. Interest is paid on the money partner's loan at the rate of 10 percent per annum.
4. Any proceeds left over are distributed equally to Brown and the money partner to return their capital contributions and pay out the profits.

Mortgage loan department

Because of the geographical extent of mortgage loan operations, the problem of organization of the mortgage loan department of a life insurance company is quite unlike that faced by its competitors in this field of operations. Investment in mortgages can be national in scope for any particular company. Their origination and servicing must be conducted at the local level to be most successful. Because of differences in practices among insurance companies, several plans of operating mortgage loan departments are in common use. The more extensive the mortgage-lending operations, the larger the number of loans outstanding and the more far-flung their geographical distribution; the more varied the kinds of property which secures them, the more complicated the mortgage loan department becomes.

The institution which has outstanding a large number of insured or guaranteed loans on residential property, widely scattered geographically without any great amount of concentration in any contiguous area, may well find one type of mortgage loan department most satisfactory. One which has a similar amount of money invested in a small number of large commercial and multifamily residence loans, concentrated in a few metropolitan areas, might find a different form of organization best adapted to its needs.

There are two major types of organization to be considered. In addition, variations and combinations of these two types are in use. These two major types are branch offices and outside correspondents. They have been known to succeed each other, following a pattern of alternation that is dictated by experience which ends in disappointment. If one system is tried continuously to the satisfaction of the management, it is not likely to be disturbed. But if its results are unsatisfactory, regardless of the reasons, it is not uncommon that a major operation is performed in order that a change of pattern may be substituted.

Where the branch office type of organization is used, it is manned by salaried employees of the insurance company. Here the control is direct. Both lending and servicing facilities can be set up by the home office, and supervisory personnel can see to it that company policies are carried out to the letter. Under this plan of organization, the lending institution can literally build a loan portfolio according to its own pattern, instead of picking and choosing among the types of loans offered for its purchase.

Branch offices may be located in the same physical quarters as the respective local offices of the insurance division of the insurance corporation, or they may occupy separate space. In either event, the employees of the mortgage loan department are under the supervision of the home-office staff engaged in mortgage loan operations. In addition, they may be subject to some measure of direction by the roving field representatives who visit them from time to time. Arm's-length supervision of small staffs needed to man branch offices may be one of the reasons that this plan of organization is less commonly used than the correspondent system next described.

Loan correspondents

As an alternative to branch offices for the purpose of making and servicing loans, some insurance companies prefer to appoint outside companies or individuals to handle this part of their mortgage business. From the standpoint of loan origination only, the service performed by such a correspondent is that of a finder, for whose service a finder's fee is paid. Here both the mortgage banker and the mortgage broker are used. Some insurance companies use either in ways that best suit their purposes. In some instances, the finder's job is completed when he points out an opportunity for making a real estate loan. Or he may take the next step and assemble information about it, leaving decisions to be made by salaried representatives of the insurance company.

Perhaps, instead, the finder assembles the information, prepares the necessary papers, and in fact does all but the closing of the loan, leaving only the latter function to be performed by the more direct representatives of the lender, if they find it desirable to complete the transaction. Finally, in the case of mortgage bankers (or mortgage companies, as they are sometimes called) the finder may use its own funds to close the loan, which is then offered for sale to the insurance company. Some of the sellers of such mortgages are properly classed as correspondents of the insurance company purchaser because of their contractual and continuing relationships. Others are not properly called correspondents, since the relationship between buyer and seller is casual and discontinuous.

Where the finder is compensated for the service of finding mortgage opportunities only, other arrangements must be made for servicing the loans which he originates. Where the correspondent is a mortgage banker, he may also service loans made by him for the insurance company or sold by him, receiving therefor a separate service fee. A variety of plans are used to provide compensation for loan correspondents. Among them are monthly payments, a percentage of collections made, and a percentage of original loans. As pointed out elsewhere in this text, a high finder's fee may be accompanied by a low servicing fee and vice versa.

Even those insurance companies that have had extensive experience with both branch offices and loan correspondents seem to encounter difficulty in deciding which plan is better. One reason for this apparent indecision is the problem of changing conditions. At one period of the business cycle, one plan appears to meet requirements best; at another period, another plan may be preferred. Some companies combine the two, using branches to establish patterns and loan correspondents to operate within patterns so established. Some companies alternate plans. Some use both at the same time. Historically speaking, correspondents appeared first. They still predominate.

Undoubtedly, branch operation provides a better opportunity for close control than does the loan correspondent plan. For that reason, times of stress are likely to emphasize the contributions of branches in contrast with those of the more independent correspondents. On the other hand, aggressive correspondents who produce results satisfactory to their principals are likely to find continued demand for their services.

Originating and service fees. Originating fees paid loan correspondents by life insurance companies vary from .25 to more than 2 percent. Probably the greatest number of cases fall within a range close to 1 percent. The maximum for FHA/VA originations is 1 percent.

Originating or finders' fees are of particular significance where mortgage loans are repaid within a relatively short period of time. If a finder's fee is paid in placing a loan on the books, this reduces the effective interest rate on the loan correspondingly. For example, if the finder's fee is 1.5 percent and the loan is repaid within five years, the 1.5 percent commission must be amortized within the five-year period, unless a corresponding penalty is charged against the borrower for the privilege of prepaying his loan. That is one reason why insurance companies frequently make no provision for mortgage loan prepayments or for such prepayments only when penalties are assessed. One common provision is to permit not more than 20 percent of the loan principal to be repaid within any consecutive period of 12 months. In the recent period of extremely high interest rates, it is not uncommon to have total "lock-in" of the loan for a minimum period, often five to seven years. Currently, finders' fees are commonly paid by the borrower.

Servicing fees commonly range from .125 to .75 percent. The rate is often related to the size of the loan to be serviced. The Federal National Mortgage Association and the Federal Home Loan Mortgage Corporation commonly allow a .375 percent servicing fee, while the Government National Mortgage Association commonly pays .44 percent. These practices tend to influence the standards for mortgage banking services to life insurance companies.

PART 2: REAL ESTATE INVESTMENT TRUSTS

Background of the real estate investment trusts

The concept of the real estate investment trust goes back to the 1880s. In the early years, trusts were not taxed if the income therefrom was distributed to beneficiaries. A Supreme Court decision in the 1930s, however, resulted in classifying all passive investment vehicles that were centrally organized and managed like corporations as "associations" taxable as corporations. This covered real estate investment trusts.

The stock and bond investment companies, also affected by the Supreme Court decision, promptly secured legislation (in 1936) which exempted regulated investment companies from federal taxation. At this time the real estate trusts were not organized to press for equal consideration and the trust did not develop into importance as a legal form for investing in real estate.

After World War II, however, the need for large sums of real estate equity and mortgage funds renewed interest in more extensive use of the real estate investment trust (which also became known as the REIT, pronounced "reet"), and a campaign was begun to achieve for the REIT special tax considerations comparable to those accorded mutual funds. In 1960 such legislation cleared the Congress.

Legal Requirements.   Effective January 1, 1961, special income tax benefits were accorded a new type of investment institution by an amendment to the Internal Revenue Code (Sections 856–858). Under this amendment, a real estate investment trust meeting prescribed requirements during the taxable year may be treated simply as a conduit with respect to the income distributed to beneficiaries of the trust. Thus the unincorporated trust or association, ordinarily taxed as a corporation, is not taxed on distributed taxable income when it qualifies for the special tax benefits. Only the beneficiaries pay the tax on such distributed income. To qualify as a "real estate investment trust" for tax purposes, the following requirements must be met:

1. Ownership must be in an unincorporated trust or association managed by at least one trustee, with transferable certificates of beneficial interest or shares, and ordinarily taxable as a domestic corporation.
2. There must be at least 100 beneficial owners.
3. The trust must not be a personal holding company even though all of its gross income constitutes personal holding company income.
4. The trust may not hold any property primarily for sale to customers in the ordinary course of business, that is, dealer property.
5. It must elect to be treated as a real estate investment trust.

At least 90 percent of the income of a real estate investment trust must come from real property rentals, dividends, interest, or gains from the sale of securities or real estate. Seventy-five percent or more of the trust income must be directly attributable to real property, and another 15 percent must be derived from real estate or any other source from which a regulated investment company would derive most of its income, such as interest and dividends. There is also a 30 percent test, which requires that not more than 30 percent of the gross income of the trust come from short-term gains on security sales and gains on the sale of real estate held for less than four years.

The trust must distribute at least 90 percent of its ordinary income to its shareholders. Any amount that the trust retains is subject to the regular corporate income tax.

When the new law initially went into effect, it appeared that if the real estate required active management and if the trustees participated in such management, the trust would not be accorded exempt status. The final Treasury regulations have defined the duties and powers of the trustees, shareholders or beneficiaries, and independent contracting managers, however, with some liberality. The property manager may perform and bill the trust for operating costs; he may hire and fire employees; he may collect rents and remit differences with proper accounting for collections and expenses. The trustee is permitted to make some important decisions, such as whether to make major repairs.

When the law was passed, real estate investment trusts where the trustee was required to be "passive" were prohibited in many states. As a result, enabling legislation was required before such trusts could be formed. At the present time, the states generally have laws on the books permitting the establishment of real estate investment trusts that may qualify for special federal income tax benefits.

Types of trusts.   The two principal types of real estate investment trusts are equity trusts and mortgage trusts. In the early years of this REIT form, the equity trust was generally used, but later the mortgage trust became the more important.

The difference between the assets held by the equity trust and those held by the mortgage trust is fairly obvious. The equity trust acquires proprietary interests, while the mortgage trust purchases mortgage obligations and thus becomes a creditor with mortgage liens given priority to equity holders. Of course, as time has progressed, more heterogeneous investment policies have been developed, combining the advantages of both types of trusts to suit specific investment objectives. Such combinations are called hybrid trusts.

For purposes of description, equity trusts have been categorized into five groups.[2] These groups, their advantages, and their disadvantages are as follows:

1. Blank check trusts.   A blank check trust is one that is organized to buy properties judged by the trustees to meet the investment goals of the trust. Participating interests in the trust are sold on the strength of the reputations of the promoters, trustees, and independent contractors with management responsibility. The advantage of this type of trust is its flexibility; but a major disadvantage results from the lapse of time between the date the investor's shares are offered to the public and the time when the funds can be profitably invested. During this period, the investor's shares tend to suffer depressed conditions in the securities market.

2. Exchange trusts.   Exchange trusts involve the exchange of property for shares in the trust immediately after its organization. Such a transfer qualifies as a tax-free exchange for income tax purposes, and the trust acquires the shareholder's cost basis with respect to the property for depreciation purposes. The disadvantage of failing to acquire a stepped-up basis for higher depreciation deductions is offset by the tax-free diversification that the investor achieves. The trust also benefits in that it obtains a seasoned property with a known income potential.

3. Purchasing trusts.   A purchasing trust is one that has been organized to purchase property described in a prospectus. The advantage of this form is that the potential investor is fully informed about the property to be acquired. Possible disadvantages to the purchasing trust may lie in the lack of diversification and, from an administrative point of view, in the difficulty of gathering sufficient historical data to meet state or federal securities registration requirements.

4. Mixed trusts.   Mixed trusts are organized to invest part of the funds raised in a specific property and the balance on a "blank check" basis. Being a hybrid, this trust will have the advantage of providing almost immediate income; but since a part of the funds will be invested over a period of time, the overall return will be relatively low until, at least, the total investment has been made.

---

[2] John C. Williamson, "The Real Estate Investment Trust Act—The Catalyst Which Is Making Real Estate 'Go Public' " *Journal of Property Management*, vol. 27, no. 2 (Winter 1961), pp. 68–79.

5. ~~Existing trusts.~~   Existing trusts are those which were in effect at the time the federal income tax law was revised to permit special treatment and which have since reorganized to qualify under the pertinent Revenue Code Sections. These trusts have the advantage of seasoned management and virtually no new organization costs. They also have an investment history to show prospective investors. Many of their properties will have been written down to the point that depreciation charges are not as great as they would like, but the trusts can cope with this problem by advantageous upgrading.

The equity trusts are distinguishable from the mortgage trusts in many respects regarding investment objectives served. Equity trusts receive rent as a primary source of income, while mortgage trust income is largely in the form of interest income and discounts earned through mortgage amortization. Capital gains in the equity trust come largely through the sale of the real estate. The mortgage trust derives its capital gains from selling mortgages at prices above cost, as a result of a change in money rates or because the mortgages have become more secure instruments. As owner of the physical property, the equity trust may obtain a depreciation deduction as a tax benefit not available to the mortgage trust, but by the same token it must assume the owner's management responsibilities. The mortgage trust income from interest and discounts is fixed in nature, whereas the rental income of the equity trust may be fixed, as in a "net lease," or volatile, where the rents are determined as a percentage of sales. Expenses of operation may also be involved in determining the return to the equity trust. Because they are constantly amortizing, the assets of the mortgage trust have been considered more liquid than the real estate owned by the equity trust. The experience of recent years, however, has demonstrated that where there are widespread delinquencies on mortgage loans, the highly leveraged mortgage trust is likely to be less viable than the equity trust.

A review of these characteristics suggests at least two distinct markets of real estate investors that the trusts serve. The equity trust has been used by the relatively small investor desiring to participate in the ownership and operation of large improved real properties—such as commerical, industrial, or apartment buildings. The mortgage trust, on the other hand, has developed as a vehicle of institutions with increasing surpluses of uninvested savings needing a fixed return or with underutilized mortgage underwriting talent that can be applied to a profitable new venture.

The appeal of equity trusts as an investment

From a negligible figure in the early 1960s, equity trust ownership of real estate grew to $7.64 billion, or 61 percent of all REIT assets (the other being principally mortgages), at the 1978 year-end. This growth was largely occasioned by investors seeking an opportunity to place funds in real estate under professional guidance as to investment selection with management provided and with somewhat greater liquidity than investment in a real estate parcel provides.

The real estate investment trust is well adapted to fulfilling these requirements. By affording the individual investor an opportunity to pool his resources with those of persons of like interests, funds are assembled to permit purchase of buildings, shopping centers, land, and developments—or whatever seems to offer the most attractive returns. Investment must be approved by a board of trustees who are ordinarily well qualified to make such decisions. The trust certificate holder buys an interest in diversified holdings, and his shares are usually readily salable in the over-the-counter market. The tax exemption places the small shareholder in a position for tax payments similar to what he might have if he had made the same investment as an individual real estate operator.

The advantage of the trust to the small private investor depends, in the final analysis, on the fundamental soundness of real estate as an investment. The attractiveness of real estate as an investment closely follows its economic value. These values are largely determined by growth in population and its purchasing power in relation to a uniquely immobile and indestructible site with improvements thereon. According to many real estate analysts, the probable physical and economic life of residential buildings is from 80 to 90 years. The economic value of land and the physical durability of buildings make it possible for the same parcel to experience diverse successive uses over a period of years or centuries. It follows that improvements with the least specialized purposes have the greatest flexibility of use and probable longest economic life.

It is a mistake to assume that land values always rise. Even in a prosperous, expanding economy certain segments of the real estate market, whether classified geographically or functionally, may experience distress. It is for this reason that if one is to take advantage of the possible physical and economic durability of real estate, investment decisions should be made by competent, foresighted appraisers with a full appreciation of local and general economic conditions. As the management counsel of mutual funds provide this judgment for investors in such funds, so also the trustees of real estate investment trusts provide this service to their investors.

Real estate as a hedge against rising price levels.   Anyone who bought real estate during or shortly after World War II realizes how rising price levels or production costs of new structures—residential, commercial, or industrial, where production is to a demand—can cause the property values to rise. A study of price levels in America from the Revolutionary War days to the present, where periods of as long as 20 years are considered as a span, has shown a steady rise.

The value of real estate that maintains its economic utility tends to move with the cost of reproduction of a new facility to render a comparable service. Particularly where leverage is used to finance ownership of a larger property subject to possibly higher reproduction cost, a properly selected, functional real estate property can serve as a hedge against higher price levels.

Tax shelters in real estate investments.   Much has been written pointing out the tax advantages that may be derived from liberal depreciation allowances deductible from taxable income. The advantage lies in the fact that the functional or economic life of a property often extends far beyond the depreciable life used for income tax purposes. In many instances, the decline in value as a result of depreciation or obsolescence has been substantially or totally offset by rising replacement costs of similar properties when demand for such properties is high in relation to supply. Thus, older properties may sell today at prices above original cost of constuction, and yet they may have been substantially depreciated for income tax purposes.

This possibility has been greatly enhanced by the use of accelerated depreciation methods. Such methods permit heavier depreciation charges in the earlier years of the life of the building, and they thus effect a deferral of income tax.

It should be pointed out, however, that to the extent a depreciation charge is taken, the investor has recognized a retieval of his capital, and not income on his investment. A statement of income and expenses may demonsrate why this is true:

Total revenues received	$100,000
Total cash expenses	60,000
Net cash earnings	$ 40,000
Depreciation charge allowable (write-off to reduce property carrying value)	30,000
Net taxable income	$ 10,000

If this property is managed by a tax-exempt real estate investment trust and the $40,000 of net cash earnings are distributed to trust certificate holders, only one fourth of the earnings (in the ratio of $10,000 to $40,000) will be taxable to the individual recipients. The other three fourths will constitute a nontaxable return of capital. For tax accounting purposes, the individual investor cannot measure his precise return on his investment by his cash receipts. Distributions paid out of depreciation (as the $30,000 above) instead of net income ($10,000 above) are considered a return of capital until the investor receives the full cost of his shares or sells them. After full recovery of costs he realizes taxable gains.

From a practical investor's standpoint, however, where the trust shares have a ready marketability, a current yield may be effectively determined by comparing the cash dividend received (trust payout) with the current market price. A history of gain or loss in capital may be derived from comparing issue price and market price. Because a large portion of real estate investment trust distributions is usually nontaxable, the aftertax value of such dividends is often substantially greater to the individual taxpaying investor than a like amount of fully taxable dividends of an ordinary corporation.

The 1974–75 reversal.   The business recession and tight money rates of the 1974–75 period brought major difficulties to the equity real estate investment trusts. Although they did not suffer the severe losses of the mortgage trusts, as will be discussed later, the value of their shares in the public markets declined substantially.

Large-scale unemployment created rental vacancies as families merged into fewer housing units. Rental overages on leases disappeared or businesses defaulted or discontinued operations. Meanwhile, maintenance costs rose under the inflationary pressures. It was generally not possible to acquire new properties under conditions of favorable leverage because of relatively higher long-term mortgage interest rates. Consequently, net income was reduced or losses were incurred and dividends were reduced or suspended.

Although banking relationships deteriorated in these years, a return to a more orderly mortgage market can do much to make refinancing and resale of properties a possibility and thus to restore liquidity to the equity trusts. Emergence from the recession will bring about a restoration of income to the trust properties. This income, in turn, will be flowed through to the equity trust shareholders.

It is a few years away, but ultimately, after the banks have dealt with the abundance of mortgages that they have had to take over, mostly from the mortgage trusts, the equity trusts may again be considered eligible borrowers, albeit under cautionary terms. As these trends develop, the equity trusts may again be in a position to offer the attractions that brought such a generous flow of funds into the real estate market during the 1960s and early 1970s.

The development of mortgage trusts.[3] The mortgage lending segment of the REIT industry by the 1974 year-end encompassed $15.29 billion, or about 72 percent, of the total industry assets of $21.18 billion. This development took place largely from 1969 through 1974. By the end of 1978 loans fell to $3.25 billion, or only 26 percent of total assets. This decline came about due to the 1974–75 reversal, causing a decline in the popularity of mortgage trusts. At year-end 1978, trust sponsor-advisors included 22 commercial banks, 32 mortgage bankers or real estate companies, and 10 insurance companies, accounting for nearly 43 percent of the total assets of the industry. Of the remainder of industry assets (57 percent), 41 percent are managed internally by REITs.

Accounting for such institutional growth, fostered by so many institutions so quickly, was the expectation of material advantages to the sponsors of the trusts. The main advantages sought were:

1. An additional source of funds to lend on mortgages that could be serviced by the sponsor or its affiliate.
2. Advisory fees.
3. An opportunity to support projects by loans beyond the legal or policy limits of the sponsoring institution.

---

[3] Financial data presented in this section were derived from *REIT Fact Book*—1979, National Association of Real Estate Investment Trusts, Inc., 1101 Seventeenth St., N.W., Washington, D.C. 20036. The current *Fact Book* is recommended supplementary reading for this chapter.

The appeal of mortgage trusts as an investment.   The mortgage trust is unlike the equity trust in that it does not own the real property. Rather, it owns mortgage paper secured by the underlying real property. Income generated by the mortgage paper is affected by the nominal interest rate on the mortgage note, the discount (or premium) at which the obligation is acquired, and the amount of funds outstanding on loan. The trust expenses applicable against this income are, generally, interest paid for the funds derived to put out on loan, management company costs, and other lesser expenses incident to the operations of this kind of investment company.

During the late 1960s and early 1970s, prior to the débacle of mortgage defaults in 1974 and 1975, this trust form held forth great promise as a source of loans, particularly for construction and development, that were beyond the legal or policy limits of the highly regulated banks, savings and loans, insurance companies, or other real estate-oriented financing institutions. Because their lending policies were relatively unregulated and because they had access to public securities markets, mortgage trusts were in a position to fill a great void in the real estate financing market.

Equity funds were raised through sale of shares to the public, and these funds were usually placed in a portfolio of FHA and VA government-backed mortgages. This investment immediately provided an effective yield on assets of 7 to 8 percent. In addition, the FHA/VA mortgages provided an equity-derived asset base that would support bank lines of credit of up to four times the amount of the equity. Thus, $1 million of shareholders' equity would support up to $4 million of bank credit lines, or similar access to the commercial paper market. Even though the cost of the short-term borrowed funds might be relatively high, there was always the reasonable expectation that the trust could put the funds out on a construction or development loan at a 3.5 to 4 percent higher rate. The spread between borrowing costs and loan income thus held promise of increasing earnings on the shareholders' equity as the loan portfolio grew. Such growth in earnings would support further sales of shares in the trust at higher prices, and so on. Following this pattern, the expansion of mortgage trusts during the early 1970s was spectacular.

However, during 1974 a general economic recession set in and the prime bank lending rate rose to an unprecedented high of 12 percent. Because of the unanticipated rise in money costs, many mortgage trusts were forced into an operating loss position because they were not able to pass on a sufficient amount of these higher costs to their borrowing customers. Their advance mortgage commitments had been made at lower rates with inadequate flexibility for upward rate adjustments. Beyond this, many developers were unable to sell their completed units or could not complete their projects because of rapidly inflating construction costs and, consequently, were thrown into default on their construction loans. The equity share values of mortgage trusts plummeted, thus foreclosing further stock sales as a source of funds.

Because of the loan default expectations, the commercial paper market dried up for the trusts and forced them to rely almost exclusively on bank credit lines. As the defaults continued to increase during 1975, many large commercial banks were placed in the position of having to extend the maturities on notes taken pursuant to these credit lines which had usually been extended by banks as a group under a revolving credit agreement. The extensions were granted to avoid the cumulative impact on the total financial system if the trusts were forced to undertake mass foreclosures in a time of serious business recession. A number of bank sponsors took large blocks of mortgages out of the trust portfolios and into their own loan and liquidation accounts to reduce trust debts where stringencies became so severe that commercial bank lines could not otherwise be reasonably renewed. Such actions had an impact on overall commercial bank liquidity and removed the mortgage trusts generally from the construction and development loan markets as a supplier of funds for the foreseeable future. There still remains, however, a real need for a significant amount of construction and development financing under proper restraints. It is possible that after the shakeout a few stronger trusts will survive and will return to this market to become viable lenders in this important field of real estate finance.

The lessons learned from this experience were costly and many. They included numerous excesses: excessive expectations of trust profitability, excessive loan-to-value ratios, excessive use of credit lines, and excessive reliance on too little expertise of too few trust executives in times of rampant inflation and confiscatory money costs.

Type of REIT mortgage loans.   Since it is reasonable to expect an eventual return of stabilized mortgage trusts to the lending markets, it is important to note the kinds of mortgage lending to which they have made a significant contribution. In order of importance, mortgage trust loans include:

1. Construction loans.
2. Development loans.
3. Long-term conventional loans on apartment and commercial properties.
4. Short- and intermediate-term loans on completed properties.
5. Junior lien loans.

Construction loans.   Nearly half of REIT mortgage loans are construction loans. This has historically been an area of great need for funds because this type of lending has been subordinated to many others by savings and loan associations, commercial banks, insurance companies, and other institutional lenders. Because the bulk of mortgage trust funds were usually raised on a short-term basis, the construction loan with high interest rates and attractive commitment fees with maturities normally falling within one to two years seemed an appropriate investment. At the 1978 year-end, about two thirds of the construction loans outstanding were for residential housing. Office buildings and shopping centers accounted for a substantial amount of the other loans for construction.

Development loans. About 13 percent of the mortgage trust loans have gone for land development. Such loans are granted a developer to make site improvements necessary with building construction. The major items of cost in development are clearing and grading the land and putting in roads and utility lines. Usually a development loan is accompanied by a construction loan on the same property.

Long-term mortgage loans. Some mortgage trusts have taken the more conservative route of investing in long-term (10 to 20 years) mortgage loans. After 1971, however, REIT long-term mortgage lending fell off markedly because the costs of long-term funds, rising along with short-term rates, rendered such commitments unprofitable.

Short- and intermediate-term loans. Loans for the short or intermediate term (up to ten years) are typically not substantially amortized. They are made on completed properties to carry the developer through an interim period during which he hopes to build a favorable operating experience, to improve significantly his bargaining position for favorable terms on his long-term mortgage loans. Particularly in recent years, loans of this type have been made when the developer found his construction loan maturing with no long-term takeout commitment to pay it off. Many such interim loans have been thrown into default because of deterioration in the real estate market and inability of the developer to obtain long-term financing.

Junior lien loans. With rising interest rates, wraparound mortgages have been used significantly in connection with financing improvements to existing properties or to refinance for purposes of raising additional funds for expansion at another site. Junior liens also arise as auxiliary forms in connection with other transactions. Liens of this type represent only about 9 percent of all trust mortgage loans.

Balance sheet of the REIT industry. The National Association of Real Estate Investment Trusts, Inc., published the balance sheet of the REIT industry as of the 1978 year-end ($ billions) shown in Exhibit 21–1.

EXHIBIT 21–1
Aggregate balance sheet data for REITs—1978 ($ billions, year-end)

Assets		Liabilities	
Land, development and construction loans	$ 1.98	Bank borrowings and commercial paper	$ 5.17
Other loans	3.25	Mortgages—owned property	2.52
Loan loss reserves	(1.12)	Other liabilities	1.97
Property owned	7.64	Total liabilities	$ 9.66
Other assets	.83	Shareholder equity	2.92
Total assets	$12.58	Total liabilities and equity	$12.58

* Source: *REIT Fact Book—1979*, p. 27.

Questions

1 Review briefly the general history of life insurance companies as lenders on real estate security.

2 Are life insurance companies more likely than savings and loan associations to invoke penalties for prepayment of mortgage loans? Why or why not?

3 How do geographical limitations on mortgage lending by insurance companies differ from those governing the operations of other types of lending institutions?

4 Evaluate life insurance companies as investors in mortgages on commercial and industrial real estate.

5 What are the most important factors considered in a decision by an insurance company whether to invest in real estate mortgages, corporate bonds, or money market securities?

6 In general, how do lending standards and restrictions relating to life insurance company mortgage loans differ from comparable criteria for savings and loan associations and banks?

7 What is a sale and buy-back agreement? A joint venture with a front money partner?

8 By what methods do insurance companies place their investable funds in real estate mortgages? What are the advantages and disadvantages of each method?

9 What is the usual range of originating fees paid by life insurance companies to loan correspondents? What is the range of servicing fees?

10 How does a real estate investment trust qualify for favored tax treatment under the Internal Revenue Code? What is that treatment?

11 Distinguish among the principal types of real estate investment trusts and show how each may be useful.

12 What are the chief differences in the tax advantages generated by the equity trust and the mortgage trust?

13 What are the major appeals of the equity trust to the public investor? What are the shortcomings of this trust as evidenced in the recent period of recession and high interest rates?

14 Answer question 13 for mortgage trusts.

15 What problems do you see to the return of equity trusts as an important institutional source of funds for financing real estate?

16 Answer question 15 for mortgage trusts.

Case problems

1 A property, with income and expenses as set forth below, has been used in examples typical of life insurance company loan arrangements.

Type of property: Apartment—144 units

Value:

Land	$ 300,000
Building improvements	1,700,000
Total	$2,000,000

Operations:

Gross income	$ 340,000
Less 5% vacancy allowance.	17,000
Effective gross income.......................	$ 323,000
Less cash operating expenses:	
40% of effective gross income...............	129,200
Net income before debt service	$ 193,800

In this case the insurance company invested in accordance with what has sometimes been called the John Hancock plan. This has often been used in development situations.

Step 1: The investor bought the land for $300,000 cash and leased it back to the developer at a 9 percent rate.

Step 2: The investor made a 75 percent loan on leasehold improvements ($1,700,000 × .75) for $1,275,000 at 9 percent for 30 years (9.66 percent constant).

Step 3: The investor contracted also to receive 30 percent of "defined net income." This is equal to the difference between effective gross income and the total of 40 percent of effective gross income taken as operating expenses, debt service, and the ground rent.

a. Compute the first-year percentage of return on investment to the insurance company.

b. Compute the first-year percentage of return on investment to the developer based on cash flow.

2   Green built a large warehouse on land that he inherited. His warehouse cost him $2 million. His land is currently appraised at $300,000. He owes $2 million on his construction loan from the local bank. Based on projected net cash inflows from the warehouse operation ($300,000), Green's appraisal of the total property is $2.8 million. To pay off the construction loan and to provide some working capital, Green seeks to sell his total project to an insurance company for $2.3 million and to buy it back over 35 years. He is willing to pay 10 percent interest and to amortize the full cost over 30 years in monthly payments. The last five years would be treated as bonus payments to the investor for his participation.

a. Under Green's sale and buy-back plan, what would his payments be annually? What would be the rate of return on his residual investment?

b. If you were the potential investor in Green's venture, what factors would you consider to evaluate the attractiveness of this offer?

3   Public Equity Real Estate Trust has assets of $2 million. Its annual revenues last year totaled $240,000. Cash expenses, exclusive of financing, were $60,000. The trust has mortgage debt of $1.2 million, with an effective interest rate of 9 percent and a loan constant of 10 percent. Annual depreciation is $50,000.

a. Compute the annual cash flow of the trust. Assuming the full amount of the cash flow was paid to the shareholders, what percentage return would they receive?

b. Determine the minimum dividend that the trustees must pay if the trust is to qualify for exemption from federal income taxes on net income paid to shareholders.

4   Mortgage Trust of America (MTA) had strong institutional sponsorship. It had bank lines permitting it to borrow up to $4 million for each $1 million of unimpaired equity

invested in government-backed mortgages. MTA sold 1 million shares to the public at $20. These funds were invested in FHA/VA mortgages to yield effectively 8 percent. Trust bank credit lines permitted borrowing at an effective rate of two points above the bank prime lending rate. The trust felt confident that it could generally lend the short-term funds for construction or development with a 4 percent spread. If demand contracted, it could pay off its bank borrowings. Operating expenses were estimated at 20 percent of total yield.

Show how the trust might expect to increase earnings and to support further equity financing as the credit lines were used. Test debt/equity ratios of 1/1, 2/1, and 3/1.

Mortgage banking

22

Meaning

Mortgage bankers are sometimes known as mortgage companies or mortgage dealers. Those included under this appellation as defined in the Constitution of the Mortgage Bankers Association of America are as follows:

> Any person, firm or corporation . . . engaged in the business of lending money on the security of improved real estate in the United States, and who publicly offers such securities, or certificates, bonds or debentures based thereon, for sale as a dealer therein, or who is an investor in real estate securities, or is the recognized agent of an insurance company or other direct purchaser of first mortgage real estate securities for investment only.

The principal activity of the modern banker is originating and servicing income property and residential mortgage loans for institutional investors. Some mortgage bankers are essentially one-man concerns, with all of the small capital owned by the manager. In other cases, the corporate form of organization is used, with more than one class of security sometimes sold to obtain capital. In some cases, operations are extensive enough to warrant the maintenance of offices in several cities by one corporation. Since mortgage bankers are essentially merchandisers of mortgages, they expect to turn their capital rapidly. Their relatively small equity capital is sometimes supplemented by the use of bank credit. Even when bonds or debentures are sold, the resulting capital of mortgage bankers is not large in comparison with the annual volume of business done.

Mortgage loan broker distinguished

Closely related to the mortgage banker, yet distinct from him, is the mortgage loan broker. The relationship is so close that there is frequent confusion among those who fail to see any major difference. On another branch of the family tree, the mortgage loan broker is closely related to the better understood real estate broker whose activity is centered around the sale of real estate. Indeed, the same individual acts frequently in a dual capacity of real estate broker and mortgage loan broker.

Unlike the mortgage banker, the mortgage loan broker never invests his own capital in a mortgage. He is strictly an agent and not a merchandiser. To be sure, he may act from time to time as an agent without a principal, since he frequently is put in the position of peddling a loan application until he finds an investor interested in it. When this is accomplished, the broker then becomes the agent of the investor for the purpose of closing the deal for a loan.

Mortgage loan brokers may operate "under their hats," from a small office devoted to this business only, or in conjunction with insurance brokerage and other related businesses. They may even use their real estate brokerage offices as their places of business. They may be individuals, partnerships, or corporations. They seldom advertise their business in any formal way, but depend upon personal contacts to secure their loan applications. Their chief function is to originate real estate loans for insurance companies, banks, and others.

Mortgage bank departments

In the smaller offices, manned by the owner and a couple of clerks, the owner-manager is a jack-of-all-trades. He takes care of all parts of the business. In the large mortgage banks, departmentalization may be carried out in some detail, with each major department operated more or less as a unit. Among the most common of such departments are: (1) the promotional department, which develops new business by calling in real estate brokers, builders, and analyzers, processes applications for loans, obtains purchase commitments, and so on; (2) the title department, which drafts papers, records them, takes care of title problems, and delivers the mortgages; (3) the servicing department which makes collections, and so forth; (4) the accounting department, which keeps all records; and (5) the insurance department, which handles all insurance problems. Sometimes separate departments handle taxes, FHA/VA transactions, and so forth.

Sideline business

Some mortgage bankers are not greatly disturbed if they fail to make a profit from mortgage loan acquisitions. By making the loan they acquire various types of sideline business. Among these are the writing of fire insurance premiums, sales commissions, property management fees, real estate brokerage, sales of leases, appraisal fees, and loan-servicing fees. The latter are normally most important. Depending upon the combination of circumstances, loan-acquisition profits and servicing profits may be alternatives. For example, one banker may be willing to accept a servicing contract at no profit if the commission from disposing of the mortgage is great enough. Another may be willing to forgo such profit if the servicing fee is large enough to show a profit.

One of the arguments used by mortgage bankers with insurance companies interested in establishing branch offices for the purpose of soliciting and servicing real estate loans is that the mortgage banker can render the service at less cost because of its sideline business operations. The branch office of the insurance company would be concerned with loans only. With approximately the same overhead costs, the mortgage banker can conduct several types of business, as listed earlier. In addition, mortgage bankers sometimes render services to real estate brokers and builders, in order to build or keep their goodwill—services which insurance companies are not permitted to render.

The emergence of real estate investment trusts during the 1960s and early 1970s provided an attractive new market for mortgage bankers. Subsequent difficulties experienced by the trusts have placed heavy demands upon these same bankers. The well-qualified and diversified mortgage banker has been viewed as a natural manager to handle the originating, servicing, and advisory functions for a mortgage trust. Some mortgage bankers saw fit to sponsor mortgage trusts themselves so that publicly derived trust funds and credit generated therefrom could be made available to them for placement. Until the recent traumatic disruption in the mortgage markets, this was considered a boon to the construction loan markets. Now it is apparent there will be a several year interval before the mortgage trusts can again become an important factor in the lending business. Meanwhile, the mortgage bankers will be called upon to exercise their highest form of expertise in liquidating the outstanding loans currently unsupported by earning assets and possibly restoring the loan portfolios to profitability.

Methods of financing mortgages

In general, mortgage banks finance real estate loans according to one of the following patterns:

1.   The loan is made only after the banker has received the prior approval of the insurance company for which it is a loan correspondent. The insurance company which agrees to take the loan may even advance to the mortgage banker the amount of money needed by the mortgagor. Otherwise the mortgage banker uses its own funds, knowing that within a short time it will recoup the amounts so invested from the institution which has contracted to take the loan. In such a transaction, the banker is, in effect, the agent for the insurance company.

2.   The mortgage banker may act as a real merchandiser, investing its own funds in the mortgage and then offering it for sale to some investor seeking this

type of outlet for its funds. In this case it may keep its own funds invested at all times, selling only such mortgages as it needs to free its funds for the purchase of a new supply. Since its capital is small in comparison with its volume of business, this is not its major objective. Whenever it makes a loan without the prior approval of some purchaser, it runs the risk of acquiring stale merchandise that no purchaser will take off its hands at an advantageous price. Then it may unwillingly find its capital tied up in nonmerchantable mortgages.

Growing significance of mortgage companies

For the volume of business performed by mortgage bankers in the United States, the number of active firms is surprisingly small. During 1978, there were 699 active firms. Yet these firms originated 17.4 percent of all mortgage debt originated by the six principal institutional originators—$33.6 of a total of $226.9 billion—in that year. Especially in regard to the federal housing programs, of $12.5 billion FHA and $14.3 billion VA loans in 1978, mortgage bankers originated $10.0 and $11.0 billion, or 80.2 percent and 77.1 percent, respectively.[1] They are, by a wide margin, the primary implementers of the federal programs.

From small beginnings before World War II, the growth in mortgage banking activities has been spectacular. The substantial postwar growth of mortgage bankers, as well as their present structure and operational methods, can be attributed largely to the federal mortgage assistance program. The Federal Housing Administration insurance and the Veterans Administration guarantee programs have offered what was needed to create a national mortgage market. These agencies provided minimum property requirements, subdivision standards, and credit review which gave insured or guaranteed mortgages a quality upon which distant lending institutions could rely with little individual review or investigation. The federal underwriting itself permitted institutional investors to make loans of higher risk than would otherwise be prudent or legally possible from the standpoint either of loan-to-value ratio or of distance from lender to liened property.

The FHA or VA mortgage has emerged as a standard article, subject to ready trade in the national marketplace. It has an additional unique feature. It is eligible, under certain limitations, for purchase by federally oriented secondary market facilities. Of particular significance to mortgage bankers in this respect is the Federal National Mortgage Association (FNMA). The availability of this resource as a buyer in the market at times of temporary credit stringency has provided a stability in the supply of mortgage funds that did not previously exist.

The mortgage banker, operating in a localized area, has been the natural

---

[1] The five other institutional mortgage originators are savings and loan associations, commercial banks, mutual savings banks, life insurance companies, and federal credit agencies. See further in *Loans Closed and Servicing Volume for the Mortgage Banking Industry, 1978.* Trends Report No. 25, Mortgage Bankers Association of America.

beneficiary of the increased need by nonresident investors for a local agency to originate and service mortgages. Accordingly, the market increase in federally underwritten mortgages has given impetus to mortgage banking.

Mortgage bankers are also deeply concerned with the support they may be able to rely upon from the Federal National Mortgage Association in a tight market. To them, this agency stands in much the same relationship as the Federal Reserve System to commercial banks or the Federal Home Loan Bank System to savings and loan associations. Yet its objectives have not been set forth with sufficient definiteness in this regard to induce reasonable reliance at all times.

Although the Federal Home Loan Mortgage Corporation (discussed in Chapter 24) has been developed in recent years as an additional secondary market facility, it was not until 1978 that it was permitted to buy directly from mortgage bankers. The addition of this resource in support of the secondary mortgage markets should be of great benefit to the mortgage banking industry.

Purchasers of mortgages

Just over half of mortgage banker loan originations during 1978 were purchased by the *Federal National Mortgage Association (FNMA)*, the *Government National Mortgage Association (GNMA)*, and *GNMA-guaranteed mortgage pools*. Nearly one half of mortgage banker loan service business was also performed for the same combined class of investors. See Exhibit 22–1.

EXHIBIT 22–1
Distribution of mortgage bankers' loans originated and serviced for customers in 1978

Customer-Investor	Originated	Serviced
FNMA	23.7%	19.7%
GNMA	3.4	0.4
GNMA mortgage pools	25.4	25.9
Life insurance companies	13.7	18.5
Mutual savings banks	4.8	9.0
Commercial banks	5.7	6.5
Savings and loan associations	8.8	11.9
Others and in inventory	14.5	8.1
Totals	100.0%	100.0%

Source: *Mortgage Banking 1978*, Trends Report No. 25, Mortgage Bankers Association of America.

Briefly, FNMA is an agency, now privately financed and operated, created by Congress to provide a secondary market for federally underwritten mortgages. GNMA is a federal guarantor of eligible mortgages to support the public market, especially for mortgage pools. Activities of these agencies in the insured mortgage market provide the most important business channels for mortgage bankers. The history and current status of FNMA and GNMA are discussed in Chapter 24.

The next most important institutional group is the *life insurance companies.* The broad geographical diversification of their mortgage lending makes them logical customers of mortgage bankers in each lending area.

Mutual savings banks, commercial banks, and *savings and loan associations* also provide important, but lesser, segments of a mortgage banker's business. Legislation expanding the lending areas for all of these classes of lenders has encouraged utilizing mortgage bankers to an increasing degree.

The demand of commercial banks for the services of a mortgage banker largely emanates from the rural areas where cash is more plentiful than local investment outlets. City banks that are interested in real estate mortgages as investments frequently originate their own mortgages or have developed their own mortgage banking facility. Country banks depend upon outside mortgage bankers instead. Frequently, if their cash resources are large, they may pay higher premiums for loans than insurance companies. Some smaller mortgage bankers cater to this trade because of the high premiums paid for loans. Larger companies usually find it more advantageous to deal instead with the few insurance companies for which each is a correspondent. Then, too, the demand for loans by country banks is likely to be intermittent, depending upon the state of their cash and upon their outlook concerning future business conditions. They are in-and-out buyers.

One further difference between commercial banks and insurance companies as purchasers of real estate mortgages is that the former are subject to fewer rules than the latter. Because the insurance companies are mass purchasers, they find it necessary to standardize the rules under which they operate. For example, a specific company may set a minimum of 720 square feet of floor space for a single residence that it will finance. In such case it is useless to offer it a loan on a smaller house, regardless of its quality. Or the insurance company may not be interested in VA loans. Commercial banks normally do not have enough mortgage experience at any one time to make them unwilling to consider the purchase of any loan which the mortgage banker may offer to them.

However, because of the restrictions under which commercial banks are forced to operate in the purchase of mortgages, the mortgage banker may make sure that he can dispose of a "bank" loan before he makes it. Some use a submission sheet in offering mortgages to commercial banks. It contains a description of the property; the terms of the loan and the price asked for it; the necessary information about the borrower—such as his occupation, annual income, and credit rating; the amount of the appraisal, FHA, or otherwise; and any other pertinent information about the application. Sometimes submission sheets are sent out on the same day to several commercial bankers. The first one to accept by telephone, telegraph, or letter gets the loan, and it is closed on that basis.

Savings and loan associations do not ordinarily purchase mortgages from mortgage bankers. They do not like to pay any premiums for the purchase of mortgages. Occasionally an individual may liquidate his mortgage holdings by selling them to a savings and loan association through a mortgage banker. Or on occasion the association may purchase an individual loan which it would have liked to make originally but which for some reason it did not have the opportunity to make. One exception to the rule about savings and loan associations' purchases of mortgages from mortgage bankers occurs when the association, like the country bank, operates in a community where savings funds greatly exceed investment opportunities. In such cases a mortgage banker, or a mortgage broker in a neighboring city which can use excess funds, serves as the investment agent for the savings and loan association.

Mortgage loans are sometimes sold to *individuals, estates, or trustees for personal trusts.* Here there is even less rigidity in purchaser requirements than in the case of commercial banks. Loans purchased by such buyers may be safe but off-color loans. Perhaps they should be called off standard. For example, insurance companies will not ordinarily consider a loan against a motel or a motor freight terminal. It may carry a high rate of return and may represent a low percentage loan. Because of the difficulty in placing such loans, the borrower usually pays all costs, including the fees to the mortgage banker.

On the other hand, some mortgage bankers prefer not to deal with individual investors except when off-standard property is involved. Volume of sales to one individual is not likely to be large. Each may have his own ideas about appraisals, location, and so on, so that the time spent in trying to sell an individual mortgage may be out of proportion to the amount of business generated. In general, the individual purchaser of mortgages expects a higher yield on his investment than does an insurance company, for example. One reason for this demand is the high-income taxes paid by the individual. To net a yield comparable to that enjoyed by an insurance company, the individual must obtain a higher interest rate.

Mortgage assembly. Occasionally a mortgage banker has found that he can get a better price for a large inventory of mortgages than for a single mortgage or a small number. Hence, by the use of his own capital, supplemented by bank loans, he accumulates whatever inventory he can carry before offering it to institutional buyers. In doing so he is taking the risk that interest rates will change before he is able to liquidate his holdings. For example, if the larger purchaser will pay a 2 percent premium on $500,000 or $1 million of 13 percent loans, the mortgage banker will work toward that amount as his goal. Meantime, if investment committees of large buyers decide suddenly that they no longer want to buy 13 percent mortgages, the mortgage banker may find sticky merchandise on his shelves. Since his bank loans are for short periods of time, he must adjust his price to the new bid price of the buyers and, if necessary, take his loss.

This type of business has become of increasing importance with the recent development and public marketing of government-backed mortgage pools through participation certificates. Mortgage bankers, both by virtue of experience and facilities, are ideally suited in many instances to move ahead in this field as mortgage assemblers. They are further abetted by the action of the Chicago Board of Trade and other exchanges in establishing a mortgage interest rate futures options market. By the purchase or sale of these options, originating mortgage bankers are able to shift their interest rate risk to speculators by hedging. These developments are discussed in detail in Chapter 24.

Pension funds.   Although as yet they have been an elusive market, pension funds offer appealing possibilities as customers of mortgage bankers. As an industry, mortgage bankers are becoming increasingly cognizant of the magnitude of the pension fund market, and they are more aware of their own excellent position to compete for fund investments.

In essence, pension funds are simply accumulations of money over the working life of an individual to provide income to him during his retirement. Before World War II, these funds were largely established by corporations or by governmental units on a voluntary basis and on a relatively small scale. In the postwar labor climate, desirable pension plans became an important method of attracting scarce workers into employment with a particular firm. Favorable tax treatment was accorded acceptable pension plans. Pensions became an important issue at the labor-management bargaining table. Under this impetus, the amount of investable funds held to underwrite retirement and related benefits grew spectacularly.

The asset volume held for investment by private pension funds alone is of the order of that of the life insurance industry. It is growing at a multibillion dollar annual rate.

The shifting of the flow of these funds from bank accounts and corporate bonds and stocks into mortgages has been a slow process. The present percentage of pension trust funds invested in mortgages is insignificant compared with the potential. The reason for the small proportion of funds invested in mortgages seems to be that investment committees and counselors, and even bank trust departments, are unfamiliar with the safety and ease with which these investments can be handled through mortgage bankers. Many trustees have been concerned that there is no market quotation on mortgages. As the secondary market for mortgages improves and their security becomes better defined, this objection can be overcome. The trustees have also had an abiding fear of additional, unanticipated costs of handling mortgage investments. In this respect the mortgage banker is admirably equipped to relieve their burden. Over a period of time, as the mortgage banker reaches the decision-making groups and dispels their fear of the unknown, he will find a lucrative market. He can demonstrate, for example, that in its important aspects a federally underwritten mortgage can be handled as safely and simply as bonds and stocks through the proper employment of mortgage banking services.

Considerable thought is constantly being directed toward the development of securities based on packages of mortgages that are serviced on a "carefree" basis by others than fund administrators. These securities are being made available in conveniently large denominations. The composite yield of the mortgage package is normally sufficient to provide a satisfactory income to the mortgage servicer as well as an attractive return to the pension fund or other institution seeking exoneration from management responsibilities and possible embarrassment with delinquencies.

Programs launched by the federal government to provide mortgage-backed securities guaranteed by the Government National Mortgage Association (GNMA) were partly inspired to lure more pension fund money into real estate financing. Details of these programs, and the allied activities of the Federal National Mortgage Association and the Federal Home Loan Mortgage Corporation, are discussed in Chapter 24.

Types of loans

Mortgage bankers typically provide their major services in arranging permanent financing for new rather than existing properties. They frequently assist builders by establishing short-term credit for new construction. This credit may be arranged for the builder directly from a commercial bank, or the mortgage banker may advance the constuction costs and borrow from the commercial bank in its own name. In either event, the funds for construction are ultimately provided by the commercial bank. Mortgage bankers usually gain an additional fee when they finance the builder themselves, but the typical 1 or 2 percent additional compensation involved often does not justify the higher risks and larger staff required in observation and supervision of the construction process. Sometimes the mortgage banker's borrowing rate is less than the lending rate generated by its inventory loan portfolio. This favorable circumstance is called a *positive carry* (referring to carrying costs of the inventory). When the borrowing rate is higher than the effective lending rate, the mortgage banker is said to be experiencing a *negative carry*. In a volatile money market this condition may quickly change, either way.

A survey of representative mortgage bankers shows a high degree of concentration of real estate loans on one- to four-family properties. By statutory limitations and practice, most FHA and VA loans are on one- to four-family dwellings; and, for the most part, the conventional mortgage loans derived by mortgage bankers are on similar properties.[2]

The small proportion of conventional loans on income properties handled through mortgage bankers can be explained in the decision of most institu-

---

[2] *Mortgage Banking 1978,* Trends Report No. 25, p. 8.

tional investors to originate such loans directly. Lending on larger building units requires specialized knowledge of appraisal techniques and legal problems, and the loans are usually large enough and in sufficient volume to justify the institutional lender in maintaining its own staff for direct negotiations with such borrowers.

A new lending pattern: Convertible mortgage. Mortgage bankers are constantly on the alert for financing techniques with good potential that also have special attraction to the mortgage banking industry. The recent development of the convertible mortgage is a good example. It is designed to deal with the diluting effect of inflation and the unadjusted return of fixed dollars at maturity.[3]

This form can offer significant advantages to both the developer and the institutional lender. From the standpoint of the developer, all financing is derived from one reliable source. The institutional lender benefits by becoming a progressively greater participant in the equity ownership by taking loan amortization through increased equity while at the same time receiving the contract rate of interest on its total investment. The mortgage company manages collections on the total investments, both mortgage loan and equity buildup. Thus, the servicing fee *does not decline* over the life of the loan.

The essentials of the arrangement provide that the institutional investor will make both mortgage and equity investments to finance a new income-producing project. The amount of the mortgage will be an acceptable percentage of the appraised economic value of the property and the remainder of the funds will be provided as equity, presumably mostly from the institutional investor, since the developer's costs are normally substantially below the economic value of the project. The investor's equity participation will be based upon the relationship between the total equity funds advanced and the total value of the project. In many cases, the developer will be able to "finance out" the total costs, thus earning his total equity position in the completed project as his profit without net cash outlay. An example will demonstrate the technique more clearly.

A shopping center is expected to generate $396,000 annual net income before financing costs. Capitalized at 11 percent, it has an economic value of $3.6 million. On the basis of the appraisal value, the investor is willing to lend $2.4 million (75 precent of an estimated loan value of $3.2 million) at 10 percent interest and will invest an additional $800,000 for a 25 percent equity position. If the developer is able to complete the project for not more than 3.2 million, he has a 75 percent initial equity with no cash outlay and a substantial income expectancy over a great many years. According to the convertible mortgage plan, the investor will receive 10 percent on his total investment

---

[3] For an excellent treatment of this subject, refer to Lois A. Vitt and Joel H. Bernstein, "Convertible Mortgages: New Financing Tool," *Real Estate Review,* vol. 6, no. 1 (Spring 1976), pp. 33–37; also Lois A. Vitt, "Convertible Mortgage Seen as New Approach to Realty Financing," *Mortgage Banker,* August 1975, pp. 5–11.

annually, but his mortgage balance is to be amortized annually by conversion to increased equity participation at any agreed rate, say 2 percent. The following table reflects the first three years of activity under such an arrangement:

(1)	(2)	(3)	(4)	(5)	(6)	(7)	(8)
Year	Mortgage balance*	Investor's equity	Financing Payments at 10 percent	Net cash flow†	Investor's share of column 5‡	Yield to investor per- cent§	Cash to developer‖
1	$2,400,000	$800,000	$320,000	$76,000	$19,000 (25%)	10.59	$57,000
2	2,352,000	848,000	320,000	76,000	20,520 (27%)	10.64	55,480
3	2,304,000	896,000	320,000	76,000	22,040 (29%)	10.69	53,960

* Reduces 2 percent of original balance annually; transferred to equity (column 3).
† $396,000 − $320,000 = $76,000 cash flow after financing costs.
‡ Investor's portion starts at 25 percent and increases 2 percent annually.
§ The sum of columns 4 and 6 divided by the sum of columns 2 and 3.
‖ Column 5 − column 6 = residential cash flow to developer.

It should be noted that both participants develop substantial tax shelter from depreciation attributable to the equity positions. Furthermore, an interesting analysis can be developed to determine reasonable expectations of benefits to be derived from the impact of earnings increases that may follow the effects of inflation over a number of years. Of course, if the developer totally finances out, his yield is infinite.

Exclusive outlets

The goal of every mortgage banker is to establish relationships with investment institutions which are so satisfactory to both the buyer and the seller of mortgages that the seller will always know where he can dispose of his inventory and the buyer will know where he can secure supplies of new mortgages. Some of these relationships crystallize into exclusive contracts. The mortgage banker agrees to sell only to one or to a very few investors; and each of these in turn agrees to buy in that market only from the mortgage banker whose name is signed to the exclusive contract. The signatures to the contract are not as important in the long run as the manner in which both parties deal with each other. If each is satisfied with the service it receives from the other, no formal contract is needed. If either is dissatisfied, a formal contract will probably be terminated at the earliest opportunity.

Most investment institutions do not object to the mortgage banker having more than one purchaser of its mortgages. In fact, they prefer such an arrangement, since it removes pressure from the investor to absorb all offerings of the seller at all times. In taking on its list of investors, however, the mortgage banker should exercise care in avoiding too much competition among them.

For example, one investor may prefer FHA or VA loans; another, conventional loans; a third, apartment or commercial; and so on.

Indemnity policies

In spite of the general practice of securing prior approval of the purchaser of the mortgage before it is granted, the mortgage banker still has a responsibility for making sure that the loans he processes do not result in a loss to the purchaser. For example, if such a loan is paid off within the first year, it is frequently replaced with another of similar amount, premium free, or the mortgage banker may return whatever premium was collected in disposing of the mortgage. At other times only the loss that is due to a negative yield will be made up. In some cases these obligations of the mortgage banker are a part of the contract between the insurance company and its correspondents. In other cases, unwritten understandings are sufficient to fix responsibility. In general, the mortgage banker is more likely to be dependent upon the continued business of the purchasing insurance company than the reverse.

The prepayment privilege in mortgages is particularly troublesome in mortgage banking because of the premiums and other fees paid by the investor in acquiring the mortgage. Because of the common practice of competitors who originate loans to include this privilege, its exclusion might result in a loss of business. From the standpoint of the investor, if he permits prepayment freely, he may lose money if the privilege is exercised early in the life of the loan. One common answer to the problem is to permit limited prepayment privilege—to become operative only after from two to five years, for example. Another is to permit prepayment on any interest date but with a penalty of a few months' interest or of a flat percentage of the amount of the mortgage. In still other cases, the amount of prepayment without penalty is limited to 20 percent per year.

Servicing department

The mortgage banker owes two obligations to the investor whose funds he handles: (1) to invest his money safely and (2) to get it back according to the loan contract. Lending money is fairly simple. Getting it back may be more difficult. Servicing involves more than serving as a clearinghouse for checks transmitted by the borrower. Adequate servicing involves at least four major operations:

1. Current payments made by the borrower must be processed and the net proceeds, after retaining tax, mortgage, and hazard insurance quotas and service fees, must be transmitted to the investor that holds the mortgage. In rare cases the investor insists that all escrow deposits for taxes, mortgage insurance, and hazard insurance be transmitted to it to be held in trust for the borrower.

2.   The security must be inspected periodically to make sure that it is not being subjected to waste or unusual depreciation.

3.   When the property changes hands and the new owner assumes the mortgage debt, a whole series of records in the office of the mortgage banker must be changed. The collection department must get the proper name and address of the new owner and set up new records to check against delinquency by him. Insurance papers must reflect the change of ownership. The tax department must change its records in order to make sure about new tax bills. The accounting department must set up new records in line with the new obligor on the loan. If the mortgage is insured by the FHA, or guaranteed by the VA, the proper governmental agency must be notified. Even where the present mortgage is completely paid off rather than assumed by the new owner, the mortgage banker must protect the interests of the holder of the mortgage by making sure that the proper amount is paid in the proper manner.

4.   Finally, in serious cases of delinquency, steps must be taken to protect the holder of the mortgage, by foreclosure if necessary.

Fees

As discussed in Chapter 21 in connection with life insurance company loan administration, mortgage bankers earn two types of fees: (1) for loan origination and (2) for servicing the loan during its existence.

Origination fees.   Origination fees are most often assessed against the borrower. They fall into two major classes: (1) All expenses of making the loan are expected to be covered. Such fees for FHA and VA loans are standard. There is no such standardization for conventional loans. Sometimes they cover out-of-pocket costs. At other times they cover what the traffic will bear. Costs cover appraisal fees, title insurance, if any, title check fees, and office expense. As pointed out elsewhere, competitive practices help to determine the amount of costs charged to the borrower. Sometimes appraisal fees are charged only if the loan is made; sometimes whether or not the loan is approved; and sometimes they are absorbed by the lender. (2) Off-standard loans—those made against properties that holders of mortgage paper do not like as security—frequently cost the borrower a fee in addition to those mentioned above. Instead of a seller's market for such mortgages, it is generally a buyer's market. Because the mortgage banker may have unusual difficulty in disposing of them, he expects the mortgagor to pay his fees.

Servicing fees.   Compensation for servicing the loan from the time it is made until it is paid off is collected by the mortgage banker out of the borrower's periodic payments. If the servicing fee is .375 percent, for example, and the contract interest rate on the mortgage note is 11.5 percent, when the borrower's payment is received by the mortgage banker, only 11.125 percent is forwarded to the lender as interest, the other .375 percent being retained as compensation for the collection service. Of course, all amortization of principal amounts is forwarded to the lender. The servicing fee is based on the unpaid loan balance and becomes less as the loan is amortized. Many loans on the books with unpaid balances too low to earn fees enough to cover the costs of carrying them can create problems for the mortgage banker.

Loan insurance and guarantee

Loans insured by the FHA or guaranteed by the VA are not necessarily free from servicing problems. On the contrary, it is probable that many such loans were made by their lenders with less than normal attention to the problems of future loan servicing. If guaranteed or insured loans are made because of the guarantee or insurance, and particularly if they would not have been granted otherwise, trouble may develop. While neither the FHA nor the VA would intentionally sanction a loan which it considered too heavy for the borrowers to carry, there is a tendency on the part of some lending institutions to assume that they have shifted their loan-servicing problems to a governmental agency when they make insured and guaranteed loans. This is not the case.

The major purpose of these governmental agencies is to be of service to the borrower. If the borrower could have obtained liberal loans without insurance or guarantee of his mortgage, there would probably never have been either an FHA or a VA lending program. Because sufficiently liberal loans were not available, these agencies were developed. Since their interest is primarily centered in assistance to the borrower, neither the VA nor the FHA will permit the borrower to lose his property by foreclosure of the mortgage until every reasonable effort to solve his financial difficulties has been made. This means loan servicing by the mortgagee.

Furthermore, much of the cost of loan servicing, even where loans are insured or guaranteed, is not recoverable from the borrower or from a governmental agency. While the principal of the loan and the delinquent interest are intended to be recoverable, the costs of working out programs of forbearance and adjustment are not.

In general, the safety but not the soundness of such loans is insured or guaranteed. This is accepted as part of the program. For example, when a mortgagee makes a guaranteed loan to a veteran, it must satisfy itself that the borrower's income, present and prospective, is sufficient to meet the carrying charges of the loan. In other words, the burden of the soundness of the loan is not shifted to the VA. In time of crisis, the VA does not undertake to make loan payments continuously, thus keeping the loan account alive on the books of the lender. While this may be done on a temporary basis, sooner or later the degree of safety of the loan will be demonstrated when foreclosure proceedings are directed, to be followed by indemnification of the lender on acount of lost principal and delinquent interest.

A forward look at mortgage banking

The exceedingly rapid rise of the mortgage banking industry over the past three decades by its very nature engendered conditions that invited correction in event of economic recession. The industry flourished in the development of a national market for federally underwritten mortgages at favorable yields to investors in new construction. Conditions were so favorable for growth in the field of mortgage origination and servicing that competition during the 1960s and early 1970s became more intense both outside the industry and from within.

Commercial banks became increasingly interested in programs of originating and servicing mortgages for investors other than themselves. In fact, commercial banks are in a particularly favorable position to move into mortgage banking because they have immediately available any funds necessary to provide interim financing or to maintain a mortgage inventory for sale. The American Bankers Association was active in pointing out the advantages of a broad mortgage program to its membership, and the commercial banks became more conscious of the advantages to be gained by offering mortgage origination and service facilities for bank-administered pension and welfare funds. These funds have been important investors through mortgage bankers in recent years.

To maximize their current opportunities, some banks acquired mortgage banking expertise by buying out mortgage banking firms. Some firms so acquired were simply absorbed into the bank assets and operations; others, secured by the one-bank holding company route, maintained their separate integrity as mortgage bankers. A great preponderance of the 100 largest mortgage bankers is now affiliated with commercial banking institutions.

Many banks even sponsored real estate mortgage investment trusts to become additional lending elements in the development and construction areas. As set forth in Chapter 21, the recession of 1974, and thereafter, placed heavy strains on most banks with this involvement, together with their mortgage servicing arms, because of massive defaults not only in their own mortgage loan portfolios but also in those of the mortgage trusts to which they had legal or moral obligations.

Savings and loan associations have also taken new cognizance of potentials in the national secondary markets. Whereas they were limited to competition in local markets in earlier days, they now find it possible to participate in loans made anywhere in the country. Through new techniques of participation and mortgage pooling, small savings and loans are enabled to originate or invest in much larger construction programs than would otherwise be possible. It is a short step from active participation in loan origination in the national market to adoption of a policy of sales of loans to other investors.

Recent studies have shown that origination and servicing costs have risen sharply in line with high inflation rates. Origination costs have been far in excess of the 1 percent maximum allowed for FHA/VA originations. Service fees, as well, have not necessarily kept up with increased servicing costs by virtue of higher average loan balances.

The obvious conclusions to be drawn from these trends are that mortgage bankers will be resorting wherever possible to higher discount points or stipulated loan origination fees. In many cases larger loans only will be sought to upgrade the overall portfolio average loan balance. Where possible, a step-up percentage for loan service fees might be arranged to take effect whenever the unpaid balance is brought down to the break-even point.

Many companies are also considering expansion into real estate operations and insurance as logical auxiliary fields which may take on primary importance when income from servicing mortgages begins to fall short. This diversification will relieve the company from such a high degree of dependence on the federal housing programs and will give it greater stability.

Questions

1   What is a mortgage banker?

2   Why are mortgage bankers important to both borrowers and lenders?

3   How does a mortgage banker originate new business?

4   What is a finder's fee? Do you approve of payment of finders' fees? Why or why not?

5   How does a mortgage banker finance the mortgages which it originates?

6   How do you account for the spectacular growth of mortgage companies since the end of World War II?

7   Who are the principal purchasers of mortgages generated through mortgage companies?

8   What types of loans are most attractive to mortgage bankers? Why?

9   How is the mortgage banker compensated for his services?

10   What are the four stages of mortgage loan servicing?

11   Loan servicing is fairly synonymous with loan collection. What are the indicia of a good loan collection policy?

12   Has the expansion of the federal loan insurance and guarantee program simplified or complicated mortgage-servicing problems? In what respects?

13   What are the obligations of a mortgage banker to the investor in the real estate mortgages which the mortgage banker originates and services?

14   If you were a mortgage banker today, what areas would you be exploring for possible expansion of your services?

Case problems

1   As an executive of the Universal Mortgage Company, you are servicing a mortgage loan for the Tinsel Makers' Pension Fund. The mortgagor is the Bi-Lo Department Store. The

department store premises burn completely to the ground, and the insurance proceeds have been received. The mortgagor desires to rebuild. What problems do you foresee and how would you act to resolve them?

2   You are asked to develop criteria for servicing an income property loan and point out how they might be different from those for servicing a loan on an owner-occupied residential unit. Be explicit in your response.

3   The Universal Mortgage Company services mortgages for a fee of .5 percent of unpaid mortgage balances annually. It collects this fee out of loan payments received from borrowers. It then remits the remaining proceeds to the Reliable Insurance Company for whom the loans are being serviced. For the past year, total servicing costs were $200,000. It has 4,000 loans to service.

a.   What is the average servicing cost per loan?

b.   What is the minimum average unpaid balance of the loans in the portfolio that the company can tolerate to break even?

c.   How can it improve its net servicing income?

4   Following the convertible mortgage model presented in the chapter, consider the returns to the institutional investor, the developer, and the mortgage banker in the following example. Note particularly, the service fee for asset management does not decline over the life of the loan.

A warehouse facility is expected to earn $220,000 annual net income before financing costs. The appropriate capitalization rate is 10.5 percent. The investor is willing to fund $2,000,000, of which $1,500,000 will be by mortgage loan and $500,000 as equity with a 10 percent rate of return to be paid on the total funding, net to investor after payment of .2 percent servicing fees to a mortgage banker to administer the investment. The initial equity participation to the investor is 25 percent, and the mortgage is to be amortized solely by a transfer to investor's equity of 2.5 percent of the initial balance annually. By virtue of this transfer, the developer's initial 75 percent claim will decrease by 2.5 percent annually.

a.   Prepare a schedule showing the investor's and developer's investment income and yield positions during the 1st, 2d, 5th, and 21st years of the plan. Assume a constant earning stream. The format for this schedule follows the explanation in the chapter.

b.   Do the same exercise as in (a) above assuming an increasing earnings stream at the rate of 3 percent annually to estimate earnings growth.

c.   Calculate the equity positions of the investor and the developer at the beginning of the 1st, 2d, 5th, and 21st years assuming that depreciation is more than offset by inflation with the result that the property increases in value at the rate of 3 percent annually (compounded monthly as per tables). Assume also that the loan agreement gives the investor his equity participation in the gross amount of the property value upon reappraisal. Thus, compute gross value less investor's equity to derive the developer's claim to assets. Then deduct the mortgage balance due investor to determine developer's residual equity value.

d.   What will the mortgage banker earn in asset management fees under requirements (a) and (b) above?

PART FIVE

Government and real estate finance

Federal assistance in housing

23

Order of discussion

Because of the complex nature of federal activities, their discussion is separated into several segments. In this chapter there is a general description of the governmental administrative organization handling various programs, a summary of the Federal Housing Administration and public housing programs, and a similar consideration of the support function of the Veterans Administration in loans to veterans.

In Chapter 24 the development of secondary markets for mortgages and federal support activities in these markets are discussed in detail. Finally, the whole question of rural real estate credit and the function of the Farmers Home Administration in aid of rural housing are dealt with in Chapter 25.

Administrative agencies

The agency principally responsible for the housing and urban development activities of the federal government is the Department of Housing and Urban Development (HUD). Its head is designated as "Secretary," who serves as a member of the President's Cabinet. The Department was created in 1965 to extend and intensify the activities and programs of the Housing and Home Finance agency.

The creation of HUD in 1965 marked the combinations of several well-known governmental agencies. The Federal Housing Adminstration (FHA) had been in operation since 1934, when it was created to handle the underwriting of federally backed mortgage insurance as a much-needed aid to real estate credit at the time. The Public Housing Administration (PHA) was established in 1937 to administer federal aid to public housing. The Urban Renewal Administration (URA) was formed in 1949 to develop and promote urban renewal programs. The Housing and Home Finance Agency was established in 1947, and it became the umbrella under which FHA, PHA, and URA functioned in loose collaboration until they were taken into HUD. The FHA is now officially designated HUD-FHA, but it is still simply referred to without the prefix. The PHA is now the Housing Assistance Administration, and the URA is now the Renewal Assistance Administration.

Certain federal housing and home finance activities have been delegated to other departments. The Department of Agriculture operates a farm housing program authorized under Title V of the Housing Act of 1949. The administrative agency handling this program is the Farmers Home Administration. The Department of Defense is responsible for certifying the need for military housing financed by mortgages insured under the federal program or for the provision of family housing where necessary in the interests of national defense. The Small Business Administration makes loans to victims of disasters so that they may restore their damaged homes or buy or build new ones. It also assists small businesses in becoming reestablished where they have suffered substantial economic injury as the result of displacement by an urban renewal program or similar government project. The Departments of Commerce and Labor are of particular assistance to the national housing program in providing housing and construction statistics and in setting standards for construction materials and labor.

Functional divisions of HUD. The major areas of HUD activities are headed by assistant secretaries. Important secretarial designations and program areas are described in a general way in the accompanying organization chart of the Department of Housing and Urban Development (Exhibit 23–1).

Functions of the FHA

Since its organization in 1934, a variety of functions have been added to the FHA program. As expressed by statutory authority, these functions involve the operation of housing loan insurance programs designed to encourage improvement in housing standards and conditions, to facilitate sound home financing on reasonable terms, and to exert a stabilizing influence in the mortgage market. The FHA is not a direct lender, nor does it plan or build houses. It does markedly affect lending terms and building plans and specifications, as well as selection of housing sites, by the conditions under which it permits insurance to be granted. The various types of loans on which insurance is issued by the FHA are defined by several titles of the National Housing Act of 1934, as amended.

Title I insures lending institutions against loss on loans which finance the alteration, repair, improvement, or conversion of existing structures and the construction of new, small, nonresidential structures. Title II covers all

EXHIBIT 23–1

DEPARTMENT OF HOUSING AND
URBAN DEVELOPMENT

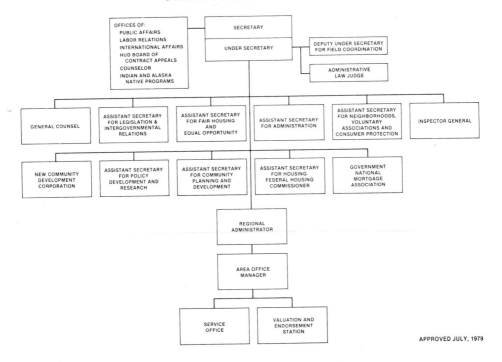

APPROVED JULY, 1979

residential mortgage insurance programs. The major programs are listed and capsulized in later paragraphs by statutory sections.

Operation of Title II. Title II of the Federal Housing Administration law set up a system of mutual mortgage insurance which at the outset was intended to encourage the construction of new homes, thus providing a market for building materials and employment for building laborers. Later it was extended to cover rental housing projects as well. In return for insurance of mortgages made by private lenders, an insurance premium was charged which was expected eventually to build reserves sufficiently large to put this title on a self-sustaining basis. The amount of insurance coverage was limited to 80 percent of the appraisal of the property insured, as set by the FHA. This insurance percentage has since been liberalized and applied to different sections of this title according to varying formulas, which usually result in insurance from 85 to 100 percent of the appraisal value. The interest rate was fixed at 5 percent, to which could be added originally .5 percent for service charge and .5 percent of the original amount of the loan for insurance premium. The net result was a charge of 6.42 percent to the borrower, computed over the life of a

20-year loan. Later the service charge was eliminated, the interest rate was reduced to 4.5 percent, and the insurance premium was reduced to .5 percent on the unpaid principal of the loan, producing a charge to the borrower of 5 percent. The interest rate has been administered following the cost of mortgage money in the free markets, but subject to statutory limits from the beginning. This practice, at times, has caused a wide divergence between FHA and conventional lending rates, and has given rise to the requirement that the seller of a property being financed through the FHA pay discount points to induce a lender to make a loan at the FHA rate. Special concession rates of interest have been authorized for certain programs.

Under the 1979 housing legislation, FHA-insured mortgages were exempted from state and local usury ceilings. New maximum mortgage amounts for FHA coverage were also established as follows:

Single-family unit...........	$ 67,500
Two-family unit.............	76,000
Three-family unit	92,000
Four-family unit	107,000

The lender must use a monthly payment direct reduction first mortgage, the maturity of which was originally limited to 20 years. This was later increased to 25 years, and then to 30 years or three fourths of the remaining economic life of the property, whichever might be less. Certain loans under sections relating to cooperative housing, slum clearance, or housing for the elderly may have repayment periods extending for as long as 40 years. In case of uncured default, the lender is entitled to receive, from the FHA, debentures equivalent to the amount of the debt then unpaid. These debentures are issued in the name of the mortgage insurance fund but are fully guaranteed as to principal and interest by the government. The interest rate varies in relation to the government's ongoing cost of money, and the maturity is three years after the maturity of the defaulted mortgage.

Approved participants.   The FHA is charged with administering the housing law in conformity with both its letter and its spirit. Both lenders and borrowers, as well as the property involved, must therefore be qualified by the FHA.

Automatic approval to become a lender is extended to members of the Federal Reserve System, the Federal Deposit Insurance Corporation, the Federal Savings and Loan Insurance Corporation, and certain other agencies. Lenders not qualified by this kind of membership must earn the specific approval of the federal housing commissioner by giving evidence of appropriate experience in making and servicing mortgage loans, sufficient capital, and capacity to continue a satisfactory business, preferably through a charter.

Once the property meets eligibility standards by type, location, and appraisal, the borrower must also be qualified for the loan. When the lender makes application for mortgage insurance, it submits information about the personal history and the financial responsibility of the mortgagor. If the FHA is not satisfied with this, it may make its own credit investigation of the borrower. Its effort is directed to a determination of the debt-paying capacity of the borrower and the degree of risk that the financial capacity of the borrower introduces into the mortgage transaction.

In attempting to measure the borrower's financial capacity to meet his obligations, the FHA is interested in the current income of the borrower and its probable continuity. It is interested also in such charges against this income as mortgage payments, insurance taxes, maintenance, and household operating expenses, as well as income taxes, life insurance premiums, payments on installment accounts, and similar payments. In the light of all these factors the borrower is given a rating denoting acceptance or rejection.

Major sections of Title II in FHA program. The most important sections of Title II that are administered by the FHA are listed in succeeding paragraphs.

Section 203 of this title provides for insuring mortgages on one- to four-family dwellings. This section has accounted for about 70 percent of all mortgage insurance written by FHA.

Section 207 authorizes the insurance of mortgages, including construction advances, on rental housing projects of eight or more family units. It also covers projects undertaken by nonprofit corporations for occupation by the elderly. Its authority further extends to insurance of loans on mobile home courts.

Section 213 authorizes the insurance of mortgages on cooperative housing projects of eight or more family units. The section provides for two types of FHA-insured cooperative housing projects—the management type and the sales type. Under the management type, the mortgagor must be a nonprofit ownership housing corporation or trust, with permanent occupancy of the housing facility restricted to members. In a sales-type project each individual member is a stockholder of the cooperative corporation, or a beneficiary of the trust, undertaking the construction of the housing project. Upon completion of the sales-type project, provision is made for the acquisition of title to an individual housing unit by each member and the insurance of an individual mortgage thereon.

Section 220 permits insurance in connection with financing the rehabilitation of existing salable housing and the replacement of slums with new housing.

Section 221 authorizes mortgage insurance on low-cost housing for relocation of families in connection with urban renewal and slum clearance programs. Its benefits are also extended to any family of low or moderate income, or individuals who are handicapped or aged 62 or over.

Section 221 (d) (2), as amended in 1968, provides for insurance of mortgages for single homes and permits a mortgagor to contribute the value of his labor to the acquisition of his dwelling. The ratio of the loan to property value can be 100 percent for an owner-occupant, except when the home was not constructed under FHA or VA inspection or over a year has passed since its completion. In the latter case, the maximum ratio is 90 percent. The minimum cash investment is $200 for a displaced family and 3 percent of acquisition cost for other families. Normal FHA ceiling interest rates apply, and a .5 percent mortgage insurance premium is charged. In the case of displaced families the term of the mortgage can be up to 40 years. For other families, it is generally 30 years.

Section 221 (d) (3) provides special terms for construction or rehabilitation of housing located in approved urban renewal areas for mortgagors approved by the Federal Housing Commissioner. Where the mortgagor accepts regulation in regard to rents, charges, and methods of operation in a manner designed to effectuate the purposes of the program, a below-market interest rate will be allowed. Under such conditions, construction financing is charged at the FHA market rate, but at time of completion of construction and final endorsement of the mortgage for insurance, the rate can be reduced to 3 percent. On mortgages carrying this rate, FHA waives its mortgage insurance premium and the mortgages will be purchased by the Federal National Mortgage Association.

The rent supplement program was also established by Section 221 (d) (3) in 1965. By this authority, low-income individuals of families who are either elderly, handicapped, displaced by government action, occupants of substandard housing, or occupants or former occupants of homes damaged by acts of God are eligible for admission as tenants to new or rehabilitated housing owned by a nonprofit organization participating in the below-market interest rate (BMIR) program. The housing owner contracts with the Secretary of HUD for federal rent supplement payments. The contracts run for terms up to 40 years. The rent supplement payments are limited to the excess of the fair rental value of the unit over one fourth of the tenant's income. When the tenant can afford to pay the whole rent by this standard he may continue to live in the unit without a rent supplement payment.

The Housing and Urban Development Act of 1968 extended the rent supplement program to owners of housing projects financed under a state or local program which provided assistance through loans, loan insurance, or tax abatements, provided the project meets the approval of the Secretary of HUD for rent supplement benefits before completion of construction or rehabilitation. Rent supplement benefits may also be extended to housing financed by direct loans under Section 202 of the Housing Act of 1959.

Section 221 (h) of the Federal Housing Act was added in 1966 to establish a program to promote homeownership for low-income families with the assistance of FHA mortgage insurance. Under this authority, the FHA insures mortgages of nonprofit organizations to finance the purchase and rehabilitation of deteriorating and substandard housing. Mortgages may also be insured to finance the resale of housing to low-income families or individuals who are eligible for rent supplements under the rent supplement program.

The mortgage to the nonprofit organization may be insured for an amount equal to the appraised value of the property plus estimated rehabilitation costs. Its maturity is set by the FHA. Under the 1966 legislation, the regular FHA ceiling interest rate was prescribed until final endorsement of the mortgage for insurance, then 3 percent. Under the 1968 admendment, the interest rate may be as low as 1 percent for purchasers whose income is low enough to warrant the lower rate. As a result, individual mortgages insured under this section may bear interest between 1 and 3 percent, depending on the individual incomes and needs of the homeowners. The mortgage of the homeowner in any individual case can be an amount equal to the unpaid balance of the mortgage of the nonprofit corporation selling the property that is allocable to the dwelling being sold. The minimum down payment required is $200, but this may be applied to closing costs. The maximum mortgage term is 25 years. The mortgage must contain a provision that the interest rate will increase to the highest rate permitted by FHA if the mortgagor does not continue to occupy the property; however, this provision is not applicable to a case of resale back to the nonprofit organization from whom the property was originally purchased, or a sale to a local housing authority or another low-income purchaser approved by the FHA.

Section 231 provides insurance for the construction or rehabilitation of rental housing for the elderly or handicapped. The facility constructed must contain at least eight units.

Section 232 authorizes FHA insurance of mortgages on urgently needed nursing homes. The insurance is applicable to convalescents who do not require hospitalization but who do need nursing care. To qualify a home for such insurance, the appropriate state agency charged with licensing and regulating such establishments must certify that the home is needed and that minimum operating standards will be enforced in the home. The property may be new or rehabilitated, but it must have at least 20 beds.

Section 233 gives the FHA authority to insure mortgages on experimental housing. This insurance is available for mortgages or home-improvement loans meeting the requirements of any of FHA's Title II programs. The program extends to all types of operations. The experimentation may involve the utilization or testing of new designs, materials, construction methods, or experimental property standards for neighborhood design. Major effort is directed toward improving low-income housing construction.

Section 234 authorizes FHA to insure a mortgage covering a family unit in a multifamily building of five or more units and an undivided interest in common areas and facilities serving the structure. This kind of ownership is known as condominium. Under the 1961 Housing Act, the insurance was limited to a mortgage on a structure carrying mortgage insurance under one of the FHA multifamily insurance programs other than Section 213. By the Housing Act of 1964, insurance was authorized for blanket mortgages to finance the construction or rehabilitation of multifamily projects to be sold as condominiums, provided the mortgagor certifies that it intends to sell the project as a condominium and will make all reasonable efforts to sell the family units to FHA-approved purchasers.

Section 235 (added in 1968) was designed to establish a homeownership assistance program for the purchase of new, single-family homes by low and moderate income families, handicapped persons, or single persons 62 years of age or older. The assistance takes the form of periodic payments to the mortgagee by the Secretary of HUD to make up the difference between 20 percent of the family's monthly income and the required monthly payment under the mortgage for principal, interest, taxes, insurance, and mortgage insurance premium. The amount of the subsidy varies according to the income of the homeowner.

Because of shoddy construction by developers under this program, further funding was halted in January 1973. The program was restarted in 1976. Changes were made to prevent some of the earlier abuses. The average incomes of participants in the program were raised somewhat by the new formula adopted for establishing eligibility. Further, to preclude the possibility of more subsidized slums, regulations were revised to require that HUD insure no more than 40 percent of the homes built in a subdivision. Higher down payments were required. The minimum down payment is now 3 percent of acquisition cost.

Example of subsidy.   As an illustration of how a subsidy works, the revised Section 235 is described herein in greater detail and by example. This section provides assistance in the form of a monthly payment to the mortgagee from HUD, reducing the interest cost to as low as 4 percent of the loan balance but not less than 20 percent of the homeowner's adjusted monthly family income. To be eligible for assistance, the family must have an adjusted income not exceeding 95 percent of the median income for the area, with appropriate adjustments for family size. A deduction of $300 is made for each family member under 21 years of age and the earnings of such minors are not included.

An assistance payment computation is made to determine the lesser of:

a. The difference between the total monthly payment under the mortgage for principal, interest at the market rate, mortgage insurance (.7 percent), taxes, and hazard insurance and 20 percent of the mortgagor's adjusted monthly income; or

b. The difference between the monthly payment of principal, interest at the market rate, and mortgage insurance premium (MIP) under the mortgage and the monthly payment that would be required at a 4 percent interest rate excluding the monthly insurance premium (MIP).

For example, assume a family has an adjusted annual income of $12,395, or a monthly income of $1,033. Other transaction items are as follows:

Sale price: $38,000

Down payment: $ 1,150
Mortgage amount: $36,850
Term in months: 360

Interest rate: 14%

Computation of monthly mortgage
    payment:
Principal and interest (see tables
    in Appendix B) $436.68
MIP = 36.85 × .5828* 21.48
Taxes and hazard insurance.............. 37.00

        Total $495.16

* FHA factor to establish mortgage insurance cost at .007 percent on a 14 percent 30-year mortgage on a monthly basis (in $ per $1,000).

Assistance calculation:
1.	Monthly mortgage payment as above........................	$495.16
2.	20% of adjusted monthly income	206.60
1.–2.	Monthly subsidy per formula (a) above	$288.56
3.	Monthly payment (principal + market interest + MIP excluding taxes and hazard insurance)	$458.16
4.	Monthly payment (principal + interest at 4%)...............	176.14
3.–4.	Monthly subsidy under formula (b) above	$282.02

Since formula (b) provides the lesser subsidy, the amount computed by that method is the authorized assistance payment. The mortgagor's monthly payment, therefore is $495.16 − $282.02 = $213.14.

Section 236 (added in 1968) was established to provide the counterpart of Section 235 for rental and cooperative housing for low and moderate income families. This section emerged from the below-market interest rate program authorized under Section 221 (d) (3) which has been successful in providing needed rental and cooperative housing for families whose incomes are too high for public housing and too low for standard housing available in the competitive market.

Section 221 (d) (3) has suffered from the limitation of depending on direct federal lending from the special assistance funds of FNMA to support its 3 percent mortgages. The limited availability of these funds greatly restricted the activity. The new subsidy program made it possible to obtain funds from the private mortgage market.

Under the Section 236 program the mortgagor-owner of the housing must make a monthly payment for principal and interest under the mortgage as though it bore a 1 percent interest rate. The difference between this amount and the monthly payment due under the mortgage, which bears the market rate of interest, for principal, interest, and mortgage insurance premium is paid to the mortgagee on behalf of the mortgagor by the federal government.

From the standpoint of the tenant, a basic rental charge is established on the basis of a 1 percent mortgage interest rate. The tenant is then required to pay either the basic rental charge or 25 percent of his income, whichever is greater.

Funding for construction under Section 236 was frozen in January 1973 for the same reasons as for the suspension of Section 235—the creation of "instant slums" by loose practices. Future operations under Section 236 are contingent upon the government making more funds available for use in this manner.

Section 237 was added in 1968 to extend FHA mortgage insurance to families of low or moderate income with impaired credit histories or irregular income patterns. Such families may become eligible if the Secretary of HUD finds them to be reasonably satisfactory credit risks and capable of home-ownership with proper financial counseling. Mortgages insured under this program must generally meet the requirements of the specific FHA program for financing under which the applicant seeks assistance. The credit and income requirements do not apply, however. Insurance will not be authorized under Section 237 unless the monthly mortgage payments for principal and interest, plus real estate taxes, can be paid with 25 percent or less of the mortgagor's monthly income, based on the last year or the past three-year average, whichever is greater.

In addition to the relaxation of credit restrictions, the 1968 legislation gave the FHA more flexible authority to accept insurance on properties in declining urban areas. Insurance may now be accepted in areas that do not meet normal eligibility requirements. Acceptance of these mortgages is permitted when the FHA is able to establish that the area is "reasonably viable," giving consideration to the need to provide adequate housing for families of low or moderate income in the area, and that the property is a reasonably acceptable risk in view of such consideration. This authority enlarges upon the 1966 amendment to Section 203 of the National Housing Act whereby the secretary of HUD was authorized to insure one- to four-family dwellings in areas fraught with riots or other disorders, without regard to economic soundness, in view of the urgent need for adequate housing for low and moderate income families in the area.

Section 238 established a Special Risk Insurance Fund to receive premiums from and pay claims under programs that are not intended to be actuarially sound. These include mortgages insured under the new Sections 235, 236, and 237, as it relates to properties in declining areas that do not pass minimum standard tests for economic soundness, as discussed in the preceding paragraph. Also included in this fund are mortgages issued under Section 233, primarily oriented to the development of new technologies for lower income housing.

New "Section 8" housing assistance program.   In the Housing and Community Development Act of 1974 a new low-income housing subsidy program was authorized by Section 8 of the Housing Act of 1937 as amended. Under this new program, designed to replace the faltering Section 236 program previously described, HUD is authorized to render aid through "assistance payments contracts." These contracts are made on behalf of eligible families occupying new, substantially rehabilitated, or existing rental units. The HUD Secretary is authorized to contract directly with private owners or public housing agencies agreeing to construct or rehabilitate housing.

Assistance payments contracts may run as long as 15 years for an existing unit and up to 20 years for a new or rehabilitated one (or up to 40 years where the project is owned by, or financed by a loan or guarantee from, a state or local agency). The contracts must specify the maximum monthly rent which is to be charged for each assisted unit. The maximum monthly rent cannot exceed by more than 10 percent the fair market rental established for comparable rental units in the area suitable for occupancy by the assisted person. However, the maximum rent can be up to 20 percent higher than fair market rental where the Secretary determines that special circumstances warrant the higher rent.

The amount of assistance provided with respect to a unit is an amount equal to the difference between the established maximum rent for the unit and the occupant family's required contribution to rent. Aided families are required to contribute between 15 and 20 percent of their total income to rent as prescribed by the Secretary. A 15 percent maximum is established for certain large families.

In general, eligible families are those who, at the time of initial renting of the units, have total incomes not in excess of 80 percent of area median income. At least 30 percent of the families assisted under all of the annual contract authority allocations must be families with gross incomes not in excess of 50 percent of area median income. These rules are subject to substantial adjustment by the Secretary to take into account construction cost variables, unusually high or low family incomes, and other factors.

From a slow start, with just $42 million in subsidies of Section 8 housing in 1974, the first year, the program has experienced enormous expansion. From 1974 through 1979 HUD commitments to this program were $130 billion in rent subsidies. Fiscal 1981 commitments to this program proposed by the federal executive branch stand at $20 billion.

The overwhelming play for this program has been brought on by a combination of factors—rent controls, declining new construction, a wave of conversions of existing apartments to condominiums, and abandonments. The program has also been greatly promoted by the liberal official definition of what constitutes a low-income family. In New York City, for example, a family of four with an income of up to $17,269 is considered low income and entitled to a subsidy that may exceed $6,000 per year. In Washington, D.C., the defined low income dividing point is $16,083; in Chicago, the amount is $15,034.

Developers have been encouraged to undertake Section 8 projects because with HUD approval they can often obtain bank financing for 90 percent of the cost of the project, in view of the HUD-guaranteed assistance payments. In addition, HUD may assume half of the loan interest cost at the market rate, leaving the developers with only the other half. HUD will also underwrite 10 percent of the cost of a project for profit. This guarantee goes a long way toward enabling a developer to borrow his down payment for the mortgage, and hence to receive a 100 percent loan.

A *new Section 245 (b)*, added to the Housing Act in 1979, authorizes a graduated payment mortgage (GPM) for the specific benefit of persons who have not owned a home in the previous three years and who otherwise have difficulty qualifying for FHA assistance. The loans are made to facilitate homeownership for households that expect their incomes to rise substantially.

These mortgages allow homeowners to make smaller monthly payments initially and to increase the payment size gradually over time. The loan balance may never exceed 113 percent of the original appraisal value of the home.

Five different payment plans are available, varying in duration and rate of increase. The size of the down payment varies in accordance with the payment program, to make certain that the total mortgage balance does not exceed maximum loan limits.

Other titles in the FHA program. Among other titles of the National Housing Act that should be mentioned are Title VII, Title X, and Title XI. Title VII—Section 701 provides for insurance of the yield from investment in rental housing projects for moderate income families. This insurance extends to commercial space and community facilities. Title X relates to land development and new communities, allowing insurance to back the financing to purchase land and develop building sites, including streets, water and sewer systems, and similar costs. Title XI authorizes mortgage insurance for financing construction and equipment of local group practice facilities for doctors, dentists, and optometrists. In certain localities, one practitioner will be sufficient to qualify.

National Corporation for Housing Partnerships. This corporation was formed pursuant to 1968 legislation authorizing the President of the United States to create one or more private corporations to engage in activities directed at providing more and better housing for low and moderate income families. The corporation was authorized to enter into and participate in all forms of partnerships and associations, to conduct research and study projects, to provide technical assistance, and to provide financing assistance to other organizations in connection with its activities. The corporation was specifically authorized to form a limited partnership in which the corporation is the general partner and each stockholder is a limited partner. The scope of activities of the limited partnership is the same as those of the corporation.

The limited partnership formed under this authority was titled the National Housing Partnership (NHP). Its initial capital was $42 million invested by 270 leading industrial corporations, utilities, financial organizations, and labor unions. Additional funds may be raised by the sale of portions of NHP's interests in projects on a continuing basis. NHP offers assistance in various ways:

1. Co-sponsorship with local sponsors in joint housing ventures.
2. Purchase of as much as 99 percent of the equity in a multifamily housing development.

3. Seed money loans.
4. Sponsorship with nonprofit and community organizations.
5. Staff services.

NHP now has projects in about two thirds of the states in a variety of locations.

Public housing

Under the U.S. Housing Act of 1937, the federal government assumed responsibility for the administration of a public housing program. Under this program, the federal government has provided financial aid for housing owned and operated by local housing authorities for the benefit of low-income families who otherwise would be unable to afford decent housing in the locality. Single elderly persons of 62 years of age or older, or persons who, regardless of age, are under disabilities which entitle them to retirement benefits under the Social Security Act, are eligible for admission as "families of low income," except when restrictive state housing laws prevail.

This segment of the federal public housing program has always been in a great measure the responsibility of the local community concerned. The actual construction and operation of housing projects is the responsibility of local housing authorities. These are nonprofit public agencies which own and operate the project. Construction is performed by private contractors under contract to the housing authority. Costs of this construction are met through the public sale of bonds by the local housing authority. Such obligations are exempt from federal income tax. To encourage further the private purchase of local housing authority obligations, the federal government guarantees the repayment of both principal and interest. All such private financing is under the control of the HUD administrator, who determines maximum maturities, interest rates, and so on. The interest rates are fixed in conformity with a formula outlined in the law which relates them to the rates on applicable government bonds.

Federal aid takes the form of (1) loans to help finance the preliminary development and (2) annual contributions to permit operation of the housing development at rents within the means of low-income families. Actually, the local housing authority pays all operating costs from rental income, and the federal contribution goes only toward bond retirement.

As a part of its complementary service, HUD also sets standards and offers technical assistance to the local housing authorities. In the consummation of new construction programs, the local authorities often undertake a simultaneous elimination of a number of substandard dwellings, either by demolition or by rehabilitation, equal to the number of units constructed for public housing.

No annual contribution will be made by the federal government unless the housing project to which it applies is exempt from all real and personal property taxes imposed by state, city, county, or other political subdivision. In lieu of such taxes, the local housing authority may contract to make payments to taxing districts not to exceed 10 percent of the annual shelter rent charged in the housing project.

Prior to 1965, public housing was geared to new construction, specifically built for the purpose. In 1965 Congress authorized local housing agencies to acquire existing housing or privately built new housing for low-rent tenants. Such programs are now known as instant housing or turnkey acquisitions. They are backed by an annual contribution contract under which HUD provides financial assistance to the local housing authority for acquisition and operation of the projects.

Also in 1965, for the first time Congress authorized the use of federal assistance to permit local housing authorities to lease private dwellings to low-income tenants. This program is initiated by the governing body of the community approving by resolution the application of this plan to the community. Upon HUD approval, listings of available homes and apartments are obtained from private owners and real estate companies. The public housing authority and the property owner usually sign a lease which provides for subleasing to eligible tenants. Other leasing arrangements are possible. The local housing authority pays the federal contribution either to the owner directly or to the tenants. If the latter, the tenant places the contribution with the balance of the rent and makes the total payment to the owner.

Local housing authorities have recently become more interested in housing specially designed to meet the need of the aging and physically handicapped. More liberal cost allowances have been allowed. In addition, in view of the low incomes of a large number of the elderly and handicapped, additional operating subsidies have been authorized for each dwelling where it is necessary to maintain project solvency.

Community development[1]

The Housing and Community Development Act of 1974 fundamentally revamped the federal government's financial assistance program for communities for physical development and improvement, including the removal and prevention of slums and blight. The change substitutes a single program of 100 percent grants (with certain related guarantees of loans) to communities on basically a formula plan for several ongoing categorical programs. Within a

---

[1] The material on community development was derived from *Evolution of Role of the Federal Government in Housing and Community Development,* Subcommittee on Housing and Community Development of the Committee on Banking, Currency and Housing, House of Representatives, 94th Cong. 1st sess. (Washington, D.C.: U.S. Government Printing Office, October 1975), pp. 201–3. This pamphlet is an excellent chronology of legislation and selected legislative actions, 1892–1974.

few restrictive limits, communities now have authority to formulate their own development plans and programs, to be assisted instead of conforming to federal programs and decisions. This approach obviously gives the communities greater authority and flexibility in determining the assisted operations to be undertaken.

Several categorical programs of several years history were terminated (as to commitment on January 1, 1975). These included:

Open space—urban beautification—historic preservation grants.

Public facility loans.

Water and sewer and neighborhood facilities grants.

Urban renewal and neighborhood development program grants.

Model cities supplemental grants.

Authority to make rehabilitation loans.

Eligible recipients.   States, cities, counties, and other units of local government (including certain designated types of public agencies) are the eligible recipients of community development block grants (and guarantee of loans). The legislation also extends this eligibility to certain private "new community" developers and citizens associations.

Eligible activities.   In general, eligible activities include the broad range of development activities typical in a community. They encompass those dealt with under the earlier programs now terminated. The activities include:

Acquisition, disposition or retention of real property that is blighted, deteriorated, or inappropriately developed; appropriation for rehabilitation or conservation activities; or appropriation for conservation of open space or historical sites and public purposes.

Acquisition, construction, or installation of most types of public works, utilities, facilities, and site and other improvements.

Code enforcement in deteriorating areas.

Clearance, demolition, removal, and rehabilitation of buildings and improvement, including interim assistance and financing of rehabilitation of privately owned property incident to other activities.

Other related activities such as public services not otherwise available, relocation payments for those displaced, and administration of the program.

Payment of the nonfederal share of other federal programs related to development.

Development of a comprehensive plan and the policy-planning-management capacity of the community.

Requirements in application for community development block grants.   To obtain HUD approval of an assisted activity, a properly prepared application must contain:

1. A summary of a three-year plan that identifies community development needs and objectives developed in accordance with area-wide development planning and national urban growth policies and which demonstrates a comprehensive strategy for meeting these needs.

2. Formulation of a program which includes activities to meet community development needs and objectives, indicates resources other than federal assistance expected to be available to meet such needs and objectives, and takes account of environment factors.

3. A description of a program to eliminate or prevent slums, blight, and deterioration where such conditions or needs exist, and provide improved community facilities and public improvements, including supporting health and social services where necessary and appropriate.

4. A housing assistance plan which accurately surveys the condition of the community's housing stock and assesses the housing assistance needs of lower income persons residing or expected to reside in the community; specifies a realistic annual goal for the number of units, or persons to be assisted, including the mix of new, existing, and rehabilitated units, and the size and types of projects and assistance best suited to the needs of the lower income persons in the area; and indicates the general locations of proposed lower income housing with a view to further revitalization, promoting greater housing choice, avoiding undue concentration of low income persons, and assuring availability of adequate public facilities and services for such housing.

Measures of applicant eligibility. Principal entitlement grantees include metropolitan cities and urban counties of at least 50,000 and 200,000, respectively. The formula on which their grants are based includes (*a*) population, 25 percent; (*b*) poverty, 50 percent; and (*c*) overcrowded housing, 25 percent. Under an alternative formula, additional assistance may be given to older, more heavily distressed areas. That formula ascribes a weight of at least 20 percent to growth lag compared to cities of similar size: to poverty, 30 percent; and to age of pre-1940 housing, 50 percent. The applicant is entitled to receive whichever sum is greater under either formula.

Small cities block grants. Small cities under 50,000 are not automatically entitled to block grants, but they may qualify. The program is competitive and designed to encourage well-planned housing and community needs consistent with the Housing and Community Development Act. About 20 percent of the Community Development Block Grant program appropriation is now set aside for small cities' development activities.

Urban Development Action Grants (UDAG). Since 1978 the Urban Development Action Grant (UDAG) program has been extremely important to severely distressed cities and urban counties. This program has been designed to encourage innovative forms of joint public/private development and to build partnerships between government and private industry. Action grants are available to support a variety of commercial, neighborhood, or industrial projects designed to help rejuvenate the local economic base; provide jobs, especially for low- and moderate-income persons; and reclaim deteriorated or aging neighborhoods.

Financing homes for veterans

When World War II ended, the deluge of returning veterans and new family formations created an acute housing shortage. A high level of economic activity provided the veteran with income sufficient to amortize a mortgage in lieu of rent, but he usually did not have the cash down payment required to permit him to buy a home under conventional lending methods. It had been the practice for many years, in compliance with investment restriction laws of the states, for institutional lenders to limit their loans to from 60 to 75 percent of the appraised value of the property. Experience had taught them to require a cushion against depreciation in value that takes place in a forced sale on foreclosure.

Legislative history.   It was therefore a revolutionary step when a grateful Congress enacted legislation providing World War II veterans a guarantee by the United States of mortgage debt incurred to acquire a home. This guarantee was intended to be sufficient to substitute, in substantial measure at least, for lack of a cash down payment. The first law, passed in 1944, provided for a 50 percent guarantee up to $2,000 with the interest rate on the loan not to exceed 4 percent.

The original construction of the guarantee law was strict. Lenders were skeptical, and few were willing to make loans except on an experimental basis. The $2,000 maximum was only sufficient to provide a substitute for the 40 percent cash down payment required by many investing institutions on a $5,000 home, and any veteran wanting to buy a home for $6,000, $8,000, or $10,000 would be faced with an increasingly prohibitive problem with the cash down payment required.

In 1945 the law was amended to raise the guarantee limit to $4,000 (the limit on nonrealty loans remaining at $2,000). The new provision permitted a $4,000 substitute for the cash down payment up to 50 percent on a $8,000 home, and a more expensive home could be obtained by an added cash down payment by the veteran; or the lender might satisfy itself with less than a 50 percent guarantee. Now, the program began to function. Furthermore, by regulation of the Veterans Administration, lenders were permitted to recoup advances made for delinquent taxes and insurance and the costs of foreclosure plus attorney fees. Lenders learned by experience that their guarantee claims were quickly honored and that the program was managed by the VA so as to honor just claims and to avoid technicalities, thereby encouraging more lenders to enter the program.

Since that time, the maximum guarantee entitlement has been raised by steps to $7,500 in 1950, to $12,500 in 1968, to $17,500 in 1974, and to $25,000 in 1978. From 1950 on, the maximum guarantee has extended to 60 percent of the total loan. On mobile home and real estate lot loans, the amount of the guaranty is limited to 50 percent of the loan, not to exceed $17,500.

Veterans who used their entitlement before October 1, 1978, may have additional entitlement for later purchases. The additional entitlement is the difference between $25,000 and the amount of entitlement used on earlier GI home loans. In 1970 the guarantee entitlement was broadened to include loans to refinance mortgages and other liens of record on homes owned and occupied by eligible veterans.

Qualified veterans.   Guaranteed or insured loans may be made to veterans of World War II or the Korean conflict who served on active duty for 90 days or more. Other veterans in active service over 180 days may also qualify. Special eligibility is granted to veterans in the above classes with less than the required service but who were separated with service-connected disabilities or to unmarried widows of veterans who died in service or as a result of service-connected disabilities. Wives of members of the armed forces who have been listed as missing in action or prisoners of war for 90 days may also qualify. In all cases, eligibility is conditioned on a separation from the service that is other than dishonorable.

All termination dates for eligibility to apply for VA-guaranteed housing were removed by the Veterans Administration Act of 1970. This act also provided that mobile homes are acceptable security for loan guarantees by the Veterans Administration.

Nature of GI obligation.   The legal nature of the VA guarantee is that of an absolute guarantee in which the Administrator becomes liable for the entire amount of the existing guarantee immediately on default. The guarantee has always been a percentage guarantee with a maximum amount fixed by law. Thus, an original loan of $40,000 made today will be guaranteed for 60 percent (or $24,000), and this percentage will adhere to the loan as the debt is decreased by payments or increased by unpaid interest.

Eligible lenders.   Any person, firm, association, corporation, or state or federal agency can be an eligible lender under the GI law. It is expected, however, that most loans will be made by commercial banks—national, state, or private; savings and loan associations; savings banks; insurance companies, credit unions; and other mortgage institutions which are subject to supervision by a governmental agency. Lenders operating under federal laws, including national banks, federal savings and loan association, and all banks, savings and loan associations, and insurance companies authorized to do business in the District of Columbia, are permitted to grant GI loans without reference to the limitations or restrictions of any other statute. These restrictions are waived in respect to ratio of loan to property value, maturity of loan, security requirements, dignity of lien, and percentage of assets which may be invested in loans against real estate as security.

Eligible lenders whose operations are supervised by a governmental agency—state or national—may make loans that are automatically guaranteed so long as they keep within the requirements of the VA. Non-supervised lenders who meet VA regulatory standards may also arrange to have their loans approved on an automatic basis. By automatic guarantee is meant that the lender need not secure the prior approval of the VA before making the loan. Most lenders, however, prefer to secure prior approval on all loans granted by them. This is their privilege. By this means they minimize the risk of having the guarantee questioned on technical grounds at a later time.

Insured loans. Any loan eligible for a guarantee under this law may be eligible for insurance as well, if made or purchased by a supervised lender. The lender which elects to use the insurance program must notify the VA of its intent at the time the loan is reported. Otherwise it is guaranteed instead of insured. When insurance is elected, the lender's insurance account is credited with 15 percent of each loan insured, provided that it keeps within the maximum amount of the guarantee. In case of default on an insured loan, the lender is entitled to obtain from the VA the full amount of its net loss, regardless of the percentage of loss to value of the property. For example, suppose that the lender has made or purchased $1 million of GI loans. Its insurance credit would be $150,000, which is 15 percent coverage. If the loans are paid down to $600,000, the coverage becomes 25 percent; to $300,000, 50 percent; and so forth. Meantime, any losses suffered by the lender would be charged against its insurance credit. If an $8,000 loan against a property resulted in an $8,000 loss, full recovery could be obtained if the balance to the insurance credit of the lender amounted to that much. Insured home loans are negligible in number and amount.

Purposes of home loan. A guaranteed home loan may be used to purchase a residential property to be occupied by the veteran as his home; for financing the construction of his home; or for paying for alterations, repairs, or improvement to the home he already owns. Loans for the purchase of real estate primarily for investment purposes are not eligible for guarantees. Residential properties may consist of not more than four-family units, provided that one is to be occupied by the veteran as his home. Where the property is to be purchased or constructed through joint ownership of two or more veterans, one additional unit may be added for each added veteran. This is being interpreted to mean that two veterans may purchase a six-family unit. In states where home appliances are included as fixtures, they can be included in the guaranteed loan. Where there is doubt, they may not be included, since Title 38 U.S. Code, Chapter 37, which establishes the guaranty, applies only to real estate loans.

GI home purchase as hedge. The purchase of homes by veterans using the liberal financing terms of the GI law has been looked upon by some of them as a kind of double hedge. In the first place, it has provided a hedge against decisions by landlords. By owning a home being financed by a GI loan, the veteran is assured a place to live at no increase in housing cost so long as he keeps up his payments. He cannot be dispossessed, and his rent cannot be increased. Only taxes, utilities, and repair costs may go higher. Financing costs are fixed for the life of the loan. These are usually no higher than rental payments for comparable accommodations.

In the second place, the ownership of his home affords the veteran a hedge against further inflation in real estate prices. If real estate prices go up substantially, the cost of housing accommodations to tenants sooner or later reflects the increase. Of course, if costs should drop, then the prices of existing properties will follow after a time. Even in such event the homeowner is in a more advantageous position than the real estate speculator or investor. The investor who retains his property after prices decline will probably suffer loss of income. The speculator who buys when prices are high and sells at a lower price will lose a part of his principal. But the owner-occupant of a home still has the use of his property.

Other lending terms. The Administrator of Veterans Affairs is authorized to establish maximum interest rates in accord with loan market demands, not to exceed limitations by Section 203 (b) (5) of the National Housing Act. The maximum term is now 30 years and 32 days; it was formerly 25 years. There is no maximum loan except that the loan cannot exceed the reasonable value of the property established by the VA. Furthermore, the VA secured amendments to state and federal laws, permitting VA-guaranteed loans as exceptions to other laws restricting loan-to-value ratios for institutional investors.

Although Congress had in mind 100 percent loans to veterans, if necessary, including all costs of making the loan, the amount of any loan is subject to negotiation with the lender selected for financing assistance. In addition, the provision of the law relating to refinancing allows the VA to guarantee a loan not to exceed the reasonable value and also the veteran is allowed to pay the discount in these cases. Furthermore, the veteran may receive cash from the transaction resulting from the difference between the loan amount (which can not exceed the reasonable value) and the mortgages or other liens or debts which are to be paid in full from the loan proceeds. Some of this cash may be used by the veteran to pay the closing costs and prepaid items which are allowable; however, these are not technically part of the loan amount. They are disclosed to the VA because only certain charges are authorized as allowable to be paid by a veteran. This disclosure is not necessary because the VA considers them to be a part of the loan. It should be emphasized that only loans provided for in 38 U.S. Code, Sec. 1803 (c), which includes refinances, carry permission to the veterans to pay discounts.

Maturity of loans. Term loans for five years or less are eligible for guarantee under the GI home-financing plan. Experience has shown, however, that most home loans are monthly payment direct reduction loans. Amortization may follow the standard plan, which provides for a level monthly payment throughout the life of the loan. Under this plan, the same monthly payment will result in a declining interest charge and an increasing proportion of the monthly payments being used to reduce the principal balance. The straight principal reduction plan is also acceptable to the VA. Under it, the same amount must be paid each month to reduce the principal balance, but the interest charge will constantly decline. As a consequence, the total monthly payment will decline month by month. Most of the loans granted follow the standard plan. The maximum maturity allowed is 30 years and 32 days.

The law provides that payments must be approximately equal; but it also provides that amortization of the indebtedness may follow established procedure in the community where the property is situated. In accordance with this provision, loan plans have been approved which call either for somewhat larger payments in the beginning with reductions later, or for small payments at the start when the borrower's expenses are great, with increases later when income applicable to the loan payments promises to be greater. Extreme variations in payments are not sanctioned by the VA.

Many lenders do not look with favor upon the maximum maturities provided under the GI law. In spite of the loan guarantee, the following reasons are set forth in support of shorter maturities for GI borrowers: (1) The shorter the maturity, the smaller is the amount of interest paid by the borrower. (2) Shorter maturities result in building equities faster at a time when family obligations are not as great as they will be later. (3) The larger the equity, the greater is the probability of forebearance if the borrower needs it.

Down payment. Under the GI law, home loans are guaranteed with or without down payment. The amount of the down payment is subject to negotiation between the borrower and the lender. Some lenders have been willing to make 100 percent loans if other factors have been favorable. Others have insisted upon at least a small down payment in order to make sure that the borrower feels a sense of ownership in the property. Even where the owner's equity is small, he may feel that this can be amortized over a period of a few years as a part of the cost of having an assurance of a place to live. As a general rule, small equities do not give the same sense of ownership that is present when the equity is larger. By the same token, an equity created by a gift is less significant in the mind of the recipient than one created from his own savings.

For the above reasons, some lenders to whom the GI loans are otherwise acceptable have insisted upon substantial down payments of 20 percent or more. Others have considered "sweat" equities as at least a partial substitute for a down payment. If some of the work needed to make the home livable is performed by the veteran, the increase in value—which also means an increase in his equity—is called a sweat equity. In some areas where loans are made with uncompleted houses as security, with the assumption that the borrower will complete the structure with his own labor and that of his friends, the name given to such a mortgage is *shell loan.* The VA requires a minimum of property improvements to qualify for guaranty, and proper escrow procedures must be followed with regard to work to be completed.

Prepayments.   All GI loans on homes must grant the privilege of prepayment of any part or all of the indebtedness at any time. The lender is not required to accept as a prepayment less than one installment or $100, whichever, is smaller. Prepayments may be used to cure defaults, unless they have been once used for this purpose. For example, if prepayments have been applied to reduce the principal balance of the loan and later the borrower defaults, the amounts prepaid may be applied, through a recalculation of the payments, to cure or to prevent a default. The veteran can thus obtain the double advantage of interest reductions and of building a cushion against possible future defaults. In addition, if prepayments are substantial, the veteran may request that the loan be reamortized, reducing future payments; assuming that the reamortization schedule will provide that the entire loan be repaid within the original loan period.

Taxes and insurance.   By mutual agreement between the veteran borrower and the lender, the latter may collect with each loan payment a proportion of taxes, assessments, and insurance premiums applicable to the property. The method of collecting and disbursing such payments should be clearly set forth in the mortgage contract. If such added payments are provided for and if the contract so stipulates, failure to meet any such payments may constitute a default just as if the borrower had failed to pay interest or principal installment when due. Custom, rather than the regulations of the VA, generally governs the collection of these added amounts. If the lender is accustomed to collect them on conventional or FHA loans, it will probably collect them on GI loans also. Some lenders have not become acquainted with the advantages of collecting taxes and insurance from their borrowers.

In 1971, VA and HUD conducted a survey of both lenders and borrowers regarding the practice of escrowing taxes and insurance as a part of the loan payment. They found this to be the common procedure. Lenders favored this policy particularly to make sure that the taxes and insurance premiums were paid in a manner not to jeopardize guaranties.

Appraisals.   Appraisal procedure under the GI law has suffered many pains. As originally written, the law prohibited the application of loan guaranties if the price paid for the property exceeded the "reasonable normal value" of the property, as determined by the appraisers responsible to the VA. Nobody ever knew how to measure "normal" value. Presumably it was intended to provide only for long-term value, from which must be eliminated elements of inflation resulting from temporary scarcity. But the veterans who needed the assistance of the guarantee most urgently were those who were homeless in a period of extreme housing shortages. To bar them from the purchase of homes, even at admittedly inflated prices, meant the practical nullification of the purposes of the GI law.

Subsequently the word *normal* was stricken from the law. Had it been omitted originally, the administrators of this law might have had equally great difficulty in defining "reasonable value." But when "normal" was dropped, its omission was interpreted to mean that reasonable value must take into account current market conditions. This change made it possible for veterans to benefit from the law. By that time, the VA defined reasonable value in its regulations as "that figure which represents the amount a designated appraiser, unaffected by personal interest or prejudice, would recommend as a proper price or cost to a prospective purchaser, whom the appraiser represents in a relationship of trust, as being a fair price or cost in the light of prevailing conditions." This concept abandons the idea of long-term value and places greatest emphasis upon prevailing conditions.

Interests covered. The GI law on home financing applies to (1) a fee simple estate, whether legal or equitable; (2) a leasehold estate, running originally for a period not less than 14 years beyond the maturity of the loan, or which is renewable for such a period; and (3) a life estate, if the remainder and reversionary interests are made subject to the lien.

Forbearance. The Congress, in passing the GI home loan provisions, sought a means of providing homes for veterans of World War II by the use of a financing program which shifts much of the risk from the shoulders of the lender to the government. It is recognized that some who take advantage of this plan will have at least temporary difficulty in living up to the obligations they assume. Lenders are expected to exercise forbearance whenever borrowers have difficulty in meeting their obligations under their mortgages. This can be accomplished by recasting the loan in such a manner as to extend the term of repayment of the principal balance. This is encouraged by the VA. Filing of notice of default with the VA still leaves the lender free to exercise patience and leniency with his delinquent borrower. He is not forced to bring foreclosure suit in order to protect his guarantee.

Hopeless cases are dealt with as such when it is determined that there is no probability that the loan will be reinstated and the default cured. When it appears that the borrower can no longer carry the property, all parties concerned are urged to find a buyer for the property. If a new buyer can take over the mortgage and pay the mortgagor something for his equity, if any, well and good. If the real estate market is not favorable; if the condition of the property is such that it does not attract buyers; and if forbearance has been carried to such a point that the sale price of the property is less than the guarantee: then the VA will consider a proposal for the sale of the property at a price that will require it to make up to the lender the difference between the mortgage indebtedness and the amount assumed by the purchaser, but not in excess of the loan guarantee.

As an alternative, the mortgagee may accept a voluntary conveyance in lieu of foreclosure, with the prior consent of the VA. The policy of the VA is to encourage the acceptance of voluntary conveyances because of the saving of time and money.

Open-end mortgages. The VA regulations authorize the use of open-end mortgages in those states that have legislation authorizing their use.

Lenders are encouraged to inspect the properties securing VA loans at least once a year for the purpose of determining their physical condition. Such an inspection may disclose evidence of intentional or unintentional waste as well as any unusual conditions that cause the property to depreciate in value more rapidly than usual. Even ordinary wear and tear needs to be offset by maintenance and repair. Mortgages protecting GI loans are permitted to contain clauses allowing the lender to make advances to cover the cost of expenditures for these purposes. As noted above, the lender is still obligated to observe due caution to make sure that in his locality such advances may not jeopardize the dignity of his lien. The VA discourages the use of open-end mortgages, and although the VA mortgage form affords a lien to the holder for advances made for taxes and insurance, none of its printed forms contains a general provision for any state. But, the view of the VA is that it cannot prevent their use, which might nevertheless be followed by a reduction of a claim on a guarantee.

Filing of claims. Should a borrower become delinquent, the lender may file a claim with the VA. The VA may elect to make good the amount of the delinquency, bringing the loan current again. Any payments made by the VA to the lender in this fashion do not reduce the amount of the debtor's obligation. The VA becomes subrogated to the amount of claim against him that is paid to the lender. Subsequently, the VA may assert this claim in any manner it sees fit. It may determine that conditions are such as to require the VA to pay off the claim of the lender and take over the mortgage. Meantime it may help the veteran and the lender to dispose of the property, in case it appears clear that the mortgagor can no longer carry it. Generally, a claim for guaranty will be submitted after liquidation of the security.

In isolated cases where for any reason a foreclosure sale is conducted, the VA does not encourage the lender to take a deficiency judgment unless it appears clear that it can probably be collected. In no event is the lender obligated to undertake to collect, by resort to legal proceedings, any debts owed by the veteran borrower to the government on account of a GI home loan.

Custody of property. As soon as the holder of a VA-guaranteed mortgage elects to convey property to the VA after acquiring it through foreclosure or voluntary deed, it must so notify the VA. Thereupon the VA expects to assume custody of the property. By this means the former lender is relieved of any responsibility for loss to the property or damage for personal injuries in connection therewith. Since the VA is a self-insurer, it has no need for any kind of commercial insurance coverage. If the holder of the title sees fit to renew any insurance policy or to place insurance against the property following its acquisition, it does so at its own risk.

In turning over property to the VA, the holder of the title has no responsibility for securing the eviction of any occupant who is a trespasser on the property. But the VA will require a showing that any occupant is not claiming to own the property, because every purchaser of property is charged with notice of all rights of all parties in possession. In case title is obtained by foreclosure action, the occupants should be joined in the suit in order to cut off whatever rights they may attempt to assert.

Title evidence.   In cases of conveyance of a property to the VA, it is the holder's responsibility (supervised or otherwise) to deliver clear title and appropriate evidence thereof to the VA. In all cases, the VA reviews the title evidence to assure itself that the title is clear. Although the VA does not directly pay for the procurement of such title evidence, the holder can be reimbursed by including those costs in the computation of the claim.

Sale of property.   A veteran who purchases a home with financial assistance afforded by a GI loan may sell his home without restrictions so far as the VA is concerned. Because of the favorable interest rate and small monthly payments, the purchaser will usually want to assume the mortgage rather than to refinance and discharge the mortgagee. But there is a pitfall in so doing, for the veteran will remain liable on the debt to the holder of the loan; and if the purchaser defaults, and the VA pays on the guarantee, the veteran will be indebted to the VA for the amount paid on the guarantee. This debt is actively enforced by both the VA and the Department of Justice. On the other hand, if the purchaser not only assumes the mortgage debt but also the obligation of the veteran to reimburse the VA in case it has to pay on its guarantee, and if the purchaser meets the VA requirements as a good credit risk, the veteran and the purchaser may apply to the VA to have the veteran released from all obligation on the debt, including reimbursement to the VA. When the VA accepts the purchaser fully in lieu of the veteran, the latter will be completely released, even though the originally guaranteed debt remains in force and effect against the purchaser. Some veterans have taken advantage of these circumstances and have sold their homes at a profit. In some cases real estate salespersons have sought out veterans interested in disposing of their homes because of the appeal of the GI financing plan. In summary, a VA mortgage is attractive as an assumption because of the ease of transfer, the absence of a prepayment penalty, and in respect to older homes, a lower interest rate. During the past ten years, in times of tight money, an assumption for many sellers was often the only means of selling a home.

Since 1950 a veteran has been able to obtain another loan even after using full entitlement provided the requirements for restoration can be met. Currently the requirements are quite simple: The veteran must have disposed of the security for the property, and the loan must have been paid in full. In some cases of assumption, if a veteran-buyer has sufficient entitlement and is willing to substitute his or her entitlement for that of the veteran-seller, restoration can be accomplished in this manner. This is known as substitution of entitlement and became effective April 1, 1975.

Direct lending.   At the time the GI bill was first discussed in Congress, there was considerable pressure to provide direct loans by the government to the veterans of World War II. Private lending guaranteed by the VA was finally

EXHIBIT 23–2

Holdings of federally underwritten mortgage debt by main types of financial institutions at December 31, 1979 ($ millions)

	FHA	VA
Commercial banks:		
One- to four-family homes	4,447	2,726
Multifamily	370	
Mutual savings banks:		
One- to four-family homes	10,797	11,397
Multifamily	2,968	
Savings and loan associations:		
One- to four-family homes	11,609	15,559
Multifamily	1,356	
Life insurance companies:		
One- to four-family homes	4,651	2,959
Multifamily	1,171	
Noninsured pension funds:		
One- to four-family homes	352	218
Multifamily	150	
Mortgage companies:		
One- to four-family homes	3,645	2,666
Multifamily	23	
Real estate investment trusts:		
One- to four-family homes	2	3
Multifamily	1	
State and local retirement funds:		
One- to four-family homes	1,839	632
Multifamily	2,228	
Federal credit agencies:		
One- to four-family homes	20,005	11,211
Multifamily	8,369	
Mortgage pools:		
One- to four-family homes	33,813	37,613
Multifamily	1,277	
State and local credit agencies:		
One- to four-family homes	2,319	560
Multifamily	542	
Totals of groups shown	111,934	85,544

Source: *The Supply of Mortgage Credit: 1970–1979,* Office of Financial Management, Financial Analysis Division, (Washington, D.C.: U.S. Department of Housing and Urban Development, April 1980).

substituted for direct lending. From time to time since the law was originally enacted, there has been pressure to add direct lending features. Finally, in 1950 the law was amended to provide that:

> Upon application by a veteran eligible for the benefit of a home loan guarantee who has not previously availed himself of this privilege, if the VA finds that private capital is not available for the purchase or construction of a home, the VA may make a loan directly under the following conditions:

    A.   That he is a satisfactory credit risk,

    B.   That the monthly payments to be required under the proposed loan bear a proper relation to the veteran's present and anticipated income and expenses,

    C.   That he is unable to obtain from private lending sources in such area at an interest rate not in excess of 4 percentum per annum a loan for such purpose for which he is qualified under Section 501—of this title.

Loans made under this amendment were to bear interest at the rate of 4 percent (increased in subsequent years consistently with the guarantee and insurance programs) and were subject to the following limitations:

    1.   The original amount of such loan shall not exceed $10,000 (since increased in steps to as much as $25,000); and

    2.   The guaranty entitlement of the veteran shall be charged with the same amount that would be deducted if the loan had been guaranteed to the maxima permitted under Section 500 (a) of this title.

The VA is authorized to sell mortgages to any private lending institution evidencing ability to service loans with the proviso that it may guarantee any loan thus sold subject to the same conditions, terms, and limitations which would be applicable to privately originated loans with an automatic guarantee.

The direct lending program has had considerable activity in capital-short areas. It has enjoyed a favorable collection experience.

Participation in FHA and VA programs.   The distribution of holdings of FHA and VA loans is now wide and substantial, as will be noted from a review of Exhibit 23–2.

Exhibit 23–2 clearly shows the relative importance of the various financial intermediaries as holders of federally underwritten mortgages. It may be noted, in particular, how extremely important the secondary markets in the form of federal credit agencies and the mortgage pools have become in support of this type of credit.

Questions

1   What are the functional divisions of HUD?

2   What are the general terms and characteristics of a Title II loan?

3   Who may participate as lenders in the FHA program? Who may participate as borrowers?

4   How do the problems involved in urban redevelopment differ from those of original city planning?

5   What are the shortcomings of complete reliance upon private capital for the elimination of substandard housing and slum areas?

6   What are the arguments for and against public housing?

7 What action has HUD taken to meet the need of housing for families with lower incomes? Distinguish the programs. How appropriate are they?

8 What is the role of the Veterans Administration in assisting GI housing?

9 It has been stated that a GI loan may provide the buyer with a "double hedge." Explain.

10 Review the relative importance of FHA-insured and VA-guaranteed mortgages to various types of financial institutions. Determine where insurance is relatively important and suggest reasons why.

Case problems

1 The Alexanders wish to purchase a single home for $65,000. They desire to qualify for a Section 203 FHA-insured mortgage. The current FHA interest rate is 11.50 percent. Assume that there are 3 discount points required for closing costs and to adjust to the current market interest rate.

   a. In 1980, current established maximum loan-to-value ratios on unsubsidized home mortgages are 97 percent of the first $25,000 of value and 95 percent of the value in excess of $25,000. What is the maximum loan the Alexanders may obtain?

   b. Compute the following:

      (1) How much cash the Alexanders would need for a down payment if they should take out a maximum mortgage loan.

      (2) Their monthly payment on a 30-year mortgage at 11.50 percent interest plus .5 percent mortgage insurance premium. Do not include taxes or hazard insurance costs. The FHA monthly insurance premium amortization factor for 30-year mortgages at 11.50 percent is .4159 in dollars per $1,000 where the mortgage insurance rate is .5 percent.

2 John Brown is applying for a homeowner's loan subsidized under Section 235 of the National Housing Act. His adjusted annual income as determined by the FHA is $12,000. He is below the area income limit of $12,500 that would exclude him. Other transaction data:

Sale price.................	$45,000	Term:	360 months
Down payment	2,000	Interest rate:	11.50%
Mortgage amount..........	43,000	Taxes and hazard insurance:	$38 monthly

   On the basis of the model included in the chapter, compute the authorized subsidy for this case and the mortgagor's required monthly payment. The FHA monthly insurance premium amortization factor for 30-year mortgages at 11.50 percent is .5823 in dollars per $1,000 where the mortgage insurance rate is .7 percent.

3 Harry Gray, a veteran, has bought his home and financed the purchase by a GI loan. He desires to sell his home. He seeks your advice. If he sells to a nonveteran, what advantages may he achieve and what are the disadvantages? How may the results be different if he sells to another veteran?

Secondary mortgage markets

24

Growth of mortgage loans

Since World War II, total mortgage debt has expanded in massive terms. During the decade of the 1950s the debt doubled, expanding about $128 billion. By January 1, 1970, outstanding mortgage loans had more than doubled again, reaching over $425 billion. At the 1979 year-end, ten years later, the outstanding mortgage debt had risen to over $1.334 trillion. This remarkable growth took place in spite of periods of extreme credit stringency during recent years.

The great increase in the demand for mortgage money can be accounted for principally as the result of three major demand factors. First, and perhaps most obvious, is the rapidly increasing national population. This factor, however, has not been as important as two others: (1) the rising unit cost of homes and (2) the higher loan-to-value ratios. For federally underwritten mortgages on single-family homes, the increased average loan between 1950 and 1980 reflected a rise in purchase price of from 4 to 10 percent per year. For the same period the loan-to-value ratio rose from 76 percent to over 90 percent. A similar trend has been confirmed for conventional loans closed by insured savings and loan associations, where the average amount of the loan more than doubled and average loan-to-value ratios rose from 58 percent to over 70 percent during the period. Another factor, longer maturity dates for loans, has also had an impact on the increased amount of borrowing.

The very policy of increased liberalization of financing terms for home-ownership as supported by the federal program has had a contradictory effect. Through stimulated demand for housing and concomitant higher prices, home market values are highly dependent upon a continuation of such liberal policies. With low down payments, conservative interest rates, and long maturities, such loans may quickly become submarginal from the point of view of the private lender. It is at this point that another need arises. That is the need for a reliable secondary market for real estate mortgages to which institutions may resort to release funds for a continuation of a lending program under continually favorable conditions in an expanding real estate construction program.

Changing character of real estate mortgages.   Until recent years investment in real estate mortgages was a highly specialized type of money commitment. Few investors were willing to undertake the risks associated with such a commitment except where they had personal knowledge of the security, based upon inspection and appraisal, and where they could keep in touch with the debt-paying habits of the borrower by performing their own servicing operations. While this is still true of conventional loans, even here the urgency of the need for personal knowledge of the security and of direct servicing is not as great as it once was.

The coming of government guarantee and insurance of mortgages, accompanied by the increasing use of title insurance, has changed the above pattern materially. No longer does the ultimate holder of a real estate mortgage think of his commitment as the financing of a real estate project. Instead he gives prime attention to the insured or guaranteed paper which he holds as a receipt for his investment. Knowledge of the security for the mortgage is subordinated to faith in the guarantee or insurance of the mortgage, supported by title insurance. This change in the concept of real estate mortgages adds greatly to their liquidity and thereby points up the need for secondary markets for mortgages.

Supply of versus demand for mortgage funds.   If the supply of funds available for mortgages were just equal to the demand for such funds in each market area, there would be little need for a secondary market for mortgages. Mortgages could be retained by the individuals and the institutions that originated them until they were amortized in an orderly fashion. There would be no occasion either to buy or sell such mortgages.

While this kind of situation obtains in some sections of the country, in large and growing areas our economy is simply not organized. In some sections we face what amounts to mortgage money surpluses. Here the supply of funds available for investment in real estate mortgages exceeds the demand for mortgage money. In other areas, where the population is growing at rates faster than the average for the entire country, the reverse is true. The demand for mortgage funds far exceeds the local supply. Means must be found to permit money-surplus areas to supplement mortgage funds in money-scarce areas; and conversely to permit money-scarce areas to provide investment outlets for a part of the funds available in money-surplus areas. Secondary markets provide one answer to this problem.

Development of a secondary mortgage market. The development of a secondary mortgage market system for all types of sound real estate mortgages has been a slow process, and it is still in an intermediate stage. Since 1913 commercial banks have been able to maintain liquidity through privileges of rediscounting certain paper with the Federal Reserve System or of receiving temporary advances from the Federal Reserve Bank in return for the pledge of acceptable collateral. Although the credit reserve principle prevailed over the mortgage discounting system in the establishment of the Federal Home Loan Bank System in 1932, there was a clearly defined purpose that the Home Loan Banks should provide liquidity to their member institutions. A serious limitation of the Home Loan Banks from a practical aspect, however, lies in the relative concentration of its membership in savings and loan associations. Although eligible, few mutual savings banks and insurance companies have joined the system, largely it may be presumed because of reluctance to become a part of a minority group in the membership. Furthermore, the use of the credit reserve principle of providing liquidity through advances rather than by purchase of mortgages has greatly limited the volume of funds that can be provided by the Home Loan Banks. The concept that the credit is temporary or that any loan with a maturity beyond one year must be amortized over the period of the advance seriously limits the use of the advanced funds in the hands of the borrowing institution.

Institutions without recourse to the Federal Reserve or Home Loan Bank systems have no direct and assured means of achieving liquidity for funds committed to real estate mortgages. Mortgage bankers, who only recently became eligible to Home Loan Bank membership and who are typically thinly margined on capital, feel a special need for a strongly supporting secondary mortgage market system. The federal government made gestures toward the setting up of a secondary market for mortgages with the establishment of the federal assistance program for real estate during the 1930s. Only fairly recently, however, has there been a secondary market worthy of the term. The secondary real estate mortgage market has been defined as the aggregate of all purchase and sale transactions in such mortgages. For such a market to be effective and worthy of acceptance, private or governmental funds must be available at all times to permit the purchase of mortgage loans meeting prescribed standards. The investor in mortgages can deal with greater confidence if he can be assured of the existence of a secondary market where he can liquidate his holdings on a reasonable basis under the conditions then current. Often the ability to sell existing mortgages in the secondary market is the only means by which the holder of such mortgages can regain the liquidity necessary to finance new housing or to recover funds for an alternative use.

A purchasing institution may acquire mortgages in the secondary market either for resale or for retention as investments. Thus, to a certain extent, private institutional investors provide a secondary mortgage market to mortgagees, investors, and other holders of mortgage loans. By far the most important factors, however, in the secondary market for mortgage loans are the Federal National Mortgage Association, the Government National Mortgage Association, and the Federal Home Loan Mortgage Corporation. These agencies will each be discussed in succeeding sections of this chapter.

Federal National Mortgage Association

Failing in its efforts to induce private capital to form national mortgage associations for the purpose of providing a secondary market for insured mortgages, Congress in 1938 authorized the Reconstruction Finance Corporation (RFC) to form a subsidiary to be known as the Federal National Mortgage Association. This institution is familiarly known as Fannie Mae, and commonly designated by its initials, FNMA.

Although established to provide a secondary market for insured mortgages, FNMA was not freely used at the time it was chartered. The restrictions it placed upon purchases tended to discourage mortgagees from selling their mortgages in this market. This was particularly true because a more satisfactory market was provided by banks, insurance companies, and so forth, which made their purchases on terms more liberal to the sellers. As a consequence, FNMA was not a major factor in the insured mortgage market until it was revived in the postwar years.

FNMA after World War II.   The principal initial objectives of FNMA were:

1. To establish a market for the purchase and sale of first mortgages insured by FHA covering properties upon which were located newly constructed houses or housing projects.
2. To facilitate the construction and financing of economically sound rental housing projects or groups of houses for rent or sale through direct lending on FHA-insured first mortgages.
3. To make FNMA bonds or debentures available to institutional and individual investors.

Since July 1, 1948, FNMA has also been permitted to purchase certain VA mortgages guaranteed under the provisions of the Servicemen's Readjustment Act of 1944, as amended. At the same time, the Association's authority to make direct FHA-insured multifamily housing loans was discontinued.

FNMA was a subsidiary of the RFC until 1950 when it was transferred to the Housing and Home Finance Agency which had been created in 1942. By becoming a part of the federal agency primarily concerned with housing and home finance, FNMA's activities in the secondary market for home mortgages could thereafter be more closely coordinated with the Home Loan Bank Board and its affiliated agencies as well as with those of the FHA.

The demand for assistance from FNMA developed after World War II because of the differential between interest rates on FHA-insured and VA-guaranteed loans and yields on government bonds. Originally VA loans were made at 4 percent and, at the same time, FHA loans were made at 4.25 percent. For some time, government bonds were selling to yield less than 2.5 percent. This differential created a favorable climate for investing in federally underwritten mortgages rather than government bonds, even considering additional risk factors and servicing costs involved with investments in mortgages. As general interest rates began to rise in the late 1940s, lenders became reluctant to make commitments to large builders because of the danger that by the time of completion of projects the current interest rates might be still higher and their mortgages worth less than face value. At this point FNMA rendered an invaluable service to both lenders and builders by entering the secondary market on a commitment basis. By its commitment, FNMA agreed to purchase at an established rate the lender's mortgage paper during the commitment period. This assured a continuing flow of funds from lenders to the mortgage market.

An additional complication has always existed with reference to both FHA and VA mortgage loans. This complication is that they have a ceiling interest rate. As the market rate of interest on government bonds, for example, rose above 3 percent, while FHA and VA loans were at 4.25 percent and 4 percent, respectively, most investors considered bonds more desirable than the federally underwritten mortgages, all costs and risks considered. At this time, FHA and VA mortgages had few takers except to the extent that FNMA made advance commitment to lenders to take such loans off their hands. Under such circumstances, FNMA placed itself virtually in the position of a primary supplier of real estate mortgage funds.

Secondary market operations since 1954. In 1954 the Congress rechartered FNMA. The new Charter Act assigned to FNMA three separate and distinct activities: (1) secondary market operations in federally insured and guaranteed mortgages, (2) management and liquidating functions, and (3) special assistance functions. Each function was carried out as though it represented the operation of a separate corporation. Each had its own assets, liabilities, and separate borrowing authority.

By a wide margin, the secondary market operations became FNMA's most important direction of activity. Furthermore, it became apparent that the operation, properly managed, could support itself.

Secondary market operations and their financing. For several years, organizations such as the National Association of Home Builders, the Mortgage Bankers Association of America, the National Association of Real Estate Boards, and the United States Savings and Loan League had advocated the formation of a new secondary market facility to be expanded from a nucleus of the FNMA mortgage portfolio. Dominant among the recommendations was the position that governmental participation in the operation of the principal secondary market facility should gradually be replaced by private enterprise. A major objective of the FNMA Charter Act was to set up a procedure whereby FNMA would over a period of time be transformed into a privately owned and managed organization. By converting FNMA to a private operation rather than setting up a new one, it was contemplated to take advantage of FNMA's years of experience in the secondary market during the transition period and eventually to concentrate the whole operation in private hands.

The Charter Act authorized issuance of nonvoting $100 par preferred and common stock for the financing of secondary market operations. The preferred stock was issued to the Secretary of the Treasury, and the common was issued only to sellers of mortgages or borrowers as they participated in FNMA's secondary market operations.

Parties utilizing the services of FNMA have been required to buy certain amounts of its capital shares in accordance with established criteria. If the purchasers of the shares have not wanted to continue to hold them, they have had a ready resale market on the New York Stock Exchange, where the shares are listed.

The Housing and Urban Development Act of 1968. Under the Housing and Urban Development Act of 1968, the assets and liabilities in connection with, and control and management of, the secondary market operations were transferred to a private corporation. This became the new Federal National Mortgage Association. Prior to this time, FNMA had been jointly financed by government and private investors. The 1968 law made it a government-sponsored corporation owned solely by private investors. All Treasury-held preferred shares were retired.

The special assistance and management and liquidating functions, largely dealing with subsidized mortgage purchases for special federal housing programs, remain in the Department of Housing and Urban Development. To perform these functions the law created another corporation titled the Government National Mortgage Association (GNMA), now familiarly known as Ginnie Mae.

The 1968 legislation expanded the purchasing power of FNMA to include certain mortgage-backed securities guaranteed by GNMA, so that, when desirable, FNMA can support the secondary market for such securities. The authority for this mutual support has provided the basis for attracting funds into the mortgage market to a far greater degree.

Besides FNMA debentures and short-term notes, two new forms of borrowing were provided for by the 1968 legislation. First, FNMA was permitted to issue subordinated notes, in a manner similar to the capital notes permitted banking institutions. These obligations are usually issued for long terms and may include provisions for convertibility to common shares.

The second new borrowing form authorized issuance and marketing of securities backed by earmarked pools of portfolio mortgages. GNMA is authorized to guarantee the payment of principal and interest on any such securities issued by FNMA. Incidentally, GNMA is authorized in a similar manner to guarantee securities issued by other agencies or private parties approved for this purpose, when the securities are backed by federally underwritten mortgages and subjected to a trust similar to that established by FNMA. The gain sought here is to create a soundly backed security that will attract new money into the mortgage market, particularly from pension and retirement funds.

The Secretary of HUD continues to have general regulatory powers to assure that the purposes of the Charter Act are served. This office must authorize all issues of corporate securities and obligations. It participates in the decision-making process regarding the levels of mortgage purchases under varying economic conditions. It may also require that a reasonable portion of FNMA mortgage purchases be related to low and moderate income housing, but only under conditions of a reasonable economic return.

Later legislation.   Authority of FNMA to buy, sell, and otherwise deal in mortgages not federally insured or guaranteed (so-called conventional mortgages) was conferred by the Emergency Home Finance Act of 1970. A conventional single-family mortgage purchase program began in February 1972. FNMA continues to recognize that its primary responsibility is to the market for federally underwritten mortgages and expects for the foreseeable future that conventional mortgages will represent a small proportion of its total mortgage portfolio. Strict qualifications will be enforced to assure proper limitations on the additional risk inherent in operating in the conventional mortgage market.

Recent legislation has also extended the powers of FNMA to permit it to deal in loans made for the construction and modernization of hospital facilities. Authority to receive federal subsidies has been further extended to allow FNMA to absorb losses from ownership and disposition of federally insured low- and middle-income mortgages acquired at prices above those warranted by the going rates in the mortgage market.

FNMA purchasing procedure.[1]   The prices paid for mortgages are competitively determined by a procedure called the Free Market System Auction. FNMA offers 4-month and 12-month forward commitments that guarantee the availability of funds to purchase mortgages at a fixed rate. Separate auctions are held for conventional and federally underwritten mortgages. The mortgages may cover either new or existing homes or condominiums. Auctions are usually held on Mondays on a biweekly basis. Sellers are lending institutions such as banks, savings and loan associations, insurance companies, and mortgage bankers. Bids on the four-month commitment are called in by telephone on a yield basis. FNMA reviews the bids and decides how much it will commit that day.

Alternatively, a seller may submit a "noncompetitive" bid. By this bid a request is made for a commitment at the average yield accepted by FNMA on that auction day. The highest acceptable commitment amount for this type of

---

[1] For an excellent discussion of purchasing procedures of all governmental secondary market agencies, see Charles E. Wiggin, "Doing Business in the Secondary Mortgage Market," *Real Estate Review,* vol. 5, no. 2 (Summer 1975), pp. 84–95.

bid is $200,000, whereas competitive bids may be accepted up to $3 million. However, the lender submitting the noncompetitive bid is assured that he will get a commitment and not lose out in the bidding.

The results of the bidding are usually announced in financial publications, such as *The Wall Street Journal,* on the Tuesday following the auction. The range of yields accepted and the average yield applicable to noncompetitive bids are stated. The yields are net to FNMA after deduction of servicing fees.

In order to convert these yields to mortgage prices, FNMA uses the *FNMA Yield Book,* which it makes available to sellers upon request. Tables contained in this book are based on the assumption of a 30-year amortization schedule with a prepayment in 12 years. Any yield premium required above the nominal mortgage rate and after the .375 percent servicing fee is made up by discount points passed on to the builder or home owner. By rule of thumb, to effect about .25 percent higher yield, the mortgage loan disbursement at original issue must be at approximately 1.75 percent discount, or 98.25 percent of the stated obligation of the note.

Under FNMA's 12-month commitment procedure, the yield at which a commitment will be made is adjusted periodically and is usually published along with the free market auction results. The 12-month yields do not necessarily follow the free market pricing.

For these commitments, FNMA charges a fee of .5 percent which is due when it issues its acceptance statement, with an additional 1/100 percent (one basis point) for a competitive bid, whether or not it is accepted. There is an additional .125 percent fee on condominium loans when they are delivered.

Prior to sale of condominium loans conventionally financed, the lender must secure approval from FNMA. Such approval requires a formal application and review of all pertinent data regarding the project, such as plans and specifications, engineering and appraisal reports, and the builder's insurance and bonding protection. Condominiums financed under a FHA program do not require the same approval.

Purchasers of commitments may choose among three alternatives during the commitment period. They may (1) exercise their right to sell to FNMA, (2) decide to retain the mortgages for their own portfolio, or (3) sell the mortgages to another buyer. If option (2) or (3) is elected, FNMA simply receives the commitment fee for its agreement to stand ready to purchase.

Servicing of mortgages. For every mortgage offered to FNMA for purchase, the seller must provide a satisfactory service agreement. If the seller is itself qualified as an eligible servicer by FNMA standards, it will ordinarily be permitted to service the mortgage upon signing a servicing agreement with FNMA. In either event, the servicer must have an office with servicing facilities satisfactory to the Association within 100 miles of the mortgaged property. FNMA provides direct servicing of mortgages on multifamily dwellings. The duties of the servicer include collecting the mortgage installments and tax and insurance deposits, paying taxes and insurance premiums when due, and handling assessments and other charges against the property in such a manner as to keep the mortgage security good. The servicer is also required to make inspections of the property, personally service accounts that have become delinquent, maintain appropriate records, make a proper accounting for the funds it receives, and report what action it has taken on delinquent accounts. After it becomes apparent that a delinquent account cannot be salvaged short of foreclosure, the account may be turned over to the Association for further action.

FNMA sales procedure.   Although the major emphasis in the FNMA programs has been in the areas of mortgage purchases, at times an equally important function may be mortgage sales. Inherent in the performance of secondary market functions is that under certain conditions it is in the best interests of an orderly market that FNMA be a seller as well as a buyer. Sales from the portfolio of the secondary market operations are made at prices based on prevailing prices for similar classes of mortgages in the general secondary market, with due regard for the impact that the contemplated sales will have on future prices. Sales of home mortgages from the special assistance portfolio are not made at less than cost, while multifamily mortgages are sold on a negotiated basis.

Lists of mortgages for sale are available to prospective purchasers in the various Association agency offices. With respect to multifamily dwellings, FNMA will issue sales options under proper circumstances. As to other mortgages, those selected by a potential buyer will be reserved for his consideration and will not be available to any other investor for a period of 15 days. This period is allowed to give the prospective purchaser an opportunity to inspect the mortgage premises and examine the notes, mortgages, and other documents related to the security at the Association agency office. A sales price is quoted in the reservation letter sent by the Association to the prospective purchaser. This price, however, is subject to change without notice during the reservation period. The actual price paid is that in effect at the time of the signing of the FNMA mortgage sales agreement when the investor consummates his purchase. Upon receipt of the sales price, the investor is assigned the mortgage without recourse, subject to the servicing agreement between the Association and the servicer, which may be canceled on 30 days' notice.

Administration of FNMA.   The board of directors of FNMA consists of 15 members, one third of whom are appointed by the President of the United States and the remainder of whom are elected by the stockholders. All terms are for one year. The presidential appointments are required to include one person each from the homebuilding, real estate, and mortgage lending industries. All directors are removable by the President but only for good cause shown.

The chief executive officer of FNMA is its president. Other officers include a vice president, general counsel, secretary, treasurer, and controller. Because of the technical nature of the functions performed, employees are usually specialists who must meet high professional standards. The Association by its very nature, in its secondary market and other operations, must be exclusively sensitive to the national need and impervious to the exhortations of special interests if it is to fulfill its highest objectives as a supplement to the existing privately financed institutions. The work is conducted out of agency offices strategically located across the country.

The Government National Mortgage Association

The Government National Mortgage Association (GNMA), as previously mentioned, performs three principal functions. Briefly, these are (1) management and liquidating of previously acquired mortgages, (2) special assistance government lending in support of federal programs, and (3) guarantee of eligible mortgages to support a public market for mortgage pools and to assist FNMA. Its operations are financed through funds from the U.S. Treasury and from public borrowing.

Management and liquidating functions. The Charter Act of 1954 authorized FNMA to manage and to liquidate the existing mortgage portfolio at the close of its former operation as of October 31, 1954. In September 1959, Congress expanded the management and liquidating functions to authorize FNMA to purchase or make commitments to purchase, service, and sell any mortgages offered it by the Housing and Home Finance Agency (now the Department of Housing and Urban Development) where the Administrator deemed their acquisition by FNMA to be in the best interest of efficient management and liquidation. This authorization has been actively used. The management and liquidating functions are directed by statute to be carried out in an orderly manner with a minimum of adverse effect upon the residential mortgage market and a minimum loss to the federal government. This responsibility is now the obligation of GNMA.

Special assistance functions. In its assumption of responsibility for government special assistance functions, GNMA has acceded to the responsibility placed upon FNMA in the Charter Act of 1954. This act charged the Association with the obligation to provide special assistance in connection with certain residential mortgages when, and to the extent that, the President of the United States determines such assistance to be in the public interest. Under this function the Association also supports special housing programs as designated by the Congress. The special assistance program is specifically intended to meet two general needs. The first need relates to housing in underdeveloped areas. GNMA is charged with the responsibility, when the President so directs, of making financing available for selected types of residential mortgages (pending establishment of their marketability) which are originated under special housing programs designed to provide housing in areas where it cannot be provided under established home financing programs. The second great need arises when a decline in mortgage lending and home building threatens the stability of a high-level national economy.

To carry out the purposes of the special assistance functions, GNMA is authorized to purchase or enter into commitments to purchase mortgages or participations therein as directed by the president or as prescribed by law. So far as practicable, mortgages purchased under these functions must meet the purchase standards imposed by private institutional investors. The crucial factor justifying the purchase by GNMA is that because of other circumstances surrounding the location of the property, the borrower, or economic conditions, the mortgages are not likely to be readily acceptable to private lenders.

As with the other operations, the special assistance functions are contemplated to be fully self-supporting. Both commitment fees and purchase and marketing fees are charged. The principal source of income, of course, is interest from mortgages held. Income earned is retained as a reserve for losses and contingencies.

The mortgage-backed security program.   GNMA is authorized by Section 06 (g) of Title III of the National Housing Act to guarantee the timely payment of the principal and interest on securities that are based on or backed by a pool of mortgages insured by the FHA or Farmers Home Administration or guaranteed by the VA. The Department of Justice has rendered an opinion that the GNMA guarantee constitutes a full faith and credit obligation of the United States, and the Secretary of the Treasury has ruled that GNMA may properly borrow from the Treasury to meet its obligations under the guarantee.

The process of pool organization is initiated by a mortgage originator who becomes the issuer of the certificates. An issuer must be an FHA-approved mortgagee and GNMA seller-servicer in good standing; it must further meet a specific net worth test. FNMA and the Federal Home Loan Mortgage Corporation are also active as issuers. The issuer applies to GNMA for permission to issue certificates against the mortgage pool that the issuer has assembled or expects to assemble. The aggregate value of the pool must usually be at least $2 million. The mortgages must meet standards of homogeneity as to type, interest rates, and maturity. For example, single-family mortgages cannot be mixed with multifamily mortgages. Furthermore, the mortgages are required to be insured or guaranteed no more than one year prior to the date on which GNMA issues its commitment to guarantee the certificates.

Upon favorable response to the issuer's application, GNMA issues a commitment to guarantee the issuer's certificates at such time as the issuer can verify that it has good title to an acceptable pool of mortgages. Documents showing proper formation of the pool are then submitted to the bank or fiduciary that is to act as custodian. Upon appropriate acknowledgment of receipt of documents by the custodian, GNMA prepares the certificates for issue.

After the certificates are issued, the issuer assumes responsibility for servicing the loans and passing through to certificate holders their proportional share of monthly interest and amortization payments. The issues must also provide accounting statements reflecting the results of the certificate holder's participation in the pool.

In addition to the GNMA guarantee, several other features commend these securities to the whole investment spectrum, including savings and loan associations, savings banks, credit union, pension funds, commercial banks, insurance companies, corporations, and partnerships, as well as individuals. Although the security has many of the characteristics normally associated with direct investment in a first mortgage loan portfolio, it has the advantage of avoiding the management problems of loan origination and servicing. The improved marketability of the GNMA certificate over individual mortgages is a decided plus factor, particularly as the secondary market is expanding through active participation of major financial institutions. The price varies, of course, with current interest rates. Hence, if prevailing interest rates for comparable securities are lower than the face rate on the certificate, the security will sell at a premium; if higher, it will sell at a discount. The Internal Revenue Service has ruled that these certificates are "loans secured by an interest in real property." This ruling is of particular interest to savings and loan associations and savings banks, since it means that such securities do not jeopardize their eligibility for special bad debt reserve deductions permitted under the Internal Revenue Code. For income tax purposes, real estate investment trusts are to treat these securities as direct mortgage investments. The Internal Revenue Service has further held that the exempt status of employees' pension and profit-sharing funds is not adversely affected by ownership of these securities.

Many developments of the mortgage-backed security program are taking place. For example, "serial maturities" and pools of FHA-insured mobile home loans are logical extensions. A mortgage-backed security guaranteeing the interim payments on a construction loan can assist substantially in the financing of multifamily projects.

There are two basic groups of mortgage-backed securities: (1) pass-through securities and (2) mortgage-backed bonds. Each group has unique appeals and some different risk characteristics.

Pass-through securities. Pass-through securities are of two types: (1) standard and (2) modified.

Under the *standard* plan the total interest payment and principal amortization are passed through to the certificate holders on a monthly basis. As any mortgages become delinquent, they are immediately replaced from a reserve pool. In the alternative, a reserve fund may be established to offset principal losses from foreclosure. This plan terminates when all mortgages in the pool are paid off.

With *modified* pass-through securities, the investor has the interest and principal passed through less frequently than monthly, perhaps quarterly, semiannually, or annually. The payment is typically made to the investor at due date whether or not the funds are actually received from the mortgagor. Excess mortgage reserve pools or guarantee reserve funds are required of issuers under the modified plan as with the standard plan. This prevents loss of principal or interest by the security holders. There is some exposure to risk, however, in the modified plan where funds need to be reinvested pending disbursement to investors. In both standards and modified plans, prepayments are passed through to investors.

Mortgage-backed bonds. There are two classifications of mortgage-backed bonds: (1) sinking fund and (2) staggered maturity.

The *sinking-fund* mortgage-backed bond is similar to the modified pass-through security in that principal repaid from the underlying pool of mortgages is accumulated in a fund from which payments are later made to bondholders. The basic distinction from the pass-through obligation is that principal is paid in predetermined specific amounts, whether or not they are accumulated from the underlying mortgages. Similarly, interest obligations on the bonds must be met without regard to interest collections on the underlying mortgages. The bond principal maturity schedule can run ahead of mortgage amortization. The possibility of interest and principal payment demands exceeding collections places a contingent demand on the reserve financial strength of the issuer.

Staggered maturity bonds come due in a pattern designed to coincide with the expected accumulation of principal from the underlying pool of mortgages. Interest and principal payments are made on the bonds as they come due without regard to the amount collected on the mortgages. If mortgagors prepay or principal funds accumulate prior to bond maturity, there is a susbstantial reinvestment risk. Interest rates may have fallen, and the issuer may be hard-pressed to reinvest at a rate sufficient to keep up bond coupon payments at the higher rate. Issuers of such bonds must have a large enough net worth to absorb potential losses created by changes in the money market. The minimum net worth requirement has been $50 million. The minimum amount permitted in a single issue is $100 million. FNMA and the Federal Home Loan Mortgage Corporation have both issued bonds backed by federally underwritten mortgages. It is interesting to note, incidentally, that the Mortgage Guaranty Insurance Corporation (MGIC) has issued mortgage-backed bonds supported by privately insured conventional mortgages.

Optional-delivery commitment for purchase of GNMA securities. Because of the lapse of time necessary to assemble eligible mortgages in required quantities, potential issuers have prevailed upon GNMA to develop a standby commitment procedure to protect them from market risk during assembly. This is called an Optional-Delivery Commitment for Purchase of GNMA Securities. The commitment is issued for a nonrefundable fee of 1 to 1.5 percent, according to its duration. The interest rate of the commitment is determined by the "asked" side of the mortgage market. In this way, if rates move higher, the issuer is protected by this upper limit standby; while, if the rates decline, he simply disregards this protection and takes his securities directly to the market as originally planned.

The tandem plan. Besides supporting a public market for mortgage pools, GNMA also has the function of purchase and sale of FHA/VA mortgages pursuant to a cooperative system with FNMA known as the "tandem plan." The program combines the GNMA guarantee with the FNMA secondary market operation to maximize the utilization of special assistance funds voted by Congress.

By this plan, the financing is afforded eligible project sponsors in two steps. In the first step, GNMA issues a commitment to buy at par a mortgage upon completion of the qualified project. By prior arrangement, FNMA has agreed to purchase a certain amount of these mortgages at market prices. As the second step, the long-term mortgage may be sold to FNMA at the market price, with GNMA making up the difference of any discount between par and the market price.

The great advantage of this arrangement is its leverage to provide government assistance. Authorities state that the tandem plan can provide as much as 30 times the financing possible if GNMA were to buy and hold the mortgages outright. This is true because the privately derived funds of FNMA actually carry the mortgage with GNMA merely absorbing the discount.

Shortly after the tandem plan developed, GNMA discovered that it could mitigate its losses by selling the mortgages directly in the open market rather than to FNMA. First, GNMA determined that all such mortgages were eligible for inclusion in GNMA pass-though pools. Second, it recognized that mortgage bankers and other institutions seeking to build loan servicing volume would be willing to pay favorable prices, accepting some front-end losses, which could be more than offset against future GNMA loan-servicing business. The GNMA loan servicing free of .44 percent is particularly attractive as compared with the .375 percent more commonly paid. By taking advantage of this program, therefore, mortgage bankers and others may develop mortgage-backed securities pools and generate loan servicing business as phases of one overall operation.

Federal Home Loan Mortgage Corporation

Title III of the Emergency Home Finance Act of 1970 provided for the establishment of the Federal Home Loan Mortgage Corporation (FHLMC), often called Freddie Mac. Its designated purpose is to serve as a secondary market facility for real estate mortgages under the sponsorship of the Federal Home Loan Bank System.

The corporation is financed by $100 million of capital shares issued to the 12 district Federal Home Loan Banks. The stock may be retired by FHLMC if such retirement will not reduce surplus and reserves below $100 million. The FHLMC board of directors is composed of the three members of the Federal Home Loan Bank Board, whose chairman is also the chairman of the FHLMC board.

FHLMC has authority to buy and sell FHA and VA loans, conventional loans, and mortgage participations. It was particularly created to improve secondary market facilities for residential conventional mortgages, which have not had the benefit of federal insurance or guarantees. In order to increase availability of mortgage credit in this direction, FHLMC has authority to purchase conventional, as well as FHA or VA, mortgages from any Federal Home Loan Bank, the Federal Savings and Loan Insurance Corporation, any member of a Federal Home Loan Bank, or any financial institution whose deposits or accounts are insured by an agency of the United States. Since 1978, mortgage bankers have also been allowed to sell to the FHLMC.

FHLMC makes no direct loans to home buyers. It merely provides funds by an intermediary process following this pattern:

1. A home buyer seeks a mortgage loan from an institution eligible to sell to FHLMC.
2. As the institution becomes short of mortgage money to lend out, it may sell some of its existing mortgages to FHLMC.
3. FHLMC may then either sell these mortgages directly or market securities backed by the mortgages in the open capital market.

Mortgage production.[2]   FHLMC has five ongoing "over-the-counter" programs whereby it contracts to buy mortgages on a continuing basis. Delivery by the seller is mandatory. Failure to deliver may disqualify a seller for up to two years. Loans delivered must meet certain quality standards as well as specific legal requirements clearly defined by the enabling statute and the corporation. For example, loan amounts, loan-to-value ratios, private mortgage insurance coverage required, term, age, and necessary documentation are all delineated. Effective January 1, 1976, FHLMC/FNMA Uniform Mortgage Documents were instituted as a general requirement. The contract amount may range between $100,000 and $5 million. There is no contract fee for a Federal Home Loan Bank System member. For nonmembers, a fee of .375 percent of the contract amount is assessed.

Over-the-counter programs.   The purchase programs are as follows:

1. *Whole loan—single-family.*   FHLMC will purchase entire interests in eligible single-family conventional residential mortgages. The deal creating the mortgage may be closed after the date of contract, but the mortgage must be delivered within 60 days of that date. The maximum purchase price can never exceed par and will be adjusted to the nominal mortgage rate and contract yield requirements to FHLMC. The servicing fee to the seller is .375 percent.

2. *Whole loan—multifamily.*   FHLMC will purchase entire interests in eligible multifamily conventional residential mortgages. Rules for the closure, delivery, and maximum purchase price are similar to the single-family loans discussed above. The servicing fee runs to .25 percent of the first $250,000 of unpaid principal balance and .125 percent of the amount in excess.

---

[2] The authors gratefully acknowledge assistance from materials developed by Ronald D. Struck, assistant vice president, in regard to FHLMC operations.

3. *Participation—Class A offering.* FHLMC will purchase from 50 to 85 percent interests in eligible multifamily conventional mortgages. Mortgages must be closed prior to date of contract and delivery must be within 30 days. In this case, mortgages are purchased at a required net yield to FHLMC, so no servicing fee is paid as such. The seller retains any interest income over FMLMC's yield requirement as servicing income.

4. *Participation—Class B offering.* Under this program single-family conventional mortgages are included along with the multifamily mortgages listed in the Class A offering. The contracts will be to purchase 50 to 85 percent participations, but the multifamily mortgages may not exceed 50 percent of the total acquired under one contract. Closing and servicing fee provisions are the same as for the Class A offering.

5. *FHA/VA loans.* FHLMC will purchase entire interests in FHA- or VA-underwritten residential mortgages. Rules for closure, delivery, maximum purchase price, and servicing fees are similar to those applied to single family conventional loans discussed above.

Loan commitments. Over and above its over-the-counter purchase programs, FHLMC has offered forward commitments to purchase mortgages with delivery of the mortgage at the seller's option. These commitments have been for periods ranging from 6 to 24 months. They have been for virtually all types of eligible conventional and FHA/VA mortgages acceptable under the purchase programs. The interest rates for all FHLMC contract and commitment programs are established on a nationwide basis in the light of current conditions in the capital markets. Commitments are issued in dollar amounts only and never for specific projects. The seller or another party must originate the loan and deal with the mortgagor/builder. In this way FHLMC avoids direct competition with any primary mortgage lender.

Mortgage marketing. To finance its operations, FHLMC relies upon four principal methods. In order of importance, these are:

1. Borrowing from the Federal Home Loan Banks.
2. Issuance of GNMA-guaranteed mortgage backed bonds.
3. Issuance of participation sale certificates.
4. Direct sale of mortgages held.

FHLMC does not view its operation as simply mortgage warehousing. Its borrowing from the Federal Home Loan Banks is rather to facilitate a flow of mortgages from sellers to buyers in the secondary market. GNMA mortgage-backed bonds have been previously discussed in this chapter as important vehicles to achieve the standardization, quality, and ease of administration so important to an efficient secondary market. Mortgages directly sold suffer in several respects by comparison and are acceptable in a much more limited market. Participation sale certificates, on the other hand, offer in a different way the aforementioned advantages of GNMA mortgage-backed securities.

Their security is broadened to encompass the area of conventional mortgages. Typical certificates represent undivided interests in specified conventional mortgage participations owned by FHLMC. The total obligation is guaranteed by FHLMC.

Automated mortgage market information network.   As another assist to the secondary market for mortgages, FHLMC has played a key role in establishing a new corporation called AMMINET (an acronym for Automated Mortgage Market Information Network). Its purpose is to establish a direct electronic communication network among subscribers to the system. Subscribers may use the service to list specific terms of offers to buy or sell mortgages. Deals may be concluded over the telephone without reliance on an intermediary.

The mortgage-interest-rate futures market

The advance commitment from investors has long been a major tool of mortgage bankers to support interim financing to allow completion of construction and loan closing. The necessity for advance commitments has not changed, although the nature of the transaction is different, in the creation and marketing of mortgage pools to public investors. In the last few years, wide fluctuations in interest rates have accentuated the risks assumed by mortgage bankers, savings and loan institutions, commercial bankers, and other financial institutions assembling underlying mortgages over time for sale at a future date. A modest interest rate change during the period of packaging can easily wipe out the narrow profit spread that the issuer seeks. If he makes a commitment in June, for example, to deliver mortgages in September at a fixed rate and the market rate decreases, he cannot acquire the mortgages at yields high enough to match his commitment and he must lose his expected profits or incur a net loss. A facility for shifting the interest rate risk to those willing to assume it has been sorely needed.

On October 20, 1975, the Chicago Board of Trade instituted trading in mortgage interest rate futures options. These options were developed primarily to provide a capability for institutional hedging against mortgate interest rate risk. This market operates on the same pattern as futures options for wheat, soybeans, cotton, shell eggs, pork bellies, and many other commodities. Hedgers are those who must accept ownership risks in these commodities and who seek to avert the risk of price fluctuation by taking an opposite position in the future market, selling against their inventories to speculators. These sales are customarily made to option buyers who are not interested in the commodities as such, merely in their price fluctuations.

The commodity-like trading unit established for trading mortgage interest rate options is a GNMA-backed modified pass-though certificate in the amount of $100,000 at 8 percent per annum. Prices are quoted as a percentage of par.

The minimum fluctuation is .03125 percent of par, or $31.25 per contract. The daily limit of price movement is $750 per contract. Contract delivery months are March, June, September, and December. Since September 12, 1978, similar options have also been traded on the American Commodity Exchange. On that exchange contract delivery months are February, May, August, and November.

To make the conversion from yield to price of the security, or vice versa, tables have been developed.[3] The yields are computed under the assumption of simple, uncompounded monthly payments of principal and interest at 8 percent on a 30-year mortgage, with prepayment in the 12th year. A partial listing of the price-yield relationship is presented in the following tabulation:

Yield (percent)	Price*
7.00	107–12
7.50	103–12
8.00	99–22
8.50	96–03
9.00	92–22
9.50	89–15
10.00	86–12
10.50	83–14
11.00	80–20
11.50	77–30
12.00	75–13
12.50	72–31
13.00	70–21
13.50	68–14
14.00	66–10
14.50	64–09

* Numbers to the right of the dash are 32ds. Thus, 107–12 means 107 12/32 percent of par. Prices are quoted as points and 32ds.

Quotations in terms of the prices shown above may be found daily in *The Wall Street Journal* and other publications carrying Chicago Board of Trade and American Commodity Exchange reports.

An example will illustrate how the hedging process may be useful to a mortgage assembler. The transaction may be summarized as follows:

Cash market	Futures market
June 1	*June 1*
He sells $1 million 8 percent GNMA-backed mortgages to a bank at a price of 80–20 to yield about 11 percent for delivery on December 1.	He buys $1 million (10) December futures contracts at 80–20.

---

[3] *GNMA Yield and Price Equivalent Tables* may be acquired through Financial Publishing Company, 82 Brookline Avenue, Boston, Mass., 02215.

If the assembler continues to originate 8 percent mortgages and the market acquisition rate drops to 10 percent for the period, assuming the options market follows the same pattern, the following theoretical result may be achieved:

Cash market	Futures market
December 1	*December 1*
He delivers the $1 million mortgages costing 86–12 to the bank at 80–20. A *loss* of 5–24 (5 24/32) points is realized. This amounts to $57,500.	He sells back his $1 million December futures contracts costing 80–20 for 86–12. He thus *gains* 5–24 points, or $57,500.

If, instead, the market acquisition rate rises to 12 percent, with a similar move in the options market, the December results would be:

Cash market	Futures market
December 1	*December 1*
He delivers the $1 million mortgages costing 75–13 to the bank at 80–20. A *gain* of 5–7 (5 7/32) points is realized. This amounts to $52,188.	He sells back his $1 million futures contracts costing 80–20 for 75–13. He therefore *loses* 5–7 points, or $52,188.

In this case, it will be seen that the mortgage assembler has successfully shifted his interest rate risk from himself to the options market. Of course, entailed in this shift is the sacrifice of any profits that might accrue from a favorable rate change during the risk period. Furthermore, it must be recognized that the futures market does not follow the cash markets precisely, and there are transactions costs. The trends and degrees of change, however, are close enough to make the exercise desirable under many conditions.

The foregoing example is known as a "long," or "buy," hedge, where the hedger seeks initially to lock in his delivery price. A different type of protection is afforded by the "short," or "sell," hedge. The latter pattern is typically used by a mortgage banker who is planning to market his pool at a future date to investors who will be willing to pay the current market rate at the time of marketing the pool certificates. He sells futures options as he acquires mortgages, thus locking in protection at his acquisition rate for each mortgage parcel of his pool.

The mortgage interest-rate futures market also holds attraction to mortgage bankers, assembling conventional mortgages for thrift institutions, FNMA, or FHLMC. When these institutions curtail their purchases and the mortgage bankers find they must warehouse their "homeless" mortgages for a while, hedging can protect them from major losses from interest rate fluctuations. The availability of the futures market further enhances the potential of the FHLMC commitment program for its approved sellers/services. For this reason, FHLMC has been a strong advocate of the development of the options market. To students of interest rates, there are numerous market strategies to which a use of the options market may be adapted.

Questions

1 What is a secondary mortgage market and why is it necessary?

2 What were the three principal activities of FNMA under its 1954 charter? How are they now administered? What is GNMA?

3 How are the secondary market operations of FNMA financed?

4 Describe the purchasing procedures whereby FNMA acquires mortgages in connection with its secondary market operations.

5 How are mortgages acquired by FNMA serviced?

6 What are the principal activities of GNMA?

7 Describe the federally insured mortgage-backed securities program as administered through GNMA. What is the tandem plan?

8 What is the Federal Home Loan Mortgage Corporation (FHLMC)? Why was it created?

9 What are the principal sources of funds from which FHLMC finances its operations?

10 What are the major FHLMC secondary market programs?

11 What are the functions of the mortgage interest rate futures market?

Case problems

1 You are an institutional mortgage lender. Your local market is too restricted to generate enough loans to utilize your facilities fully. You seek out a mortgage banker with an active market in a neighboring locality. He agrees to close $500,000 of mortgage loans meeting FHLMC specifications in your name at 9 percent plus 2 points. To accomplish this for you, it is agreed that he is to receive 1 point and out-of-pocket costs in connection with loan origination.

How may the secondary market provided by FHLMC be used to your advantage?

2 Trace through the consequences and compute the yield to the mortgage assembler from the following transaction:

Assume you have $1,176,470 in mortgages yielding an aggregate of 8 percent—about 50 percent single-family and 50 percent multifamily and eligible for FHLMC Class B participation—available for sale. FHLMC purchased 85 percent of the total ($1,000,000) under its participation plan to yield 7.75 percent to FHLMC.

3 *a.* On August 1, a mortgage assembler sells $1 million 8 percent GNMA-backed mortgages to a bank to yield 10 percent. Delivery was contracted for December 1. How may he establish a hedge to protect himself against the possibility of a drop in interest rates during his acquisition period?

b. Assuming that the market acquisition rate did in fact drop to 9.5 percent for the period, and that the cash and options markets moved together, what will be the results of a hedge transaction entered into on the August 1st date?

4 *a.* On March 1, a mortgage banker makes a commitment to acquire a $1 million mortgage pool, based on current GNMA-backed 8 percent certificates, at 83.14 (approximately 10.5 percent yield). How may he hedge to protect himself if he will not be marketing the mortgages until September 15?

b.   Assuming the yield on this class of mortgages rises to 11.5 percent by September 15, what will be the results as the mortgage pool certificates are sold in the market and the hedge is closed?

5   Several brokerage houses and banks have worked as dealers in GNMA-backed securities. Obtain a prospectus of a GNMA-backed security issue marketed through one of your local houses, and study it in depth. You may particularly want to study the functions of origination, trading, and management of the security position (long or short), sales activities to thrift institutions and others, and cashier obligations, as well as the terms of the issue itself.

Rural real estate credit and the Farmers Home Administration

25

Meaning of farms

The American farm combines both residential and business uses in its real estate relationship. It affords a place for the owner-operator and his family to live while it provides them with their means of livelihood. In times past, the farmer has been looked upon as a grower of crops and farm animals. To an increasing extent he has become a business executive. Like any other type of business, farming requires capital. Requirements for this purpose cover real estate capital, machinery, working capital, and contributions to cooperative ventures.

Real estate capital, with which we are primarily concerned in this study, covers the cost of land and its more or less permanent improvements. The latter include the home, various types of farm buildings, fences, drainage, and, in some cases, irrigation and terracing. These costs add up to the greatest proportion of the capital investment of the farmer.

Determinants of amount of investment

The amount invested by an individual farmer in his real estate is governed by several unrelated factors. The type of farming, of course, helps to set the pattern of investment. The size of the farm in turn helps to determine the use made of it. The period of the business cycle is a major factor in the pricing of farms. The price paid measures the kind and amount of financing needed. One interesting feature of farm financing that has assumed greater importance in recent years is the competition of city folk in the purchase of farms. There has always been a feeling on the part of many city dwellers that ownership of a farm is quite desirable. More recently, several new factors have accentuated this feeling. In groping for security in an uncertain world, people seem to feel that farming offers a better than usual sense of protection to farm owners. Many people feel that nothing can happen to interfere materially with farm ownership. Some city people have purchased farms as a hedge against inflation. Others have purchased rundown farms as a means of equalizing income tax burdens. Whatever the incentive that impels city people to purchase farms, the effects of their competition complicate the financial problems of farmers who hope to make a business of farming.

Sources of farm capital

Traditionally, the typical cycle that eventually leads to farm ownership, by those who make farming a business as owner-operators, begins with the small savings of a boy on the farm. These are added to as the young man works as a hired hand until the equity capital necessary for a venture on his own takes form. Seldom can a young man hope to own a farm unless he inherits it. Ownership comes in the middle life of the farmer who buys a farm. Until the person ambitious to become a farm owner acquires some capital through savings, he will probably maintain his status as a laborer working for someone else.

With some capital accumulated through savings, the farmer may become his own manager through one of the following processes: (1) He may enter into partnership with someone else. (2) He may become a tenant instead of a laborer for hire. (3) He may use some kind of credit arrangement to add to his equity capital the amount needed for acquiring a farm.

Partnership. Partnerships are commonly used in farm operation. One partner, frequently the inactive one, owns the farm and takes into partnership a younger man with experience and usually some capital. Sometimes even the capital is absent. The owner of the farm matches his capital against the skill of the younger man. Father and son and father and son-in-law partnerships are very common. Two brothers may become partners. Or partnerships are arranged in which no blood or marital relationship exists between the participants.

Farm partnerships have the advantage of encouraging long-range planning which may end in a transfer of title to the land at the death of the older member of the firm. They are frequently entered into without written or formal agreement. The imposition of personal income taxes probably did more to require an accounting of income between partners than had ever been done before. As a general rule, farmers have not been accustomed to distinguishing sharply between income and capital investment. This has been true of partnerships as well as of other types of business organization on the farm.

Because of the prevalence of the father-son origin of farm partnerships, the problem of lines of authority takes on interesting patterns. The older man tends to make the decisions at the outset, but, if all goes well, more and more he defers to the wishes of the younger partner, until finally the original position is reversed. Eventually, the son may, to all intents and purposes, become the owner, with the father being supported by the son as his share in the fruits of the partnership.

Leasing. In the absence of a father-son partnership, and particularly if the farm owned by the father is not large enough to support two families, the younger man may lease a farm instead. Although he is expected to have some capital, he can enter the farming business by using the real estate capital of someone else. In return for the use of this capital, he pays a share of the crops, or a cash rental, or a combination of the two. Some farmers prefer a lease to farm ownership, especially in times when the price of land is very high. By renting land owned by someone else, they can continue to add to their savings, pending a decline in prices.

Some farmers own the place that provides them with a home and lease additional land for productive purposes. Sometimes that partnership arrangement discussed above is made possible by leasing adjoining or nearby land. By this means not only is additional land acquired, but a home needed for the younger member of the partnership is made available also. Some city people who own farms but are unacquainted with their operation are very glad to shift the burdens of management to a tenant skilled in farm operation.

The lease arrangement avoids some of the difficulties occasionally encountered in partnerships. Under a proper form of lease, the landlord is concerned only with end results. Meantime, management is centered in the tenant. At the same time, tenancy lacks the stability of a partnership arrangement. Leases are likely to run one year at a time or on a year-to-year basis. Some of the work on a farm and some of the investment by the tenant must necessarily look beyond this short period for results.

A modification of farm leasing takes the form of a manager-operator agreement. The owner of the farm hires a manager who operates the farm, with all capital being supplied by the owner. By a kind of profit-sharing plan, the hired manager is permitted to share in the results of his labors over and above a stipulated salary for his services.

Like partnerships, leases are frequently informal and oral rather than written. As in other business matters, a more formal written lease is recommended. Like other leases, farm leases should include all practicable provisions to make sure of complete meeting of minds between the tenant and the landlord. In general, a lease that leans too far in the direction of protecting either party to the disadvantage of the other is not likely to endure for long or to produce satisfactory results.

Use of credit. As a business loan, the financing of farm real estate is expected to be repaid from the income from farm operations. While the lender will look to the appraisal of the security for the loan as a basis for his decisions, neither he nor the borrower expects to have the loan repaid from the proceeds of the sale of the property. Here, as elsewhere in real estate finance, a distinction must be made between a safe loan and a sound one. A lender may feel safe in making a loan if the liquidating value of the security will be at least equal to the amount of the loan. But a borrower who would expect to use this means of meeting his obligations would not be making a sound business commitment.

Because most farms are family operated, the personal equation in farm loans is particularly significant. The lender gives great weight to the moral hazard. An ambitious, experienced farmer can obtain real estate financing of greater advantage to him than he could if his reputation for integrity and skill were less favorable. The lender knows that he is taking the risk of managerial ability and acts accordingly. In analyzing the moral hazard, the family is included in the lender's calculations. As a family-operated business, farming reflects the type of family as well as the type of head of the household. The attitude of the wife toward farming and farm life may be nearly as important as that of the borrower. Farm productivity, in terms of dollar income, is frequently definitely related to the interest taken by the wife in farm operations.

Increasing demand for credit. In looking into the future, it seems probable that farmers will depend more upon credit facilities in financing their operations than has been true in the past. The reasons for this change are: (1) The average size of farms is increasing. Increased mechanization makes possible the handling of more acres with the same man power. (2) This increased mechanization calls for larger capital investment. (3) Soil exhaustion requires greater attention to and investment in rehabilitation and conservation programs. (4) Many farmers are reaching an age when they are no longer able to continue to handle their acreage. With higher prices of farms, the transfer of these holdings to younger men will call for more credit than was needed when the present farmers acquired their holdings.

Factors considered by lender. In addition to the moral hazard, the lender on farm real estate takes into account various factors that may not be present in considering urban real estate as security for loans. Loans are made not on acres alone but upon the productivity of those acres. Erosion and wastage as well as fertility must be studied, since the loan will be repaid over a long period of time. The lender must look to the productivity of the farm over a series of years as the source of repayment of his loan. Hence, he tries to measure it as best he can.

The size of the farm is important. Since it must first afford a living to its owners, the lender wants to make sure that there will be enough left to pay taxes and operating expenses—including reasonable allowances to maintain the productivity of the land—and still leave a balance of income from which the mortgage can be amortized. Even a well-operated small farm might be a poor lending risk because of the absence of a debt-paying balance of income.

As a business executive seeking a business loan, the farmer must be able to demonstrate his efficiency as a manager. Operating costs should be consistent with a productive unit of the kind that a borrower should offer as security for a loan. Evidence of lack of balance in the investment of capital or in the use of labor will not produce a high credit rating for lending purposes. For example, some farms are inefficiently operated because their owners or operators economize too much in the use of laborsaving machinery; others lean in the opposite direction and are burdened with more mechanization than the particular farm can support.

To an increasing extent farmers are required, for one reason or another, to keep accounting records of their operations. When the owner of a farm makes an application for a real estate loan, he must be in a position to tell what he owns and what he owes. His net worth will go a long way toward determining his borrowing capacity. Not only will the lender be interested in the use of a microscope but he will want to use his telescope also. He will want to know in detail the current condition of the business and also the progress of the operations as compared with those in preceding periods. An increase in assets or a decrease in debts indicates an increase in net worth. The opposite tendency in either would speak against an extension of too much credit to the applicant for a real estate loan. Changes in price levels are taken into account in measuring changes in net worth.

In some respects an income statement is even more useful in measuring debt-paying capacities than is a balance sheet. The latter is somewhat of a liquidation measure; the former tests the farm operation as a going concern. As might be expected, adequate and accurate income statements for farm operations are more rare than balance sheets. They are becoming more common. County extension agents are rendering worthwhile service in encouraging accounting records. The farmer who keeps them is a better credit risk than one who does not.

Types of farm mortgages.   As stated above, farm mortgages should be paid out of income. The type of mortgage most likely to meet the needs of most farmers runs for a long period of time—10, 20, 30, or, in some cases, as long as 40 years; is payable in annual or semiannual installments; and carries a low rate of interest, since the average return on farm capital is low. Some years may show higher than average returns, but others will show lower rates of return, depending upon prices of farm products, crop yields, and other factors.

Term loans fail to meet the needs of most farmers. If a lump-sum mortgage falls due at an inopportune time, when renewals are not favored and refinancing is unavailable, trouble for the borrower may result. Foreclosure marks the end of the trail for many such mortgages.

Sinking fund for future payments.   Because of the irregularity of farm income, some farm mortgages provide that the borrower may build up in high-income years what amounts to a sinking fund to take care of installments in lean years. If such funds are credited with the same rate of interest as is charged on the mortgage, the effect is about the same as if prepayments had been allowed. The difference lies in the fact that prepayments might not be considered by the lender as an offset to no payments when farm income is low. Both the Federal Land Bank System and some private lenders on farm security encourage the practice of developing a fund to take care of some future payments.

Timing of payments. Unlike mortgage payments on residential properties in urban areas, where the monthly payment direct reduction loan plan has become the common pattern, farmers make their payments less frequently. Payments are most commonly made on an annual, semi-annual, or quarterly basis. Which of these plans is followed is determined by the nature of the farming operations. In areas where cash crops are harvested once a year, annual payments best meet the requirements of the borrower. Where tradition dictates a semiannual contract, borrowers frequently become six months in arrears unless their cash income permits payments more often than once a year. In the infrequent cases where income is collected more frequently, the payments may even be met quarterly without inconvenience to the borrower. For example, dairy farmers might readily meet quarterly payments on their mortgages.

Rehabilitation financing. Where farmers undertake a program of soil rehabilitation or a conservation program, the amounts so invested cover a series of years. Some mortgages are so written as to provide for advances as needed for this purpose. The repayment of these advances is arranged in such a manner as to permit the anticipated increase in yield to pay the cost of the program. In order to play safe, only a portion of the anticipated increased yield—perhaps 75 percent—is required to repay the loan. In some cases only a small part of the advances is required to be repaid annually until the entire program is completed. Then the repayments are increased to amortize the advances over a period comparable to those of ordinary farm mortgage loans.

In financing any such operations, the lender must make sure that the borrower proceeds under the guidance of experts, so that the funds advanced will be spent in such a manner that their recovery within a reasonable time may be expected. The usual period for repayment of such loans runs from 5 to 15 years. This is an area of financing in which neither the lender nor the borrower is presumed to be expert. Both need the advice and guidance of specialists capable of fitting a conservation program to the needs of a specific farm.

Appraisals for farm loans. The average appraiser who appraises property for the purpose of making loans on urban real estate would be of little use to lenders on farm property. Since farm loans are made on the business of farming, the appraiser must be able to set loan values on more than land and permanent improvements. He must be able to measure the selling price of the land and also its earning capacity. The latter is conditioned by the character of the management of the farm, so that this must be reviewed also.

Unlike loans against urban real estate, farm mortgages do not really constitute the first private claim against the property offered as security. Since the farmer-borrower and his family make their living from the operation of the farm, their living expenses constitute the first deduction from farm income. To be sure, their standard of living will probably be lowered in times of reduced income, but they nevertheless depend upon farm income to pay their family expenses. Then, unless the lender is willing to foreclose his mortgage at the first sign of default, he must allow the borrower enough to continue to pay operating expenses, including ordinary repairs and maintenance costs. All of these considerations must be taken into account in appraising farms for lending purposes.

Because the lender must always take into account the possibility of foreclosure as a last resort, he must consider the problem of future salability of the farm. Here even apparently extraneous factors must be studied. Among them are such subjects as the condition of roads, the proximity of schools, and the availability of markets.

Sources of funds for farm mortgages

The sources of funds for loans on farm mortgages as security are, in order of volume: individuals and others, Federal Land Banks, insurance companies, and commercial banks. The miscellaneous group of individuals and others account for approximately 40 percent of farm mortgage loans. Individual lenders are present when the seller of a farm takes back a purchase-money mortgage as part payment for his property, when a father or other relative sets up a young man in the farming business, or when the funds needed by the borrower are obtained for a person of means who is willing to invest funds in farm mortgages.

In spite of the prevalence of farm mortgages held by individuals, this class of loans is ordinarily made with less attention to safeguarding the interests of both mortgagor and mortgagee than is true of institutional lenders. In many cases no expert appraiser is asked to give an opinion of value. The borrower and the lender agree upon the value of the property for lending purposes. Particularly if a purchase-money mortgage is involved, the needs of the borrower rather than the value of the property may determine the amount of the loan. This may later cause trouble for both borrower and lender.

As a general rule, the term of mortgages made by individuals is shorter than is that of mortgages held by financial institutions. Interest rates are relatively high where no family relationships are involved, with wide variations in specific cases. Short terms and high interest rates result in higher than average installment payments. Unless the payments are carefully geared to the income-producing capacity of the farm, trouble may result.

Included in the miscellaneous category of farm mortgage lenders are the usual sources of real estate finance with urban land as security. They cover savings and loan associations, mortgage loan companies which represent life insurance companies and other institutional investors, and so forth. In some localities, school funds are invested in farm mortgages. Endowment funds of educational and charitable institutions provide sources of farm mortgage finance. As with individuals who invest in farm mortgages, there is no common pattern of mortgage lending by miscellaneous sources. Expert appraisals may be lacking, and attention to the details of sound mortgage lending may be overlooked.

In general, individual and miscellaneous lenders do not hold enough mortgages to give them a wide distribution of risks. With limited resources they may not be able to pursue policies more flexible than those set forth in the mortgage instrument. Under the best of circumstances, they may not be able to help the borrower meet unusually difficult financial problems. Since the lender usually dictates the terms of an unstandardized loan pattern, he is likely to make sure that his interests rather than those of the borrower are taken care of.

Life insurance companies. Life insurance companies have experienced a long and varied history as holders of farm mortgages. They tend to concentrate their farm loans in the best-developed areas and upon relatively large individual loans. In some cases they make loans directly through their branch offices, and in other cases they purchase farm mortgages from mortgage bankers and others. Even commercial banks sometimes have purchase agreements with life insurance companies by which the bank may hold a mortgage for a short period of time—as much as two years—and then dispose of it to an insurance company.

Some insurance companies offer long-term farm financing at low rates of interest. Some of these loans may run as long as 40 years. Several amortization plans are used, most of which provide for some kind of prepayment privileges, provided that these advance payments arise from farm income.

Commercial banks. In their real estate lending operations, commercial banks are subject to various kinds of limitations. The laws and regulations under which they operate set standards that must be observed. In addition to legal restrictions, policies established by boards of directors of commercial banks limit their real estate lending operations. Some will make no farm loans under any circumstances; others favor this type of lending. Still others prefer a balanced program in which farm loans play some part.

In rural areas, commercial banks constitute the largest segment of institutional lenders who hold farm mortgages. Here again, governmental restrictions determine the kinds of loans made. National banks may make unamortized five-year loans up to 50 percent of appraised value. They may also make amortized loans. On such loans they may lend up to 66.67 percent of the appraisal value on a ten-year maturity if 40 percent of the principal amount is to be amortized over the life of the loan. As an alternative, they may lend up to 90 percent of the appraised value for a term not longer than 30 years if the loan is secured by an amortized mortgage, deed of trust, or other instrument under the terms of which the installment payments are sufficient to amortize the entire principal of the loan within the period ending on the date of its maturity. Most commercial bank loans on farm mortgages tend to be of the relatively shorter maturities.

Federal Land Banks.   The 12 Federal Land Banks, through national farm loan associations, make long-term mortgage loans to farmers and ranchers. As of the end of 1979, the amount of farm mortgages held by Federal Land Banks was slightly more than $31.2 billion.

Such loans are limited to 65 percent of the normal value of the security when used for agricultural purposes. Only those who derive the principal part of their income from farming operations are eligible for Land Bank loans. Such persons may obtain loans to purchase land for agricultural purposes, to make improvements in the form of buildings or otherwise, to refinance debts at least two years old, and to provide funds for long-term agricultural purposes.

Land Bank loans may be made for periods of from 5 to 40 years. Appraisals are made by experienced Land Bank appraisers. All such loans must be collateralized by first mortgages. In addition, each borrower must purchase stock in the Land Bank which makes the loan equal to 5 percent of the amount of the loan. This, too, is held as collateral to protect the loan. Finally, the national farm loan association which recommends the loan must endorse the note given by the borrower.

Interest rates on Land Bank loans are conservative. Farmers obtaining loans from this source are required to pay interest at rates based on the cost of money in the investment market and the cost of operations.

Servicing of Land Bank loans.   Land Bank loans are serviced through the national farm loan associations. When the borrower gets into financial difficulty, forbearance is exercised whenever the borrower is deemed to have a reasonable opportunity to catch up on his obligations. Deferments, extensions, and suspended-payment plans have been developed for this purpose. Loans are sometimes recast, and a new plan of amortization is set up. When foreclosure has been necessary, deficiency judgments have not been enforced for amounts greater than the difference between the fair value of the property and the amount of investment shown on the books of the lender. As soon as full recovery is realized, any additional claims are voluntarily released, provided there is no evidence of bad faith on the part of the borrower.

Farmers Home Administration

In 1946 Congress set up the Farmers Home Administration (FmHA) to insure or guarantee private loans or to lend appropriated funds to farmers unable to obtain financial assistance from any other source. Since that time the agency has grown and its functions have expanded to include many areas of rural real estate financing. Currently, rural people may look to the FmHA to help purchase or operate farms, provide new employment and business opportunities, buy homes, and improve the environment or general community living standards. Some loans are strictly for individuals and their families. The concept of "individual" may, however, extend to agriculture-related partnerships and corporations. Other loans are made only to groups, such as associations, partnerships, corporations, or public bodies. The purposes may be nonprofit or for profit subject to limitations.

By classification, the principal types of loans for individuals, as broadly defined, are:

Farm ownership loans.	Farm operating—youth loans.
Rural housing loans.	Farm emergency loans—economic and disaster.
Soil and water loans.	Business and industrial loan guaranties.
Recreation loans.	

Loan programs for groups include:

Rental and cooperative housing loans.
Rural housing site development loans.
Self-help technical assistance grants.
Loans for community facilities.
Grants to energy-impacted communities.
Planning grants.
Industrial development grants.
Indian land acquisition loans.
Grazing association loans.
Rural conservation and development and watershed loans.
Irrigation and drainage loans.

A common requirement, as indicated above, is that the applicant is unable to obtain credit on reasonable terms elsewhere. The agency's function is to provide a supplemental source of credit, augmenting the efforts of private lenders rather than competing with them. Furthermore, under most of the FmHA programs the borrowers are required to refinance with commercial credit conventionally when they become able to do so.

In most programs the credit may be provided alternatively in the form of an insured loan from a private lender or a direct FmHA loan. Because of the limited appropriation of government funds, loans made under the insurance operation greatly predominate over the direct loans. In either case, the credit arrangements are generous when the FmHA assists the borrower, and he often ends up with better terms than could be obtained from a private lender alone if he had been able to meet ordinary credit standards.

Of the numerous loan programs listed, the most significant are those for farm ownership, rural housing, business and industrial purposes, and rental and cooperative housing. These programs are therefore described in greater detail.

Farm ownership loans.   Insured and direct farm ownership loans are made to help farmers and ranchers acquire and operate family farms. Operations, however, may include establishment and operation of nonfarm enterprises to supplement farm income. The enterprise must be located or headquartered on the borrower's farm, but the operations may be so widely variant as to include a repair shop, service station, grocery store, sporting goods store, beauty or barber shop, cabinet shop, or other viable business.

Who may borrow.   To be eligible, the loan applicant must:

1. Be a U.S. citizen of legal age.
2. Have sufficient farm experience and training to assure reasonable prospects of success. If the loan is for a nonfarm enterprise, the same standard is applied for that activity, although he need not have personally operated this type of business previously.
3. Be of good character.
4. Be unable to obtain credit from other sources on reasonable terms.

Terms and security.   The rate on these loans is conservative, with maturities not to exceed 40 years. The maximum FmHA real estate loan is $200,000, with the total real estate debt against the security limited to $225,000, or the market value of the farm, whichever is less. Farm ownership loans must be secured by a mortgage on land owned or purchased by the borrower. The borrower is expected to refinance the unpaid balance due on his loan as soon as he is able to do so on reasonable terms from another lender.

Rural housing loans.   The objective of rural housing loans is to assist eligible individual rural residents, farmers, and senior citizens to obtain adequate housing. Funds from these loans may be used to buy, build, repair, improve, or relocate homes and to buy minimum adequate sites.

Who may borrow.   To be eligible, the borrower must:

1. Be a U.S. citizen or permanent resident of good character.
2. Be of moderate or low income without adequate housing; or be a farm owner without adequate housing for his family or his tenant, share croppers, farm laborers, or farm manager.
3. Have sufficient income prospects to meet a reasonable projection of expenses and loan repayment requirements.
4. Be unable to obtain credit elsewhere.
5. Seek housing located in rural areas, open country, towns, villages, and places without more than 20,000 population that are rural in character and not associated with an urban area.

Terms and security.   Loans may be up to 100 percent of FmHA appraised value. Interest rates are established by the FmHA. An interest credit may be granted on loans to low-income families that may reduce the effective rate to the borrower to as low as 1 percent. Co-signers may be used, and the repayment period may extend up to 33 years. Loans may be made on owned land or on leased land where the lease is for a sufficient term. On loans for regular housing purposes, the lease should be for at least 50 years. Repair loans are generally approved if the term of the lease is at least one and one half times the repayment period of the loan.

Business and industrial loan guaranties. In the interest of broadening the economic bases of rural areas and towns up to 50,000 population, the FmHA guarantees business and industrial loans made by private lenders on real estate and other security. Such loans may be used for the acquisition, improvement, or control of rural businesses or industries.

Who may borrow? These loan guaranties from the FmHA are available to individuals, cooperatives, corporations, partnerships, Indian tribal groups, municipalities, counties, and other state political subdivisions. The borrower must first meet the credit tests of the private lender, and its credit worthiness is then reviewed by the FmHA.

Terms and security. Since the loans are made by a private lender, the interest rates and maturities are negotiated, within limits, by the borrower and the lender. The FmHA then guarantees up to 90 percent of the loan for a fee. This fee is .5 percent if the initial maturity date is one year or less. For a guaranty on business or industrial, operating, and production-type emergency loans, the fee is 1 percent for each three-year period or part thereof. Mortgage security on real estate and other assets satisfactory to both the lender and the FmHA is required.

Rental and cooperative housing loans. Another objective of the FmHA is to increase the amount of available and adequate rental and cooperatively owned housing designed and constructed for occupancy by low- and moderate-income families and senior citizens. There is, in particular, a serious shortage of good rental housing in rural areas and small towns. To help reduce this shortage, the FmHA assists individuals and both nonprofit and profit organizations in financing new rental units or bringing existing properties up to standard.

To qualify for FmHA assistance, the applicant for a loan must establish that three conditions exist:

1. There must be a need for rental housing in the area.
2. The housing contemplated fits the needs of prospective tenants from the standpoint of design, location, and cost.
3. Good management of the project will be provided.

To answer the questions posed by the requirements listed above, the FmHA looks at:

1. Economic conditions and trends in the community.
2. Estimate of number of houses or apartments in the area currently for rent.
3. Characteristics of available rental housing, such as location, quality and size of units, type of building, age of structure, vacancy rate, reasons for vacancies, and rental levels.

4. Characteristics of the eligible occupants, such as single or couples, male or female, size and composition of family, and number of senior citizens and nonsenior citizens.
5. Income and financial condition of the people in the area who would be eligible to occupy the housing as planned.
6. Present living arrangements of eligible occupants in the area and the extent to which inadequate housing is associated with health or financial conditions.
7. Estimate of the number of eligible occupants who are willing and financially able to occupy the proposed housing.
8. Financial responsibility and managerial competency of the applicant.
9. Architectural planning.
10. Site selection.
11. Financial planning.

Financial planning.   Since the financial arrangements are of great concern to potential organizers of a rural rental project, the terms, limitations, and inducements are discussed in greater detail. An example is also presented.

Terms and security.   Interest rates are set in accordance with current market conditions and can be obtained by calling a local FmHA office. Borrowers agreeing to rent to low-income tenants may receive interest credits to reduce the effective rate to as low as 1 percent. Although the government will require that the loan be secured adequately, the loan-to-value ratio may run as high as 95 percent. Furthermore, only 2 percent of the remaining 5 percent equity requirements must be deposited in cash as initial operating expense. The other 3 percent may be earned as architectural or legal fees, or by performance of other services, such as engineering, and so on. An additional advantage to the applicant may be granted in appropriate cases in the form of a waiver of individual personal liability. In this instance, the government looks exclusively to the project value for recovery of the loan balance. Where FmHA administrators approve limited profit partnerships, this form, in particular, can be profitably used despite a limitation of 8 percent return on equity investment. An attractive tax shelter is provided the investor in the depreciation deductible by the partners in such a venture. Corporations are generally less popular because the operating losses generated by the depreciation cannot be passed through the corporate entity and the prescribed return allowable to a stockholder has been found to be inadequate.

To induce more construction of this type of housing, the FmHA underwrites rent concessions to low-income tenants who occupy the units. The tenant is required to pay only a basic rental adjusted for possible overage determined by his monthly family income. This basic rental is determined by the amount required to operate the project with payments of principal and interest on the loan amortized over 40 or 50 years with interest at 1 percent per annum. All new projects have a 50-year amortization. In determining overage, any tenant

Budgets—Schedule I

Budget for market rent	*Budget for basic rent*

Budget for market rent

Operations and maintenance expenses, vacancy and contingency allowances, reserve and return allowable on investors' equity . . . . $ 5,277

Loan repayment at 9% interest ($100,000 × .09123)*   9,123

    Total annual requirement. . . . $14,400

$14,400 ÷ 12 = $1,200 monthly requirement:
Market rent for two-bedroom units = $160
Market rent for one-bedroom units = $140
($160 × 4) + ($140 × 4) = $1,200—monthly income requirement

Budget for basic rent

Operations and maintenance expenses, vacancy and contingency allowances, reserve and return allowable on investors' equity $5,277

Loan repayment at 1% interest ($100,000 × .02552)*   2,552

    Total annual requirement. . . . $7,829

$7,829 ÷ 12 = $652 (rounded) monthly requirement:
Basic rent for two-bedroom units = $91
Basic rent for one-bedroom units = $72
($91 × 4) + ($72 × 4) = 652—monthly income requirement

* Initial mortgage balance multiplied by appropriate loan constant for 50 years.

Calculation of overage—Schedule II

Apt. No.	Type	Occupant	Basic monthly rental	Market monthly rental	25 per cent of adjusted monthly family income*	Tenant's monthly rental payment	Overage
1	1 Br.	Jones	$ 72	$ 140	$ 70	$ 72	$ 0
2	1 Br.	Smith	72	140	80	80	8
3	1 Br.	Brown	72	140	97	97	25
4	1 Br.	Wilson	72	140	60	72	0
5	2 Br.	Bryan	91	160	150	150	59
6	2 Br.	Fontana	91	160	120	120	29
7	2 Br.	Jackson	91	160	71	91	0
8	2 Br.	Morales	91	160	90	91	0
Totals.			$652	$1,200	$738	$773	$121

* The rural rental housing program also has a deep subsidy called rent assistance. The tenants whose rent and utilities will exceed 25 percent of adjusted income may be assisted. The difference between what the tenant pays and the basic rent is paid to the owner under a separate agreement with the FmHA.

Interest credit calculation–Schedule III

1.	Annual payment by borrower at 9% interest (Schedule I)		$9,123
2.	Annual payment by borrower at 1% interest (Schedule I)	$2,552	
	Add overage ($121 × 12)—per Schedule II).	1,452	
3.	Annual basic rental adjusted for overage.		4,004
4.	Annual interest credit allowed by FmHA		$5,119

is required to pay as rent whichever is the higher of (1) the basic monthly rental or (2) 25 percent of the tenant's adjusted family income where utilities are not included in the rent.

The market rental for the project is determined on the basis of operating the project with payments of principal and interest which the borrower is obligated to pay under the terms of the promissory note. The difference between the rental collectible at market rates and that determined under the concession rules becomes the interest credit allowed by the FmHA.

Computation of interest credit. A hypothetical example may contribute to a better understanding of the application of the interest credit to a real situation. In this case, assume a $100,000 loan at 9 percent for 50 years for rural rental housing. The project contains 4 one-bedroom units and 4 two-bedroom units.

Volume of farm debt. The farm mortgage debt at the end of 1979 was $92.3 billion. This amount is up from $4.8 billion, 20 times since the end of 1945. The relative importance of various loan sources at the end of 1979 is shown in Exhibit 25–1. The great significance of federal agencies and individuals to rural credit is readily apparent.

EXHIBIT 25–1
Distribution of farm mortgage loans by principal lenders as of December 31, 1979 ($ billions)

Type of lender	Amount	Percentage
Commercial banks	$10.3	11.1
Life insurance companies	12.1	13.1
Federal and related agencies	36.6	39.7
Individuals and others	33.3	36.1
Total	92.3	100.0

Source: *Federal Reserve Bulletin,* March 1980, p. A41.

Although a large portion of farm mortgages are in support of the farming business, there is a new thrust under way toward living in rural communities. The Farmers Home Administration is becoming an increasingly important agency to help fulfill the housing demands created by the new population flow.

Questions

1 What are the common sources of farm capital?

2 Why are partnership and leasing arrangements relatively common in financing farm operations?

3 What are the chief purposes of farm mortgages and how should mortgage terms be arranged to fulfill these purposes?

4   Discuss the applicability of the following provisions in a farm mortgage: (*a*) amortization, (*b*) prepayment privileges, and (*c*) sinking fund for future benefits.

5   What criteria should be used in appraisals for farm loans?

6   Why are individuals the principal source of mortgage loan funds utilized in financing farms?

7   Discuss the commercial bank as a source of funds for financing farm real estate?

8   Under what conditions may a farmer borrow funds through the Federal Land Bank System?

9   How does the Farmers Home Administration offer financial assistance to farmers in buying farms? To nonfarming owners?

10 With the recent population trend toward the rural areas, do you see any special opportunities for the developer or investor to work with the FmHA to their mutual advantage?

Case problems

The FmHA is contemplating a $150,000 loan at 9 percent for 50 years for rural rental housing. All income requirements to cover annual expenses of operation and maintenance, allowances, reserves, and return to investors were estimated at $6,716. Compute the market and basic rental requirements for eight one-bedroom units. If the tenants' total monthly overage for the first year should be $60, what would be the FmHA interest credit? Assume that the appropriate constants for a 50-year loan are at 9 percent, 0.09123, and at 1 percent, .02552.

Selected references

<hr>
<hr>

**PART ONE: INSTRUMENTS USED IN REAL ESTATE FINANCE:
LEGAL AND FINANCIAL CHARACTERISTICS**

Books

Atteberry, William; Pearson, Karl G.; and Litka, Michael P. *Real Estate Law.* Columbus, Ohio: Grid, Inc., 1974.

Bohon, Davis T. *Complete Guide to Profitable Real Estate Leasing.* Englewood Cliffs, N.J.: Prentice-Hall, Inc., 1969.

Cribbet, John E. *Principles of the Law of Property.* Mineola, N.Y.: Foundation Press, Inc., 1975.

Friedman, M. R. *Friedman on Leases.* New York: Practicing Law Institute, 1974.

Grange, William J., and Woodbury, T. C. *Manual of Real Estate Law and Procedures.* New York: Ronald Press Co., 1968.

Kratovil, Robert. *Modern Mortgage Law and Practice.* Englewood Cliffs, N.J.: Prentice-Hall, Inc., 1972.

————. *Modern Real Estate Documentation.* Englewood Cliffs, N.J.: Prentice-Hall, Inc., 1975.

————. *Real Estate Law.* Englewood Cliffs, N.J.: Prentice-Hall, Inc., 1979.

Lusk, Harold, and French, William. *Law of the Real Estate Business.* Homewood, Ill.: Richard D. Irwin, Inc., 1975.

McMichael, Stanley L., and O'Keefe, Paul T. *Leases: Percentage, Short and Long Term.* Englewood Cliffs, N.J.: Prentice-Hall, Inc., 1974.

Rabin, Edward H. *Fundamentals of Modern Real Property Law.* Mineola, N.Y.: The Foundation Press, Inc., 1974.

Seidel, George J. III. *Real Estate Law.* St. Paul, Minn.: West Publishing Co., 1979.

Semenow, Robert W. *Questions and Answers in Real Estate.* Englewood Cliffs, N.J.: Prentice-Hall, Inc., 1975.

Thompson, George W. *The Law of Real Property.* Vols. 1–12. Indianapolis, Ind.: The Bobbs-Merrill Co., Inc., 1941 (with later supplements).

Periodicals

Halper, Emanuel M.   "What Is a New Net Net Net Lease?" *Real Estate Review,* Winter 1974, pp. 9–14.

————.   "People and Property: Negotiating the Operating Leasehold." *Real Estate Review,* vol. 5 (Summer 1975), pp. 77–83.

Johnstone, Quintin.   "Title Insurance." *The Yale Law Journal,* vol. 66, no. 4 (February 1957), pp. 492–524.

Kempner, Paul, S.   "Investments in Single-Tenant Net Leased Properties." *Real Estate Review,* Summer 1974, pp. 121–24.

Levy, David S.   "ABC's of Shopping Center Leases." *Real Estate Review,* Spring 1971, pp. 12–16.

Lynch, James D.   "New Uniform Laws Are Proposed that Will Affect Real Estate Transactions." *Mortgage Banker,* August 1979.

McKillop, Hart.   "Title Insurance." *University of Florida Law Review,* vol. 8, no. 4 (Winter 1955), pp. 447–64.

Starr, John O.   "Lease Guarantee Insurance." *The Appraisal Journal* April 1972, pp. 175–87.

"Title Insurance. New Horizons for the 1980's" Special issue of *Mortgage Banker,* August, 1980.

PART TWO: MORTGAGES AND RESIDENTIAL FINANCING

Books

Beaton, William R.   *Real Estate Finance.* Englewood Cliffs, N.J.: Prentice-Hall, Inc., 1975.

Clurman, David, and Hebard, Edna L.   *Condominiums and Cooperatives.* New York: Wiley-Interscience, 1970.

Federal Home Loan Bank Board.   *Alternative Mortgage Instruments Research Study.* Vol. I–III. Washington, D.C.: FHLBB (November 1977).

Lessard, Donald and Modigliani, Franco.   "Inflation and the Housing Market: Problems and Potential Solutions." *New Mortgage Designs for an Inflationary Environment.* Boston: Federal Reserve Bank of Boston, January 1975.

Maisel, Serman J., and Roulac, Stephen E.   *Real Estate Investment and Finance.* New York: McGraw-Hill Book Co., Inc., 1976.

Von Furstenberg, George.   *The Economics of Mortgages with Variable Interest Rates.* Washington, D.C.: FHLMC Monograph No. 2 (February 1973).

Periodicals

Brueggeman, William B., and Baesel, Jerome B.   "The Mechanics of Variable Rate Mortgages and Implications for Home Ownership as an Inflation Hedge." *Appraisal Journal,* April 1976, pp. 236–46.

Brueggeman, William B., and Peiser, Richard.   "Housing Choice and Relative Tenure Prices." *Journal of Financial and Quantitative Analysis,* November 1979.

Cassidy, Henry, and McElhone, Josephine.   "The Flexible Payment Mortgage." *Journal of the Federal Home Loan Bank Board,* vol. 7 (August 1974), pp. 7–11.

————. "The Pricing of Variable Rate Mortgages." *Financial Management,* vol. 4 (Winter 1975), pp. 37–55.

Epley, Donald. "Can Variable-Rate and Fixed-Rate Mortgages Coexist?" *Real Estate Review,* vol. 5 (Winter 1976), pp. 119–21.

Friedman, Harris. "Variable Interest Rates and Variable Balance Mortgages." *Journal of the Federal Home Loan Bank Board,* vol. 3 (January/February 1970), pp. 15–18.

Kaufman, George. "The Case for Mortgage Rate Insurance," *Journal of Money, Credit, and Banking,* vol. 7 (November 1975), pp. 515–59.

Liew, C. K. "Lending Behavior and the Nature of Default Loans in the Case of the Savings and Loan Industry." *Journal of Finance,* vol. 25 (June 1970).

Meltzer, Allan H. "Credit Availability and Economic Decisions: Some Evidence from the Mortgage and Housing Markets." *Journal of Finance,* June 1974, pp. 763–77.

Millar, James, and Stansell, Stanley. "A Comparison of the Characteristics of Fixed and Variable Mortgages." *The Appraisal Journal,* vol. 44 (January 1976), pp. 63–68.

————. "An Empirical Study of Mortgage Payment to Income Ratios in a Variable Rate Mortgage Program." *Journal of Finance,* vol. 31 (May 1976), pp. 415–25.

————. "How Variable Rate Mortgages Would Affect Lenders." *Real Estate Review,* vol. 5 (Winter 1976), pp. 116–18.

————. "Variable Rate Mortgage Experience of the Farm Credit System." *Financial Management,* vol. 4 (Winter 1975), pp. 46–57.

————. "Variable Rate Mortgage Lending: Some Empirical Results." *American Real Estate and Urban Economics Association Journal,* vol. 3 (Winter 1975), pp. 95–109.

————. "Settlement Costs and You." *A HUD Guide for Homebuyers,* June 1976.

Stansell, Stanley, R., and Millar, James A. "How Variable-Rate Mortgages Would Affect Lenders," *Real Estate Review,* Winter 1976, pp. 116–18.

Tucker, Donald P. "The Variable-Rate Graduated-Payment Mortgage." *Real Estate Review,* Spring 1975, pp. 71–80.

von Furstenberg, George M. "Default Risk on FHA-Insured Home Mortgages as a Function of the Terms of Financing, a Quantitative Analysis." *Journal of Finance,* June 1969, pp. 455–65.

von Furstenberg, George M., and Green, R. Jeffrey. "Home Mortgage Delinquencies: A Cohort Analysis." *Journal of Finance,* December 1974, pp. 1545–48.

Weinrobe, Maurice. "Whatever Happened to the Flexible Payment Mortgage." *Journal of the Federal Home Loan Bank Board,* vol. 8 (December 1975), pp. 16–24.

PART THREE: ANALYZING INCOME-PRODUCING PROPERTIES

Books

Akerson, Charles B. *Study Guide, Course I-B Capitalization Theory and Techniques.* Chicago: American Institute of Real Estate Appraisers, 1973.

Beaton, William, and Robertson, Terry. *Real Estate Investment.* 2d ed. Englewood Cliffs, N.J.: Prentice-Hall, Inc., 1977.

Bierman, Harold, and Smidt, Seymour. *The Capital Budgeting Decision.* New York: Macmillan Publishing Co., Inc., 1975.

Britton, James A., Jr., and Kerwood, Lewis O. *Financing Income-Producing Real Estate.* New York: McGraw-Hill Book Co. 1977.

Cohen, J.; Zinbarg, E.; and Zeckel, A. *Investment Analysis and Portfolio Management* 3d ed. Homewood. Ill.: Richard D. Irwin, Inc., 1977.

Downs, J. C., Jr. *Principles of Real Estate Management.* Chicago: Institute of Real Estate Management, 1970.

Federal Home Loan Mortgage Co. *Home Mortgages Underwriting Guidelines,* Washington, D.C.: FHLMC, March 1976.

Graaskamp, J. A. *A Guide to Feasibility Analysis.* Chicago: Society of Real Estate Appraisers, 1970.

Kahn, Sanders A., and Case, Frederick E. *Real Estate Appraisal and Investment.* New York: The Ronald Press Co., 1976.

Kinnard, William N. Jr. *Industrial Real Estate.* Washington, D.C.: Society of Industrial Realtors of the National Association of Real Estate Boards, 1967.

————. *Income Property Valuation.* Lexington, Mass.: Lexington Books, D. C. Heath & Co., 1971.

Messner, Stephen D.; Schreiber, Irving; and Lyon, Victor L. *Marketing Investment Real Estate: Finance Taxation Techniques.* Chicago: Realtors National Marketing Institute, 1975.

Mossburg, Lewis, G. Jr. *Real Estate Syndicate Offerings, Law and Practice.* San Francisco: Real Estate Syndication Digest, 1974.

Prentice-Hall. *Federal Tax Course—1979.* Englewood Cliffs, N.J.: Prentice-Hall, Inc., 1978.

————. Special Supplement to *Federal Tax Course—1979, Revenue Act of 1978 and Energy Tax of 1978.* Englewood Cliffs, N.J.: Prentice-Hall, Inc., 1978.

Roulac, S. E. *Real Estate Syndicate Digest.* San Francisco: Real Estate Syndicators Digest, Inc., 1972.

————. *Real Estate Venture Analysis 1974.* New York: Practicing Law Institute, 1974.

Sumichrast, Michael, and Seldin, Maury. *Housing and Markets: The Complete Guide to Analysis and Strategy for Builders, Lenders, and Other Investors.* Washington, D.C.: Homer Hoyt Institute, 1976.

Tax Management Portfolios. Washington, D.C.: Bureau of National Affairs, Inc., 1976.

Van Horne, James. *Financial Management and Policy.* 4th ed. Englewood Cliffs, N.J.: Prentice-Hall, Inc., 1977.

Wendt, Paul F. *Real Estate Appraisal: Review and Outlook.* Athens: U. of Georgia Press, 1974.

Wendt, Paul F., and Cerf, Alan R. *Real Estate Investment Analysis and Taxation.* New York: McGraw-Hill Book Co., 1969.

Willis, A. B. *Willis on Partnership Taxation.* New York: McGraw-Hill Book Co., 1976.

Periodicals

Aronsohn, Alan J. B. "The Real Estate Limited Partnership and Other Joint Ventures." *Real Estate Review,* Spring 1971, pp. 43–49.

Barrett, J. E. "Use of the Wrap-Around Mortgage in Realty Sales: Tax Advantages and Problems." *Journal of Taxation,* vol. 40 (May 1974), pp. 274–77.

Bell, Robert. "Negotiating the Purchase-Money Mortgage." *Real Estate Review,* vol. 7 (Spring 1977), pp. 51–58.

Bradley, David. "Ellwood through Algebra—New Horizons." *Appraisal Journal,* vol. 44 (January 1976), pp. 98–110.

Brannon, G., and Sunley, E. "The Recapture of Excess Depreciation on the Sale of Real Estate." *National Tax Journal,* December 1976, pp. 413–21.

Chesborough, Lowell D. "Do Participation Loans Pay Off?" *Real Estate Review,* Summer 1974, pp. 95–100.

Dolman, John. "Real Estate Counseling: Some Distinctions from and Relationships with Real Estate Valuation." *Appraisal Journal,* vol. 41 (October 1973), pp. 453–63.

Downs, Anthony. "Characteristics of Various Economic Studies." *Appraisal Journal,* July 1966, pp. 329–39.

————. "Investing in Housing Rehabilitation Can Be Successful." *Real Estate Review,* Summer 1976.

Elledge, Harold. "Case Study: A Limited Partnership for Syndication." *Real Estate Today,* January 1976.

Fass, Peter M. "The Regulated World of the Real Estate Syndicates." *Real Estate Review,* Winter 1972, pp. 52–56.

Friedman, H. C. "Real Estate Investment and Portfolio Theory." *Journal of Financial and Quantitative Analysis,* March 1971, pp. 861–74.

Gau, George, and Kohlhepp, Daniel. "Reinvestment Rates and the Sensitivity of Rates of Return in Real Estate Investment." *American Real Estate and Urban Economics Association Journal,* Winter 1976.

Graaskamp, James. "Rational Approach to Feasibility Analysis." *Appraisal Journal,* vol. 40 (October 1972), pp. 513–21.

Gunning, Francis. "The Wrap-Around Mortgage . . . Friend or U.F.O." *Real Estate Review,* vol. 2 (Summer 1972), pp. 35–48.

Handorf, William, et al. "Land Development Acceptability: A Capital Budgeting Analysis." *Journal of the Federal Home Loan Bank Board,* vol. 9 (June 1976), pp. 9–12.

Handorf, William, and May, Gordon. "Making Fixed Assets Work: Sell Your Building and Lease it Back? It's a Possible Source of Investable Funds." *Journal of the Federal Home Loan Bank Board,* vol. 9 (October 1976).

Hemmer, Edgar, H. "How a Computer 'Thinks' about Real Estate." *Real Estate Review,* Winter 1975, pp. 113–23.

Hertz, David. "Investment Policies That Pay Off." *Harvard Business Review,* vol. 46 (January–February 1968), pp. 96–108.

Jackol, Howard T. "A Lender Looks at Condominium Conversions." *Real Estate Review,* vol. 4 (Spring 1974), pp. 70–77.

Jordan, John. "How to Account for Real Estate Joint Ventures." *Real Estate Review,* vol. 4 (Spring 1974), pp. 119–25.

Kelleher, D. "How Real Estate Stacks Up to the S & P 500." *Real Estate Review,* vol. 6 (Summer 1976).

Klink, James. "How to Account for Real Estate Joint Ventures." *Real Estate Review,* vol. 4 (Spring 1974), pp. 119–25.

Lawless, Harris. "Living with the Deal, or How to Manage the Real Estate Syndicate." *Real Estate Review,* vol. 3 (Winter 1974), pp. 84–88.

Leider, Arnold. "Wrap-Around Mortgage Financing by a Commercial Bank." *Journal of Commercial Bank Lending,* vol. 56 (April 1974), pp. 2–22.

————. "How to Wrap-Around a Mortgage." *Real Estate Review,* Winter 1975, pp. 29–34.

Levin, Michael R. "Financing the Commercial Condominium." *Real Estate Review,* Winter 1975, pp. 71–77.

Lex, R. "Marketing Studies for Office Buildings." *Real Estate Review,* vol. 5 (Summer 1975).

McCrary, Dennie. "Standby Permanent Financing for Condominium Development." *Real Estate Review,* vol. 4 (Spring 1974), pp. 74–77.

Messner, Stephen D., and Findlay, M. Chapman III. "Real Estate Investment Analysis: IRR versus FMRR." *The Real Estate Appraiser,* July–August 1975.

Miller, R. A. Stuart, and James Kafes. "How to Value Real Estate Subject to an Equity Participation." *Real Estate Review,* vol. 2 (Spring 1972), pp. 89–95.

"New Perspectives in Real Estate Financing" Special issue of *Mortgage Banker,* July 1980.

Opperman, John C. "Lender-Developer Participation," *The Mortgage Banker,* September 1968.

Ordway, Nicholas. "Controlling for Uncertainty through Computer Application of PERT/CPM to Real Estate Project Analysis." *American Real Estate and Urban Economics Association Journal,* vol. 4 (Fall 1976).

Parisse, Alan J. "How Not to Analyze a Syndication." Real Estate Review, Winter 1974, pp. 89–96.

Pellat, P. G. K. "The Analysis of Real Estate Investments under Uncertainty." *Journal of Finance,* vol. 27, no. 2 (May 1972), pp. 459–71.

Pyhrr, Stephen. "A Computer Selection Model to Measure the Risks in Real Estate Investment." *American Real Estate and Urban Economics Association Journal,* vol. 1 (June 1973), pp. 48–78.

————. "A Computer Simulation Model to Measure the Risk in Real Estate Investment." *The Real Estate Appraiser,* May–June 1973.

Reilly, F.; Marquandt, R.; and Price, D. "Real Estate as an Inflation Hedge." *Review of Business and Economic Research,* vol. 12 (Spring 1977).

Ricks, R. Bruce. "Imputed Equity Returns on Real Estate Financed with Life Insurance Company Loans." *Journal of Finance,* December 1969, pp. 921–37.

Roberts, Paul E. "Working Out the Construction Mortgage Loan." *Real Estate Review,* Summer 1975, pp. 53–57.

Rose, Cornelius, C. Jr. "Equity Participations." *The Mortgage Banker,* June 1968, pp. 44–47.

Roulac, Stephen. "Giving the Syndicator His Just Reward." *Real Estate Review,* vol. 3 (Winter 1974), p. 89–96.

————. "Life Cycle of a Real Estate Investment." *Real Estate Review,* Fall 1974, pp. 113–47.

Schulkin, Peter A. "Construction Lending at Large Commercial Banks." *Real Estate Review,* Spring 1971, pp. 54–60.

Schwind, Robert L. "Land Trusts—A Real Estate Syndication Device." *Trusts and Estates,* July 1962, pp. 350–52.

Sillcocks, H. Jackson. "Financial Sense in Sales and Real Estate Leasebacks." *Real Estate Review,* vol. 5 (Spring 1975), pp. 89–95.

Simpkins, John, and Nielsen, Gordon. "The Rise of Project/Construction Management." *Real Estate Review,* vol. 6 (Winter 1977), pp. 47–53.

Sonnenblick, Jack E. "Shopping Center Financing." *Journal of Property Management,* vol. 30, no. 6 (November–December 1965), pp. 303–06.

Strung, Joseph. "The Internal Rate of Return and the Reinvestment Presumptions." *Appraisal Journal,* vol. 44 (January 1976), pp. 22–33.

Tockarshewsky, Joseph. "Reducing the Risks in Construction Lending." *Real Estate Review,* vol. 7 (Spring 1971), pp. 59–63.

Trowbridge, Charles. "What Is a Wrap-Around Mortgage?" *Real Estate Today,* vol. 8 (December 1975), pp. 44–53.

Valachi, Donald. "Calculating True Yields on Wrap-Arounds." *Real Estate Review,* vol. 6 (Winter 1977), pp. 92–99.

————. "The Internal Rate of Return: A Note on the Arithmetic of Multiple and Imaginary Rates." Real Estate Appraiser, vol. 43 (March–April 1977), pp. 39–42.

Weil, S. Douglas. "Land Leasebacks Move Up Fast as Financing Technique." *Real Estate Review,* Winter 1972, pp. 65–71.

Wendt, Paul F., and Wong, S. N. "Investment Performance: Common Stock, versus Apartment Houses." Journal of Finance, December 1965, pp. 633–46.

Wilner, Alfred. "Five Trouble Spots in Construction." *Real Estate Review,* vol. 6 (Winter 1977), pp. 54–57.

PART FOUR: THE MORTGAGE MARKET AND SOURCES OF REAL ESTATE CREDIT

Books

Federal Reserve Bank of Cleveland. *Money Market Instruments.* Cleveland: Federal Reserve Bank, September 1971.

Friend, I., et al. *Study of the Savings and Loan Industry.* Vols 1–4. Washington, D.C.: Federal Home Loan Bank Board, 1969.

Gramlich, E. M., and Jaffee, D. M., eds., *Savings Deposits, Mortgages and Housing: Studies from the FRB-MIT-Penn Model.* Lexington, Mass.: Lexington Books, 1972.

Gup, Benton E. *Financial Intermediaries.* Boston: Houghton Mifflin Co., 1980.

Guttentag, Jack M., and Beck, Morris. *New Series on Home Mortgage Yields since 1951.* New York: National Bureau of Economic Research, Columbia University Press, 1970.

Klaman, Saul B. *The Postwar Rise of Mortgage Companies.* New York: National Bureau of Economic Research, Inc., 1959.

Kroos, Herman E., and Blyn, Martin R. *A History of Financial Intermediaries.* New York: Random House, 1971.

Morris, Peter. *State Housing Finance Agencies.* Lexington. Mass.: Lexington Books, 1974.

Mortgage Guarantee Insurance Corporation. *MGIC Fact Book.* Milwaukee, Wisc., 1975.

National Association of Mutual Savings Banks. *Mutual Savings Banks Annual Report.* New York: National Association of Mutual Savings Banks, 1976.

_____. *Mutual Savings Banks: Basic Characteristics and Role in the National Economy.* Englewood Cliffs, N.J.: Prentice-Hall, Inc., 1962.

Reeb, Donald J., and Kirk, James T. Jr. *Housing the Poor.* New York: Praeger Publishers, 1973.

Office of Economic Research, Federal Home Loan Bank Board. *A Financial Institution for the Future.* Washington, D.C: Federal Home Loan Bank Board, 1975.

Pease, Robert H., and Kerwood, Lewis O. *Mortgage Banking.* New York: McGraw-Hill Book Co., Inc., 1965.

Rose, Peter S., and Fraser, Donald R. *Financial Institutions.* Dallas: Business Publications, Inc., 1980.

Schwarz, Edward W. *How to Use Interest Rate Futures Contracts.* Homewood, Ill.: Dow Jones-Irwin, 1979.

Silber, W. L. *Portfolio Behavior of Financial Institutions.* New York: Holt, Rinehart and Winston, 1970.

Spolan, Harmon S. *Banker's Handbook of Federal Aids to Financing.* Boston, Mass.: Warren, Gorham & Lamont, Inc., 1974 (with 1976 supplement by the staff editors of the Banking Law Journal).

Starr, Rodger. *Housing and the Money Market.* New York: Basic Books, Inc., 1975. 1975.

U.S. Commission on Financial Structure and Regulation. *Report.* Washington, D.C.: Hunt Commission, 1971.

Van Horne, James C. *Function and Analysis of Capital Market Rates.* Englewood Cliffs, N.J.: Prentice-Hall, Inc., 1970.

Periodicals

Alberts, William. "Business Cycles, Residential Construction Cycles, and the Mortgage Market." *Journal of Political Economy,* June 1962, pp. 263–87.

Allen, Charles. "The Mortgage-Backed Bond Regulations: How They Work." *Journal of the Federal Home Loan Bank Board,* vol. 8 (June 1975), pp. 13–15.

Bradley, Eugene. "A Sectorial Econometric Study of the Postwar Residential Housing Market." *Journal of Political Economy,* April 1967, pp. 274–78.

Dockson, Robert. "Marketing Mortgage-Backed Bonds." *Journal of the Federal Home Loan Bank Board,* vol. 8 (November 1975), pp. 3–11.

Earnhardt, Roger. "Construction Lending Via a Mortgage Backed Security." *Real Estate Review,* vol. 3 (Fall 1973), pp. 30–31.

Englebrecht, Ted, and Kramer, John. "Tax Breaks for REITs under the Tax Reform Act." *Real Estate Review,* vol. 7 (Spring 1977), pp. 30–32.

Fitzhugh, Gilbert W. "The Life Insurance Companies' Urban Investment Program." The Mortgage Banker, June 1968, pp. 13–24.

Ganis, David. "All About the GNMA Mortgage Backed Securities Market." *Real Estate Review,* vol. 4 (Summer 1974), pp. 55–65.

_____. :"GNMA Futures Market Has Advantages, but Not a Way to Make or Take Delivery." *Mortgage Banker,* vol. 36 (January 1976), pp. 16–23.

Guttentag, Jack. "Mortgage Warehousing," *Journal of Finance,* vol. 12, no. 4 (December 1957), pp. 438–50.

————. "The Short Cycle in Residential Construction: 1946–59." *American Economic Review,* June 1961, pp. 275–98.

Harrington, Phillip N. "FREDDIE Mac: Big Man in Mortgages." *Real Estate Review,* vol. 3 (Winter 1974), pp. 102–04.

Haverkampf, Peter T. "The Pension Trusts Move into Real Estate—Slowly." *Real Estate Review,* Spring 1974, pp. 426–29.

Hines, Mary Alice. "The REIT Shakeout in 1974." *Real Estate Review,* Winter 1975, pp. 56–59.

Jacobs, Steven F. "Mortgage Bankers Must Develop Knowledge and Strategy to Use GNMA Futures Market." *Mortgage Banker,* vol. 37 (April 1977).

————, and Kozuch, James "Is There a Future for a Mortgage Futures Market." *Mortgage Banker,* vol. 34 (June 1974), pp. 5–13.

Kaplan, Donald. "Mortgage-Backed Bonds: A New Source of Funds for the Savings and Loan Industry." *Journal of the Federal Home Loan Bank Board,* vol. 8 (March 1975), pp. 13–24.

Miller, Thomas C. "Mortgage Bankers Must Know Basics of Pension Fund Investments." *Mortgage Banker,* vol. 36 (September 1976), pp. 32–37.

————. "GNMA Options Market—A Proposed New Marketing Tool." *Mortgage Banker,* vol. 37 (April 1977), pp. 58–60.

"Mortgage Banking in the 1980's," Special issue of *Mortgage Banker,* April, 1980.

Murray, James E. "Fannie Mae Goes Shopping for Conventional Mortgages." *Real Estate Review,* vol. 1 (Fall 1971), pp. 54–60.

Silber, William L. "A Model of Federal Home Loan Bank System and FNMA Behavior." *Review of Economics and Statistics,* vol. 55 (August 1973), pp. 303–320.

Smith, David. "Regional Impact of Disintermediation." *Journal of the Federal Home Loan Bank Board,* vol. 10 (June 1977), pp. 20–24.

Smith, Lawrence. "A Sectorial Econometric Study of the Postwar Residential Housing Market: An Opposite View." *Journal of Political Economy,* March/April 1970, pp. 284–89.

Stefaniak, Norbert J. "Management Policies of Real Estate Investment Trusts." *Journal of Property Management,* vol. 22, no. 2 (March–April 1968), pp. 63–67.

Stevenson, Eric. "A Commitment Made and Kept: The (Life Insurance Companies') Urban Investment Program." *The Mortgage Banker,* May 1970, pp. 18–27.

Struck, Ronald. "The Mortgage Corporation." *Journal of the Federal Home Loan Bank Board,* vol. 9 (March 1976), pp. 47–49.

Taylor, Harold. "The REITs Are Sorting Themselves Out." *Real Estate Review,* vol 4 (Spring 1974), pp. 102–5.

"The GNMA Story: Important Facts for Investor and Issuer." Three articles in *Mortgage Banker,* vol. 37 (February 1977), pp. 8–36.

Vitt, Lois A., and Berstein, Joel H. "Convertible Mortgages: New Financing Tool?" *Real Estate Review,* Spring 1976, pp. 33–37.

Wentmore, John. "Inflation Hits Mortgage Banking—Origination and Servicing." *Mortgage Banker,* vol. 34 (February 1974), pp. 85–87.

Wiggin, Charles. "Doing Business in the Secondary Mortgage Market." *Real Estate Review,* vol. 4 (Spring 1974), pp. 126–29.

PART FIVE: GOVERNMENT AND REAL ESTATE FINANCE

Books

Aaron, Henry J. *Shelter and Subsidies: Who Benefits from Federal Housing Policies?* Washington, D.C.: The Brookings Institution, 1972.

Board of Governors of the Federal Reserve System. *Ways to Moderate Fluctuations in Housing Construction.* Washington, D.C., 1972.

Downs, Anthony. *Federal Housing Subsidies: How Are They Working?* Lexington, Mass.: Lexington Books, 1973.

Farmers Home Administration. *This Is FmHA.* Washington, D.C.: USDA, February 1974.

Federal Land Bank Association. *Federal Land Banks: How They Operate,* April 1973.

Harrison, Bennett. *Urban Economic Development: Suburbanization, Minority Opportunity, and the Condition of the Central City.* Washington, D.C.: The Urban Institute, 1974.

Institute for Contemporary Studies. *Government Credit Allocation: Where Do We Go from Here?* San Francisco, Calif., 1975.

Nelson, Aaron G., and Murray, William G. *Agricultural Finance.* Ames: Iowa State University Press, 1967.

Netzer, Dick. *Economics and Urban Problems: Diagnoses and Prescriptions.* New York: Basic Books, Inc., 1974.

Schaevitz, Robert C., and Van, Elizabeth A., eds. *Handbook of Federal Assistance—Financing, Grants, and Technical Aids.* Boston and New York: Warren, Gorham & Lamont, 1980.

Swackhamer, Gene L., and Doll, Raymond J. *Financing Modern Agriculture.* Kansas City, Mo.: Research Department, Federal Reserve Bank of Kansas City, 1969.

U.S. Department of Housing and Urban Development. *Housing in the Seventies.* Washington, D.C., 1974.

Periodicals

Brueggeman, William B. "Federal Housing Subsidies: Conceptual Issues and Benefit Patterns." *Journal of Economics and Business,* Winter 1975, pp. 141–149.

Brueggeman, William B., and Zerbst, Robert. "FHA and VA Discount Points and Housing Prices." *Journal of Finance,* December 1977.

Colean, Miles. "Crucial Year Looms for FHA Future." *Mortgage Banker,* vol. 35 (January 1975), pp. 21–29.

Halperin, Jerome Y., and Brenner, Michael J. "Opportunities under the New Section 8 Housing Program." *Real Estate Review,* Spring 1976, pp. 67–75.

Kidd, Phillip. "Decline in Use of FHA Programs Signals Major Industry Change." *Mortgage Banker,* May 1974, pp. 12–19.

Marcis, Richard G. "The Conventional Pass-through Security: A Star Is Born." *Real Estate Review,* Summer 1979.

Marr, John A. "Financing Subsidized Housing with Municipal Bonds."*Real Estate Review,* Summer 1979.

Mason, W. Beverly. "An Independent FHA Could Help Ease Housing Crisis." *Mortgage Banker,* December 1974, pp. 12–18.

Penner, R. G., and Silber, W. I. "The Interaction between Federal Credit Programs and the Impact on the Allocation of Credit." *American Economic Review,* December 1973, pp. 338–52.

Wentmore, John. "FHA-VA Mortgage Costs—Bargains in Capital-Short Areas." *Mortgage Banker,* April 1974, pp. 5–16.

Wolff, Robert G. "The FmHA 502 Rural Housing Guaranteed Loan Program." *Mortgage Banker,* June 1980.

APPENDIXES

* Reprinted from Paul Wendt and Alan R. Cerf, *Tables for Investment Analysis* (Center for Real Estate and Urban Economics, 1966; reprinted by the Institute of Business and Economic Research, 1977 and 1979, University of California, Berkeley).

† Reprinted from: Paul Wendt and Alan R. Cerf, *Tables for Investment Analysis*, Berkeley, California. Institute for Business and Economic Research, University of California, Berkeley, 1979.

4.00%   ANNUAL COMPOUND INTEREST TABLES   4.00%
                    EFFECTIVE RATE 4.00

	1	2	3	4	5	6
	AMOUNT OF $1 AT COMPOUND INTEREST	ACCUMULATION OF $1 PER PERIOD	SINKING FUND FACTOR	PRESENT VALUE REVERSION OF $1	PRESENT VALUE ORD. ANNUITY $1 PER PERIOD	INSTALMENT TO AMORTIZE $1
YEARS						
1	1.040000	1.000000	1.000000	0.961538	0.961538	1.040000
2	1.081600	2.040000	0.490196	0.924556	1.886095	0.530196
3	1.124864	3.121600	0.320349	0.888996	2.775091	0.360349
4	1.169859	4.246464	0.235490	0.854804	3.629895	0.275490
5	1.216653	5.416323	0.184627	0.821927	4.451822	0.224627
6	1.265319	6.632975	0.150762	0.790315	5.242137	0.190762
7	1.315932	7.898294	0.126610	0.759918	6.002055	0.166610
8	1.368569	9.214226	0.108528	0.730690	6.732745	0.148528
9	1.423312	10.582795	0.094493	0.702587	7.435332	0.134493
10	1.480244	12.006107	0.083291	0.675564	8.110896	0.123291
11	1.539454	13.486351	0.074149	0.649581	8.760477	0.114149
12	1.601032	15.025805	0.066552	0.624597	9.385074	0.106552
13	1.665074	16.626838	0.060144	0.600574	9.985648	0.100144
14	1.731676	18.291911	0.054669	0.577475	10.563123	0.094669
15	1.800944	20.023588	0.049941	0.555265	11.118387	0.089941
16	1.872981	21.824531	0.045820	0.533908	11.652296	0.085820
17	1.947900	23.697512	0.042199	0.513373	12.165669	0.082199
18	2.025817	25.645413	0.038993	0.493628	12.659297	0.078993
19	2.106849	27.671229	0.036139	0.474642	13.133939	0.076139
20	2.191123	29.778079	0.033582	0.456387	13.590326	0.073582
21	2.278768	31.969202	0.031280	0.438834	14.029160	0.071280
22	2.369919	34.247970	0.029199	0.421955	14.451115	0.069199
23	2.464716	36.617889	0.027309	0.405726	14.856842	0.067309
24	2.563304	39.082604	0.025587	0.390121	15.246963	0.065587
25	2.665836	41.645908	0.024012	0.375117	15.622080	0.064012
26	2.772470	44.311745	0.022567	0.360689	15.982769	0.062567
27	2.883369	47.084214	0.021239	0.346817	16.329586	0.061239
28	2.998703	49.967583	0.020013	0.333477	16.663063	0.060013
29	3.118651	52.966286	0.018880	0.320651	16.983715	0.058880
30	3.243398	56.084938	0.017830	0.308319	17.292033	0.057830
31	3.373133	59.328335	0.016855	0.296460	17.588494	0.056855
32	3.508059	62.701469	0.015949	0.285058	17.873551	0.055949
33	3.648381	66.209527	0.015104	0.274094	18.147646	0.055104
34	3.794316	69.857909	0.014315	0.263552	18.411198	0.054315
35	3.946089	73.652225	0.013577	0.253415	18.664613	0.053577
36	4.103933	77.598314	0.012887	0.243669	18.908282	0.052887
37	4.268090	81.702246	0.012240	0.234297	19.142579	0.052240
38	4.438813	85.970336	0.011632	0.225285	19.367864	0.051632
39	4.616366	90.409150	0.011061	0.216621	19.584485	0.051061
40	4.801021	95.025516	0.010523	0.208289	19.792774	0.050523
41	4.993061	99.826536	0.010017	0.200278	19.993052	0.050017
42	5.192784	104.819598	0.009540	0.192575	20.185627	0.049540
43	5.400495	110.012382	0.009090	0.185168	20.370795	0.049090
44	5.616515	115.412877	0.008665	0.178046	20.548841	0.048665
45	5.841176	121.029392	0.008262	0.171198	20.720040	0.048262
46	6.074823	126.870568	0.007882	0.164614	20.884654	0.047882
47	6.317816	132.945390	0.007522	0.158283	21.042936	0.047522
48	6.570528	139.263206	0.007181	0.152195	21.195131	0.047181
49	6.833349	145.833734	0.006857	0.146341	21.341472	0.046857
50	7.106683	152.667084	0.006550	0.140713	21.482185	0.046550

5.00%   ANNUAL COMPOUND INTEREST TABLES   5.00%
                                             EFFECTIVE RATE   5.00

	1	2	3	4	5	6
	AMOUNT OF $1 AT COMPOUND INTEREST	ACCUMULATION OF $1 PER PERIOD	SINKING FUND FACTOR	PRESENT VALUE REVERSION OF $1	PRESENT VALUE ORD. ANNUITY $1 PER PERIOD	INSTALMENT TO AMORTIZE $1
YEARS						
1	1.050000	1.000000	1.000000	0.952381	0.952381	1.050000
2	1.102500	2.050000	0.487805	0.907029	1.859410	0.537805
3	1.157625	3.152500	0.317209	0.863838	2.723248	0.367209
4	1.215506	4.310125	0.232012	0.822702	3.545951	0.282012
5	1.276282	5.525631	0.180975	0.783526	4.329477	0.230975
6	1.340096	6.801913	0.147017	0.746215	5.075692	0.197017
7	1.407100	8.142008	0.122820	0.710681	5.786373	0.172820
8	1.477455	9.549109	0.104722	0.676839	6.463213	0.154722
9	1.551328	11.026564	0.090690	0.644609	7.107822	0.140690
10	1.628895	12.577893	0.079505	0.613913	7.721735	0.129505
11	1.710339	14.206787	0.070389	0.584679	8.306414	0.120389
12	1.795856	15.917127	0.062825	0.556837	8.863252	0.112825
13	1.885649	17.712983	0.056456	0.530321	9.393573	0.106456
14	1.979932	19.598632	0.051024	0.505068	9.898641	0.101024
15	2.078928	21.578564	0.046342	0.481017	10.379658	0.096342
16	2.182875	23.657492	0.042270	0.458112	10.837770	0.092270
17	2.292018	25.840366	0.038699	0.436297	11.274066	0.088699
18	2.406619	28.132385	0.035546	0.415521	11.689587	0.085546
19	2.526950	30.539004	0.032745	0.395734	12.085321	0.082745
20	2.653298	33.065954	0.030243	0.376889	12.462210	0.080243
21	2.785963	35.719252	0.027996	0.358942	12.821153	0.077996
22	2.925261	38.505214	0.025971	0.341850	13.163003	0.075971
23	3.071524	41.430475	0.024137	0.325571	13.488574	0.074137
24	3.225100	44.501999	0.022471	0.310068	13.798642	0.072471
25	3.386355	47.727099	0.020952	0.295303	14.093945	0.070952
26	3.555673	51.113454	0.019564	0.281241	14.375185	0.069564
27	3.733456	54.669126	0.018292	0.267848	14.643034	0.068292
28	3.920129	58.402583	0.017123	0.255094	14.898127	0.067123
29	4.116136	62.322712	0.016046	0.242946	15.141074	0.066046
30	4.321942	66.438848	0.015051	0.231377	15.372451	0.065051
31	4.538039	70.760790	0.014132	0.220359	15.592811	0.064132
32	4.764941	75.298829	0.013280	0.209866	15.802677	0.063280
33	5.003189	80.063771	0.012490	0.199873	16.002549	0.062490
34	5.253348	85.066959	0.011755	0.190355	16.192904	0.061755
35	5.516015	90.320307	0.011072	0.181290	16.374194	0.061072
36	5.791816	95.836323	0.010434	0.172657	16.546852	0.060434
37	6.081407	101.628139	0.009840	0.164436	16.711287	0.059840
38	6.385477	107.709546	0.009284	0.156605	16.867893	0.059284
39	6.704751	114.095023	0.008765	0.149148	17.017041	0.058765
40	7.039989	120.799774	0.008278	0.142046	17.159086	0.058278
41	7.391988	127.839763	0.007822	0.135282	17.294368	0.057822
42	7.761588	135.231751	0.007395	0.128840	17.423208	0.057395
43	8.149667	142.993339	0.006993	0.122704	17.545912	0.056993
44	8.557150	151.143006	0.006616	0.116861	17.662773	0.056616
45	8.985008	159.700156	0.006262	0.111297	17.774070	0.056262
46	9.434258	168.685164	0.005928	0.105997	17.880066	0.055928
47	9.905971	178.119422	0.005614	0.100949	17.981016	0.055614
48	10.401270	188.025393	0.005318	0.096142	18.077158	0.055318
49	10.921333	198.426663	0.005040	0.091564	18.168722	0.055040
50	11.467400	209.347996	0.004777	0.087204	18.255925	0.054777

	1 AMOUNT OF $1 AT COMPOUND INTEREST	2 ACCUMULATION OF $1 PER PERIOD	3 SINKING FUND FACTOR	4 PRESENT VALUE REVERSION OF $1	5 PRESENT VALUE ORD. ANNUITY $1 PER PERIOD	6 INSTALMENT TO AMORTIZE $1
YEARS						
1	1.060000	1.000000	1.000000	0.943396	0.943396	1.060000
2	1.123600	2.060000	0.485437	0.889996	1.833393	0.545437
3	1.191016	3.183600	0.314110	0.839619	2.673012	0.374110
4	1.262477	4.374616	0.228591	0.792094	3.465106	0.288591
5	1.338226	5.637093	0.177396	0.747258	4.212364	0.237396
6	1.418519	6.975319	0.143363	0.704961	4.917324	0.203363
7	1.503630	8.393838	0.119135	0.665057	5.582381	0.179135
8	1.593848	9.897468	0.101036	0.627412	6.209794	0.161036
9	1.689479	11.491316	0.087022	0.591898	6.801692	0.147022
10	1.790848	13.180795	0.075868	0.558395	7.360087	0.135868
11	1.898299	14.971643	0.066793	0.526788	7.886875	0.126793
12	2.012196	16.869941	0.059277	0.496969	8.383844	0.119277
13	2.132928	18.882138	0.052960	0.468839	8.852683	0.112960
14	2.260904	21.015066	0.047585	0.442301	9.294984	0.107585
15	2.396558	23.275970	0.042963	0.417265	9.712249	0.102963
16	2.540352	25.672528	0.038952	0.393646	10.105895	0.098952
17	2.692773	28.212880	0.035445	0.371364	10.477260	0.095445
18	2.854339	30.905653	0.032357	0.350344	10.827603	0.092357
19	3.025600	33.759992	0.029621	0.330513	11.158116	0.089621
20	3.207135	36.785591	0.027185	0.311805	11.469921	0.087185
21	3.399564	39.992727	0.025005	0.294155	11.764077	0.085005
22	3.603537	43.392290	0.023046	0.277505	12.041582	0.083046
23	3.819750	46.995828	0.021278	0.261797	12.303379	0.081278
24	4.048935	50.815577	0.019679	0.246979	12.550358	0.079679
25	4.291871	54.864512	0.018227	0.232999	12.783356	0.078227
26	4.549383	59.156383	0.016904	0.219810	13.003166	0.076904
27	4.822346	63.705766	0.015697	0.207368	13.210534	0.075697
28	5.111687	68.528112	0.014593	0.195630	13.406164	0.074593
29	5.418388	73.639798	0.013580	0.184557	13.590721	0.073580
30	5.743491	79.058186	0.012649	0.174110	13.764831	0.072649
31	6.088101	84.801677	0.011792	0.164255	13.929086	0.071792
32	6.453387	90.889778	0.011002	0.154957	14.084043	0.071002
33	6.840590	97.343165	0.010273	0.146186	14.230230	0.070273
34	7.251025	104.183755	0.009598	0.137912	14.368141	0.069598
35	7.686087	111.434780	0.008974	0.130105	14.498246	0.068974
36	8.147252	119.120867	0.008395	0.122741	14.620987	0.068395
37	8.636087	127.268119	0.007857	0.115793	14.736780	0.067857
38	9.154252	135.904206	0.007358	0.109239	14.846019	0.067358
39	9.703507	145.058458	0.006894	0.103056	14.949075	0.066894
40	10.285718	154.761966	0.006462	0.097222	15.046297	0.066462
41	10.902861	165.047684	0.006059	0.091719	15.138016	0.066059
42	11.557033	175.950545	0.005683	0.086527	15.224543	0.065683
43	12.250455	187.507577	0.005333	0.081630	15.306173	0.065333
44	12.985482	199.758032	0.005006	0.077009	15.383182	0.065006
45	13.764611	212.743514	0.004700	0.072650	15.455832	0.064700
46	14.590487	226.508125	0.004415	0.068538	15.524370	0.064415
47	15.465917	241.098612	0.004148	0.064658	15.589028	0.064148
48	16.393872	256.564529	0.003898	0.060998	15.650027	0.063898
49	17.377504	272.958401	0.003664	0.057546	15.707572	0.063664
50	18.420154	290.335905	0.003444	0.054288	15.761861	0.063444

7.00%   ANNUAL COMPOUND INTEREST TABLES   7.00%
                                  EFFECTIVE RATE 7.00

	1 AMOUNT OF $1 AT COMPOUND INTEREST	2 ACCUMULATION OF $1 PER PERIOD	3 SINKING FUND FACTOR	4 PRESENT VALUE REVERSION OF $1	5 PRESENT VALUE ORD. ANNUITY $1 PER PERIOD	6 INSTALMENT TO AMORTIZE $1
YEARS						
1	1.070000	1.000000	1.000000	0.934579	0.934579	1.070000
2	1.144900	2.070000	0.483092	0.873439	1.808018	0.553092
3	1.225043	3.214900	0.311052	0.816298	2.624316	0.381052
4	1.310796	4.439943	0.225228	0.762895	3.387211	0.295228
5	1.402552	5.750739	0.173891	0.712986	4.100197	0.243891
6	1.500730	7.153291	0.139796	0.666342	4.766540	0.209796
7	1.605781	8.654021	0.115553	0.622750	5.389289	0.185553
8	1.718186	10.259803	0.097468	0.582009	5.971299	0.167468
9	1.838459	11.977989	0.083486	0.543934	6.515232	0.153486
10	1.967151	13.816448	0.072378	0.508349	7.023582	0.142378
11	2.104852	15.783599	0.063357	0.475093	7.498674	0.133357
12	2.252192	17.888451	0.055902	0.444012	7.942686	0.125902
13	2.409845	20.140643	0.049651	0.414964	8.357651	0.119651
14	2.578534	22.550488	0.044345	0.387817	8.745468	0.114345
15	2.759032	25.129022	0.039795	0.362446	9.107914	0.109795
16	2.952164	27.888054	0.035858	0.338735	9.446649	0.105858
17	3.158815	30.840217	0.032425	0.316574	9.763223	0.102425
18	3.379932	33.999033	0.029413	0.295864	10.059087	0.099413
19	3.616528	37.378965	0.026753	0.276508	10.335595	0.096753
20	3.869684	40.995492	0.024393	0.258419	10.594014	0.094393
21	4.140562	44.865177	0.022289	0.241513	10.835527	0.092289
22	4.430402	49.005739	0.020406	0.225713	11.061240	0.090406
23	4.740530	53.436141	0.018714	0.210947	11.272187	0.088714
24	5.072367	58.176671	0.017189	0.197147	11.469334	0.087189
25	5.427433	63.249038	0.015811	0.184249	11.653583	0.085811
26	5.807353	68.676470	0.014561	0.172195	11.825779	0.084561
27	6.213868	74.483823	0.013426	0.160930	11.986709	0.083426
28	6.648838	80.697691	0.012392	0.150402	12.137111	0.082392
29	7.114257	87.346529	0.011449	0.140563	12.277674	0.081449
30	7.612255	94.460786	0.010586	0.131367	12.409041	0.080586
31	8.145113	102.073041	0.009797	0.122773	12.531814	0.079797
32	8.715271	110.218154	0.009073	0.114741	12.646555	0.079073
33	9.325340	118.933425	0.008408	0.107235	12.753790	0.078408
34	9.978114	128.258765	0.007797	0.100219	12.854009	0.077797
35	10.676581	138.236878	0.007234	0.093663	12.947672	0.077234
36	11.423942	148.913460	0.006715	0.087535	13.035208	0.076715
37	12.223618	160.337402	0.006237	0.081809	13.117017	0.076237
38	13.079271	172.561020	0.005795	0.076457	13.193473	0.075795
39	13.994820	185.640292	0.005387	0.071455	13.264928	0.075387
40	14.974458	199.635112	0.005009	0.066780	13.331709	0.075009
41	16.022670	214.609570	0.004660	0.062412	13.394120	0.074660
42	17.144257	230.632240	0.004336	0.058329	13.452449	0.074336
43	18.344355	247.776496	0.004036	0.054513	13.506962	0.074036
44	19.628460	266.120851	0.003758	0.050946	13.557908	0.073758
45	21.002452	285.749311	0.003500	0.047613	13.605522	0.073500
46	22.472623	306.751763	0.003260	0.044499	13.650020	0.073260
47	24.045707	329.224386	0.003037	0.041587	13.691608	0.073037
48	25.728907	353.270093	0.002831	0.038867	13.730474	0.072831
49	27.529930	378.999000	0.002639	0.036324	13.766799	0.072639
50	29.457025	406.528929	0.002460	0.033948	13.800746	0.072460

8.00%   ANNUAL COMPOUND INTEREST TABLES   8.00%
                              EFFECTIVE RATE 8.00

	1 AMOUNT OF $1 AT COMPOUND INTEREST	2 ACCUMULATION OF $1 PER PERIOD	3 SINKING FUND FACTOR	4 PRESENT VALUE REVERSION OF $1	5 PRESENT VALUE ORD. ANNUITY $1 PER PERIOD	6 INSTALMENT TO AMORTIZE $1
YEARS						
1	1.080000	1.000000	1.000000	0.925926	0.925926	1.080000
2	1.166400	2.080000	0.480769	0.857339	1.783265	0.560769
3	1.259712	3.246400	0.308034	0.793832	2.577097	0.388034
4	1.360489	4.506112	0.221921	0.735030	3.312127	0.301921
5	1.469328	5.866601	0.170456	0.680583	3.992710	0.250456
6	1.586874	7.335929	0.136315	0.630170	4.622880	0.216315
7	1.713824	8.922803	0.112072	0.583490	5.206370	0.192072
8	1.850930	10.636628	0.094015	0.540269	5.746639	0.174015
9	1.999005	12.487558	0.080080	0.500249	6.246888	0.160080
10	2.158925	14.486562	0.069029	0.463193	6.710081	0.149029
11	2.331639	16.645487	0.060076	0.428883	7.138964	0.140076
12	2.518170	18.977126	0.052695	0.397114	7.536078	0.132695
13	2.719624	21.495297	0.046522	0.367698	7.903776	0.126522
14	2.937194	24.214920	0.041297	0.340461	8.244237	0.121297
15	3.172169	27.152114	0.036830	0.315242	8.559479	0.116830
16	3.425943	30.324283	0.032977	0.291890	8.851369	0.112977
17	3.700018	33.750226	0.029629	0.270269	9.121638	0.109629
18	3.996019	37.450244	0.026702	0.250249	9.371887	0.106702
19	4.315701	41.446263	0.024128	0.231712	9.603599	0.104128
20	4.660957	45.761964	0.021852	0.214548	9.818147	0.101852
21	5.033834	50.422921	0.019832	0.198656	10.016803	0.099832
22	5.436540	55.456755	0.018032	0.183941	10.200744	0.098032
23	5.871464	60.893296	0.016422	0.170315	10.371059	0.096422
24	6.341181	66.764759	0.014978	0.157699	10.528758	0.094978
25	6.848475	73.105940	0.013679	0.146018	10.674776	0.093679
26	7.396353	79.954415	0.012507	0.135202	10.809978	0.092507
27	7.988061	87.350768	0.011448	0.125187	10.935165	0.091448
28	8.627106	95.338830	0.010489	0.115914	11.051078	0.090489
29	9.317275	103.965936	0.009619	0.107328	11.158406	0.089619
30	10.062657	113.283211	0.008827	0.099377	11.257783	0.088827
31	10.867669	123.345868	0.008107	0.092016	11.349799	0.088107
32	11.737083	134.213537	0.007451	0.085200	11.434999	0.087451
33	12.676050	145.950620	0.006852	0.078889	11.513888	0.086852
34	13.690134	158.626670	0.006304	0.073045	11.586934	0.086304
35	14.785344	172.316804	0.005803	0.067635	11.654568	0.085803
36	15.968172	187.102148	0.005345	0.062625	11.717193	0.085345
37	17.245626	203.070320	0.004924	0.057986	11.775179	0.084924
38	18.625276	220.315945	0.004539	0.053690	11.828869	0.084539
39	20.115298	238.941221	0.004185	0.049713	11.878582	0.084185
40	21.724521	259.056519	0.003860	0.046031	11.924613	0.083860
41	23.462483	280.781040	0.003561	0.042621	11.967235	0.083561
42	25.339482	304.243523	0.003287	0.039464	12.006699	0.083287
43	27.366640	329.583005	0.003034	0.036541	12.043240	0.083034
44	29.555972	356.949646	0.002802	0.033834	12.077074	0.082802
45	31.920449	386.505617	0.002587	0.031328	12.108402	0.082587
46	34.474085	418.426067	0.002390	0.029007	12.137409	0.082390
47	37.232012	452.900152	0.002208	0.026859	12.164267	0.082208
48	40.210573	490.132164	0.002040	0.024869	12.189136	0.082040
49	43.427419	530.342737	0.001886	0.023027	12.212163	0.081886
50	46.901613	573.770156	0.001743	0.021321	12.233485	0.081743

9.00%   ANNUAL COMPOUND INTEREST TABLES   9.00%
                   EFFECTIVE RATE 9.00

	1 AMOUNT OF $1 AT COMPOUND INTEREST	2 ACCUMULATION OF $1 PER PERIOD	3 SINKING FUND FACTOR	4 PRESENT VALUE REVERSION OF $1	5 PRESENT VALUE ORD. ANNUITY $1 PER PERIOD	6 INSTALMENT TO AMORTIZE $1
YEARS						
1	1.090000	1.000000	1.000000	0.917431	0.917431	1.090000
2	1.188100	2.090000	0.478469	0.841680	1.759111	0.568469
3	1.295029	3.278100	0.305055	0.772183	2.531295	0.395055
4	1.411582	4.573129	0.218669	0.708425	3.239720	0.308669
5	1.538624	5.984711	0.167092	0.649931	3.889651	0.257092
6	1.677100	7.523335	0.132920	0.596267	4.485919	0.222920
7	1.828039	9.200435	0.108691	0.547034	5.032953	0.198691
8	1.992563	11.028474	0.090674	0.501866	5.534819	0.180674
9	2.171893	13.021036	0.076799	0.460428	5.995247	0.166799
10	2.367364	15.192930	0.065820	0.422411	6.417658	0.155820
11	2.580426	17.560293	0.056947	0.387533	6.805191	0.146947
12	2.812665	20.140720	0.049651	0.355535	7.160725	0.139651
13	3.065805	22.953385	0.043567	0.326179	7.486904	0.133567
14	3.341727	26.019189	0.038433	0.299246	7.786150	0.128433
15	3.642482	29.360916	0.034059	0.274538	8.060688	0.124059
16	3.970306	33.003399	0.030300	0.251870	8.312558	0.120300
17	4.327633	36.973705	0.027046	0.231073	8.543631	0.117046
18	4.717120	41.301338	0.024212	0.211994	8.755625	0.114212
19	5.141661	46.018458	0.021730	0.194490	8.950115	0.111730
20	5.604411	51.160120	0.019546	0.178431	9.128546	0.109546
21	6.108808	56.764530	0.017617	0.163698	9.292244	0.107617
22	6.658600	62.873338	0.015905	0.150182	9.442425	0.105905
23	7.257874	69.531939	0.014382	0.137781	9.580207	0.104382
24	7.911083	76.789813	0.013023	0.126405	9.706612	0.103023
25	8.623081	84.700896	0.011806	0.115968	9.822580	0.101806
26	9.399158	93.323977	0.010715	0.106393	9.928972	0.100715
27	10.245082	102.723135	0.009735	0.097608	10.026580	0.099735
28	11.167140	112.968217	0.008852	0.089548	10.116128	0.098852
29	12.172182	124.135356	0.008056	0.082155	10.198283	0.098056
30	13.267678	136.307539	0.007336	0.075371	10.273654	0.097336
31	14.461770	149.575217	0.006686	0.069148	10.342802	0.096686
32	15.763329	164.036987	0.006096	0.063438	10.406240	0.096096
33	17.182028	179.800315	0.005562	0.058200	10.464441	0.095562
34	18.728411	196.982344	0.005077	0.053395	10.517835	0.095077
35	20.413968	215.710755	0.004636	0.048986	10.566821	0.094636
36	22.251225	236.124723	0.004235	0.044941	10.611763	0.094235
37	24.253835	258.375948	0.003870	0.041231	10.652993	0.093870
38	26.436680	282.629783	0.003538	0.037826	10.690820	0.093538
39	28.815982	309.066463	0.003236	0.034703	10.725523	0.093236
40	31.409420	337.882445	0.002960	0.031838	10.757360	0.092960
41	34.236268	369.291865	0.002708	0.029209	10.786569	0.092708
42	37.317532	403.528133	0.002478	0.026797	10.813366	0.092478
43	40.676110	440.845665	0.002268	0.024584	10.837950	0.092268
44	44.336960	481.521775	0.002077	0.022555	10.860505	0.092077
45	48.327286	525.858734	0.001902	0.020692	10.881197	0.091902
46	52.676742	574.186021	0.001742	0.018984	10.900181	0.091742
47	57.417649	626.862762	0.001595	0.017416	10.917597	0.091595
48	62.585237	684.280411	0.001461	0.015978	10.933575	0.091461
49	68.217908	746.865648	0.001339	0.014659	10.948234	0.091339
50	74.357520	815.083556	0.001227	0.013449	10.961683	0.091227

10.00%   ANNUAL COMPOUND INTEREST TABLES   10.00%
                         EFFECTIVE RATE 10.00

	1 AMOUNT OF $1 AT COMPOUND INTEREST	2 ACCUMULATION OF $1 PER PERIOD	3 SINKING FUND FACTOR	4 PRESENT VALUE REVERSION OF $1	5 PRESENT VALUE ORD. ANNUITY $1 PER PERIOD	6 INSTALMENT TO AMORTIZE $1
YEARS						
1	1.100000	1.000000	1.000000	0.909091	0.909091	1.100000
2	1.210000	2.100000	0.476190	0.826446	1.735537	0.576190
3	1.331000	3.310000	0.302115	0.751315	2.486852	0.402115
4	1.464100	4.641000	0.215471	0.683013	3.169865	0.315471
5	1.610510	6.105100	0.163797	0.620921	3.790787	0.263797
6	1.771561	7.715610	0.129607	0.564474	4.355261	0.229607
7	1.948717	9.487171	0.105405	0.513158	4.868419	0.205405
8	2.143589	11.435888	0.087444	0.466507	5.334926	0.187444
9	2.357948	13.579477	0.073641	0.424098	5.759024	0.173641
10	2.593742	15.937425	0.062745	0.385543	6.144567	0.162745
11	2.853117	18.531167	0.053963	0.350494	6.495061	0.153963
12	3.138428	21.384284	0.046763	0.318631	6.813692	0.146763
13	3.452271	24.522712	0.040779	0.289664	7.103356	0.140779
14	3.797498	27.974983	0.035746	0.263331	7.366687	0.135746
15	4.177248	31.772482	0.031474	0.239392	7.606080	0.131474
16	4.594973	35.949730	0.027817	0.217629	7.823709	0.127817
17	5.054470	40.544703	0.024664	0.197845	8.021553	0.124664
18	5.559917	45.599173	0.021930	0.179859	8.201412	0.121930
19	6.115909	51.159090	0.019547	0.163508	8.364920	0.119547
20	6.727500	57.274999	0.017460	0.148644	8.513564	0.117460
21	7.400250	64.002499	0.015624	0.135131	8.648694	0.115624
22	8.140275	71.402749	0.014005	0.122846	8.771540	0.114005
23	8.954302	79.543024	0.012572	0.111678	8.883218	0.112572
24	9.849733	88.497327	0.011300	0.101526	8.984744	0.111300
25	10.834706	98.347059	0.010168	0.092296	9.077040	0.110168
26	11.918177	109.181765	0.009159	0.083905	9.160945	0.109159
27	13.109994	121.099942	0.008258	0.076278	9.237223	0.108258
28	14.420994	134.209936	0.007451	0.069343	9.306567	0.107451
29	15.863093	148.630930	0.006728	0.063039	9.369606	0.106728
30	17.449402	164.494023	0.006079	0.057309	9.426914	0.106079
31	19.194342	181.943425	0.005496	0.052099	9.479013	0.105496
32	21.113777	201.137767	0.004972	0.047362	9.526376	0.104972
33	23.225154	222.251544	0.004499	0.043057	9.569432	0.104499
34	25.547670	245.476699	0.004074	0.039143	9.608575	0.104074
35	28.102437	271.024368	0.003690	0.035584	9.644159	0.103690
36	30.912681	299.126805	0.003343	0.032349	9.676508	0.103343
37	34.003949	330.039486	0.003030	0.029408	9.705917	0.103030
38	37.404343	364.043434	0.002747	0.026735	9.732651	0.102747
39	41.144778	401.447778	0.002491	0.024304	9.756956	0.102491
40	45.259256	442.592556	0.002259	0.022095	9.779051	0.102259
41	49.785181	487.851811	0.002050	0.020086	9.799137	0.102050
42	54.763699	537.636992	0.001860	0.018260	9.817397	0.101860
43	60.240069	592.400692	0.001688	0.016600	9.833998	0.101688
44	66.264076	652.640761	0.001532	0.015091	9.849089	0.101532
45	72.890484	718.904837	0.001391	0.013719	9.862808	0.101391
46	80.179532	791.795321	0.001263	0.012472	9.875280	0.101263
47	88.197485	871.974853	0.001147	0.011338	9.886618	0.101147
48	97.017234	960.172338	0.001041	0.010307	9.896926	0.101041
49	106.718957	1057.189572	0.000946	0.009370	9.906296	0.100946
50	117.390853	1163.908529	0.000859	0.008519	9.914814	0.100859

11.00%   ANNUAL COMPOUND INTEREST TABLES   11.00%
                    EFFECTIVE RATE 11.00

	1	2	3	4	5	6
	AMOUNT OF $1	ACCUMULATION	SINKING	PRESENT VALUE	PRESENT VALUE	INSTALMENT
	AT COMPOUND	OF $1	FUND	REVERSION	ORD. ANNUITY	TO
	INTEREST	PER PERIOD	FACTOR	OF $1	$1 PER PERIOD	AMORTIZE $1

YEARS

1	1.110000	1.000000	1.000000	0.900901	0.900901	1.110000
2	1.232100	2.110000	0.473934	0.811622	1.712523	0.583934
3	1.367631	3.342100	0.299213	0.731191	2.443715	0.409213
4	1.518070	4.709731	0.212326	0.658731	3.102446	0.322326
5	1.685058	6.227801	0.160570	0.593451	3.695897	0.270570
6	1.870415	7.912860	0.126377	0.534641	4.230538	0.236377
7	2.076160	9.783274	0.102215	0.481658	4.712196	0.212215
8	2.304538	11.859434	0.084321	0.433926	5.146123	0.194321
9	2.558037	14.163972	0.070602	0.390925	5.537048	0.180602
10	2.839421	16.722009	0.059801	0.352184	5.889232	0.169801
11	3.151757	19.561430	0.051121	0.317283	6.206515	0.161121
12	3.498451	22.713187	0.044027	0.285841	6.492356	0.154027
13	3.883280	26.211638	0.038151	0.257514	6.749870	0.148151
14	4.310441	30.094918	0.033228	0.231995	6.981865	0.143228
15	4.784589	34.405359	0.029065	0.209004	7.190870	0.139065
16	5.310894	39.189948	0.025517	0.188292	7.379162	0.135517
17	5.895093	44.500843	0.022471	0.169633	7.548794	0.132471
18	6.543553	50.395936	0.019843	0.152822	7.701617	0.129843
19	7.263344	56.939488	0.017563	0.137678	7.839294	0.127563
20	8.062312	64.202832	0.015576	0.124034	7.963328	0.125576
21	8.949166	72.265144	0.013838	0.111742	8.075070	0.123838
22	9.933574	81.214309	0.012313	0.100669	8.175739	0.122313
23	11.026267	91.147884	0.010971	0.090693	8.266432	0.120971
24	12.239157	102.174151	0.009787	0.081705	8.348137	0.119787
25	13.585464	114.413307	0.008740	0.073608	8.421745	0.118740
26	15.079865	127.998771	0.007813	0.066314	8.488058	0.117813
27	16.738650	143.078636	0.006989	0.059742	8.547800	0.116989
28	18.579901	159.817286	0.006257	0.053822	8.601622	0.116257
29	20.623691	178.397187	0.005605	0.048488	8.650110	0.115605
30	22.892297	199.020878	0.005025	0.043683	8.693793	0.115025
31	25.410449	221.913174	0.004506	0.039354	8.733146	0.114506
32	28.205599	247.323624	0.004043	0.035454	8.768600	0.114043
33	31.308214	275.529222	0.003629	0.031940	8.800541	0.113629
34	34.752118	306.837437	0.003259	0.028775	8.829316	0.113259
35	38.574851	341.589555	0.002927	0.025924	8.855240	0.112927
36	42.818085	380.164406	0.002630	0.023355	8.878594	0.112630
37	47.528074	422.982490	0.002364	0.021040	8.899635	0.112364
38	52.756162	470.510564	0.002125	0.018955	8.918590	0.112125
39	58.559340	523.266726	0.001911	0.017077	8.935666	0.111911
40	65.000867	581.826066	0.001719	0.015384	8.951051	0.111719
41	72.150963	646.826934	0.001546	0.013860	8.964911	0.111546
42	80.087569	718.977896	0.001391	0.012486	8.977397	0.111391
43	88.897201	799.065465	0.001251	0.011249	8.988646	0.111251
44	98.675893	887.962666	0.001126	0.010134	8.998780	0.111126
45	109.530242	986.638559	0.001014	0.009130	9.007910	0.111014
46	121.578568	1096.168801	0.000912	0.008225	9.016135	0.110912
47	134.952211	1217.747369	0.000821	0.007410	9.023545	0.110821
48	149.796954	1352.699580	0.000739	0.006676	9.030221	0.110739
49	166.274619	1502.496534	0.000666	0.006014	9.036235	0.110666
50	184.564827	1668.771152	0.000599	0.005418	9.041653	0.110599

12.00%   ANNUAL COMPOUND INTEREST TABLES   12.00%
EFFECTIVE RATE 12.00

	1	2	3	4	5	6
	AMOUNT OF $1 AT COMPOUND INTEREST	ACCUMULATION OF $1 PER PERIOD	SINKING FUND FACTOR	PRESENT VALUE REVERSION OF $1	PRESENT VALUE ORD. ANNUITY $1 PER PERIOD	INSTALMENT TO AMORTIZE $1
YEARS						
1	1.120000	1.000000	1.000000	0.892857	0.892857	1.120000
2	1.254400	2.120000	0.471698	0.797194	1.690051	0.591698
3	1.404928	3.374400	0.296349	0.711780	2.401831	0.416349
4	1.573519	4.779328	0.209234	0.635518	3.037349	0.329234
5	1.762342	6.352847	0.157410	0.567427	3.604776	0.277410
6	1.973823	8.115189	0.123226	0.506631	4.111407	0.243226
7	2.210681	10.089012	0.099118	0.452349	4.563757	0.219118
8	2.475963	12.299693	0.081303	0.403883	4.967640	0.201303
9	2.773079	14.775656	0.067679	0.360610	5.328250	0.187679
10	3.105848	17.548735	0.056984	0.321973	5.650223	0.176984
11	3.478550	20.654583	0.048415	0.287476	5.937699	0.168415
12	3.895976	24.133133	0.041437	0.256675	6.194374	0.161437
13	4.363493	28.029109	0.035677	0.229174	6.423548	0.155677
14	4.887112	32.392602	0.030871	0.204620	6.628168	0.150871
15	5.473566	37.279715	0.026824	0.182696	6.810864	0.146824
16	6.130394	42.753280	0.023390	0.163122	6.973986	0.143390
17	6.866041	48.883674	0.020457	0.145644	7.119630	0.140457
18	7.689966	55.749715	0.017937	0.130040	7.249670	0.137937
19	8.612762	63.439681	0.015763	0.116107	7.365777	0.135763
20	9.646293	72.052442	0.013879	0.103667	7.469444	0.133879
21	10.803848	81.698736	0.012240	0.092560	7.562003	0.132240
22	12.100310	92.502584	0.010811	0.082643	7.644646	0.130811
23	13.552347	104.602894	0.009560	0.073788	7.718434	0.129560
24	15.178629	118.155241	0.008463	0.065882	7.784316	0.128463
25	17.000064	133.333870	0.007500	0.058823	7.843139	0.127500
26	19.040072	150.333934	0.006652	0.052521	7.895660	0.126652
27	21.324881	169.374007	0.005904	0.046894	7.942554	0.125904
28	23.883866	190.698887	0.005244	0.041869	7.984423	0.125244
29	26.749930	214.582754	0.004660	0.037383	8.021806	0.124660
30	29.959922	241.332684	0.004144	0.033378	8.055184	0.124144
31	33.555113	271.292606	0.003686	0.029802	8.084986	0.123686
32	37.581726	304.847719	0.003280	0.026609	8.111594	0.123280
33	42.091533	342.429446	0.002920	0.023758	8.135352	0.122920
34	47.142517	384.520979	0.002601	0.021212	8.156564	0.122601
35	52.799620	431.663496	0.002317	0.018940	8.175504	0.122317
36	59.135574	484.463116	0.002064	0.016910	8.192414	0.122064
37	66.231843	543.598690	0.001840	0.015098	8.207513	0.121840
38	74.179664	609.830533	0.001640	0.013481	8.220993	0.121640
39	83.081224	684.010197	0.001462	0.012036	8.233030	0.121462
40	93.050970	767.091420	0.001304	0.010747	8.243777	0.121304
41	104.217087	860.142391	0.001163	0.009595	8.253372	0.121163
42	116.723137	964.359478	0.001037	0.008567	8.261939	0.121037
43	130.729914	1081.082615	0.000925	0.007649	8.269589	0.120925
44	146.417503	1211.812529	0.000825	0.006830	8.276418	0.120825
45	163.987604	1358.230032	0.000736	0.006098	8.282516	0.120736
46	183.666116	1522.217636	0.000657	0.005445	8.287961	0.120657
47	205.706050	1705.883752	0.000586	0.004861	8.292822	0.120586
48	230.390776	1911.589803	0.000523	0.004340	8.297163	0.120523
49	258.037669	2141.980579	0.000467	0.003875	8.301038	0.120467
50	289.002190	2400.018249	0.000417	0.003460	8.304498	0.120417

13.00%

ANNUAL COMPOUND INTEREST TABLES
EFFECTIVE RATE 13.00

13.00%

	1 AMOUNT OF $1 AT COMPOUND INTEREST	2 ACCUMULATION OF $1 PER PERIOD	3 SINKING FUND FACTOR	4 PRESENT VALUE REVERSION OF $1	5 PRESENT VALUE ORD. ANNUITY $1 PER PERIOD	6 INSTALMENT TO AMORTIZE $1
YEARS						
1	1.130000	1.000000	1.000000	0.884956	0.884956	1.130000
2	1.276900	2.130000	0.469484	0.783147	1.668102	0.599484
3	1.442897	3.406900	0.293522	0.693050	2.361153	0.423522
4	1.630474	4.849797	0.206194	0.613319	2.974471	0.336194
5	1.842435	6.480271	0.154315	0.542760	3.517231	0.284315
6	2.081952	8.322706	0.120153	0.480319	3.997550	0.250153
7	2.352605	10.404658	0.096111	0.425061	4.422610	0.226111
8	2.658444	12.757263	0.078387	0.376160	4.798770	0.208387
9	3.004042	15.415707	0.064869	0.332885	5.131655	0.194869
10	3.394567	18.419749	0.054290	0.294588	5.426243	0.184290
11	3.835861	21.814317	0.045841	0.260698	5.686941	0.175841
12	4.334523	25.650178	0.038986	0.230706	5.917647	0.168986
13	4.898011	29.984701	0.033350	0.204165	6.121812	0.163350
14	5.534753	34.882712	0.028667	0.180677	6.302488	0.158667
15	6.254270	40.417464	0.024742	0.159891	6.462379	0.154742
16	7.067326	46.671735	0.021426	0.141496	6.603875	0.151426
17	7.986078	53.739060	0.018608	0.125218	6.729093	0.148608
18	9.024268	61.725138	0.016201	0.110812	6.839905	0.146201
19	10.197423	70.749406	0.014134	0.098064	6.937969	0.144134
20	11.523088	80.946829	0.012354	0.086782	7.024752	0.142354
21	13.021089	92.469917	0.010814	0.076798	7.101550	0.140814
22	14.713831	105.491006	0.009479	0.067963	7.169513	0.139479
23	16.626629	120.204837	0.008319	0.060144	7.229658	0.138319
24	18.788091	136.831465	0.007308	0.053225	7.282883	0.137308
25	21.230542	155.619556	0.006426	0.047102	7.329985	0.136426
26	23.990513	176.850098	0.005655	0.041683	7.371668	0.135655
27	27.109279	200.840611	0.004979	0.036888	7.408556	0.134979
28	30.633486	227.949890	0.004387	0.032644	7.441200	0.134387
29	34.615839	258.583376	0.003867	0.028889	7.470088	0.133867
30	39.115898	293.199215	0.003411	0.025565	7.495653	0.133411
31	44.200965	332.315113	0.003009	0.022624	7.518277	0.133009
32	49.947090	376.516078	0.002656	0.020021	7.538299	0.132656
33	56.440212	426.463168	0.002345	0.017718	7.556016	0.132345
34	63.777439	482.903380	0.002071	0.015680	7.571696	0.132071
35	72.068506	546.680819	0.001829	0.013876	7.585572	0.131829
36	81.437412	618.749325	0.001616	0.012279	7.597851	0.131616
37	92.024276	700.186738	0.001428	0.010867	7.608718	0.131428
38	103.987432	792.211014	0.001262	0.009617	7.618334	0.131262
39	117.505798	896.198445	0.001116	0.008510	7.626844	0.131116
40	132.781552	1013.704243	0.000986	0.007531	7.634376	0.130986
41	150.043153	1146.485795	0.000872	0.006665	7.641040	0.130872
42	169.548763	1296.528948	0.000771	0.005898	7.646938	0.130771
43	191.590103	1466.077712	0.000682	0.005219	7.652158	0.130682
44	216.496816	1657.667814	0.000603	0.004619	7.656777	0.130603
45	244.641402	1874.164630	0.000534	0.004088	7.660864	0.130534
46	276.444784	2118.806032	0.000472	0.003617	7.664482	0.130472
47	312.382606	2395.250816	0.000417	0.003201	7.667683	0.130417
48	352.992345	2707.633422	0.000369	0.002833	7.670516	0.130369
49	398.881350	3060.625767	0.000327	0.002507	7.673023	0.130327
50	450.735925	3459.507117	0.000289	0.002219	7.675242	0.130289

14.00%   ANNUAL COMPOUND INTEREST TABLES   14.00%
                              EFFECTIVE RATE 14.00

	1 AMOUNT OF $1 AT COMPOUND INTEREST	2 ACCUMULATION OF $1 PER PERIOD	3 SINKING FUND FACTOR	4 PRESENT VALUE REVERSION OF $1	5 PRESENT VALUE ORD. ANNUITY $1 PER PERIOD	6 INSTALMENT TO AMORTIZE $1
YEARS						
1	1.140000	1.000000	1.000000	0.877193	0.877193	1.140000
2	1.299600	2.140000	0.467290	0.769468	1.646661	0.607290
3	1.481544	3.439600	0.290731	0.674972	2.321632	0.430731
4	1.688960	4.921144	0.203205	0.592080	2.913712	0.343205
5	1.925415	6.610104	0.151284	0.519369	3.433081	0.291284
6	2.194973	8.535519	0.117157	0.455587	3.888668	0.257157
7	2.502269	10.730491	0.093192	0.399637	4.288305	0.233192
8	2.852586	13.232760	0.075570	0.350559	4.638864	0.215570
9	3.251949	16.085347	0.062168	0.307508	4.946372	0.202168
10	3.707221	19.337295	0.051714	0.269744	5.216116	0.191714
11	4.226232	23.044516	0.043394	0.236617	5.452733	0.183394
12	4.817905	27.270749	0.036669	0.207559	5.660292	0.176669
13	5.492411	32.088654	0.031164	0.182069	5.842362	0.171164
14	6.261349	37.581065	0.026609	0.159710	6.002072	0.166609
15	7.137938	43.842414	0.022809	0.140096	6.142168	0.162809
16	8.137249	50.980352	0.019615	0.122892	6.265060	0.159615
17	9.276464	59.117601	0.016915	0.107800	6.372859	0.156915
18	10.575169	68.394066	0.014621	0.094561	6.467420	0.154621
19	12.055693	78.969235	0.012663	0.082948	6.550369	0.152663
20	13.743490	91.024928	0.010986	0.072762	6.623131	0.150986
21	15.667578	104.768418	0.009545	0.063826	6.686957	0.149545
22	17.861039	120.435996	0.008303	0.055988	6.742944	0.148303
23	20.361585	138.297035	0.007231	0.049112	6.792056	0.147231
24	23.212207	158.658620	0.006303	0.043081	6.835137	0.146303
25	26.461916	181.870827	0.005498	0.037790	6.872927	0.145498
26	30.166584	208.332743	0.004800	0.033149	6.906077	0.144800
27	34.389906	238.499327	0.004193	0.029078	6.935155	0.144193
28	39.204493	272.889233	0.003664	0.025507	6.960662	0.143664
29	44.693122	312.093725	0.003204	0.022375	6.983037	0.143204
30	50.950159	356.786847	0.002803	0.019627	7.002664	0.142803
31	58.083181	407.737006	0.002453	0.017217	7.019881	0.142453
32	66.214826	465.820186	0.002147	0.015102	7.034983	0.142147
33	75.484902	532.035012	0.001880	0.013248	7.048231	0.141880
34	86.052788	607.519914	0.001646	0.011621	7.059852	0.141646
35	98.100178	693.572702	0.001442	0.010194	7.070045	0.141442
36	111.834203	791.672881	0.001263	0.008942	7.078987	0.141263
37	127.490992	903.507084	0.001107	0.007844	7.086831	0.141107
38	145.339731	1030.998076	0.000970	0.006880	7.093711	0.140970
39	165.687293	1176.337806	0.000850	0.006035	7.099747	0.140850
40	188.883514	1342.025099	0.000745	0.005294	7.105041	0.140745
41	215.327206	1530.908613	0.000653	0.004644	7.109685	0.140653
42	245.473015	1746.235819	0.000573	0.004074	7.113759	0.140573
43	279.839237	1991.708833	0.000502	0.003573	7.117332	0.140502
44	319.016730	2271.548070	0.000440	0.003135	7.120467	0.140440
45	363.679072	2590.564800	0.000386	0.002750	7.123217	0.140386
46	414.594142	2954.243872	0.000338	0.002412	7.125629	0.140338
47	472.637322	3368.838014	0.000297	0.002116	7.127744	0.140297
48	538.806547	3841.475336	0.000260	0.001856	7.129600	0.140260
49	614.239464	4380.281883	0.000228	0.001628	7.131228	0.140228
50	700.232988	4994.521346	0.000200	0.001428	7.132656	0.140200

15.00%   ANNUAL COMPOUND INTEREST TABLES   15.00%
                                   EFFECTIVE RATE 15.00

	1 AMOUNT OF $1 AT COMPOUND INTEREST	2 ACCUMULATION OF $1 PER PERIOD	3 SINKING FUND FACTOR	4 PRESENT VALUE REVERSION OF $1	5 PRESENT VALUE ORD. ANNUITY $1 PER PERIOD	6 INSTALMENT TO AMORTIZE $1
YEARS						
1	1.150000	1.000000	1.000000	0.869565	0.869565	1.150000
2	1.322500	2.150000	0.465116	0.756144	1.625709	0.615116
3	1.520875	3.472500	0.287977	0.657516	2.283225	0.437977
4	1.749006	4.993375	0.200265	0.571753	2.854978	0.350265
5	2.011357	6.742381	0.148316	0.497177	3.352155	0.298316
6	2.313061	8.753738	0.114237	0.432328	3.784483	0.264237
7	2.660020	11.066799	0.090360	0.375937	4.160420	0.240360
8	3.059023	13.726819	0.072850	0.326902	4.487322	0.222850
9	3.517876	16.785842	0.059574	0.284262	4.771584	0.209574
10	4.045558	20.303718	0.049252	0.247185	5.018769	0.199252
11	4.652391	24.349276	0.041069	0.214943	5.233712	0.191069
12	5.350250	29.001667	0.034481	0.186907	5.420619	0.184481
13	6.152788	34.351917	0.029110	0.162528	5.583147	0.179110
14	7.075706	40.504705	0.024688	0.141329	5.724476	0.174688
15	8.137062	47.580411	0.021017	0.122894	5.847370	0.171017
16	9.357621	55.717472	0.017948	0.106865	5.954235	0.167948
17	10.761264	65.075093	0.015367	0.092926	6.047161	0.165367
18	12.375454	75.836357	0.013186	0.080805	6.127966	0.163186
19	14.231772	88.211811	0.011336	0.070265	6.198231	0.161336
20	16.366537	102.443583	0.009761	0.061100	6.259331	0.159761
21	18.821518	118.810120	0.008417	0.053131	6.312462	0.158417
22	21.644746	137.631638	0.007266	0.046201	6.358663	0.157266
23	24.891458	159.276384	0.006278	0.040174	6.398837	0.156278
24	28.625176	184.167841	0.005430	0.034934	6.433771	0.155430
25	32.918953	212.793017	0.004699	0.030378	6.464149	0.154699
26	37.856796	245.711970	0.004070	0.026415	6.490564	0.154070
27	43.535315	283.568766	0.003526	0.022970	6.513534	0.153526
28	50.065612	327.104080	0.003057	0.019974	6.533508	0.153057
29	57.575454	377.169693	0.002651	0.017369	6.550877	0.152651
30	66.211772	434.745146	0.002300	0.015103	6.565980	0.152300
31	76.143538	500.956918	0.001996	0.013133	6.579113	0.151996
32	87.565068	577.100456	0.001733	0.011420	6.590533	0.151733
33	100.699829	664.665525	0.001505	0.009931	6.600463	0.151505
34	115.804803	765.365353	0.001307	0.008635	6.609099	0.151307
35	133.175523	881.170156	0.001135	0.007509	6.616607	0.151135
36	153.151852	1014.345680	0.000986	0.006529	6.623137	0.150986
37	176.124630	1167.497532	0.000857	0.005678	6.628815	0.150857
38	202.543324	1343.622161	0.000744	0.004937	6.633752	0.150744
39	232.924823	1546.165485	0.000647	0.004293	6.638045	0.150647
40	267.863546	1779.090308	0.000562	0.003733	6.641778	0.150562
41	308.043078	2046.953854	0.000489	0.003246	6.645025	0.150489
42	354.249540	2354.996933	0.000425	0.002823	6.647848	0.150425
43	407.386971	2709.246473	0.000369	0.002455	6.650302	0.150369
44	468.495017	3116.633443	0.000321	0.002134	6.652437	0.150321
45	538.769269	3585.128460	0.000279	0.001856	6.654293	0.150279
46	619.584659	4123.897729	0.000242	0.001614	6.655907	0.150242
47	712.522358	4743.482388	0.000211	0.001403	6.657310	0.150211
48	819.400712	5456.004746	0.000183	0.001220	6.658531	0.150183
49	942.310819	6275.405458	0.000159	0.001061	6.659592	0.150159
50	1083.657442	7217.716277	0.000139	0.000923	6.660515	0.150139

16.00%   ANNUAL COMPOUND INTEREST TABLES   16.00%
                                    EFFECTIVE RATE 16.00

	1	2	3	4	5	6
	AMOUNT OF $1 AT COMPOUND INTEREST	ACCUMULATION OF $1 PER PERIOD	SINKING FUND FACTOR	PRESENT VALUE REVERSION OF $1	PRESENT VALUE ORD. ANNUITY $1 PER PERIOD	INSTALMENT TO AMORTIZE $1
YEARS						
1	1.160000	1.000000	1.000000	0.862069	0.862069	1.160000
2	1.345600	2.160000	0.462963	0.743163	1.605232	0.622963
3	1.560896	3.505600	0.285258	0.640658	2.245890	0.445258
4	1.810639	5.066496	0.197375	0.552291	2.798181	0.357375
5	2.100342	6.877135	0.145409	0.476113	3.274294	0.305409
6	2.436396	8.977477	0.111390	0.410442	3.684736	0.271390
7	2.826220	11.413873	0.087613	0.353830	4.038565	0.247613
8	3.278415	14.240093	0.070224	0.305025	4.343591	0.230224
9	3.802961	17.518508	0.057082	0.262953	4.606544	0.217082
10	4.411435	21.321469	0.046901	0.226684	4.833227	0.206901
11	5.117265	25.732904	0.038861	0.195417	5.028644	0.198861
12	5.936027	30.850169	0.032415	0.168463	5.197107	0.192415
13	6.865791	36.786196	0.027184	0.145227	5.342334	0.187184
14	7.987516	43.671987	0.022898	0.125195	5.467529	0.182898
15	9.265521	51.659505	0.019358	0.107927	5.575456	0.179358
16	10.748004	60.925026	0.016414	0.093041	5.668497	0.176414
17	12.467685	71.673030	0.013952	0.080207	5.748704	0.173952
18	14.462514	84.140715	0.011885	0.069144	5.817848	0.171885
19	16.776517	98.603230	0.010142	0.059607	5.877455	0.170142
20	19.460759	115.379747	0.008667	0.051385	5.928841	0.168667
21	22.574481	134.840506	0.007416	0.044298	5.973139	0.167416
22	26.186398	157.414987	0.006353	0.038188	6.011326	0.166353
23	30.376222	183.601385	0.005447	0.032920	6.044247	0.165447
24	35.236417	213.977607	0.004673	0.028380	6.072627	0.164673
25	40.874244	249.214024	0.004013	0.024465	6.097092	0.164013
26	47.414123	290.088267	0.003447	0.021091	6.118183	0.163447
27	55.000382	337.502390	0.002963	0.018182	6.136364	0.162963
28	63.800444	392.502773	0.002548	0.015674	6.152038	0.162548
29	74.008515	456.303216	0.002192	0.013512	6.165550	0.162192
30	85.849877	530.311731	0.001886	0.011648	6.177198	0.161886
31	99.585857	616.161608	0.001623	0.010042	6.187240	0.161623
32	115.519594	715.747465	0.001397	0.008657	6.195897	0.161397
33	134.002729	831.267059	0.001203	0.007463	6.203359	0.161203
34	155.443166	965.269789	0.001036	0.006433	6.209792	0.161036
35	180.314073	1120.712955	0.000892	0.005546	6.215338	0.160892
36	209.164324	1301.027028	0.000769	0.004781	6.220119	0.160769
37	242.630616	1510.191352	0.000662	0.004121	6.224241	0.160662
38	281.451515	1752.821968	0.000571	0.003553	6.227794	0.160571
39	326.483757	2034.273483	0.000492	0.003063	6.230857	0.160492
40	378.721158	2360.757241	0.000424	0.002640	6.233497	0.160424
41	439.316544	2739.478399	0.000365	0.002276	6.235773	0.160365
42	509.607191	3178.794943	0.000315	0.001962	6.237736	0.160315
43	591.144341	3688.402134	0.000271	0.001692	6.239427	0.160271
44	685.727436	4279.546475	0.000234	0.001458	6.240886	0.160234
45	795.443826	4965.273911	0.000201	0.001257	6.242143	0.160201
46	922.714838	5760.717737	0.000174	0.001084	6.243227	0.160174
47	1070.349212	6683.432575	0.000150	0.000934	6.244161	0.160150
48	1241.605086	7753.781787	0.000129	0.000805	6.244966	0.160129
49	1440.261900	8995.386873	0.000111	0.000694	6.245661	0.160111
50	1670.703804	10435.648773	0.000096	0.000599	6.246259	0.160096

20.00%   ANNUAL COMPOUND INTEREST TABLES   20.00%
                                    EFFECTIVE RATE 20.00

	1 AMOUNT OF $1 AT COMPOUND INTEREST	2 ACCUMULATION OF $1 PER PERIOD	3 SINKING FUND FACTOR	4 PRESENT VALUE REVERSION OF $1	5 PRESENT VALUE ORD. ANNUITY $1 PER PERIOD	6 INSTALMENT TO AMORTIZE $1
YEARS						
1	1.200000	1.000000	1.000000	0.833333	0.833333	1.200000
2	1.440000	2.200000	0.454545	0.694444	1.527778	0.654545
3	1.728000	3.640000	0.274725	0.578704	2.106481	0.474725
4	2.073600	5.368000	0.186289	0.482253	2.588735	0.386289
5	2.488320	7.441600	0.134380	0.401878	2.990612	0.334380
6	2.985984	9.929920	0.100706	0.334898	3.325510	0.300706
7	3.583181	12.915904	0.077424	0.279082	3.604592	0.277424
8	4.299817	16.499085	0.060609	0.232568	3.837160	0.260609
9	5.159780	20.798902	0.048079	0.193807	4.030967	0.248079
10	6.191736	25.958682	0.038523	0.161506	4.192472	0.238523
11	7.430084	32.150419	0.031104	0.134588	4.327060	0.231104
12	8.916100	39.580502	0.025265	0.112157	4.439217	0.225265
13	10.699321	48.496603	0.020620	0.093464	4.532681	0.220620
14	12.839185	59.195923	0.016893	0.077887	4.610567	0.216893
15	15.407022	72.035108	0.013882	0.064905	4.675473	0.213882
16	18.488426	87.442129	0.011436	0.054088	4.729561	0.211436
17	22.186111	105.930555	0.009440	0.045073	4.774634	0.209440
18	26.623333	128.116666	0.007805	0.037561	4.812195	0.207805
19	31.948000	154.740000	0.006462	0.031301	4.843496	0.206462
20	38.337600	186.688000	0.005357	0.026084	4.869580	0.205357
21	46.005120	225.025600	0.004444	0.021737	4.891316	0.204444
22	55.206144	271.030719	0.003690	0.018114	4.909430	0.203690
23	66.247373	326.236863	0.003065	0.015095	4.924525	0.203065
24	79.496847	392.484236	0.002548	0.012579	4.937104	0.202548
25	95.396217	471.981083	0.002119	0.010483	4.947587	0.202119
26	114.475460	567.377300	0.001762	0.008735	4.956323	0.201762
27	137.370552	681.852760	0.001467	0.007280	4.963602	0.201467
28	164.844662	819.223312	0.001221	0.006066	4.969668	0.201221
29	197.813595	984.067974	0.001016	0.005055	4.974724	0.201016
30	237.376314	1181.881569	0.000846	0.004213	4.978936	0.200846
31	284.851577	1419.257883	0.000705	0.003511	4.982447	0.200705
32	341.821892	1704.109459	0.000587	0.002926	4.985372	0.200587
33	410.186270	2045.931351	0.000489	0.002438	4.987810	0.200489
34	492.223524	2456.117621	0.000407	0.002032	4.989842	0.200407
35	590.668229	2948.341146	0.000339	0.001693	4.991535	0.200339
36	708.801875	3539.009375	0.000283	0.001411	4.992946	0.200283
37	850.562250	4247.811250	0.000235	0.001176	4.994122	0.200235
38	1020.674700	5098.373500	0.000196	0.000980	4.995101	0.200196
39	1224.809640	6119.048200	0.000163	0.000816	4.995918	0.200163
40	1469.771568	7343.857840	0.000136	0.000680	4.996598	0.200136
41	1763.725882	8813.629408	0.000113	0.000567	4.997165	0.200113
42	2116.471058	10577.355290	0.000095	0.000472	4.997638	0.200095
43	2539.765269	12693.826348	0.000079	0.000394	4.998031	0.200079
44	3047.718323	15233.591617	0.000066	0.000328	4.998359	0.200066
45	3657.261988	18281.309940	0.000055	0.000273	4.998633	0.200055
46	4388.714386	21938.571928	0.000046	0.000228	4.998861	0.200046
47	5266.457263	26327.286314	0.000038	0.000190	4.999051	0.200038
48	6319.748715	31593.743577	0.000032	0.000158	4.999209	0.200032
49	7583.698458	37913.492292	0.000026	0.000132	4.999341	0.200026
50	9100.438150	45497.190751	0.000022	0.000110	4.999451	0.200022

4.00% MONTHLY COMPOUND INTEREST TABLES 4.00%
EFFECTIVE RATE 0.333

	1 AMOUNT OF $1 AT COMPOUND INTEREST	2 ACCUMULATION OF $1 PER PERIOD	3 SINKING FUND FACTOR	4 PRESENT VALUE REVERSION OF $1	5 PRESENT VALUE ORD. ANNUITY $1 PER PERIOD	6 INSTALMENT TO AMORTIZE $1	
MONTHS							
1	1.003333	1.000000	1.000000	0.996678	0.996678	1.003333	
2	1.006678	2.003333	0.499168	0.993367	1.990044	0.502501	
3	1.010033	3.010011	0.332225	0.990066	2.980111	0.335558	
4	1.013400	4.020044	0.248753	0.986777	3.966888	0.252087	
5	1.016778	5.033445	0.198671	0.983499	4.950386	0.202004	
6	1.020167	6.050223	0.165283	0.980231	5.930618	0.168617	
7	1.023568	7.070390	0.141435	0.976975	6.907592	0.144768	
8	1.026980	8.093958	0.123549	0.973729	7.881321	0.126882	
9	1.030403	9.120938	0.109638	0.970494	8.851815	0.112971	
10	1.033838	10.151341	0.098509	0.967270	9.819085	0.101842	
11	1.037284	11.185179	0.089404	0.964056	10.783141	0.092737	
12	1.040742	12.222463	0.081817	0.960853	11.743994	0.085150	
YEARS							**MONTHS**
1	1.040742	12.222463	0.081817	0.960853	11.743994	0.085150	12
2	1.083143	24.942888	0.040092	0.923239	23.028251	0.043425	24
3	1.127272	38.181562	0.026191	0.887097	33.870766	0.029524	36
4	1.173199	51.959601	0.019246	0.852371	44.288834	0.022579	48
5	1.220997	66.298978	0.015083	0.819003	54.299069	0.018417	60
6	1.270742	81.222564	0.012312	0.786942	63.917437	0.015645	72
7	1.322514	96.754159	0.010335	0.756136	73.159278	0.013669	84
8	1.376395	112.918536	0.008856	0.726536	82.039332	0.012189	96
9	1.432472	129.741474	0.007708	0.698094	90.571761	0.011041	108
10	1.490833	147.249805	0.006791	0.670766	98.770175	0.010125	120
11	1.551572	165.471452	0.006043	0.644508	106.647648	0.009377	132
12	1.614785	184.435477	0.005422	0.619278	114.216744	0.008755	144
13	1.680574	204.172126	0.004898	0.595035	121.489536	0.008231	156
14	1.749043	224.712876	0.004450	0.571741	128.477623	0.007783	168
15	1.820302	246.090488	0.004064	0.549360	135.192149	0.007397	180
16	1.894464	268.339057	0.003727	0.527854	141.643824	0.007060	192
17	1.971647	291.494067	0.003431	0.507190	147.842937	0.006764	204
18	2.051975	315.592448	0.003169	0.487335	153.799376	0.006502	216
19	2.135575	340.672634	0.002935	0.468258	159.522640	0.006269	228
20	2.222582	366.774626	0.002726	0.449927	165.021858	0.006060	240
21	2.313134	393.940053	0.002538	0.432314	170.305800	0.005872	252
22	2.407374	422.212242	0.002368	0.415390	175.382893	0.005702	264
23	2.505454	451.636283	0.002214	0.399129	180.261235	0.005548	276
24	2.607530	482.259104	0.002074	0.383505	184.948607	0.005407	288
25	2.713765	514.129547	0.001945	0.368492	189.452483	0.005278	300
26	2.824328	547.298441	0.001827	0.354067	193.780048	0.005160	312
27	2.939396	581.818687	0.001719	0.340206	197.938203	0.005052	324
28	3.059151	617.745341	0.001619	0.326888	201.933580	0.004952	336
29	3.183786	655.135702	0.001526	0.314091	205.772552	0.004860	348
30	3.313498	694.049404	0.001441	0.301796	209.461240	0.004774	360
31	3.448495	734.548511	0.001361	0.289982	213.005529	0.004695	372
32	3.588992	776.697613	0.001288	0.278630	216.411071	0.004621	384
33	3.735213	820.563935	0.001219	0.267722	219.683298	0.004552	396
34	3.887391	866.217439	0.001154	0.257242	222.827427	0.004488	408
35	4.045770	913.730937	0.001094	0.247172	225.848475	0.004428	420
36	4.210601	963.180208	0.001038	0.237496	228.751259	0.004372	432
37	4.382147	1014.644119	0.000986	0.228199	231.540408	0.004319	444
38	4.560682	1068.204748	0.000936	0.219265	234.220372	0.004269	456
39	4.746492	1123.947521	0.000890	0.210682	236.795424	0.004223	468
40	4.939871	1181.961340	0.000846	0.202434	239.269671	0.004179	480

5.00%   MONTHLY COMPOUND INTEREST TABLES   5.00%
                                     EFFECTIVE RATE 0.417

	1 AMOUNT OF $1 AT COMPOUND INTEREST	2 ACCUMULATION OF $1 PER PERIOD	3 SINKING FUND FACTOR	4 PRESENT VALUE REVERSION OF $1	5 PRESENT VALUE ORD. ANNUITY $1 PER PERIOD	6 INSTALMENT TO AMORTIZE $1	
MONTHS							
1	1.004167	1.000000	1.000000	0.995851	0.995851	1.004167	
2	1.008351	2.004167	0.498960	0.991718	1.987569	0.503127	
3	1.012552	3.012517	0.331948	0.987603	2.975173	0.336115	
4	1.016771	4.025070	0.248443	0.983506	3.958678	0.252610	
5	1.021008	5.041841	0.198340	0.979425	4.938103	0.202507	
6	1.025262	6.062848	0.164939	0.975361	5.913463	0.169106	
7	1.029534	7.088110	0.141081	0.971313	6.884777	0.145248	
8	1.033824	8.117644	0.123188	0.967283	7.852060	0.127355	
9	1.038131	9.151467	0.109272	0.963269	8.815329	0.113439	
10	1.042457	10.189599	0.098139	0.959272	9.774602	0.102306	
11	1.046800	11.232055	0.089031	0.955292	10.729894	0.093198	
12	1.051162	12.278855	0.081441	0.951328	11.681222	0.085607	
YEARS							**MONTHS**
1	1.051162	12.278855	0.081441	0.951328	11.681222	0.085607	12
2	1.104941	25.185921	0.039705	0.905025	22.793898	0.043871	24
3	1.161472	38.753336	0.025804	0.860976	33.365701	0.029971	36
4	1.220895	53.014885	0.018863	0.819071	43.422956	0.023029	48
5	1.283359	68.006083	0.014705	0.779205	52.990706	0.018871	60
6	1.349018	83.764259	0.011938	0.741280	62.092777	0.016105	72
7	1.418036	100.328653	0.009967	0.705201	70.751835	0.014134	84
8	1.490585	117.740512	0.008493	0.670877	78.989441	0.012660	96
9	1.566847	136.043196	0.007351	0.638225	86.826108	0.011517	108
10	1.647009	155.282279	0.006440	0.607161	94.281350	0.010607	120
11	1.731274	175.505671	0.005698	0.577609	101.373733	0.009864	132
12	1.819849	196.763730	0.005082	0.549496	108.120917	0.009249	144
13	1.912956	219.109391	0.004564	0.522751	114.539704	0.008731	156
14	2.010826	242.598299	0.004122	0.497308	120.646077	0.008289	168
15	2.113704	267.288944	0.003741	0.473103	126.455243	0.007908	180
16	2.221845	293.242809	0.003410	0.450076	131.981666	0.007577	192
17	2.335519	320.524523	0.003120	0.428170	137.239108	0.007287	204
18	2.455008	349.202022	0.002864	0.407331	142.240661	0.007030	216
19	2.580611	379.346715	0.002636	0.387505	146.998780	0.006803	228
20	2.712640	411.033669	0.002433	0.368645	151.525313	0.006600	240
21	2.851424	444.341787	0.002251	0.350702	155.831532	0.006417	252
22	2.997308	479.354011	0.002086	0.333633	159.928159	0.006253	264
23	3.150656	516.157528	0.001937	0.317394	163.825396	0.006104	276
24	3.311850	554.843982	0.001802	0.301946	167.532948	0.005969	288
25	3.481290	595.509709	0.001679	0.287250	171.060047	0.005846	300
26	3.659400	638.255971	0.001567	0.273269	174.415476	0.005733	312
27	3.846622	683.189213	0.001464	0.259968	177.607590	0.005630	324
28	4.043422	730.421325	0.001369	0.247315	180.644338	0.005536	336
29	4.250291	780.069922	0.001282	0.235278	183.533283	0.005449	348
30	4.467744	832.258635	0.001202	0.223827	186.281617	0.005368	360
31	4.696323	887.117422	0.001127	0.212933	188.896185	0.005294	372
32	4.936595	944.782889	0.001058	0.202569	191.383498	0.005225	384
33	5.189161	1005.398630	0.000995	0.192709	193.749748	0.005161	396
34	5.454648	1069.115587	0.000935	0.183330	196.000829	0.005102	408
35	5.733718	1136.092425	0.000880	0.174407	198.142346	0.005047	420
36	6.027066	1206.495925	0.000829	0.165918	200.179632	0.004996	432
37	6.335423	1280.501402	0.000781	0.157843	202.117759	0.004948	444
38	6.659555	1358.293140	0.000736	0.150160	203.961555	0.004903	456
39	7.000270	1440.064850	0.000694	0.142852	205.715609	0.004861	468
40	7.358417	1526.020157	0.000655	0.135899	207.384291	0.004822	480

6.00%   MONTHLY COMPOUND INTEREST TABLES   6.00%
                              EFFECTIVE RATE 0.500

	1	2	3	4	5	6
	AMOUNT OF $1 AT COMPOUND INTEREST	ACCUMULATION OF $1 PER PERIOD	SINKING FUND FACTOR	PRESENT VALUE REVERSION OF $1	PRESENT VALUE ORD. ANNUITY $1 PER PERIOD	INSTALMENT TO AMORTIZE $1

MONTHS
1	1.005000	1.000000	1.000000	0.995025	0.995025	1.005000
2	1.010025	2.005000	0.498753	0.990075	1.985099	0.503753
3	1.015075	3.015025	0.331672	0.985149	2.970248	0.336672
4	1.020151	4.030100	0.248133	0.980248	3.950496	0.253133
5	1.025251	5.050251	0.198010	0.975371	4.925866	0.203010
6	1.030378	6.075502	0.164595	0.970518	5.896384	0.169595
7	1.035529	7.105879	0.140729	0.965690	6.862074	0.145729
8	1.040707	8.141409	0.122829	0.960885	7.822959	0.127829
9	1.045911	9.182116	0.108907	0.956105	8.779064	0.113907
10	1.051140	10.228026	0.097771	0.951348	9.730412	0.102771
11	1.056396	11.279167	0.088659	0.946615	10.677027	0.093659
12	1.061678	12.335562	0.081066	0.941905	11.618932	0.086066

YEARS   MONTHS
1	1.061678	12.335562	0.081066	0.941905	11.618932	0.086066	12
2	1.127160	25.431955	0.039321	0.887186	22.562866	0.044321	24
3	1.196681	39.336105	0.025422	0.835645	32.871016	0.030422	36
4	1.270489	54.097832	0.018485	0.787098	42.580318	0.023485	48
5	1.348850	69.770031	0.014333	0.741372	51.725561	0.019333	60
6	1.432044	86.408856	0.011573	0.698302	60.339514	0.016573	72
7	1.520370	104.073927	0.009609	0.657735	68.453042	0.014609	84
8	1.614143	122.828542	0.008141	0.619524	76.095218	0.013141	96
9	1.713699	142.739900	0.007006	0.583533	83.293424	0.012006	108
10	1.819397	163.879347	0.006102	0.549633	90.073453	0.011102	120
11	1.931613	186.322629	0.005367	0.517702	96.459599	0.010367	132
12	2.050751	210.150163	0.004759	0.487626	102.474743	0.009759	144
13	2.177237	235.447328	0.004247	0.459298	108.140440	0.009247	156
14	2.311524	262.304766	0.003812	0.432615	113.476990	0.008812	168
15	2.454094	290.818712	0.003439	0.407482	118.503515	0.008439	180
16	2.605457	321.091337	0.003114	0.383810	123.238025	0.008114	192
17	2.766156	353.231110	0.002831	0.361513	127.697486	0.007831	204
18	2.936766	387.353194	0.002582	0.340511	131.897876	0.007582	216
19	3.117899	423.579854	0.002361	0.320729	135.854246	0.007361	228
20	3.310204	462.040895	0.002164	0.302096	139.580772	0.007164	240
21	3.514371	502.874129	0.001989	0.284546	143.090806	0.006989	252
22	3.731129	546.225867	0.001831	0.268015	146.396927	0.006831	264
23	3.961257	592.251446	0.001688	0.252445	149.510979	0.006688	276
24	4.205579	641.115782	0.001560	0.237779	152.444121	0.006560	288
25	4.464970	692.993962	0.001443	0.223966	155.206864	0.006443	300
26	4.740359	748.071876	0.001337	0.210954	157.809106	0.006337	312
27	5.032734	806.546875	0.001240	0.198699	160.260172	0.006240	324
28	5.343142	868.628484	0.001151	0.187156	162.568844	0.006151	336
29	5.672696	934.539150	0.001070	0.176283	164.743394	0.006070	348
30	6.022575	1004.515043	0.000996	0.166042	166.791614	0.005996	360
31	6.394034	1078.806895	0.000927	0.156396	168.720844	0.005927	372
32	6.788405	1157.680906	0.000864	0.147310	170.537996	0.005864	384
33	7.207098	1241.419693	0.000806	0.138752	172.249581	0.005806	396
34	7.651617	1330.323306	0.000752	0.130691	173.861732	0.005752	408
35	8.123551	1424.710299	0.000702	0.123099	175.380226	0.005702	420
36	8.624594	1524.918875	0.000656	0.115947	176.810504	0.005656	432
37	9.156540	1631.308097	0.000613	0.109212	178.157690	0.005613	444
38	9.721296	1744.259173	0.000573	0.102867	179.426611	0.005573	456
39	10.320884	1864.176825	0.000536	0.096891	180.621815	0.005536	468
40	10.957454	1991.490734	0.000502	0.091262	181.747544	0.005502	480

	1	2	3	4	5	6	
	AMOUNT OF $1 AT COMPOUND INTEREST	ACCUMULATION OF $1 PER PERIOD	SINKING FUND FACTOR	PRESENT VALUE REVERSION OF $1	PRESENT VALUE ORD. ANNUITY $1 PER PERIOD	INSTALMENT TO AMORTIZE $1	
MONTHS							
1	1.005833	1.000000	1.000000	0.994200	0.994200	1.005833	
2	1.011701	2.005833	0.498546	0.988435	1.982635	0.504379	
3	1.017602	3.017534	0.331396	0.982702	2.965337	0.337230	
4	1.023538	4.035136	0.247823	0.977003	3.942340	0.253656	
5	1.029509	5.058675	0.197680	0.971337	4.913677	0.203514	
6	1.035514	6.088184	0.164253	0.965704	5.879381	0.170086	
7	1.041555	7.123698	0.140377	0.960103	6.839484	0.146210	
8	1.047631	8.165253	0.122470	0.954535	7.794019	0.128304	
9	1.053742	9.212883	0.108544	0.948999	8.743018	0.114377	
10	1.059889	10.266625	0.097403	0.943495	9.686513	0.103236	
11	1.066071	11.326514	0.088288	0.938024	10.624537	0.094122	
12	1.072290	12.392585	0.080693	0.932583	11.557120	0.086527	
YEARS							MONTHS
1	1.072290	12.392585	0.080693	0.932583	11.557120	0.086527	12
2	1.149806	25.681032	0.038939	0.869712	22.335099	0.044773	24
3	1.232926	39.930101	0.025044	0.811079	32.386464	0.030877	36
4	1.322054	55.209236	0.018113	0.756399	41.760201	0.023946	48
5	1.417625	71.592902	0.013968	0.705405	50.501993	0.019801	60
6	1.520106	89.160944	0.011216	0.657849	58.654444	0.017049	72
7	1.629994	107.998981	0.009259	0.613499	66.257285	0.015093	84
8	1.747826	128.198821	0.007800	0.572139	73.347569	0.013634	96
9	1.874177	149.858909	0.006673	0.533568	79.959850	0.012506	108
10	2.009661	173.084807	0.005778	0.497596	86.126354	0.011611	120
11	2.154940	197.989707	0.005051	0.464050	91.877134	0.010884	132
12	2.310721	224.694985	0.004450	0.432765	97.240216	0.010284	144
13	2.477763	253.330789	0.003947	0.403590	102.241738	0.009781	156
14	2.656881	284.036677	0.003521	0.376381	106.906074	0.009354	168
15	2.848947	316.962297	0.003155	0.351007	111.255958	0.008988	180
16	3.054897	352.268112	0.002839	0.327343	115.312587	0.008672	192
17	3.275736	390.126188	0.002563	0.305275	119.095732	0.008397	204
18	3.512539	430.721027	0.002322	0.284694	122.623831	0.008155	216
19	3.766461	474.250470	0.002109	0.265501	125.914077	0.007942	228
20	4.038739	520.926660	0.001920	0.247602	128.982506	0.007753	240
21	4.330700	570.977075	0.001751	0.230910	131.844073	0.007585	252
22	4.643766	624.645640	0.001601	0.215342	134.512723	0.007434	264
23	4.979464	682.193909	0.001466	0.200825	137.001461	0.007299	276
24	5.339430	743.902347	0.001344	0.187286	139.322418	0.007178	288
25	5.725418	810.071693	0.001234	0.174660	141.486903	0.007068	300
26	6.139309	881.024426	0.001135	0.162885	143.505467	0.006968	312
27	6.583120	957.106339	0.001045	0.151904	145.387946	0.006878	324
28	7.059015	1038.688219	0.000963	0.141663	147.143515	0.006796	336
29	7.569311	1126.167659	0.000888	0.132112	148.780729	0.006721	348
30	8.116497	1219.970996	0.000820	0.123206	150.307568	0.006653	360
31	8.703240	1320.555383	0.000757	0.114900	151.731473	0.006591	372
32	9.332398	1428.411024	0.000700	0.107154	153.059383	0.006533	384
33	10.007037	1544.063557	0.000648	0.099930	154.297770	0.006481	396
34	10.730447	1668.076622	0.000599	0.093193	155.452669	0.006433	408
35	11.506152	1801.054601	0.000555	0.086910	156.529709	0.006389	420
36	12.337932	1943.645569	0.000514	0.081051	157.534139	0.006348	432
37	13.229843	2096.544450	0.000477	0.075587	158.470853	0.006310	444
38	14.186229	2260.496403	0.000442	0.070491	159.344418	0.006276	456
39	15.211753	2436.300456	0.000410	0.065739	160.159090	0.006244	468
40	16.311411	2624.813398	0.000381	0.061307	160.918839	0.006214	480

8.00%   MONTHLY COMPOUND INTEREST TABLES   8.00%
EFFECTIVE RATE 0.667

	1 AMOUNT OF $1 AT COMPOUND INTEREST	2 ACCUMULATION OF $1 PER PERIOD	3 SINKING FUND FACTOR	4 PRESENT VALUE REVERSION OF $1	5 PRESENT VALUE ORD. ANNUITY $1 PER PERIOD	6 INSTALMENT TO AMORTIZE $1	
MONTHS							
1	1.006667	1.000000	1.000000	0.993377	0.993377	1.006667	
2	1.013378	2.006667	0.498339	0.986799	1.980176	0.505006	
3	1.020134	3.020044	0.331121	0.980264	2.960440	0.337788	
4	1.026935	4.040178	0.247514	0.973772	3.934212	0.254181	
5	1.033781	5.067113	0.197351	0.967323	4.901535	0.204018	
6	1.040673	6.100893	0.163910	0.960917	5.862452	0.170577	
7	1.047610	7.141566	0.140025	0.954553	6.817005	0.146692	
8	1.054595	8.189176	0.122112	0.948232	7.765237	0.128779	
9	1.061625	9.243771	0.108181	0.941952	8.707189	0.114848	
10	1.068703	10.305396	0.097037	0.935714	9.642903	0.103703	
11	1.075827	11.374099	0.087919	0.929517	10.572420	0.094586	
12	1.083000	12.449926	0.080322	0.923361	11.495782	0.086988	
YEARS							**MONTHS**
1	1.083000	12.449926	0.080322	0.923361	11.495782	0.086988	12
2	1.172888	25.933190	0.038561	0.852596	22.110544	0.045227	24
3	1.270237	40.535558	0.024670	0.787255	31.911806	0.031336	36
4	1.375666	56.349915	0.017746	0.726921	40.961913	0.024413	48
5	1.489846	73.476856	0.013610	0.671210	49.318433	0.020276	60
6	1.613502	92.025325	0.010867	0.619770	57.034522	0.017533	72
7	1.747422	112.113308	0.008920	0.572272	64.159261	0.015586	84
8	1.892457	133.868583	0.007470	0.528414	70.737970	0.014137	96
9	2.049530	157.429535	0.006352	0.487917	76.812497	0.013019	108
10	2.219640	182.946035	0.005466	0.450523	82.421481	0.012133	120
11	2.403869	210.580392	0.004749	0.415996	87.600600	0.011415	132
12	2.603389	240.508387	0.004158	0.384115	92.382800	0.010825	144
13	2.819469	272.920390	0.003664	0.354677	96.798498	0.010331	156
14	3.053484	308.022574	0.003247	0.327495	100.875784	0.009913	168
15	3.306921	346.038222	0.002890	0.302396	104.640592	0.009557	180
16	3.581394	387.209149	0.002583	0.279221	108.116871	0.009249	192
17	3.878648	431.797244	0.002316	0.257822	111.326733	0.008983	204
18	4.200574	480.086128	0.002083	0.238063	114.290596	0.008750	216
19	4.549220	532.382966	0.001878	0.219818	117.027313	0.008545	228
20	4.926803	589.020416	0.001698	0.202971	119.554292	0.008364	240
21	5.335725	650.358746	0.001538	0.187416	121.887606	0.008204	252
22	5.778588	716.788127	0.001395	0.173053	124.042099	0.008062	264
23	6.258207	788.731114	0.001268	0.159790	126.031475	0.007935	276
24	6.777636	866.645333	0.001154	0.147544	127.868388	0.007821	288
25	7.340176	951.026395	0.001051	0.136237	129.564523	0.007718	300
26	7.949407	1042.411042	0.000959	0.125796	131.130668	0.007626	312
27	8.609204	1141.380571	0.000876	0.116155	132.576786	0.007543	324
28	9.323763	1248.564521	0.000801	0.107253	133.912076	0.007468	336
29	10.097631	1364.644687	0.000733	0.099033	135.145031	0.007399	348
30	10.935730	1490.359449	0.000671	0.091443	136.283494	0.007338	360
31	11.843390	1626.508474	0.000615	0.084435	137.334707	0.007281	372
32	12.826385	1773.957801	0.000564	0.077964	138.305357	0.007230	384
33	13.890969	1933.645350	0.000517	0.071989	139.201617	0.007184	396
34	15.043913	2106.586886	0.000475	0.066472	140.029190	0.007141	408
35	16.292556	2293.882485	0.000436	0.061378	140.793338	0.007103	420
36	17.644824	2496.723526	0.000401	0.056674	141.498923	0.007067	432
37	19.109335	2716.400273	0.000368	0.052330	142.150433	0.007035	444
38	20.695401	2954.310082	0.000338	0.048320	142.752013	0.007005	456
39	22.413109	3211.966288	0.000311	0.044617	143.307488	0.006978	468
40	24.273386	3491.007831	0.000286	0.041197	143.820392	0.006953	480

8.50%   MONTHLY COMPOUND INTEREST TABLES   8.50%
                              EFFECTIVE RATE 0.708

	1	2	3	4	5	6
	AMOUNT OF $1 AT COMPOUND INTEREST	ACCUMULATION OF $1 PER PERIOD	SINKING FUND FACTOR	PRESENT VALUE REVERSION OF $1	PRESENT VALUE ORD. ANNUITY $1 PER PERIOD	INSTALMENT TO AMORTIZE $1
MONTHS						
1	1.007083	1.000000	1.000000	0.992966	0.992966	1.007083
2	1.014217	2.007083	0.498235	0.985982	1.978949	0.505319
3	1.021401	3.021300	0.330983	0.979048	2.957996	0.338067
4	1.028636	4.042701	0.247359	0.972161	3.930158	0.254443
5	1.035922	5.071337	0.197187	0.965324	4.895482	0.204270
6	1.043260	6.107259	0.163740	0.958534	5.854016	0.170823
7	1.050650	7.150519	0.139850	0.951792	6.805808	0.146933
8	1.058092	8.201168	0.121934	0.945098	7.750906	0.129017
9	1.065586	9.259260	0.108000	0.938450	8.689356	0.115083
10	1.073134	10.324846	0.096854	0.931850	9.621206	0.103937
11	1.080736	11.397980	0.087735	0.925296	10.546501	0.094818
12	1.088391	12.478716	0.080136	0.918788	11.465289	0.087220

YEARS							MONTHS
1	1.088391	12.478716	0.080136	0.918788	11.465289	0.087220	12
2	1.184595	26.060437	0.038372	0.844171	21.999453	0.045456	24
3	1.289302	40.842659	0.024484	0.775613	31.678112	0.031568	36
4	1.403265	56.931495	0.017565	0.712624	40.570744	0.024648	48
5	1.527301	74.442437	0.013433	0.654750	48.741183	0.020517	60
6	1.662300	93.501188	0.010695	0.601576	56.248080	0.017778	72
7	1.809232	114.244559	0.008753	0.552721	63.145324	0.015836	84
8	1.969152	136.821455	0.007309	0.507833	69.482425	0.014392	96
9	2.143207	161.393943	0.006196	0.466590	75.304875	0.013279	108
10	2.332647	188.138416	0.005315	0.428698	80.654470	0.012399	120
11	2.538832	217.246858	0.004603	0.393882	85.569611	0.011686	132
12	2.763242	248.928220	0.004017	0.361894	90.085581	0.011101	144
13	3.007487	283.409927	0.003528	0.332504	94.234798	0.010612	156
14	3.273321	320.939504	0.003116	0.305500	98.047046	0.010199	168
15	3.562653	361.786353	0.002764	0.280690	101.549693	0.009847	180
16	3.877559	406.243693	0.002462	0.257894	104.767881	0.009545	192
17	4.220300	454.630657	0.002200	0.236950	107.724713	0.009283	204
18	4.593337	507.294589	0.001971	0.217707	110.441412	0.009055	216
19	4.999346	564.613533	0.001771	0.200026	112.937482	0.008854	228
20	5.441243	626.998951	0.001595	0.183782	115.230840	0.008678	240
21	5.922199	694.898672	0.001439	0.168856	117.337948	0.008522	252
22	6.445667	768.800112	0.001301	0.155143	119.273933	0.008384	264
23	7.015406	849.233766	0.001178	0.142543	121.052692	0.008261	276
24	7.635504	936.777024	0.001067	0.130967	122.686994	0.008151	288
25	8.310413	1032.058310	0.000969	0.120331	124.188570	0.008052	300
26	9.044978	1135.761595	0.000880	0.110559	125.568199	0.007964	312
27	9.844472	1248.631307	0.000801	0.101580	126.835785	0.007884	324
28	10.714634	1371.477676	0.000729	0.093330	128.000428	0.007812	336
29	11.661710	1505.182546	0.000664	0.085751	129.070487	0.007748	348
30	12.692499	1650.705711	0.000606	0.078787	130.053643	0.007689	360
31	13.814400	1809.091800	0.000553	0.072388	130.956956	0.007636	372
32	15.035468	1981.477780	0.000505	0.066509	131.786908	0.007588	384
33	16.364466	2169.101112	0.000461	0.061108	132.549457	0.007544	396
34	17.810936	2373.308640	0.000421	0.056145	133.250078	0.007505	408
35	19.385261	2595.566257	0.000385	0.051586	133.893800	0.007469	420
36	21.098742	2837.469426	0.000352	0.047396	134.485244	0.007436	432
37	22.963679	3100.754635	0.000323	0.043547	135.028655	0.007406	444
38	24.993459	3387.311862	0.000295	0.040010	135.527934	0.007379	456
39	27.202654	3699.198142	0.000270	0.036761	135.986665	0.007354	468
40	29.607121	4038.652333	0.000248	0.033776	136.408142	0.007331	480

9.00%   MONTHLY COMPOUND INTEREST TABLES   9.00%
                              EFFECTIVE RATE 0.750

	1	2	3	4	5	6
	AMOUNT OF $1 AT COMPOUND INTEREST	ACCUMULATION OF $1 PER PERIOD	SINKING FUND FACTOR	PRESENT VALUE REVERSION OF $1	PRESENT VALUE ORD. ANNUITY $1 PER PERIOD	INSTALMENT TO AMORTIZE $1
MONTHS						
1	1.007500	1.000000	1.000000	0.992556	0.992556	1.007500
2	1.015056	2.007500	0.498132	0.985167	1.977723	0.505632
3	1.022669	3.022556	0.330846	0.977833	2.955556	0.338346
4	1.030339	4.045225	0.247205	0.970554	3.926110	0.254705
5	1.038067	5.075565	0.197022	0.963329	4.889440	0.204522
6	1.045852	6.113631	0.163569	0.956158	5.845598	0.171069
7	1.053696	7.159484	0.139675	0.949040	6.794638	0.147175
8	1.061599	8.213180	0.121756	0.941975	7.736613	0.129256
9	1.069561	9.274779	0.107819	0.934963	8.671576	0.115319
10	1.077583	10.344339	0.096671	0.928003	9.599580	0.104171
11	1.085664	11.421922	0.087551	0.921095	10.520675	0.095051
12	1.093807	12.507586	0.079951	0.914238	11.434913	0.087451

YEARS						MONTHS
1	1.093807	12.507586	0.079951	0.914238	11.434913	0.087451	12
2	1.196414	26.188471	0.038185	0.835831	21.889146	0.045685	24
3	1.308645	41.152716	0.024300	0.764149	31.446805	0.031800	36
4	1.431405	57.520711	0.017385	0.698614	40.184782	0.024885	48
5	1.565681	75.424137	0.013258	0.638700	48.173374	0.020758	60
6	1.712553	95.007028	0.010526	0.583924	55.476849	0.018026	72
7	1.873202	116.426928	0.008589	0.533845	62.153965	0.016089	84
8	2.048921	139.856164	0.007150	0.488062	68.258439	0.014650	96
9	2.241124	165.483223	0.006043	0.446205	73.839382	0.013543	108
10	2.451357	193.514277	0.005168	0.407937	78.941693	0.012668	120
11	2.681311	224.174837	0.004461	0.372952	83.606420	0.011961	132
12	2.932637	257.711570	0.003880	0.340967	87.871092	0.011380	144
13	3.207957	294.394279	0.003397	0.311725	91.770018	0.010897	156
14	3.508886	334.518079	0.002989	0.284991	95.334564	0.010489	168
15	3.838043	378.405769	0.002643	0.260549	98.593409	0.010143	180
16	4.198078	426.410427	0.002345	0.238204	101.572769	0.009845	192
17	4.591887	478.918252	0.002088	0.217775	104.296613	0.009588	204
18	5.022638	536.351674	0.001864	0.199099	106.786856	0.009364	216
19	5.493796	599.172747	0.001669	0.182024	109.063531	0.009169	228
20	6.009152	667.886870	0.001497	0.166413	111.144954	0.008997	240
21	6.572851	743.046852	0.001346	0.152141	113.047870	0.008846	252
22	7.189430	825.257358	0.001212	0.139093	114.787589	0.008712	264
23	7.863848	915.179777	0.001093	0.127164	116.378106	0.008593	276
24	8.601532	1013.537539	0.000987	0.116258	117.832218	0.008487	288
25	9.408415	1121.121937	0.000892	0.106288	119.161622	0.008392	300
26	10.290989	1238.798494	0.000807	0.097172	120.377014	0.008307	312
27	11.256354	1367.513924	0.000731	0.088839	121.488172	0.008231	324
28	12.312278	1508.303750	0.000663	0.081220	122.504035	0.008163	336
29	13.467255	1662.300631	0.000602	0.074254	123.432776	0.008102	348
30	14.730576	1830.743483	0.000546	0.067886	124.281866	0.008046	360
31	16.112406	2014.987436	0.000496	0.062064	125.058136	0.007996	372
32	17.623861	2216.514743	0.000451	0.056741	125.767832	0.007951	384
33	19.277100	2436.946701	0.000410	0.051875	126.416664	0.007910	396
34	21.085425	2678.056697	0.000373	0.047426	127.009850	0.007873	408
35	23.063384	2941.784473	0.000340	0.043359	127.552164	0.007840	420
36	25.226888	3230.251735	0.000310	0.039640	128.047967	0.007810	432
37	27.593344	3545.779215	0.000282	0.036241	128.501250	0.007782	444
38	30.181790	3890.905350	0.000257	0.033133	128.915659	0.007757	456
39	33.013050	4268.406696	0.000234	0.030291	129.294526	0.007734	468
40	36.109902	4681.320272	0.000214	0.027693	129.640902	0.007714	480

9.50%   MONTHLY COMPOUND INTEREST TABLES   9.50%
                                   EFFECTIVE RATE 0.792

	1	2	3	4	5	6
	AMOUNT OF $1 AT COMPOUND INTEREST	ACCUMULATION OF $1 PER PERIOD	SINKING FUND FACTOR	PRESENT VALUE REVERSION OF $1	PRESENT VALUE ORD. ANNUITY $1 PER PERIOD	INSTALMENT TO AMORTIZE $1
MONTHS						
1	1.007917	1.000000	1.000000	0.992146	0.992146	1.007917
2	1.015896	2.007917	0.498029	0.984353	1.976498	0.505945
3	1.023939	3.023813	0.330708	0.976621	2.953119	0.338625
4	1.032045	4.047751	0.247051	0.968950	3.922070	0.254967
5	1.040215	5.079796	0.196858	0.961340	4.883409	0.204775
6	1.048450	6.120011	0.163398	0.953789	5.837198	0.171315
7	1.056750	7.168461	0.139500	0.946297	6.783496	0.147417
8	1.065116	8.225211	0.121577	0.938865	7.722360	0.129494
9	1.073548	9.290328	0.107639	0.931490	8.653851	0.115555
10	1.082047	10.363876	0.096489	0.924174	9.578024	0.104406
11	1.090614	11.445923	0.087367	0.916915	10.494940	0.095284
12	1.099248	12.536537	0.079767	0.909713	11.404653	0.087684

YEARS							**MONTHS**
1	1.099248	12.536537	0.079767	0.909713	11.404653	0.087684	12
2	1.208345	26.317295	0.037998	0.827578	21.779615	0.045914	24
3	1.328271	41.465760	0.024116	0.752859	31.217856	0.032033	36
4	1.460098	58.117673	0.017206	0.684885	39.803947	0.025123	48
5	1.605009	76.422249	0.013085	0.623049	47.614827	0.021002	60
6	1.764303	96.543509	0.010358	0.566796	54.720488	0.018275	72
7	1.939406	118.661756	0.008427	0.515622	61.184601	0.016344	84
8	2.131887	142.975186	0.006994	0.469068	67.065090	0.014911	96
9	2.343472	169.701665	0.005893	0.426717	72.414648	0.013809	108
10	2.576055	199.080682	0.005023	0.388190	77.281211	0.012940	120
11	2.831723	231.375495	0.004322	0.353142	81.708388	0.012239	132
12	3.112764	266.875491	0.003747	0.321258	85.735849	0.011664	144
13	3.421699	305.898776	0.003269	0.292253	89.399684	0.011186	156
14	3.761294	348.795027	0.002867	0.265866	92.732722	0.010784	168
15	4.134593	395.948628	0.002526	0.241862	95.764831	0.010442	180
16	4.544942	447.782110	0.002233	0.220025	98.523180	0.010150	192
17	4.996016	504.759939	0.001981	0.200159	101.032487	0.009898	204
18	5.491859	567.392681	0.001762	0.182088	103.315236	0.009679	216
19	6.036912	636.241570	0.001572	0.165648	105.391883	0.009488	228
20	6.636061	711.923546	0.001405	0.150692	107.281037	0.009321	240
21	7.294674	795.116775	0.001258	0.137086	108.999624	0.009174	252
22	8.018653	886.566731	0.001128	0.124709	110.563046	0.009045	264
23	8.814485	987.092874	0.001013	0.113450	111.985311	0.008930	276
24	9.689302	1097.595994	0.000911	0.103207	113.279165	0.008828	288
25	10.650941	1219.066282	0.000820	0.093888	114.456200	0.008737	300
26	11.708022	1352.592202	0.000739	0.085412	115.526965	0.008656	312
27	12.870014	1499.370247	0.000667	0.077700	116.501054	0.008584	324
28	14.147332	1660.715658	0.000602	0.070685	117.387195	0.008519	336
29	15.551421	1838.074212	0.000544	0.064303	118.193330	0.008461	348
30	17.094862	2033.035174	0.000492	0.058497	118.926681	0.008409	360
31	18.791486	2247.345541	0.000445	0.053216	119.593820	0.008362	372
32	20.656495	2482.925693	0.000403	0.048411	120.200725	0.008319	384
33	22.706602	2741.886606	0.000365	0.044040	120.752835	0.008281	396
34	24.960178	3026.548765	0.000330	0.040064	121.255097	0.008247	408
35	27.437415	3339.462955	0.000299	0.036447	121.712011	0.008216	420
36	30.160512	3683.433122	0.000271	0.033156	122.127671	0.008188	432
37	33.153870	4061.541498	0.000246	0.030162	122.505803	0.008163	444
38	36.444312	4477.176216	0.000223	0.027439	122.849795	0.008140	456
39	40.061322	4934.061676	0.000203	0.024962	123.162729	0.008119	468
40	44.037311	5436.291914	0.000184	0.022708	123.447408	0.008101	480

	1 AMOUNT OF $1 AT COMPOUND INTEREST	2 ACCUMULATION OF $1 PER PERIOD	3 SINKING FUND FACTOR	4 PRESENT VALUE REVERSION OF $1	5 PRESENT VALUE ORD. ANNUITY $1 PER PERIOD	6 INSTALMENT TO AMORTIZE $1	
MONTHS							
1	1.008333	1.000000	1.000000	0.991736	0.991736	1.008333	
2	1.016736	2.008333	0.497925	0.983539	1.975275	0.506259	
3	1.025209	3.025069	0.330571	0.975411	2.950686	0.338904	
4	1.033752	4.050278	0.246897	0.967350	3.918036	0.255230	
5	1.042367	5.084031	0.196694	0.959355	4.877391	0.205028	
6	1.051053	6.126398	0.163228	0.951427	5.828817	0.171561	
7	1.059812	7.177451	0.139325	0.943563	6.772381	0.147659	
8	1.068644	8.237263	0.121400	0.935765	7.708146	0.129733	
9	1.077549	9.305907	0.107459	0.928032	8.636178	0.115792	
10	1.086529	10.383456	0.096307	0.920362	9.556540	0.104640	
11	1.095583	11.469985	0.087184	0.912756	10.469296	0.095517	
12	1.104713	12.565568	0.079583	0.905212	11.374508	0.087916	
YEARS							MONTHS
1	1.104713	12.565568	0.079583	0.905212	11.374508	0.087916	12
2	1.220391	26.446915	0.037812	0.819410	21.670855	0.046145	24
3	1.348182	41.781821	0.023934	0.741740	30.991236	0.032267	36
4	1.489354	58.722492	0.017029	0.671432	39.428160	0.025363	48
5	1.645309	77.437072	0.012914	0.607789	47.065369	0.021247	60
6	1.817594	98.111314	0.010193	0.550178	53.978665	0.018526	72
7	2.007920	120.950418	0.008268	0.498028	60.236667	0.016601	84
8	2.218176	146.181076	0.006841	0.450821	65.901488	0.015174	96
9	2.450448	174.053713	0.005745	0.408089	71.029355	0.014079	108
10	2.707041	204.844979	0.004882	0.369407	75.671163	0.013215	120
11	2.990504	238.860493	0.004187	0.334392	79.872986	0.012520	132
12	3.303649	276.437876	0.003617	0.302696	83.676528	0.011951	144
13	3.649584	317.950102	0.003145	0.274004	87.119542	0.011478	156
14	4.031743	363.809201	0.002749	0.248032	90.236201	0.011082	168
15	4.453920	414.470346	0.002413	0.224521	93.057439	0.010746	180
16	4.920303	470.436376	0.002126	0.203240	95.611259	0.010459	192
17	5.435523	532.262780	0.001879	0.183975	97.923008	0.010212	204
18	6.004693	600.563216	0.001665	0.166536	100.015633	0.009998	216
19	6.633463	676.015601	0.001479	0.150751	101.909902	0.009813	228
20	7.328074	759.368836	0.001317	0.136462	103.624619	0.009650	240
21	8.095419	851.450244	0.001174	0.123527	105.176801	0.009508	252
22	8.943115	953.173779	0.001049	0.111818	106.581656	0.009382	264
23	9.879576	1065.549097	0.000938	0.101219	107.853730	0.009272	276
24	10.914097	1189.691580	0.000841	0.091625	109.005045	0.009174	288
25	12.056945	1326.833403	0.000754	0.082940	110.047230	0.009087	300
26	13.319465	1478.335767	0.000676	0.075078	110.990629	0.009010	312
27	14.714187	1645.702407	0.000608	0.067962	111.844605	0.008941	324
28	16.254954	1830.594523	0.000546	0.061520	112.617635	0.008880	336
29	17.957060	2034.847259	0.000491	0.055688	113.317392	0.008825	348
30	19.837399	2260.487925	0.000442	0.050410	113.950820	0.008776	360
31	21.914634	2509.756117	0.000398	0.045632	114.524207	0.008732	372
32	24.209383	2785.125947	0.000359	0.041306	115.043244	0.008692	384
33	26.744422	3089.330596	0.000324	0.037391	115.513083	0.008657	396
34	29.544912	3425.389448	0.000292	0.033847	115.938387	0.008625	408
35	32.638650	3796.638052	0.000263	0.030639	116.323377	0.008597	420
36	36.056344	4206.761236	0.000238	0.027734	116.671876	0.008571	432
37	39.831914	4659.829677	0.000215	0.025105	116.987340	0.008548	444
38	44.002836	5160.340305	0.000194	0.022726	117.272903	0.008527	456
39	48.610508	5713.260935	0.000175	0.020572	117.531398	0.008508	468
40	53.700663	6324.079581	0.000158	0.018622	117.765391	0.008491	480

11.00%   MONTHLY COMPOUND INTEREST TABLES   11.00%
EFFECTIVE RATE 0.917

	1	2	3	4	5	6
	AMOUNT OF $1 AT COMPOUND INTEREST	ACCUMULATION OF $1 PER PERIOD	SINKING FUND FACTOR	PRESENT VALUE REVERSION OF $1	PRESENT VALUE ORD. ANNUITY $1 PER PERIOD	INSTALMENT TO AMORTIZE $1

MONTHS

1	1.009167	1.000000	1.000000	0.990917	0.990917	1.009167
2	1.018417	2.009167	0.497719	0.981916	1.972832	0.506885
3	1.027753	3.027584	0.330296	0.972997	2.945829	0.339463
4	1.037174	4.055337	0.246589	0.964158	3.909987	0.255755
5	1.046681	5.092511	0.196367	0.955401	4.865388	0.205533
6	1.056276	6.139192	0.162888	0.946722	5.812110	0.172055
7	1.065958	7.195468	0.138976	0.938123	6.750233	0.148143
8	1.075730	8.261427	0.121044	0.929602	7.679835	0.130211
9	1.085591	9.337156	0.107099	0.921158	8.600992	0.116266
10	1.095542	10.422747	0.095944	0.912790	9.513783	0.105111
11	1.105584	11.518289	0.086818	0.904499	10.418282	0.095985
12	1.115719	12.623873	0.079215	0.896283	11.314565	0.088382

YEARS | | | | | | | MONTHS

1	1.115719	12.623873	0.079215	0.896283	11.314565	0.088382	12
2	1.244829	26.708566	0.037441	0.803323	21.455619	0.046608	24
3	1.388879	42.423123	0.023572	0.720005	30.544874	0.032739	36
4	1.549598	59.956151	0.016679	0.645329	38.691421	0.025846	48
5	1.728916	79.518080	0.012576	0.578397	45.993034	0.021742	60
6	1.928984	101.343692	0.009867	0.518408	52.537346	0.019034	72
7	2.152204	125.694940	0.007956	0.464640	58.402903	0.017122	84
8	2.401254	152.864085	0.006542	0.416449	63.660103	0.015708	96
9	2.679124	183.177212	0.005459	0.373256	68.372043	0.014626	108
10	2.989150	216.998139	0.004608	0.334543	72.595275	0.013775	120
11	3.335051	254.732784	0.003926	0.299846	76.380487	0.013092	132
12	3.720979	296.834038	0.003369	0.268747	79.773109	0.012536	144
13	4.151566	343.807200	0.002909	0.240873	82.813859	0.012075	156
14	4.631980	396.216042	0.002524	0.215890	85.539231	0.011691	168
15	5.167988	454.689575	0.002199	0.193499	87.981937	0.011366	180
16	5.766021	519.929596	0.001923	0.173430	90.171293	0.011090	192
17	6.433259	592.719117	0.001687	0.155442	92.133576	0.010854	204
18	7.177708	673.931757	0.001484	0.139320	93.892337	0.010650	216
19	8.008304	764.542228	0.001308	0.124870	95.468685	0.010475	228
20	8.935015	865.638038	0.001155	0.111919	96.881539	0.010322	240
21	9.968965	978.432537	0.001022	0.100311	98.147856	0.010189	252
22	11.122562	1104.279485	0.000906	0.089907	99.282835	0.010072	264
23	12.409652	1244.689295	0.000803	0.080582	100.300098	0.009970	276
24	13.845682	1401.347165	0.000714	0.072225	101.211853	0.009880	288
25	15.447889	1576.133301	0.000634	0.064734	102.029044	0.009801	300
26	17.235500	1771.145485	0.000565	0.058020	102.761478	0.009731	312
27	19.229972	1988.724252	0.000503	0.052002	103.417947	0.009670	324
28	21.455242	2231.480981	0.000448	0.046609	104.006328	0.009615	336
29	23.938018	2502.329236	0.000400	0.041775	104.533685	0.009566	348
30	26.708098	2804.519736	0.000357	0.037442	105.006346	0.009523	360
31	29.798728	3141.679369	0.000318	0.033558	105.429984	0.009485	372
32	33.247002	3517.854723	0.000284	0.030078	105.809684	0.009451	384
33	37.094306	3937.560650	0.000254	0.026958	106.150002	0.009421	396
34	41.386816	4405.834459	0.000227	0.024162	106.455024	0.009394	408
35	46.176050	4928.296368	0.000203	0.021656	106.728409	0.009370	420
36	51.519489	5511.216961	0.000181	0.019410	106.973440	0.009348	432
37	57.481264	6161.592447	0.000162	0.017397	107.193057	0.009329	444
38	64.132929	6887.228627	0.000145	0.015593	107.389897	0.009312	456
39	71.554317	7696.834582	0.000130	0.013975	107.566320	0.009297	468
40	79.834499	8600.127195	0.000116	0.012526	107.724446	0.009283	480

12.00%   MONTHLY COMPOUND INTEREST TABLES   12.00%
                         EFFECTIVE RATE 1.000

	1 AMOUNT OF $1 AT COMPOUND INTEREST	2 ACCUMULATION OF $1 PER PERIOD	3 SINKING FUND FACTOR	4 PRESENT VALUE REVERSION OF $1	5 PRESENT VALUE ORD. ANNUITY $1 PER PERIOD	6 INSTALMENT TO AMORTIZE $1	
MONTHS							
1	1.010000	1.000000	1.000000	0.990099	0.990099	1.010000	
2	1.020100	2.010000	0.497512	0.980296	1.970395	0.507512	
3	1.030301	3.030100	0.330022	0.970590	2.940985	0.340022	
4	1.040604	4.060401	0.246281	0.960980	3.901966	0.256281	
5	1.051010	5.101005	0.196040	0.951466	4.853431	0.206040	
6	1.061520	6.152015	0.162548	0.942045	5.795476	0.172548	
7	1.072135	7.213535	0.138628	0.932718	6.728195	0.148628	
8	1.082857	8.285671	0.120690	0.923483	7.651678	0.130690	
9	1.093685	9.368527	0.106740	0.914340	8.566018	0.116740	
10	1.104622	10.462213	0.095582	0.905287	9.471305	0.105582	
11	1.115668	11.566835	0.086454	0.896324	10.367628	0.096454	
12	1.126825	12.682503	0.078849	0.887449	11.255077	0.088849	
YEARS							**MONTHS**
1	1.126825	12.682503	0.078849	0.887449	11.255077	0.088849	12
2	1.269735	26.973465	0.037073	0.787566	21.243387	0.047073	24
3	1.430769	43.076878	0.023214	0.698925	30.107505	0.033214	36
4	1.612226	61.222608	0.016334	0.620260	37.973959	0.026334	48
5	1.816697	81.669670	0.012244	0.550450	44.955038	0.022244	60
6	2.047099	104.709931	0.009550	0.488496	51.150391	0.019550	72
7	2.306723	130.672274	0.007653	0.433515	56.648453	0.017653	84
8	2.599273	159.927293	0.006253	0.384723	61.527703	0.016253	96
9	2.928926	192.892579	0.005184	0.341422	65.857790	0.015184	108
10	3.300387	230.038689	0.004347	0.302995	69.700522	0.014347	120
11	3.718959	271.895856	0.003678	0.268892	73.110752	0.013678	132
12	4.190616	319.061559	0.003134	0.238628	76.137157	0.013134	144
13	4.722091	372.209054	0.002687	0.211771	78.822939	0.012687	156
14	5.320970	432.096982	0.002314	0.187936	81.206434	0.012314	168
15	5.995802	499.580198	0.002002	0.166783	83.321664	0.012002	180
16	6.756220	575.621974	0.001737	0.148012	85.198824	0.011737	192
17	7.613078	661.307751	0.001512	0.131353	86.864707	0.011512	204
18	8.578606	757.860630	0.001320	0.116569	88.343095	0.011320	216
19	9.666588	866.658830	0.001154	0.103449	89.655089	0.011154	228
20	10.892554	989.255365	0.001011	0.091806	90.819416	0.011011	240
21	12.274002	1127.400210	0.000887	0.081473	91.852698	0.010887	252
22	13.830653	1283.065278	0.000779	0.072303	92.769683	0.010779	264
23	15.584726	1458.472574	0.000686	0.064165	93.583461	0.010686	276
24	17.561259	1656.125905	0.000604	0.056944	94.305647	0.010604	288
25	19.788466	1878.846626	0.000532	0.050534	94.946551	0.010532	300
26	22.298139	2129.813909	0.000470	0.044847	95.515321	0.010470	312
27	25.126101	2412.610125	0.000414	0.039799	96.020075	0.010414	324
28	28.312720	2731.271980	0.000366	0.035320	96.468019	0.010366	336
29	31.903481	3090.348134	0.000324	0.031345	96.865546	0.010324	348
30	35.949641	3494.964133	0.000286	0.027817	97.218331	0.010286	360
31	40.508956	3950.895567	0.000253	0.024686	97.531410	0.010253	372
32	45.646505	4464.650519	0.000224	0.021907	97.809252	0.010224	384
33	51.435625	5043.562459	0.000198	0.019442	98.055822	0.010198	396
34	57.958949	5695.894923	0.000176	0.017254	98.274641	0.010176	408
35	65.309595	6430.959471	0.000155	0.015312	98.468831	0.010155	420
36	73.592486	7259.248603	0.000138	0.013588	98.641166	0.010138	432
37	82.925855	8192.585529	0.000122	0.012059	98.794103	0.010122	444
38	93.442929	9244.292938	0.000108	0.010702	98.929828	0.010108	456
39	105.293832	10429.383172	0.000096	0.009497	99.050277	0.010096	468
40	118.647725	11764.772510	0.000085	0.008428	99.157169	0.010085	480

13.00%   MONTHLY COMPOUND INTEREST TABLES   13.00%
                                  EFFECTIVE RATE 1.083

	1	2	3	4	5	6
	AMOUNT OF $1 AT COMPOUND INTEREST	ACCUMULATION OF $1 PER PERIOD	SINKING FUND FACTOR	PRESENT VALUE REVERSION OF $1	PRESENT VALUE ORD. ANNUITY $1 PER PERIOD	INSTALMENT TO AMORTIZE $1

MONTHS						
1	1.010833	1.000000	1.000000	0.989283	0.989283	1.010833
2	1.021784	2.010833	0.497306	0.978680	1.967963	0.508140
3	1.032853	3.032617	0.329748	0.968192	2.936155	0.340581
4	1.044043	4.065471	0.245974	0.957815	3.893970	0.256807
5	1.055353	5.109513	0.195713	0.947550	4.841520	0.206547
6	1.066786	6.164866	0.162210	0.937395	5.778915	0.173043
7	1.078343	7.231652	0.138281	0.927349	6.706264	0.149114
8	1.090025	8.309995	0.120337	0.917410	7.623674	0.131170
9	1.101834	9.400020	0.106383	0.907578	8.531253	0.117216
10	1.113770	10.501854	0.095221	0.897851	9.429104	0.106055
11	1.125836	11.615624	0.086091	0.888229	10.317333	0.096924
12	1.138032	12.741460	0.078484	0.878710	11.196042	0.089317

YEARS						MONTHS
1	1.138032	12.741460	0.078484	0.878710	11.196042	0.089317	12
2	1.295118	27.241655	0.036708	0.772130	21.034112	0.047542	24
3	1.473886	43.743348	0.022861	0.678478	29.678917	0.033694	36
4	1.677330	62.522811	0.015994	0.596185	37.275190	0.026827	48
5	1.908857	83.894449	0.011920	0.523874	43.950107	0.022753	60
6	2.172341	108.216068	0.009241	0.460333	49.815421	0.020074	72
7	2.472194	135.894861	0.007359	0.404499	54.969328	0.018192	84
8	2.813437	167.394225	0.005974	0.355437	59.498115	0.016807	96
9	3.201783	203.241525	0.004920	0.312326	63.477604	0.015754	108
10	3.643733	244.036917	0.004098	0.274444	66.974419	0.014931	120
11	4.146687	290.463399	0.003443	0.241156	70.047103	0.014276	132
12	4.719064	343.298242	0.002913	0.211906	72.747100	0.013746	144
13	5.370448	403.426010	0.002479	0.186204	75.119613	0.013312	156
14	6.111745	471.853363	0.002119	0.163619	77.204363	0.012953	168
15	6.955364	549.725914	0.001819	0.143774	79.036253	0.012652	180
16	7.915430	638.347406	0.001567	0.126336	80.645952	0.012400	192
17	9.008017	739.201542	0.001353	0.111012	82.060410	0.012186	204
18	10.251416	853.976825	0.001171	0.097548	83.303307	0.012004	216
19	11.666444	984.594826	0.001016	0.085716	84.395453	0.011849	228
20	13.276792	1133.242353	0.000882	0.075319	85.355132	0.011716	240
21	15.109421	1302.408067	0.000768	0.066184	86.198412	0.011601	252
22	17.195012	1494.924144	0.000669	0.058156	86.939409	0.011502	264
23	19.568482	1714.013694	0.000583	0.051103	87.590531	0.011417	276
24	22.269568	1963.344717	0.000509	0.044904	88.162677	0.011343	288
25	25.343491	2247.091520	0.000445	0.039458	88.665428	0.011278	300
26	28.841716	2570.004599	0.000389	0.034672	89.107200	0.011222	312
27	32.822810	2937.490172	0.000340	0.030467	89.495389	0.011174	324
28	37.353424	3355.700690	0.000298	0.026771	89.836495	0.011131	336
29	42.509410	3831.637843	0.000261	0.023524	90.136227	0.011094	348
30	48.377089	4373.269783	0.000229	0.020671	90.399605	0.011062	360
31	55.054699	4989.664524	0.000200	0.018164	90.631038	0.011034	372
32	62.654036	5691.141761	0.000176	0.015961	90.834400	0.011009	384
33	71.302328	6489.445641	0.000154	0.014025	91.013097	0.010987	396
34	81.144365	7397.941387	0.000135	0.012324	91.170119	0.010969	408
35	92.344923	8431.839055	0.000119	0.010829	91.308095	0.010952	420
36	105.091522	9608.448184	0.000104	0.009516	91.429337	0.010937	432
37	119.597566	10947.467591	0.000091	0.008361	91.535873	0.010925	444
38	136.105914	12471.315170	0.000080	0.007347	91.629487	0.010914	456
39	154.892951	14205.503212	0.000070	0.006456	91.711747	0.010904	468
40	176.273210	16179.065533	0.000062	0.005673	91.784030	0.010895	480

14.00% MONTHLY COMPOUND INTEREST TABLES 14.00%
EFFECTIVE RATE 1.167

	1 AMOUNT OF $1 AT COMPOUND INTEREST	2 ACCUMULATION OF $1 PER PERIOD	3 SINKING FUND FACTOR	4 PRESENT VALUE REVERSION OF $1	5 PRESENT VALUE ORD. ANNUITY $1 PER PERIOD	6 INSTALMENT TO AMORTIZE $1	
MONTHS							
1	1.011667	1.000000	1.000000	0.988468	0.988468	1.011667	
2	1.023469	2.011667	0.497100	0.977069	1.965537	0.508767	
3	1.035410	3.035136	0.329475	0.965801	2.931338	0.341141	
4	1.047490	4.070546	0.245667	0.954663	3.886001	0.257334	
5	1.059710	5.118036	0.195387	0.943654	4.829655	0.207054	
6	1.072074	6.177746	0.161871	0.932772	5.762427	0.173538	
7	1.084581	7.249820	0.137934	0.922015	6.684442	0.149601	
8	1.097235	8.334401	0.119985	0.911382	7.595824	0.131651	
9	1.110036	9.431636	0.106026	0.900872	8.496696	0.117693	
10	1.122986	10.541672	0.094862	0.890483	9.387178	0.106528	
11	1.136088	11.664658	0.085729	0.880214	10.267392	0.097396	
12	1.149342	12.800745	0.078120	0.870063	11.137455	0.089787	
YEARS							**MONTHS**
1	1.149342	12.800745	0.078120	0.870063	11.137455	0.089787	12
2	1.320987	27.513180	0.036346	0.757010	20.827743	0.048013	24
3	1.518266	44.422800	0.022511	0.658646	29.258904	0.034178	36
4	1.745007	63.857736	0.015660	0.573064	36.594546	0.027326	48
5	2.005610	86.195125	0.011602	0.498601	42.977016	0.023268	60
6	2.305132	111.868425	0.008939	0.433815	48.530168	0.020606	72
7	2.649385	141.375828	0.007073	0.377446	53.361760	0.018740	84
8	3.045049	175.289927	0.005705	0.328402	57.565549	0.017372	96
9	3.499803	214.268826	0.004667	0.285730	61.223111	0.016334	108
10	4.022471	259.068912	0.003860	0.248603	64.405420	0.015527	120
11	4.623195	310.559535	0.003220	0.216301	67.174230	0.014887	132
12	5.313632	369.739871	0.002705	0.188195	69.583269	0.014371	144
13	6.107180	437.758319	0.002284	0.163742	71.679284	0.013951	156
14	7.019239	515.934780	0.001938	0.142466	73.502950	0.013605	168
15	8.067507	605.786272	0.001651	0.123954	75.089654	0.013317	180
16	9.272324	709.056369	0.001410	0.107848	76.470187	0.013077	192
17	10.657072	827.749031	0.001208	0.093834	77.671337	0.012875	204
18	12.248621	964.167496	0.001037	0.081642	78.716413	0.012704	216
19	14.077855	1120.958972	0.000892	0.071034	79.625696	0.012559	228
20	16.180270	1301.166005	0.000769	0.061804	80.416829	0.012435	240
21	18.596664	1508.285522	0.000663	0.053773	81.105164	0.012330	252
22	21.373928	1746.336688	0.000573	0.046786	81.704060	0.012239	264
23	24.565954	2019.938898	0.000495	0.040707	82.225136	0.012162	276
24	28.234683	2334.401417	0.000428	0.035417	82.678506	0.012095	288
25	32.451308	2695.826407	0.000371	0.030815	83.072966	0.012038	300
26	37.297652	3111.227338	0.000321	0.026811	83.416171	0.011988	312
27	42.867759	3588.665088	0.000279	0.023328	83.714781	0.011945	324
28	49.269718	4137.404360	0.000242	0.020296	83.974591	0.011908	336
29	56.627757	4768.093468	0.000210	0.017659	84.200641	0.011876	348
30	65.084661	5492.970967	0.000182	0.015365	84.397320	0.011849	360
31	74.804537	6326.103143	0.000158	0.013368	84.568442	0.011825	372
32	85.975998	7283.656968	0.000137	0.011631	84.717330	0.011804	384
33	98.815828	8384.213826	0.000119	0.010120	84.846871	0.011786	396
34	113.573184	9649.130077	0.000104	0.008805	84.959580	0.011770	408
35	130.534434	11102.951488	0.000090	0.007661	85.057645	0.011757	420
36	150.028711	12773.889539	0.000078	0.006665	85.142966	0.011745	432
37	172.434303	14694.368869	0.000068	0.005799	85.217202	0.011735	444
38	198.185992	16901.656479	0.000059	0.005046	85.281792	0.011726	456
39	227.783490	19438.584900	0.000051	0.004390	85.337989	0.011718	468
40	261.801139	22354.383359	0.000045	0.003820	85.386883	0.011711	480

15.00%   MONTHLY COMPOUND INTEREST TABLES   15.00%
                                       EFFECTIVE RATE 1.250

	1 AMOUNT OF $1 AT COMPOUND INTEREST	2 ACCUMULATION OF $1 PER PERIOD	3 SINKING FUND FACTOR	4 PRESENT VALUE REVERSION OF $1	5 PRESENT VALUE ORD. ANNUITY $1 PER PERIOD	6 INSTALMENT TO AMORTIZE $1	
MONTHS							
1	1.012500	1.000000	1.000000	0.987654	0.987654	1.012500	
2	1.025156	2.012500	0.496894	0.975461	1.963115	0.509394	
3	1.037971	3.037656	0.329201	0.963418	2.926534	0.341701	
4	1.050945	4.075627	0.245361	0.951524	3.878058	0.257861	
5	1.064082	5.126572	0.195062	0.939777	4.817835	0.207562	
6	1.077383	6.190654	0.161534	0.928175	5.746010	0.174034	
7	1.090850	7.268038	0.137589	0.916716	6.662726	0.150089	
8	1.104486	8.358888	0.119633	0.905398	7.568124	0.132133	
9	1.118292	9.463374	0.105671	0.894221	8.462345	0.118171	
10	1.132271	10.581666	0.094503	0.883181	9.345526	0.107003	
11	1.146424	11.713937	0.085368	0.872277	10.217803	0.097868	
12	1.160755	12.860361	0.077758	0.861509	11.079312	0.090258	
YEARS							MONTHS
1	1.160755	12.860361	0.077758	0.861509	11.079312	0.090258	12
2	1.347351	27.788084	0.035987	0.742197	20.624235	0.048487	24
3	1.563944	45.115506	0.022165	0.639409	28.847267	0.034665	36
4	1.815355	65.228388	0.015331	0.550856	35.931481	0.027831	48
5	2.107181	88.574508	0.011290	0.474568	42.034592	0.023790	60
6	2.445920	115.673621	0.008645	0.408844	47.292474	0.021145	72
7	2.839113	147.129040	0.006797	0.352223	51.822185	0.019297	84
8	3.295513	183.641059	0.005445	0.303443	55.724570	0.017945	96
9	3.825282	226.022551	0.004424	0.261419	59.086509	0.016924	108
10	4.440213	275.217058	0.003633	0.225214	61.982847	0.016133	120
11	5.153998	332.319805	0.003009	0.194024	64.478068	0.015509	132
12	5.982526	398.602077	0.002509	0.167153	66.627722	0.015009	144
13	6.944244	475.539523	0.002103	0.144004	68.479668	0.014603	156
14	8.060563	564.845011	0.001770	0.124061	70.075134	0.014270	168
15	9.356334	668.506759	0.001496	0.106879	71.449643	0.013996	180
16	10.860408	788.832603	0.001268	0.092078	72.633794	0.013768	192
17	12.606267	928.501369	0.001077	0.079326	73.653950	0.013577	204
18	14.632781	1090.622520	0.000917	0.068340	74.532823	0.013417	216
19	16.985067	1278.805378	0.000782	0.058875	75.289980	0.013282	228
20	19.715494	1497.239481	0.000668	0.050722	75.942278	0.013168	240
21	22.884848	1750.787854	0.000571	0.043697	76.504237	0.013071	252
22	26.563691	2045.095272	0.000489	0.037645	76.988370	0.012989	264
23	30.833924	2386.713938	0.000419	0.032432	77.405455	0.012919	276
24	35.790617	2783.249347	0.000359	0.027940	77.764777	0.012859	288
25	41.544120	3243.529615	0.000308	0.024071	78.074336	0.012808	300
26	48.222525	3777.802015	0.000265	0.020737	78.341024	0.012765	312
27	55.974514	4397.961118	0.000227	0.017865	78.570778	0.012727	324
28	64.972670	5117.813598	0.000195	0.015391	78.768713	0.012695	336
29	75.417320	5953.385616	0.000168	0.013260	78.939236	0.012668	348
30	87.540995	6923.279611	0.000144	0.011423	79.086142	0.012644	360
31	101.613606	8049.088447	0.000124	0.009841	79.212704	0.012624	372
32	117.948452	9355.876140	0.000107	0.008478	79.321738	0.012607	384
33	136.909198	10872.735858	0.000092	0.007304	79.415671	0.012592	396
34	158.917970	12633.437629	0.000079	0.006293	79.496596	0.012579	408
35	184.464752	14677.180163	0.000068	0.005421	79.566313	0.012568	420
36	214.118294	17049.463544	0.000059	0.004670	79.626375	0.012559	432
37	248.538777	19803.102194	0.000050	0.004024	79.678119	0.012550	444
38	288.492509	22999.400698	0.000043	0.003466	79.722696	0.012543	456
39	334.868983	26709.518627	0.000037	0.002986	79.761101	0.012537	468
40	388.700685	31016.054774	0.000032	0.002573	79.794186	0.012532	480

20.00%   MONTHLY COMPOUND INTEREST TABLES   20.00%
                                      EFFECTIVE RATE 1.667

	1 AMOUNT OF $1 AT COMPOUND INTEREST	2 ACCUMULATION OF $1 PER PERIOD	3 SINKING FUND FACTOR	4 PRESENT VALUE REVERSION OF $1	5 PRESENT VALUE ORD. ANNUITY $1 PER PERIOD	6 INSTALMENT TO AMORTIZE $1	
MONTHS							
1	1.016667	1.000000	1.000000	0.983607	0.983607	1.016667	
2	1.033611	2.016667	0.495868	0.967482	1.951088	0.512534	
3	1.050838	3.050278	0.327839	0.951622	2.902710	0.344506	
4	1.068352	4.101116	0.243836	0.936021	3.838731	0.260503	
5	1.086158	5.169468	0.193444	0.920677	4.759408	0.210110	
6	1.104260	6.255625	0.159856	0.905583	5.664991	0.176523	
7	1.122665	7.359886	0.135872	0.890738	6.555729	0.152538	
8	1.141376	8.482551	0.117889	0.876136	7.431865	0.134556	
9	1.160399	9.623926	0.103908	0.861773	8.293637	0.120574	
10	1.179739	10.784325	0.092727	0.847645	9.141283	0.109394	
11	1.199401	11.964064	0.083584	0.833749	9.975032	0.100250	
12	1.219391	13.163465	0.075968	0.820081	10.795113	0.092635	
YEARS							MONTHS
1	1.219391	13.163465	0.075968	0.820081	10.795113	0.092635	12
2	1.486915	29.214877	0.034229	0.672534	19.647986	0.050896	24
3	1.813130	48.787826	0.020497	0.551532	26.908062	0.037164	36
4	2.210915	72.654905	0.013764	0.452301	32.861916	0.030430	48
5	2.695970	101.758208	0.009827	0.370924	37.744561	0.026494	60
6	3.287442	137.246517	0.007286	0.304188	41.748727	0.023953	72
7	4.008677	180.520645	0.005540	0.249459	45.032470	0.022206	84
8	4.888145	233.288730	0.004287	0.204577	47.725406	0.020953	96
9	5.960561	297.633662	0.003360	0.167769	49.933833	0.020027	108
10	7.268255	376.095300	0.002659	0.137585	51.744924	0.019326	120
11	8.862845	471.770720	0.002120	0.112831	53.230165	0.018786	132
12	10.807275	588.436476	0.001699	0.092530	54.448184	0.018366	144
13	13.178294	730.697658	0.001369	0.075882	55.447059	0.018035	156
14	16.069495	904.169675	0.001106	0.062230	56.266217	0.017773	168
15	19.594998	1115.699905	0.000896	0.051033	56.937994	0.017563	180
16	23.893966	1373.637983	0.000728	0.041852	57.488906	0.017395	192
17	29.136090	1688.165376	0.000592	0.034322	57.940698	0.017259	204
18	35.528288	2071.697274	0.000483	0.028147	58.311205	0.017149	216
19	43.322878	2539.372652	0.000394	0.023082	58.615050	0.017060	228
20	52.827531	3109.651838	0.000322	0.018930	58.864229	0.016988	240
21	64.417420	3805.045193	0.000263	0.015524	59.068575	0.016929	252
22	78.550028	4653.001652	0.000215	0.012731	59.236156	0.016882	264
23	95.783203	5686.992197	0.000176	0.010440	59.373585	0.016843	276
24	116.797184	6947.831050	0.000144	0.008562	59.486289	0.016811	288
25	142.421445	8485.286707	0.000118	0.007021	59.578715	0.016785	300
26	173.667440	10360.046428	0.000097	0.005758	59.654512	0.016763	312
27	211.768529	12646.111719	0.000079	0.004722	59.716672	0.016746	324
28	258.228656	15433.719354	0.000065	0.003873	59.767648	0.016731	336
29	314.881721	18832.903252	0.000053	0.003176	59.809452	0.016720	348
30	383.963963	22977.837794	0.000044	0.002604	59.843735	0.016710	360
31	468.202234	28032.134021	0.000036	0.002136	59.871850	0.016702	372
32	570.921630	34195.297781	0.000029	0.001752	59.894907	0.016696	384
33	696.176745	41710.604725	0.000024	0.001436	59.913815	0.016691	396
34	848.911717	50874.703013	0.000020	0.001178	59.929321	0.016686	408
35	1035.155379	62049.322767	0.000016	0.000966	59.942038	0.016683	420
36	1262.259241	75675.554472	0.000013	0.000792	59.952466	0.016680	432
37	1539.187666	92291.259934	0.000011	0.000650	59.961018	0.016678	444
38	1876.871717	112552.303044	0.000009	0.000533	59.968032	0.016676	456
39	2288.640640	137258.438382	0.000007	0.000437	59.973784	0.016674	468
40	2790.747993	167384.879554	0.000006	0.000358	59.978500	0.016673	480

		4.00%		5.00%		6.00%	
		BAL 25 YR LOAN	BAL 30 YR LOAN	BAL 25 YR LOAN	BAL 30 YR LOAN	BAL 25 YR LOAN	BAL 30 YR LOAN
YR	MOS						
	1	.9981	.9986	.9983	.9988	.9986	.9990
	2	.9961	.9971	.9966	.9976	.9971	.9980
	3	.9941	.9957	.9949	.9964	.9956	.9970
	4	.9922	.9942	.9932	.9952	.9942	.9960
	5	.9902	.9927	.9915	.9939	.9927	.9950
	6	.9882	.9913	.9898	.9927	.9912	.9940
	7	.9862	.9898	.9881	.9915	.9897	.9929
	8	.9843	.9883	.9864	.9902	.9883	.9919
	9	.9823	.9869	.9846	.9890	.9867	.9909
	10	.9803	.9854	.9829	.9878	.9852	.9898
	11	.9782	.9839	.9811	.9865	.9837	.9888
	12	.9762	.9824	.9794	.9852	.9822	.9877
2	24	.9515	.9641	.9577	.9697	.9633	.9747
3	36	.9257	.9450	.9349	.9534	.9432	.9608
4	48	.8989	.9251	.9110	.9363	.9219	.9461
5	60	.8710	.9045	.8858	.9183	.8993	.9305
6	72	.8420	.8830	.8593	.8993	.8753	.9140
7	84	.8118	.8606	.8315	.8794	.8498	.8964
8	96	.7804	.8373	.8023	.8585	.8228	.8777
9	108	.7476	.8131	.7715	.8365	.7940	.8579
10	120	.7136	.7878	.7392	.8134	.7635	.8368
11	132	.6781	.7616	.7053	.7891	.7311	.8145
12	144	.6413	.7343	.6696	.7636	.6967	.7908
13	156	.6029	.7058	.6321	.7367	.6602	.7656
14	168	.5629	.6762	.5926	.7085	.6215	.7389
15	180	.5213	.6454	.5511	.6788	.5803	.7105
16	192	.4781	.6134	.5076	.6476	.5366	.6803
17	204	.4330	.5800	.4617	.6149	.4903	.6483
18	216	.3861	.5453	.4136	.5804	.4410	.6144
19	228	.3374	.5091	.3630	.5442	.3887	.5783
20	240	.2866	.4715	.3098	.5061	.3332	.5400
21	252	.2338	.4324	.2538	.4661	.2743	.4994
22	264	.1788	.3916	.1950	.4240	.2118	.4562
23	276	.1215	.3493	.1332	.3798	.1453	.4104
24	288	.0620	.3051	.0683	.3333	.0748	.3617
25	300	.0	.2592	.0	.2844	.0	.3101
26	312	.0	.2114	.0	.2331	.0	.2553
27	324	.0	.1617	.0	.1791	.0	.1970
28	336	.0	.1099	.0	.1223	.0	.1352
29	348	.0	.0560	.0	.0627	.0	.0696
30	360	.0	.0	.0	.0	.0	.0
31	372	.0	.0	.0	.0	.0	.0
32	384	.0	.0	.0	.0	.0	.0
33	396	.0	.0	.0	.0	.0	.0
34	408	.0	.0	.0	.0	.0	.0
35	420	.0	.0	.0	.0	.0	.0
36	432	.0	.0	.0	.0	.0	.0
37	444	.0	.0	.0	.0	.0	.0
38	456	.0	.0	.0	.0	.0	.0
39	468	.0	.0	.0	.0	.0	.0
40	480	.0	.0	.0	.0	.0	.0

YR	MOS	7.00% BAL 25 YR LOAN	7.00% BAL 30 YR LOAN	8.00% BAL 25 YR LOAN	8.00% BAL 30 YR LOAN	8.50% BAL 25 YR LOAN	8.50% BAL 30 YR LOAN
	1	.9988	.9992	.9989	.9993	.9990	.9994
	2	.9975	.9984	.9979	.9987	.9981	.9988
	3	.9963	.9975	.9968	.9980	.9971	.9982
	4	.9950	.9967	.9958	.9973	.9961	.9976
	5	.9938	.9959	.9947	.9966	.9951	.9969
	6	.9925	.9950	.9936	.9959	.9941	.9963
	7	.9912	.9942	.9925	.9952	.9931	.9957
	8	.9899	.9933	.9914	.9945	.9921	.9950
	9	.9886	.9924	.9903	.9938	.9910	.9944
	10	.9873	.9916	.9892	.9931	.9900	.9937
	11	.9860	.9907	.9880	.9924	.9890	.9931
	12	.9847	.9898	.9869	.9916	.9879	.9924
2	24	.9683	.9789	.9727	.9826	.9747	.9842
3	36	.9507	.9673	.9574	.9728	.9604	.9753
4	48	.9318	.9547	.9407	.9622	.9448	.9655
5	60	.9116	.9413	.9227	.9507	.9279	.9549
6	72	.8899	.9269	.9032	.9382	.9094	.9434
7	84	.8667	.9115	.8821	.9248	.8893	.9308
8	96	.8417	.8949	.8592	.9102	.8674	.9171
9	108	.8150	.8772	.8345	.8944	.8436	.9022
10	120	.7863	.8581	.8076	.8772	.8177	.8860
11	132	.7556	.8377	.7786	.8587	.7895	.8684
12	144	.7226	.8158	.7471	.8386	.7588	.8492
13	156	.6873	.7923	.7130	.8169	.7254	.8283
14	168	.6494	.7672	.6761	.7933	.6890	.8056
15	180	.6087	.7402	.6361	.7678	.6494	.7808
16	192	.5651	.7112	.5928	.7402	.6064	.7539
17	204	.5184	.6802	.5459	.7103	.5595	.7246
18	216	.4683	.6469	.4952	.6778	.5084	.6927
19	228	.4145	.6112	.4402	.6428	.4529	.6579
20	240	.3569	.5730	.3806	.6048	.3924	.6201
21	252	.2951	.5319	.3161	.5636	.3267	.5790
22	264	.2289	.4880	.2463	.5190	.2550	.5342
23	276	.1578	.4408	.1706	.4707	.1771	.4855
24	288	.0816	.3902	.0887	.4185	.0923	.4325
25	300	.0	.3360	.0	.3618	.0	.3747
26	312	.0	.2778	.0	.3005	.0	.3119
27	324	.0	.2154	.0	.2341	.0	.2435
28	336	.0	.1485	.0	.1622	.0	.1691
29	348	.0	.0768	.0	.0843	.0	.0881
30	360	.0	.0	.0	.0	.0	.0
31	372	.0	.0	.0	.0	.0	.0
32	384	.0	.0	.0	.0	.0	.0
33	396	.0	.0	.0	.0	.0	.0
34	408	.0	.0	.0	.0	.0	.0
35	420	.0	.0	.0	.0	.0	.0
36	432	.0	.0	.0	.0	.0	.0
37	444	.0	.0	.0	.0	.0	.0
38	456	.0	.0	.0	.0	.0	.0
39	468	.0	.0	.0	.0	.0	.0
40	480	.0	.0	.0	.0	.0	.0

		9.00%		9.50%		10.00%	
		BAL 25 YR LOAN	BAL 30 YR LOAN	BAL 25 YR LOAN	BAL 30 YR LOAN	BAL 25 YR LOAN	BAL 30 YR LOAN
YR	MOS						
	1	.9991	.9995	.9992	.9995	.9992	.9996
	2	.9982	.9989	.9984	.9990	.9985	.9991
	3	.9973	.9983	.9975	.9985	.9977	.9987
	4	.9964	.9978	.9967	.9980	.9969	.9982
	5	.9955	.9972	.9958	.9975	.9962	.9978
	6	.9945	.9967	.9950	.9970	.9954	.9973
	7	.9936	.9961	.9941	.9965	.9946	.9968
	8	.9927	.9955	.9933	.9960	.9938	.9964
	9	.9917	.9949	.9924	.9954	.9930	.9959
	10	.9908	.9943	.9915	.9949	.9922	.9954
	11	.9898	.9938	.9906	.9944	.9914	.9949
	12	.9888	.9932	.9897	.9938	.9905	.9944
2	24	.9766	.9857	.9784	.9871	.9801	.9883
3	36	.9633	.9775	.9660	.9796	.9685	.9815
4	48	.9487	.9686	.9523	.9714	.9557	.9740
5	60	.9327	.9588	.9373	.9624	.9416	.9657
6	72	.9153	.9491	.9208	.9525	.9261	.9566
7	84	.8961	.9364	.9027	.9416	.9088	.9465
8	96	.8752	.9236	.8827	.9297	.8898	.9353
9	108	.8524	.9096	.8608	.9165	.8688	.9230
10	120	.8274	.8943	.8367	.9021	.8456	.9094
11	132	.8000	.8775	.8102	.8862	.8200	.8943
12	144	.7701	.8592	.7811	.8687	.7916	.8777
13	156	.7374	.8392	.7491	.8495	.7604	.8593
14	168	.7016	.8173	.7139	.8284	.7258	.8390
15	180	.6625	.7933	.6752	.8052	.6876	.8166
16	192	.6196	.7671	.6327	.7797	.6454	.7919
17	204	.5728	.7384	.5859	.7517	.5988	.7645
18	216	.5216	.7070	.5345	.7209	.5473	.7343
19	228	.4655	.6727	.4781	.6870	.4905	.7009
20	240	.4042	.6351	.4160	.6498	.4276	.6640
21	252	.3372	.5941	.3477	.6089	.3582	.6233
22	264	.2639	.5492	.2727	.5639	.2816	.5783
23	276	.1836	.5001	.1902	.5144	.1969	.5286
24	288	.0959	.4463	.0996	.4601	.1033	.4736
25	300	.0	.3876	.0	.4003	.0	.4130
26	312	.0	.3233	.0	.3346	.0	.3459
27	324	.0	.2530	.0	.2624	.0	.2719
28	336	.0	.1760	.0	.1831	.0	.1901
29	348	.0	.0919	.0	.0958	.0	.0997
30	360	.0	.0	.0	.0	.0	.0
31	372	.0	.0	.0	.0	.0	.0
32	384	.0	.0	.0	.0	.0	.0
33	396	.0	.0	.0	.0	.0	.0
34	408	.0	.0	.0	.0	.0	.0
35	420	.0	.0	.0	.0	.0	.0
36	432	.0	.0	.0	.0	.0	.0
37	444	.0	.0	.0	.0	.0	.0
38	456	.0	.0	.0	.0	.0	.0
39	468	.0	.0	.0	.0	.0	.0
40	480	.0	.0	.0	.0	.0	.0

		11.00%		12.00%		13.00%	
YR	MOS	BAL 25 YR LOAN	BAL 30 YR LOAN	BAL 25 YR LOAN	BAL 30 YR LOAN	BAL 25 YR LOAN	BAL 30 YR LOAN
	1	.9994	.9996	.9995	.9997	.9996	.9998
	2	.9987	.9993	.9989	.9994	.9991	.9995
	3	.9981	.9989	.9984	.9991	.9987	.9993
	4	.9974	.9986	.9978	.9988	.9982	.9991
	5	.9968	.9982	.9973	.9985	.9977	.9988
	6	.9961	.9978	.9967	.9982	.9973	.9986
	7	.9954	.9974	.9962	.9979	.9968	.9983
	8	.9948	.9971	.9956	.9976	.9963	.9981
	9	.9941	.9967	.9950	.9973	.9958	.9979
	10	.9934	.9963	.9944	.9970	.9953	.9976
	11	.9927	.9959	.9938	.9967	.9948	.9973
	12	.9920	.9955	.9932	.9964	.9943	.9971
2	24	.9831	.9905	.9856	.9923	.9879	.9938
3	36	.9731	.9849	.9771	.9877	.9805	.9900
4	48	.9620	.9786	.9674	.9825	.9722	.9857
5	60	.9495	.9716	.9565	.9766	.9627	.9808
6	72	.9357	.9639	.9443	.9700	.9518	.9752
7	84	.9202	.9552	.9304	.9626	.9395	.9689
8	96	.9030	.9455	.9149	.9542	.9255	.9617
9	108	.8834	.9347	.8973	.9448	.9095	.9535
10	120	.8623	.9226	.8776	.9342	.8914	.9442
11	132	.8384	.9092	.8553	.9222	.8707	.9336
12	144	.8117	.8941	.8302	.9087	.8472	.9215
13	156	.7818	.8774	.8019	.8935	.8204	.9077
14	168	.7486	.8587	.7700	.8763	.7900	.8921
15	180	.7115	.8378	.7341	.8570	.7553	.8743
16	192	.6701	.8146	.6936	.8353	.7159	.8540
17	204	.6239	.7886	.6480	.8107	.6710	.8309
18	216	.5724	.7597	.5966	.7831	.6199	.8047
19	228	.5149	.7274	.5387	.7520	.5618	.7748
20	240	.4507	.6913	.4734	.7169	.4956	.7408
21	252	.3792	.6511	.3999	.6774	.4203	.7021
22	264	.2993	.6062	.3170	.6328	.3347	.6581
23	276	.2102	.5561	.2237	.5826	.2371	.6080
24	288	.1108	.5003	.1185	.5261	.1262	.5510
25	300	.0	.4379	.0	.4623	.0	.4861
26	312	.0	.3684	.0	.3905	.0	.4122
27	324	.0	.2908	.0	.3096	.0	.3282
28	336	.0	.2042	.0	.2184	.0	.2325
29	348	.0	.1076	.0	.1156	.0	.1237
30	360	.0	.0	.0	.0	.0	.0
31	372	.0	.0	.0	.0	.0	.0
32	384	.0	.0	.0	.0	.0	.0
33	396	.0	.0	.0	.0	.0	.0
34	408	.0	.0	.0	.0	.0	.0
35	420	.0	.0	.0	.0	.0	.0
36	432	.0	.0	.0	.0	.0	.0
37	444	.0	.0	.0	.0	.0	.0
38	456	.0	.0	.0	.0	.0	.0
39	468	.0	.0	.0	.0	.0	.0
40	480	.0	.0	.0	.0	.0	.0

		14.00%		15.00%		20.00%	
		BAL 25 YR LOAN	PAL 30 YR LOAN	BAL 25 YR LOAN	BAL 30 YR LOAN	BAL 25 YR LOAN	BAL 30 YR LOAN
YR	MOS						
	1	.9996	.9998	.9997	.9999	.9999	*****
	2	.9993	.9996	.9994	.9997	.9998	.9999
	3	.9989	.9994	.9991	.9996	.9996	.9999
	4	.9985	.9993	.9987	.9994	.9995	.9998
	5	.9981	.9991	.9984	.9993	.9994	.9998
	6	.9977	.9989	.9981	.9991	.9993	.9997
	7	.9973	.9987	.9978	.9989	.9991	.9997
	8	.9969	.9985	.9974	.9988	.9990	.9996
	9	.9965	.9983	.9971	.9986	.9989	.9996
	10	.9961	.9981	.9967	.9985	.9987	.9995
	11	.9957	.9979	.9964	.9983	.9986	.9995
	12	.9953	.9977	.9960	.9981	.9984	.9994
2	24	.9898	.9950	.9914	.9960	.9966	.9987
3	36	.9835	.9919	.9861	.9935	.9942	.9979
4	48	.9763	.9884	.9799	.9906	.9914	.9968
5	60	.9680	.9843	.9727	.9872	.9880	.9956
6	72	.9585	.9796	.9643	.9833	.9838	.9940
7	84	.9476	.9743	.9546	.9787	.9787	.9921
8	96	.9350	.9681	.9434	.9735	.9725	.9898
9	108	.9205	.9610	.9303	.9673	.9649	.9870
10	120	.9039	.9528	.9151	.9602	.9557	.9836
11	132	.8848	.9434	.8975	.9520	.9444	.9794
12	144	.8628	.9327	.8771	.9424	.9306	.9744
13	156	.8376	.9203	.8534	.9313	.9139	.9682
14	168	.8086	.9060	.8258	.9184	.8934	.9606
15	180	.7753	.8897	.7939	.9034	.8685	.9514
16	192	.7369	.8709	.7568	.8860	.8380	.9402
17	204	.6929	.8493	.7137	.8658	.8010	.9264
18	216	.6423	.8244	.6637	.8424	.7557	.9097
19	228	.5841	.7959	.6057	.8152	.7006	.8894
20	240	.5173	.7631	.5383	.7837	.6334	.8645
21	252	.4404	.7253	.4601	.7470	.5514	.8342
22	264	.3521	.6820	.3694	.7045	.4514	.7973
23	276	.2506	.6322	.2640	.6551	.3295	.7522
24	288	.1340	.5749	.1418	.5978	.1908	.6973
25	300	.0	.5091	.0	.5313	.0	.6303
26	312	.0	.4334	.0	.4541	.0	.5486
27	324	.0	.3465	.0	.3645	.0	.4490
28	336	.0	.2466	.0	.2605	.0	.3275
29	348	.0	.1317	.0	.1398	.0	.1794
30	360	.0	.0	.0	.0	.0	.0
31	372	.0	.0	.0	.0	.0	.0
32	384	.0	.0	.0	.0	.0	.0
33	396	.0	.0	.0	.0	.0	.0
34	408	.0	.0	.0	.0	.0	.0
35	420	.0	.0	.0	.0	.0	.0
36	432	.0	.0	.0	.0	.0	.0
37	444	.0	.0	.0	.0	.0	.0
38	456	.0	.0	.0	.0	.0	.0
39	468	.0	.0	.0	.0	.0	.0
40	480	.0	.0	.0	.0	.0	.0

Index